D1367330

Refiguring Revolutions

Refiguring Revolutions

Aesthetics and Politics from the English Revolution
to the Romantic Revolution

EDITED BY

Kevin Sharpe and Steven N. Zwicker

UNIVERSITY OF CALIFORNIA PRESS
Berkeley   Los Angeles   London

University of California Press
Berkeley and Los Angeles, California

University of California Press, Ltd.
London, England

Library of Congress Cataloging-in-Publication Data

Refiguring revolutions : aesthetics and politics from the English revolution to the Romantic
  revolution /edited by Kevin Sharpe and Steven N. Zwicker.
      p. cm.
  Includes bibliographical references and index.
  ISBN 0-520-20919-2 (cloth : alk. paper). — ISBN 0-520-20920-6 (pbk. : alk. paper)
      1. Revolutionary literature, English—History and criticism.   2. Great Britain—Politics and
  government—19th century.   3. Great Britain—Politics and government—18th century.
  4. Great Britain—Politics and government—1603–1714.   5. Politics and literature—Great
  Britain—History.   6. Revolutions—Great Britain—Historiography.   7. Literature and revolutions—History.   8. Romanticism—Great Britain.   9. Revolutions in literature.   10. Aesthetics, British.   I. Sharpe, Kevin.   II. Zwicker, Steven N.
      PR25.R44   1998
      820.9'358—dc21   97-24626
                                                                                        CIP

Printed in the United States of America
9 8 7 6 5 4 3 2 1

The paper used in this publication meets the minimum requirements of American National
Standard for Information Sciences—Permanence of Paper for Printed Library Materials,
ANSI Z39.48-1984.

CONTENTS

LIST OF ILLUSTRATIONS / *vii*
PREFACE / *ix*

Introduction: Refiguring Revolutions
Kevin Sharpe and Steven Zwicker / *1*

REPUBLIC AND MONARCHY

"An Image Doting Rabble": The Failure of Republican Culture
in Seventeenth-Century England
Kevin Sharpe / *25*

Queen Anne Makes Provision
Toni Bowers / *57*

Sad Stories: Louis XVI, George III, and the Language of Sentiment
John Barrell / *75*

READING AND WRITING

Reading the Margins: Politics and the Habits of Appropriation
Steven Zwicker / *101*

The Politics of Song in Wordsworth's *Lyrical Ballads*
Gerald Izenberg / *116*

COMMERCE AND SOCIETY

Performing the Passions in Commercial Society: Bernard Mandeville
and the Theatricality of Eighteenth-Century Thought
Edward Hundert / *141*

"These Neuter Somethings": Gender Difference and Commercial Culture
in Mid-Eighteenth-Century England
Harriet Guest   /   *173*

BODY AND SELF

Bathing and Baptism: Sir John Floyer and the Politics of Cold Bathing
Mark Jenner   /   *197*

Medicine, Politics, and the Body in Late Georgian England
Roy Porter   /   *217*

NATURE AND CULTURE

A Natural Revolution? Garden Politics in Eighteenth-Century England
Stephen Bending   /   *241*

The Pastoral Revolution
Michael McKeon   /   *267*

NOTES   /   *291*
LIST OF CONTRIBUTORS   /   *361*
INDEX   /   *363*

ILLUSTRATIONS

1. Oliver Cromwell (1651) / *31*

2. Frontispiece to *Eikon Basilike* (1649) / *34*

3. *Pious Instructions* / *38*

4. Charles I defends the tree of religion / *40*

5. The Dragon of the Commonwealth's Standing Army / *41*

6. Anne of Denmark (1688) / *63*

7. Anne of Denmark with the Duke of Gloucester / *65*

8. Gillray, *Louis XVI Taking Leave of His Wife and Family* (1792) / *82*

9. *The King's Departure from His Disconsolate Family* / *84*

10. *The Last Interview between Louis the Sixteenth and His Disconsolate Family* / *85*

11. *The Final Interview of Louis the Sixteenth* / *86*

12. British medal by Küchler that depicts the final interview (1793) / *88*

13. Hogarth, *The Company of Undertakers* / *223*

14. Rowlandson, *The Tooth-Ache, or Torment and Torture* (1823) / *225*

15. Hogarth, *The Reward of Cruelty* / *226*

16. Rowlandson, *Medical Dispatch, or Dr. Doubledose Killing Two Birds with One Stone* / *227*

17. Hogarth, *Cunicularii, or The Wise Men of Godliman in Consultation* (1726) / *229*

18. Gillray, *Taking Physick, or The News of Shooting the King of Sweden!* (1792)   /   233

19. "A View of Lord Bute's Erections at Kew" (1767)   /   250

20. "A View of the Princess Dowagers Palace at Kew" (1769)   /   251

21. "A View of the Wilderness with the Alhambra, the Pagoda, and the Mosque" (Kew Gardens) (1763)   /   253

22. Frontispiece to volume 3 of *The Spiritual Quixote,* second edition, by Richard Graves (1773)   /   260

23. "The Sad Historian of the Pensive Plain," title page of Oliver Goldsmith's *The Deserted Village* (1770)   /   263

PREFACE

In this volume we have set out to broaden and, more important, to redirect the interdisciplinary exploration of the political culture of early modern England. Ten years ago, as we planned *Politics of Discourse*, the moment suggested a new address to the relations between literature and politics. At that time the interrogation focused on canonical texts and high politics; but the conversation stimulated by that collection and by other volumes began to question and transform the very categories of and the boundaries between politics and literature. Yet for all this, the traditional periodization of dynasty and century still dominates the chronologies of not only political but even cultural history. What we must recognize is that traditional dynastic chronologies, even our current usage "early modern," often occlude and distort cultural and aesthetic history. The conventional periodization that separates the Puritan Revolution and the Romantic Revolution forecloses aesthetic and cultural histories enacted between and by those revolutions. We seek to return aesthetic history to the center of politics, to argue that the aesthetic writes the political—even that the subjugation of the aesthetic is an attenuation of political narrative itself. For politics between these revolutions was a set of social and aesthetic practices, a narrative of representations, exchanges, and performances as much as a story of ministries and dynasties. Our volume, as its title announces, urges a reconstitution, a refiguration of both chronology and politics. Still more, these essays explore the relations between the chronological and the figurative, between political and aesthetic change.

Kevin Sharpe would like to thank Martin Ridge, Roy Ritchie, and the Huntington Library for a stimulating year in which some of these questions were explored; the University of Southampton for time and funds for research; and colleagues and friends, especially Gerald Aylmer, George

Bernard, Heidi Brayman, Ian Donaldson, Peter Lake, David Riggs, Mark Stoyle, Hugh Trevor-Roper, and Greg Walker, for all their stimulating suggestions and criticisms. Steven Zwicker would like to thank Washington University for research support; students and colleagues at Washington University, including Anne Cotterill, Derek Hirst, Gerald Izenberg, and Naomi Lebowitz; the National Endowment for the Humanities and the Folger Shakespeare Library, Washington, D.C., for research support in 1994–1995; and friends and colleagues over the years at the Folger, including Sabrina Baron, Constance Jordan, David Kastan, Kathleen Lynch, Michael Mendle, Barbara Mowat, Lena Orlin, John Pocock, Gordon Schochet, and Lois Schwoerer; he would like to thank as well the superb staff of the Folger Library. We both wish to express thanks to Stanley Holwitz of the University of California Press for his enthusiasm for this collection; Judy Zwicker for sustenance, friendship, and wonderful good humor; and Aaron Zwicker for the entertainments that in quite different ways gave both editors welcome diversion and good cheer.

St. Louis, 1996

Introduction

Refiguring Revolutions

Over a decade ago, when *Politics of Discourse* was initially planned, the state of scholarship in historical and critical studies seemed to urge an interdisciplinary program that could explicate the relations between text and moment, relations central to each discipline.[1] That program, it might be thought, has richly fulfilled its promise. Under the banner of new historicism, a whole panoply of literary texts, and especially the theater, have been resituated in history and critically reconceived.[2] Where once the literary text, even most notoriously Shakespeare himself, was transported above time and circumstance or romanticized into the alternative history of "heritage," now critical fashion dictates that the text has its meaning only in history.[3]

The rich promise of new historicism, however, has only been partly fulfilled. Not least because scholars trained as historians have ignored or slighted its practices and very premises, new historicism has remained almost wholly within the boundaries of a single discipline. In consequence, the history in new historicism has often seemed serendipitous rather than deeply researched, casually anecdotal, in short, insufficiently historical.[4] Moreover, the move to interdisciplinarity seemed to promise more than the marriage of history and literature. In new historicist theory, after all, the category of text itself was redefined to embrace not only verbal records but paintings and prints, carnival and procession, ritual and festival, a myriad of cultural practices.[5] And the most stimulating of new historicist scholarship has provided the occasional example: the brilliant explication of an individual portrait, the full historical reading of courtly festival. On the whole, however, new historicism has remained intensely literary in its theorizing and practice.

But there has been no shortage of other advocates for a broader interdisciplinary agenda in the academy. Those pursuits newly gathered under the banner of cultural studies enjoy a remarkable prominence, the very name "Cultural Studies" appropriating interdisciplinarity in all its possibilities. Indeed, cultural studies has opened for inquiry a dazzling array of neglected cultural artifacts and sites—the advertisement and the soap opera, rap and the comic book—and invigorated feminist and materialist agendas. Much of the impetus and energy of cultural studies has come, quite naturally, from the interrogation of our own culture. But the very source of this energy, presentism, has occluded its capacity to be historical. It is one thing to unpack the baggage of the Marlboro Man or the shifting politics of Palmolive, quite another to decode the performance of advertisements in eighteenth-century serials. The obvious problem of cultural studies is its failure to historicize, to historicize both present and past. In cultural studies, perhaps more than in any other field, the past has been elided, history replaced by theory. And the claim to theory itself is not unproblematic; rather than a coherent methodology, cultural studies has fragmented into a myriad of moves and locutions. The promise of a fruitful eclecticism and interdisciplinarity has in fact collapsed altogether into a failure of discipline.[6] What in reality has driven cultural studies has been neither history nor theory but contemporary politics and commitments. No scholars, of course, work free of their own circumstances and values, but some feminist and postcolonialist critics, rather than endeavoring to recapture the past, quite consciously appropriate history to validate contemporary theories and agendas.[7]

Whatever then its value in the explication of the contemporary, cultural studies has offered no satisfactory method or practice for the interrogation of aesthetics and politics in the past. Some of the very best work both in new historicism and cultural studies has developed and refined the anthropological method of thick description: the explication of one incident as a point of entry into a broader system of values and beliefs.[8] But often thick description is insufficiently historical in two senses, neither attending enough to the moment nor to change over time.[9] There is nothing intrinsically or necessarily ahistorical in this approach, and some of the best cultural history of late has demonstrated how the carefully documented case study can spread far more light than the generalizations of cultural criticism.[10] Empiricism and history have for some time appeared endangered pursuits, derided by the higher practitioners of theory and suspect as the props of a humanist scholarship that was the ally of a political as well as intellectual conservatism. Rightly we have been led to question, problematize, and historically situate scholarship and history themselves.[11] Yet in their more sophisticated deployment, empirical research and the case study that explores the construction or deconstruction of meaning in an historical moment seem to hold the greatest promise for an understanding of the culture of politics and the politics of the aesthetic both in the past and in our own age.[12]

Such case studies, for all their potential in a reconfiguring of the past, have yet to be realized. While the scholarly article in such fields as garden history, the history of medicine, or gender now fully engages with the ideological and political, specialized journals (and academic institutions) still tend to address discrete and confined intellectual communities. In consequence, and somewhat paradoxically, their capacity, perhaps even their intention, to write a truly interdisciplinary history is foreclosed by traditional intellectual practices and paradigms. For all the broader import of individual studies, gender history, for example, remains largely confined to a specialized readership, and much of our political history is still written from the conventional materials of high politics.[13]

It is only when these histories enter into conversation that the vocabulary and conceptual apparatus emerge for reimagining the past. And conversation here is very much the appropriate metaphor. As in the Restoration coffeehouse, it is the congress of various individuals and groups with their own particular histories which begins to transform the historical narrative itself. The history of the Restoration coffeehouse, after all, is not merely that of the club or commodity; it is the site of the transformation of the public sphere—of the histories of party, taste, and polite society.[14] The coffeehouse powerfully demonstrates how the history of politics must, for this age, also be that of politeness and fashion.

Each of our contributors speaks in a particular historical voice. But the conversation that takes place in this volume not only adjusts those individual stories in light of each other; it also compels a history of society and public life in which the garden, hygiene, reading, and sensibility form the conversation of politics. And it is not merely the idioms and discursive practices of politics that are thus reconsidered. It is even political chronology—the old periodicity of dynasty, battle, and event—that, we now see, reduces and confines the history of politics itself.

I

Scholars of the Renaissance state have recently demonstrated, and with increasing sophistication, the interpenetration of the aesthetic and political, how dynasty and diplomacy themselves demand aesthetic as well as political histories. Who would now question the essentially aesthetic in Queen Elizabeth's rule or the Field of the Cloth of Gold?[15] Indeed, it is difficult to conceive the Renaissance state without the aesthetic language of magnificence, splendor, and display.[16] In England, then, there can be no doubt that the demise of Renaissance monarchy in 1649 marked an aesthetic as well as a political revolution. Some scholars indeed have concluded that the aesthetic and the political themselves, like the body politic, were rent asunder.[17] The historian of the 1650s has felt little need to embrace the aesthetic in the narrative of the republic and Protectorate, even confining iconoclasm, that violent demonstration of the politics of the aesthetic, to the narrative of church and faith.[18] For the Restoration the assumption of this disjuncture, the severing of the political and aesthetic, has impoverished both their histories. Remarkably there is no study of court ritual and festival, of chivalry and honor for the decades after 1660; it is as though a sudden modernity had swept away the Renaissance state.[19] In part, such historiography responds to a gradual and faltering move by contemporaries to assign the political and the aesthetic to separate spaces, indeed, their own autonomy. Yet such a move itself needs searching interpretation and a recognition that the separation of the political and the aesthetic is a political story that must also be told as an aesthetic history. For all the apparent and achieved autonomy of politics in the late seventeenth century, the Advice-to-Painter poem and satirical print announce, as if paradoxically, the most obvious integrity of the aesthetic to the political.[20] In fact, between the demise of the Renaissance state and the obviously aestheticized politics of romanticism, we endlessly confront the ambiguity of aesthetic and political narratives, distinct and autonomous yet integrated and dependent. It is precisely in confronting and exploring that ambiguity that we venture a new history of the Augustan state.

Such a new history begins with recharting chronology itself. Conventional history has situated the English revolution and the romantic revolution not only in divided periods but also in separate disciplines. In consequence it has forced into categories delineated by the dynastic, genres, economies, and sensibilities with their own other histories and narratives. A recognition of 1649 and 1789 as both aesthetic and political moments discloses a narrative quite different from the disjunctures and vicissitudes of dynastic change, party fortune, and factional intrigue. It suggests a long historical trajectory from the collapse of one model of a naturalized polity to the construction of another organic conception of the social, perhaps too a history of romanticism inscribed in part by civil war.[21] This is neither the traditional narrative of commerce, rationalism, and individualism nor the revisionist insistence on the continuities of authority, deference, and Anglicanism.[22] In both these stories the aesthetic has been wholly marginalized.[23] But only when the aesthetic is returned to the center do we understand that these rival historiographical interpretations are neither antagonistic nor exclusive. The slow unraveling of traditional orders and the gradual emergence of different, competing systems must not be alternative interpretations but integrated into one narrative. The very synchronicity and integrity of, yet dissonance and tension within and between, these histories can best be appreciated and interpreted in what we delineate as aesthetic sites and cultural practices.

It is no accident that it was scholars of the Elizabethan and early Stuart theater who finally discredited the thesis of an ideally ordered and harmonious commonweal.[24] The very form of drama, we now see, exposes the fault lines between order and its subversion and the contemporary struggles to contain contradiction.[25] We have no such exegesis of Restoration theater. We are just beginning to comprehend the shaping force of political circumstance and political memory on the generic mixture of the Restoration tragicomedy.[26] The heroic drama, that boldest of experiments on the Restoration stage, remains strange and unyielding, largely because criticism has been preoccupied with an unpoliticized aesthetic genealogy of Restoration drama, blind to the incoherence and instabilities of its political moment.[27] Nor is the stage the only theater of such cultural ambiguity and contradiction. Can we not discern in the regalia of the commonwealth and Protectorate both an acquiescence in and wrestling against the authority of royal form?[28] The aesthetics of the eighteenth-century English landscape cannot be read apart from its political and national performance in Hanoverian England, nor can its history from formality to naturalism be charted independent of the politics of the gothic and the sublime.[29]

As we review particular moments and sites in which the aesthetic and political newly explicate each other, aesthetics and politics not only lose their determinacy in such explication, they are themselves revealed as categories constructed and named out of particular moments and ideological circumstances. Indeed, we may begin to discern the shadowy outline of a larger history, a *longue durée* in which social order and political community are successively constructed, deconstructed, and refigured through what we would now consider aesthetic performance and practice. We open in 1649 with violent assault on the iconicity of Renaissance monarchy. Thereafter, whatever the force of royalist polemics and however limited the success of republican representation, the mystery of kingship was irreparably fractured. Though he touched for the king's evil, Charles II himself appears to have recognized that his authority could not simply be reconstituted out of the old pieties.[30] Along with feudal incidents and homage, the Court masque, that cynosure of kingly power and mysteries, demised.[31] Rather, the Restoration comedy and Rochester's satires themselves announce and perform a process of demystification, indeed of the most brutal realism. Restoration politics appears to have been deaestheticized. In fact, the accommodation of difference and the emergence of party take place in sites that were every bit as aesthetic as political: in Marvell's *Last Instructions,* in Purcell's *Dido and Aeneas,* in Kneller's Kit Kat Club portraits.[32] In turn, a new culture of difference in matters of politics as in critical taste just contained civil violence. James II's failure was unquestionably one of representation as well as policy: his Catholicism an alien aesthetic as well as a tainted faith.[33] And it was the Whigs' construction of an aesthetic as well as political culture that secured their dominance.[34] What sustained Whig hegemony and the appearance, to some degree the reality, of stability was not merely the political arts of patronage and management but the construction of a new culture of commerce and politeness and a new aesthetic of refinement and taste.[35] There were strains and divisions in this society, but the culture long glossed and contained them. What destabilized and ultimately fractured this culture was the intrusion of marginalized and different sensibilities outside its political semiotics and aesthetic codes.

With the rise of religious enthusiasm, the reopening of fundamental constitutional issues in the American colonies, and finally the onset of revolutionary populism on the Continent, a culture of political contest, indeed a politicized culture, came to appear vulnerable and dangerous. Toward the close of the eighteenth century, artists as well as politicians, fearful of just such threats, again worked to contain the forces of disruption. Once more the state was aestheticized, indeed renaturalized; and the forces of dissent were reinscribed onto the realms of spirit and art, pacified and neutered. Accordingly, the notion of the individual changed from Locke's active political agent to Wordsworth's existential subject and Rousseau's citizen participating in the general will.[36]

If the English Revolution demystified kingship, deconstructed the unitary commonweal, and overtly politicized culture, by the romantic revolution we have returned to a cultural re-creation of organic politics. Radical individualism had been refigured into the unthreatening realm of the aesthetic. The recognition of 1649 and 1789 as starting and ending points suggests not only a new history but a new terrain of aesthetics and politics, a terrain yet to be explored and mapped. Its surveying will not only reveal interior contours and ecologies, it may redraw the very borders we have begun to sketch.

Modern theory has of course made us conscious of the indeterminacy and constructedness of all social meaning and categories; the map itself we now clearly recognize as an ideological as well as material composition. Nevertheless, for all the skepticism of the postmodern, inquiry demands some prospect of meaning and definition. For our refiguring of the territory between the Puritan/(English?) Revolution and the romantic/(French?) revolution we might in fact think in terms of a number of explorations: of the commercial, of the literary, of the sexual and psychological, and of the colonial.

II

Historians have long identified commerce as the defining characteristic of Augustan society. When we think of Augustan England we immediately think of the Bank, the Stock Exchange, the Insurance Company.[37] The New Oxford History of this age takes as its title *A Polite and Commercial People*. And that title reminds us that commerce extends far beyond the economic into social life and social order, into manners and behavior, and so into the cultural and aesthetic. Scholars of language have shown us that commerce permeated beyond the material and social exchange into the very discourse, hence the imagination, of this age. John Pocock's work writes the discursive history of the seventeenth and eighteenth centuries as a transformation from the idioms of custom and grace to the language of commerce and interest.[38] But at the juncture of the material and the discursive there is still a history to be written of transformation from a society of honor and patronage to a new world of self-advancement and contractual exchange. The decline of chivalry is emblematic of this transformation.[39] One might even suggest that Renaissance ideas of honor emerge by the end of the seventeenth century as codes of politeness and manners.[40] Far from heralding the feared disintegration of the commonweal, commerce and exchange wrote a new order in which, as Voltaire intuited, material interest cemented the social community.[41] This is not to say that old values simply disappeared or that the new were unequivocally celebrated. The language of the "country," long the idiom of a landed culture and stoic virtue, remained the most potent source of social critique and opposition politics.[42] Throughout the eighteenth century we discern ambivalence about commerce and commercialization: Defoe's gendered and politicized figure of the despotic Lady Credit echoes all the anxieties and revulsion evoked by Machiavelli's capricious goddess Fortuna.[43] What overrode such anxieties was not only spectacular material gain but a language that, eliding the pejorative, rewrote commerce into the moral discourse of progress.[44] The central terms of that discourse were politeness and civilization. What we need to appreciate is that as well as expressing the new coherence of commercial society, politeness was a vital agent of its transformation and sustenance. Politeness as language and social practice endowed commerce with a validating discourse and tempered the vulgarity of exchange and the shame of usury.[45] In the same process polite culture refashioned and broadened elite society. Where chivalry had been the preserve of courtly culture, the exclusive linguistic and moral property of landed aristocracy, politeness seductively posed as an attainable commodity.[46] The academy and books of manners, education, and instruction in the social graces, in deportment, and in dalliance, once mysteries revealed only to an aristocratic coterie, were now published promiscuously to the world.[47] Their purchase promised entry into a refigured elite. Politeness, in rendering more permeable the boundaries of class, facilitated the frequent intermarriages of land and money which are so common a motif of Augustan society and literature.[48] The coffeehouse, that academy of politeness, is also the site of the miscegenation of land and money. Moreover, not only an exchange for commerce, scandal, and political news, the coffeehouse became the locus of aesthetic and critical judgment: commercial society with its self-validating language of politeness and claims to arbitrate taste looked to be establishing cultural and political hegemony.

The Tory objection to commerce was of course always cultural and moral stigma as well as political opposition. Such moral critique, never restricted to the narrow confines of party interest, now developed into an alternative program and ideology, with its own community, language, and aesthetic.[49] For those outside the newly constituted elite—the small freeholder, the village laborer—the decay of the old landed values of hospitality and paternalism rendered life harsher and more brutal rather than more civilized and polite. As E. P. Thompson has argued, for all its apparent coherence and veiling of dissonance, polite commercial society was itself the agent of a deeper fissure between the elite and the plebeian. Not surprisingly the land itself remained the moral high ground, the central motif in opposition rhetoric.[50] The old country critique of the court—of its corruption and decadence—is recycled by and through social change into a vituperative condemnation of commerce itself.[51] Luxury, effeminacy, superficiality, the erosion of social integrity and personal authenticity became the linguistic and conceptual apparatus that demonized urbanity and destabilized commercial society.

What fused the social issues of poverty and dispossession with the rhetoric of corruption and decadence was finally an aesthetic as much as a political move. For it was romanticism that gave representation to the vagrant and marginal and raised the language of corruption into an utter repudiation of commercial society. At the center of romanticism was a sacrilizing of the land itself: the old moral and political geography of pastoral was here endowed with spiritual valence.[52] The country became the site not just of social and political honesty but of psychological integrity.[53]

As romanticism powerfully reminds us, the most forceful critique of commercial society was aesthetic, and in that recognition we discern the need for a fully aesthetic history of commerce and politeness themselves.[54] Politics is the story of ethereal ambitions as well as struggles for place; commerce is structured by desire and fantasy as well as by currency and credit. It is then in aesthetics, perhaps in aesthetics alone, that such aspiration has full personal as well as social articulation.

III

Aesthetics has its most material expression in the production and consumption of texts. The later seventeenth and eighteenth centuries, as we know, was the period in which letters developed into a profession and literature into commercial practice.[55] This is not to deny that there are examples of the professional writer in earlier years, nor to claim the sudden death of patronage and the creation of a full market economy of the book.[56]

Yet we recognize that by the closing decades of the seventeenth century, even the most exalted aesthetic texts, Tonson's issue of *Paradise Lost* and Dryden's *Virgil,* were conceived as commercial ventures.[57] Indeed in Dryden's case the *Virgil* signals a moment at which a career founded in the marketplace became a real possibility. Nor was the commercialization of literature a story exclusive to its highest modes. We are familiar with Grub Street, with penny journalism, with the pamphlet and periodical that exploded in the 1690s.[58] But where traditional literary histories saw Grub Street as a reflection of commercial society, we emphasize the performance of literature, its scripting of the new culture of commerce. Literature was that mirror in which polite society identified and defined itself, as books of manners, manuals of conversation, Restoration comedy, and the new forms of fiction offered the images that fashioned social performance.[59]

The relationship of literature to politics needs to be similarly rearticulated. The movement of the author from dependence on courtly and aristocratic patronage and the gradual institutionalization of the literary in its own societies and clubs began to endow writing with its own autonomy and a new authority.[60] And it was an authority that writers were quick to exercise in the political as well as aesthetic arena. As emerging parties scripted their programs, they competed to recruit to their cause the skills and reputations of writers. It is clear that the literary was constituted as a fully authoritative political agent in the newly constituted public sphere at a time when party fortunes and reputations were made by rhetorical skills.[61] Nor is the political performance of the literary merely a matter of recruitment to party causes. Literary debate, and more largely aesthetic conversation and contest, became an alternative site to the violent conflict of the battlefield: the battle of the books is only the most obvious metamorphosis of bloody into verbal engagement.[62] Not only a product of commercial and polite society, the literary and aesthetic were agents of the civilizing process. The story of political change in Augustan England is broader than the narrative of emerging party and partisanship. Theories of individual rights, challenges to patriarchalism, the active participation of women in political society are familiar topoi of the political narrative. But it is important to emphasize how literary forms and practices enacted such political developments.[63] Female authorship itself challenged patriarchal authority, and it was through writing that the female voice was more broadly articulated and heard in the public sphere.[64] At a time when political theory was written on the foundations of individual property rights and agency, the developing legal and conceptual apparatus of copyright advanced the idea of intellectual property and prefigured the authorship of the self.[65]

The self in literature is a consuming as well as producing subject, and the Augustan moment was a time of crucial transition in literary consumption. A central feature of this transition is unquestionably the change in the locations and habits, hence experience, of reading. Whereas in the earlier modern period the experience of the text was commonly that of public locution from the pulpit and by head of household, by the end of the seventeenth century architectural and social change made reading a more private and unmediated experience. This is a transition that, though no less important than that from manuscript to print culture, is only now being analyzed and charted.[66] What is already clear is that private reading licenses the construction of private meaning, hence an autonomy of the self. It is no accident that this is the age in which readers, as if inscribing their ownership of meaning on the material book itself, engaged in fierce marginal glossing, debating and contesting the text in a newly strenuous and politicized fashion. The debate reminds us that though increasingly a private activity, reading was still—perhaps more now than ever—an intensely social and socialized practice. Our very notion of the reading public, as distinguished from the Renaissance coterie, emerges as part of the commercialization of print; and it develops in relation to the central place of press, publishing house, bookseller, and lending library in commercial and polite culture.[67] The coffeehouse provided the most obvious site for social reading, a reading that took place in the context of a variety of social exchanges: between text and conversation, between stage and event, poem and politics.[68] And in these exchanges consuming readers begin to participate in the shaping and production of the text. Where once allegory and its mysteries were decoded only by the few, the book with printed key graphically illustrates the demands and social activities of the consuming reader.[69] We have remarked on the literature of manners and mores, the nearly sacrosanct texts of this society. What we also need to consider is the role of the consuming reader in the history of the transition of this genre from courtesy book to manual of self-improvement. Surely the novel as a form only makes sense in the context of a consumer culture of self-development.[70]

Hitherto we have discerned the active performance of the text in the world. The text itself, however, was also permeated by, marked by the world. And literally so. As well as a site for literary debate, the margin was a battleground of political skirmish and party warfare. Even in the privacy of the study, the imagination might be invaded by the sign of another reader, a hand from the outside world.[71] Reading has become part of the political process—part of division and contest. Interestingly, however, we might think of the margin simultaneously as the place of pacification and containment. Contest in the margin is not only conceptually marginal; the limited space on the page functions in the most material way to delimit difference. Would it be fanciful to think of the material form of the book as a chapter in the history of the socialization of difference and political pacification?[72]

The most obvious way in which politics drives the literary, we now know, is in the history of genre and form. And the most familiar and well-told chapters of that history have been the development of the country house poem, the rise of the novel, the mutation of epic into burlesque.[73] What we would wish to urge is that there is no history of literary forms outside of social and political history. The Restoration tragicomedy clearly took its form from its moment of political ambivalence and contradiction; Augustan pastoral is rewritten across the eighteenth century by the history of land-holding and agricultural labor, less obviously by gender and colonial exploration; the decline and recovery of devotional lyric follows the cadences of the history of religious enthusiasm.[74] Even when it remains unyielding and unfathomable, we must suspect the pressure of politics on literary form. Though no critic has yet explored the translation of cavalier lyric from erotic dalliance to hardcore pornography, it is not only in the obvious politics of gender that the political will be discovered as shaping force.[75] In this age the political is all-pervasive not only in the content but in the very form and design of text—of lyric verse, of landscape garden, of engraved cartoon.

For some time the romantics' claim to visionary imagination, to a poetics of transcendence, was taken at face value.[76] The rejection of inherited literary values, hierarchies, and forms, the spurning of the academy, the flaunting of social as aesthetic convention appeared to substantiate the claims for an autonomous aesthetic and personal space. But the very claim to such autonomy was fundamentally political. If not as immediately apparent as the drive of partisanship in Swift and Pope, the revival of religious enthusiasm, the resurgence of radical voices at home and in the colonies, and the revolutionary populism of the Jacobins were every bit as much the motor of romantic lyric. The election of the vagrant and solitary wanderer as subjects of representation was the exercise of political as well as aesthetic franchise. Politics drove every gesture of lyric expression: its openness of form, its meters and rhythms as well as its prophetic urgencies and declamations of self.[77]

IV

The history of the self has in recent years been reconstituted as a history of gender and sexuality. Feminist history and gender studies have provided among the most provocative and innovative perspectives onto the eighteenth century.[78] No history of this period can now be written without address to the ambivalences of gender or sensitivity to the gendering of language. And yet the master narrative of most surveys and histories, while gesturing to gender, prohibits its entry into the dominant story of politics, diplomacy, and public address. In the Renaissance state the central political representation is, of course, the body politic.[79] The very materials of Renaissance culture—from Elizabeth's self-fashioning as Virgin Queen to the platonic love culture of the Carolines—announce the interpenetration of the political and the sexual.[80] After the Restoration, however, it is not the figurative representation of the sexual but the literalized and graphically sexual body that is at the center of politics: not the metaphoric body politic but the fully sexualized body of Charles II. The history of gender in the court of this king is a fully political history.[81] Most obviously the representation of Charles as progenitor and procreator, from succession through Exclusion, charts the familiar politics of dynasty, more important, announces a move to explicit sexuality.[82] And the celebration of the king's whoring and debauchery marks not only a reaction to Puritan asceticism and the repression of the 1650s but a revolutionary change from an etherialized to a brutalized sexual representation. Not merely sexually explicit, this is the first, perhaps only, court that could be characterized as pornographic. Rochester after all was Gentleman of the Bedchamber as well as chief pornographer, and the king's whores, we hardly need reminding, enjoyed political influence as well as royal intimacy.[83]

The king's body and royal debauchery are the most obvious demonstrations of sexual politics. What we need to appreciate is that in Restoration England changes in sexuality must be told as a larger story of cultural, social, and political history. The social histories of this age immediately remark the more obvious presence of women throughout Restoration culture: on the stage, as writers, in Hyde Park, in the coffeehouses, in representation on canvas and engraved print. At first the greater visibility of women might lead us to plot a continuity from the protofeminism of some radical movements of the 1650s, especially when we discern a newly erotic portrayal of women, a public recognition of female sexual agency.[84] But the Restoration narrative is hardly one of sustained radicalism, either sexual or political. The acknowledged sexuality of women is structured as much a site of male gaze and desire as of female liberation. Restoration pornography subjects and commodifies rather than liberates female sexuality. Moreover, images of the female in this period were exoticized as well as eroticized. As we view the portraits of aristocratic females surrounded by palms, exotic fruits, and parrots we cannot but contemplate the exchange between the feminization of the colonial Other and the colonization of the exoticized female body.[85]

Indeed the process of representation as domestication is common to both. As the large panoply of colonial life is reduced to artifact and curio, so the experience and agency of female sexuality, rather than liberated, appears trivialized by the erotic. We might read in the eighteenth-century preoccupation with manners and morals some negotiation with the issue of an acknowledged female sexuality, perhaps even some gesturing to its containment.[86] In the aesthetic, for all the high visibility of the female subject, the conventions of form—the picaresque and epistolary novel, for example—emplot masculine authority. The picaresque novel writes the heroine, after all, into a traditionally male adventure, while Hogarth's *Harlot's Progress* charts a moral narrative of descent from female chastity to debauchery, a narrative at once conventional and misogynistic.[87] But in many ways the heroine breaks forth from form and convention: as Clarissa triumphs over masculine domination and sexual violence, Moll Flanders manipulates masculine desire itself to female advantage. The novel in fact graphically demonstrates the failure to confine the female to the private sphere. Far from being delimited, the feminine penetrates to the very center of male society and culture. The shift from a culture of honor and martial prowess to a society of commerce and consumption was figured by contemporaries in gendered language and as a process of feminization. Dame Credit is only one term in a lexicon of feminizing vocabulary that characterizes the commercial. The cosmetic and the paraphernalia of the boudoir in reconfigured masculine space deconstruct masculinity itself.[88] The sentimental hero, that composite of masculine form and feminine sensibility, appears almost hermaphrodite. Beneath the veneer of politeness, mid-eighteenth-century society reveals fracture and incoherence in sexual identity, an instability that resonates in the commercial and political culture at large.[89]

In the sexual as in the political, the story of romanticism is one of a yearning for healing and wholeness. The romantic spiritualized body, at the farthest remove from the grotesque torsos of Restoration sexuality, seems to elide the very issue of sexual identity. The menace of sexual appetites is muted by translation to the realm of spirit. The process of spiritualization and etherialization served also to soothe anxiety about the feminization of the masculine. In romantic aesthetics the "man of feeling" is a figure of celebration rather than anxiety as sentiment and softness are appropriated from exclusively female space.[90] With the physical body etherialized and gender anxieties eased, romantic culture could rejoice in sexual union and ecstasy. Given the political freighting of the sexual, the pleasure celebrated is that of social and political reintegration as well as sexual union.

V

Our very terms *pleasure* and *integration* are the vocabulary of modern psychology. In a real sense, the origins of what we call psychology can be traced to the beginnings of our period, to civil violence and the fracturing of the body politic. Thomas Hobbes's revolutionary political theory rested on a personal and social psychology: a figuration of society as an artificial coherence of atomized passions and interests. For all the contemporary repudiation of Hobbes's political theory, the old commonweal was irreparably damaged by the new psychology.[91] After Hobbes the challenge to political philosophy, the problem for political order itself, was that of accommodating an acknowledged individual agency. That accommodation was famously achieved by John Locke. In *The Second Treatise* Locke takes individual ownership of the self as well as real property as the fundamental of the state. Locke's argument was epistemological and psychological as well as political theory. For all his distance from Hobbes's politics, Locke too took the impulses of pleasure and pain as defining principles of the self.[92] The *Treatise on Education* assumes a self capable of development and progress, what we might call a personality. Accordingly, Locke appropriates to the individual what was idealized and theorized as a common and shared conscience.[93] The privatization of conscience was a first step in the constitution of the self as the locus of order.

Bourgeois manners and polite society, theorists have argued, were both the expressions and the instruments of the interiorization of order in late seventeenth- and early eighteenth-century England.[94] Bernard Mandeville provided the political theory that structured and validated this process. In *The Fable of the Bees* Mandeville utterly rewrote the social figure of the hive, refashioning the argument of organic community into advocacy of individual passion and interest. In Mandeville's politics as in polite society the individuated subject is not just accommodated but fully socialized. Fashion appears to fulfill the fantasy of infinite self-expression.[95] Renaissance scholars have characterized a psychological as well as material moment insightfully as one of "self-fashioning."[96] In Augustan England commodity culture, no longer the privilege of an aristocratic elite, democratized the opportunities for self-presentation.[97] At this moment costume became more visible on the stage as well as on the street.[98] The *theatrum mundi* was one of the oldest metaphors of social and political representation, a figure brilliantly extended throughout Renaissance political and literary discourse. But for the Augustans the metaphor of theatricality diffused into common social discourse and even social practice. Like the donning of dress, the adoption of personae and performance of roles were characteristics, and recognized as characteristics, of the social theater.[99]

The notion of the autonomous actor commanding the social stage was a conceit, reluctantly acknowledged, perhaps never easily abandoned. Yet fashion and role, seemingly vehicles for self-expression, are also the instruments for the social inscribing of the self: social role and persona in the end fabricate personality. The creation of the self, we might discern, is a process of interiorizing all the instability and incoherence of society and state. The anxiety of the Augustan age derived from the inherent instability of personal as well as social constructions. The period between the privatization of conscience and the birth of psychology lacked conceptual and institutional apparatus for analysis and care of the psyche. The medical profession took a remarkably long time to acknowledge and diagnose the psychological implications of cultural and political change. Still dominated by the Cartesian theory of disjuncture between mind and body, the Hanoverian doctor applied his arts to the material body, as if abandoning the ghostly psyche to the curate and cunning man. It was the madness of George III that critically expressed that abandonment and compelled attention to the psyche as well as body of the polity.[100]

The yearning to heal and integrate is a defining impulse of romanticism. We understand romanticism in the first impulse as a move to withdraw the individual from social artifice and masquerade into the healing space of solitude and the balm of nature. The failure of the medical profession, itself tarnished by the social ills of commerce and corruption, turned the romantics to the homeopathy of nature. In nature alone lay the promise of wholeness and integrity.[101] The romantic self, however, proved to be a more complicated narrative than joyful discovery of psychic harmony and wholeness. Wordsworth's mounting anxiety about the tyranny of the sovereign self discloses not coherence and integration, but fracture and dislocation.[102] His politicized language demonstrates the self as inevitably social. And it is a language that points to a psychology indelibly marked by social moment and political event. Where the English Civil War had fractured the Renaissance body politic, the French Revolution deconstructed the romantic self. In that simultaneous dissolution of the self and state, we may even discern the origins of Freudian analysis and social psychology.

VI

Our explorations of aesthetics and politics then trace a trajectory not only from the English revolution to the French Revolution but an arc from the most socialized arena of commerce to what we still conceive as the most private terrain of the self. We claim not simply the interrelatedness of the aesthetic and the political; we insist that there can be no history of the one independent of the other, that, in short, political history must be aesthetic history. At its most theoretical, political history has been written as the history of political thought and philosophy. Yet for all the current ferment in theory, no critical practice has yet examined the canonical political text as aesthetic performance. This is an omission all the more remarkable when we consider the deep rhetorical self-consciousness, the sensitivity to figure and form, that characterize this age. We require studies not just of the argument and discourse but of, say, the fantasies of More's *Utopia,* the poetics of *Leviathan,* the deep structures of *Two Treatises,* or the figurations of *The Social Contract.*[103] For all the linguistic turn, we await study informed by the aesthetics of political language.

Political theory after all imagines and interrogates political arguments through metaphor and representation. Political theory is itself a master narrative of representation, its very language of structure and relation, a reifying, indeed humanizing, of its artifice and abstractions. The engraved frontispiece of *Leviathan* is only the most obvious device for making the state visible, imaginable. It is no coincidence that Hobbes felt the need to represent, to reliteralize, the ancient figure of the body politic at the revolutionary moment of its deconstruction. From Hobbes onward, the project of political theory was either the reconstitution or reinvention of that representation that might accommodate individual will to political order. The metaphor of the body had for long not simply described but had drawn the social imagination to organic community. The metaphor had such authority that even after 1649, the political community was reluctant to surrender it. One of the earliest gestures of the Restoration was to reclaim the metaphoric body and head from commonwealth and republic for Crown and kingdom. And the metaphor continued for decades thereafter to circulate as royalist language. But repeated failures of the royal body personal—Charles II's failure to beget a legitimate heir, Queen Anne's political infertility, George III's breakdown—drained the body political of metaphoric power.[104]

Accordingly, and parallel to that decline, we may sense a contemporary quest for an alternative idiom that might structure the imagination of politics. Mandeville's commonwealth of bees and his theatrical language offer such figurative alternatives, with the hive and the stage as sites of the strictest regulation and containment.[105] But Mandeville's metaphors do not sustain a vivid life in eighteenth-century political discourse, nor in consequence do they refashion an organic state or political order. No controlling metaphor had fully displaced that of the body politic before its demise with the decapitation of Louis XVI.[106] The romantic metaphor rejects the boundaries of the body altogether. The etherialized body releases the subject from corporeality and the state from the political script of the organic body. The full panorama of nature, unbounded and infinite, becomes the romantic figuration of the political; and in turn the metaphor renaturalizes the mechanistic and artificial commonwealth of Hobbes and Mandeville.[107] At the very moment of its hegemony, however, the metaphor of nature for politics is complicated and destabilized by history. The French Revolution not only marks the death of the body politic, it also stains the romantic landscape and its political vision with the blood of violence and terror. For Wordsworth the nature that promised to nurture a new order transmutes into a landscape of menace and fear.[108] It is no coincidence that in France the romantic move was to a reconstitution of the organic state. While Rousseau's *Émile* stands for a naturally constructed and fully realized self, the despotism of individuality must be regulated and contained. The *Social Contract,* after all, takes its title and being from a terminology that expresses legal obligations as well as commercial bond.

VII

The representation, the imagining of the state was not constructed only out of indigenous materials. The colonies that came under British rule during

this period were not just the prizes of commercial acquisition or the ultimate trappings of state power. They were extensions of (a still largely)
English culture and politics, the projections of an English imagination onto
new and other landscapes and communities.[109] The construction of India
as an imperial domain was and remains a larger story than that of constitutions and institutions; English imaginings and anxieties were transported to
the very interior of colonial land and psyche, into their own aesthetic as
political histories. We have of course long appreciated that the traffic was
not one-way. The exchange between mother country and colonial offspring
imported the materials of mysterious Other into fashionable commercial
society.[110] Exotic objects—animals, fruit, and especially porcelain—became
the subjects of fascination, of fashion and fetish, artifacts of commercial
consumption and aesthetic refinement in England. And they carried more
than commercial import. Oriental medical practices were enacted on the
very body of the English; in plays about the Indies and Peru English actors
costumed in exotic garb and ventriloquizing the voices of the alien performed before the paying spectators of the London theater.[111] The fashion
for the exotic garden brought the colony to the traditional heart of English
politics, the aristocratic country house.[112] As we review the paintings and
prints of this age, we see the English landscape, that site of national self-
imagining and construction, become porous to the Eastern, no longer
determinate. It is a visual instability that represents a large canvas of uncertainty and ambivalence—both about the colonial Other and the indigenous
English. For one, the colonial act expressed contradiction at the heart of
commercial society. What was morally validated as the gift of polite civilization could also be perceived as a violent act of greed and plunder; slavery
wrenched the veil from politeness to expose commerce and commodification in their most dehumanized and dehumanizing form.[113]

Nor was the colonial romance, as it first seemed, that fundamentally masculine narrative of adventure and power. As delicate porcelain and Oriental unguent invaded the male boudoir, as the tattoo, first encountered in
the Cook Islands, became a fashionable male decoration, John Bull
appeared not strengthened by colonial conquest but feminized by colonial
encounter.[114] The patriotic empire of Englishness itself appeared, ironically, diluted by colonial experience. And the anxiety about that dissolution
was political as well as cultural and aesthetic. For where the colonies were
first imagined and represented as a new Eden, a paradisial landscape of natural innocence, the fitting plantation for English personal and public
virtue, they were also perceived as sites of licentious sexual degeneracy and
despotic politics.[115] Such paradoxical figuring perhaps addressed anxieties
about the delicate construction of social and political order at home. Native
ambivalences and anxieties about commerce and the constitution, about
patriarchy and gender, even about "civilization" and "nature," we might

suggest, were interrogated, at one remove, in the writing and representation of the colonies. The artifacts and texts of colonialism, the imagining of the foreign, we come to see, script not only the conventional narrative of commercial expansion and global power but of English aesthetics and politics, of the exploration and interrogation of domestic no less than foreign terrain.

VIII

Our explorations of the society of Augustan England and the landscape of the Augustan imagination have followed a number of journeys that we might see, in directional terms, as longitudinal lines. Our mappings, however, at a number of points, have opened onto the equal promise of alternative routes and directions. The very language we have encountered and deployed exposes the crosscurrents that inevitably complicate any perception of narrative flow. We have sketched the outlines of commerce and literature, sexuality and empire, as constituents of a large design for an aesthetic and political history of this period. But language is not exclusive to any one of these idioms: the terms constitution and consumption inhabit at once the commercial and political. Desire signals both commercial and sexual fantasy; sentiment becomes a discourse for family love, social disposition, aesthetic experience and, in fine, political representation.[116] *The Spectator* institutionalizes the multivalent performance of a term that evokes regard, self-representation, theatricality, fashion, and vanity as well as critical taste and political judgment. Language has its own longitude and latitude:[117] it performs not only widely across the contemporary moment; it carries the freight of meanings in the process of decay and constitution.[118] Did those who took pleasure from the Georgian scatological cartooning of "Broad Bottoms" recall the political history of the Rump and its desecration?[119]

The Rump suggests not only a chronology from the 1650s to Georgian England but also a narrative of a process common to the stories we have told. Demystification is a counterplot to all our narratives. The events of 1649 obviously mark a crucial stage in the demystification of power. The Restoration Court, as we have argued, was far removed from the magic of Renaissance monarchy. And in Augustan political debate the mysteries of power and politics are exposed to argument and analysis. Packing and party management locate politics in the world of business and exchange; electoral bribery and rotten boroughs publicize corruption and decay; unsurprisingly the high mysteries of state are reduced to vulgar squib and gross cartoon.[120] Such a process is no simple teleology of debasement and rationalization. At some level, after all, the mysteries of state had always articulated the subject's desire as well as the arts of rule. Throughout the eighteenth century there remained the vestiges of mystical politics, even a cultural desire for those mysteries: Boswell, for one, relates the story of Dr. Johnson being touched for the king's evil.[121] Yet for all the power of cultural memory, Johnson was among the last to be touched, and the demise of touching with Anne's reign is emblematic of a larger story of desacralization. By the mid-eighteenth century politics is articulated in the language of reason and science rather than mystery. In some ways the age of romanticism appears to be the culmination of this story: the ferment in the American colonies reverberated through English radical consciousness; the revolution in France toppled the iconicity of power. But romanticism also gave voice to a cultural desire to remove, to elevate, even to remystify power; it transported authority from the rational individualized subject to the unfathomable reaches of the sublime.

The narrative of demystification in this period is traditionally related as a process of secularization. Revisionist scholarship has exposed the anachronism and teleology of that history, powerfully arguing the continuity of the confessional state.[122] Yet at the same time this was an age in which the mysteries of Christianity were laid bare and the rationality of faith celebrated.[123] The historiography appears to present us with alternative and contradictory narratives. We might suggest that a trajectory from demystification to respiritualization helps to resolve this paradox. The ossification of the Anglican church and the rationalization of established religion diffused religiosity into the broader confessional community and released the spirit into exaltation.

This crosscurrent of demystification not only plots a new story of politics and spirituality in this age, we might venture more broadly that our crosscurrent may also suggest other histories: of the desacralized female body, the demystified colonial Other.

Another current that flows across our charted landscape is, to use a contemporary language, democratization. Democratization is not simply the history of the enlargement of the franchise and the process of ballot and election. It is the dispersal of authority and agency, the diffusion of power into the public imagination, even a public capacity to conceive itself as a political actor. The cultural and political history of the Augustan age might be refigured as a story of such dispersals and diffusions. Most obviously, policy itself begins to reach beyond Whitehall and Westminster to be constituted in an enlarged public sphere.[124] Commerce enables that enlarged constitution of the political: as a solvent of rigid social stratification, it releases politics from aristocratic privilege and commodifies politics itself and so transforms the consuming subject into political agent. Acquisition— the commercialization of culture and its vocabulary of taste—democratizes the aesthetic. Even the story of colonial acquisition and empire is as well one of democratization. Where foreign policy was once the ultimate of *arcana imperii,* the importation and display of exotica implicated consuming society in the traffic of colonial enterprise.[125]

The terrain of politics and aesthetics is crossed by many more currents than those we have identified as demystification and democratization. As other currents are followed, some will demand different and longer chronologies than those marked by the English revolution and the romantic revolution. Yet our chronology itself has gestured to some fertile rehistoricizing of the conventional histories of commerce, sexuality, and the self. Moreover it is this very periodizing that discloses a new configuration of the aestheticizing of politics and the political performance of the aesthetic. Our period begins after all at the moment when politics emerges into its own sphere and is validated as a practice free from the opprobrium of Machiavellianism.[126] And it ends with the naming of that very category, the aesthetic. The autonomy and definition of the aesthetic is unquestionably a social and political history. And far above intrigue, cabal, and interest, politics emerges as aesthetic terrain, "that sublime science which embraces for its object the happiness of mankind."[127]

IX

Any historicizing of culture confronts the methodological conundrum of text and moment. Theory has insistently problematized text and moment but offered no satisfactory working method for historical exegesis of their relationship. Historians, in the main, have retreated from theory to the familiar craft of the case study, a working practice that necessarily isolates and contains. The case study delimits not only the larger chronology but often the intertextuality of meaning in any historical moment. Rather than the case study, we would reconfigure text and moment as a point intersected by a number of axes and on a number of planes. The conventional trajectory plots the axis of chronology, be it politics, economics, or gender. We urge a three-dimensional model that opens the point to the synchronicity of its other trajectories and histories. The meeting of text and moment, to change the metaphor, is no single fault line but a series of reverberations— of politics into the psychological and aesthetic, of the sexual into commerce and warfare. The year 1649 is a point not only on the traditional trajectory of dynastic history; it is also a critical moment in the histories of sexuality and aesthetics, even in the history of romanticism.[128] To neglect these reverberations is to fail to write any of these histories; it is a failure of history.

These axes of meaning are, of course, cultural constructions. To return to our idiom, the map that imposes design on the infinite vagaries of landscape is the ultimate ideological construction. But our design responds to the construction of contemporaries who themselves conceived not only the commercial and the political but, by the end of our period, the psychological, the aesthetic, and the sexual as terrains of meaningful discourse. That said, the recovery of these terrains as themes for historical exploration undoubtedly responds to our own political moment, our own aesthetic and cultural constructions. The alleged crisis of capitalism has demanded a new history of consumerism; contemporary deconstructions of family and gender are the conditions of a new history of sexuality; the postcolonial era has brought the idea of empire to the center of cultural studies. Very much to our purposes, the Internet and MTV question the institution of the book and fragment and deconstruct the constitution of the aesthetic. And for some the post–cold war era and "new world order" herald the end of history itself.[129]

To confront the ideational force of our own time, however, is not to return to the presentism of cultural studies. It is rather to begin to discern another history of our aesthetic and political culture with its own echoes and memories, its commerce and exchange with the Augustan moment— an exchange between Augustanism, modernity, and the postmodern. This is a history as yet unexplored; but only such a history will enable us not only to comprehend the past but to situate the present and to begin to imagine the future.

Republic and Monarchy

"An Image Doting Rabble"

The Failure of Republican Culture in Seventeenth-Century England

Kevin Sharpe

Only a short time ago almost all historians agreed with E. W. M. Tillyard that Tudor ideas of order and harmony presented monarchy as the natural, divine mode of government and rendered alternative polities literally unimaginable.[1] More recently, however, scholars have detected in repeated homilies on obedience anxieties about dissenting views. In particular, it has been argued, a republic in early modern England was not only thinkable but was thought.[2] Radical Calvinists facing persecution on the Continent read in the Bible of resistance to ungodly tyrants and were in turn read in English Puritan circles.[3] And all educated Englishmen learned from the Greek and Roman past the achievements and virtues of the classical republics and studied their contemporary and later humanist historians and apologists. Toward the end of Elizabeth's reign, some suggest, as criticism of the regime intensified, republican ideas became fashionable in the intellectual circles of Sidney and Essex and bequeathed a language and a vision of politics that remained to critique and contest the official discourse of monarchy and state.[4]

Such suggestions and revisions prompt questions that have yet to be pondered. If the languages of tyrannicide and republic ran current in early modern England, was civil war and regicide the violent and incomprehensible shock to Englishmen that we have traditionally presented it as being? Was a commonwealth erected in 1649 not because of unforeseen and unintended events but because the idea was already established in the political and cultural imagination? Or, alternatively, have recent revisions exaggerated the power and importance of republican languages and beliefs? In pursuing these questions, I shall argue that, not least because they have largely ignored the visual, the symbolic, and the emblematic, historians of republican discourse have underestimated the pervasiveness of monarchy in the culture of early modern England. In early modern England government was not just a matter of institutions or rational arguments but a nexus of customs and cultural practices. The forms through which authority had traditionally expressed itself became the forms through which any authority must express itself. Since these were forms shaped by kings, then something essential of the royal remained, whatever the constitution, policies, or personnel. And I shall suggest that it was because the culture was so inscribed and colored with monarchism that a commonwealth was never established as the government of seventeenth-century Englishmen. The failure of republican politics was a failure to forge a republican culture that erased or suppressed the images of kingship, images that sustained a monarchical polity, even in the absence of the king.

THE COMMONWEALTH ESTABLISHED?

The Commonwealth was not established when the axe separated Charles I's head from his body on the scaffold at Whitehall. A king had been executed but the institution of monarchy had not been abolished. Not until March did the Rump pass an act "for abolishing the kingly office" as "burdensome and dangerous to the liberty, safety and public interest of the people" and even then somewhat ambiguously decreed that "the office of a king in this nation shall not henceforth reside in . . . any one single person."[5] The faltering tone expressed the fundamental questions of 1649: What was the nature and authority of the new government? What were the people to expect from Parliament and what, as Isaac Pennington put it, from "their supreme governor or governors"?[6] Novelty and uncertainty, it was recognized, threatened the new regime. As John Goodwin put it in his *Defence of the Honourable Sentence Passed upon the Late King,* "the first apparition of things new and strange, especially when the reasons and causes of them are unknown . . . are usually disturbing and offensive to their apprehensions."[7] The new commonwealth had to construct its own authority in 1649. This, in part of course, was a question of time. Apologists for the regime, arguing that all could not be "perfected with one swap," believed that "a year or two will habituate the present government."[8] In *The Case of the Commonwealth Stated,* Marchamont Nedham predicted confidently: "Let the Commonwealth have leave to take breath a little in the possession of a firm peace, then they would soon find the rivulets of a free state much more pleasing than the troubled oceans of kingly tyranny."[9] Time undoubtedly could dull the sense of shock and gradually dispel the feeling that the new government was a temporary aberration. But time in itself was not enough. To establish the authority of the new regime, the language and image of a republic had to be instilled in and the language and image of monarchy erased from the political culture of early modern England. The kingdom of England had to be "turned into a commonwealth."[10]

Much Commonwealth propaganda was necessarily defensive, a justification of the shocking events that had brought it into being. *A Declaration of the Parliament* rejected the right of a son to succeed to a father who had forfeited the crown, condemned the prodigality of kings and courts, and asserted the right of the people to determine the fate of kings as they had originally instituted them.[11] The *Obstructors of Justice* denied any obligations to kings who did not discharge their trust.[12] Many writers cited necessity as the reason for the rejection of monarchy.[13] More originally, *The Case of the Commonwealth*, pointing to European neighbors who had cast off the yoke of kingship, suggested that the cycle of history itself had turned against monarchy.[14] Most famously, in *The Tenure of Kings and Magistrates* (and in *Eikonoklastes*), Milton attacked "lawless kings," justified the trial and regicide, and defended the Commonwealth. Milton's texts, however, exemplify the problem of such propaganda: the *Tenure*, still more *Eikonoklastes*, "operate within terms of reference" defined by Charles I, his trial, and his own book.[15] As such they, as much as royalist polemic, vividly sustained the memory of the king and too narrowly discussed the new commonwealth in relation to (corrupted) monarchy.

Some, quick to see that the negative arguments against kingship did not establish the authority of the new regime, shifted to more pragmatic justification. Urging all to submit to those who now possessed power, *The Bounds and Bonds of Public Obedience* argued that "so soon as one supreme power is expelled by another, law, life and estate fall into the hands of the succeeding power."[16] Authority, others concurred, came from power. When Scripture, some argued, enjoined obedience to authority, it meant any who possessed power.[17] Yet more boldly *The Case of the Commonwealth* asserted that "the sword creates a title"; as a result of the defeat of the king "the old allegiance is cancelled and we are bound to admit a new."[18] Though the de facto arguments moved the debate away from the monarchy, they also threatened to take it outside the discourse of history, law, and divinity in which all politics had been conducted. As such they were vulnerable to the counterarguments of royalists and other enemies who could more easily deploy the power of those legitimating vocabularies and familiar tropes.

More positive polemics, therefore, rather than ignoring traditional history and language, endeavored to rewrite them. From 1649 pamphlets like *King Charles' Trial Justified* argued that the historical origins of power lay in the people.[19] The 1650 tract *The Government of the People of England Precedent and Present the Same* not only pursued the historical argument of its title but proclaimed as its slogan: "All government is in the people, from the people and for the people."[20] The author of *The True Portraiture of the Kings of England*, tracing the power of the people to determine government from the time of the Saxons, claimed that now Parliament had returned affairs "to their first natural and right principle."[21] The force of these arguments, however, was undercut not only by the persistence of arguments against or about monarchy in their pages and titles.[22] As the agitation in the army and Leveller pamphleteering had graphically demonstrated, the language of popular sovereignty could undermine as well as underpin the government of the Rump and sustain a radical politics that alienated elites, parliamentarian as much as old royalist.[23] Significantly this was an argument that was used with caution in official circles and one that faded as the regime survived the anxious first months of existence.

There is perhaps one surprising silence in the Commonwealth propaganda of 1649 and 1650. Although Nedham drew on the classical past to argue that Rome's greatness stemmed from the overthrow of kings and to expound the virtues of republican democracy, classical arguments for republican government are hard to find in the pamphlets collected by George Thomason.[24] *A Short Discourse between Monarchical and Aristocratical Government* of October 1649 cited Tacitus as evidence of the fundamental incompatibility between liberty and monarchy, but in defense of the middle way the author appealed to the Netherlands and Venice rather than to Rome.[25] While the language used to describe Roman heroes and emperors was early applied to Cromwell, classical antiquity scarcely featured in arguments for the new republic.[26] If anything, classical republican language developed in reaction to Cromwell's (as some saw it) imperialism in an English context in which the republic had died in all but name.[27]

It was in Scripture rather than the classics that Commonwealth propagandists found justification for their existence. The revealingly titled *Logical Demonstration* directly stated that both king and Parliament had appealed to God and that he had passed his sentence.[28] Scripture, claimed the author of *Monarchy No Creature of God's Making*, showed that the people should be governed by parliaments and that Providence so directed events to reestablish godly government.[29] The mutations of commonwealths, the case went, followed God's will and, fearful Englishmen were consoled, "a bright star of Providence leads us."[30] Cromwell, of course, was from the beginning the most famous spokesman of the providentialist arguments for regicide and republic.[31] These victories, he wrote to Parliament after successful campaigns in Ireland, "are seals of God's approbation of your great change of government."[32] But the argument from Providence was a dangerously malleable rhetoric and an instrument that could, as circumstances changed, be wielded by enemies as well as friends. Just as Oliver used this argument to support his Protectorate, his critics asserted that the Lord's will ordained a free commonwealth for his people.[33] And it is important to note that after Charles II's "miraculous" escape from the battle of Worcester, royalists appropriated the language of Providence to contest republic and to claim God's protection of the king.

One of the weaknesses of republican polemics was—understandably—an uncertainty about the strategies for argument and justification. Was the government after 1649, as some had it, a continuation of the true constitution after the pruning of a corrupt excrescence from the body politic? Or was the Commonwealth the outcome of a revolution effected by Providence? Were the arguments for obedience pragmatic—the need for some authority—or religious: the obligation to follow God's decree? Such dilemmas and uncertainties expressed a still greater problem that faced the regime and its apologists: the problem of language itself.

Language is inextricably interwoven with the structures of power and the culture of authority. Words derive their force from the institutions, personalities, customs they describe, but in addition words as validating terms can endow with power and construct and create authority. A successful new regime in 1649 had not only to undermine the language/power of its enemies but to speak and write a new discourse that would utter and inscribe its own authority.[34] There is some indication—and if there is anything in the suggestion it would repay further investigation—that this was a situation that Cromwell sought to address. For in his letters to Parliament in 1650 we can hear him endeavoring to write a new community, a new commonwealth into existence.[35] Avoiding the authorial *I*, Cromwell wrote as the voice of the army ("We thought fit to take the field"),[36] as the servant of the public ("your instruments," "you whom we serve"),[37] and as God's soldier against his "enemy" "for England and his people."[38] And, perhaps acknowledging the importance of these letters as language, the Rump ordered them printed and read from the pulpits as a new litany of state. But even as he struggled for a new discourse, Cromwell's speeches and letters at times resonate—"We beg of you not to own us but God alone"—with the rhetoric of warrior kings like Shakespeare's Henry V.[39] And because Cromwell always addressed his letters to Speaker William Lenthall, the wider issues of the nomenclature appropriate to the new government were left unaddressed. Petitions to "the present visible Supreme Power Assembled at Westminster" indicate that at the most fundamental level—its own name—language was a problem for the Commonwealth government.[40] And the problem permeated language and metaphor used to it, of it, and by it. In 1650 *The Government of the People of England* slipped naturally into metaphors with royal valence in discussing the vigilant physicians of the Commonwealth, as the author of *The Fundamental Right of the People* (1651) perhaps not innocently wrote of "the head and the members" that existed in every body politic.[41] Such usages were not trivial. Did the very metaphors and language of politics which kept the memory of monarchy alive imply that language itself was royal(ist)?[42] The issue is graphically illustrated in an account of the reception of the new republic's ambassadors in the United Provinces. Relieved that the Dutch government was willing to recognize the regime, the apologist for the Commonwealth in *Joyful News from Holland* celebrated the validation of its ambassadors and its authority in the "*Royal* entertainment given by the States."[43] While such language ran current (in both republics), monarchy was never erased from the perceptions of power. Throughout the republic's brief life the problem of language undermined its authority. With another change and challenge in 1653, one pamphleteer, uneasy about how to describe the regime, attempted to brush aside the problem: "What is the matter of words," he asked, "or how the Supreme Authority be called, provided the country be well-governed?"[44] But as more astute polemicists discerned, it did matter. In his *History of Britain* Milton recognized both the absence of an indigenous language to describe the new commonwealth and the need for such a language to create it. "Many civil virtues," he maintained, must "be imported into our minds from foreign writings and examples of best ages, we shall else miscarry."[45] Nedham made some effort to translate those foreign examples into English idioms before he turned "Protectorian." And in Milton's case, as Blair Worden has argued, "his reading . . . freed him from the conceptual limitations of contemporary political debate."[46] Most, however, remained citizens of an English discursive commonweal ignorant of foreign writings and the civil virtues they advanced.[47] Milton's hopes were dashed not only by his elitism. In his disdain for an "image doting rabble," he not only showed contempt for the uneducated; he exhibited his blindness to a need perhaps greater than that of language itself: the need for a new government, in an intensely visual and emblematic culture, to supplant the image of monarchy and construct effective representations of its authority.[48]

It was a need that the Rump government failed to meet. For all the power of satiric cartoons lampooning the Court in the 1620s and 1630s and the importance attached to standards and banners during the war, few visual representations of Commonwealth government were produced, whether we survey paintings, engravings (which were reaching a wide audience by mid-century), or engraved or woodcut illustrations in books or on broadsides.[49] At a time when a powerful and evocative image of the king was, as we shall see, polemically colored and widely disseminated, the near absence of a contesting representation of the Commonwealth is striking. In part the explanation lies in Puritan iconophobia: certainly the word was to be the foundation of the new commonwealth's representation as it was of its justification. But, as important, was the absence of any model for a visual representation of republic suitable for the English polity. There is evidence of the odd gesture toward its construction. In 1650 the *Government of the People of England* carried on its title page an engraving of two hands clasping a bound bundle of arrows (with individual broken arrows on the ground) to symbolize the strength that lay in the unity of the people. But neither the Thomason tracts nor a major collection of engravings yields many such positive images of republican government.[50] Artists painted and engraved godly figures or military heroes of campaigns in Ireland and Scotland— Fairfax, Essex, most of all Cromwell—but in many such cases the image was more regal than republican. In 1651 *A Perfect List of All the Victories Obtained by Oliver Cromwell* was dominated by an engraving of Oliver (figure 1) with

Figure 1. Oliver Cromwell (1651)

his left hand on his sword and his right holding a baton of command. The page who ties a sash around his waist adds to the courtly air—a regal impression reinforced by his standing between the act of Parliament constituting him Captain General and the propositions sent by Charles II to the pope.[51] Such an image, in the traditional iconography of royalty, evoked the absent king and Court. In visual representation the image of the Commonwealth never broke free of the cult of personality and dynasty, nor of the genres and forms of courtly iconography.

With seals and coins the regime took more trouble to mark the change of government. The new great seal of the Commonwealth, removing the representation of a single person who had given documents their authority, had the arms of England and Ireland (not yet conquered) on one side and a representation of the House of Commons in session on the other, with a motto that endeavored to rewrite history: as the 1651 seal has it, "in the third year of freedom by God's Blessing Restored."[52] New coins were minted depicting the St. George Cross, the harp of Erin, the palm of victory and peace, and bearing mottos in the vernacular such as "God with Us" or simply "The Commonwealth of England."[53] Such images skillfully associated Parliament with the nation and promoted the idea of an English state, forged in victory and protected by God.[54] Though these representations were important, several factors limited their effectiveness in erasing the royal image. Not least because it had many other pressing matters to handle, the Rump took some time to issue the new seal and coins.[55] Moreover, the regime never had enough bullion to replace royal coins so "at no point . . . did the output of new style coinage threaten to swamp the circulation of coin issued by the Royal mints"; because few coins of small denomination were minted, little of the new money circulated among the ordinary people.[56] Most of all the life of the new images was short. Cromwell as Protector swiftly reverted to a regal style on seals and coins—a decision that may tell us as much about the hold of a royal image (and the failure of republican forms to replace it in the imagination of the nation) as about the ambitions or preferences of Cromwell himself.[57]

THE ROYAL PRESENCE

In many ways the early years of the Commonwealth evoke the old royal Presence Chamber: the accoutrements of monarchy were there; the king was symbolically present even in his absence. Through all the discussion of his person, deeds, and trial, negative as well as positive, Charles I dominated the political discourse for some time after his death. And the issue of monarchy remained the central subject of political debate throughout the 1650s. "The King's person in England never dies says the law," the *Second Part of a Religious Demurrer* reminded readers.[58]

There can be little doubt that his manner of dying was the most popular thing Charles I ever did. The king's bravery in battle, his deportment at his trial, and his accomplished performance on the scaffold did much to erase earlier failings, and criticisms, from the national memory. As one writer claimed, even Charles's critics and enemies admired his fortitude of spirit and stand on conscience.[59] As for the people, Arise Evans believed they "knew not the sweetness of King Charles his Nature and Love to them until he declared it upon the scaffold."[60] Royalist panegyrics in 1649 proclaimed that the king would never be forgotten. The sheer quantity of royalist hagiography ensured that the king was remembered. But the most eloquent testimony to the power of the royal memory comes from those who opposed it. *The Life of King Charles, or The Pseudo Martyr Discovered,* for example, exhibits an unease that even denunciations contributed to the "frequent occasions to rake over his ashes."[61] An apologist for the Commonwealth, acknowledging the force of the axiom that the king can do no wrong, rued "how hard it hath been to make the people think the king could offend or was liable to any guilt."[62] It is revealing that the Commonwealth government did not attempt to make January 30 a commemoration day on the ritual calendar. Though literature critical of the king began to be more effective from 1652 or 1653, the memory of Charles as a virtuous martyr survived his detractors. Throughout the years of the Commonwealth, the king, as a monument of 1649 had put it, did "live in each true subject's heart."[63] That he did was largely a result of the power of the king's image in the culture and imagination of the nation.

Only recently has close attention been paid to the extraordinary rhetorical power of the *Eikon Basilike*, "the image of the king."[64] The *Eikon* towered over the literature of 1649 and the continuing debate over the authorship not only kept Charles I at the center of political discussion, it pointed up the need to deprive the king of a language that carried such authority. The king's book, however, succeeded in (re)claiming a number of validating vocabularies for the royalist cause: as one elegist put it with astute use of possessive pronouns: "Thy book is our best language."[65] Not least on account of its own appropriations of biblical language, the *Eikon* was held by many to be "next to hallowed writ and sacred page."[66] Testament to its authority, the *Eikon* spawned an industry of extracts, copies, and imitations. And it continued, seemingly unabated. As late as 1657 the *Psalterium Carolinum,* which rendered in verse and music "the devotions of His Majesty in his solitude and sufferings," was sold at the Bell in Paul's yard.[67] The *Eikon Basilike* did what Charles had foreseen his martyrdom would do: it raised the king above the polemical fray, enshrined his memory, and so denied the fruits of victory to his conquerors. As *Virtus Redeviva* was to put it, "by Thy Book thou gainst the greatest victory."[68] Milton was not the only one to appreciate the need to contest its power and royal authorship.[69] The *Eikon Alethine,* anxious about the damage the *Eikon* inflicted on the new regime, systematically analyzed the book to prove that it was neither the king's work nor even a fair reflection of his views or style, then closed with the caution that if this had not persuaded the readers, they should realize that it is "not writing but acting well that adorns a king."[70]

What most dismayed the critics of the *Eikon Basilike*, however, was what has received least scholarly attention: its visual evocation and the power of its emblematic frontispiece (figure 2). The author of *The Portraiture of Truths Most Sacred Majesty,* recognizing that "multitudes biased by affection to the late king would readily and very credulously take for current anything stamped with his effigies," asked his readers why the book so prevailed with them: "Will you be frighted by his image whose person could neither frown

Figure 2. Frontispiece to *Eikon Basilike* (1649)

nor flatter you from fidelity to your country?"[71] The answer, as he suspected, lay in the question. Or, as *The Pseudo Martyr Discovered* put it, the royalists had won the victory "by presenting this book with his picture praying on the frontispiece purposefully to catch . . . the people . . . canonizing him for a saint, and idolizing his memory for an innocent martyr."[72] The principal artifice of the impostor who compiled the *Eikon*, he continues, was that he "garnished the approaches to his collections with the king's picture in some places standing, in others kneeling, and as it were ejaculating his prayers to God and those dressed with sundry devices and mottos and all this to invite the eye if not the understanding of the silly beholder to a belief that he died an innocent martyr."[73] The pamphleteer accepted the power of the appeal to "the eye," as he acknowledged in suitably military language that it had "so much taken in the opinion of the vulgar belief and [was] esteemed to be such an impregnable rampier encircling his innocency that it hath been thought not accountable," that is, above reproach.[74] The visual power of the

Eikon, ignored by logocentric historians, was clearly obvious to contemporaries, whether they were enemies or allies. And royalists ensured that the image, like the text, continued to circulate in a number of different forms. For one, there were many copies and variants of the famous frontispiece, sold as engravings and reproduced in books and polemical tracts. Some engravings carried verse explaining the symbolism or biblical passages glossing its meaning.[75] Artists entered the disputes over authorship by depicting the king seated, writing.[76] Badges of emblems from the *Eikon* were circulated, one depicting a skull inscribed "CR" and a celestial crown of glory.[77] There was almost no visual response to these images. Though the *Eikon Alethine* reinforced its argument that the king's book was a prelatical forgery by an illustration of a curtain drawn aside to reveal a priest writing, the opportunity to mock or desecrate the image—by caricature or cartoon, for example—was not taken.[78] If Milton's contempt for images expressed a broader reluctance to engage on these terms, it was a polemical disaster. The image of the king dominated the visual culture of the Commonwealth; given the force of symbols and emblems the absent king, as we shall argue, remained a presence and power in the political culture too.

We must also recall that the *Eikon Basilike* addressed in general the nation, in particular a figure who, more than any emblem, bore the king's image: his son. The *Eikon Basilike* closed with an address to the prince; by the time of publication he was the new king. Charles II and his supporters were quick to imitate the discursive and visual polemics of the king's book in speeches, declarations, and engravings that proclaimed the succession. At Scone in 1651 a ceremony marked Charles's coronation as king of Scotland (in contrast to the uncelebrated change of government in England in 1649) and thereafter raised not only the royal profile but the threat of invasion to restore the Stuarts to the throne of England.[79]

The continuous presence, symbolic and physical, of the two kings also ensured that traditional political and religious ideas remained alive in the national consciousness and the nation's conscience. Albeit debated and contested, theories of divine right, the duty of obedience, and the sanctity of oaths survived the battles of civil war; indeed the *Eikon Basilike* and royalist propaganda successfully reclaimed the divine for Charles I and his son. Immediately after the execution, *A Serious and Faithful Representation of Ministers of the Gospel* was presented to the General Council and published to the nation. "You cannot but know," the London ministers asserted as though it was indisputable, "how fully and frequently God's word commandeth and enforceth obedience and submission to magistrates."[80] "No necessity," they continued, anticipating Commonwealth counterarguments, "can . . . dispense with lawful oaths"; to oppose princes, they concluded, was the doctrine of Jesuits, not Protestant Englishmen.[81] In a similar vein *The Rebels Looking Glass, or The Traitors Doom,* echoing James I's words that "Kings are God's vice-gerents," accused M.P.s of breaking their oath not only to the king but to God and recalled God's punishments on Corah, Absalom, Achitophel, Shimei, and Shiba for the sin of rebellion.[82] Several pamphlets took up the themes of the divine nature of monarchy, the binding religious obligation of oaths, the sin perpetrated by the regicides, and the divine judgment that awaited them. The point here is not that such arguments and beliefs were new or original: they were traditional and commonplace. What is important is that having been questioned and contested they were reinforced and reappropriated by the *Eikon Basilike* and by skillful royalist polemics and sustained throughout the short life of the Commonwealth. And they planted in the consciences of many the fear that to fall in with the new government was to sin.

Monarchy in England was not only sanctioned by Scripture, it was at the heart of the nation's law and of its history—of its identity. "I have late heard much of a Commonwealth," Robert Sprye wrote in *The Rules of Civil Government*, "but know not what it meaneth."[83] History had determined what government was. *A Brief Chronology of Great Britain* made a powerful ideological point in its one-page history from biblical times to Charles I, as did royalists who depicted the Stuarts as the thread that connected England to six hundred years of history.[84] Commonwealth writers could respond to the historical case in two ways. One was to press a different reading of history.[85] Accordingly, *The True Portraiture of the Kings of England* exposed the myth of seamless continuity to show that the succession in England had often been interrupted since Saxon times, leaving but a "broken and usurped title."[86] *The Number and Names of the Kings of England* began a catalog of the monarchs from Brutus, with brief entries starkly listing all those "killed," "beheaded," or "murdered."[87] More positively, *The Continuation of a Historical Discourse* argued that the nation had been in ancient Saxon times a commonwealth and "as I found this nation a commonwealth, so I leave it."[88] The alternative strategy was to reject history altogether. So *The Royalist Reformed* sought to sweep aside tradition by asserting simply that "the chief books about governments were written in old dark times when tyrants were the only kings."[89] History in itself was not what mattered, the author of *A Short Discourse* agreed: "Antiquity is an argument for nothing but truth and goodness."[90] History, however, could not be so easily dismissed in a seventeenth-century England where gentlemen's education, titles, houses, and lands as well as the nation's institutions were defined by it, where custom was the very basis of the common law. Because Commonwealth apologists could never overcome a feeling that history (destiny) was against them, the weapon of history remained in the hands of the royalists, who used it to effect: "Our realm is a Monarchy," the author of *The Immortality of the King* proclaimed, "successive by inherent birthright"; "*were* there an interregnum there would be a time, like the present with us, in which the statutes and common law should neither be of force or use."[91]

Neither the law nor Scripture, of course, were royalist property. Yet though the Commonwealth justified itself from readings of the Bible, the constitution, and the English past, it was royalist propaganda that was most effective when it evoked these normative languages. "The God of order," *A Dissection of All Governments* put it, "intended . . . monarchical government" and kings had linearly descended since the Conquest in fulfillment of God's will.[92] In a similar blend of legal and divine discourse, another announced: "England in her best and loudest language the law hath largely declared the sacred sovereignty of her kings."[93] Christian time, history, they were claiming, was the time of kings: "Monarchy was created with and will end with the world."[94] Such rhetoric, not least the appropriation of the apocalyptic, undercut pragmatic defenses of the new regime and made it appear an "interruption" to history itself—illegitimate and ungodly.[95] Other vocabularies and metaphors, seemingly effortlessly but often artfully employed, served to connect God, king, and nation. When the elegist of *Jeremias Redevivus* spoke of a regicide that had "widdowed our whole nation," he evoked not only the political marriage of king and realm but the mystical union of Christ and his church.[96] References to "nursing fathers" and to biblical kings bound monarchy, Scripture, and church.[97] And such representations of monarchs as divine, natural rulers, the protectors of church and law, are not only a commonplace of royalist texts; they were the recurring motif of the skillfully polemical paintings and engravings that may have reached an even wider audience.

We have glanced at the frontispiece to the *Eikon Basilike* and its importance for that text. More generally, we need to examine the images of Charles I and Charles II which both kept them in the public eye and continued the argument for restoration by different means. First, we should note the very large number of portraits of the royal family in aristocratic and country houses. For every known great master (many were sold and dispersed widely in the 1650s), there were scores of copies, "afters," and imitations in a society that still venerated the image more than the artist. There was scarcely a country house in which some image of the king or Court did not hang, daily observed by family, visitors, retainers, and servants.[98] More important, because neglected, many formed the templates of hundreds more engravings and woodcuts, a surprising number of which have survived—perhaps because they became treasured possessions. Such portraits of king and courtiers evoked memories, doubtless sustained royalist communities, and retained mystical, iconic power with plain folk.[99] (Not for nothing did radical soldiers shoot at the paintings of kings.)[100] Appearing in a wide range of contemporary books, these portraits sustained the connection of royalty with a number of cultural practices. Engravings, moreover, were often directly polemical and partisan. Sometimes the argument resided in a simple juxtaposition of image and words: the *Pious Instructions* (figure 3) found hanging

PIOUS INSTRUCTIONS,

Which were found | hanging up in a
Black Ebony Frame, | written in Gold, in
King Charles I's | C L O S E T,
soon after his Death, | *Ann. Dom.* 1648.

CHARLES.I.KING OF ENGLAND, &c.
*His Sufferings & his Death with truth proclaim :
Fr He not Glory, but the Nd... Shame*

1 Thoughts	Heavenly, Timerous, Religious.	6 Diet	Moderate, Meet, Frugal.
2 Will	Firm, Obedient, Mature.	7 Apparel	Comely, Clean, Decent.
3 Words	Few, Honeſt, Unfeigned.	8 Sport	Honeſt, Short, Seldom.
4 Works	Profitable, Godly, Pure.	9 Prayer	Brief, Faithful, Frequent.
5 Behaviour	Diſcreet, Courteous, Chearful.	10 Sleep	Temperate, Quiet, In due Time.
	Remembrance of	Death, Judgment, Puniſhment.	

In the Chariot of Wiſdom, the firſt Step is, to know thy ſelf. | *A ſpecial Reſpect of thy Ways, is to be had ; Cuſtom will make it pleaſant.*

Figure 3. *Pious Instructions*

in Charles I's closet consisted of an engraving of the king above injunctions concerning daily life, diet and apparel, thoughts ("heavenly"), prayer ("faithful," "frequent") and remembrance ("judgement");[101] Simon's engraving of the king's trial was captioned "the picture of the royal martyr . . . in the pretended High Court of Justice."[102] Often the image provided its own symbolic meaning. The frontispiece to *The Subjects Sorrow,* to take a case, depicted Charles on his deathbed above which angels held a crown, while in the distance a cross stood on a hill, associating the king's sacrifice with Christ's.[103] Other engravings represented Charles coming to the defense of the tree of religion against ruffians who lopped at its branches (figure 4) or reaching out to raise a fainting figure of Ecclesia, crowned and bearing the scepter in one hand, Magna Carta in the other.[104] In some cases the image encapsulated the symbolic presence of the king even in his absence. The engraving of Judge Jenkins, who opposed the regicide, holding Magna Carta or the map of London churches with a prominent St. Paul's bearing the device "O Theater of Royal Love," visually conjoined king, church, and law.[105] The toppled oak, with water from heaven pouring down on its stump, promised restoration.[106] And the promise was made real in the portrayals of Charles II. A simple engraving of Charles I giving thanks for the birth of his son underpinned the succession, as less subtly did that of Charles II with the sword of faith in his hand, a book with "In Verbo Tuo Spes Mea" (the words of Charles I in the *Eikon*), looking heavenward to a crown inscribed "Carolus ad Carolum."[107] As many Englishmen contemplated their sin, a complex engraving showed the Scots presenting a pistol to an armored Charles II behind whom a monster trampled Charles I. On top of the Banqueting House the figure of justice with uneven scales and broken sword associates regicide with the destruction of law, as the whole calls on the English to join the fight for the newly proclaimed king.[108] Engravings of the coronation in Scotland in themselves gave visual reinforcement to Charles II's legitimate succession;[109] Hollar's Jupiter and Minerva crowning Charles as he triumphed over the dragon of rebellion announced a new St. George, a king blessed by wisdom and the gods themselves.[110]

Royalist visual propaganda, as well as authorizing the royalist cause, lampooned the Commonwealth in graphic cartoons. In one (figure 5) the Commonwealth is depicted ruling with a standing army represented as a large dragon whose tail is a chain and which shits out excise and taxes.[111] Caricatures of ministers like Hugh Peters show him as avaricious and lascivious, while tub preachers in general fanned fear of parity in state as well as church.[112] Where the Commonwealth failed to draw on the tradition of the scatological cartoon, in defeat the royalists employed this as other visual genres to polemical effect. By 1653 the visual had almost become identified with the royal—perhaps a point made in the portrait of Charles I in armor that illustrated William Sanderson's *Graphice . . . or The Most Excellent Art of*

Figure 4. Charles I defends the tree of religion

Painting.[113] Certainly as the Cromwellian Protectorate began to take more pains over its image, its style too became more regal.

Visuals held such sway in early modern culture because symbols were held to represent truths. It is important therefore to understand that even after the execution of the king, the universe of symbols—coins, heraldic escutcheons, processions, card games, and a myriad of social practices—were inscribed with and by monarchy. In a woodcut of 1649, *The King's Last Farewell*, the royal coffin is flanked by two standard-bearers whose banners are blank, without escutcheons.[114] Can, the image leads us to ask, there be a universe of signs, meaning, without a king? And, as if by answer, *The Royal Charter* reminded readers that the throne, the crown, and the scepter stood

Figure 5. The Dragon of the Commonwealth's Standing Army

for justice, honor, and strength and that there was need for "the signs *and* the things signified."[115] To be fair, the Rumpers, not least because they were part of this culture, recognized the authority of signs. As well as a new seal, they ordered a new parliamentary mace, new civic maces, with more republican motifs, new arms for courts, naval yards, and ships, and new liveries for coachmen and watermen.[116] But the endeavor to create a new symbolic system was faltering and problematic. When the Rump planned a medal to commemorate the victory at Dunbar, Cromwell advised a picture of Parliament on the one side, the army on the other, but Parliament insisted on Cromwell's bust after his portrait by Walker.[117] As well as flattery of the Lord General, their decision also points up the difficulty of symbols detached from persons in a heraldic culture. Significantly, when Oliver became Lord Protector the arms of the Commonwealth, detached from any dynasty or family, were replaced by a new device incorporating his own escutcheon.[118]

If new symbols were hard to create, it was even more difficult to remove the old. When the Commonwealth witnessed citizens "going a whoring after the [king's] image set up in the old Exchange" they took it down and placed there the words "Exit Tyrannus Regum ultimus Anno Libertatis Angliae Restituto primo AD 1648 Jan 30."[119] Words, however, did not replace such icons; statues removed were preserved and engraved. Moreover, the site remained in the national memory as the *Royal* Exchange.[120] In the capital and in the provinces daily life involved daily encounter with the symbols of royalty. Many had purchased royal goods, from great paintings to close stools; more fingered the king's coin.[121] Aristocrats and gentlemen bore arms crossed with royal emblems, more humble folk drank or shopped in "The King's Head in The Old Bailey" and such like.[122] There, no doubt, they continued to drink the king's health, since drinking the Rump's was neither ordered nor mentioned.[123] Some played the "Royal Game at Pickett"; any who played cards could share the lament that "I lost the game for lack of a king."[124] At every game chess players were reminded that their whole purpose as a player was to protect the king.

The historian does not have to imagine the connections contemporaries made between such play and politics.[125] The *Game at Chess* used the board as a political allegory in 1623; thirty years later the author of *The Royal Game at Pickett* satirized Cromwell and his generals by means of an imagined card game. Images of monarchy continued to pervade the visual and symbolic universe. The material culture, which is also the political culture, remained a royal culture, and the royal icon continued to shape the forms and genres of social and political life.

"It is easy," the author of *A Short Discourse* wrote in 1649, "to frame the idea of a new government . . . but not so easy to alter an old one."[126] This was true not just of the institutions but of the customary practices and forms that had themselves become inextricably associated, indeed endowed, with authority. Let us consider acts and proclamations. These partook of a set visual form, with decorated initial letters and Gothic script, a standard form of address and a language peculiar to the genre. So identified did the act become with its generic markers that the new regimes found it necessary to continue the old forms. Though, as royalists protested, the Rump altered "the ancient, regal and legal style of writs" to remove oaths of allegiance, they retained the regalia of form.[127] An Act for bestowing the powers of the Lord Warden and Lord Admiral on the Council of State deployed Gothic script, a large ornamental B on "Be it enacted," angels and cornucopia, even a crowned (Tudor) rose.[128] When the Protector was invested, he was proclaimed at the familiar London landmarks—the Strand, Temple Bar, the Exchange.[129] Cromwell's own proclamations adopted a distinctly regal style and in letters patent he resumed the royal address "Right trusty and well beloved Counsellor."[130] Proclamations for fast days and commemorations (of Dunbar, for example) connect the familiar form to a continued familiar practice; the commemoration of Guy Fawkes' Day in particular could not but evoke a king, a Stuart saved by the hand of God.[131]

Whatever the Commonwealth's desire to silence the bells of some festivals and birthdays, such rituals were (and are) integral to government. Indeed, so was the culture of the aristocracy and the Court. *Honor Redevivus* was consciously royalist in stating that the king was "the true fountain from whence all these rivulets and swelling streams of honour spring"; but even a bare list of the dukes, earls, and barons in 1652 could hardly avoid mentioning the "especial grace and favour of the several kings" who had "admitted [them] into the honour of their ancestors."[132] The House of Lords may have been abolished, but the aristocracy remained—in London and on their estates—the heads of local society and patronage. Any permanent political settlement needed to embrace them and, as part of his quest for settlement, Cromwell felt it increasingly necessary to reestablish a court as a centre of display and a point of contact between Whitehall and the shires.[133]

With an aristocracy and a court went aristocratic pastimes and courtly culture. Cromwell, as John Adamson put it, may have preferred to read of the zeal of Phineas to chivalric romances and the like, but most aristocrats did not share his preference.[134] In 1653 *The Card of Courtship, or The Language of Love* published a guide to writing amorous letters and to forms of compliment that, for all Puritan objections, reminds us of the continuing symbiosis of love and politics.[135] By 1658 *The Accomplished Courtier* was advising on all modes of behavior at court, asking "Qui enim non vivit in Aula?"[136] *The Mysteries of Love and Eloquence* meanwhile addressed terms used at horse races and balls, how to woo fair ladies, "the choice of a gentleman usher," and included love poems, cavalier carpe diem songs, and (often vulgar) jests.[137] By 1658 the open revival of such practices was seen by contemporaries to presage a return to monarchy. But they had never gone away. Throughout the 1650s courtly literature was read and courtly practices pursued, all pointing to the absence at the center: the absence of the king.

The same is true of plays. It is often wrongly believed that because the public theaters were closed all experience of drama ended during the republic. Certainly the republic's opposition to theater was political as well as religious. As the prologue to the first play revived at the Cockpit in 1660 put it: "They that would have no king would have no play" for fear that the ghosts of Harries and Edwards would "still on the stage a march of glory tread" and "teach the people to despise their reign."[138] Yet, for all that, across the decade old plays were still read, new ones published, some performed with official sanction and, doubtless in aristocratic houses, many more without. In 1653, for example, five new plays by Richard Brome were published, including *The Court Beggar*.[139] Two years later *Hymen's Praeludia,* the third part of the romance *Cleopatra,* was translated and published—with a preface rich in political language.[140] William Davenant staged a number of entertainments for Cromwell, while in 1653 James Shirley, author of the famous *Triumph of Peace,* devised the masque *Cupid and Death* for the entertainment of the Portuguese ambassador.[141] Davenant, we now know, was advancing schemes for a new reformed drama that might inculcate civic virtues through "heroic representations," but he and Shirley were playwrights to the former king and, as the 1660 prologue stated, plays were about courts and kings.[142] In one case a play drew dramatic attention to a living king and dynasty: *The Nuptials of Peleus and Thetis* (1654), published in English, to be sold at the Anchor in the lower walk of the New Exchange, a masque performed at Paris by the king, the Duke of Anjou, Henrietta Maria, and the Duke of York. It closed with the lines: "By this we find adversity to be / The surest road to true felicity."[143]

Like play, procession was integral to the political culture of early modern England but because of its associations with royal festival presented a difficulty to the Commonwealth government. The new regime had to express itself ceremonially but was never certain how. The years 1649–1653 were not devoid of procession and celebration. There were several receptions for Cromwell after returns from victories in Ireland, in Scotland, and at Worcester. There were state funerals for Isaac Dorislaus, Henry Ireton, and others. But stripped of the allegories, myths, pageants, and tableaux vivants scorned by Puritan iconoclasts, such occasions became little more than military parades.[144] Still too focused on personality for staunch republicans, denuded of the mysteries and spectacles that awed the mob, the Rump celebrations failed to find "a suitable vehicle for spectacular presentation of itself."[145] Significantly, there were no Lord Mayor's shows from 1643 to 1655.[146] Joyful, grand celebration and pageant therefore remained in the public mind as regal occasions, and those who rued their end could not but be led to regret too the demise of their raison d'être. When in 1656 *London's Triumph* described and defended the mayoral pageant that did "dazzle and amaze the common eye . . . to make them know there is something more excellent in magistracy than they understand," its author linked "those ancient customs of joy and entertainment" to princes who delighted to behold them.[147]

Across a broad spectrum of genres, surviving cultural forms kept kingship at the center of political and social life and undermined the Commonwealth's establishment not just in the institutions but in the material culture of England. Time might have made the difference, but one of the reasons that the Rump government did not enjoy more time was because it failed to establish itself as the government of the nation. There was no great public outcry when Cromwell dissolved Parliament in April 1653. There is, however, something revealingly poignant about his trifling with the mace, his dismissing as a "bauble," "a jester's staff," one of the symbols of its authority to which the Commonwealth had devoted attention.[148] After 1653 the style of government as well as the constitution was to change profoundly. The Oliver Cromwell who as Lord General in the early 1650s had endeavored to write a new script for a republic became—from the start, then progressively more so—a monarchical figure. Whether he aped the king out of ambition or came to a sense that there was no real alternative image for government we do not need to judge. The question that matters is whether his appropriation of royal words and idioms erased the memory and power of monarchy itself or whether it turned men to thinking that the thing signified was as necessary as the signs.

THE PROTECTORATE

When Cromwell dissolved the Rump he knew that it had failed to establish a republic or erode the hold of kingship on the nation. As he explained in his *Declaration . . . Showing the Grounds and Reasons for the Dissolution of the Late Parliament,* the supreme authority had been entrusted to "men fearing God and of approved integrity" "hoping thereby the people might forget monarchy."[149] The experiment was an even greater failure. As one panegyrist wrote, when the Barebones assembly dissolved itself, they were saying, "Cromwell we are deserted. You only remain: the finishing of all our affairs is returned to you: on you it relies."[150] The battery of second person singular pronouns makes the point: from 1653 government by a single person was effectively reestablished in England. The year 1653 marked a major shift in the form and style of government, bringing the monarchical, albeit not the monarchy, back to center stage. By no means did all contemporaries see things this way or intend that they should be. Going through the constitution line by line, Nedham presented the Protectorate as the mean between extremes, the best of all governments. Nedham, however, throughout felt the need to make a case against the Stuarts and to press the distinctions between a monarch and a Protector.[151] That he felt such a need from the very beginning is not surprising when we read *A Declaration concerning the Government of the Three Nations* (1653).[152] For this account of Cromwell's investiture as Protector sketched a ceremony that, as we shall see, appeared familiarly regal, with oaths, a chair of state, the surrender of the seal and sword, a procession to the Banqueting House, and a grand feast.[153] Contemporaries of all political shades saw significance in the occasion. Supporters believed revealingly that the ceremony at last validated the government: "*Now* this commonwealth is become the wonder and emulation of Europe."[154] But others, the same writer admitted, "begin to breathe forth a disowning and dislike of this great and unparalleled change."[155]

The sense on all parts that a major change had taken place is manifested—what else would we expect—in the issue of nomenclature and language. Some thought the title General, as honorable to the Romans as Imperator to the Germans, the best for the Protector; others thought of him as the head of a Sanhedrin or noted that the title Protector was given to governors of Israel, like Joshua and Moses.[156] Some accepted the title was known "but little" but knew what a Protector should be.[157] Others, however, had no doubt that it was a form of kingship. The royalist *Character of a Protector* mocked the title and office as a debased monarchy:

> What's Protector, tis a stately thing
> That Apes it in the non-age of a King.

A Protector was counterfeit and insubstantial: "a brasse farthing stamped with a Crowne," the "fantastick shaddow of the Royal head."[158] But it was not only royalists who feared Cromwell had appropriated the kingship. Critics were quick to charge that "the pomp and vanity in court is now up again" and to jeer at the title.[159] Almost all who defended the Protectorate felt the need to reply to accusations that it was but an ersatz monarchy. Cromwell himself in his speeches to Parliament, drawing attention to his dislike of the hereditary principle, defended the protectoral constitution as the mean between kingship and democracy, effected by God's providence.[160] Whatever their interests or bias, however, contemporaries were right to suspect that, notwithstanding the constitution, the culture of monarchy was returning and the few tender shoots of a new republican style withering before they were even established.

From its inception the Protectorate involved the restoration of a court and courtly life. The republican *Picture of a New Courtier* sneered at the "gentlemen ushers and gentlemen waiters, the grooms of the stool, gentlemen sewers besides the fiddlers and others . . . which shine in their gold and silver."[161] As the author rightly observed, Cromwell occupied old royal palaces and enhanced them with "new rivers and ponds," enclosed parks for sport outside and employed "trumpet, harp, lute and organ" for recreation within.[162] Sweetmeats and delicious wines were served and the pomp, it was claimed, outstripped that of the king. Nor was pomp and ceremony confined within the precincts of the Protector's palaces. Days after his investiture, the City invited Cromwell to a grand feast at Grocers' Hall, to which he set forth in "great . . . pomp and magnificence."[163] When, soon after, he called his first Parliament, Cromwell rode to Westminster in a full procession, with his gentlemen "very richly clad," followed by the Captain of the Guard, Commissioners of the Seal, and members of the Council, and he entered the abbey with four maces and the sword and purse of state borne before him.[164] To celebrate the peace with the Dutch in April 1654, an elaborate entertainment was prepared by Oliver Fleming, Master of Ceremonies. The Dutch envoys having passed through the city in the Protector's coach, attended by fifty other coaches of the nobility, were greeted by trumpets in Palace Yard. The next day they were brought in similar style to the Banqueting House, "which was hung with extraordinarily rich hangings," where, after formal audience, an elaborate dinner was served which greatly impressed the visitors.[165]

On such occasions the style adopted to and by Cromwell was regal and it therefore comes as no surprise to hear contemporaries soon using royal language to discuss the Protectorate and the Protector. From the beginning Cromwell was celebrated by panegyrics that revived the traditional genres, language, and metaphors of paeans to kings. The Protector was called "Sovereign," "Prince," in Latin "Maxime Princeps." He was described as "Sun," "husband," "father of your country," "nursing father," "pilot," "universal medicine," "the body politic's doctor."[166] In one panegyric, metaphor extends to fully developed royal simile: "As the world looks gay with rays everywhere diffused over it by the Sun, so all England was exhilarated by the news of your welfare."[167] The author of *The Unparalleled Monarch* took such language and praise to its heights, applying all the standard symbols of monarchy to Cromwell: the pilot, the oak, the physician.[168] But this tract praises Cromwell in a language and style that borrows directly from royal panegyric and that makes an important departure from any language employed since 1649. Cromwell is described as a natural ruler who bore regality in his looks, a heroic prince whose very actions seemed the stuff of fable and romance. Beyond mere mortal celebration, "Methinks," the author wrote, "I see a kind of dawning of celestial beauty in his courts as if some rays and little glories of heaven were descending on earth."[169] Cromwell's glory, he continued, "cannot be fully illustrated unless I could use the sunbeams for my pencils and blend the virtues and graces with the angelical beauties," for such a man appeared to have "the general applause and acclamations of angels."[170] Such extravagant vocabulary extends far beyond the discourse of Providence to present Cromwell as a prince who carried some kind of divinity in his person—as the "anointed of God," a "saint."[171] Against the spirit of regicide and Commonwealth it mystifies (his) power, as an authority possessed of supernatural, even magical, qualities: "his sovereignty is mysterious."[172] And significantly *The Unparalleled Monarch* deploys the language of masque: an intensely symbolic, visual language and a form in which the very presence of the prince has transformative and transcendent power.

This tendency to more regal forms is seen clearly in the visual representations of Oliver Cromwell as Protector. At the simplest level this renewed vision is manifest in the larger number of paintings, miniatures, and engravings that date from the Protectorate. But it is manifest also in the style of such portraits and the use to which they were put. Interestingly and significantly, in May 1653, shortly after Cromwell had dissolved the Rump and during a period when it might have seemed logical for him to assume power, a portrait of the Lord General was put up at the Royal Exchange, with verses beneath enjoining him "Ascend these thrones . . ."[173] The visual, in other words, was associated with the regal. And for all the gestures to a different, more Roman image portraying Oliver, toga'd as a Roman military hero, for all the resistance to idealizing implied in Cromwell's famous preference for "warts and all," the images of the Protector were predominantly royal images. Indeed the Faithorne engraving of "Oliverus Britannicum Heros" depicted Cromwell mounted as St. George in a manner that appropriated for the Protector not only a traditional English royal icon but one that had been reinvested with symbolic power by Charles I himself.[174] In a still more striking and audacious appropriation of the royal, the engraver Peter Lombart reworked the plates of Van Dyck's *Charles I on Horseback with Mr. St.*

Antoine and substituted Cromwell's head for that of the king.[175] Such images not only reflected but endeavored to effect a change in the government and culture—the birth of a new kingship of, as one engraving by Faithorne was titled, "Oliverus Primus."[176] Evidently the change was approved if not directed by Cromwell himself, for in devising his seal as Protector Oliver fundamentally rejected the Commonwealth model and directly copied royal antecedents. On one side the great seal bore Oliver bare-headed and mounted, his right hand on the baton of command; behind lay the Thames and London and around the edge was written once more in Latin "Olivarius Dei Gra Reip Angliae Scotiae et Hiberniae &c Protector." On the obverse the shield topped with the imperial crown and quartered for St. George's cross, St. Andrew's cross, and the harp of Errin also carried Cromwell's family arms, the white lion, and his motto "Pax Quaeritur bello."[177] Here, in the new great seal, which became the model for others, the joining of Cromwell's with the nation's arms symbolized the return to personal, even dynastic rule. Cromwell indeed changed his crest as Protector from a demi-lion holding a halbert to the demi-lion with a diamond ring in his paw "to signify his political marriage to the imperial crown of the three kingdoms."[178] Not for nothing did Thomas Simon, chief engraver at the Mint, submit his account for work on seals executed "in imitation of Charles Stuart."[179] Coins similarly abandoned the republican style and adopted the royal. The representation of Parliament—the central image of the old commonweal—disappeared to be replaced by an imperial bust of Cromwell, the fifty-shilling piece bearing a large imperial crown "nearly exactly resembling the one used by Charles I."[180] Cromwell's medals and coins, like his sign manual with its large signature and flourish, appeared to herald the return of monarchy.

Not surprisingly contemporaries began to regard Cromwell as a king—and by descent as well as desert. In 1656 the writer of *The Unparalleled Monarch* argued that Cromwell was "the offspring of some worthy ancient descended of great and mighty kings."[181] "He is a king," he added, "and will not put on a crown."[182] Since 1653, however, Cromwell had symbolically put on a crown. And from 1653 the discourse was no more of the nature of a republic. More than historians have recognized, the political debate and political culture were dominated by the question of kingship.

Historians such as Sir Charles Firth and Roy Sherwood have seen the issue of kingship as one that came to the fore after 1656.[183] Yet we know that Cromwell and Bulstrode Whitelocke debated the importance of the title as early as 1652, and recent scholarship has shown that the question remained vital thereafter and throughout the life of the Protectorate.[184] Those who in 1653 erected the picture of Cromwell at the Royal Exchange, urging him to be king, were not alone.[185] The same year the author of *The Only Right Rule for Regulating the Laws and Liberties of the People of England* felt it necessary to counter the prevailing view that the only way to reestablish the law and government was to restore monarchy.[186] In *A True State of the Case of the Commonwealth*, Nedham, while he concentrated on defending the new regime against the charge that it reintroduced monarchy, appeared also to want to keep his options open, simultaneously reminding readers that they had fought Charles I not because he was a king but because he was a tyrant. Rather than a desire for monarchy it was "hankering after that family" he was most eager to dispel.[187] Did his ambivalence express an uncertainty in official circles, even a wavering in Cromwell's own mind as early as 1654? While the evidence does not permit a clear answer to that question, it does yield many other examples of uncertainties, anxieties, and hedged bets. The pseudonymous Cornubiensis, for example, in *The Grand Catastrophe* set out to persuade readers that "it is a gross mistake" to regard the Protectorate as "monarchical or kingly government."[188] It was not a single person but the distribution of power, he contended, that made a monarchy, and there was no reason to suspect the Protector of a desire for more power. Yet between the lines, as well as in its very title, *The Grand Catastrophe, or The Change of Government* revealed its anxieties that kingship was returning. Some, the author had heard, had drawn up a pedigree to prove Cromwell's descent from Cadwallader as part of a design to make him king. "There are those," he told Oliver, "who suspect you'll king it"—and he may well have deep down been among them as he prayed: "Let him be the shame of men . . . if he make his Protectorship a step to kingship."[189] Similarly George Wither, though he called on all to obey the new government, could not disguise his doubts about the title and its holder, nor his fears that all might return again to the monarchy against which he had "put on arms."[190] During 1654 and 1655, as the failure of parliaments signaled the broader failure to settle, royalists and others called for a return to monarchy and urged Cromwell to be the instrument for the restoration of the Stuarts.[191] During the winter of 1654 there was even a rumor circulating that Cromwell's daughter Frances might marry Charles II and so unite their families in royal rule.[192] Time—and the developing regal style of the Protector's Court—strengthened the calls from several quarters for Cromwell to accept the crown. *A Copy of a Letter Written to an Officer of the Army*, purportedly by "a true commonwealthman and no courtier" who supported the Protectorate, was frank in its admission that most desired the old government back and were happier with hereditary rule.[193] John Hall in *The True Cavalier* had no doubt that "the present government . . . is monarchy" and assured Cromwell that old royalists would find no difficulty in obeying him as a king.[194] The author of *The Unparalleled Monarch*, as the title indicated, thought Cromwell a "matchless prince" already, lacking only the "crowning" that the envy of a few had denied him.[195]

Only in the context of these debates and positions can we fully understand Parliament's offer of the crown to Cromwell in 1657. Whether Oliver himself desired it has been the subject of a contentious historical debate in his own day and ever since, one that goes to the core of Cromwell's complex personality and one we cannot hope to resolve here. But the remark in one later vindication of the Protector that Cromwell "well [knew] that the power of a king was universally understood and reverenced by the people of this nation" is helpfully suggestive.[196] Oliver had once said that he would not contest over forms of government.[197] But as his own changing rhetoric and representation hints, he may have come to see that the forms were an essential adjunct of any authority, that to continue to enact his ideals and programs he needed to adopt and adapt the familiar forms of the old (royal) government. So, leaving aside his personal ambition, Cromwell may easily have been led to the view that only a royal style enabled the settlement he so desperately sought. And though he rejected the crown, he did all to mitigate his refusal and further symbolically to portray himself as the monarch in all but name. This was dramatically apparent in the ceremony that marked Cromwell's second investiture as Lord Protector, with the power (one he had earlier denounced) now descending in his family. Into Westminster Abbey, with M.P.s and aldermen seated around "like a theatrum," marched the great officers of the household and heralds before His Highness, "richly dressed, habited with a costly mantle of estate, lined with ermines and girt with a sword of great value." With "loud acclamation" the Protector was "enthroned" and, with his son and successor standing behind, was presented with the Bible, sword, and scepter, the symbolism of each explained as they were bestowed on him. The Speaker then administered the oath, after which the trumpets sounded and the shout of the spectators proclaimed him: "Long live his Highness."[198] As Roy Sherwood long ago argued, "The only significant ingredients of a true coronation that were missing at the reinvestiture . . . were the anointing and the crowning";[199] in all other respects Cromwell was invested as a king and the objections against the office were subtly circumvented. The language of contemporaries reveals that many saw the occasion as in essence a coronation.[200] Fittingly then an anagram of 1658, greeting him as a new monarch and St. George, turned Cromwell's name into "Rule welcome Roy."[201]

Most of all, the signs that the Protector had become a king were manifested at every point in the state funeral that followed Cromwell's death in September 1658. *The Commonwealth Mercury* for November 18 describes how the actual body of his late Highness was privately removed from Whitehall to Somerset House, but there an effigy was displayed to public view. After passing through the Presence Chamber, the Privy Chamber, and the Withdrawing Chamber, all hung with black and with a chair and cloth of estate symbolizing the king's presence even in death, the mourners came to the room where lay the effigy "apparelled in a rich suit of uncut velvet, being robed first in a kirtle robe of purple velvet, laced with a rich gold lace and furred with ermine."[202] On 23 November the effigy, looking for all like the icon of a medieval king, was placed on a hearse and "vested with royal robes, a sceptre in one hand, a globe in the other and *a crown on the head.*"[203] Covered with a canopy of state "very rich," the carriage, adorned with plumes and escutcheons, conveyed the effigy "all along the way from the Strand to Westminster," attended by the household, the Council, public officers and private servants, the mayor and aldermen, judges, ambassadors, "a great part of those of the nobler sort," and heralds. As thousands watched, the procession made its slow way to Westminster Abbey, where the effigy was placed with elaborate ceremony "in a most magnificent structure built to the same form as one before had been . . . for King James, but much more stately."[204] There in the abbey too Cromwell's body was laid in the chapel of Henry VII, the resting place of kings. Not only was this the most magnificent state funeral of the century, with thousands spent on building, painting, gilding, and the hundreds of escutcheons, shields, banners, badges, and crests that decorated lying-in rooms, coaches, and streets.[205] Careful attention to detail, to the politics of places, the conjunction of escutcheons, the situation of objects (most of all the crown) and the pose and appearance of the effigy lying and standing in state, ensured that, however he had lived, Cromwell died a king. As one astute observer put it, "The senate hath deservedly adorned him dead with a crown and other regal ensigns which living he refused."[206] After 1657 few panegyrists denied him the title that the funeral rituals had at last bestowed on him. In his *Plea for the Lords,* newly revised in 1658, William Prynne did not hesitate to write of the "new king" established recently.[207] A poem of 1658 foresaw deified amid a heavenly throng "so rare a monarch"; the next year a panegyrist after hymning his virtues wrote simply: "Such was our prince."[208]

Understandably, amid the pomp and the panegyrics, from 1657 some began to hope and others to fear that the Humble Petition and Advice had increased the possibility that the Stuarts might be restored. It was said that Charles II himself believed that Cromwell had laid the foundations for restored monarchy—by which, of course, he meant Stuart monarchy.[209] As a 1659 pamphlet reminded readers, Oliver Cromwell himself had once argued against the hereditary principle and government by one, and the author added that "if first they bring in a single person and grant that, the next dispute will be whether the one family or the other has most right."[210] Despite the uncertainties, however, Richard Cromwell succeeded his father without trouble. On September 3, 1658, not only the day of Dunbar and Worcester but the same day as the accession of Richard I, Richard Cromwell was installed in a ceremony in London.[211] Much augured well for the perpetuation of the hereditary Protectorship, which some still praised as the best "midway between a monarchical and democratical," which others would readily see become a crown.[212] In the country the peaceful succession appears to have been a cause of joy. Richard was proclaimed with trumpets, feasts, running claret, bonfires and bells, salutes and cheers throughout the provincial towns of England. From many came addresses of condolence and congratulation that they had a "rightful successor," new "prince and ruler" to whom they happily rendered homage and obedience.[213] In the autumn of 1658 it might have seemed that Cromwell had at last succeeded in erasing monarchy from the canvas of politics and establishing protectoral government. But the regime was unstable and indeed destabilized, albeit from two quite contrary positions, by the question of monarchy. Because he was not quite a king, Richard could not rely on those who wished for a monarchy. Because he was too much one, he soon attracted the suspicion and opposition of sections of the army for whom his succession seemed to signal another step toward monarchy. "Have you not given way to the monarchical foundation of government," the apologists for Richard were asked, with vehement disapproval.[214] And the revival of hagiographical lives of Charles I and panegyrical characters of Charles II in 1659 appeared to answer the question in the affirmative.[215] But the demise of Richard Cromwell did not, as we know, lead smoothly to the Restoration of Charles Stuart. That it did not owed much to the powerful articulation of arguments and voices that for long had been silent or but faintly heard: the voices of the commonwealthmen and republicans, of the champions of the Good Old Cause.

THE GOOD OLD CAUSE
AND THE SURVIVAL OF REPUBLICAN DISCOURSE

The Good Old Cause has, as its name implies, a long history. Even if we do not accept a story that goes back to Saxon times, the cause was one for which many had fought in 1649. But what I wish to argue is that it was the *reaction* to the monarchism of the Protectorate that cohered and strengthened a party and position that had failed to establish itself in the early years after regicide. From his appearance as a military leader and commanding personality, Cromwell attracted the charge that he was an ambitious schemer who grasped at the crown. Royalist propaganda depicted all the regicides, and Cromwell in particular, as greedy for power.[216] But unease about Cromwell's designs was not confined to royalists. A new regime that was endeavoring to revise the government of a single person was concerned (as, ironically, was Cromwell himself) to play down the cult of personality. Cromwell felt the need to defend himself against accusations that he pursued his own ambition rather than the Good Old Cause. Yet from the time of his brutal suppression of the Levellers, there were those in the army and the nation who feared Cromwell would betray their trust; and the dissolution of the Rump in 1653 dramatically confirmed those fears. His taking the title Protector in a government in which much executive power returned to a single person threatened to surrender all the victories for which so much blood had been spilled. As an apologist for the Protectorate admitted in 1653, Cromwell drew from some quarters "a dislike of this great and unparalleled change."[217] With the investiture of "His Highness" the Lord Protector, the author of *An Honest Discourse* lamented the betrayal of all their protestations and declarations against the king: "Now proud monarchy seems to step up again as high if not higher than before."[218] Moreover the talk was of "the Protector's secret aim and drift to make himself and family great."[219]

After the dismissal of the first Protectorate Parliament, such attacks on Cromwell intensified. The developing Court and regal style of the Protectorate gave further ammunition to its opponents' fire. *The Picture of a New Courtier* deployed the old "country" dialogue between "Mr. Time Server" and "Mr. Plain Heart" to deride the pride, pomp, and extravagance of a Protector who violated the laws and cozened the people.[220] In 1656 *An Appeal from the Court to the Country,* by an M.P. excluded from the Commons, called for forceful resistance, claiming it would have been "much better . . . for us patiently to have borne the yoke of kingly government" than Cromwell's.[221] By 1656, of course, the revival of kingly government was very much in the air. And as it looked as though King Oliver I might soon be enthroned, the champions of the old commonwealth waged a powerful—and successful— campaign against it.[222] Effectively returning to the evidence of Scripture, *English Liberty and Property Asserted* demonstrated "that God did never institute or approve the office of a king" and that "this new modelled kingship" was directly opposed to the will of Christ.[223] A direct petition *To the Parliament of the Commonwealth of England* asked, "What is in your minds that ye are now about to set up a king over us again?" and it warned against reentangling the nation in a tyrannical bondage.[224] *A Narrative of the Late Parliament* railed against the ambitions of an upstart Protector and his courtiers and condemned "the hot attempts to build again the cursed ruins of kingship."[225] Cromwell's death checked what some still feared, even after his refusal of the crown: an inexorable drift toward monarchy. George Wither believed that the Lord "took hence our Protector" because Cromwell had planned to take the crown the day he died. And in *Salt upon Salt* he penned an attack on a Cromwell who had reerected the idols of monarchy he had pulled down and on "the costly puppet play" of a funeral at which his "Image" had literally been "crowned in his place."[226]

Rather than the events of 1649, it was the Protectorate, still more the threat of the kingship, that galvanized the republican cause and case. James Harrington's *Oceana,* published in the autumn of 1656, and Henry Vane's *Healing Question* of the same year are only the most famous manifestos of a republicanism now more forcefully argued and articulated.[227] From then until the very eve of restoration—and beyond—pamphleteers not only mustered a powerful argument against kingship but the case for a perpetual Commonwealth. Yet the author who argued that all who desired a monarchy should be sent to Bedlam also epitomizes the tone of desperation that sounds in many republican treatises of the late 1650s—desperation borne of a fear that, far from being erased from popular memory, consciousness, and culture, monarchy would be the choice of the people of England.[228] It is a desperation everywhere audible in that last great call to erect a republic. Milton's *Readie and Easie Way to Establish a Free Commonweal* was published in February 1660 and revised by the first week of April during elections to Parliament.[229] Following Harrington and Vane, Milton laid out a constitution for government by an elite, an aristocracy of virtue and a Sanhedrin of the godly. As for the multitude who, he knew, were now "so mad upon" a king, he despised an abject people's "perpetual bowing and cringings" to a monarch, their "deifying and adoring him" as a "demigod."[230] Ten years earlier, in *Eikonoklastes,* he had similarly derided the "image doting rabble" as he had struggled against the power of the royal image.[231] The repetition of bitter invective evidences not only Milton's frustration on the eve of the Restoration but perhaps also his own awareness that the failure of republican politics lay, as much as anything, in the failure of republican culture.

CONCLUSION

The events of January 1649 removed the head from a king and monarchy from the constitution. But the languages, still more the symbols and images of kingship remained and were not replaced by republican discourse and representations that imprinted themselves on the imagination or the culture of Englishmen. Indeed from the early 1650s a cult of personality began to develop around Cromwell and contemporaries began to apply to him the language familiarly used of a royal head of state. From 1653, when his emergent authority was officially recognized in the title "His Highness the Lord Protector," Cromwell increasingly adopted the rhetoric and style of a king. And in turn that style prompted the offer of the crown—a gesture that reflected a cultural change more than created it. Language and image were central to the exercise of power and the short-lived Commonwealth never succeeded in rewriting and redrawing them as republican vocabularies and signs. The Cromwell who sent his portrait to Queen Christina of Sweden acted not just out of ambition but from a pragmatic grasp of the power of such signs and the semiotics of power.[232]

On the eve of the offer of the kingship to Oliver, one apologist for a republic put forward an acute analysis of what had gone wrong. Despondent again at the "high and ranting discourse of personal prerogative and unbounded monarchy," the author of *The Excellency of a Free State* set out to answer why the people had not learned what true freedom was.[233] He recalled, in a passage of wonderful insight, that Gracchus had advised the Romans about "the negligence of their ancestors who when they drove out kings forgot to drive out the mysteries and inconveniences of kingly power."[234] And, he continued, "Not only the name of King but the thing King (whether in the hands of one or many) was plucked up root and branch, before ever the Romans could attain to a full establishment in their rights and freedoms."[235] Those who ousted Tarquin took care therefore "to imprint such principles in men's minds as might actuate them with an irreconcilable enmity to the former power, in so much that the very name of king became odious to the Roman people."[236] They brought up their youth to dislike royal government and Brutus "brake all the images and statues of the Tarquins and he levelled their houses with the ground that they might not remain as temptations to any ambitious spirits."[237] Cromwell instead lived in those houses, (Whitehall and Hampton Court) and was surrounded by those royal images—the paintings, tapestries, and silver of kings.[238] Because the "thing king" was never "plucked up root and branch" from the culture of England, the principles of a free commonwealth were never fully established.

If the Commonwealth failed, however, and the discourse of a republic was never dominant, that is not to argue that they were of no importance. That England had been stably governed at home and won spectacular victories abroad without a king was an ineradicable fact of history. And for all the failure of a republican image, a republican language had been created for and spoken in an indigenous English context. As a sermon delivered at Lyme Regis in 1660 was to put it, for some years the name of a commonwealth had been "beaten into us."[239] It would no longer be sufficient for a new king to stand as "silent rhetoric" for kingship: the case would have to be argued.[240] And behind all the scenes of pageant and celebration, between the lines of panegyric lauding the monarchy as historic, natural, divine, the king as Sun, head, and father, one discerns an anxiety: that more than ever the case for monarchy needs to be repeated because it cannot be assumed.[241] If the Protector had felt the need to appropriate royal rhetoric and metaphor, the royalists in 1660 thought it prudent to boast that it was "kingly government" that "incorporated the perfections of a free Commonwealth."[242] And if the royal regalia, melted in the civil war, had to be remade, that was true, to a degree, of the monarchy itself.

The memories of civil war and regicide were not erased at the Restoration. None would ever forget that the title itself could not save the king's head.[243] The trials and speeches of the regicides—of Harrison, Peters, and Scott, of Jones and Carew—were forceful reassertions of the principles of the Good Old Cause of which, they claimed, "their blood will make many more hundreds persuaded."[244] Though their enemies tried "to suppress and destroy those that did not think the king's person sacred," the republican cause, Carew prophesied, would live on.[245] The inscription "Exit Tyrannus" that had been placed where Charles I's picture stood had now been erased, "yet," Charles II was warned, "it was written with the pen of a diamond on the hearts of many thousands."[246] A republican cause and a Commonwealth party were born from 1649 and, though they failed to establish a dominant culture and government, they remained to destabilize the English royal regimes of 1660 to 1668 and, both chronologically and geographically, some beyond.

More than forging a minority party, those who did not think the king's person sacred won a bigger victory still. For all the prevailing "mysteries" of kingship that dogged the republican cause, something had imperceptibly but fundamentally changed in the 1650s. As a consequence, gradually but undoubtedly, authority—not just monarchy—became demystified, and all governments had to argue their case. The process of demystification and (provided we are wary of anachronism) rationalization is part of a bigger story and a broader change in the political culture of late Stuart England. That story—of the decline of chivalry and emblems, the demise of masque and metaphysical poetry, the changes in portraiture and prose—has yet to be told and cannot be told here. But it begins in the 1650s and continues even through the euphoria of the Restoration. Charles II touched for the king's evil, and his coronation pageant was rich in the symbols and mysteries of monarchy.[247] Yet his personal style was—consciously?—down to earth, physical and coarse. By the end of his reign he was described—even by allies—as debauched and poxed. If the king's body was slowly demystified, so too his power was plunged into the maelstrom of debate and contest, the subject of pamphlet polemic and party politics. Perhaps because he adapted so well to a new world, even shaped his rhetoric and representation to it, Charles II died peacefully in his bed and left a strong monarchy at his death. But it was never quite the old monarchy. If the English revolution never fully forged a republican culture and government, the republic nevertheless effected a radical transformation of royal culture and power.

Queen Anne Makes Provision

Toni Bowers

On October 29, 1708, Great Britain went into mourning. The occasion was the death of Prince George of Denmark, Queen Anne's husband of twenty-five years and the father of her many deceased children.[1] The prince, it is true, had been something less than a vivid presence in public life. When they noticed him at all, contemporaries invariably remarked on his indolence and lack of interest in politics, and they often implied that the royal spouse might be something of an intellectual lightweight. Swift's view of Prince George is politely representative: "The Prince being somewhat infirm and inactive, neither affected the Grandeur of a Crown, nor the Toils of Business."[2] King Charles II put it rather less tactfully: "I have tried him, drunk and sober," Charles is said to have declared, "but . . . there was nothing in him."[3] Nevertheless, the marriage between Queen Anne and Prince George had been a harmonious one, and contemporaries unanimously praised theirs as a model companionate marriage.[4] As Anne's biographer observes, the queen "remain[ed] blindly devoted to her husband throughout their married life" and grieved long and heartily over his death.[5] Her suffering did not, however, prevent her from making one highly controversial response to George's death: in one of her first official acts as royal widow, Anne ordered removed from the collect for the Anglican service for March 8 these words: "And that these blessings may continue to after ages, make the queen, we pray thee, a happy mother of children, who . . . may happily succeed her in the government of these kingdoms."[6]

The excision seems reasonable enough, under the circumstances. Not only had she lost her beloved Prince George, but by 1708 Queen Anne was forty-three years old. Her health, never good, was visibly deteriorating. Besides, as the veteran of seventeen pregnancies (once with twins), Anne had already done more than her duty by way of attempting to provide the nation with heirs. That not one of Anne's children was alive when she assumed the throne in 1702 was tragic, to be sure, but by the time of Prince George's death there was little reason to think the situation might change. Nevertheless, Parliament objected to the queen's decision to remove the prayer for heirs from the prayerbook. The House of Commons went so far as to request "that your Majesty would not so far indulge your just Grief, as to decline the Thoughts of a second Marriage. This would be an unspeakable Joy to your People, who would join their most fervent Prayers to Almighty God, to bless your Majesty with royal Issue."[7]

Anne's reply at this juncture silenced Parliament forever on the issue of remarriage. "The provision I have made for the Protestant Succession," she wrote, "will always be a proof, how much I have at my heart the future happiness of the kingdom. The subject of this Address is of such a nature, that I am persuaded you do not expect a particular Answer."[8] It is a strangely opaque reply: the queen responds by refusing to respond, and in the process employs oddly self-canceling language. What "provision," after all, *had* Queen Anne made for the succession? True, measures had been taken to ensure Protestant succession on the queen's death. The Act of Succession, passed under William III in 1701, named the electress Sophia of Hanover and her sons as heirs after Anne; and as recently as 1706 the Regency Act had established a council of officers who after the queen's death would exercise sovereignty until the arrival of the Hanoverian successor. But the Act of Succession had been William's project, not Anne's, and the Regency Act was a compromise measure designed largely to placate the queen's fury at those who wished to invite the designated heir to reside in England even before Anne's death. In neither case might Queen Anne be credited with active "provision" for the succession. And in what was most important—the production of heirs—Anne had failed resoundingly. Under such circumstances, it is surprising that the queen should have called attention to "the provision I have made for the Protestant Succession."

Faced with Queen Anne's odd reply to Parliament's request that she remarry, commentators have tended to look for ways to excuse her. Anne, we are reminded, was devastated over the loss of Prince George. And Parliament's timing was tactless, to say no more: the brutal haste of the request did not escape the notice of the Augustan popular press, where broadsides quickly appeared bearing such titles as "The Hasty Widow, or the Sooner the Better." But there is more to Anne's response than the tender feelings of a bereaved wife and more to Parliament's hurry than insensitivity to those feelings. No part of the exchange, after all—neither the words Queen Anne wanted to delete from the collect, Parliament's request, nor the Queen's reply to Parliament—is primarily concerned with Anne as a *wife*. More fundamentally—and more preposterously—the "subject of the address" is the aging queen's potential to be a *mother*. Though everyone knew the queen's maternal history and though there was no realistic possibility that Anne might at such a late date be physically capable of bearing a child, Parliament pretended to ask for an heir; Anne, in her grief, refused to pretend.

Why, we might ask, should Parliament have engaged in such a pretense at all? And why should Queen Anne have responded with this particular mixture of ambiguity and acerbity? The first question need not puzzle us for long. Ever since the 1701 Act of Succession (when William's government officially despaired that Anne, then Princess of Denmark, would ever provide a healthy heir), right up until George's death in 1708, Tory factions in Parliament had been trying to bring to London a representative of the house of Hanover. Supporters of "the invitation," as this initiative was called, argued that a Hanoverian presence would preempt Jacobite pretensions and ensure a seamless transition at Queen Anne's death. The queen, after all, was not getting any younger; she seemed to be always unwell; and the Hanoverian electress expressed herself willing, even eager, to reside in London.[9] But at the same time it was no secret that the presence of a successor would humiliate the childless queen, and many of the disaffected Tories who advanced the invitation as an obvious, necessary step would have been only too delighted for such an opportunity. Anne herself felt strongly that a Hanoverian presence would fatally undermine her always precarious authority. According to the earl of Dartmouth, the queen said that "whoever proposed bringing over her successor in her lifetime, did it with a design to depose her."[10]

As it happened, Whig leaders were able to exploit the queen's anxiety over the invitation as well as her disgust with the Tories who promoted it. Making much of their loyalty in hopes of obtaining power, the Whigs engineered and passed the Regency Act in February 1706, specifying that on the queen's death a committee of seven officers of state (and certain others to be named by the Hanoverian successor) would govern until the successor arrived in Britain.[11] The hope was that this measure might both mollify the queen and put to rest Protestant worries about the succession; but such hope was unrealistically optimistic.[12] For the matter of the invitation by no means went away after 1706. Pamphlets almost immediately appeared arguing that any opposition to the invitation necessarily revealed Jacobite sympathies, and for the rest of her life the queen was suspected of supporting the "Pretender."[13] Indeed, bitter division over the matter of the invitation continued until the very last month of the queen's life.

It is important to see Parliament's 1708 request that the widowed queen remarry as part of this protracted (and for Anne very painful) debate. The renewal of the issue in the fall of 1708 put the queen in a particularly difficult position, as the duke of Marlborough understood and observed to his wife Sarah in February of 1709: "As to the adress made to the Queen to lay aside grief and to think of marrying, [it] is a very good antidote against the invitation for this sessions, but may be a strong argument for it at another time."[14] The parliamentary request, in other words, might temporarily slow down efforts to install a Hanoverian representative, but no matter how Anne responded she could not hope to bring such efforts to an end. Her refusal to entertain the idea of remarriage would certainly backfire on her, enhancing the perceived urgency of the invitation and fueling rumors of the Queen's Jacobitism. Yet acquiescence to Parliament's disingenuous proposal could only result in yet more humiliation for the queen, who would in effect be publicly offering herself as a potential childbearer—though aging, ailing, and famous throughout Europe for her inability to bear healthy children.

In short, in the eyes of many of her subjects, Anne's "provision" for the Protestant succession was anything but the manifest, indubitable accomplishment the queen purported to consider it. On the contrary, it was a gaping absence, a festering wound, the site of perennial contention and anxiety. Some past act of "provision," the queen's statement implies, "proves" that she has the nation's best interests "at my heart," and relieves her of responsibility for whatever undesirable events might follow her reign, including (as many feared) invasion, civil war, the imposition of Catholicism, and French annexation. She leaves it up to her auditors to define what that "provision" might have entailed and to decide where, in case of the worst, responsibility might actually lie.

"MAKING PROVISION" IN QUEEN ANNE'S ENGLAND

Anne's language, though in one sense disturbingly and deliberately vague, also carried very specific resonances for her original auditors. For in Augustan England "making provision" was a precise, legally operative term. It denoted an expectant mother's preparation of childbed linen before delivery, an action assumed to indicate maternal affection and often successfully cited in defense of mothers prosecuted for infanticide. Transcripts of Old Bailey sessions throughout the early eighteenth century show juries relying heavily on the demonstration that accused mothers did (or did not) lay aside childbed linen before delivery, and handing down sentences accordingly.[15] Indeed, throughout Queen Anne's reign, when physical violence was not clearly in evidence, the so-called "benefit-of-linen" argument virtually guaranteed acquittal for mothers accused of the murder of newborns.[16]

The "benefit-of-linen" defense was not only likely to clear a woman of the charge of infanticide, it also helped to strengthen her defense against the related supposition of prostitution. In Augustan England unmarried mothers accused of infanticide were routinely assumed to be prostitutes.[17] But the fact that an accused woman had "made provision" militated against this possibility: a whore, it was reasoned, would not lavish money on the rituals of lying-in, and a woman able to lay aside linen was likely to have a husband somewhere paying the bill. So a mother who could demonstrate that she had "made provision" for a deceased child had gone a long way toward establishing both her innocence of the child's fate and her own social legitimacy.

So convinced was Augustan society by the benefit-of-linen argument, in fact, that in 1728 Defoe chastised his contemporaries for their gullibility in this particular. "I wonder," Defoe wrote,

> [that] so many Men of Sense, as have been on the Jury, have been so often impos'd upon by the stale Pretence of a Scrap or two of Child-Bed Linnen being found in the Murderer's box, &c., when alas! perhaps it was ne'er put there till after the Murder was commited; or if it was, but with a view of saving themselves by that devilish Precaution; for so many have been acquitted on that Pretence, that 'tis but too common a Thing to provide Child-Bed Linnen beforehand for a poor Innocent Babe they are determined to murder.[18]

A few years earlier, Defoe had set the same critique into motion when his Moll Flanders laid aside linen for a child she would shortly abandon, fully expecting it to be misused or murdered. To be sure, the episode has its ambiguities: Moll is neither unequivocally well intentioned nor wholly corrupt.[19] But no matter how we interpret Moll Flanders's duplicitous motives, Defoe is pointing out that "making provision" does not *necessarily* indicate maternal virtue, an argument he clearly thought worth making in a day when everyone from the neighborhood gossip to the city magistrate seemed to think it did.[20]

So "making provision" had very specific meanings and functions in Queen Anne's day. In defending herself against Parliament's request that she again embark on marriage and childbearing, Anne implicitly cast herself as a well-meaning mother who had already made adequate provision for her "offspring," the Protestant succession; should there be a miscarriage or an accident at delivery—as some hoped and many feared—it would not be the queen's fault. Yet Anne's claim to have "made provision" for the succession is subject to a much darker interpretation. Though many of her contemporaries trusted the queen's sincerity when she declared herself eager to facilitate the smooth delivery of the Hanoverian succession, many others did not. These latter saw a cynical and scheming Queen Anne—one of Defoe's evil mothers who make provision "for a poor innocent babe they are determined to murder." A number of pamphlets from the last years of Anne's reign complain of political "miscarriages" and hint that these are not entirely accidental.[21] "Making provision," apparently the touchstone of queenly (as maternal) rectitude, turns out to be subject to contradictory interpretations, not all the reliable "proof" of good intentions that Queen Anne claimed it was.

MATERNAL SYMBOLISM AND POLITICAL AUTHORITY

What is perhaps most interesting about the exchange between Queen Anne and Parliament in 1708, however, is that when faced with Parliament's hostile and cynical suggestion that she remarry and bear children, the queen took refuge, by implication at least, in the trope of motherhood. This is worthy of notice, first of all, because motherhood is precisely what Anne is resisting in her response. And it becomes considerably more remarkable when we recall that the representation of herself as mother was the central image Anne had relied on throughout her career at moments when she most needed to bolster her authority, and that by 1708 that representation had become intensely problematic, even embarrassing.

Anne's implicit self-presentation in 1708 as a wrongly accused, provident mother must have called to her listeners' minds two distinct periods in her public career, each of which we shall examine in detail. The first period lasted from her marriage in 1683 until the death of her son William, Duke of Gloucester, in 1700. Princess Anne began this period as a fertile young wife and controversial heir apparent; she consciously traded on her body's potential for childbearing to maintain political viability. But by the turn of the century Anne had been bitterly disappointed on many fronts and had undergone a dramatic physical decline: by the time she ascended the throne in 1702, she had become a virtual invalid, far from the vigorous breeder of earlier days. The second period of Queen Anne's public career began at her accession in 1702 and continued until her death. During this time Anne attempted to build political authority from symbolic, rather than physical, maternity, with unfortunate results. Both early and late, then, Anne relied on maternal self-representation as her primary means of building and maintaining political power. What changed at the turn of the century was the quality of the maternity Anne claimed as well as the tone of her maternal self-representations. At the beginning of her career Anne was on the offensive, determined to produce a Protestant heir; she ended her reign isolated and exhausted, deeply embittered against those she had formerly trusted, profoundly disappointed in her effort to reshape physical failure into symbolic success.

During the first part of Anne's public career, motherhood proved a powerful political tool indeed. For many years "the teeming Princess of *Denmark*," as she was called, enjoyed fame across Europe as the Protestant Stuart whose offspring would effectively eliminate Jacobite pretensions.[22] Anne's political authority was routinely represented in maternal terms at this time, as we see in a portrait from 1688 (figure 6). The political nature

Figure 6. Anne of Denmark (1688)

of Anne's maternity and the public authority it provided are evident in the captions to this portrait, where Anne proclaims herself (in faulty French) one who would be either queen or the mother of a king—significantly, it does not seem to matter which.[23] The declamatory Dutch at the bottom of the portrait ("O Virtue and Courage Reward My Hope and Crown It with Glory"[24]) reinforces the message that Anne's motherhood was a public phenomenon of international importance, at least as great a political force as her own potential to be queen.

Princess Anne, moreover, clearly understood motherhood to be her ticket to political authority, and she exploited the political potential of her maternal body at every opportunity.[25] During 1687, when Anne wished to avoid a potentially damaging association with her unpopular father without openly offending him, she excused herself from attending James's court by pleading problems related to pregnancy.[26] In 1688 she again used pregnancy for political ends, this time to avoid hearing the report of the council James appointed to verify the legitimacy of the newborn James Edward Stuart (later known as the Pretender[27]). King James himself recounted this incident in his memoirs: "On the fifteenth [of October 1688] the prince of Wales was named. His birth was proved, in a council extraordinary, on the twenty-second. The princess Anne waved [*sic*] being at it; pretending danger in coming abroad, being with child."[28] "None believed that [pregnancy] to be the true reason," Bishop Gilbert Burnet informs us, "so it was looked on as a colour that shewed she did not believe" in the child's legitimacy.[29] Throughout that autumn Anne continued to plead pregnancy to avoid appearing in public or seeing her father; but in December, when Princess Anne and Prince George had safely defected to the Prince of Orange, George revealed to Clarendon that Anne had not been pregnant at all. "Good God bless us!" Clarendon wrote in his diary, "Nothing but lying and dissimulation in the world."[30]

Anne's maternal stratagems continued under William and Mary. When William maneuvered to cashier Sarah Churchill as Anne's principal attendant, the princess used her current pregnancy to create public sympathy and to put reciprocal pressure on the childless king and queen.[31] Even as late as 1701, when the Act of Settlement had been passed and William (by then ruling alone) wanted to invite a Hanoverian representative to reside in England, Anne prevented the invitation "by falsely informing the king that she was again pregnant."[32] It was no secret to Princess Anne, in other words, that political leverage lay in her ability to reproduce and in the secrets and mysteries surrounding pregnancy. Throughout the treacherous years surrounding the Glorious Revolution, through the joint reign of William and Mary, and then during seven years under William (who always remained hostile to his sister-in-law, jealous of her superior hereditary claim to the throne) Anne managed to retain her position as heiress-apparent by means of carefully timed exploitations of the political possibilities of physical motherhood.

Anne's efforts were strengthened immeasurably on July 24, 1689, when she gave birth to a son, William Henry (later Duke of Gloucester) to widespread Protestant rejoicing. The child's birth, coming as it did on the heels of the so-called Glorious Revolution, when parliamentary factions ousted James and settled the throne on William and Mary, was viewed by many as an auspicious sign of God's blessing on that unprecedented and profoundly controversial event. Little William's relative health promised a smooth Protestant succession in the Stuart line, seemed to vindicate the revolution, and—not least—dramatically enhanced Princess Anne's political importance *as a mother* (figure 7). Decades later Thomas Salmon would

Figure 7. Anne of Denmark with the Duke of Gloucester

recall not only that the nation reached consensus on the revolution settlement after Gloucester's birth but also that Anne's many years of maternal
promise seemed finally to have paid off. "Upon the Birth of a Son," Salmon
wrote, "the Interest of the Princess of *Denmark* seemed to be much
advanced, and all the World began to make their Court that Way, how much
soever they had slighted her before."[33]

Gradually it became clear, however, that, as one contemporary put it,
"though there was a child born every year for many years, yet they have all
died: So that the fruitfullest marriage that has been known in our age, has
been fatally blasted as to the effect of it."[34] In 1700 the "fatal blast" of royal
bereavement was felt especially keenly. For in that year the nation lost
Gloucester, always the most promising and now the last remaining of Anne's

children, just five days after his eleventh birthday. Gloucester's birth in 1689 had strengthened both his mother's political importance and Whiggish justifications for the Glorious Revolution; when the child died he took with him the confidence of many in his mother's right to reign and a large part of her public authority. Two years later, when Anne at last assumed the throne, she did so as a paradoxical and unprecedented figure: a "childless parent"[35] chronically ill from almost continuous childbearing and a disputed heir whose authority rested on a betrayed father and a failed maternal body.

Obviously, a powerful self-representation was called for. It is therefore striking that at her accession Anne chose not to *replace* maternal imagery but to *redefine* it as a symbolic rather than a literal undertaking. She cast herself not as the physical mother of a particular heir (now an untenable image) but as the symbolic mother of the entire nation. The goal, apparently, was to exploit the authority of maternal figuration while minimizing any connection between that authority and the queen's maternal failure. Accordingly, as early as her coronation in 1702—her first chance to represent herself publicly as queen—Anne adopted symbolic motherhood as the privileged sign of royal legitimacy and power, choosing for the text of the coronation sermon Isaiah 49:23: "Kings shall be thy nursing fathers, and their queens thy nursing mothers."

In attempting to tap the political and iconographic potential of symbolic motherhood, Anne consciously followed the example of Elizabeth I, who from the first days of her reign had exploited the power of maternal symbolism. At her accession Elizabeth had made it clear immediately that she did not wish to marry and have children;[36] she deliberately sublimated relational intimacy, including maternal experience, into her public relationship with her people, as she told her first Parliament on February 4, 1559.

> The House of Commons addressed the Queen in a very dutiful manner, and represented to her, how necessary it was for the happiness of the Nation, that she should think of marrying. The Queen graciously thanked the Commons, and . . . added, that by the Ceremony of her Inauguration, she was married to her People, and her Subjects were to her instead of Children: They would not want a Successor when she died, and for her part, she would be well contented, that the Marble should tell Posterity, HERE LIES A QUEEN THAT REIGNED SO LONG, AND LIVED AND DIED A VIRGIN.[37]

When nagged by her second Parliament to marry, Elizabeth instead intensified her symbolic maternal image: "I assure yow all that though after my death yow may have many stepdames, yet shall yow never have any, a more naturall mother, than I meane to be unto yow all."[38]

Anne was keenly aware of the many similarities between Elizabeth's situation on her accession in 1558 and Anne's own delicate position when she assumed the throne in 1702. Elizabeth was unquestionably the daughter of Henry VIII, but her legitimacy had been undermined by her maternal inheritance: Henry had divorced and then executed her mother, Anne Boleyn—whose position had been controversial in any case during her brief tenure as Henry's queen—and had drawn up a will stating that his heirs in the Suffolk line should take precedence over Anne Boleyn's daughters. When Elizabeth came to the throne, therefore, she was haunted by a contradictory legacy much like Queen Anne's: her right to rule was disputed by her own father, from whom that right also derived. And crucially, Elizabeth was also childless. An eighteenth-century chronicler's description of Elizabeth's precarious position might well have been written with Anne also in mind: "Her Right to the Crown was always contested openly or tacitly . . . the Papists in general considering her but as a Queen *de facto,* believed they might with a safe Conscience assist in dethroning her."[39]

Faced with problems very like those Elizabeth had surmounted—especially her contestable right to rule and her childlessness—Anne cannily modeled both her iconography and her policy on that of the Virgin Queen. The costume Anne wore for her own first address to Parliament on March 11, 1702, for instance, precisely reproduced a famous ensemble worn by Elizabeth,[40] and before the end of the first year of her reign Anne had adopted Elizabeth's motto (adopted from her mother, Anne Boleyn), *semper eadem:* "Always the same."[41] As late as 1713 Anne wrote to England's Dutch allies that "she had ever in her Eye the Example and wise Conduct of that great Queen her Predecessor," and she said she considered her emulation of Elizabeth to be "one of the greatest Glories of her Reign."[42] In the year of her death Anne resisted a proposed bill that would have limited religious toleration, arguing that it had always been "the Glory of her Reign" to follow "the Steps of Queen *Elizabeth.*"[43] Like Elizabeth, Anne declared herself the mother of the nation rather than of birth children and she effaced as much as possible her own complicated and tenuous place in patriarchal inheritance.

In this way Queen Anne attempted to use symbolic maternity as Elizabeth had used it, as an escape from a legitimation crisis, a way of stepping out (or appearing to step out) of the issue of patriarchal inheritance altogether to create a kind of alternate matriarchal order instead. The move had worked for Elizabeth, at least in the short term and as far as her own retention of power was concerned; but it did not work for Anne. A combination of problems made it difficult for Queen Anne to bolster her authority by means of maternal symbolism.[44]

For one thing, there were not only striking similarities but also great differences between Anne's situation and Elizabeth's, differences that Anne underestimated to her cost. Take the crucial problem childlessness, for instance. Elizabeth repeatedly made it clear that she wanted to live single and chaste: "I hapelie chose *this kynde of life* in which I yet lyve," she explained, not for the last time, in the 1559 speech we have already considered.[45] When Elizabeth said "her Subjects were to her instead of Children," "instead of" carried a message of choice, the willed exclusion of one option (physical motherhood) in favor of another (symbolic motherhood).[46] So Elizabeth's maternity was always *designedly* symbolic—as indeed was Elizabeth's entire persona: she was to a great extent an icon, a sign of the nation.[47] She made what might have been her most vulnerable spot—motherhood—work in her own interests by transforming it from physical absence to symbolic presence. It was a strategy calculated to outwit patriarchy on its own ground, so to speak, by magnifying rather than denying or ignoring the importance of maternity for queenly authority while redefining maternity as a symbolic matter separate from Elizabeth's particular female body.

But everyone knew that for Anne symbolic maternity was not a first choice but a last resort. Anne's public persona, unlike Elizabeth's, had always been constituted in maternal terms. From her birth Anne's life had held significance—not only for others but for Anne herself—largely because she might produce an heir. By the time of her accession, however, Anne's physical motherhood was a public failure. The figure of symbolic motherhood, a personal innovation and an act of resistance for the twenty-five-year-old Elizabeth, had become the sign of weary defeat for the middle-aged Anne. Maternal symbolism ironically accentuated Anne's unwilling childlessness and so undermined, instead of bolstering, her authority as monarch.

It may also be that Elizabeth was able to exploit figural motherhood successfully because certain symbolic resonances were available to her which were not available to Anne. Critic Margaret Homans has argued that women have traditionally been identified with the debased literal—the body and its needs, the mundane routines of housekeeping, and literal meaning—while men are traditionally associated with more highly valued figural constructions, especially metaphorical language. The "differential valuations of literal and figurative," Homans says, have implications for "the way our culture constructs masculinity and femininity." For "to take something literally is to get it wrong, while to have a figurative understanding of something is the correct intellectual stance. [The masculine] symbolic order, both the legal system and language, depends on the identification of the woman with the literal, and then on the denial that the literal has any connection with masculine figurations."[48] Homans's arguments cannot be applied equivalently to all historical periods. They are far less relevant to Elizabethan England, when images of the Virgin and the queen *were* strongly associated with the figural, than to Augustan England, when the kinds of gendered associations Homans describes had begun to take hold in British imaginations, delimiting representational and interpretive possibilities for both women and men. Indeed, this historical distinction is precisely the point: keeping it in mind, we can follow Homans's insights to a better understanding of Anne's representational predicament.

As we have seen, Anne initially tried to deploy literal motherhood as a means toward political power, and when that strategy failed she tried to exploit the power of maternal figuration instead. But in fact *both* procedures were doomed. To insist so strenuously on physically bearing a child was, for Anne, "to get it wrong"—not only because she proved unable to bear healthy children but because literal motherhood, even if it had lasted, would always have been already coopted by patriarchy. The point of Anne's maternity, after all, was the continuation of a Protestant Stuart line to forestall the Jacobite menace; her motherhood was not fundamentally "about" Anne at all. Indeed, the greatest fiction surrounding Anne's maternal experience may well have been the idea that successful physical motherhood really would have engendered political authority for Anne or freed her from the reductions and exploitations of androcentric culture. Ironically enough, it was perhaps only because she never was literally a maternal queen that Anne was able to cherish the cold comfort that things might have been different. Her failure to sustain heirs, in other words, did not in any simple sense *cause* Queen Anne's failure to construct and maintain royal authority in her female person; the more fundamental problem was the imbeddedness of all maternal authority—literal or figurative, queenly or not—in gendered (that is, politicized) systems of meaning.[49]

Unlike Anne, Elizabeth had shrewdly recognized maternity to be not an end in itself but one of many signs pointing toward the real signified: her own power. As a result, she was able to keep everyone guessing. Against all expectations, for instance, Elizabeth chose not to attempt a vindication of her mother, and so she avoided resuscitating the issue of her own much-contested maternal inheritance. And Elizabeth was cunning enough to shift the grounds of her self-representation, manipulating signals, playing off popular hopes. When figural maternity no longer served her purposes, she manipulated other images instead.[50] Anne more naively chose maternal self-representation and stuck to it. And perhaps because of her many maternal losses, Anne—unlike Elizabeth—saw literal and symbolic maternity as distinct, mutually exclusive options. (This belief may have partly fueled her refusal in 1708 to cooperate with Parliament's pretenses about her maternal potential.) Anne seems to have realized too late what Elizabeth knew all along: that maternity's relation to political authority was neither inevitable nor consistent, and that neither symbolic nor physical motherhood would ever be enough.

Any symbol, of course, is subject to multifarious, even anarchic deployments, and no monarch engaging in symbolic self-representation can expect fully to control the resonances of the symbols she selects. Queen Anne's use of symbolism, however, and her particular choice of maternal symbolism, were especially vulnerable to exploitation by enemies. For representational habits had undergone considerable change between Elizabeth's first parliamentary address in 1559 and Anne's coronation in 1702. Elizabeth was able to exploit allegories, analogies, and symbols in her effort to create her own political legitimacy and authority because those forms carried extraordinary and widely perceived representational (that is, political) power. Further, though there were certainly points of epistemological strain throughout the sixteenth and seventeenth centuries, Elizabeth could still assume that many of her subjects saw the universe as a system of meaningful and interrelated signs. This sign system guaranteed ontological significance to empirical experience and practical political importance to ideational forms; and it made possible Elizabeth's exploitation of the sign of motherhood without imposing on her the burden of mimetic accuracy.[51]

By the time of Anne's reign the cultural assumptions that made Elizabeth's self-representations powerful had undergone significant revision. Indeed, it is not too much to say that Anne assumed the throne not only in the wake of political revolution but in the midst of profound revolutions of sensibility, cultural direction, and representational possibility. At the end of Elizabeth's lifetime there was still consensus on "the essential and god-given integrity of words and things,"[52] but by 1700 rejection of an organic and necessary connection between words and the things they stand for had become a familiar if still somewhat unorthodox gesture with far-reaching epistemological and political repercussions.[53] The natural world was no longer a reliable indicator of a supernatural world, any more than the monarch was assumed to be a sublunary version of God. Symbols could no longer be relied on to signify in predictable (if not entirely univocal) ways or to evoke reliable responses. Communication and interpretation became problematic activities, and effective representation increasingly came to be understood more as a matter of faithfulness to materially verifiable, empirical detail than as the deployment of a set of reliably decipherable symbols.

Such change, of course, was hardly straightforward. In fact, the seventeenth century's new emphasis on representational and interpretive instability was not really a single change at all but many related developments— gradual, multiple, and in all likelihood scarcely observable shifts in purpose and emphasis, shifts in which various genres, speakers, and audiences shared unevenly. Elizabeth was never able to exploit symbolic codes for political ends *without* being vulnerable to constructions other than those she desired any more than Anne was *entirely* unable to use received symbols to construct and bolster her political authority. But in comparative terms Elizabeth was better positioned than Anne successfully to create political authority from symbolic self-representation.

Not only had symbolic representation itself become newly problematic. In addition, the particular symbol of Anne adopted—that of the nation's figural mother—was an especially unstable sign: maternal authority per se was being vigorously contested throughout Anne's reign. In novels, visual art, conduct literature, and printed ephemera of all kinds, questions about maternal agency and the scope of maternal authority took center stage in the early eighteenth century as never before. The maternal became a discursive obsession, a crucial site on which battles over agency and authority were fought. And the struggle to define maternal rectitude and responsibility was critical to the broader project of constructing political authority in Augustan England; it participated in Britain's urgent need to define the changed relationships of authority and subordination that had emerged in the wake of the tumultuous seventeenth century. So when Anne doggedly stuck to maternal symbolism as the means for representing her political authority, she built her house on shifting sand.[54]

When Elizabeth represented herself as the nation's symbolic mother, she benefited from the powerful influence that Marian imagery still held in English culture.[55] But for Anne's subjects the "ritual resource" of Marian mythology[56] was less important—and less appealing—than for Elizabeth's; what traces did remain may have done more to undermine than to bolster the authority of a queen who represented herself as a symbolic mother. Besides, even if Marian symbolism *had* carried the positive charge in Anne's day that it did in the sixteenth century, the attributes of the maternal icon par excellence simply could not have worked for Anne as they did for Elizabeth. Anne could figure herself, with some difficulty and limited success, as queen-mother; but by no means could a woman who had been pregnant seventeen times represent herself as a *virgin* queen-mother. Anne's iconography was like Elizabeth's in many of its features, often deliberately so; but it necessarily lacked the element of divine mystery, the unique, magical immanence of the "virgin scepter-swaying mother" that Elizabeth's all-encompassing imagery had been able to recoup for Protestantism and for queenly authority.[57]

For all these reasons, though Queen Anne carefully emulated Elizabeth's successful self-representation as symbolic national mother, she was never able to forge political authority from that representation. Anne presided over a culture in which relations of authority and reciprocity were undergoing critical revision at every level; and although she gained much from those revisions, Anne also misunderstood them.[58] For "the Second Elizabeth,"[59] symbolic maternity failed to generate political power. Indeed, Anne's choice of maternal imagery as the representation of her royal authority turned out to be not only ineffective but actually damaging to the queen's interests. For by the time of the exchange between Anne and her Parliament in 1708 with which we began, the figure of maternal monarch had become less an enabling and life-giving image than a tragic specter: in Anne's England, after all, any woman reduced to pleading that she had "made provision" was by definition the accused mother of a dead child.

CHILDLESS QUEEN AS PROVIDENT MOTHER

"The subject of this Address is of such a nature," the queen further declared to Parliament in 1708, "that I am persuaded you do not expect a particular Answer." On the surface Anne's meaning is straightforward enough: her grief for Prince George is none of Parliament's business. Surely they do not really expect serious consideration of such a request at such a time; surely this request is a political gesture, not a serious recommendation.

Indeed, that may well have been the problem: that Parliament was merely making a political statement may have been precisely the issue that provoked the queen. For in Anne's day "particular" meant, among other things, "private" and "personal," the opposite of "public." What was *particular* in Augustan England concerned only one individual, uniquely; hence Steele's complaint in 1709, one year after Anne's exchange with Parliament: "We live in an Age wherein Vice is very general, and Virtue very particular."[60] When Queen Anne decided that Parliament didn't really want a "particular" answer, she not only registered dissatisfaction with the transgression of her privacy but at the same time, paradoxically, objected that the request was *not particular enough.* Though it demanded access to and exposure of the queen's most private feelings, Parliament's petition was not really personal. On the contrary, it constituted a well-considered move on the public chessboard of Augustan politics—strategic, indifferent, expedient.

In her desire for "particularity," however—as in so much else—Queen Anne was to be frustrated. Worse, she would have to share responsibility for her own disappointment. For as we have seen, at her accession in 1702 it had been Anne herself, not Parliament, who led the way in subordinating the particularities of her maternity to a vision of abstract, symbolic motherhood. In 1708 Anne made the bitter discovery that Parliament could exploit the strategy to her disadvantage, making of royal maternity a mere counter in a larger debate in which the Queen herself had little part. Like her physical motherhood, symbolic maternity turned out to be a kind of political boomerang, beyond Queen Anne's control and capable of reducing, rather than augmenting, her authority.

When Queen Anne declined to give Parliament a "particular answer," she did more than refuse to consider the possibility of marriage and procreation. She also registered her frustration with being cast in the role of political red herring. Recognizing and resenting her position as "royal cipher,"[61] Anne refused to join Parliament in pretending that she might still make physical provision for the Protestant succession. But at the same time the language of the queen's reply—particularly the implied reference to the phenomenon of "making provision"—complicates her refusal. For while disallowing Parliament's cynical exploitation of her new position as single female monarch, Anne continued to cast herself in a provident, maternal role, despite the notorious failure of her maternal body. Perhaps then this is the truest reason why Queen Anne abstained from giving Parliament a more "particular answer": because she already had specified her provision. Her many pregnancies, lyings-in, and bereavements had made Anne permanently and irreducibly a provident mother, both to her own children and to the nation, despite the fact that the children had all died. To say otherwise would be to assume that maternity depends on the continued existence of offspring and thus to enforce a manifestly patriarchal definition of motherhood and, finally, of womanhood.

So, on the one hand, the suggestion of tragedy and the taint of guilt implied in Queen Anne's oblique identification of herself, the guardian of the Protestant succession, with the desperate mother of a dead child demonstrate that the functions of maternal symbolism went far beyond the control of any single agent in Augustan England, even (or perhaps, especially) the monarch. The language of symbolic maternity, sad to say, was no more under Anne's control than her physical motherhood had been. Furthermore, the dialogue between queen and Parliament in 1708 demonstrates more than the peculiar vulnerability of Queen Anne's symbolic maternal self-representation; it also makes disturbingly vivid the queen's position as royal outsider—her entrapment, her sense of redundancy, depletion, and waste, her resentment against being used as a convenience. But at the same time, paradoxically, Anne's self-defense rings true and powerful. After all, Queen Anne *did* do her utmost for the Protestant succession. And at her death Protestant interests—which would certainly have foundered had she betrayed them—did prevail.[62]

Perhaps then when Queen Anne insisted that she had "made provision" for the Protestant succession, she was more aware of the resonances of her language than we have assumed, and more deliberate in its use. Perhaps the queen was demanding that her reproductive efforts be acknowledged as significant despite the deaths of her children—that Parliament recognize her as a particular woman, blamelessly provident, and irreducibly a mother though she would never leave an heir. If so, her contemporaries disappointed her: as we have seen, Queen Anne's reply did little to ease popular concerns that the nation's symbolic mother would betray and abandon the Protestant succession; on the contrary, the queen's words fueled such concerns. And even today, while the idea that Queen Anne was a secret Jacobite has been largely discredited, the queen herself is often still seen as little more than a cipher.[63] In particular, Anne's maternal experience goes unrecognized except as a means of denigrating her abilities and denying her the credit she deserves for the achievement of the Hanoverian succession after her death.

Perhaps, after all, history's failure to recognize Queen Anne as provident mother persists not merely because Anne failed to provide heirs but also because her unique position and history demanded new ways of thinking about inheritance itself. A childless mother, a fatherless daughter, a married queen unsubordinated to the authority of a king/husband—in all these roles Anne embodied transgression and paradox and made plain the most revolutionary results of the political upheavals witnessed by her generation: patriarchal inheritance had become interpretable and negotiable, less important than social consensus to the establishment of public authority. When Parliament asked the queen to remarry, it was asking her to *pretend to believe* that her maternal body held significance. Anne insisted instead on *really believing* in the political significance of her own maternal history, refusing to accept Parliament's definition of her maternity as a mere decoy or token. In Anne's estimate the result of her efforts to provide the nation with an heir was not simply nothing at all: she had, despite everything, "made provision."

And what had Queen Anne provided? By my reckoning, at least two legacies of great value have remained unappreciated from that day to this. First, the possibility of imagining a kind of (re)production that doesn't add up to anything measurable yet is not waste. And second, the example of a public woman who resisted those who would erase her particularity in the name of the political and who called that resistance a political act. Queen Anne left us, in other words, with the possibility of refiguring legitimate inheritance and political significance as matters not necessarily dependent on patriarchal systems of exclusion, and with the chance to transform familiar patterns of dominance and subordination into something new.

Sad Stories

Louis XVI, George III, and the Language of Sentiment

John Barrell

I

This essay is about the use of the language of sentiment in political discussion in the mid-1790s. It focuses on representations of the last interview of the former Louis XVI with his family on the evening of January 20, 1793, the day before his execution, and the reflection which they cast upon the representation of George III and the terms in which the monarchy could be discussed in Britain. It ends by suggesting that it is of the nature of the language of sentiment that its effects could not be controlled; and that its use in the language of loyalist political argument in the 1790s should be seen not simply as a response to a real or imagined republican threat but also as in some sense the cause of loyalist alarmism about the intentions of the popular reform movement in Britain.

It will help if I offer here a few of the defining characteristics of the language of sentiment, whether we find it in the novels, plays, poetry, periodical essays, or in the political writing of the late eighteenth and early nineteenth centuries. One such characteristic is well described by Tom Paine, in his discussion of what he called Burke's "tragic paintings" of the events of October 5 and 6, 1789, which were calculated to produce, says Paine, "through the weakness of sympathy, a weeping effect."[1] The language of sentiment is a highly pathetic language, the aim of which is indeed to reduce the reader to tears; tears of pain at representations of suffering, tears of joy at moments of reconciliation. And as Paine says it was imagined to operate by inviting readers to sympathize with the pathetic emotions it displays, by a process of sympathetic identification with those whose pains and pleasures it describes. If the discourse of the division of labor, for example, proposes that humans are distinguished from animals by their propensity to truck and barter, the discourse of sentiment grounds that distinction no less firmly on a universal propensity to sympathy.

The language of sentiment was gendered as feminine, as against the languages in which political or economic affairs were usually discussed. It placed a high value on sensibility, on delicacy of sentiment, supposed to be an especially feminine characteristic; it understood the processes by which men are softened, or melted by sympathy, or broken by suffering, as a process of feminization; in the great crises of pathos it described and produced, male sympathizers, male objects of sympathy, were temporarily "unmanned." Indeed it seems true to say that in the terms of the language of sentiment, men have to be in some degree feminized in order to attract the sympathy of the reader; and that the more powerful the man, the more he must be represented as *un*manned, as feminized by suffering, if he is to become the object of sympathetic identification.

The language of sentiment sought to represent all virtues as private, indeed as domestic virtues, all affective relations as aspiring to the condition of family relations. The family, as imagined in the language of sentiment, could still include domestic relations which were not ties of blood; it could include the servants of a household, for example, but in doing so it represented the love they were supposed to feel for their employers as something far exceeding the love which it was their *duty* to feel. It was this language, and not the age of chivalry, as Burke suggested, which had "incorporated into politics the sentiments which beautify and soften private society":[2] the introduction of the language of sentiment into politics necessarily had the effect of blurring the distinction between public and private, and representing the ties which bound the nation and state as the affective ties which bound the family. Family affection became, if not the first qualification for citizenship, at least the sine qua non of good citizenship: "We begin our publick affections in our families," wrote Burke. "No cold relation is a zealous citizen."[3] "The unkindest brother," wrote the loyalist divine John Whitaker, "the sternest husband, the most imperious wife, the most despotic father, is commonly a violent partisan for liberty."[4]

The language of sentiment was rarely used as the only, or even the primary, language in which the institution of monarchy was vindicated by loyalist writers of the 1790s, who were well aware of the danger of making the legitimacy of the monarchy appear to depend too heavily on the private virtues and affections of the monarch for the time being. It seems to have been regarded, indeed, by some loyalist writers—by Whitaker, for example, and perhaps especially by John Reeves—as a largely inappropriate language in which to describe the authority of the Crown. It was an especially useful language, however, in which to respond to imagined threats to the personal safety of the king, and also to defend the king from real or imagined insults to his authority, for it proposed limits to political discussion which were set not by the freedom, but by the decencies and delicacies of private inter-course. The language of sentiment was especially useful for this purpose during the Regency crisis, but it was equally serviceable in the years when popular radicalism was at its most vocal and well-organized. For example, during the trial of Paine, the attorney-general Sir Archibald Macdonald secured the permission of the court to read a letter he had received from the absent defendant, in which Paine had asked whether it was "possible that you or I can believe, or that reason can make any other man believe, that the capacity of such a man as Mr. Guelph, or any of his profligate sons, is necessary to the government of a nation?" In reply, Macdonald exclaimed:

> He is a barbarian, who could use such profligate expressions . . . If giving me pain was his object, he has that hellish gratification. . . . Gentlemen, there is not perhaps in the world a more beneficial analogy, nor a finer rule to judge by in public matters, than by assimilating them to what passes in domestic life. A . . . kingdom is a large family. Suppose this to have happened in private life, judge of the good heart of this man, who thrusts into my hands, the grateful servant of a kind and beneficent master . . . slander upon that master, and slan-der upon his whole offspring.—Lay your hands on your hearts, and tell me what is your verdict with respect to his heart.—I see it![5]

Or here is the next attorney-general, Sir John Scott, prosecuting Daniel Isaac Eaton for publishing Paine's *Letter Addressed to the Addressers*. Arguing that the pamphlet was an "indecent account" of the king's behavior, and that the tiny profits that accrued to the publishers of such pamphlets did not make the publication of them any less criminal, Scott exclaimed:

> If a man . . . chooses, for two-pence, to run the risk of publishing a work, the purport of which is to make wives and children detested of husbands and fathers,—[and] is he not to be brought to justice, because he happens to have a wife and children? I know what you would have said to the officer of the crown, if he had negligently permitted the continuance of such publications: I know you would have said, that if a guillotine was to be found in this coun-try, his head ought to be the first that should be severed.[6]

Scott speaks as if the worst thing about libels on the king is that they some-how sow dissension in private families—they make husbands hate their wives and fathers hate their children. I won't attempt here to unravel the process by which this suggestion gives rise to Scott's third-person fantasy of his own decapitation, and by a guillotine, but perhaps as my essay continues it will unravel itself.

Unsurprisingly, the introduction of this language into political debate was resisted by many radical and opposition writers, who rightly saw that no discussion of the authority of the king could be conducted if the distinction between the king's private and public character was not clearly defined.

Thus one anonymous pamphleteer exclaimed against loyalist attempts to exploit "admiration of the private virtues of an ill-advised King" as an obstacle in the way of "progress to truth."[7] Other commentators attempted to discredit loyalist uses of the language of sentiment by emphasizing the mismatch between the delicacy of feeling it affected and the squalid interests it concealed: Paine did so continually, and so did Thomas Erskine. In his defense for example of John Frost, who had avowed his republican sympathies in a London coffeehouse, Erskine remarked to the jury: "The three estates of the kingdom are co-ordinate, all alike representing the dignity, and jointly exercising the authority of the nation; yet all our loyalty appears to be wasted upon one of them.—How happens it . . . that we are so exquisitely sensible, so tremblingly alive to every attack upon the CROWN, OR THE NOBLES that surround it, yet so completely careless of what regards THE ONCE RESPECTED AND AWFUL COMMONS OF GREAT BRITAIN?"[8] The language of Erskine's question, though not its tone, appears to invite an equally sentimental answer, to do no doubt with the ineffable tenderness everywhere evident in the relation between the king and his subjects. The answer Erskine in fact offers is that the Crown is the object of special tenderness as the source of honors, pensions, and sinecures.

A number of writers among the host of those who wrote replies to Burke's *Reflections on the Revolution in France* behave as if this political language of sentiment, this privatized language of politics, suddenly emerged, fully articulate, in that text. In fact its emergence was a gradual process, though subject to sudden accelerations in moments of political danger, in particular in the American war of independence, so regularly described as the destruction of the dear domestic ties between parent and offspring. The implication of Linda Colley's writings on George III, however, and I agree, is that the anxieties surrounding the king's illness of 1788–1789 and the Regency crisis gave a new kind of power to this language.[9] They did so in two ways in particular. They gave rise to newly affective descriptions of the relation of the king to his people: the description, to give just one example, of the king as "inexpressibly dear," "unutterably dear" to his people, a phrase which repeats one of the most common of sentimental notions, that there is no language—*not even* the language of sentiment itself—to express the depth of our deepest private affections. The king's illness also gave, as Colley has argued, a newly immediate power to the rhetorical figures by which the king was represented as the father of his people, and by which the nation, the constitution, and the king could all be conflated within the image of a mild, tender, and above all a vulnerable father, whose illness had unmanned, had feminized him, and had inspired in his people a love similar to that which it arguably revealed in his family. The point is made by the repeated reference in the early 1790s to the king's paternal "tenderness" for his people, for example; the phrase had had a long life before 1788, but thereafter it seems to be used in a way which emphasises the reciprocity of the word; the king's tenderness is itself tender, easily hurt, and therefore must be warmly, passionately reciprocated if his feelings are not to be wounded.

It seems reasonable to suppose that Burke's invocation of the language of sentiment in the *Reflections,* and of the nation as a family bound by emotions too profound to be fully understood, owed much of its affective power to the much more immediate sense in which George III was so generally represented as the tender "father" of his people in the period during and following his illness. I am thinking for example of the representation in the *Reflections,* of the constitution as a father, not just vulnerable but actually wounded, and whose wounds must be tended "with pious awe and trembling solicitude."[10] But Burke's attempt to use the same language to evoke similar sentiments in favor of the French royal family, in particular in favor of Marie Antoinette, notoriously met with a much more cynical response, so vast was the gap between his account of Marie Antoinette and what was known or believed of her private life. As John Brewer has pointed out, it was not until the imprisonment of the royal family in the Temple in 1792, and the execution of Louis and Marie Antoinette the following year, that the royal family could be rehabilitated *as* a family, and their sudden display of domestic virtues could be mobilized to reveal the inhumanity of republican attitudes to the natural family affections, and to emphasize therefore the unnaturalness of republican government.[11] Understood in those terms, the sufferings of the French royal family inevitably evoked the memory of 1788–1789 and the vulnerability of George; and his own exemplary private character, the ineffable love he inspired in his subjects, and the especially sympathetic national character of the British people, could all be tied together in an argument to demonstrate that the British neither would nor should follow the French along the path to a republic.

II

The news of the execution of Louis XVI reached London on January 24, 1793, and accounts of it, derived from the Paris press, from government intelligence, and the letters of correspondents, appeared in the London newspapers on the two following days. Detailed news about what transpired in the hours before his execution was scanty, however, and only the *World,* on January 26, had sufficient information to begin the process of building what became, in the ensuing weeks and months, the elaborate three-part narrative of the events of January 20 and 21. This narrative, as it came to be amplified first in pamphlet accounts of Louis's trial and execution and later in a host of different accounts and images, began in the Temple, with the last meeting between Louis and his family on the evening of January 20, a scene in which Louis was represented in his private character as a family man. It ended in the Place de la Révolution, where he appeared in his public character, as a monarch illegally dethroned and condemned, meeting his death in some versions with heroic defiance, in others with the anxieties of a good patriot or with meek resignation. Between its pathetic opening and tragic closure the narrative came to include a scene of preparation for death, as Louis divested himself of his private character as if to take on the role of Christian martyr or Roman hero.

During the period of his trial, Louis had been held in an apartment of the Temple on the floor below that occupied by his wife Marie Antoinette, his sister Elisabeth, and his children Marie-Thérèse Charlotte, just fourteen years old, and Louis, who was not quite nine. On the afternoon of January 20, the former king was told that he would be executed on the morning of the following day; shortly afterwards, the other members of the family were similarly informed. The family then met for the last time. According to most accounts of the meeting, no one apart from the five members of the family was present during most of what came to be known as "the last interview," and it is not clear how far the earliest reports of what passed are simply invented or derive, at whatever remove, from the oral accounts of the municipal officers guarding the prisoners, or of Edgeworth, Louis's confessor, who later claimed that he overheard much of the family's conversation while waiting in an adjoining room. Edgeworth also recorded that the interview took place in a room with a glass door, through which the municipal officers who guarded the prisoners could "see and hear" the whole scene; but according to Cléry, Louis's valet, who himself claimed to have watched the scene through the same glass door, "It was impossible to hear any thing."[12] The lack of reliable information about what took place made opposition newspapers such as the *Morning Chronicle* wary of offering any lengthy account of the interview. It did not, however, prevent loyalist newspapers and pamphleteers from reporting the scene at length: sometimes in tableau, as if seen but not heard; sometimes with snatches of dialogue.[13]

It goes without saying that all extended accounts of the interview are pathetic in the extreme; the grief of the royal family is described in harrowing detail, its effect heightened by the repeated assertion that it was quite indescribable. Marie Antoinette, in particular, is almost invariably represented as wholly "distracted," though the word was interpreted in two ways, probably because of the ambiguity of the French *distraite* in the reports of correspondents. Sometimes her "distraction" is taken to suggest that she was almost removed from the scene, as if unable to focus on what was happening, sometimes that her emotions were so violent that she fainted, or fell into a "delirium of anguish" or "convulsive hysteric fits."[14]

In most accounts, Marie-Thérèse Charlotte too, who was known to be unwell, is described as fainting with grief. Descriptions of her sufferings developed a particular pathos from the rumor which circulated in Paris following the execution that she had died on the evening of January 20. The longest of the newspaper reports, which appeared in the loyalist *World* of January 26, reported that during the course of the interview Louis had visited the apartment where his daughter lay "insensible" and "struggling with death"; finally she exclaimed, "O my Father! O my tender Father!" and expired immediately after. Revised versions of the *World's* report of the scene later appeared in a number of pamphlets. In these the princess does not die, but what had formerly been her last words became her last breathless speech before she collapsed at her father's feet.[15]

These pathetic images of the grief of the royal family provided the context in which Louis's own deportment in the last hours of his life was to be represented. Different reports have him conducting himself very differently. According to some, at the sight of his family Louis's "fortitude," which had enabled him to hear the news of his sentence without dismay, was quite "overcome";[16] he was "unmanned"; "accumulated tenderness overpowered him—the big drop rolled down his cheek—he seemed nearly senseless!"[17] In James Gillray's extraordinary satire of the interview scene, *Louis XVI Taking Leave of His Wife and Family* (figure 8), published two months after the execution, Louis is depicted as a terrified sot, gripping a decanter and glass of wine in what seems to be an attempt more to forget his impending death than to fortify his spirits to face it. The image was no doubt partly intended to throw contempt and ridicule on the sentimental attitude to monarchy so evident in other representations of those last hours.[18] Other versions of the scene, however, which show Louis as "unmanned," as briefly less than a man, do so both in order to show him as more human, more vulnerable, than we expect kings to be, and to enable us to measure the moral achievement by which, in the later scenes of the drama or even before the end of the interview itself, he confronts his death with a resolution and firmness of spirit entirely superhuman. In William Preston's verse tragedy *Democratic Rage,* for example, published some months after the execution, Louis appears in the long interview scene as an exemplary father, teaching his family resignation to God's will, and giving advice and instruction to his wife, sister, daughter, and (especially) his son. Eventually, however, Marie Antoinette breaks down, and begins to speak in a broken syntax, punctuated with the frequent dashes that in the language of sentiment signify madness or unendurable mental agony. She faints under the weight of her feelings, and only now does Louis's nerve falter. He is, however briefly, "unmanned," and for the first time we are invited to recognize with what difficulty, with what manly courage, he had controlled himself thus far. Within a few lines, however, he has recovered to the point where he can even demand that his own life be cut short in order to spare his wife the anguish of seeing him again.[19]

Figure 8. James Gillray, *Louis XVI Taking Leave of His Wife and Family* (1792)

Most accounts, however, of Louis's behavior during the interview show him as displaying throughout a deep familial tenderness and an astonishing self-restraint, and as managing—if only just—to prevent himself from being overwhelmed by feelings no less intense than those evinced by his family. In John Bartholomew's tragedy *The Fall of the French Monarchy*, for example, Louis appears throughout the interview as a perfect husband and father, full of kindly advice, adorned by every private virtue, thinking least of himself, and concerned only to soothe the wild emotions of his womenfolk.[20] "The king," announced the loyalist writer John Gifford, "although affected at different times beyond the power of expression, retained his recollection to the last."[21] In some representations of the interview, the interpretation of Louis's immense calmness becomes the object of a dispute between two different discourses which compete to establish the significance of his execution, though the value language of these discourses is not so incompatible as to preclude traces of both appearing in the same text. Sometimes Louis's behavior appears as a saintlike resignation, a "heavenly serenity" as the *World* describes it, derived from Louis's unshakable belief in the reality of life after death. Sometimes it appears as a stoic heroism which owes less to his religious faith than to a sense, in himself or the reporters, of the exemplary behavior appropriate to his public character.[22] I shall say more about these competing but overlapping discourses in a while; but the differences between the various accounts and images of Louis's demeanor at the last interview are altogether less striking than what they have in common. In every account that treats the interview at any length,[23] Louis appears as model father, the head and center of a family about to be divided, but still held together by the deepest love and tenderness. Louis's great affection for his family is equally evident whether he is shown collapsing under the weight of his impending sense of loss, or struggling not to do so, or apparently without difficulty devoting his last hours with his family to an attempt to soothe and reassure them.

The representation of Louis as a perfect father, so little concerned about his own fate, so anxious for his family, was reinforced by the publication of the will he had written on Christmas Day 1792. This had been read to the Commune of Paris immediately after the execution; it was published in the London newspapers on January 26, and was repeatedly reprinted, most notably in a broadside published by William Lane, beneath an engraving of Louis elevated *in altis*.[24] The will was mainly concerned with Louis's hopes and wishes for the future of his wife, sister, and children, and everywhere testified to the immense and loving concern he felt for them. Together with accounts of the last interview, it represented Louis not as a king, a public hero or martyr exalted above the reach of the grief and sympathy of his former subjects and present admirers, but as a private individual whose chief concerns as he contemplated his end were such as those who thought of themselves as ordinary people would expect to feel.

III

Daniel Arasse has shown that in France the terms on which Louis's death was to be represented were the object of a competition—it would be surprising if it were not so—between Catholic and loyalist commentators on the one hand, and republicans on the other; a competition which turned especially on the precise text of Louis's last words.[25] In Britain, there was also a competition, though a more benign one, to establish the terms on which his execution was to be described; a competition which, as David Bindman has pointed out, turned rather on the appropriate terms in which his heroism was to be described; whether as Catholic martyr, his concern entirely for his future state, or as Roman hero, deliberately divesting himself of whatever comforts might serve to palliate his fate.

In these terms Bindman distinguishes between three engravings of the interview published in the two years immediately following the execution.[26] In *The King's Departure from His Disconsolate Family*, after Domenico Pellegrini (figure 9), the competition is played out between the image itself and the inscription beneath it. According to the latter, Louis "alone seems superior to the horror and despair that surrounds him, and tears himself from every

Figure 9. M. Bovi after D. Pellegrini, *The King's Departure from His Disconsolate Family*

endearing tye with the fortitude of a Martyr." In fact, however, as Bindman points out, Louis is shown standing above his largely prostrate family in the attitude less of a Christian martyr than of an antique hero: "a Hector parting from his affectionate family for a higher purpose, a man of action who rises above the emotions which touch him deeply and to which lesser mortals would surrender." The mood is close to those paintings by David which represent a heroic but essentially secular renunciation of private concerns in favor of a stern public duty. In a second engraving, by Luigi Schiavonetti after Charles Benazech, *The Last Interview between Louis the Sixteenth and His Disconsolate Family* (figure 10), Louis is seated at the center of his family, embracing his daughter, and allowing his kneeling son (in the words of the account on which the design is apparently based) to make "an absolute monopoly of one of his Royal Parent's hands."[27] Louis's gaze, however, is turned away from the family, and fixed upon a small crucifix in the far left of the picture, in front of which a Bible is propped open and Edgeworth half stands, half kneels, in an attitude of prayer. *The Final Interview of Louis the Sixteenth,* after Mather Brown (figure 11), manages to suggest the composure of Louis, surrounded by his frantic family, in terms which appear to favor neither of the two discourses; according to the description issued with

Figure 10. Luigi Schiavonetti after Charles Benazech, *The Last Interview between Louis the Sixteenth and His Disconsolate Family*

the print, it displays the "resigned virtue and heroic fortitude" of Louis, phrases which do not seem to differentiate classical from Christian heroism.

To some extent, this competition may have been the more or less accidental result of the mixture of sources relied upon by the London newspapers from which most later accounts and images of the events of January 20 and 21 seem ultimately to derive; to some extent also, however, it may have been a reflection of a certain poverty in the linguistic and imaginative resources of the late century, its inability to produce a language adequate to the representation of public tragedy. We can't as easily read off, as Arasse does, the politics of representations of Louis's death from the terms in which that death is represented in Britain, for, as the engravings suggest, too often the languages of martyrdom and of civic heroism seem to compete within *individual* representation in an attempt to find a language adequate to the occasion. The notion of martyrdom was too irredeemably Catholic; the language of civic virtue, already tainted with democratic republicanism, was experienced as too cold; as Johnson had remarked, some years earlier, about Addison's tragedy of *Cato,* it communicates "no vibration to the heart."[28]

Figure 11. P. W. Tompkins after Mather Brown, *The Final Interview of Louis the Sixteenth*

If Louis's execution was experienced by many in Britain, as most evidently it was, as an appalling, an overpoweringly pathetic event, this was because the linguistic vacuum was filled—was already filled, before the narrative of his last hours reached the Place de la Révolution—by the language of sentiment in which the last interview had been described; a language entirely adequate to the pathos of the event, but at the price—or with the advantage—of representing Louis's death as first and foremost a domestic tragedy. For the British, the Louis who died under the guillotine was a father wrenched from the bosom of his loving family; if he was a religious martyr, his piety was understood and felt as an essentially private virtue; if he was a Roman hero, he was so because of the awesome courage with which he parted from his family. On the morning of his execution, Louis divested himself of the objects of sentimental value that remained to him—a ring, locks of his children's hair, and so on—as if divesting himself of sentiment itself. He refused a further interview with his wife, as if refusing further communication, also, with his own private identity. Whatever the effect of these painfully deliberate actions on Louis himself, their rhetorical effect must have been to insist upon the terrible private cost of public heroism.[29]

The pathos of Louis's death, wrote one memorialist, was made all the greater by the fact that "it was reserved for Louis the Sixteenth . . . when pursued to death as a king, to be exempt from no suffering as a private man."[30] And it was repeatedly as a private man, "the kindest Patron, the most affectionate Friend, the most amiable of Men!" that Louis was especially memorialized, in the verses, sermons, and other elegies and obituaries that appeared in the year following his death.[31] The point is made most clearly perhaps by Henry Hunter, in a sermon preached at the Scots Church, London Wall, in early February. Contrasting the reactions to Louis's death in France, which "revels in the blood of her native prince," and in Britain, which "mourns, sincerely mourns" his loss, Hunter claimed that Britain "loses all thought of the enemy and the king, in respect for the virtues, and sympathy in suffering, of the man."[32] This effusion of national sympathy, as Helen Maria Williams suggested, was especially an effect produced by the narrative of the last interview:

> Alas! when imagination pictured the anguish of such an interview, it was not necessary to look back upon the former elevation of the sufferer, in order to pity the gloomy transition in his fate! it was not necessary to recollect, that he who was the following morning to suffer death upon the scaffold, was once the first monarch of Europe, and would be led to execution through the streets of his own capital! It was enough to consider this unfortunate person as a man, a husband, a father![33]

"A man, a husband, a father": especially striking in representations of the last interview is the repetition, from account to account, of the various relations, "father, husband, and brother," in which Louis stood to the members of his family. A version of the phrase first appears in the *Morning Herald* report of January 25; a version of it appeared the next day in the *World*, in the last words of the family to their father: "'We will see you by and bye— Adieu Husband! Adieu Brother! Adieu Father!'" Thereafter it turns up in text after text,[34] finally perhaps in Gifford's *Reign of Louis the Sixteenth* the following year: "A sister, children, a wife in a prison, taking their last leave of a brother, father, husband, and a king, rendered more dear by his past sufferings, their common calamity, and the dreadful fate awaiting him the following day."[35]

The wave of sympathy for Louis and his family produced in Britain by accounts of the last interview may have owed much to the repetition, from text to text, of this litany of the familial relations through which in the language of sentiment all affective relationships are figured. Sentimental narratives represented these relationships as functioning entirely by means of the sympathetic identification of one person with another; they were believed to owe their special affective power to their ability to persuade the reader to perform a similar act of identification. The point is reinforced by

Figure 12. British medal by C. H. Küchler that
depicts the final interview (1793)

one of the medals illustrating the last interview, designed by the refugee
Conrad Heinrich Küchler and issued by Matthew Boulton in July 1793 (figure 12).[36] The image of the grieving family is surmounted by the legend
"An est dolor par dolori nostro?"—"Is their grief as great as ours?" At first
reading this may seem an embarrassingly insensitive question, for it apparently ignores one of the essential decencies of the language of sympathy by
suggesting that we feel the pains of others every bit as sharply as they do.
Küchler must have believed however that the effect of the question would
have been to magnify the sense of loss claimed to be suffered by the public
at large, without diminishing that felt by Louis's immediate family; and the
silent logic which justified this belief must have been that Louis was as much
our father as he was the father of Marie-Thérèse and little Louis; as much
our husband as Marie Antoinette's; as much our brother as Elisabeth's.

Husband, wife, brother, sister, father, child—the list so often repeated
provides multiple opportunities for sympathetic identification with the
characters in the narrative, multiple points of entry into the scene and
thereby into the sufferings of a family. By invoking the members of the royal
family as often by the names of the relations between them as by their personal names, the family itself is represented as typical, and the obstacle
which royalty interposes to the propensity to sympathy is more easily overcome. The list may also have reinforced the effect by which accounts of the
last interview may be supposed to have attached the subjects of George III

more firmly to their own king; for it was a rhetorical device already, by 1793, familiar to the British by its repeated use in descriptions of his virtues. Here, for example, is the Reverend William Hett's loyalist oration published under the title *The Genuine Tree of Liberty; or the Royal Oak of Great Britain* in January 1793: "In his private character, our most gracious sovereign holds up to his subjects a model of every social . . . virtue. He is a kind husband, a tender parent, and a faithful friend."[37] Or here is Mary Wollstonecraft, reminding Burke of his notorious failure during the Regency crisis to sympathize with the sufferings of George, "a father torn from his children,—a husband from an affectionate wife,—a man from himself!"[38]

Another point of entry into the scene of the last interview was provided in the engravings after Brown and Pellegrini which represent Cléry as present at the interview, distraught with grief but still the staunch servant who would not desert his master, and to whom in his will Louis entrusted the day-to-day care of his son. As we have seen, Cléry was not present at the interview, and indeed I have found no written account which places him in the room with the royal family. His inclusion in the scene can have had no other purpose than to provide a further channel of identification and sympathy, and one which at the same time reinforced the value of the ties between those of different social rank which the French had so rashly severed: ties of obedience, of deference, and of that grateful affection of servant for master still regularly described as "love." For female spectators, Marie Antoinette's maidservant Tison, who was also absent from the interview but is present in Brown's image of it, may have served a similar purpose.

There were accounts and images of the interview in which Edgeworth, too, is shown as giving comfort to the afflicted family, and which increased still further these opportunities for sympathetic identification and vicarious participation in the scene—identification with Edgeworth not as Catholic Priest, but as the owner of a reassuringly English name. In a number of early accounts of the events of January 20 and 21, Edgeworth was described as English,[39] though in fact he was a member of an Irish family; his father had converted to Catholicism, and Edgeworth himself, who was known in Paris as De Fermond, was brought up in France, and had a poor command of English. Edgeworth remained with Louis to the very moment of his death; in narratives of the execution, especially, which depended heavily on nonjuring Catholic sources, he played a crucial role in ensuring that Louis's life was represented as an imitation of Christ, his death as a Christian martyrdom. For British audiences, however, the main effect of the role accorded him in the narrative may have been to enforce the contrast between the "sanguinary, ferocious, and resentful" character of the French,[40] and the characteristic sensibility of the English, which, as a number of accounts and discussions of Louis's death suggest, gave them an especially immediate access to the tragedy—the domestic tragedy—of the royal family.[41]

IV

The potential of the story of Louis's last hours to be used as propaganda was evident as soon as it reached Britain. When William Lane of the Minerva Press published his broadside account of the execution on January 29, he priced it at sixpence, with a discount for bulk purchases of one hundred;[42] a few days later he halved the original price, and offered a still more generous discount to those willing to act as agents to distribute the sheet, expressing the hope that it would be circulated "in every village throughout the three kingdoms." In a long advertisement announcing these reductions, Lane described his wish that

> this horrid and unjust sacrifice . . . should be known to all classes of people, and in particular to the honest and industrious Artisan and manufacturer, who might be deluded by the false and specious pretences of artful and designing persons . . .
> And as the spirit of this country is rouzed, in loyalty to our most excellent King, to add support to Government, and our happy Constitution[,] It is highly necessary the conduct of France, in their destruction of monarchy, should be publicly and universally known.[43]

As propaganda, it was imagined that the story would have an immediate effect, in finally providing what the opposition *Morning Chronicle* described as a "popular argument" for war with France; indeed, on the very day that news of the execution reached London, the pro-government *Times* greeted it, with an indecent eagerness, as an event from which considerable "advantage" could be expected, as a justification for Britain's entry into the war.[44] The timing of Louis's death had an additional advantage for loyalists; it ensured that very few of the sermons delivered in Anglican churches five days later, on the anniversary of the death of Charles the Martyr, would fail to compare the work of the English regicides with that of the French, so as to give a new immediacy to the now over-familiar lessons taught by the traditional January 30 texts: "Fear God. Honour the King"; "meddle not with them that are given to change." The anniversary of Charles I's death, wrote the reviewer of one such sermon, "will acquire consequence, we had almost said immortality, from a similar event in a neighbouring kingdom . . . It is impossible that the one event should not revive the remembrance of the other."[45] And the continuing production for a year and more of variously priced narratives and images of Louis's last hours—in handbills and broadsides, chapbooks, plays, poems, histories, travel books, polite and popular engravings, transfer-printed pottery—makes it clear that the story was imagined to have a more permanent propaganda value, beyond its convenience in providing a "popular argument" for war with the French republic. As late as 1821 John Clare remarked that "the reading a small pamphlet on the

Murder of the French king many years ago . . . cured me very early from thinking favourably of radicalism."[46]

Some idea of how it was supposed that the story would influence the sensibilities of Lane's "honest and industrious Artisan and Manufacturer" was given by George Crabbe in the poem he began writing in about 1799, and eventually published in 1807 as *The Parish Register*. In its long verse introduction, the poem contrasts the habitations of the idle and dissolute poor with the cottage of an "industrious swain," which is hung with the enviable collection of engravings he has managed to assemble and, despite his poverty, to keep and even to augment. These include various heads of heroes, lovers, and kings; images of the Lancashire ox, of Daniel Mendoza, of Lady Godiva; a couple of comic prints; a panorama of the Battle of the Nile, with room beside it for another, of Trafalgar, not yet purchased; and, most important for my purposes, a print of Charles the Martyr, a group portrait of the British royal family, and two engravings of Louis XVI. The first of these shows Louis on his throne; the second represents the last interview of Louis with his family on the evening before his execution.

The poem spends more time on this last engraving than on any other, concerned not so much with how it looks as with how it is used. These are the lines in question:

> Here the last Lewis on his throne is seen,
> And there he stands imprison'd, and his Queen;
> To these the mother takes her child, and shows
> What grateful duty to his God he owes;
> Who gives him to a happy home, where he
> Lives and enjoys his freedom with the free;
> When kings and queens, dethroned, insulted, tried,
> Are all these blessings of the poor denied.[47]

The mother of the household, it appears, uses this engraving to teach her son a lesson in the beliefs and attitudes appropriate to his situation in life: a lesson in religion, in patriotism, in gratitude, in contentment, and in domestic values. It also teaches that each of these lessons is inextricable from the others; Crabbe's sentence binds them into a complex manifold, most evident in the ambiguous use of the word "home" to suggest at once the happy household of this virtuous family as distinct from the miserable homes of the undeserving poor, and the happy condition of Britain as opposed to the miserable state of France.

Crabbe does not say so in so many words, but the print may well be thought of as teaching both mother and child a further lesson, one which operates not only by contrast but by comparison. Seen in the context of the neighboring image of the British royal family, reinforcing George III's identity as family man, it invites a close comparison between his mild domestic virtues and those of Louis XVI. If accounts of the private virtues of both men minimized the distinction between their private and public characters by insisting on the mild paternal love both felt, not just for their immediate family but for their people, accounts and images of the last interview invited an implicit but sharp contrast between how this love was reciprocated by their subjects. By depicting at once the overpowering strength and the pathetic vulnerability of the domestic affections of the French royal family, in the context of this continually implied comparison and contrast with the British, representations of the last interview may have been more effective than any image of George III could have been, in enabling the love a subject was enjoined to feel for the king to be experienced not as a duty but as a spontaneous, if not as a simple, emotion.

I have suggested that representations of the last interview, whether verbal or visual, depicted the French royal family much more as a family than as royal; and Crabbe's poem offers a particularly useful insight into the sympathy such representations were supposed to evoke. The poem visualizes the picture as being studied by mother and son together, in the absence of the father of the family; in this context, the power of the picture to invite them to imagine the grief they too would feel if their husband and father were about to die becomes particularly apparent. It invites them both to identify with members of royal families, and to understand, by this act of sympathetic identification, that royal families and ordinary families, though divided by rank, are equalized by the love each is supposed to feel for the father, and by the grief each would feel at his death.

V

Writers who supported the French republic, if not the execution of Louis, were not much more immune from the pathos of this language than monarchists and loyalists, and they responded to the event not by minimizing its pathos as a domestic tragedy, but by attempting to insist that it did not justify a politically ungrammatical elision of the distinction between the public and political nature of the event and the private pathos in which it was saturated.[48] Faced by the overwhelming private tragedy, wrote Helen Maria Williams for example, "the feelings of the heart, which run a faster pace than the reasonings of the head, reject for a while all calculation of general good or evil, and melt in mournful sympathy . . . But, when we consider the importance which the event may have in its consequences, not only to this country, but to all Europe, we lose sight of the individual sufferer, to meditate upon the destiny of mankind."[49] For most commentators, however, the meaning of Louis's death was so far determined by the only language which could lend it an appropriate pathos, that its political significance could not easily be separated from the private tragedy; and it would not have served the purposes of government or of loyalism in Britain if it could have been.

In his speech to the Commons on February 1, on preparations for war, Pitt insisted that British relations with France should be governed by "reason and reflection," not by "sentiment and feeling," but took every opportunity to use the "sympathies," the "tears," the "sighs" of the British as a "popular argument" for war. Other ministers, constitutionally less frigid than Pitt by reputation was, were still more willing, as the attorney and pamphleteer William Fox put it, "to suffuse our eyes with tears, that they may lead us blindly" into the war.[50]

If radicals were not immune from the power of the language of sentiment to excite their sympathy for the sufferings of kings, the effects of this saturation, this appropriation of the public by the private, may well have made it more difficult for English republicans to contemplate the assassination of the king as a possibly necessary step towards the establishment of a British republic. In the years following Louis's execution, among all the songs, the pasquinades, the caricatures produced in Britain that recommend the guillotining of tyrants, and George among them, no attempt seems ever to have been made or planned on the king's life; and one reason for this may be the success with which George was presented to his people as an object of sympathy, and his family as the objects of sympathetic identification. If the language of sentiment ensures that we "lose all thought" of the king in the sufferings of the man, it may have made it too difficult to separate the assassination or judicial execution of cruel tyrants from the cruel murder of tender fathers. The figure by which the political crime of regicide was traditionally represented as parricide, the most unnatural crime of all, was given a new immediacy by being translated into the language of domestic sentiment.

William Fox's pamphlet on the death of Louis was perhaps the most intelligent commentary on the attempt to define public policy in the language of private sentiment.

> It might possibly be doubted whether our own virtue were not rather a more rational ground of glory, than any *emotion* or *feeling* respecting the crimes of others. It must indeed be acknowledged, that to express the warmest emotions, and the most indignant feelings against *them*, is a far easier task than to pursue the thorny path of virtue, and steadily resist the temptations to which we are exposed. Thus we execrate an Inkle, and we sob and sigh at the tragedy of Oroonoko; yet we could not only perpetrate the facts themselves, but, through every revolving hour from age to age, we can realize the scenes, and re-act them on the wide theatre of the world, for the sake of gratifying our appetite with a despicable luxury. Let it then be asked, if we have no other, no clearer evidence of our purity, than our amazement and our horror, our feeling and our emotion, on the death of the King of France.[51]

Fox was an eloquent opponent of the slave trade, and the first point he is concerned to make is that if private emotion is to be used as the justification of public action, there are crimes enough within the jurisdiction of Britain which call for vengeance, without our searching Europe for criminals. The more general point of his pamphlet, however, is that the violent feelings and emotions aroused by tragic events have no necessary basis in morality and that the sensibility which is outraged by the representations of suffering also finds pleasure and gratification in them. By pointing out that we sympathize with the victims of the same crimes as we perpetrate ourselves, Fox was raising the most awkward question of all about the nature of the sympathy, and the pleasure, evoked by the spectacle of the death of Louis XVI.

Fox is entirely typical in attempting to think about the death of Louis by invoking the effects of sentimental drama; there was probably no other way either of representing many of the events of 1789–1794 in their full horror, or of trying to describe the affective power of how they had been represented.[52] It's not surprising therefore that at least three tragedies were written in 1793 and 1794 about the execution;[53] that the various engravings of the last interview should represent it so obviously as a theatrical event taking place in a stage-like space; or that Paine, attacking Burke's account of October 1789, should insist on the dangers of representing what were essentially political events as the actions in a sentimental tragedy—as tragic drama, tragic painting. The question raised by Fox—that we may take a pleasure in the pain of others—was an apparent paradox which in the eighteenth century was discussed primarily in terms of the aesthetics of tragedy and the psychology of the emotions it aroused, and was of especial interest in the late eighteenth century because it seemed to offer an especially productive way of thinking about the effects of sympathy.

The paradox was addressed in terms particularly relevant to this essay by Joanna Baillie, in the introduction to the *Series of Plays* she published in 1798. Though she does not say so, Baillie's thinking about tragedy sets out from a remark by Burke, in his *Philosophical Enquiry* of 1757, that no one would stay to watch a tragedy if an execution were going on outside.[54] It seemed to Baillie that the sensibilities of the polite had become altogether more delicate by the 1790s; though they still took great pleasure in the sufferings of those about to be executed, she argued, it was a pleasure most could enjoy only vicariously. Even among the polite, however, this pleasure, even if necessarily enjoyed at second hand, is the most intense pleasure there is. "There are very few," she argues, "who will not be eager to converse" with those who have witnessed an execution at first hand, "and to learn, very minutely, every circumstance connected with it"—how the victim behaved, his expression, and so on—everything, in short, "except the very act itself of inflicting death."[55] "To lift up the roof of his dungeon," she wrote,

> and look upon a criminal the night before he suffers, in his still hours of privacy, when all that disguise, which respect for the opinion of others, the strong

motive by which even the lowest and wickedest of men still continue to be moved, would present anx object to the mind of every person, not withheld from it by great timidity of character, more powerfully attractive than any other.[56]

Some sense of the attraction exerted by the exhibition of suffering, and of the excitement with which this passage is written, may be communicated by its fractured syntax, as well as by the slippage of terms on which Baillie's argument depends. Baillie cannot surrender the notion that this pleasure has nothing to do with any "natural love of cruelty"; it arises, she insists, entirely from "the sympathetick propensity of our minds." As her argument develops, however, this propensity to sympathize with suffering no longer seems to be the sole motive for the "strong curiosity" to observe its effects: even the practice among the "savages of America" of inflicting the most appalling tortures on their prisoners of war is adduced as evidence of this universal sympathy and curiosity. But the effect of this example is to suggest something altogether more disturbing: that though in modern, polite societies the pleasure we take in the pain of others may best be tasted vicariously, in a more natural state, where the passions claimed to be universal are more easily observed, it may even be fed by the pleasure of inflicting pain.[57]

But however single-mindedly eighteenth-century theorists of tragedy attempted to explain its effects in terms of sympathetic identification, the concept of sympathy rarely seems adequate even to their own accounts of the pleasures we take in observing the pain of others. Burke's version of the argument, for example, founders on the issue of the direction of our sympathetic identification when we are confronted with men of power. There was no more secure proposition in eighteenth-century theories of tragedy than that the sufferings of kings were particularly fitted to evoke sympathy, by the appalling contrast between their former prosperity and their subsequent misery. According to Adam Smith, we have a predisposition to sympathize with kings in their prosperity as well as in their sufferings. According to Burke, however, our natural response to the institution of monarchy is one of dread, and for most people this response could be overcome only "by using," as he put it, "no small violence to their natural dispositions."[58] This seems to imply that though we may sympathize with, we may also exult in the distresses of unhappy kings, for though kings are human like us, and never more so than when brought to grief, they are also alien objects of terror whose destruction we can hardly help desiring.

The process by which the suffering, the vulnerability of George were used to reinforce his claim to his subjects' love might at first sight appear to have represented him as entirely an object of pity, not of fear. But the image of George as tender, wounded, feminized, if it was always intimately dependent on the notion that his subjects would lose all recollection that he was also the king, was equally dependent on the assurance that they could never for a moment forget it. Both his vulnerability and his authority depended on being represented in a language that, while blurring the distinction between them, still kept them both in play. The king came to be presented as a kind of drag queen, whose feminized exterior did not quite conceal the man beneath, and was not quite intended to.[59] The figure of George was required to evoke both pity and fear, a doubling of emotions in which the identity of the victim of suffering, the object of sympathetic identification, could be as readily discovered in the terrified subject as in the wounded king. Burke's argument, it seems, like the figure of the king himself, can be read two ways. We may take pleasure in the sympathetic emotion aroused in us when the king is wounded; but how can we be sure that this pleasure is not, or is not also, a pleasure at the wound he suffers?

The instability, the ambiguity of the feelings evoked by the double character of George III was intensified by the fact that the language of sentiment represented him so insistently as a father; the very word by which his power was masked was one which may have made it more immediate, more disturbingly, as well as more reassuringly familiar. One source of the excitement the language of sentiment was able to generate was its tendency to represent unequal familial relations—husband and wife, father and child, brother and sister, master and servant—as somehow equalized by a reciprocity of tenderness, yet in such a way as not to abolish the fear attendant upon them but to suspend, even to increase it. Erskine's phrase, quoted earlier, is exact here: the language of sentiment represents the weaker parties in such relations as "tremblingly alive" to the passions of the stronger (and remember Burke's "pious *awe*," "*trembling* solicitude"). The language of sentiment masks power with weakness, fear with tenderness, hate with love, but the mask is always transparent, and like the stocking pulled down over the features of the bank robber it makes the face beneath still more frightening than it would be without the disguise.

It's possible, I have suggested, that the language of sentiment, by representing the king as a vulnerable father, may have made it more difficult, in the language of the law of treason, to "imagine" his death, in the sense of designing or intending it. It seems equally likely, however, that especially after the death of Louis, this language may have made it easier to "imagine" the king's death in the sense of fantasizing about it. I am thinking here partly of the explosive outbursts of republican sentiment which often led to trials for seditious words, such as those uttered in May 1794 by Edward Swift of Windsor: "Damn the King and Queen They ought to be put to Death the same as the King and Queen of France were . . . / Damn and bugger the King and all that belong to him . . . / Damnation blast the King. I would as soon shoot the King as a Mad dog."[60] I am thinking partly too of those jocular radical projections of the king's death I referred to earlier: pasquinades like the one produced in 1794 at the trial of Thomas Hardy, advertising the drama of "GEORGE'S HEAD IN A BASKET"; fables like John Thelwall's of the cock King Chaunticlere, decapitated by one of his rebellious subjects; songs like Robert Crosfeild's "Plant, Plant the Tree," in which the liberty tree is watered by the blood of the royal family.[61] I am thinking also of the prophecies of the king's death published in 1795 by Richard Brothers and Sarah Flaxmer, which involved imagining, in scenes reminiscent of the crisis of 1788–1789 the grief it would bring upon the royal family.[62] But I am thinking especially of the alarmism of loyalists, so "tremblingly alive," not only to the real threat to the unreformed constitution posed by the popular radical movement, but also to the series of threats to the king's own person which existed, as numerous commentators insisted, only in the imagination of loyalists themselves.

The phenomenon of loyalist alarmism cannot easily be considered except in the context of the language in which it found utterance. Was the anxiety continually expressed by ministers and by the ministerial press for the safety of the king's life a cynical maneuver, as so many radical commentators argued, to discredit the popular radical movement as one dedicated to king-killing? Did loyalists really believe in the guilt of the would-be regicides they claimed to have discovered, or that attempts to reform the House of Commons would inevitably lead to the king's execution? Were they projecting on to those charged with or suspected of imagining the king's death a guilty desire they could not acknowledge as their own? These questions don't seem to me to be mutually exclusive; the likely answer to all of them seems to be yes; for the effects of the language in which the alarm was propagated were always bound to exceed its effect as propaganda.

I am attempting to argue, then, that the particular anxieties surrounding the person of the king in the period from 1788 to the mid-1790s need to be understood as an effect of the institution of monarchy having become so heavily invested in the language of sentiment. The processes by which this language had been adopted as a political language, as apparently the only language now trusted with the task of uniting a divided and stratified society, are too complex to be discussed here; what is clear, however, is that they antedate the revolution. The language of sentiment was the only language available to communicate a sense of the dangers of revolution to the heart. In a different age, the evocation of warm beer and long shadows on the cricket field might have done the job less messily, though perhaps less effectively. The language of sentiment, however, by evoking sympathy for kings and love of country in the powerfully affective language of family love, necessarily evoked also a range of more disturbing emotions.

When we read the imaginative literature of this period—a novel such as *Caleb Williams,* or a poem such as the *Prelude*—it's easy to recognize the extraordinary power of the language of sentiment, its tendency to exceed its apparent brief to describe the depth of family love, and to call up as well the guilt and hatred of family life, or of social life conceived of in familial terms. We recognize this easily enough, too, where the language of politics itself becomes self-consciously literary—in the ease for example by which Burke's figure of the constitution as a wounded father moves into the fantasy of his being hacked to pieces. What I am trying to argue is that the effects of the language of sentiment were no easier to control *whenever* it was mobilized to describe the nature of political affiliation. There is no need to search the sentimental language of the alarmists for symptoms of the kind represented by Burke's vertiginous slippage; the language was itself the symptom.

Reading and Writing

Reading the Margins

Politics and the Habits of Appropriation

Steven Zwicker

In 1661 Archibald Campbell, marquis and eighth earl of Argyll, wrote to his son to advise him on books and their cultivation:

> Your own choice and judgment will best direct you to what Books you shall read, and to what Science you shall chiefly apply your self, though I think it pedantical, and unworthy and unhandsome for a Nobleman or Person of Honour to be affectedly excellent in any one, it seems as ridiculous as Nero's mad Ambition of being counted the chief Fidler and best Singer in the World. . . .
>
> Think no cost too much in purchasing rare Books; next to that of acquiring good Friends I look upon this purchase; but buy them not to lay by, or to grace your library, with the name of such a Manuscript, or by such a singular piece, but read, revolve him, and lay him up in your memory where he will be far the better Ornament.
>
> Read seriously whatever is before you, and reduce and digest it to practice and observation, otherwise it will be Sysyphys his Labour to be always revolving Sheets and Books at every new Occurence which may require the Oracle of your reading.
>
> Trust not to your Memory, but put all remarkable, notable things you shall meet with in your Books *sub salva custodia* [under the sound care] of Pen and Ink, but so alter the property by your own Scholia and Annotations on it, that your memory may speedily recur to the place it was committed to.
>
> Review frequently such memorandums, and you will find you have made a signal progress and proficiency, in whatever sort of Learning you studied.[1]

Reflective and philosophical scholia occupy an important position in the spectrum of early modern habits of reading. Books might be mined for wisdom, and the philosophical cast of early modern literature, its cultivation of morals and parables, of the oracular and the epigrammatic, is evidence of such an understanding of the uses of books and the nature of reading.[2] But the marquis of Argyll might have suggested that by the 1660s there were more timely, indeed more contemporary, ways to read, concerned less with exemplarity than with passionate contest, less with study than with the correction of malignant opinion and the repudiation of fools. His son, in turn, might have observed something old-fashioned about the world of books his father had imagined, not simply privileged and aristocratic but perhaps backward-looking in its emphasis on practice and self-fashioning.[3] After years of civic turmoil, of the raising of arms and the destruction of monarchy, of social agitation and spiritual experiment, not only had the commonweal been turned upside down but all the forms and offices of literary culture had been pressed toward polemical service.

In such a world it was not only the production of texts but as well their consumption that was driven by partisanship; with the raising of arms, reading was commandeered by parties and faction and the apprehending of books was shaped by political urgencies and religious passions. Years of polemical debate had transformed genres and literary modes—pastoral, romance, theater itself—but the capacity of literary forms fully to enter civic life was premised on interpretive practices, habits of commentary and contest that might fill a library of books read between the civil wars and the close of the seventeenth century.[4] The scholia are often fleeting—an insult scrawled across the title page, an aspersion cast on an author who might be exposed for schism or delinquency, an opinion denounced as impious and profane. But there are other, more substantial demonstrations of the habits of mind that such readers brought to texts, and these can be found in manuscript notations written down the margins of printed pages. The interpretive habits that shaped the understanding and appropriation of books might also be found occupying a crucial role in the courtroom, and I want to begin with the legal cases because they illustrate habits of reading and contest in such a brilliant and economical way.

In 1683 Algernon Sidney, Whig theorist and republican martyr, was brought to trial at King's Bench on charges of compassing and imagining the death of Charles II. Part of the Crown's evidence came from manuscript pages, supposedly in Sidney's hand, on which he had written of "the expulsion of Tarquin, the insurrection against Nero; [and] the slaughter of Caligula."[5] The Crown argued that the examples from antiquity revealed Sidney's thinking on the death of the king. Sidney's words make Roman tyrannicide his ostensible subject, but allegory and innuendo could be used to point his republican passions at Charles II. Sidney denied the application, protesting "the dark and slippery places" where the court's innuendos would make him run;[6] but he could not have been surprised by the Crown's case. From our point of view the Crown was merely covering judicial murder with the thin veil of allegory. But Judge Jeffreys was hardly alone in these habits of reading. A culture steadily alert to reflection and innuendo, read-ers who knew, delicately and dangerously, to draw parallels and seek appli-cations, quickly discerned the school of reading to which the Crown's jus-tice and chief allegorist belonged. Nor was it a minority position. In 1660 the publisher of *Salmasius His Dissection and Confutation of the Diabolical Rebel Milton* reminded Charles II "of that time when Salmasius's learned Writings against Sedition and Rebellion were evermore deemed malignant and unsufferable, insomuch that to see one of his Books was a Crime almost unpardonable; or to read one, a sufficient proof for Sequestration."[7] And in 1664 the Crown mounted a campaign against the printer John Twyn, not for composing but simply for reading treason.[8] When compassing and imagining the death of the king could be hung on a thread of evidence so thin as proofing a scandalous text, reading might prove almost as lethal a practice as raising arms or writing against the king. The game repeatedly turned on the interpretation of that mysterious phrase "compassing and imagining," language that allowed wide latitude to a judiciary that may have lacked bureaucratic heft but understood the exemplary force of judicial murder.

The habits of reading that made possible the Crown's conviction of Sid-ney and Twyn are broadly evident across later seventeenth-century literary culture. And we discover these habits displayed in a variety of textual sites: in epics and mock-epics like *The Davidies* and *The Dispensary*, but also in satires like *Tarquin and Tulia*, allegories like *The Sicilian Usurper*, and anthologies like *Poems on Affairs of State*. Restoration broadsides, ballads, songs, litanies, theatrical prologues and epilogues, and those "Sessions of Poets" that make such a superb hash of contemporary verse and versifiers have come down to us in copies covered with manuscript notation. Here we can discover the identities, often veiled, of the courtiers, poets, and patrons inscribed in the present tense (and on occasion in the eternity) of these works. When Dry-den sighed, tongue in cheek, that the tedium of rehearsing titles and names was below the dignity of verse, and then sketched those brilliant images of Shemei, Corah, Calab, and Agag, his audience had no trouble supplying the names of the poet's contemporaries. Dryden's readers do not always agree on the identity of minor characters, but the habit was endemic and the plea-sures of this recreation obvious in the number of printed keys and surviving copies of *Absalom and Achitophel* with manuscript notation.[9]

The polemical reading of texts was not, of course, limited to print. Man-uscripts themselves were marked with writing against the center, and audi-ences that delighted in the heroic drama (for us, that most mysterious of tastes) knew exactly how to read the arguments and parallels written into the exotic sites of this theater. These plays were no idle exercises in cultural anthropology. Mexico, the Indies, and Peru reflected—in their fabulous sets, their costumes and machines—the politics and culture not of the New

World but of the Old. What animated this theater was not merely visual spectacle (though we should not underestimate the appetite for spectacle after nearly two decades of closet drama) but more pointedly its capacity to throw the shadow of epic across allegories of policy and intrigue. And when such plays were delayed in production, censored, or even banned, it was clear that contemporary nerves had been touched. In 1692 Queen Mary—not known for particularly shrewd habits of reading—demanded that the performance of Dryden's *Cleomenes* be banned.[10] Not even the poet, despite his claim "tis now seven or eight Years since I design'd to write this Play,"[11] could have been surprised that Mary construed the tragedy of Egyptian usurpation and exile as a play whose politics were concerned less with the Orient and antiquity than with Whitehall and the present.[12]

As the Crown's justice affirmed in Sidney's trial, the meaning of texts would be delimited neither by the moment of their creation nor by the antiquity of their idiom. For those who found in Aesop's fables a text for dangerous times or discerned in Virgil's *Aeneid* either a vindication of or a melancholy reflection on the Glorious Revolution, dates of composition, transcription, translation, or publication would neither determine nor delimit the parallels and reflections to be discovered in histories and epics, or in fables and theater. Algernon Sidney had claimed that it was "a right of mankind . . . exercised by all studious men, that they write in their own closets what they please for their own memory, and no man can be answerable for it, unless they publish it."[13] But the Crown's justice was hardly interested in the rights of privacy and closeted reflection: "Pray do not go away with that right of mankind, that it is lawful for me to write what I will in my own closet, unless I publish it; I have been told, Curse not the king, not in thy thoughts, not in thy bedchamber, the birds of the air will carry it."[14] The free play of meanings and intentions across a wide spectrum of literary texts and intellectual modes made writing and reading, even meditating and reflecting, vivid but dangerous acts in the decades that followed the English civil wars.

READING IN THE HEAT OF CRISIS

In the early 1640s we can follow the manuscript notations of the antiquary and royalist lawyer Sir Roger Twysden on the tracts of Philip Hunton and Sir Robert Filmer as he delicately negotiated a space for himself between theories of mixed government and royal absolutism, dissenting from Hunton's insistence on limitations but as well denying Filmer's conflation of regal and patriarchal authority.[15] And at the end of the decade, I suspect shortly after the execution of Charles I, one angry reader of William Prynne's *New Discovery of the Prelates Tyranny* (1641) covered the pages of this book with accusations of treachery, deceit, and sedition.[16] In the 1650s the widespread suspicion of Cromwell's motives can be followed in the manuscript commentary written down the margins of Cromwell's published parliamentary addresses.[17] And in a copy of the 1654 edition of *Cabala,* a royalist collection of ministerial letters on affairs of state, next to the bishop of Lincoln's apostrophe to James I as "the only heaven wherein my soul delighted," a reader retorted, "impious, prophane, atheisticall."[18]

We can gauge contemporary responses to the Anglo-Dutch wars in the marginal annotations on Richard Hawkins's *Discourse of the National Excellencies of England.* The book was published in 1658, but one reader in 1667 extended the chronicle of Anglo-Dutch conflicts, remarking the current English failures: "We made no preparations but were cowed by ye Dutch without any to appear for defence."[19] And when dissenters were harassed in the 1660s and hoped to assert their political innocence, they first recorded "without any addition, alteration or correction" and then printed and distributed their sermons to create a public record, vindicating the dissenting "hearers" by creating witnessing readers.[20]

From the 1670s we can follow, in an interleaved copy of *The Rehearsal,* the marquis of Halifax's transcriptions, identifications, and corrections of every passage that the duke of Buckingham ridiculed in his mocking anthology of the heroic drama.[21] On the title page of Edward Howard's 1674 *Poems and Essays,* the poet was dismissed by an anonymous reader as "a degraded, unblushing shameless Profligate";[22] and on a copy of Clement Walker's *Compleat History of Independency* (1661) a reader in 1671 denounced the book's former owner as a "spitefull fanatick . . . as appears by the malevolent marginal notes."[23] The years of popery and plots supply us with a feast of manuscript commentary. Narcissus Luttrell's notes on what are now known as the Bindley Pamphlets are a storehouse of exactly contemporary responses to the texts and events of the Exclusion Crisis, but it was not only collectors like Luttrell who responded to and explicated the polemical force of this literature.[24] Texts of political theory like Filmer's *Patriarcha* and James Tyrrell's *Patriarcha non Monarcha* were read in the heat of the Exclusion Crisis and annotated accordingly. In a copy of *Patriarcha* one reader underscored Filmer's discussion of divines as "Pleaders for Absoluteness of Monarchical Power" and wrote in the margin: "Judases."[25] When Bishop Burnet went on his travels at James II's accession and published in 1686 a set of letters on the politics, economics, and social culture of France, Switzerland, and Italy, one contemporary tracked Burnet through "all his designs," exposing contradictions, denying observations, refuting arguments. Burnet wrote of the marks of extreme poverty of rural France, and the reader comments, "I saw the contrary in 1685";[26] when Burnet celebrated the wealth and ease of the Swiss cantons, the reader exclaims, "This false remark is the author his chief design in all this book";[27] and when Burnet derided the Venetians as "generally ignorant of the matters of Religion to a Scandal"[28] and scorned Venetian religion as superstition and atheism, our annotator rejoins, "Like Cato, they have Two Religions, one public, another private . . . their secret religion is Socinianism or Deism: not Atheism."[29] And in what looks like a swipe at Burnet for his role in the revolution, the reader remarks, "Whatever be the secret perswasion of the Venetians in matters of Religion, yet they are great Enemies to Innovation; [and] they are enemies to Churchmens medling with the Civile government."[30]

In the next decade, on the flyleaves of a copy of Edward Dacres's translation of Machiavelli, the *Discourses* are brought close to home:

> By History & observation it may be proved that its an Easy thing for to change A nations Religion & to prove ye change does strengthen our Authors interest. But it may be changed & effected after some publick Revolution. The people are subject to expect great advantage of both Religion & policy from such changes . . . Thus Q El. Brought in the Reformation & established it, which thing confirmed & supported her indifferent Title. The Long parliament turned out the Church of Eng: & Brought in Presbytery [then] independency. King James might have restord the Church of Rome but that he wanted courage to execute his designs & was not wicked enough for such an attempt. W[ha]t King William will or may do in this: Time will show.[31]

Could Machiavelli have been read in the 1690s without the shadow of the English Reformation and revolution crossing the page?

A COMMUNITY OF PRACTICES

Not so long ago we were often instructed—and on occasion we are still urged to believe—that seventeenth-century readers exercised an utterly free hand in elevating texts of civic theory, philosophy, and literature above political circumstance.[32] Such readers, the argument goes, might have admired a poem like Dryden's *Absalom and Achitophel* as much for the light it cast on Scripture as for the heat it generated in exposing the design of Exclusion. But the traces that contemporary readers left on their texts scarcely suggest such voluntarism. Of course, acts of interpretation and application occur in the private space between the reader and the page. But reading is also situated within a community of interpretive and hence political practices. The evidence that we can recover from late seventeenth-century readers leaves little doubt about the force and direction of those polemical currents that absorbed such texts as *Venice Preserv'd, Absalom and Achitophel,* and *Patriarcha* in the Exclusion Crisis or *The Two Treatises of Government* and *Don Sebastian* in the aftermath of 1688. Moreover, these texts, and not only Locke's *Two Treatises,* retained their political force for some years beyond their initial publication. On a copy of *Patriarcha non monarcha* (1681) annotated in the 1690s, a reader glossed Tyrrell's discussion of sovereignty: "Mark those which doat on Arbitrary power; and you'll find them either hot brain'd fools; or needy bankrupts."[33] And from the same decade a reader of *Absalom and Achitophel* remarked of Dryden's lines "Thus, heaping Wealth, by the most ready way / Among the Jews, which is to Cheat and Pray": "tis much in practis at this verey day Aug: 16: 96."[34] Of David's ironic self-description "And Kings are onely Officers in Trust," the same reader comments: "in Eng: the Law makes them so and no more."[35] And in the same copy the commentary of the 1696 reader is itself contested and defaced. Next to Dryden's line "Yet, grant our Lords the People Kings can make," the earlier commentary "as was lately done by Parliament . . . to the . . . of ye Kingdome" is rendered partly illegible by the cross-hatching of a contesting reader.[36] Similar contestation can be found in a copy of William Prynne's 1643 *Treachery and Disloyalty of Papists to their Soveraignes*, where page after page of marginal annotation is so carefully defaced that every line of marginalia is rendered wholly illegible.[37] The language of sovereignty, contract, and covenant retained its capacity to engage political sensibilities and to inflame partisan opinion well beyond the crises of the 1640s or the 1680s, when such idioms excited a display of the full armory of political contest.

The experience of the printed text as palimpsest can be repeated with a number of books. A polemical masterpiece like *Absalom and Achitophel* drew powerful commentary, a layering of contemporary and near contemporary responses. It may be difficult for us to recover the exact nuance of contemporary gossip in this piece; surely the jokes and bits of sacred and sexual irony scattered through the poem could have been understood only as part of the public scandals and private rumors that saturated the discourse of court and city politics and politicians. But for readers in 1681 the language of scriptural righteousness had an exact polemical edge and a long historical reach. Of course, to allegorize political crisis as sacred history in 1681 was hardly to present an original template; it was rather to insist on an idiom that not only excited the memory of familiar ways but indeed risked, and perhaps willingly courted, platitude rather than novelty. Politics allegorized as Scripture could only have recalled the days of "dreaming saints," of insurrection and enthusiasm. That was of course the point: to suggest to the whole of the poem's readership that the ill-affected were once again stirring civil war and that the history of the Jews applied to English politics allowed more than one party to claim narratives of exile and election as their own.

But what could it have meant to cover idioms of sacred history with the studied negligence of courtly wit, with the bedroom jokes of a besotted and sterile Court, a mode of irony now itself rather beside the point in a time not of procreative liberty but of feminized luxury? Clearly, the poem drew much of its energy from the mocking encounter with scriptural sobriety. For those willing to identify themselves with spiritual enthusiasm, the fleering wit of this poem would have constituted a steady insult, every gesture in its rewriting of II Samuel to accommodate the forms and postures of Stuart monarchy an outrage. But for wits and courtiers, the wry amusements over sexual abundance were themselves a form of nostalgia, perhaps even wishful thinking, about a not so distant past. And yet, for all the mockery and irony, this counterpointing of past and present—of Israel with England but as well of '41 with '81—constituted a crucial mode of political reflection in the months surrounding the Exclusion Crisis and for some years beyond. Tory partisans would have eagerly played at the naming of names; but the desire to participate in unmasking political identities easily crossed party lines, and we know both from attacks on the poem and from annotation that it was not only loyalists who found the contests and engagements and entertainments of this text worth their while.

What could have been more obvious in 1681 than the contemporary identities of the figures in its opening lines?

> In pious times, e'r Priest-craft did begin,
> Before *Polygamy* was made a sin;
> When man, on many, multiply'd his kind,
> E'r one to one was, cursedly, confind:
> When Nature prompted, and no law deny'd
> Promiscuous use of Concubine and Bride;
> Then *Israel*'s Monarch after Heaven's own heart,
> His vigorous warmth did, variously, impart
> To Wives and Slaves: And, wide as his Command,
> Scatter'd his Maker's Image through the Land.
> *Michal,* of Royal blood, the Crown did wear,
> A Soyl ungratefull to the Tiller's care:
> Not so the rest; for several Mothers bore
> To Godlike *David,* several Sons before.
> But since like slaves his bed they did ascend,
> No True Succession could their seed attend.
> Of all this Numerous Progeny was none
> So Beautifull, so brave as *Absalon.*[38]

Were Dryden's contemporaries writing Charles II for David, Queen Catherine for Michal, Monmouth for Absalom, and Shaftesbury for Achitophel lest they forget who these characters were? The keys were surely no reader's glossary like those provided for English-language editions of Tolstoy's novels. Manuscript notations and keys suggest neither an unsteady grasp of design nor an equivocal reader; they suggest nothing so much as that powerful drama of partisanship that constituted the world of popery and Exclusion. And if there were mysteries in the design, so much the better. Amnon's identity has never been discovered. Having caught the imagination of his readers, was Dryden likely to have played out a wholly predictable hand? In later years the poet would darken such puzzles, as when he toyed with readers of *Don Sebastian,* insisting that the play's moral was "couch'd under every one of the principal Parts and Characters, which a judicious Critick will observe."[39] No one has yet observed that moral, but Dryden knew very well how to use enigma in challenging his readers to discover the abundant morals of this Jacobite tragedy and tragedian in a world of revolution and usurpation.

Indeed, the poet understood exactly what his contemporaries were about to do with his poems, his allegories, his prefaces, and his dedications because he had heard from them often and, more important, because he was one of them; because he, like Milton and Marvell and Rochester, had gone to school in the politics, poetics, and hermeneutics of a world turned upside down by pamphlets and poems and the force of arms. Dryden engaged and solicited his readers; he also gulled and abraded and mocked them. And when he began to unwind the ironies and politics of *Absalom and Achitophel,* he knew there would be no escaping the particular applications he had up his sleeve. Whatever else the Whigs and Birmingham Protestants would do with his text, they would hardly fail to make and understand the applications he had in mind. The intimacies and abrasions of their mutual embrace can be felt in the poet's every move in preface and poem, from his mocking anonymity to his threatening suggestions of judicial vengeance and civil war. Like so much else from these years, *Absalom and Achitophel* was written with an exact and delicately graded sense, indeed, one is tempted to add, with the complicity of its hostile and polemicized readers. And are we wrong to hear the poet's relish when he turned again to take up his encounter with contesting readers, prefacing *The Medall* with an epistle to the Whigs: "For to whom can I dedicate this Poem, with so much justice as to you?"[40]

Of course, Dryden was hardly alone in this work. One finds a similar contrapuntal density on the pages of any number of seventeenth-century allegories, parallels, and fables that allured and abraded and confronted, then steadily engaged their readers in acts of decoding and application. The printer's device of connecting the first and last letters of proper names with dashes, partially veiling but also inviting the discovery of contemporary identities, appears in scores of later seventeenth-century pamphlets, broadsides, and satiric verse. Perhaps libel laws, or on occasion something approaching delicacy, or a pretense of coyness encouraged such veiling. But the dashes look rather like an invitation to fill in the blanks, an institutionalizing of manuscript notation. We might find the mechanical adoption of the device a trivializing of annotation, a reduction to puzzle and enigma of what is in other settings a fuller, more impassioned polemical and ideological engagement. But we should also allow that the habits of mind and indeed the long-held habits of reading, glossing, and commonplacing that encouraged annotation and topical application have now become absorbed in the material and aesthetic properties of the text itself. Manuscript marginalia have been written into the textual and the literary systems of this moment when the twinning of the mythic and the topical and the insistent clamor for gossip and slander as well as the desire for sublimity drove the epic gestures of Marvell, Rochester, Dryden, Swift, and Pope. The particular registers in which epic and satire dwelled during these years were determined by a readerly culture that inscribed, in the most literal sense, its politics, its often bitter partisanship, and its fascination with the most intimate kinds of topicality in the margins of printed texts of everything from pamphlets and broadsides to aesthetic theory and epic poetry.

Nor should we ignore the complicity of booksellers, who understood the relation between scandal and market. If gossip and intimacies of political and sexual scandal might limit the shelf life of certain texts—of broadsides and satirical squibs—their dense particularity and their invitation to play at unmasking names might also guarantee a brisk trade. Once baited in this way, readers would occupy an easily calculated position in the pamphlet market and in more elevated reaches of the book trade as well. The entertainment provided by partially concealed and suggestively revealed identities reached a particularly brilliant apogee in the first edition of Alexander Pope's *Dunciad* (1728) with its gallery of initialed fools and hacks. But by the late 1720s Pope was writing and publishing in a changing market and in a different aesthetic and ideological world. The names he may have feared wholly to reveal had little to do with the corruption of place or with the scandals, plots, and occasionally lethal politics of Exclusion, Rye House, or the Glorious Revolution. Pope had scores to settle, but the stakes had fallen dramatically in the decades between the revelations of the Popish Plot and Theobald's exposure of Pope's skills as an editor of Shakespeare. Nor was Pope patient enough to play long on the secrets of *The Dunciad*. The 1728 edition with its initial letters, hints, and puzzles was followed by the 1729 *Dunciad variorum*, which named the offending names. Pope claimed that the 1728 edition was unauthorized, and that to correct errors and avoid misunderstandings Lawton Gilliver printed a corrected text with identities revealed. More surely Pope was eager to intervene, to manage from every possible angle the production and consumption of his masterly vendetta. There may have been legal, but surely there were no political, reasons to conceal names when the stakes were as low as those that dominated this astonishing poem. And did anyone other than Pope's victims care enough to uncover all those names hinted at in the first issue of *The Dunciad?* In 1728 Jonathan Swift had said of those names: "The Notes I could wish to be very large, in what relates to the persons concerned; for I have long observed that twenty miles from London no body understands hints, initial letters, or town-facts and passages; and in a few years not even those who live in London."[41] Such was hardly the case in 1681. Nor is it surprising that in the decades that separate *Absalom and Achitophel* from *The Dunciad* certain habits of annotation have begun to decline or that from the evidence of that decline we can speculate not only on modes of reading and understanding but on the relation between the position of the aesthetic in the early eighteenth century and the structural fixity of its politics.

Of course, scandal and partisanship form only part of the elaborate system of annotation that early modern books reveal. Anyone who has spent time with these books has come across a variety of traces left by earlier readers. We find their underscoring, their pointing fingers and signs of return, their brackets, corrections, and cross-hatching; their scribbles, ciphers, and codes; their repeated signatures and alphabets, accounts, and sums; their acquisition dates and purchase prices as well as their more substantive engagements with printed texts and, on occasion, with earlier readers as they confute and confirm or deface and delete one another. Fully verbalized commentary has the most to tell us about the transactions that took place between readers and their texts; and this seems especially so when we eavesdrop on those whose writings or lives are already familiar: Jonson as he marked his Martial;[42] Charles I reading *Richard III*;[43] Francis Atterbury annotating *Paradise Lost*;[44] Swift reading Clarendon.[45] At one end of the century Sir Edward Coke wrote on his copy of Bacon's *Great Instauration,* "It deserveth not to be read in schooles / but to be fraughted in the ship of fooles";[46] a century later Defoe can be discovered similarly mocking Bacon's *Advancement of Learning.*[47] And when Lord Burghley's library was sold at auction in 1687, Cecil's fame was not to be overlooked in marketing the collection:

> If the Catalogue, here presented, were only of Common Books, and such as were easie to be had, it would not have been very necessary to have Prefac'd any thing to the Reader: But since it appears in the World with two Circumstances, which no Auction in England (perhaps) ever had before . . . it would seem an Oversight, if we should neglect to advertise the Reader of them. The first is, That it comprises the main part of the Library of that Famous Secretary William Cecil, Lord Burleigh. . . . The second is, That it contains a greater number of Rare Manuscripts . . . many of which are rendered the more valuable by being remark'd upon by the hand of the said great Man.[48]

But most traces of early readers were not this glamorous, either for immediate or for later consumers. More often they were anonymous and elusive, not so easy of intellectual and social access. And yet, taken as a whole, the network of marginal activity that we discover by surveying a cross section of early modern books allows us to think about the interplay between the composing and consuming of texts with a sense of the forces that shaped and the passions that drove readers in their acquisition and appropriation of texts.

Even under a complicated system of statutes, ordinances, monopolies, licensing laws, and other forms of policing that were intended—and at times functioned—to regulate the creation and dispersal of texts, the writing, printing, publishing, vending, and finally reading of books in this age was astonishingly varied and prolific. The library and auction catalogs of the later seventeenth century suggest the energy and industry of seventeenth-century writers, printers, publishers, and booksellers as well as the appetites and habits of collectors and consumers in these years. As texts were various, so were readers, and the experience of books was determined by many forces: by intellect and education; by social status and memory; by religion and politics; by gender, age, and geography; and by friendship, alliance, and dependency. Yet allowing all the varieties that can help us sort and categorize early modern readers, there emerge, in the period that I have been describing, some powerful habits that repeatedly shaped readers' encounters with their texts and that seem to shadow the reading experience across a wide variety of genres and modes. Those habits were determined partly by the ways early modern readers were taught to gloss and apply Scripture, to listen to and read sermons, and to practice commonplacing. But it was the collective experience of politics that left the deepest imprint, not only on the making of books but on their consumption as well.

Is it any wonder to find a 1680 primer "containing plain and easie directions for spelling and reading English, with all the necessary rules for the true reading of the English tongue: together with a brief and true account of the bloody persecutions, massacres, plots, treasons, and most inhuman tortures committed by the papists upon Protestants for near six hundred years past, to this very time."[49] What arrests our attention is not the anti-Catholicism—we are, after all, in the midst of the Popish Plot—but rather the seamless continuity between the two projects of this "how to" book. The naïveté of the conjunction is striking, a seamless link between the two parts of the enterprise, as if learning to read led one naturally to those brief and true accounts of plots, treasons, and tortures.

But it will be some decades before the position of politics in this literary culture and all that is implied by that geography will shift. The Sacheverell riots in 1710 and the furious pamphleteering in the months prior to the settlement in 1714 suggest the volatility of politics and the virulence of party culture in the first years of the new century. And the grip of polemic in the midst of Pope's art can still surprise; but the center of that enterprise is more certainly aesthetics than civics. The passions may not have dimmed, but they have narrowed. It was one sort of enterprise for Dryden to reimagine Virgil in the unsteady aftermath of the Glorious Revolution;[50] it was quite another for Pope to construct and steadily to revise the empire of dullness over two decades of Hanoverian rule.

And what of our deeply engaged readers in the 1740s as Pope prepared his final extension of *The Dunciad*? By the middle of the eighteenth century it is not so much the traces of readers we discover in their books but more often their absence that is striking, for those habits of reading and understanding expressed in manuscript marginalia have begun to disappear from the margins of books by the time Pope had made his final revisions on *The Dunciad,* a fantastic structure in which every name was named in the printed text and glossed in that wilderness of notes that at once threaten to overwhelm Pope's verse and so brilliantly organize every move the reader might make or imagine in acquiring Pope's text. But it was not only the domineering temperament of the poet that had reorganized the space readers might hope to occupy in his text. By the mid-eighteenth century political culture and the position of the book within that culture had undergone a sea change. What nicer demonstration of the transformation of habits and understanding than the career of Milton's major poetry: at first soiled by association with regicide, held in suspicion even as it was envied or reluctantly admired by those who sought to refashion literary art in the first years of the Restoration; then appropriated by Whiggery after 1688;[51] glossed, annotated, and explained by Hume, Bently, and Richardson in the first decades of the eighteenth century;[52] canonized in the marmoreal editions of Newton and Wharton and finally transformed into an object of fully aestheticized contemplation, an icon of the literary sublime.[53]

READING AND INTERIORITY

We have been tracing an arc in habits of reading that spans a hundred years and more, from the outbreak of civil war and the surge of pamphleteering in the 1640s through Pope's last edition of *The Dunciad.* I want to close by looking back on the habits and figures of reading over this hundred years, but not by contemplating a margin or an editorial scheme but now a scene of reading, and this from a late eighteenth-century novel, known in its 1784 translation as *The Sorrows and Sympathetic Attachments of Young Werter.*[54] Goethe's novel allows us to imagine yet another metamorphosis in habits of reading, but it also enables us to look back on earlier scenes of reflective and contestative reading, deepening our sense of the cultural and historical constitution of reading and helping us gauge transformations in those forces that shape and shadow reading along the way.

Toward the end of the novel, just before Werther's suicide, Goethe places the final and forbidden clarification of the lovers' passion, a clarification that takes place as the hero reads his translation of the Gaelic bard Ossian to his beloved. Charlotte, in a slight pique and quandary over Werther's moods, tries to settle the atmosphere of the last visit:

"'Have you nothing to read,' said she. He answered, 'No.' 'Then open that drawer, and you will find your own translation of some of the songs of Ossian—I have not yet read it, as I hoped to hear you read it yourself; but you have been fit for nothing lately.' He smiled, with his eyes full of tears, took out the manuscript, and began to read." What follows in Goethe's text are James Macpherson's Ossian fragments. We can leave aside the oddity of an English audience in 1786 reading an English translation of a German book in which Werther was supposed to have translated the Ossianic fragments into a German now supposedly translated back into English. The translation of Werther's translation is simply a verbatim reproduction of passages from Macpherson's *Fragments of Ancient Poetry* (1760), itself a supposed translation from Gaelic. The conundrum over translation raises questions about translation and authenticity that might well bear on our understanding of late eighteenth-century reading, but what most interests me in the passage is the response of the lovers to the reading of Ossian. Following Werther's melancholy recital, the scene closes as

> a flood of tears streamed from the eyes of Charlotte, and gave some relief to her oppressed heart. Werter stopped, threw down the paper, seized her hand, and wept bitterly. Charlotte leaned on the other arm, and applied her handkerchief to her eyes. They were both in the greatest agitation. In this story, they saw all their own misfortunes, mutually felt them—and their tears flowed from the same source. She trembled, and wished to go from him; but sorrow and soft compassion pressed her down. She sighed to recover herself, and sobbing, desired him to proceed. Werter, with his heart almost bursting, took up the manuscript and in broken accents continued. . . . The unhappy Werter was quite overwhelmed by the power of these words.[55]

No one coming across these passages in the 1780s would image Charlotte now retiring to her study to commonplace the scenes from Ossian, nor would we expect a late eighteenth-century reader to abstract or to contest, perhaps not even to mark the text, at least not with pen and ink. Goethe is dramatizing the discovery of the self at the moment of most passionate readerly discourse. For all the scenes of sentiment and sympathy in the novel, it is in the act of readerly subjectivity that these characters reach most deeply within, to discern or to discover or indeed, through the idioms of their text, to construct the self—an event that Goethe's contemporaries repeated often and at times in shocking ways. Some of Goethe's contemporaries found the book alarming because it could be understood as a defense of suicide. But the novel was also shocking because of the kind of psychic work that Goethe recorded in this scene and because that work was repeated by readers outside the text but clearly within the grip of its fictions and discernments. Werther and Charlotte reading and discovering the deepest self not only authorized self-discovery as a mode of reading but acted as its model.

The capacity to imagine the self as psychological or passional subject marks a disjunction in the cultural and intellectual history of reading. Nor should we neglect the powerful relations between the emergence of the self as a subject of reading and the gradual discovery of the self as a political subject, a turn in the civic culture that would reach one climax with the revolutionary events in France in the next decade. The French Revolution reminds us again of the political and ideological constitution of reading, of the ways in which the narrative of reading practices is not only an intellectual but a social and aesthetic history as well, with all the particularity and contingency that word implies.

But Goethe's scene not only looks forward to the reflexivity of romanticism; it might also be used to look back over that long revolutionary moment in England that began with the pamphleteering of the civil wars and whose contestations, whose polemical fervor and partisan force, dominated the creation and consumption of texts for the next half century and beyond. We might begin to feel a release from that partisan and partied domination after the settlement of 1714, but of course the rhythms of intellectual habit do not turn exactly on political events though just as surely they are driven and constituted by public life.

I have insisted throughout on the circumstantial, on the constructedness of habits and practices of reading and interpretation, but I want to end by acknowledging, at least for a moment, the transcendental. Goethe's lovers may not put us in mind of seventeenth-century readers, but they might just remind us of an earlier pair of lovers driven to destruction by their absorption in a text; the scene is Canto V of *The Inferno,* and the lovers are Paolo and Francesca, who discover in the pages of a book the passional self. What the pairs of lovers ask us to pause over is not the distance between Dante and Goethe, though there is distance enough to remark between the poet of sacred cosmologies and the universal genius of the German Enlightenment, or the distinctions between reading a vernacular epic in a manuscript culture and an epistolary novel in a world of print and leisure, but rather the commonality of reading. Like Dante's and Goethe's lovers, like those who first read Dante and Goethe as their contemporaries, and like those who marked their Spenser and Shakespeare or wrote in the margins of their Milton, and Dryden, and Swift, when we sit down to read we can only do so in the present tense. We are of course shaped and driven by the imperatives of our own time. But as we reconstitute the moment of reading in the past— and we do so with an alertness to all the signs and traces of that readerly world—and hold it in a suspension with the contingences of the present, we allow a dialectic that truly opens the possibilities of imagining the past, offering a perspective that is difficult otherwise to conjure, a sudden apprehension of the past that at once intrudes on the present and insists not on continuities or homogeneity but on differences and distance.

The Politics of Song in Wordsworth's
Lyrical Ballads

Gerald Izenberg

Wordsworth's poetry was from its very beginnings, in the apt phrase of James Averill, "poetry of human suffering."[1] Despite the autobiographical itinerary he offers in *The Prelude,* it did not take the French Revolution to open Wordsworth to "love of mankind." It could in fact be argued that his reformist enthusiasm represented an aberration from a more fundamental attitude to human misery which predated the revolution; after the brief moment in the early 1790s when he held that such distress was produced and could be alleviated by politics, he reverted to his previous concern with suffering as an ontological condition. In this bald formulation, however, the contention would only be partly right. There was no simple reversion: Wordsworth's revolutionary experience did leave a permanent mark on the poetic treatment of suffering that followed it. *Lyrical Ballads,* however, represents neither the linear sublimation of democratic sympathies that critics from Hazlitt to Gill have found in their rustic subjects and "plain" style nor the conservative "apostasy" that historicists old and new have seen in their nostalgic, aestheticized ruralism or in their "displacement" of politics by aesthetics *tout court.*[2]

Not that a social vision is lacking in *Lyrical Ballads.* Much of what recent historicist critics have said about the work seems valid. The poet himself could be quite explicit about his politics, as he was in his letter of January 14, 1800, to Charles James Fox, commending *Lyrical Ballads* to the statesman as social criticism, lamenting with particular reference to *Michael* and *The Brothers* the rapid disappearance of the "small independent *proprietors* of land" in the face of a rising manufacturing and urban economy, and implying the need for changes in social policy to counteract these adverse developments.[3] The precise ideological coloration of Wordsworth's social vision may be a matter of dispute. In the theory of poetic language he advances in the "Preface," for example, Wordsworth couples an explicitly modernist, egalitarian defense of the value of the common with a critique of the modernity out of which that value emerged.[4] The social ideal implied by the critique looks less like the Burkean hierarchical traditionalism it later became than a chastened democratic agrarian republicanism shorn of its recent radical political implications.[5] David Simpson is surely right in arguing that Wordsworth's writings in the years after 1797 "contain a sophisticated (if often implicit) reformulation of the traditional defense of civic or public virtue against the dangerous effects of a commercial and industrial society."[6] Gary Harrison, however, offers a persuasive qualification of the often associated view that Wordsworth's romance of independent proprietors had purely conservative implications with regard to the poor because it suppressed the socioeconomic conflicts that were destroying the very society he idealized and thus blinded him to the political measures necessary to cope with the realities of rural poverty. While agreeing with Simpson that "Wordsworth's poetry is implicated in an ideology that confirms and perpetuates the pauperization of the agricultural laborer and the idealization of rustic poverty," Harrison argues that there are also radically utopian elements in Wordsworth's representation of the poor, who function in the poetry as mirrors of the reader's own vulnerabilities.[7] These and other critics have done much historical mapping to locate Wordsworth's social views within the context of contemporary debates about such issues as urbanization and pauperization in England in the 1790s and the first decade of the nineteenth century. But however Wordsworth's social ideal is characterized, its significance for the project of *Lyrical Ballads* has been misunderstood in the recent efforts to historicize the poetry.

To an extent Wordsworth himself is responsible for the misunderstanding. Having committed himself to a social ideal that was no longer historically viable, he appears to have made himself vulnerable to charges that he willfully ignored contrary social realities or that, in an even more radical evasion, he displaced social concerns altogether onto ambitions for poetry (the two criticisms are, of course, incompatible).[8] But to attribute to Wordsworth a need to be anachronistic in his politics or to aestheticize politics altogether as the mainspring of his poetic project is to mistake the point of the social arrangements he indisputably evokes in *Lyrical Ballads*. Those arrangements do not eliminate, they were not intended to eliminate, human suffering; Wordsworth did not believe that any social arrangements could. Rather Wordsworth believed that only one social form can create the kind of society that allows human beings to receive from and offer to one another as much support and consolation as there is to be had in the face of inevitable aloneness, decrepitude, and death. This is a not inconsiderable end; it is worthy of the sharp polemics Wordsworth occasionally engages in on behalf of the social forms he believes could accomplish it and against those that would undermine it. For the rest, however—that is, for what Wordsworth considered the essential—what humans require is the right attitude to their fate, and that ultimately meant the right relationship to nature. Indeed, a good part of the reason Wordsworth insisted on his social utopia in the teeth of an adverse reality—are not critics inconsistent in arguing that Wordsworth both emphasized that reality and evaded it?—was that his ideal imagined the social conditions most conducive to nurturing the proper—nonexploitive—attitude to nature. As Wordsworth's own itinerary had shown, however, these conditions were not necessary ones; they could, for example, be poetically imagined, rather than actually lived. And he could be quite explicit that these social arrangements were not ends in themselves. He was drawn to the story of the shepherds recounted in "Michael," he says in the poem itself, not because he loved such men "For their own sakes, but for the fields and hills / Where was their occupation and abode." The real subject of the poem is nature, rightly conceived. Furthermore, the evocation of a threatened world is not meant to inspire social action but the poetry that will echo Wordsworth's own; he writes

> for the sake
> Of youthful Poets, who among these Hills
> Will be my second Self when I am gone.[9]

It was Wordsworth's conceit that personal experience had brought him the knowledge of the right attitude to nature; moreover, he felt that he could not only transmit but create that attitude with his song, in the face of the powerful poetic countertendencies of the age. But here precisely was the source of the difficulty. There was a deep tension between attitude and conceit, for the essence of the right attitude was "wise passiveness," resignation in the face of human transience and receptivity toward nature's eternal Being, while the conceit ultimately meant poetry's triumph over fate. Poetry, in a word, could accomplish what social arrangements could not. It is the paradoxical stances of passivity and poetic absolutism that *Lyrical Ballads* wrestles with. Both were legacies of Wordsworth's encounter with the French Revolution. The poetic will was the postrevolutionary transformation of the ideal of absolute autonomy Wordsworth had defined at the peak of his political radicalism, "wise passiveness" the retreat from that absolute autonomy as a norm for living in the face of the personal and political havoc it could wreak. I want to trace their evolution in the development of Wordsworth's poetry, but by way of a prelude I will illustrate their significance within Wordsworth's immediate postrevolutionary work through a reading of one of the ballads.

THE PARADOX OF SONG

Part two of "Hart-leap Well," the poem that opens the second volume of the 1800 edition of *Lyrical Ballads,* begins with a striking and curious disclaimer:

> The moving accident is not my trade,
> To curl the blood I have no ready arts;
> 'Tis my delight, alone in summer shade,
> To pipe a simple song to thinking hearts.[10]

Coming where they do, these lines seem wholly unmotivated, their illocutionary force quite unclear. One interpretation would link them to an ostensibly strong tension within the poetic program Wordsworth lays out in "Preface." There he acerbically attacks literature that stokes the emotions with melodramatic plots full of lurid detail, the "frantic novels, sickly and stupid German Tragedies, and deluges of idle and extravagant stories in verse" of such literary purveyors of sensationalism as Matthew Lewis and Gottfried Bürger. Yet at the same time he himself asserts that "the end of Poetry is to produce excitement in coexistence with an overbalance of pleasure."[11] James Averill suggests that Wordsworth's own desire to stir up the emotions may be dangerously similar to the craving for the extraordinary and outrageous in the poetry he wishes to contrast with his own;[12] the force of his disclaimer is thus defensive.

The danger Wordsworth feared seems to materialize, in part one of "Hart-leap Well," where the narrator relates the story of Sir Walter's pursuit of the hart and his building of a "pleasure-house" to honor the prodigious leaps by which the animal gallantly tried to escape his pursuer. The chase is exciting, the hart's death pathetic; and there is even a clear echo of Bürger's *Der Wilde Jäger,* with its overtly supernatural events, in the portentous suggestion the narrator makes about the hunt: "This race it looks not like an earthly race."[13] In this reading the disavowal that opens part two is meant to signal the reader that, despite apparent similarities, the narrator's intentions in telling Sir Walter's story are far different from those of Bürger. It thus prepares the reader for the second narrative, the poet's encounter with the shepherd at the ruins of Sir Walter's pleasure-house, which culminates in a moral lesson about the inappropriateness of Sir Walter's response to his triumph: in reducing Sir Walter's commemorative edifices to barely recognizable ruins, nature teaches us "Never to blend our pleasure or our pride / With sorrow of the meanest thing that feels."[14] With his disclaimer the poet thus also distances himself as artist from the creative act of Sir Walter, whose building of the pleasure-house on the spot he killed the hart meant precisely exploiting the occasion of the hart's pain for his own pride and pleasure. Sir Walter is thus linked with the aesthetics of the literature Wordsworth repudiates: "Blending pleasure and pride with the sorrow of others," Averill writes, "is the primary enterprise of sentimental and tragic fiction."[15]

There is a problem, however, with the sharp distinction that both poet and critic posit between the first and second parts of the poem. Averill himself points out that Bürger's supernaturalism is evoked only to be dismissed by the narrative itself. The hint of the supernatural is never realized; the tale is told objectively and dispassionately, without sentimentality or melodrama. The narrator in fact explicitly eschews emotive detail in describing the fate of the hart: "I will not stop to tell how far he fled / Nor will I mention by what death he died."[16] It would seem too that the apologia is textually misplaced. Although a case can be made for hooking the reader with an exciting tale before pointing a moral, the possibility of misunderstanding would have been obviated altogether had a disavowal of sensationalist intent preceded the narrative rather than followed it. The most telling point is that the concluding moral implicates the "simple song" the narrator claims as his preferred mode just as much as it does the ballad that titillates with melodramatic plot and sensationalist detail. For the moral condemns blending pleasure with the pain of others, and the program of the "Preface" defines the task of poetry as exactly that: outweighing the pain of the emotional events that the poem describes with an "overbalance" of poetic pleasure.

It is the pursuit of poetic pleasure rather than the arousal of excitement which links Wordsworth to sensationalist literature. He is, after all, quite clear about the difference between the situations his poetry was concerned with and those exploited by the literature he despises. "The human mind," he claims, "is capable of excitement without the application of gross and violent stimulants."[17] A crucial point of the "Preface" is precisely that it is possible to evoke powerful emotions through homely situations plainly described without recourse to the artificial, the grotesque, the supernatural. Wordsworth was not likely to be concerned that the subjects of *Lyrical Ballads* would be confused with those of the writers he scorned. But the appeal of pleasure, however differently motivated and produced, unavoidably connects his work directly with theirs—and thus with the pleasure-house of Sir Walter. If Sir Walter's artistic endeavor represents the "imperialism" of the aggressive imagination openly aggrandizing itself at the expense of the suffering of others,[18] the more sympathetic and humane song of the narrator is another if less immediately obvious face of that imperialism. It is in fact appropriate that the defensive remarks appear at the beginning of the section in which the narrator gives the lesson of the tale. The conflict between poetic forms and intentions is not simply between Wordsworth and the sensationalists but within Wordsworth himself, between Wordsworth the sufferer and Wordsworth the poet. It is in that conflict, that contradiction, that the true politics of *Lyrical Ballads* inheres.

THE VICISSITUDES OF SUFFERING

Already in "An Evening Walk," the suffering outcast, in particular the poor and abandoned vagrant woman, was the figure through whom Wordsworth represented the agony of exile from the ordered world, the very embodiment of human vulnerability and fragility. She was also the figure through whom he connected himself with the social world in a complex network of identification, displacement, and sympathy.[19] Though she would yield in Wordsworth's revolutionary phase to the "hunger-bitten girl" who could be rescued from poverty and despair by the creation of an egalitarian polity, the vagrant of "An Evening Walk" is not simply a prepolitical figure. Her situation has indeed been affected by historical events—she is alone and destitute because her husband is off fighting the American colonists—but Wordsworth neither attacks nor even seriously attends to the sociopolitical causes of poverty and misery, as other contemporary poems of the same genre do. It is crucially significant that the woman and her children appear in the loco-descriptive poem not as figures observed, like every other person or object in the poem, but as ones visualized, irrupting unsummoned and uncontrolled from the poet's imagination into the poem in terrifying contrast to the family of mother swan and cygnets he has just observed at home in their world. The disruption of the ordered harmony of the world comes from within the observer rather than from without. While it is impossible to say precisely just what are the existential referents for the poetic choice of a destitute mother and her children, the central experience they evoke is the fear of aloneness, helplessness, and utter annihilation. The vagrant's plight is an unhealable rupture in the fullness of being created by the play of contrasts in the preceding descriptions of the natural and human environment which constructs the landscape as a harmony of opposites. The poem finds no way of integrating the dissonance of the vagrant's awful fate in that picturesque plenitude because it is the very negation of the picturesque.

Wordsworth's prerevolutionary poetry was unable to conjure an image of natural harmony powerful enough to contain the terror of the vagrant's annihilation because the terror of the sublime was also associated for him with lawless, destructive rage, a rage that came out of his own sense of aloneness and exile. He had experimented with the sublime in the gothic landscape description of "The Vale of Esthwaite," and frightened by its potential for violence and destruction he exiled it from his early poetry.[20] It was the French Revolution that made it possible for Wordsworth to reappropriate the sublime because under the aegis of revolutionary idealism he could reconceive, and thus legitimize, power and violence as serving the cause of justice and integration, of creation rather than destruction. In "Descriptive Sketches" he refigured nature in its Alpine manifestation as an awesome power with the capacity to destroy and create, hence able to contain destruction as a moment of creation. Humans in turn could appropriate the destructive power of nature through their identification with "god-like" heroes of old, wild dwellers in the mountains such as William Tell who had sublimated their wild energy in the service of human liberation.[21] When the vagrant woman reappears during this phase in "A Night on Salisbury Plain," her plight is the product of oppression rather than an emblem of nothingness. She is now not only the object of the narrator's strong identification but an object lesson of the power of the ruling elites to dispossess smallholders and reduce them to beggary through control and manipulation of the political system. Such illegitimate power justifies the use of force against it, though by the time "Salisbury Plain" was written Wordsworth was already beginning to shrink from the revolutionary violence he had defended just a short time before in the regicidal *Letter to the Bishop of Llandaff.*

I have traced in some detail the process by which Wordsworth soon turned not only against political violence but against political radicalism itself. Frightened by the violence of the Terror he took refuge in William Godwin's political theory, which rested its hopes for reform on reason rather than action. Paradoxically, the turn to theory radicalized Wordsworth even more. Trying to articulate and refine Godwin's idea of the supremacy of private judgment over all other forms of authority, he went a crucial step beyond his political mentor, for whom the authority of judgment was still rooted in Dissenting theology and justified by conscience's sure knowledge of absolute truths. For Wordsworth autonomy came to mean a free mind "Which, *to the blind restraints of general laws / Superior,* magisterially adopts / One guide—the light of circumstances, flashed / Upon an independent intellect"[22]—a mind, that is, unrestrained by any principles other than the "law" of its unique individuality, which was no law at all. The establishment of the foundationless self as a new absolute opened up an abyss of freedom and doubt and led Wordsworth to the crisis of moral skepticism which almost undid him.

It was, however, through the figure of Rivers in his play *The Borderers* that Wordsworth revealed the most frightening implications of the criterion of freedom he had devised at the peak of his theoretical radicalism. For Rivers the idea of the mind as its own warrant for belief and action becomes the rationale for a readiness to defy the strongest moral taboos and the most powerful feelings of love and connection:

> Now for the cornerstone of my philosophy:
> I would not give a denier for the man
> Who would not chuck his babe beneath the chin
> And send it with a fillip to its grave.[23]

The idea of the absolute authority of the self does not entail the nihilistic satanism of Rivers's philosophy; it only permits it. But for Wordsworth

Rivers's "philosophical" conclusion seemed a natural one; it was a psychologically warranted extrapolation of the injured, angry, self-feeling that he came to suspect and fear lay at the bottom of his own revolutionary fervor. It had made him the too acquiescent ally of violence that could go as terribly wrong as it did in the Terror; earlier, and more personally, it had made possible the "defiance of law and custom" that had led to his fathering and abandoning a bastard child.[24] Generalized into a philosophical principle, that self-feeling was more than the destructive narcissism of a single individual, it was also a new legitimization for the greatest public and social enormities. If the figure of Rivers was not wholly congruent with Wordsworth, Rivers unquestionably represented a part of him, a potential sufficiently realized in his own behavior to be generalizable as a character type. Wordsworth came to see that type as the greatest danger of revolutionary idealism.[25] It was the Revolution, with the implications of its ideologies of freedom for a new concept of selfhood, which offered the conditions for the possibility of that kind of generalization. The moral-psychological result of the radically "independent intellect" was a self-divinization whose aim, far from Godwinian benevolence, was destructive omnipotence. Combating *this* legacy of revolution became one of Wordsworth's most pressing drives.

But in abandoning revolution Wordsworth also abandoned the political solution to alienation he had temporarily adopted. He thus had to address once again the problem of the vagrant, which had been the mainspring of his poetic project from the very beginning. In "The Ruined Cottage" Wordsworth effected his poetic recovery from his revolutionary crisis by offering a new solution. The treatment of Margaret in the poem shows that the politicized understanding of poverty had never been adequate to the dilemma the vagrant symbolized for him all along. As in the case of the vagrant woman in the politically charged "Adventures on Salisbury Plain," Margaret's desperate economic situation has been brought about by poor harvests and war, both conceivably remediable by more just political and social institutions. But Margaret is finally undone less by objective conditions than by her own response to them, a response of complete passivity; she can only wait for her husband's return, utterly unable to act, even on behalf of her child. Her expression of guilt for having wronged the child would seem to acknowledge that action of some sort was within her power. Yet neither the Pedlar nor the traveler to whom he tells her tale holds her responsible for her immobility; in her all-consuming, paralyzing longing and her passive waiting for her husband they see not remediable pathology but the symbol of irremediable human lack of self-sufficiency and ultimate aloneness. Where the contemporary critic Thomas De Quincy impatiently found "criminal indulgence" in Margaret's refusal to go on living, Wordsworth saw finitude and the legitimacy of longing. And in the eternity of nature, in the weeds that overgrew the ruins of Margaret's cottage and seemed the very symbol of human decay, he found ultimate consolation for them:

> What we feel of sorrow and despair
> From ruin and from change, and all the grief
> The passing shews of being leave behind,
> Appeared as an idle dream that could not live
> Where meditation was.[26]

Nature is one, and transient, suffering humanity is also part of its eternity and tranquil beauty—"She sleeps in the calm earth and peace is here." The longing that has been unappeased and unappeasable when directed at a mortal love is fulfilled when its object is displaced onto nature herself.

HOW SONG REMEDIES THE IRREMEDIABLE

Lyrical Ballads unfolds the implications of the image of nature and of the right human relationship to her adumbrated in "The Ruined Cottage." There is, however, a subtle though crucial difference between them, implicit in the first edition of the ballads, programmatically explicit in the "Preface" to the second. The Pedlar in "The Ruined Cottage" pays homage to nature with philosophical argument. The poet of *Lyrical Ballads,* and even more the polemicist of the "Preface," turns self-consciously to the labor of the poet as poet. Where "The Ruined Cottage" celebrates nature, *Lyrical Ballads* cele-brates song. And for all that the celebration of nature creates the kind of problems for Wordsworth we have come to appreciate since the work of Geoffrey Hartman, the celebration of song creates even more. For song, unlike nature, is self-evidently the creation of the poet, and Wordsworth's argument for the power of song is an assertion of poetic mastery which con-tradicts the philosophical consolation of "The Ruined Cottage."

What had made the consolation of nature possible in "The Ruined Cot-tage" was a transformation in Wordsworth's figuration of it, a transforma-tion that had initially been effected in his revolutionary poetry and that was originally the counterpart of his political activism. Before the Revolution, as I have noted, he had consciously rejected the sublime for the picturesque, securing safety at the expense of impotence; the domesticated and benign landscape of "An Evening Walk" was completely effaced by the terror of the vagrant's situation. At the extreme of Wordsworth's political development, the human mind had taken over the attributes of the sublime from nature, and nature was temporarily left behind. The autonomy that was superior to general laws had shaken off with "resolute mastery . . . the accidents of nature, time and place, / That make up the weak being of the past."[27] Wordsworth was rescued from the dangers that the terrible aloneness of absolute autonomy threatened by a return to nature effected through the ministrations of his sister Dorothy. But while the nature to which he returned was the absolute power that it had become for him through the Revolution, his relationship to it could no longer be the innocent appropriation or identification it had been in the first flush of revolutionary enthusiasm; that was too close to the angry self-divinization that had almost destroyed him. First through the figure of the Pedlar, later much more fully in *The Prelude,* Wordsworth worked out the contradictory relationship that became the hallmark of his great work: a relationship in which the mind is an absolute and autonomous creative force and yet derives its power from its dependence on, its fusion with, the absolute power of (a maternally figured) nature. This inherently unstable equilibrium was disrupted in each poem and passage that tried to assert it. But the celebration of song provided a much more fragile occasion for this disruption than descriptions of nature. If the evocation of sublime nature inevitably but unwittingly led back to the sublime imagination that constructed it, the celebration of song, an inescapably human creation, necessarily and consciously referred back to the human creator. The dangers of self-aggrandizement were all the more obvious and troublesome when the singer, however much in the service of nature he knew his song to be, promoted it as superior to the art of others and ultimately to nature herself. The figure of the revolutionary monster Rivers continued to haunt *Lyrical Ballads* even as Wordsworth tried to call up through these poems a vision of independence-preserving fusion with nature and the set of social relations that would best promote it.

Much of Wordsworth's own emphasis in the "Preface"—and his commentators have generally followed him in this—is on the difference between his subject matter and language and those of the sensationalist writers and stilted formalists whose work he excoriates. But more significant for Wordsworth's project were the more purely "poetic" aspects of poetry, that which made them song; hence the emphasis on the "lyrical" nature of his ballads which produced what has sometimes seemed the redundancy of the title. Wherein lay the peculiar power of song for Wordsworth? "The music of harmonious metrical language," he claimed, together with memories of pleasure from past reading of poetry, "make up a complex feeling of delight, which is of the most important use in tempering *the painful feeling which will always be found intermingled with powerful descriptions of the deeper passions.*"[28] The assumptions here are crucial yet far from self-evident. *Are* powerful descriptions of the "deeper passions" *always* accompanied by painful feelings? Why should they be? Wordsworth also says that the pleasure of meter derives from the perception of "similitude in dissimilitude" and that this principle is the driving force of the sexual appetite and all the passions deriving from it.[29] Are the sexual passions then *not* "deeper passions"? In the sense in which Wordsworth uses that term, they are not. His sense, never explicitly stated, emerges from the partial listing of the passions and the poems illustrating them which appears a little earlier in the "Preface." *Lyrical Ballads,* Wordsworth tells his readers, accomplishes his aim of illustrating the way our feelings and ideas are associated in a state of excitement by, for example, "tracing the maternal passion . . . as in the poems of the IDIOT BOY and the MAD MOTHER"—poems in which one mother copes with possible fatal danger to her retarded son and another, deranged mother tries to comfort the helpless infant fatally dependent on her; by "accompanying the last struggles of a human being, at the approach of death, cleaving in solitude to life and society, as in the Poem of the FORSAKEN INDIAN," or "by showing, as in Stanzas entitled WE ARE SEVEN the perplexity and obscurity which in childhood attend our notion of death."[30] The passions he mentions are those of extreme situations and final things, where human frailty and helplessness are made manifest: madness, aloneness, and death, the reality of utter annihilation. While the list also includes poems concerned with ostensibly less desperate emotions, for example, *The Brothers,* which in Wordsworth's own words displays "the strength of fraternal or . . . moral attachments when early associated with the great and beautiful objects of nature," these affects are significant in the poetry precisely in relation to the more tragic situations it depicts, as humane, sympathetic responses to the pain of loss and fate. And to Wordsworth's list there could be added many other poems that deal with vulnerability, finitude, and death, with the loss of love which leaves one utterly bereft or inspires consolation, for example, and notably, the "Lucy poems."

The tragedy of the human situation, Wordsworth believed, was enough to evoke the deepest emotions; no artificial stimulus was needed. What enraged him about the sensationalist poetry he so reviled in the "Preface" was that it excited strong emotions with melodramatic and supernatural events for the sake of cheap entertainment and the writer's self-aggrandizement. Such literature did not take the realities of life and emotion seriously. For Wordsworth, life's blood was at stake in the pain of the extreme situations of human reality. "Extreme," however, did not mean for Wordsworth rare, unusual, or dramatic. Human fragility showed itself closest to home in the humblest circumstances—in the plight of an aging man unable to perform the tasks necessary for his own survival, of a mad woman unable to care for her child, of a child defending against the pain of premature death. Harrison has pointed out that Wordsworth's poetry did not treat rustic paupers and sufferers the way eighteenth-century loco-descriptive or pastoral poetry did, as distanced aesthetic objects. "Wordsworth's reader," he says, "encounters the poor as mirrors of his or her own precarious subjectivity and as reminders of the fragility of the reader's own social status."[31] While Harrison overemphasizes the importance of social vulnerability amid all the vulnerabilities the flesh is heir to, he correctly points to the emotional immediacy of Wordsworth's figures and situations. And Harrison's emphasis on readers should not obscure the fact that if Wordsworth was able to hold a mirror up to his readers, it was because he was able to bring to his figures the painful knowledge of his own "precarious subjectivity" reflected in them. Art that toyed with pain by rousing it artificially for fun sadistically exacerbated the real pain of life.

And worse, art that melodramatically exploited the simulacra of extreme situations for purposes of titillation threatened to displace art that could help us cope with them. For if we could not be cured of our deepest pain, we could be assuaged by facing it, recognizing it, and evoking it poetically, obtaining that "overbalance of pleasure" with which the right kind of poetry alone could counter it. *Lyrical Ballads* is nothing less than a manifesto that, *at the boundary,* poetry does indeed succeed politics in dealing with the human condition.

Lyrical Ballads extends the repertoire of figures of suffering to include retarded adolescent boys, elderly and impoverished men, innocent young girls, even flora and fauna ("Nutting"), though the vagrant or abandoned woman is still central. And insofar as the poetry moralizes—and it does so bluntly and unembarrassedly—it does so in a way different from the philosophical moralizing of "The Ruined Cottage," criticizing those who fail to sympathize with the plight of the needy either by ignoring them or actively refusing assistance. But sympathy and even material help do not change the ultimate realities. On the contrary, given those realities, sympathy and help are not even unalloyed goods. While morally demanded, they are also morally equivocal. Harry Gill is punished for refusing to allow Goody Blake to pull sticks from his hedge for her fire, but, as "Simon Lee" suggests, kind deeds create their own pain.

It is, of course, possible from the vantage point of contemporary political debates to see a conservative social ideology in the call for private and paternalistic acts of charity rather than formal social assistance as an entitlement, which is implicit in the story and moral of "Goody Blake and Harry Gill."[32] Indeed, such a judgment is not wholly anachronistic. Wordsworth himself in his radical phase took a Painite position that combined individualistic economics and politics with a readiness to ameliorate the condition of the poor,[33] though his own sketchy suggestions about how to do that were less interventionist than Paine's own; they were largely negative and focused almost exclusively on the need to destroy the aristocratic control of politics which created "the present *forced* disproportion of . . . possession" through such measures as enclosure acts and the setting of arbitrarily low wages for workers.[34] Having abandoned radical republicanism, Wordsworth had no other political solution for poverty. An anachronistic importation of current debates, however, ought not to blind us to the fact that from a contemporary perspective "Goody Blake and Harry Gill" could look very radical indeed. Mary Jacobus quotes the complaint of a contemporary, Dr. Charles Burney, that "if all the poor are to help themselves, and supply their wants from the possessions of their neighbours, what imaginary wants and real anarchy would it not create?"[35] Burney in fact noticed what has escaped some modern commentators, that Wordsworth was not simply recommending benevolent acts of charitable giving on the part of possessors but their acknowledgment of Goody Blake's right to take what she wanted. This is a moral entitlement that leads to a social obligation, even if not one enacted by law and enforced by government, and it is precisely the ethical presupposition that underlies the contemporary welfare-state mentality conservatives reject.

But however one judges the social ideology implied in "Goody Blake and Harry Gill," "Simon Lee" shows Wordsworth's sense of the limitations of any social philosophy, no matter how benevolently inspired. In terms of the issues raised by that poem, the difference between morally enforced individual obligation to the weak and helpless and legally enforced public obligation is irrelevant. Even considering only the ideal of independence within the classical republican tradition, the need for assistance, in making someone dependent on others, renders him unfit for participation in self-governance and incapable of civic virtue. In relation, however, to the ideal of absolute self-sufficiency that since the Revolution haunted Wordsworth's ideal of freedom like a resident specter, the need for assistance of any kind, private or public, was the ultimate humiliation.

In his reading of the poem David Simpson makes the poet's discomfort in helping the old hunter rest almost wholly on the social differences between them. He traces "Simon Lee" back to its biographical occasion, when Wordsworth was a tenant of the manor house at Alfoxden and encountered the real-life prototype of Simon Lee, a poor old man by the name of Christopher Tricky living at the dog pound just outside the manor grounds. While pointing to Wordsworth's identification with the old man as one who himself knew all too well the predicament of not being able to earn a living of his own, Simpson emphasizes the social status that made possible Wordsworth's wishful identification with the old hierarchy that inhabited manor houses, an identification that also enabled him to deny his own precarious finances and to perform an act of "contingent condescension." "The instability of [Wordsworth's] position," Simpson concludes, "makes him at once a man of the people—a man assisting a fellow man—and a proxy of the old hierarchy. Wordsworth occupies the classic bourgeois site, an unstable and amorphous middle ground which disables him from validating *any* orthodox social role in a wholehearted manner."[36]

Whether or not this is a plausible reading of a universal bourgeois guilt in the face of lower-class poverty—many a bourgeois then and now would, I think, reject it—or an accurate speculation about Wordsworth's state of mind in meeting Christopher Tricky, Simpson ignores the *poem's* emphasis on Simon Lee's physical infirmity, brought on by age. In view of his social interpretation, Simpson is puzzled by the fact that while the real Christopher Tricky either never had a cottage or lost it, Wordsworth makes Simon Lee an owner-occupier. He does so, however, precisely to *rule out* the force of difference based on class in order to focus on the inevitable decline of aging and thus the fragility of the human condition as such. The difference between the poet-narrator and the once-proud old owner-huntsman is in nothing more than their age and sheer physical strength—but that is everything. Verse after verse contrasts what Simon Lee once was to what he is now, as Wordsworth piles up the details of his current sad decrepitude:

> And he is lean and he is sick;
> His body, dwindled and awry,
> Rests upon ankles swoln and thick;
> His legs are thin and dry.

In the face of his age and physical condition, ownership and economic independence mean virtually nothing:

> This scrap of land he from the heath
> Enclosed when he was stronger;
> But what to them avails the land
> Which he can till no longer?[37]

When the narrator, with subtly emphasized pride, severs "with a single blow" the root that the old man could barely unearth, and for his act receives Simon's heartfelt gratitude, he does not record embarrassment or discomfort; his emotion is more precise and more powerful. He is left mourning—for the fate of the old man, no doubt, but for himself as well, since despite his pride he recognizes in Simon Lee at the very least his own future self, which will know similar helplessness and fear, and perhaps even his present self, which already knows the helplessness of childhood and is constantly aware of the permanent precariousness of existence.

Simon Lee's fate—perhaps more precisely the emotion created by empathizing with it—is the kind of extreme situation Wordsworth wanted to deal with and face up to in *Lyrical Ballads,* a situation for which there is no ultimate remedy even if human kindness—personal or social—can make it somewhat more bearable. And while Wordsworth insisted—within whatever limitations his social vision may have created for seeing the full possibilities of social action—that everything human beings could do to alleviate misery they should do, the greater ambition of his poetry was to meet the feelings generated by the irremediable. Because this was his central concern, he insisted that pain always accompanies deep feeling; by definition, the deepest feelings were the inevitably painful responses to the irremediable. And it is in light of his beliefs about the irremediable that one can appreciate the enormity of his claim that there is remedy in song, that is, in the work of the poet. The poet accomplishes the apparently impossible. Wordsworth attributed this magic to the objective, natural power of meter. "The co-presence of something regular," he argued, "something to which the mind has been accustomed in various moods and in a less excited state, cannot but have a great efficacy in tempering and restraining the passion by an intertexture of ordinary feeling, and of feeling not strictly and necessarily connected with the passion."[38] But there is another aspect of meter to which Wordsworth attributes its power and which appears rather the function of consciousness than nature: "the tendency of metre to divest the language in a certain degree of its reality, and thus to throw a sort of half consciousness of unsubstantial existence over the whole composition," a tendency that means that "more pathetic situations and sentiments, that is, those which have a greater proportion of pain connected with them, may be endured in metrical compositions, especially in rhyme, than in prose."[39] Meter works by derealizing tragedy; and this is accomplished by throwing an "unsubstantial existence," a fiction or fantasy of regularity, over it. Wordsworth's derivation of metrical pleasure from sexual passion gives some sense of what this fantasy might be—the fantasy of fusion, of perfect belonging and the eternity and wholeness that it produces, that is possible in sexual union. The pleasure of meter is thus not one of mere "dumb" feeling but of a fantasy whose content, conveyed by formal rather than semantic means, by rhythm and rhyme—which thus become signifiers—is the negation of the tragic content conveyed by the meaning of the narrative. The irregularity of life, its jagged nonlinearity terminated by the ultimate break that is death, is suspended in the regularity of meter and rhyme.

The creative process by which this effect is produced is more complex than is commonly appreciated in brief summaries of Wordsworth's "romantic" definition of poetry. When against the first part of that definition— "Poetry is the spontaneous overflow of powerful feelings"—we are warned to remember the qualifying clause that immediately follows—"it takes its origin from emotion recollected in tranquillity,"—the warning usually omits the next and crucial step. "The emotion," Wordsworth says, "is contemplated till by a species of reaction the tranquillity gradually disappears, and an emotion, kindred to that which was before the subject of contemplation, is gradually produced." Once again the poet is in a state of powerful emotion. The difference, however, is that this second time the emotion has been voluntarily reproduced, which makes it possible for it to be "qualified by various pleasures, so that in describing any passions whatsoever [that is, even the most painful] . . . the mind will upon the whole be in a state of enjoyment."[40]

The process sounds uncannily like the one that Freud describes in the famous "*fort-da*" episode in *Beyond the Pleasure Principle:* mastering trauma— not coincidentally the trauma of separation and loss—by conscious symbolic repetition. Like the little boy who overcomes his anxiety at his mother's absence by repeatedly throwing a wooden reel out of his bed and retrieving it, the poet rehearses the emotion that when inflicted on him from the outside threatened to overwhelm him with the pain of annihilation, and he thus masters the danger by a fictive act that denies power to the other. Wordsworth asserts that it is nature that sees to it that voluntary repetition is accompanied by pleasure and that the poet who would overmaster pain with pleasure is imitating nature's effect. Once again, however, Wordsworth is attributing to nature the creation of fictions, the work of the mind, or the poet. More important, nature herself is the Other over whom the poet's fiction triumphs, just as the young boy declares his superior ontological power over the mother on whom he depends for his very being by soothing himself with the symbolic control of her comings and goings. Poetry declares its victory over "fate," that is, over the cosmos that would seem to deny to the human permanent belonging because of human transience, by displaying the power of pleasure to overcome the pain of the denial.

Wordsworth's veneration of nature always contained an element of reaction-formation which contributed to its characteristic overidealization in his work. This reaction-formation was not only an effort to house and tame the potentially destructive power of his own autonomy, as I have suggested before; what must also be seen is that the rage that fueled the destructive urge was aimed at the very same source to which he subordinated his power in order to make it safer. It was his alienation from that source which his poetry from the beginning had aimed at overcoming, an alienation that he also experienced as active exclusion. The power of poetry, though partially derived from nature, was also in an agonistic relationship with her, a relationship of conflict and competition in which the stakes were the highest imaginable, being itself.

SONG AND AGGRESSION

This agonistic relationship with nature illuminates an aspect of "Hart-leap Well" that ought to seem more puzzling than it has. The moral at the end of the story makes the hart seem merely a pathetic and helpless creature, but if the stag were only that, Sir Walter would seem like the sadist sometimes caricatured by opponents of hunting; he would hardly be the worthy subject of a morality tale. Sir Walter is proud of conquering the hart; his pride would make no sense if he did not regard the hart as a worthy opponent, and the poem would make no sense as a whole if the narrator did not share that point of view to the extent that he regards pride under the circumstances as a plausible temptation. To this same extent, the narrator is associated even more closely with Sir Walter, with the hunt, with competition, and with conquest than I suggested earlier. There is not only a parallel between the pride of the poet in his "simple song" and the pride of the hunter, there is a direct identification with him. The hart has two faces. He is a mere creature, "one of the meanest things that feels." But he is at the same time the representation of nature itself, a mysterious power able to perform unimaginable feats. Sir Walter's reaction to the hart's leaps, "Till now / Such sight was never seen by human eyes," must be taken within the poem at face value or his grand commemorative and celebratory gesture is inexplicable. Seen in this light, the narrator's remark that "this chase it looks not like an earthly chase" is not just an allusion to Bürger's supernaturalism. It points rather to a reality for Sir Walter and narrator alike—not that the hart has a supernatural dimension but that it represents the totality of nature. That makes the hunt a more than earthly chase and a worthy competition indeed. Yet the hart-as-nature is always shadowed by the hart-as-creature, which makes of the chase an act of cruelty and exploitation and of the conquest an act of domination rather than of overcoming.

Recent commentators have noted Wordsworth's own competitiveness and self-aggrandizing tendencies, even in the publishing history of *Lyrical Ballads,* which shows a sustained effort on his part to diminish Coleridge's part in the enterprise.[41] The "Preface" to the second edition of *Lyrical Ballads* is a sustained polemic aimed at a number of different targets, but it focuses principally on eliminating two kinds of rival writers. Wordsworth's quarrel with the sensationalists, in particular, had a personal edge to it which is not apparent from the issues of principle raised in an admittedly sharp way in the "Preface." The year prior to the publication of the first edition of *Lyrical Ballads,* his play *The Borderers* had been rejected for production at Covent Garden despite initially positive indications, while a gothic play by Matthew Gregory Lewis, one of the bêtes noires of the "Preface," was enjoying great popular success in Drury Lane. In a letter to his friend James Tobin, Wordsworth bitingly indicated how much this bothered him: "If I had no other method of employing myself Mr. Lewis's success would have thrown me into despair. The Castle Spectre is a Spectre indeed. Clothed with the flesh and blood of £400 received from the treasury of the theatre it may in the eyes of the author and his friend appear very lovely."[42] The insinuation that Lewis was concerned with money rather than art is of a piece with Wordsworth's attack in the "Preface" on the commercial civilization of the city which was destroying the sensibilities of its inhabitants. But Wordsworth's "despair" was not void of competitive vanity in light of his own failure. Wordsworth's vanity, however, must not be understood or dismissed as "mere" vanity, that is, as something purely personal. What was at stake for him in the rejection of *The Borderers* was the failure to appreciate the fundamental nature of its concerns, which were precisely about the immense dangers of a certain kind of vanity made possible by contemporary historical events. More to the heart of the issue, it is impossible to separate the personal from the principled in Wordsworth's reaction to Lewis's success. For what Wordsworth proposed to substitute in place of River's malevolent self-sufficiency was an ideal that bore an uncomfortably close resemblance to it. The Pedlar, the hero of *The Recluse*, which Wordsworth announced as the successor work to *The Borderers* (that is, the new work whose employment kept him from despair at Lewis's success), was like Rivers a man who created his own world, a "chosen son" who could pass beyond the barriers of the merely visible to endow it with powers and qualities emanating from himself. Unlike Rivers, however, the Pedlar tried to retain his links to those mighty forms of nature from which they both learned of the powers of their own minds. In this way he could maintain a meek dependence on nature, contradictory indeed but a necessary defense against the dangers inherent in world-making autonomy as Wordsworth understood it, as Wordsworth had lived it during the Revolution.[43] Rivers and the Pedlar are twinned figures, one the constantly hovering negative potential of the other. They make a joint appearance as Sir Walter and the narrator in "Hart-leap Well." But in the poem "Ruth" they are joined together as the two aspects of the "Youth from Georgia," one of the most remarkably telling figures in *Lyrical Ballads*.

Commentators have long been agreed that the Youth who seduces and abandons Ruth is a figure of the poet—Mary Moorman suggests that he is in fact a representation of *the* poet, "Wordsworth's picture of what he himself might have been if he had grown up in a savage society."[44] The developmental context I have argued for Wordsworth's poetry, as well as evidence from "Ruth" itself and other poems, indicate that the resemblance is closer than hypothetical projection. Some early lines describing the Youth's childhood link him with the young Wordsworth of the 1799 *Prelude* nurtured by the Derwent, the "fairest of all rivers," that "loved / To blend his murmurs with my nurse's song":

> —While he was yet a Boy
> The moon, the glory of the sun,
> And streams that murmur as they run
> Had been his dearest joy.[45]

In connecting the Youth with the poet-to-be of *The Prelude*, these lines also establish the benign possibility of a poetry deriving from a healthy relationship to nature, a relationship like that ascribed to the Pedlar and described or assumed in many of the poems of *Lyrical Ballads*. For the most part it is this aspect of the Youth that seduces Ruth with the promise of a paradisial existence away from the woe of the world in "quiet bliss." Other lines, however, while also pointing to the connection between the Youth and the author of *The Prelude*, represent the poet's malign potentiality:

> Whatever in these climes he found
> Irregular in sight or sound

> Did to his mind impart
> A kindred impulse, seem'd allied
> To his own powers, and justified
> The workings of his heart.[46]

This language not only closely approximates the terms in which the mental formation of both Rivers and the Pedlar are described; they point forward to the Snowdon vision of the 1805 *Prelude* in which Nature is kindred to the mind,

> the express resemblance . . .
> . . . a genuine counterpart
> And brother of the glorious faculty
> Which higher minds bear with them as their own.[47]

Except that for the Youth from Georgia it is not the regular, hence unifying but the "irregular," potentially disruptive and destructive aspects of nature which are kindred to the self and which are used to justify similar impulses within him:

> The wind, the tempest roaring high,
> The tumult of a tropic sky
> Might well be dangerous food
> For him, a Youth to whom was given
> So much of earth so much of heaven,
> And such impetuous blood.[48]

The use of a structure parallel to the one that describes the beneficently creative mind in *The Prelude* to describe the "lawless" mind of the Youth carries with it the clear implication that both are potentialities of the same autonomy, that the same being can slide from creation to destruction at will:

> But ill he liv'd, much evil saw
> With men to whom no better law
> Nor better life was known;
> Deliberately and undeceiv'd
> Those wild men's vices he receiv'd,
> And gave them back his own.[49]

The "wild men" of these lines seem to refer to the "vagrant bands of Indians" with whom the Youth had roamed about in the West, though no specifics are given of their evil acts. It is tempting to see in these lawless, perhaps murderous Indians of Wordsworth's imagination the French revolutionaries who had let loose their own bloody impulses in the Terror. The most evil thing the Youth does in the poem, of course, is to abandon Ruth, and it is hard not to see here an echo of Wordsworth's own act of lawlessness and irresponsibility during the Revolution, his impregnation and subsequent abandonment of Annette Vallon. It was the parallelism between the revolutionaries' destructive arrogation of power to themselves and Wordsworth's own transgression, seen subsequently through the lens of the philosophy of lawless autonomy he developed as the logical conclusion of the revolutionary idea of freedom, that ultimately drove Wordsworth away from the Revolution. But at the outset of the poem his activity with the Indians is in the past; in the present, however, the Youth is still a hunter, and hunting is of course killing in the interests of conquest. In fact, the prospect of "driving the flying deer," with which the Youth also tempts Ruth, is the one appeal that seems to give her a moment's pause about marrying him and going to America to share his life. Her brief reservations, of course, turn out to be fully justified; it is the spirit of self-absorption and self-aggrandizement which lead him to abandon her and go off "to live as lawless as before."[50]

It is the idea of hunting that links the Youth of "Ruth" not only with the hunter-creator Sir Walter of "Hart-leap Well" but with the poet-author of *Lyrical Ballads*. Hunting is the conquest of nature, and "nature," as I have suggested, was for Wordsworth both the exclusionary power to be overcome and the power that, in a species of denial, makes possible the overcoming. In a verse that refers to the grief-stricken reaction that drives Ruth mad, there is a jarring, apparently unmotivated reference to nature as the cause of her sadness:

> The engines of her grief, the tools
> That shap'd her sorrow, rocks and pools,
> And airs that gently stir
> The vernal leaves, she loved them still,
> Nor ever tax'd them with the ill
> Which had been done to her.[51]

In the limited context of the poem alone, these lines are surprising; nothing in the story has suggested that "nature," at least the gentle, harmonious nature of the verse, was the "engine of her grief" or in any way deserved to be "tax'd" for what had been done to her. The verse reveals the poet's identification not only with the abandoner but with the abandoned; it is the poet's abandonment by nature that is projected onto Ruth. By the same token, the consolation of the song of "Ruth" is the overcoming of the pain caused by that abandonment through the pleasure of poetic conquest.

In the figure of the Youth there come together all the aspects of Wordsworth's poetic persona: the abandoned self, the soldier of freedom, the lawless marauder, the hunter, the abandoner, and the singer of songs of the one life with nature. The spirit of the lawless rebel, the self-sufficient humanist of revolutionary ideology is not exorcised by the rejection of political radicalism, the withdrawal to a "wise passiveness" in the face of nature or to a vision of an agrarian society of owner-occupiers unseduced by luxury and diversion from a knowing oneness with nature. After the Revolution in the light of the new sense of self it helped to produce, even the lyrical singer is a revolutionary in that he proclaims the triumph of the individual will over any power that would diminish, exclude, or humiliate it. This power continued to frighten Wordsworth even as he wrote polemics against the new urban commercial social conditions that he believed exacerbated it. *Lyrical Ballads* shows Wordsworth fighting two enemies, the social enemy without and the new self within. Perhaps Wordsworth's most telling representation of the Janus faces of song is offered in the marvelous fragment about the "Danish Boy," with its clear implication of the compartmentalized but not wholly unconscious sense of the compulsion to conquest in the most apparently benign communion:

> There he sits:—in his face you spy
> No trace of a ferocious air,
> Nor ever was a cloudless sky
> So steady or so fair.
> The lovely Danish Boy is blest
> And happy in his flower cove;
> From bloody deeds his thoughts are far;
> And yet he warbles songs of war;
> They seem like songs of love,
> For calm and gentle is his mien;
> —Like a dead Boy, he is serene.[52]

In the wake of the revolution and the new concept of self it had helped to produce, the lyrical gesture is not only political, it is warlike, an assertion of the absolute supremacy of the poet's voice. This is clearly for the poet a dangerous assertion, dangerous not least politically. It would be an error to think that the only revolutionary or postrevolutionary politics is a politics of class and social interest. Wordsworth was not unaware that it was as a member of an aggrieved social group that he protested aristocratic depredations and manipulations of the legal system in 1793. But it was as an *individual* that he felt *he* had transgressed against others in his revolutionary years, whether lover or king, authorized by a new concept of the individual and his entitlements. Wordsworth was not alone in this feeling. He was a member of a transnational generation of young European writers and thinkers who, from parallel backgrounds, parallel needs, and parallel political-personal experiences, came to similar definitions of a new individuality and similar appreciations of its dangers. This was as much a historical and political event as the demand for a free and equal society—or as the retreat from it. In the case of the romantics, in fact, it was the prospects and then the problems of the new individuality that lay behind both.

The French Revolution was not only a chapter in the liberation of groups, it was a chapter in the liberation of the individual as such. When the logical implications of the idea of the rights and dignity of the individual drove those bold enough to make the appropriate inferences to the notion of infinite, ungrounded individual autonomy, the young romantics recoiled, terrified by the implications of this freedom as revealed by the uses they had put it to in their own lives. But they could not put the genie back into the bottle, not only because the inference seemed inescapable but because they did not wish to surrender the new self completely. Wordsworth's *Lyrical Ballads* is telling evidence of this refusal to surrender that self just because the poems make an effort to do so. In evoking the tragedy of finitude, they call for mutual consolation in the face of fate, a consolation made possible by the belief in our oneness with infinite nature that holds us dependently in its eternal embrace. But in that very same construction nature must also be the oppressor, the very emblem of the otherness that has the power to exclude, that is the power that excludes; and the voice that consoles does so by pronouncing the superiority of its poetic uniqueness over that apparently absolute power. The poems of *Lyrical Ballads* are, despite themselves, songs emanating from a sense of the power of human selfhood utterly new in history.

Commerce and Society

Performing the Passions in Commercial Society

Bernard Mandeville and the Theatricality of Eighteenth-Century Thought

Edward Hundert

It has become something of a commonplace to refer to Hanoverian Britain as a society notable for the theatricality of its public life, one in which "grandees stage-managed a . . . theatre of power," one distinguished by "conspicuous menace (and mercy) from the Judge's Bench; exemplary punishment tempered with silver linings of philanthropy, largesse and selective patronage; a grudging and calculating display of *noblesse oblige.*"[1] While contemporary republicans criticized this histrionic manipulation of the signs of power by an oligarchical elite that sought to "show and parade to fascinate the vulgar,"[2] modern historians of British society have emphasized the ways in which both rulers and ruled performed in public with "the studied consciousness of public theatre."[3] If, following the example of the court at Versailles, the visible accoutrements of continental states were conspicuously fashioned as instruments of monarchical absolutism in polities sustained by their capacity to fascinate the obedient and arrest rebellion by the production of awe,[4] in the limited and unreformed British parliamentary monarchy even elections themselves were theatrical events, public spectacles in which crowd and patrician adopted highly stylized roles, just as they did in various forms of public disorder and during the criminal proceedings that followed in their wake.[5]

Standard explanations of these practices refer to the continuing vitality of traditional patterns of behavior among the ruling orders in a premodern polity and to the persistence of ancient ceremonial forms of communal solidarity, especially among a partially literate population seeking to resist the intrusion of market relationships into the heart of social life. Within these perspectives the theater serves as a useful construct for the analysis of the ways in which persons inhabited and reshaped largely traditional roles even as they responded to challenges to the social arrangements within which these roles were coherently sustained. Little attention, however, has been paid to an equally significant aspect of British (and European) cultural history: theatricality as a distinguishing feature of the self-understanding of commercial modernity, of the actor taken as a representative man, a figure symbolizing a public sphere whose altered conventions mirrored those of the stage in what has been called the first consumer society.[6] In what follows I focus on the work of Bernard Mandeville, commercial society's first celebrant, in order to show how an aesthetic of theatricality, transposed into a form of social understanding, functioned in the eighteenth-century discourse of morals as a form of anxious uncertainty about stable ethical norms and a unitary personal identity.

SOCIABILITY AND SELF-LOVE

The eighteenth-century notion of persons as social actors engaged in purely self-interested and instrumental relations with others emerged as part of a European-wide shift in moral psychology in late seventeenth-century France, largely within a context of theological dispute. This enterprise was part of a well-known subversive tradition of continental philosophy, the morally skeptical doctrines of Pierre Bayle and Bayle's allies in the Republic of Letters and the Augustinian rigorism of La Rochefoucauld and the most prominent Jansenist divines, particularly Pierre Nicole, most of whose major works had been translated into English during the first decades of the eighteenth century.[7] In complementary fashion both groups sought to anatomize forms of moral behavior with the express object of showing that a person's apparent practice of Christian virtue offered no guarantees about the underlying motives informing it. Since apparently virtuous acts were rewarded by public esteem, it was in the obvious interest of the vicious majority to mime the conventional signs of Christian piety in order to win the approval of their fellows. The majority of men, in other words, could be understood as relentless egoists. They behaved according to the socially prescribed conventions of propriety not because of their moral content but because, in the expectation of these skilled social actors, such behavior would win the approbation of their fellows. Moreover, if virtue could reasonably be understood as one of the masks available to fallen men in their pursuit of selfish interests, so these writers concluded, then the difference between virtue and vice would have nothing to do with behavior. Instead, the distinction between an act that stemmed from selfish desire and one whose source was Christian charity would of necessity depend entirely on the judgment of God as he inspected each human heart.

Two unsettling consequences followed from these influential arguments. First, it was assumed that the great majority of mankind merely feigned Christian commitments while in reality being driven by self-love. Yet the fact that the behavior of the majority was in principle indistinguishable from true Christian behavior challenged the conventional assumption that believers who feared hell and yearned for salvation were more powerfully motivated toward virtuous action than were pagans, Jews, or atheists. Bayle drew the obvious conclusion: any man, atheist or believer, could make a good subject, since civil conduct required only outward conformity to standards of propriety produced by social pressure and intersubjective expectations, underwritten by law. The rectitude of a citizen required no spiritually enriched conscience.[8] Second, as was famously suggested by Pierre Nicole in his *Moral Essays,* just as the selfish, and thus conflicting, wants of individuals could be harnessed to politically beneficial ends, so too could competing social and economic interests be made to obey similar systematic constraints. Social utility and communal benefit could correctly be understood as unintended consequences of certain historically domesticated forms of self-aggrandizement. The seemingly anarchic tendencies of the scramble for wealth, for example, revealed themselves at a deeper level to be structured social regularities attending the common pursuit of material gratification. Gross cupidity and never satisfied material interest created secret social bonds, for the intersubjective sources of commercial exchange in goods and money provided "no less peace, security, and comfort, than if one were in a Republic of Saints."[9] Moral beliefs and shared habits of life differed from place to place because they were the contingent historical products of diverse cultural experiences. Both individual and communal expressions of self-regard could best be understood not simply as varied examples of the essential propensity of Adam's heirs to sin but as dependent features of the discrete practices by virtue of which egoism had been locally disciplined.

The decisive transposition of this mode of moral argument into a secular instrument of social understanding was undertaken by the London-based Dutch physician and satirist Bernard Mandeville in *The Fable of the Bees* (1714, 1723, and 1728),[10] a work that retained its reputation as the epitome of immorality for over two generations after its publisher was charged in 1723 with printing a book designed "to run down Religion and Virtue as prejudicial to Society . . . and to recommend Luxury, Avarice, Pride and all vices, as being necessary to *Public Welfare*" (1:385). "Private Vices, Publick Benefits," the *Fable*'s notorious maxim, encapsulated Mandeville's thesis that contemporary society is an aggregation of self-interested individuals driven by passions for gain and approbation that necessarily bind persons together neither by shared civic commitments nor by moral rectitude but, paradoxically, by the tenuous bonds of envy, competition, and exploitation. According to Mandeville, each individual is a compound of various passions, which "govern him by turns, whether he will or no" (1:39). The distinctive amalgam of philosophy and satire he erected on this basis had both a critical and constructive intention: to "pull off the disguises of artful men," as he wrote in response to Bishop Berkeley, and to expose "the hidden springs" of human action to analytic inspection.[11]

Mandeville's project of "anatomizing the invisible part of man" (1:136) was designed to demonstrate that the vocabularies of formal systems of ethics served the essentially political and socializing purpose of deflecting critical attention from the irreducibly passionate and utterly self-regarding sources of actual human wishes. Only passions can move one to act, and the object of any passion is nothing other than one's own interest, "since it is impossible that Man . . . should act with any other View but to please himself " (1:348). Aside from the natural passions like fear and grief, two distinct forms of self-interest are uppermost: self-love, directing one's attention to self-preservation, and, crucially, self-liking, the "instinct, by which every Individual values himself above its real worth. . . . It is this that makes us so fond of the Approbation, Liking and Assent of others; because they strengthen and confirm us in the good Opinion we have of ourselves" (2:230). Mandeville thus adopted what in the French lexicon of moral psychology was termed *amour-propre* as a central feature of the analysis of contemporary social practices.

Mandeville had only a passing interest in the rigorously exclusive social arena of the Court and of those noble elites whose threatened habits of life was the compelling subject of Nicole, La Rochefoucauld, and their contemporaries. *The Fable*'s inquiry centered instead on what was at once a wider, rapidly expanding, and relatively novel domain—the social dynamics of moneyed wealth in modern commercial societies, of which Britain had become the exemplar. Mandeville reshaped his French ideological inheritance by giving prominence to the role of the demands made by the social environment in shaping the emotions of *all* actors into expressive conjunctions of judgment and passion whose local embodiments could only be realized and understood within the established conventions and beliefs of a given public sphere. If the demands of pride and the need for esteem were constant and universal features of the human constitution, desires themselves were nevertheless realized or thwarted only in socially structured, rule-governed interactions with others. In contemporary polities, Mandeville claimed to have discovered, the conditions of commercial modernity had made the Christian saint, the classical citizen, as well as the noble warrior anachronistic mental deposits of long vanished or quickly eroding social formations.

In the recently constituted commercial societies on which *The Fable* concentrated, persons were obliged to respond to a revised structure of priorities if they were to satisfy their impulses. These persons were driven not merely by the universal appetites for authority and esteem: in the centers of European commercial societies outward displays of wealth were now widely accepted as a direct index of social power. "People, where they are not known," he observed,

> are generally honour'd according to their Clothes and other Accoutrements they have about them; from the riches of them we judge of their Wealth, and by their ordering of them we guess at their Understanding. It is this which encourages every Body . . . to wear Clothes above his rank, especially in large and populous cities where obscure men may hourly meet with fifty strangers to one acquaintance, and consequently have the pleasure of being esteemed by a vast majority, not as what they are, but what they appear to be. (1:127–128)

The Fable consolidated a revolution in the understanding of the relationship between motives and acts largely begun in France by viewing commerce and sociability as reciprocal and historically decisive features of the modern dynamics of self-regard. Mandeville showed that the aggressive pursuit of wealth had now to be understood not as an activity properly confined to marginalized minorities but as central to the self-definition of large urban and commercial populations. Mandeville for the first time systematically comprehended from the perspective of society itself the consequences of the behavior of persons for whom opportunities for consumption and display encouraged forms of self-presentation which were in effect the vehicles through which individuals established their identities. Here,

> The Fickle Strumpet that invents new Fashions every Week . . . the profuse Rake and lavish heir, that scatter about their Money without Wit or Judgement, buy everything they see, and either destroy or give it away the next Day, the Covetous and perjur'd Villain that squeezed an immense Treasure from the Tears of Widows and Orphans, and left the Prodigals the money to Spend: It is these . . . that we stand in need of. . . . And it is folly to imagine that Great and Wealthy nations can subsist, and be at once Powerful and Polite without. (1:355–356)

Repositioning the conceptual materials he first found in Bayle and his Augustinian predecessors in this altered commercial context, Mandeville argued that if moral judgments were in fact nothing other than expressions of feeling (passion), then the operative traditions of Christian moral psychology could not be enlisted to explain the status and workings of human desire. These judgments had to be set in a different problem-space from the one typically assumed by Mandeville's contemporaries. Moral codes themselves were then not expressions of universal principles but historically inscribed ideological products established in the course of the civilizing process. According to Mandeville, all civilized nations owed their very foundations not to morally empowered acts of virtuous legislators of the sort populating European national myths but to the ability of strong, cunning minorities to tame and discipline the fractious passions of savage multitudes

(1:41–57). Mandeville located the "origin of moral virtue" within the context of his reconstruction of the formation of societies. He then recast the notion of "the rational ambition of Being Good" (1:49) as a psychologically implausible standard of virtue designed to manage irreducibly passionate egoists through shame and guilt. Mandeville was therefore free to argue that the actual workings of desire in any given community could in principle be accounted for by a sociology of its members' emotions. He placed the expression of supposedly moral sentiments in the context of responses to locally generated opportunities for private satisfaction. And once Mandeville was able to demonstrate that a good action (socially considered) need not be the action of a good man but the unintended result of his "private vice," he could then also make the telling point that what constituted happiness for any given individual was independent of the officially sanctioned moral standards that supposedly regulated public life. Social action could be strictly conceived in terms of an individual's search for pleasure and the degrees to which he managed to satisfy his desires. And since these desires had self-liking as their foundation, which depended on public esteem and approbation, Mandeville more cogently explains why persons so often spoke and acted in ways that *appeared* moral (since in so doing they would be publicly rewarded); he could further argue that both speech and action could most usefully be understood purely as instruments employed by self-interested actors in order to achieve their ends. Behavior in public was a species of performance designed to win approval, a series of performances whose success depended on no genuine moral standard but on how well a social actor could satisfy his desires within the given, socially structured conventions of rewards and punishments.

For Bayle and Nicole the primary purpose of unmasking egoism was to show that while sinners could lead a serviceable life by following the socially useful principles of *honnêteté,* they could never sufficiently free themselves from vice to escape eternal damnation. The unregenerate were forever bound to the power of their sinful wills, their acts devoid of the charity that spiritually distinguished God's elect. The social utility of an action could never for either Bayle or Nicole earn the title of virtuous. Virtue was not a social category but rather an absolute quality of purely personal decisions, a matter of individual conscience wholly irrelevant to the requirements of society. Though it was an admirable, if paradoxical, fact that men might succeed in living together amicably by following their interests under the guidance of the law, this in no way implied that morality should therefore be understood in terms of social utility alone. For strictly to identify morality with legislation and public prosperity would be to render religion superfluous and to deprive men of the possibility of salvation.[12] For Mandeville, by contrast, the distance between appearance and motivation, between the individual's public face and private moral identity, was the ideal conceptual space within which to examine the hidden theatrical dynamics of commercial sociability.

Mandeville expected his readers to recognize that "the rules of politeness" with which he equated "virtue" in an established commercial British elite had acquired an importance much greater than the mere "points of small morals" that Hobbes, for example, had dismissed as largely irrelevant to civil polities. In the philosopher's view these practices were nothing more than social decencies, "as how one man should salute another, or how a man should wash his mouth, or pick his teeth before company."[13] Nor were the rules to which Mandeville referred merely a codification of the *politesse* featured in Renaissance courtesy books like Castiglione's *The Courtier,* further refined in seventeenth-century Parisian salons, then becoming the social legislation of an aristocratic elite for whom the norms of acceptable conduct at Court would be labeled immoral in urban and commercial settings.[14] Rather, for Mandeville and his intended audience, "politeness" had come to refer precisely to the manners of "the Town" rather than of the Court, to the contemporary writings on manners and civility of Shaftesbury, Addison, and Steele rather than the sermons of strict moralist divines. Acceptable forms of behavior by moneyed commoners rather than the titled alone embodied the rules of politeness, formed as they were amid the rapidly expanding commercialization of leisure, especially in the West End of London, the exemplary site for his own and for the most disturbing social observations of his contemporaries.

Central to Mandeville's argument was the thesis that the growth of commerce, increased consumption, and the expansion of a class of leisured commoners were all powerful civilizing agents. Together they enlarged the consciousness of the individual's dependence on others. But in direct opposition to public moralists like Addison and Steele or to the philosophy of polite sociability enunciated in Shaftesbury's *Characteristics* (1711 and 1714),[15] Mandeville celebrated rather than bemoaned the contradictions of modern societies, where the polish and civility that necessarily accompanied commercial opulence had created a decidedly secular world in which publicly proclaimed standards of propriety paid mere lip service to the Christian or antique ideals that the triumph of modernity had rendered vestigial. Nothing exemplified this point for Mandeville so forcefully as the examination of "Good Manners," which have "nothing to do with Virtue or Religion; instead of extinguishing, they rather inflame the passions," which "the Man of Sense and Education . . . hides . . . with the greatest Dexterity . . . [and] enjoys a Pleasure altogether unknown to the Short-sighted" (1:79). Revised "methods of making ourselves acceptable to others, with as little prejudice to ourselves as possible" (2:147), were required as the "bond of society" among persons whose wealth and security enabled them to distinguish themselves by and thus take delight in the "tokens and badges" of affluent living instead of the trophies of conquest and the submissions of war. Social pretense had largely supplanted physical aggression in commercial societies, in which clothes, ornaments, equipages, servants, furniture, buildings, and titles had come to offer the psychological satisfactions necessary to stifle the violent, "odious part of pride" (2:126). Through the agency of approbation, which Mandeville termed "flattery" in *The Fable*'s "Enquiry into the Origin of Moral Virtue" (1:41–57), the social legislation of a once rude but recently tamed and reconstituted warrior caste, together with the elaborate codes of decorum that distinguished all modern elites, licensed the emotional compensations for living with others which previously could be gained only by the prospect of force. Increasingly internalized as they were formally codified, these rules licensed the satisfaction of pride through public approbation.

Mandeville, then, effectively redescribed the scene of moral activity as an arena that was not populated by rationally endowed, undivided consciousnesses inquiring into those choices that directly affected their own souls and the good of their community. The moral actor anatomized in *The Fable* was, by contrast, an intersubjectively defined, socially situated participant in a communal drama, a person driven by passions who of necessity competed with those around him in a public market for tokens of esteem. This individual's desires alone formed the premises of his practical reasoning, while the material and symbolic rewards of the social order to which he happened to belong constituted inescapable features of his own identity. These rewards were socially defined prizes whose acquisition and loss were signs of no intrinsically moral qualities but merely an index of the ethically indifferent process governing the rise and fall of persons and groups in which the individual was obliged to participate.

Mandeville insisted that any useful discussion of contemporary morals and manners could only be undertaken by reference to the socially sanctioned devices through which contemporary social elites publicly performed the roles they played in order to maximize their private satisfactions. As Mandeville's spokesman Cleomenes declared in *The Fable:* "In the very Politeness of Conversation, the Complacency, with which fashionable People are continually soothing each other's Frailties, and in almost every part of a Gentlemen's Behavior . . . there was a disagreement between the outward Appearances, and what is felt within, that was clashing with Uprightness and Sincerity" (2:17). Styles of behavior deemed virtuous, polite, and honorable, so he asserted in what amounted to *The Fable*'s third volume, served as a model for the decidedly histrionic quality of modern social transactions:

> When *A* performs an Action which, in the Eyes of *B*, is laudable, *B* wishes well
> to *A;* and, to shew him his Satisfaction, tells him, that such an Action is an

Honour to Him, or that He ought to be Honoured for it: By saying this, *B*, who knows that all Men are affected with Self-liking, intends to acquaint *A*, that he thinks him in the Right to gratify and indulge himself in the Passion of Self-liking. In this sense the Word Honour, whether it is used as a Noun or a Verb, is always a Compliment we make to Those who act, have or are, what we approve of; it is a term of Art to express our Concurrence with others, our Agreement with them in their Sentiments concerning the Esteem and Value they have for themselves. . . . So that the Highest Honour which Men can give to Mortals, whilst alive, is in Substance no more, than the most likely and most effectual Means that Human Wit can invent to gratify, stir up, and encrease in Him, to whom that Honour is paid, the Passion of Self-liking.[16]

In so locating the space of moral approbation within the context of what he pointedly described in the *Fable* as a "Comedy of Manners" (1:79), Mandeville adopted the stance of the skeptical observer of worldly folly who recognized that the content of actions standardly understood as virtuous can, from this detached perspective, be redescribed as enacting a drama; and that once so redescribed, these actions immediately lose their distinctly moral character, transformed as they are into features of merely prudential attempts to win the approbation ("applause") of the specifically circumscribed audience to whom they are directed. By subsuming the moral codes governing communal behavior under the headings of what he repeatedly called mere "ceremonies" and "customs," Mandeville succeeded in placing the "general practices" of polite society in a theatrical context, within whose histrionic conventions the negotiations of public life necessarily took place.

THE DYNAMICS OF PERFORMANCE

For Augustinians like Pierre Bayle the image par excellence of a social world characterized by passionate striving without end was a "spectacle of marionettes," which most charitably could be seen as a diversion for the Creator.[17] In the *Maxims* La Rochefoucauld set the habits of the court within a conceptual environment of histrionic falsity, of deceitfulness and covert exhibitionism, in which masks must always be worn, and players "end by disguising ourselves from ourselves." Here, sadly for his wordly prospects, "a wise man thinks it more advantageous not to join the battle than to win."[18] Theatrical conventions themselves provided Nicole with the most telling metaphors through which to depict the duplicities governing social exchange among an unregenerate elite. "We are like those dancers at a masked ball," he wrote,

who hold one another by the hand affectionately without recognizing one another, and part a moment later, never to see each other again. . . . To see how men use one another one might think of human life and the affairs of the world as a serious game where any moves are permitted to seize the goods of another at our own risk, and where the lucky players despoil with all honor, the more unfortunate or less skilled.[19]

For each of these writers the ancient figure of the *theatrum mundi* served in their social criticism as a compelling device for the representation of and response to grave spiritual uncertainties about the constitution of a stable, undivided, and thus morally responsible self. Public life understood as little more than a theater of outward display and moral dissimulation at once provided for them instantly comprehensible metaphors for the depiction of elite, particularly aristocratic, social space and compelling idioms for the examination of an individual sinner's actions within it. Trading on the rhetorical symbiosis of the vocabularies of stage and society in Western languages, they were particularly responsive to the stress placed by aggressively demythologizing accounts of the body politic on the classical association of the person with the figure of the masked actor. As Hobbes, from whom Jansenists especially derived many of their political insights, put it in *Leviathan:*

> The word Person is latine . . . as *Persona* in latine signifies the *disguise,* or *outward appearance* of a man, counterfeited on the Stage; and sometimes more particularly that part of it, which disguiseth the face, as a Mask or Visard: And from the Stage, hath been translated to any Representer of speech and action, as well in Tribunals, as Theatres. So that a *Person,* is the same that an *Actor* is, both on the Stage and in common Conversation; and to *Personate,* is to Act, or Represent himself, or an other.[20]

Heightened fears about exposing one's true character to the world, and thus being revealed to others, were at the heart of the French moralists' concerns as they concentrated on a Court society characterized by what they took to be the rampant growth of unbelief, by merely ceremonial religious observance, and by the spread of immorality. All could adopt a theatrical perspective on this morally suspect world because each in his own fashion adhered to the Augustinian view that motives alone determine the quality of any act and that regardless of an individual's success in concealing his motives from those around him, God would always penetrate behind the curtain of the world's theater and judge individuals accordingly.[21]

This French inflection given to the Augustinian language of morals in the late seventeenth century served the critical purpose of enabling Mandeville to expose the irreducible gap between natural impulse and virtuous action while employing the rigorous moral rhetoric shared by his many critics. By speaking in their language, he could satirically pose as an advocate of the most severe ethical standards and then from an elevated rhetorical position insist that "be we Savages or Politicians, it is impossible that Man, mere Fallen Man, should act with any other View but to please himself . . . [for] we are always forc'd to do what we please, and at the same time our

Thoughts are free . . . it is impossible we could be sociable Creatures without Hypocrisy" (1:348–349). This mock-Augustinian stance further enabled Mandeville to situate the distance between motive and act within the theatrical perspective that served his French predecessors. In so doing he was able to place in a commercial context the ancient insight that actions on the stage and in society each have as part of their content the possibility of being variously performed and understood as features of a role. He could then show that the meaning of these performances can never be transparent—an actor's overt professions notwithstanding—since roles are filled by persons who must, as a condition of success, perform them in certain socially specified ways to the exclusion of others. Not only do public acts invite but they always demand interpretation by members of the audience, who by their responses alone certify success or failure. As in John Gay's *The Beggar's Opera* (1728), to which Mandeville compared his own unmasking efforts (2:6), actors may play the roles of criminals, who themselves play roles as "gentlemen," "merchants," and "ladies" before an audience meant to read their own values into these impostures. Public life portrayed as a theater of deceit dramatically served to reveal Mandeville's intentionally unsettling claim, later bemoaned by Rousseau in the *Discourse on the Origins of Inequality* (1755), that the difference between being and appearing is the most psychologically significant characteristic of public life in commercial societies (1:127–130).

For Mandeville's French predecessors, along with the Elizabethan and Jacobean dramatists who so distinguished the English theater before the civil wars, the metaphor of world-as-stage derived from the Stoic conception of the theater as a paradigm of human life. This classical trope was standardized in Latin literature by Petronius's *Satyricon,* whose motto "Totus mundus agit histrionem" ("All the world plays the actor") ran above the newly erected Globe theater in London in 1599. Its zone of applicability was later extended to the entire sublunary world in John of Salisbury's influential *Polycraticus* (1159), a discourse on "the frivolities of courtiers and the footprints of philosophers," much reprinted during the sixteenth and seventeenth centuries.[22] The metaphor was intended to expose the artificial, because merely conventional, boundaries placed on acceptable public behavior and to throw into skeptical relief the formal regularities of social existence. Like the popular medieval imagery of the Wheel of Fortune and the Ship of Fools, the theatrical metaphor was a rhetorical device employed to unmask worldly ambition and pretense. For Bayle and Nicole, as for Jacques in *As You Like It,* the reminder that "all the world's a stage" served the traditional and essentially conservative function of recalling to individuals the fact that they are subject to the scrutiny of a higher power into whose care their souls were entrusted. Within the conceptual ambit of the theater, men could be viewed as puppets in a drama of which they remained unaware, as unwitting actors who inhabited roles that had an illusory, because merely secular, importance. For this very purpose Don Quixote announced "that there is nothing that shows us more clearly, by similitude, what we are and what we ought to be than do plays and players." He told Sancho Panza, who had already heard "this fine comparison . . . many times before," that "in the comedy that we call life" we "play . . . all the characters that a drama may have—but when it is all over, that is to say when life is done, death takes from each the garb that differentiates him, and all are at last equal in the grave."[23]

The metaphor of the *theatrum mundi* retained its conventional ethical force for Mandeville's seventeenth-century Jacobean and Augustinian predecessors because it served to underwrite their deeply held belief in the existence of a moral identity independent of and prior to a person's status and occupation. As in Thomas Heywood's *Apology for Actors* (1612), the most substantial commentary to come out of the Elizabethan theater, in Webster's commentaries on the role of character on the stage,[24] as well as in Hamlet's instruction to his players (III.ii.19–24), the self is viewed as existing apart from its embodied relationships. The allegorical figure of the world as a stage functioned for French *moralistes* and English dramatists as an instrument of social intelligibility only in the restricted though important sense that it reasserted the central Christian doctrine of the spiritual role-nakedness of all persons, regardless of the social stations to which they may have been assigned by birth or good fortune. For these writers the notion of "playing a part" essentially signified the accomplishment of a task, a sense easily extended to the notion of a person's social as distinct from spiritual role as that part given to an individual to play either well or badly. In this conceptual environment, where no body of acting theory was produced, even great actors like Edward Alleyn and Richard Burbage were conceived of primarily as rhetoricians with a mimetic talent for impersonating ideal moral types, often derived from the Theophrastian *Characters,* through the presentation of concrete examples.[25] Any "self-fashioning" on the model of the theater was constrained by a shared and virtually unchallenged belief that the stage, unlike the journal, letter, or essay, was an inappropriate setting for the examination of singular identities.[26]

Mandeville's purposes in emphasizing the theatricality of public life and the context within which he portrayed commercial societies as theatrical worlds were significantly different. Theatricality served for him as a conceptual instrument for the examination of modern consciousness rather than merely as a convenient metaphor for social relations that derived from the playhouse. As with contemporaries writing in the Epicurean vein with which *The Fable* was associated,[27] Mandeville employed theatricality not so much to expose the vanity of human aspirations from a celestial perspective as to highlight the distance between genuine knowledge and mere appearance in the minds of social actors themselves. Thomas Burnaby's well-known translation of the *Satyricon* in 1694 was so understood by contemporary Epicureans like Charles de Marguetel de Saint Denis, seigneur de Saint-Evremond,[28] while the enemies of Lucretius and Epicurus as heralds of irreligion typically pointed to the London stage as a sign of the moral degeneracy of the age.[29] The *theatrum mundi* became a conceptually enabling device by the early eighteenth century with which philosophical radicals like Mandeville could examine the gulf between the detached observer of the world and the mass of men who remained imaginatively ensnared by its public rituals. "The Wise Man," in John Digby's rendition of the Epicurean maxim, "shall reap more Benefit, and take more Satisfaction in the public Shews, than other Men. He there observes the different Characters of the Spectators; he can discover by their looks the effect of the Passions that moves 'em, and amidst the Confusion that reigns in these places . . . he has the Pleasure to find himself the only person undisturb'd, and in a State of Tranquility."[30]

Digby's translation was meant to evoke the famous passage that begins book 2 of *De Rerum Natura,* where Lucretius writes of the pleasure of beholding a ship in peril at sea from the safety of the shore. The passage not only illustrates the pleasure (literally, the sweetness) of watching suffering or danger from a safe distance but compares this delight to that which the true philosopher experiences in his security from worldly illusion. As Bacon rendered Lucretius in his essay "Of Truth":

> It is a pleasure to stand upon the shore, and to see ships tossed upon the sea; a pleasure to stand in the window of a castle, and to see a battle and the adventures thereof below: but no pleasure is comparable to standing on the vantage ground of Truth and to see the errors, and the wanderings, and tempests, in the vale below.

Mandeville adopted a Baconian perspective when he interpreted this passage, a perspective he identified with that of the modern forms of scientific inquiry in which he participated as a physician.[31] In the fashion of Bacon, Mandeville engaged in "serious satire" by writing a "treatise into the inner nature of things," to take the titles of two of Bacon's works, in order to describe "what men do, and not what they ought to do."[32] He understood the false beliefs of his contemporaries, particularly those socially stabilizing myths Bacon had called the *idola* of the marketplace, as distorting ideological residues generated by commercial society's unwritten conventions. The wise man became a student of this society by virtue of his ability to stand aloof from those public spectacles through which these myths were enacted. "To me," Mandeville said, alluding to Lucretius,

> it is a great Pleasure, when I look on the Affairs of human Life, to behold into what various and often strangely opposite Forms the hope of Gain and

thoughts of Lucre shape Men, according to the different Employments they are of, and Stations they are in. How gay and merry does every Face appear at a well-ordered Ball, and what a solemn Sadness is observ'd at the Masquerade of a Funeral! But the Undertaker is as much pleas'd with his Gains as the Dancing-Master. . . . [Likewise,] those who have never minded the Conversation of a spruce Mercer, and a young Lady his Customer . . . have neglected a Scene of Life that is very Entertaining. . . . Reader[s] [should] . . . examine these People separately, as to their Inside and the different Motives they act from. (1:349–350)

A prominent line of early eighteenth-century moral argument regarding the theatricality of public life followed from the conventions of the immensely popular contemporary London stage where, as Hume remarked, "the curiosity of several more is excited, than when our prime minister is to defend himself from a motion of impeachement."[33] This essentially declamatory theater was distinguished by a sedate, controlled, and minutely polished adherence to the classical rules of oratory, of which acting was understood to be a subgenre. Acting technique was marked by small, exact gestures, a precise vocal cadence, and an emphasis on formal restraint in both actor and audience, with facial expression and stance often derived from historical painting. "Tho the Passions are very beautiful in their proper gestures," said Thomas Betterton, the greatest actor of his day, "yet they ought never to be so extravagantly immoderate to transport the Speaker out of himself."[34] Both the procedures and objectives of this theater, in which tragedy was the dominant form, were effectively articulated into aesthetic principles by the prominent eighteenth-century literary critic John Dennis. Following the Christianized Aristotelianism of the French critic André Dacier, who saw in classic drama a means to give morally flawed men "instructions, disguised under the charmes of pleasure, as physicians guild and sweeten the bitter pilles they administer to their patients,"[35] Dennis argued that the stage should be understood as at once entertaining and moving, yet essentially harmless and possessing the potential for moral instruction.[36] Because the passions evoked in the theater were necessarily inspired under conditions in which the audience remained aware of its self-imposed distance from the dramatic action, even the arousal of painful feelings, Dennis claimed, could be controlled and so rendered pleasurable. This view depended on a strict conceptual division, derived from Descartes, between the various passions. Passions were understood as physiological humors prone to excitement, either from external sources or from will and cognition. They were conceived as higher powers in principle able to guide and control these perturbations. Thus even the evocation of sadness in the playhouse could produce pleasure in the spectator, so Descartes argued in *The Passions of the Soul* (1649), for "when passions are only caused by the stage adventures which we see represented in the theatre, or by other similar means which, not being able to harm us in any way, [they] seem pleasurably to excite our soul in affecting it."[37]

Writers on aesthetics and students of the stage could then accept a modern, mechanist account of the relationship of the passions to the actions of the human body associated with Harvey as well as Descartes and yet retain a classical understanding of theatrical engagement that stressed the governing power of consciousness to shape and control the emotions. Just as guides to manners took the passions, in the popular writer Abel Boyer's words, to be "Nature's never-failing Rhetoric, and the only Orators that can master our Affections,"[38] contemporary artists and critics similarly concentrated on the representation of the passions as the crucial element in the portrayal of character.[39] A true "painting of the passions" was taken to be the highest praise one could bestow on any attempt to depict the vicissitudes of human nature. It was thought to be the pictorial and dramatic artist's business to know the best way of representing each passion so as to make the audience respond appropriately, while an intricate set of rules provided for artists the affective conventions through which the passions could be portrayed.

These conventions were drawn in part from classical authorities like Cicero and Quintillian, but they primarily derived from recent formulations of a grammar of passions that could be represented pictorially. The most important of these guidebooks was the *Conférence de M. Le Brun sur l'expression générale et particulière* (1667) by Charles Le Brun, chancellor of the Académie Royale de Peinture et de Sculpture, who codified the principles of Cartesian philosophical psychology in a catalog of instructions, accompanied by drawings, on how properly to depict the influence of each passion on the human face.[40] The pervasive influence of Le Brun's treatise extended beyond the audience of painters to whom it was addressed. Translated into English in 1701, *A Method to Learn to Design the Passions* was reprinted throughout the century. Hume began his essay "Of Tragedy" (1757) with a consideration of Le Brun, whose work was still cited as authoritative by the actor Henry Siddons over a century later.[41] The most important nonpictorial consequence of the idea that there were universal and invariant norms of expression was its effect on theatrical practices, a transmission encouraged by Shaftesbury's arguments affirming the parallels between the pictorial and dramatic arts and then codified into principles of literary criticism.[42] In contemporary acting treatises, like those of Aaron Hill and Samuel Foote, which together formed the first systematic body of writing on the theory and practice of the art of acting in the West (and whose "English" principles transformed European thinking about performance practices), the stage was conceived as a *tableau vivant* where actors drew on a standardized gestural "language" for the expression of the passions.[43] Even more strongly after the naturalistic revolution in acting technique associated with the convulsive triumphs of Charles Macklin and David Garrick as Shylock and Richard III at Covent Garden in 1741, in which active gesture and studied pose displaced declamation as the central tool in an actor's repertoire, audiences engaged with actors in a contract of performance and response wherein they were presumed to be thoroughly familiar with nature's rhetoric of emotional representations.[44] Here the focus was on theater as performance rather than drama conceived as literature, with plays primarily understood as vehicles for the actor's virtuosity. Indeed, the details of facial aspect, gesture, and tone of voice, which Garrick put forward as the essential elements of a "scientifical" account of acting,[45] had already begun to be cataloged in the *Thesaurus Dramaticus* (1724), an account of the "poetical beauties" of the English stage.

The abbé Du Bos's seminal work on aesthetics, *Critical Reflections on Poetry and Painting* (1719), in which Lucretius's words were cited in support of an argument placing the audience of theatrical entertainments at a safe imaginative remove from the performances enacted before it, became the authoritative statement of aesthetic principles associated with the stage during the first half of the eighteenth century.[46] For Du Bos, whose work was translated into English by Montesquieu's translator Thomas Nugent in 1748, each passion had its particular natural expression, tone, and gesture, which "rise, as it were, mechanically within us."[47] The principal merit of dramatic poetry, he argued, consists in the imitation of just those objects that excite our passions, and it is the business of the actor to revive these passions within himself in order more effectively to convey their natural signs to his audience. Spectators are moved in the theater when the "artificial" (as opposed to naturally occurring) passions are aroused; and in providing us with the best representation of the "symptoms and nature" of the passions, drama serves as a vehicle of moral instruction and emotional refinement. The inherently distancing conditions of the theater, however, "where everything shows itself in the nature of a copy," and the separation of the audience from the stage and setting of the play ensure that the spectator's pleasure in viewing Racine's *Phaedre*, for example, "is never attended with those disagreeable consequences, which [would] arise from the serious emotions caused by the [dramatic] object itself."[48] Du Bos argued, after Dennis, and in a manner similar to Shaftesbury, whose writings deeply impressed him, that an enlightened "public" can properly assess the value of a spectacle because its sentiments are refined by education and experience to form a kind of sixth sense, *le sentiment*.[49] An audience is thus enabled to form disinterested judgments (*sans intérêt*), particularly about those powerfully moving expressions of emotion which, on the stage as in society, could not effectively be conveyed in words.[50] "The spectator therefore preserves his understanding, notwithstanding the liveliest emotion. He receives the impression of the passions, but without . . . falling into extravagances."⁵¹ In a directly related vein, one of Addison's purposes in *The Spectator* (1711–1714) was to help constitute just such a public, a "Fraternity of Spectators," as his spokesman announced in one of the early numbers, composed of "every one that considers the World as a Theatre, and desires to form a right Judgement of those who are actors in it." These "impartial spectators," whose cultivated taste could conquer hypocrisy and encourage Christian virtue, would be able to "consider all the different pursuits and Employments of Men, and . . . will [be able to] find [that] half [of] the[ir] Actions tend to nothing else but Disguise and Imposture; and [realize that] all that is done which proceeds not from a Man's very self is the Action of a Player."⁵²

Mandeville, as we have seen, fully subscribed to the position that an individual's character could best be understood as a distinct amalgam of discrete passions; but he was a thorough-going physiological materialist who strenuously denied the view, taken from Descartes, whom he called a "Vain reasoner" (1:181), that the passions were subject to purely rational control, either on the stage or in the street, as Du Bos had insisted. One of Mandeville's primary purposes was to expose this view as self-serving nonsense. It was itself an example of the "Practical Part of Dissimulation" (2:77) and hypocrisy that contemporary doctrines of politeness and, he pointedly said, supposedly refined aesthetic prejudices (2:40) were meant to conceal by describing the "Arts of rendring . . . Behaviour agreeble to others, with the least Disturbance to themselves" (2:11).

Members of an expanding *beau monde* who constituted the elite of commercial societies could never, Mandeville insisted, strictly adhere to the codes of polite intercourse promoted by Addison, Steele, Shaftesbury, and Du Bos while at the same time remaining independent and undeluded moral agents. These individuals were required to adopt highly stylized public personae as they regularly confronted virtual strangers whose approbation they sought, especially in the widening urban spaces whose rituals had become the privileged subjects of popular art—the coffeehouse, club, square, park, and, as Voltaire pointedly remarked, the London stock exchange, where material interest alone formed a social bond and promoted civilized intercourse among unrelated persons with otherwise incommensurable habits and beliefs.⁵³ In populous cities, Montesquieu said, directly alluding to Mandeville, "men are motivated by an ambition of distinguishing themselves by trifles—strangers to one another, their vanity redoubles because there is greater hope of success." "The more people communicate with each other," he continued, citing *The Fable* as his authority, "the more easily they change their manners, because each becomes to a greater degree a spectacle to the other.⁵⁴ Along with other contemporary observers, Mandeville was quick to notice that the enlarged public at London's theaters themselves (2:39), which were and would remain the most commercially successful public entertainments in Europe during the eighteenth century, provided a microcosm (in Dennis's words) of a novel social universe, an arena in which people who had risen from obscurity and who had recently made their fortunes from speculation could pretend to polite habits and aspire "to a condition of distinction and plenty." As Dennis wrote in his own attack on *The Fable,* Mandeville's work embodied the threat of moral degeneration posed to British society by the newly moneyed.[55]

When Mandeville's adversary William Law attacked Dennis for defending the moral propriety of the stage, he observed that the patrons at London's theaters were convinced of their right to judge a play simultaneous with its production, a point famously made again by Dr. Johnson in mid-century and typified by Boswell, for whom the theater was the exemplary site for the practiced display of states of feeling.[56] As Boswell argued in *On the Profession of a Player* (1770), his own consideration of the stage, forms of public presentation had been refined into art by the cultivation of "double feeling" of actors themselves. When he went to a packed Drury Lane Theatre to see Garrick play Lear, followed by a popular comedy, Boswell testified how for both actor and spectator performance had come to be understood as a discontinuous series of heightened moments of affective engagement, directed to others prepared by their emotional expectations and theatrical public habits to respond in a similarly discontinuous fashion. "I kept myself at a distance from all acquaintances, and got into a proper frame. Mr. Garrick gave the most satisfaction. I was fully moved, and shed an abundance of tears. The farce was *Polly Honeycomb,* at which I laughed a good deal."[57] As plays themselves increasingly considered the active role of the audience in the dynamics of theatrical performance, audiences enlarged the idea of performance to include the auditorium as well as the stage. Theatrical encounters offered an opportunity for the rehearsal of public expression, in which the individual could conceptually remove himself from his companions and then, in imaginative isolation, experience those nuances of feeling whose appropriately performed outward signs distinguished his sensibility. Little wonder that for Law one "must . . . abhor the Thoughts of being at a Play, as of being a player your self."[58]

Mandeville strictly adhered to the ancient view, shared by his critics but enriched by his Augustinian perspective, that theatricality had a necessarily hostile relationship to all forms of moral intimacy and that individuals would become divided personalities as the social pressures of civil society required them to adopt the strategic poses of actors in public life. But he abandoned entirely the effective, and originally Platonic, corollary of this view, namely, that public theatrics were necessarily destructive of the political body and the social fabric. Mandeville abandoned this understanding since a genuine sense of duty could hardly be expected of persons whose public professions were always mediated by masks of propriety, just as the classical figure of the masked actor, the *hypocrates* who merely impersonates by playing a role, could never be relied on to treat his fellows as brothers. Instead, Mandeville celebrated theatrical relations as inherent attributes of political and economic life in advanced societies. One could, for example, best understand the failure of the British state to enforce social discipline among the swelling London populace by viewing the "festival atmosphere" of the procession from Newgate to Tyburn as a "spectacle" in which crimes the law purportedly punished were transformed into acts of popular heroism through the political mismanagement of what in effect was a "public theatre."[59] It is the business of the skillful politician to "extract good from the very worst, as well as the best" by assigning appropriate social roles to those individuals most competent to play them (1:49–52, 208–210). The management of appearances in fact lay at the heart of governing egoists, whether these were devout believers, which "Popes . . . by a Strategem of the Church . . . have made great Men the chief Actors in . . . childish Farces," common soldiers captivated by Cromwell's zealous professions of faith, which he "made use of . . . accordingly," or members of the moneyed and educated classes, who "conform to all Ceremonies that are fashionable" and "make a Shew outwardly of what is not felt within, and counterfeit what is not real."[60] On a more mundane but socially decisive level, Mandeville argued that the envy and emulative propensities characteristic of fallen men had in commercial societies become the propulsive features of civil life itself, despite the standard disapproval of self-indulgence which remained the prevailing moral orthodoxy. In nations shaped by commerce, the self-regard that characterized all persons everywhere took the form of man as a consuming and especially a displaying animal—a creature whose boundless appetites are governed by the desire for esteem within an expanding world of marketable goods. An ethos of public display fired an economy of conspicuous consumption, which in turn depended on the promotion of unstable fashion and social fantasy. Here, even a "poor common Harlot . . . must have Shoes and Stockings, Gloves, the Stay and Mantuamaker, the Seamstress, the Linnen-draper, all must get something by her, and a hundred different Tradesmen dependent on those she laid her Money out with, may touch part of it before a Month is at an end" (1:88).

Little wonder that for Mandeville's adversaries like the social critic George Bluett, a society so understood as an aggregation of purely self-interested individuals competitively bound to one another by greed, vanity, and imagination immediately evoked the image of a perverse masquerade.[61] Mandeville had previously exploited this image in his satiric account of government politics when he had a fictional opponent of the Whigs charge them with being "admirably qualified for Poetry and the Stage: you first forgo Harpies, Sphinxes, Dragons, and Chimeras, that never were in Nature, and then put them off [as] Realities upon the People."[62] He insisted that under modern conditions public life was of necessity theatrical, resembling in considerable detail the masquerades put on by Count Heidegger, the Flemish adventurer whose spectacles featuring masks, cross-dressing, and purportedly illicit liaisons at The Haymarket were the toast of London society and the object of fear and revulsion among contemporary moral reformers.[63] As Mandeville mockingly said of one of the bishop of London's sermons against immoral practices, his was a "most edifying Anti-Heidegger Discourse."[64]

Mandeville's most anxiety-provoking claim was neither that his contemporaries were immoral nor that the springs of their actions could be shown to contradict their professed ideals. It was rather that fiction and fantasy profoundly influenced the fashioning of selves in commercial society and that the primary stabilizing forces of this society were those inherent in the essentially theatrical relations through which it regulated itself. He expressed in heightened form the legitimation anxieties of a recently disenchanted community in which the content of inherited moral commitments had become detached from the tacit picture of the world inhabited by individuals unavoidably situated in a community whose practices stand at some remove from its professed beliefs. Mandeville was a dangerous author throughout the eighteenth century because his argument threatened to subvert the historically moralized structures of deference and obedience on which traditional society rested. "Suppose every body knew as much as the Author of *The Fable of the Bees* and that Virtue and Vice were but Bugbears invented for the uninterrupted indulging of the Appetites of some certain Persons," the anonymous author of *The True Meaning of the Fable of the Bees* asked his readers, "or suppose they had made the Discovery that it was in the Essence of the *Politician* to consult nobody but himself. How would you keep People in awe?"[65]

HENRY FIELDING'S CHALLENGE

As Mandeville's anatomy of the passions and his theatrical account of their harnessing as social instruments demanded from his readers a dramatic perspective on the conventions of civil life, *The Fable* symbolized for a significant segment of his audience the triumphant principles of a recently debased public sphere, where the sentiments of love, honor, friendship, and civic virtue were all too plausibly redescribed and then celebrated in terms of pure theatrical contrivance. While many were shocked and revolted by the prospect of such a world—and the works attacking Mandeville came to amount to a small library—the most direct confrontation in the eighteenth century with these images of a theatricalized modern moral subject was the work of Henry Fielding, who self-consciously adopted a position in diametric opposition to those "political philosophers," particularly Mandeville and La Rochefoucauld, who represented man as a "depraved, and totally bad" creature.[66] In *Tom Jones* he condemned "that modern doctrine" that alarmed the world by declaring "that there were no such things as virtue or goodness really existing in human nature, and . . . deduced our best actions from pride."[67] The greatest, because the most influential, representative of this modern doctrine of cynical egoism, said the *Covent-Garden Journal*, was "that charming fellow Mandevil . . . who hath represented human nature in a picture of the highest deformity."[68] Fielding occasionally invented disreputable characters to express Mandeville's views, like Thwackum and Square in *Tom Jones*, while his apostrophe to vanity in *Joseph Andrews* is in fact a summary of *The Fable*.[69] Likewise, the "Modern Glossary" of vice in the *Covent-Garden Journal* is a compendium of Mandeville's arguments about the role of self-love, in which *The Fable*'s discussion of dress as a primary mark of social worth is similarly satirized.[70] Throughout his career Fielding alternatively sought to ridicule or demolish Mandeville's psychological views, even when his diagnosis of contemporary social ills, like the increase of robbery in London, was virtually identical to those in *The Fable*.[71]

Were Fielding's opposition to Mandeville confined to these criticisms of Mandeville's doctrines, his views would simply be part of the general chorus of complaint *The Fable* continued to elicit in the two generations after its publication. But, as William Hazlitt said, Fielding sought to offer an imaginative picture of the "moral, political, and religious feeling" in the England of George II.[72] He attempted directly to counter the world Mandeville described because it riveted the imagination of his contemporaries, a world in which distinctions between the real and the merely apparent, the felt and the feigned, are features of an ensemble of dispositions whose articulation is entirely public. Because Fielding fully accepted Mandeville's challenge to orthodox ethical reasoning as a defining focus of his fiction, he is important for an understanding of *The Fable*'s significance in forging a theatrical language of social intelligibility. Fielding sought to depict the public sphere as a spectacle of competing characters dominated by ruling passions, an imaginative realm in which he, like Mandeville, could count on his readers' consciousness of role distance as a pervasive category of their own social perceptions. Fielding wished to reveal and decipher the code that underlay this spectacle and then claim for his enterprise a moralizing function that vitiated the premises on which Mandeville's understanding of it was based. He sought imaginatively to reveal that "there is in some human Breasts, a kind and benevolent Disposition, which is gratified by contributing to the Happiness of others."[73] Fielding moreover, who wrote extensively for the London stage until the Licencing Act of 1737 and who took Garrick as his performing ideal, accepted the fully theatricized public domain Mandeville had portrayed as his representative subject, one in which "the Hypocrite may be said to be the player, [as] . . . indeed the Greeks called them both by one and the same name." As the narrator of *Tom Jones* says, departing from the telling of his hero's story to reflect on the colonization of public discourse by theatrical metaphor,

> [The] comparison between the world and the stage has been carried so far and become so general that some words proper to the theatre and which were at first metaphorically applied to the world are now indiscriminately and literally spoken of both: thus stage and scene are by common use grown as familiar to us, when we speak of life in general, as when we confine ourselves to dramatic performances; and when we mention transactions behind the curtain, St. James's is more likely to occur to our own thoughts than Drury-Lane.[74]

Readers of *Tom Jones* were told that the characters of the novel should be considered actors in a double sense. Their performances enact roles understood as such by the generalized "audience" of society, a public divided into the socially segregated "boxes, stalls, and balconies" where theatrical responses form essential aspects of the spectacle on view. Fielding's conceptual object was to situate these spectators as the central characters "at this great drama." His fictions were meant to serve as appropriate vehicles for the representation of their consciousness, aware of the possibility of a theatrical detachment from any particular social embodiment, and for the understanding of character as a circumscribed feature of this self-awareness. Like Mandeville, Fielding conceived of his readers as the audience at a drama in which they participated and as persons who would be provided with sets of instructions necessary to decode its rules.

Fielding's object was to translate the signs and concepts formerly at home in an aristocratic moral and discursive environment into the codes of a moneyed and mobile culture where they bore altered intersubjective meanings. His "comic prose epic" rendered the actions of men as performances necessarily undertaken within discrete behavioral styles. The artist would represent these forms of public personality stereotypically in order to expose their unwritten protocols. Once in conscious possession of these rules, the audience could, as Shaftesbury and Du Bos had argued, emotionally detach itself from the roles persons played, precisely because the performative requirements of these roles had been revealed as merely the outward conformity of otherwise free moral agents to pre-scripted social demands. Fielding sought to disperse the passionate attachments these stylized social performances were meant to engender in an audience for whom styles of behavior had become objects of dramatic art. He wished to re-create Addison's impartial spectator, the participant-observer who could in effect systematically separate the form of an act—its socially specified and easily mimed behavioral requirements—from its ethical import and thus from the moral sources of action on which men ought properly to be judged.

Fielding feared the impending demise of the classical ideal of virtuous self-sacrifice in the name of the public good because, as he put it in Mandeville's idiom, this standard of moral propriety was fast becoming in the minds of his audience a "political maxim" by which the cunning advanced their private interests. Yet he sympathized with this response, believing that

> it is impossible that any man endowed with rational faculties, and being in a state of freedom, should willingly agree, without some motive of love or friendship, absolutely to sacrifice his own interest to that of another. . . . Thus, while the crafty and designing part of mankind, consulting only their own separate advantage, endeavor to maintain one constant imposition on the others, the whole world becomes a vast masquerade where the greatest part appear disguised . . . a very few only showing their own faces, who become by so doing, the astonishment and ridicule of all the rest.[75]

Like Mandeville, Fielding here deployed one of the most ubiquitous Augustan images of social subversion and the decay of public identity;[76] and it is important to notice that in exposing to ridicule the moral duplicities of this "vast masquerade" he was also intent on showing how even those honest souls for whom love bridged the gulf between motive and act still necessarily followed the theatrical imperatives that governed communal behavior. Suppose these individuals were distinguished by genuinely moral, other-regarding sentiments. As social creatures they were obliged nevertheless to act within the formal conventions demanded by all social roles, to appear in one of "those disguises" worn on "the greater stage" of society.[77] Yet if one maintains that all men are players and that even the highest forms of moral sensibility remain extrinsic to the performative demands of the ethical act, how then can the theatrically embodied persons who appear on society's stage truly be known, save perhaps in those rare and privileged moments when the force of circumstance may lead to a collapse of dramaturgical ingenuity? This crucial question was previously raised by Thomas Blackwell in his influential *An Inquiry into the Life and Writings of Homer* (1735), a comparison of the transparent emotional expression of the ancients with duplicitous modern sensibilities, and then later in the century by John Brown, another of Mandeville's critics, who argued that the modern performing arts morally corrupted their audiences by encouraging techniques of dissimulation and disguise.[78] It was the abiding question Fielding and his contemporaries had inherited from Mandeville, and he explicitly sought to resist the force of Mandeville's motto "Private vices, public benefits" in order to deny the morally skeptical conclusions of *The Fable* because of their licentious implications. Fielding argued instead that the true scene of meaningful human action, and thus of morals, was not the mere backdrop of conventional social arrangements in which, he agreed with Mandeville, the skillful deceived less talented players. It was rather a universe of supposedly natural signs of divine inscription, a world populated by beings whose very features revealed their genuine sentiments. In such a moral universe, even the most practiced performer could be unmasked, for

> however cunning the disguise which a masquerader wears; however foreign to his age, degree or circumstances; yet if closely attended to he very rarely escapes the discovery of an accurate observer; for Nature, which unwillingly submits to the imposture, is ever endeavoring to peep forth and show herself; nor can the cardinal, the friar, or the judge, long conceal the sot, the gamester or the rake.
>
> In the same manner will those disguises which are worn on the greater stage generally vanish, or prove ineffectual to impose the assumed for the real character upon us, if we employ sufficient diligence and attention in the scrutiny.[79]

Fielding was committed to the view, shared by Jansenists and Calvinists alike, that truly moral acts could only be performed by genuinely virtuous actors. He believed as well that goodness was a property of the soul, given through grace, though not by the *Deus absconditus* of La Rochefoucauld, Bayle, and Nicole whose workings could nowhere be seen with any certainty. Rather, Fielding thought that the purposes of an Enlightenment God "peep forth" from the "Nature" in which he inscribed them. This precept, he said, gave him the courage to "defy the wisest man in the world to turn a true good action into ridicule."[80] For even if in their theatrically encoded performances all persons became fit subjects for Mandevillian satire, Fielding was convinced that the property of virtue was Nature's stamp, "imprint[ed] on men with] sufficient marks," and permanently available for the properly instructed to decipher.[81]

Nature "imprint[ed] sufficient marks in the countenance to inform an accurate and discerning eye," Fielding claimed, echoing Betterton and Le Brun, and in his *Essay on the Knowledge and the Characters of Men* he sought to "set down some few rules" to guide the discernment of men of open dispositions, the sure indication, he said, "of an honest and upright heart."[82] He sometimes thought that these principles, cited with Shaftesbury's authority, offered a way for the morally worthy to remain impartial spectators of their own social drama. These persons could achieve the critical distance necessary to comprehend the global character of theatrical behavior. Then, by judging dissimulation with charity, they could reduce the anxieties generated by their own performances and begin a morally informed process of harmonizing public representations with private insight. "A single bad act no more constitutes a villain in life, than a single bad part on the stage," the narrator says in *Tom Jones:* "Thus the man as well as the player may condemn what he himself acts; nay it is common to see vice sit as awkwardly on some men as the character of Iago would on the honest face of [the popular actor] Mr William Mills."[83] Like Tom Jones, who knows that "appearances . . . are often deceitful," but who is seldom so deceived, and unlike

Jonathan Wild, author of "Maxims for the Great Man," the hypocrite's handbook, it could be hoped that good men, no matter how ordinary, might know their fellows and in that knowledge forgive them.

Yet, Fielding recognized, as the self-regarding passions drove the players of a theatricized world, they similarly distorted the judgment of its spectators, "for as affectation always overacts her part, it fares with her as with a farcical actor on the stage . . . while the truest and finest strokes of Nature, represented by a judicious and just actor, pass unobserved and disregarded."[84] Although in possession of rules by which to decipher nature's inscriptions, men nevertheless remained vulnerable to the passionately distorted images of their own creation and failed to encounter the man performing behind the mask. Even in a world of natural signs "a more reliable guide" was needed for their decoding. This guide, Fielding said, is to be found in "the *actions* of men,"[85] a piece of advice that could only give small comfort to his discerning reader, so intimately acquainted by Mandeville's *Fable* and by Fielding's own fictions with the endlessly interpretable, because never unmediated, transactions between audience and masquerade, reader and player, in what Fielding himself described as a mere pantomime of critical communication.[86] As the century's greatest mime told a philosopher who, like Fielding, sought to defend the principles of virtue and penetrate by reason the masks of vicious actors, "The man who must have a manual won't ever go far, [for] society offers many more [poses] than . . . art can imitate."[87]

THE APOTHEOSIS OF THE ACTOR

As with virtually all of Mandeville's critics, Fielding's dilemma arose from the traditions of moral psychology informing eighteenth-century techniques for representing the person. He assumed that the modern writer's task was to classify and embody the visible signs of the invisible powers from which action sprang, critically distancing the reader from his own motives by satirically rendering their effects. As he said early on in *Joseph Andrews:* "Passions operate differently on the human mind, as diseases on the body, in proportion to the strength or weakness, soundness or rotteness, of the one and the other."[88] In his fictions Fielding combined the "various atoms" that comprise "all human particles"—passions, dispositions, social position, education, habit, occupation—in different ways, in order to discover, as he says of the human spectacle in *Tom Jones,* what their result would be. The rhetoric of the theater eminently suited these purposes. Fielding exploited the metaphorical equation of the world as a stage for the comprehension by persons experiencing a dislocation of the traditional nexus between status and economic power, persons whose expanded opportunities for profit and social promotion in an increasingly mobile world heightened the distance between their private moral intuitions and the requirements of public performance. The relatively stable system of expression, pose, gesture, and plot which Fielding adopted from the contemporary stage permitted him to depict for an enlarged and diverse reading public those universal features of the human drama whose representations were previously confined to the socially elevated. As Fielding said, his novels sought to embody the spirit of the epic under modern, prosaic conditions.

The response that Diderot placed in the mouth of Rameau's nephew, whose Mandevillian maxims reduced his philosophical adversary to astonished silence,[89] highlights how these representational practices, which supported a theatrical view of social action and which were contingent on particular assumptions about what constitutes psychological realism, became problematic during the course of the eighteenth century.[90] Fielding already had an inkling of this shift when he rejected those "immense Romances of the modern Novel . . . [which,] without any assistance from Nature or History, records persons who never were, or will be, and facts which never did nor possibly can happen."[91] His point, here famously made against Richardson, was that the narrative of a given identity could only successfully be charted against the background of its governing passions. Such a life, he believed, could move and instruct an audience only if it were placed in imaginative contact with precisely these unvarying characteristics of human nature, publicly expressed on the dramatic surface of social action. Mandeville began from identical premises, as did Chesterfield and Burke. Hume and Gibbon wrote their histories from a similar perspective, one also shared by the eighteenth-century biographers of Garrick, Siddons, the Barrys, and Kemble, actors who for the first time became celebrated public icons.[92] So did Smollett, whose fictions, like Fielding's, are populated with Mandevillian figures of wickedness. Like these writers, Fielding thought it absurd that the peculiarities of a character's emotional response, historical or fictive, could or should compel the reader somehow to "identify" with him—a usage, it is worth noting, that did not become common until late in the eighteenth century.[93] Like Mandeville, Fielding wanted to encourage the reader's conceptual distance from his creations, not the suspension of disbelief. He wished to dissect the theatrical demands of all roles, so that in an encounter with the performance of such roles spectators could detach, not identify, and remain self-consciously free moral agents.

Fielding's understanding of social action as theatrical rests on the assumption, first made explicit in *The Fable* and later bemoaned by Rousseau in his encounter with Mandeville ("the most excessive detractor of human virtue")[94] that contemporary societies were distinguished by the encouragement given their members to conduct their lives in ways designed for studied self-misrepresentation. As Rousseau put it in his polemic against the the theater, "When we are purely spectators we immediately take the side of justice," but when we enter into theatrical relations, "only then [do] we prefer the evil that is useful to us to the good that makes us love."[95] Mandeville gave theoretical expression to this common concern among eighteenth-century observers of public life that, as one of them noted, "Greatness is so Theatrical, and the actors change so often that really I was at a loss where to fix."[96] The modern reign of fashion was at once an instrument of and spur to these deceptive practices, depending as it did on an explosion of mobile wealth and its associated ideology of manners, recently elevated by Shaftesbury to the status of moral philosophy. Social actors, most especially those recently propelled into the higher orbits of society, were seen repeatedly to conceal their intentions because the exposure of these wholly self-regarding purposes would make their achievement impossible. From this perspective, hypocrisy emerged at once for both Mandeville and Fielding as a defining feature of human conduct, as it did in much of eighteenth-century thought, while the astute social observer in Fielding's fictions assumed the role of an impartial spectator—a detached decoder of ubiquitous practices of concealment. Fielding unmasked the intentions of men in order to give full sense to their performances, conceived as elements of social practices that cannot, in principle, be understood from the point of view of the fully engaged, theatrically situated participant in public life.

The awareness of others as beholders complicit in accepting the necessity of representing themselves as their fellows wished to see them engendered a commonly shared psychological perspective on the sources of social conduct. In the language that Addison and Shaftesbury did so much to construct, persons of refinement were both actors and spectators in relation to their own lives, lives understood as moral careers shaped by the techniques of politeness for monitoring and controlling one's public persona. A primary object of this language was to normalize the relations of persons self-conscious of the apparent gulf between inherited standards of propriety and contemporary requirements for social success. It is for this reason that writers, like Hume, who employed this language, so often expressed perplexity about identity and moral agency and so strenuously devoted their intellectual energies to the discovery of those features of a self that could be said to possess undistorted moral sentiments.[97] *The Fable* articulated the assumptive background against which this language developed, as Hume recognized when he named Mandeville as one of "the late philosophers in England, who have begun to put the science of man on a new footing."[98]

Mandeville did not simply deny that exclusively moral sentiments could coherently be imagined for persons driven by self-regard. His significant ideological accomplishment consisted in providing an argument about the centrality of the passions which effectively set the terms in which the eighteenth-century language of sociability addressed the problem of moral autonomy by considering the prospect that the modern self had acquired the opinions of others as part of its content. As he put it, "We need not look for . . . the Origin of Politeness . . . any further than in the Self-Liking, which I have demonstrated every individual Man to be poss'd of " (2:138). Modern sociability, Mandeville continued,

[has] nothing to do with virtue or Religion. . . . It is a Science that is ever built on the same steady Principle in our Nature, and we shall find, that Luxury and Politeness ever grew up together, and were never enjoyed assunder; that Comfort and Delight upon Earth have always employ'd the Wishes of the *Beau Monde;* and that, as their chief Study and greatest Solicitude, to outward Appearance, have ever been directed to obtain Happiness in the World, so what would become of them in the next seems, to the naked Eye, always to have been the least of their Concern. (2:146–147)

After the controversy about the nature of egoism begun by the storm of controversy surrounding *The Fable*'s appearance in 1723, virtually all socially engaged British critics, philosophers, and theologians of the following two generations were obliged to confront Mandeville's claim that reason's essential practical role is to answer those questions that the passions provide the only motives for asking—questions concerning the existence and nature of those objects that the passions impel all persons to want or to be. If reason's purpose is to prescribe means for the achievement of the ends set by the passions and if reason judges those means only in terms of their efficacy, then, as Mandeville insisted, any plausible account of morals would have to be undertaken within the context of a hierarchy of indelible desires. An epistemology of sense impressions and ideas, wedded to a psychology of passions, shaped in the eighteenth century a conception of personality molded solely through interaction with the objects it encounters. Within this conceptual space, where the person is understood as a strictly arranged ensemble of dispositions, all actions may coherently be considered in terms of the divided personality's need to establish an "outward appearance" for the approval of others while attempting to satisfy its hidden impulses. When Hume asserted that "reason is and ought only to be the slave of the passions and can never pretend to any other office than to serve and obey them,"[99] he effectively distilled this precept into a philosophical principle and drew from it an account of the development of morals founded on the intersubjective, histrionic relationships Mandeville located at the heart of commercial sociability. "In general," Hume said,

the minds of men are mirrors to one another, not only because they reflect each other's emotions, but also because those rays of passions, sentiments and opinions may often be reverberated, and may decay away by insensible degrees. Thus the pleasures which a rich man receives from his possessions being thrown upon the beholder, causes a pleasure and esteem; which sentiments again, being perceived and sympathized with, increase the pleasure of the possessor; and being once more reflected, become a new foundation for pleasure and esteem in the beholder. . . . But the possessor has also a secondary satisfaction in riches arising from the love of esteem he acquires by them, and this satisfaction is nothing but a second reflection of that original pleasure, which proceeded from itself. The secondary satisfaction of vanity becomes one of the principal recommendations of riches, and is the chief reason we either desire them for ourselves or esteem them in others.[100]

Beginning his inquiry from the spectator's point of view and presuming with Mandeville that the individual's judgments are governed by the compound of his passions, Hume not only viewed the self as a kind of theater, "where several perceptions successively make their appearance, pass, repass, glide away, and mingle in an infinite variety of postures and situations";[101] he also sought to show that the individual's limited sympathies for the welfare of others could be furthered and fully accounted for in terms of an essentially self-interested beholder's responses to the postures and demands of his fellows. Montesquieu had previously made a related point in *The Persian Letters* (1721), which Hume noted, when his Persian visitors to Paris saw in the theater and its audience the model of contemporary European culture, one in which individuals are obliged continually to interact with other social actors in order to secure public approbation and may advance their private ambitions only by respecting the rules of civility.[102] Similarly, for Adam Smith social life of necessity resembles a masquerade,[103] despite the discreditable ends to which players ply their talents,[104] for the approbation and disapprobation of oneself which we call conscience is but a mirror of feeling—a social product that is an effect of each of us judging others as a spectator while finding others as spectators judging ourselves. We then come to judge our own conduct, Smith argued in direct opposition to the "indulgent and partial spectator" of Mandeville's "licentious system," in which the opinion of others is the arbiter of our performances, when "we examine it as we imagine an impartial spectator would."[105] Smith sought to show that unlike the spectator of Mandevillian provenance who seeks applause, the man of genuine self-command could be governed not by the desire for praise but for praiseworthiness itself. Yet most men, the ambitious or deferential in Smith's account, are moved by the universal desire to be at the center of the scene where "the abstract idea of a perfect and happy state" is being staged.[106] Here persons expose themselves to "the public admiration," either by playing or by competing for roles, and admiration is bestowed on the condition that allows for visibility: "to be observed, to be attended to, to be taken notice of with sympathy, complacency and approbation."[107] Men require mirrors, for without society, a man "could no more think of his own character . . . than of the beauty or deformity of his own face," and the only mirror in which he can view his character "is placed in the countenance and behaviour of those he lives with."[108] Smith argued that if "we begin . . . to examine our own passions and conduct, and to consider how these must appear to [others] . . . we [must] suppose ourselves the spectators to our own behavior, and endeavor to imagine what effect it would, in this light, produce upon us. This is the only looking-glass by which we can, in some measure, with the eyes of other people, scrutinize the propriety of our own conduct."[109]

These thinkers, like so many of their Enlightenment contemporaries, not only accepted Mandeville's initial challenge that the abiding problem posed by commercial sociability was to show how individuals could be considered moral if they were irreducibly proud and vain and that the inherent dynamics of commerce depended on the encouragement of these frightening natural propensities. Like him, but without his satiric glee, they confronted the possibility that, as Smith put it, "society may subsist among different men, as among different merchants, from a sense of its utility, without any mutual love or affection; and though no man in it should owe any obligation, or be bound in gratitude to any other, it may still be upheld by a mercenary exchange of good offices, according to agreed valuation."[110] They confronted, in other words, the possibility that in commercial societies, where social standing and public identity so intensely depended on the opinion of others, the individual's moral autonomy threatened always to be compromised. Practical reason had few defenses in a social world where beliefs were decisively shaped by economic contingencies.[111]

Eighteenth-century intellectuals were thus faced with the argument, most clearly associated with *The Fable*, that character itself was in essence a social artifact, a construct of the demands of others which existed in an intersubjective space and within which a person's public identity was of necessity devised. Once Mandeville's challenge was addressed in the idiom of the passions which *The Fable* elevated into a dominant vocabulary among post-Protestant (or post-Augustinian), prerevolutionary intellectuals, persons could immediately be understood as players pressured by circumstance and goaded by opportunity to perform in ways designed to elicit that public approbation demanded by their dominant passions. As Kant observed when lecturing to his students for the last time in 1797, "The more civilised men become, the more they become actors. They want to *put on a show* and fabricate an illusion of their own persons."[112] As if to address Smith's worry about the connection between modern morals and mercenary exchange, Kant continued, in the idiom of *The Fable*, which he much admired,[113] "all human virtue in circulation is small change. Only a child would take it for real gold. But it is better to have small change in circulation than no means of exchange at all."[114] The language of an efflorescent European theater and of theories of acting first crafted in England (and then adopted on the Continent in works like Diderot's *Paradox of Acting*, Lessing's *Hamburg Dramaturgy*, and Goethe's *Rules for Actors*), ideally suited the purposes of intellectuals determined to comprehend what they understood to be a wholly new and culturally revolutionary social formation, in which personation was required for public identity. As Rousseau protested in the *Letter to d'Alembert,* his contemporaries sought "to present virtue to us as a theatrical game,"[115] for in commercial societies characterized by persons driven by the "furor to distinguish themselves," mere "opinion" had become "the queen of the world."[116]

Rousseau's antitheatrical animus was an expression of two incompatible positions. In the first, derived from a long-standing republican opposition to the stage found in both classical authors like Solon (as reported by Plutarch) and Tacitus and in early modern writers such as Machiavelli and Sidney, Rousseau viewed the theater as a symbol of the growth of morally debilitating luxury, of "discontent with one's self, the burden of idleness, [and] the neglect of simple and natural tastes."[117] Theaters were institutions in which the simplicity of manners required of active and independent citizens was threatened by a powerful encouragement of the habits of dissimulation, display, and anticivic egoism which characterized modern commercial life.[118] Rousseau was intimately aware of these temptations, and often despised himself when he succumbed to them. In January 1766, during his visit to England, Garrick played two characters especially for Jean-Jacques at a packed Drury Lane Theatre. In response, Garrick's wife reported, Rousseau "was so very anxious to display himself, and hung so foward over the box," that she had to "hold him by the skirt of his coat, that he might not fall over into the pit."[119] In the theater and through the dispersion of its habits, the modern self, so Rousseau thought, had become a heteronomous residue of its reflection in the mirror of strangers, themselves in constant need of public reminders of their own identities. In the preface to his play *Narcissus, or The Lover of Himself,* Rousseau defended his own dramatic efforts by arguing that since the "dangerous doctrines" of egoism and self-regard spawned by "Mandeville had more than succeeded," the theater itself should properly be employed, not for the now impossible resurrection of virtue among a population committed to luxury and bereft of nondissimulating communication, but by legislators who might tame vice by manipulating the public opinion that imparted to socialized and deracinated metropolitans the sentiment of their own existence.[120]

Rousseau's other mode of argument conceived of the theater not so much as a vehicle for the promotion of self-regard but as a set of devices for the diminution of individuality. From this perspective, he viewed the playhouse as an arena in which the feelings of individuals were manipulated and normalized, for in the theater "we give our tears" only to fictions "while our heart closes itself for fear of being touched at our expense."[121] Writing in this mode during the last decade of his life, Rousseau began to take leave of that body of assumptions about the relationship of the passions to both character and behavior which informed Mandeville's work and the eighteenth-century reflection on morals and their relationship to public life which followed from it. Instead, Rousseau searched for those features of an individual's history, exemplified by his own, that could never fully be captured by typifying theatrical conventions, either on the stage or in the street. They were expressions of an inner life that resisted all attempts to encode it as a feature of social practices theatrically conceived, precisely because such a life was singular and self-defining. As he wrote in the first page of *The Confessions,* "I know my own heart . . . I am made unlike anyone I have ever met. I will even venture to say that I am like no one in the whole world. I may be no better, but at least I am different."

This claim to indubitable introspective knowledge of states of feeling and response which certified the individual's uniqueness not only departed absolutely from the arguments of *The Fable.* It soon became foundational both for an emerging narrative of romantic identities and for the practices of representing and understanding the self which would characterize the nineteenth-century novel as well as the stage.[122] Hegel, who gave philosophical statement to this transformed conception of self, understood that it presumed a revision of theatricality's primary zone of applicability from the footlights to backstage. "It is manifest that behind the so-called curtain, which is supposed to conceal the inner world," he wrote in *The Phenomenology of Spirit,* "there is nothing to be seen unless *we* go behind it ourselves, as much in order that we may see, as that there may be something behind there which can be seen."[123] But until the eighteenth-century vocabulary of the passions was succeeded by a new language of the emotions, which are seen to rest on judgments and modifying passion itself, a language in which persons could understand themselves as moved by integrated patterns of feeling which shape a unique identity, the theatrical plasticity of the self that Mandeville so powerfully anatomized would retain its central place on the horizon of social understanding.

"These Neuter Somethings"

Gender Difference and Commercial Culture in Mid-Eighteenth-Century England

Harriet Guest

I

"There are few things by which a man discovers the weakness of his judgement more, than by retailing scraps of common-place sentiment on the trite and thread-bare topic, the degeneracy of the times," remarked Adam Fitz-Adam in the issue of *The World* for February 26, 1756. But for most of the periodical essayists of the mid century, this "trite and thread-bare topic" is the stock in trade, and the narrative of corruption and degeneration is continually alluded to, with ironic acceptance or humorous despair, but above all with a familiarity that indicates the persuasiveness of its account of the times. His tongue pushing more visibly against his cheek, Fitz-Adam goes on to defend modernity, complaining that "really it is a great breach of good-manners, that modern fine gentlemen cannot put a little *rouge* on their faces, but the saucy quill of some impertinent author immediately rubs it off." For, he points out, "Juvenal informs us, that the Roman beaux did the same." Finally, Fitz-Adam cites a correspondent who argues that the present age is preeminently uncorrupt because it has achieved that "Conquest over the affections and passions" which philosophers have always advocated, for now Englishmen do not marry for love but, more prudently, for money.[1] The paper, I think, is typical of mid-eighteenth-century social satire, in that it deplores the pervasiveness of what it identifies as degeneracy, but sees its progress as inevitable and manages to convey almost a perverse pleasure in the absurdities it produces. For periodical papers of the mid century return repeatedly to the theme of Britain's inevitable imitation of the decline and fall of the Roman Empire and to the representation of a metropolitan culture as caught up in the historical process where "as the Men became mercenary and effeminate, the Women grew lewd and luxurious,"[2] where errant sexuality and the culture of commercial prosperity are perceived as the intertwined manifestations of national degeneration.

The sense, by mid century, that the process of degeneration may be as much a matter for wry humor or ironic detachment as for alarm or disgust seems to indicate the extent to which the narrative on corruption has become dissociated from that on commercial progress. For commerce can of course be celebrated with increasing ease in these decades as the source of a culture distinguished by its own characteristic set of virtues and social benefits. Samuel Johnson argues, for example, in *The Adventurer,* that "he, whose mind is engaged by the acquisition or improvement of a fortune, not only escapes the insipidity of indifference, and the tediousness of inactivity, but gains enjoyments wholly unknown to those who live lazily on the toil of others; for life affords no higher pleasure than that of surmounting difficulties, passing from one step of success to another, forming new wishes, and seeing them gratified."[3] In Johnson's account the endless promotion of desire that characterizes commercial culture seems wholly removed from and uninfected by the heady mixture of avarice and licentious sexuality that mark desire as the symptom of degeneracy. The processes of this moralization of desire are obviously complex. But in the periodical papers I am concerned with it seems to be effected by a relatively simple maneuver of representing fashionable society in both a synecdochic and antithetical relation to commercial society. So a correspondent observes to Adam Fitz-Adam that "the luxury and corruption of any nation is just in proportion to its wealth, and the largeness of its metropolis." He asserts that "one great cause of the excessive luxury that prevails amongst us" is the "infinite number of people that resort hither, [who] naturally rival each other in their tables, dress, equipage, furniture, and in short, extravagances of all sorts." The move from an inclusive "us," absorbed in luxury, to the metropolis, and then to a "them" who engage their minds in "constant hurry and dissipation" speedily resolves the luxury and corruption that attend commercial prosperity into the problems of "that part of the human species which calls itself the world," or fashionable society.[4] Fashionable society represents, often in the same breath, the same sentence, both the desirous and competitive energies that are seen to characterize commercial progress, and the indolence, frivolity, and dissipation to which commercial industry is opposed.

In the first half of this essay I will explore some of the implications of the ambivalent relation I have outlined between commerce and fashion, first in some more periodical essays, and then in Sarah Fielding's novel *The Adventures of David Simple*. In particular, I am interested in the way problems about the morality of commercial culture come to be represented as anxieties about sexual difference. In the second half of my essay, I look at the relation between those anxieties and the instability of the distinction between notions of the public and private and the different kinds of morality appropriate to them. What interests me, broadly speaking, is the question of the kind of moral ascendancy women, or perhaps notions of femininity, seem to gain in the mid century. It is obvious, I think, from, for example, the essays of David Hume, where women are represented as "much better Judges of all polite Writing than Men,"[5] or from the kind of reception that the works of Elizabeth Carter and other learned ladies gained, that during the middle decades of the century more was demanded of women—affluent or middle-class women were able to do more—by way of a contribution to the notion of the superiority of British culture. By the late 1760s and 1770s publications by women could be welcomed simply because they were by women, and it became commonplace to claim that Britain was more civilized than other European nations because women were better treated in this culture as well as better educated. This is a considerable cultural shift that needs to be thought about in a range of different terms and contexts. This essay will look only at a limited selection of texts and issues, but I hope it will provide a way into thinking about some of the wider implications of this cultural shift, as well as how it came about.

The kinds of anxieties that fashion provokes in the periodical essayists of the mid century seem to stem from its capacity to blur differences seen as necessary to the preservation of the social structure: differences of age— cosmetics make the old appear young and age the youthful prematurely; differences of nation—as the fashionable adopt the modes, manners, and language of Paris; differences of gender—men are feminized by their absorption in appearance, their desire for trivia, while women are masculinized by the boldness of fashionable manners; and differences of social station, which are no longer clearly indicated by modes of dress and which give way to differences of wealth or ready cash rather than inherited position.[6] Dress in particular is perceived to have become a system of masquerade, which disguises the differences of social station or class to which it had once been a legible index. But anxieties about dress, of course, which are the subject of numerous periodical essays, function as a means to discuss (or draw a veil over) what are perhaps more profound instabilities in the hierarchy of social difference—instabilities that may be perceived as matter for ambivalent regret. Bonnell Thornton's periodical *The Connoisseur,* for example, remarks mockingly on the appearance of what it calls "second-hand gentry":

> When I see the wives and daughters of tradesmen and mechanics make such attempts at finery, I cannot help pitying their poor fathers and husbands, and at the same time am apt to consider their dress as a robbery on the shop. Thus, when I observe the tawdry gentility of a tallow-chandler's daughter, I look upon her as hung round with long sixes, short eights, and rush-lights; and

> when I contemplate the aukward pride of dress in a butcher's wife, I suppose
> her carrying about her surloins of beef, fillets of veal, and shoulders of mutton.

Like so many essayists of the period, Mr. Town the connoisseur is here deploring the availability of the fashions of the noble and/or wealthy to women of the artisanal or shopkeeping classes, the "red-armed belles that appear in the park every Sunday." But the humor is complicated: it is ridiculous for the women to dress up and rob the shop when Mr. Town can so readily perceive them untransformed by their purchases or can indeed reverse the reproduction of value and perceive them to be made absurd by their adornment in the goods they sell. But he seems to accept the aspiration this implies to accept that the red arms of labor need transforming. He is "vastly diverted" when "going upon some business to a tradesman's house, I surprised in a very extraordinary deshabille two females, whom I had been frequently used to see strangely dizened out in the Mall. . . . One, who always dresses the family dinner, was genteely employed in winding up the jack, while the other was up to the elbows in soap-suds." It is ludicrous that tradesmen's daughters should wish to be taken for "fine ladies" but their household chores are not wrapped up in any notion of the dignity of labor or proper feminine domesticity—in the eyes of the connoisseur their work is absurdly vulgar, contemptibly demeaning.[7] Politeness demands that women of this class should not be perceived to work, in the same breath as it disparages their "tawdry gentility."

The connoisseur expresses a common complaint of the period when he remarks that "there is scarce one woman to be met with, except among the lowest of the vulgar. The sex consists almost entirely of Ladies."[8] Catherine Talbot lamented, in her essay "On true Politeness," that "regard to the different stations of life is too much neglected by all ranks of people. . . . All sorts of people put themselves on a level."[9] But the desire for exclusive distinction conflicted with the sense, so important to the cultural ascendance of the manners and aspirations of the middle classes, that politeness is a universal code. In this context exclusivity could seem to be a kind of residual idiosyncrasy inherited from the association of fashion with courtly nobility. Henry Fielding, for example, in the *Covent-Garden Journal*, mocks the attempts of the fashionable "to preserve their circle safe and inviolate . . . against any intrusion of those whom they are pleased to call the vulgar." He suggests that they are obliged to continue to favor the hoop petticoat because it has been "found impossible . . . to slide with it behind a counter." But the point of his satire is to emphasize the permeability of distinctions of station within the middle classes, and between them and a nobility distinguished by no more than the absurdities of fashionable excess. So, for example, he notes that on "observing that several of the enemy had lately exhibited arms on their vehicles, by which means those ornaments became vulgar and common," fashionable people replaced their own coats of arms with ciphers, "cunningly contrived to represent themselves instead of their ancestors"; they replace the signs of aristocratic rank with those of individual difference.[10]

The fashionable and trading classes are, then, ambiguously identified in their aspiration to polite leisure, and the desires of the fashionable are represented in a doubled and ambivalent relation to the energies of commerce. The uneasiness of the perceived relation between the two may be indicated by the frequency with which gambling, which parodies the activities and energies of trade, is represented as central to anxieties about fashionable life. James Fordyce, in his influential *Sermons to Young Women* (1765), cites the view that gambling tends "to destroy all distinctions both of rank and sex; to crush all emulation, but that of fraud; to confound the world in a chaos of folly." Gambling is perceived to function like fashion and like trade, and Fordyce agrees that it is an exceptionally laborious calling, for "this trade goes on when all the shops are shut."[11] Adam Fitz-Adam is resigned to the fact that "it is my lot to live in an age when virtue, sense, conversation, all private and public affections are totally swallowed up by the single predominant passion of gaming,"[12] and it is of course appropriate that "Commerce" should be the name of a once-fashionable card game. In periodical essays the difference between the habits of expenditure and consumption necessary to commerce and fashion—the difference between good and bad taste—is represented not only as a matter of class difference but as a matter of the ability of consumers smoothly to assimilate the goods they purchase, preserving their own personalities from becoming dissipated in the variety of objects they desire. Much of the humor of the papers, however, depends precisely on the inability of purchasers to digest what they consume (to borrow the language of Shelley's *Defence*). So, for example, Thornton concludes the discussion of "second-hand gentry" from which I have quoted with the observation that "true oeconomy does not merely consist in not exceeding our income, but in such judicious management of it, as renders our whole appearance equal and consistent." He dwells on the notion that fashionable cosmetics make women appear to be "bedaubed, like an old wall, with plaister and rough-cast" or that makeup resembles the paint on portraits offered for sale, but "the picture fails to charm, while my thoughts are engrossed by the wood and canvas."[13] Those who fail to assimilate or digest their purchases to their own consistency expose the mechanics of the reproduction of value, they disclose their own status as things to be bought and sold, units of exchange. Indeed, in an extended fantasy the connoisseur proposes to "open a shop or warehouse . . . under the name of a Mind-and-body-Clothier: two trades which . . . are, in their nature, inseparable." From this establishment he will market personality to the fashionable packaged in its moral or professional accoutrements.[14]

Fashionable appearance and personality is characterized as an assemblage of bits, "their red, their pompons, their scraps of dirty gauze, flimsy sattins, and black callicoes; not to mention their affected broken English, and mangled French, which jumbled together compose their present language."[15] It is in these terms that the *World* repeatedly and vehemently attacks the fashion for chinoiserie, and censures fashionable dress, remarking, for example, of a young lady seen at Ranelagh: "I could not help condemning that profusion of ornament, which violated and destroyed the unity and τὸ ὅλον [wholeness or completeness] (a technical term borrowed from the toilette) of so accomplished a figure."[16] This fear of severalness, of a dissipation that violates ideal unity, is clearly a language of sexual anxiety, a sort of defensive shoring-up of phallic power and taste which finds expression in the frequent satires on the fashionable erosion of sexual difference. And gendered identity emerges in these papers as something either differentiated or confused, even denied, by patterns of consumption. Eliza Haywood's *Female Spectator* comments in fairly typical terms in a paper of 1744:

> let it not be said we are the only thoughtless, gawdy flutterers of the human world:—there are *men*-butterflies, as well as *women:*—*things* that are above the trouble of reflection, and suffer themselves to be blown about by every wind of folly.—Whatever has the name of novelty will carry them through thick and thin;—led by that restless charm, no matter if the chair be overturned, the gilded chariot broke, and the coachman's neck into the bargain, still they press on a mingled motley crowd.[17]

The endless pursuit of novelties, the business of continually "forming new wishes" which Johnson saw as the highest pleasure, is here represented (as is gambling in so many essays of the period) as so absorbing a preoccupation that it erases the gendered and indeed moral or human nature of those engaged in it, who become "*things . . .* blown about by every wind" of fashionable desire.

The periodicals do, of course, acknowledge with some regularity that, in the words of the *World,* "novelty and fashion are the support and source of trade. . . . By increasing the wants, they increase the connections of mankind." This argument emphasizes that the vagaries of desire can "occasion many advantages to the public,"[18] to produce a kind of compromise between the ethics of commerce and a more severe civic ideal, but it does so by displacing onto the workings of fashion the sense in which commerce is perceived to threaten the fantasy of masculinity central to the civic ideal of public virtue.[19] Fashionable objects of desire are repeatedly represented as both the symptom and the cause of an alarming degeneration of manliness, of a specifically British and heterosexual masculinity. The *Connoisseur*, for example, writes that

> it is too notorious, that our fine gentlemen, in several other instances be-
> sides the article of paint, affect the softness and delicacy of the fair sex. The
> male beauty has his washes, perfumes, and cosmetics. He has his dressing-
> room . . . a neat little chamber, hung round with Indian paper, and adorned
> with several little images of pagods and bramins, and vessels of Chelsea china,
> in which were set various-coloured sprigs of artificial flowers.[20]

The fine gentleman is surrounded by imported luxuries, which may mark his degeneracy,[21] but it seems to be the size of his possessions, his "little chamber" and "little images," perhaps more than their un-Christian diversity, that signals their unmasculine character. In Hogarth's *Marriage à la Mode* a similar collection of goods is "irrefutable evidence of crude lack of taste, coarse sensuality, and of thriftlessness in buying, for want of a better occupation";[22] they are a sign of the kind of abandon that Henry Fielding implies in his account of the beau, "his body dressed in all the tinsel which serves to trick up a harlot."[23] Mr. Town seems rather to perceive these goods as signs of infantilism, but he nevertheless expresses his own homophobic passion in deducing from them that their owner is one of "these equivocal half-men, these neuter somethings between male and female."[24]

The progress of commerce and the notion of its general utility may be acknowledged in mid-century periodicals to offer a kind of justification of fashionable consumption, but if anything that perception seems to increase the essayists' hostility to particular examples of fashionable taste. Fashionable manners seem to prompt an antagonism that indicates the persistence of anxiety about inhabiting a culture dominated by commerce. In this culture, the periodicals suggest, notions of the public become peripheral, almost accidental to the private interests that are the motor of commercial progress, and within the apparently expanding sphere of the private that is governed by commerce, distinctions—between social stations, between national identities, or between vice and virtue—seem increasingly evasive, seem to melt into air. Gender difference, these papers imply, may provide the means, the basis on which all those other distinctions can be reinstated: if only men can be made less effeminate and women less lewd or bold, then national degeneration may be checked, and what seems to be mercenary or luxurious, but inseparable from commercial prosperity, may be moralized and made compatible with civilized politeness or the ideals of public and private virtue. Anxiety about gender difference is not only, of course, the province of the periodicals. Even Samuel Richardson's Sir Charles Grandison, himself no nonpareil of British virility, questions whether "there be characters more odious than those of a masculine woman, and an effeminate man."[25] The relation between fashion and commerce which I have been trying to draw out, however, suggests that commercial culture may require tolerance alongside antagonism toward some forms of blurring of gender difference, that the erosion of gendered identity may crop up so frequently because that identity requires redefinition as well as confirmation. I want now to focus my discussion on a small group of novels by women: Sarah Fielding's *Adventures of David Simple* (published in two volumes in 1744, with the additional *Volume the Last* appearing in 1753) and Sarah Scott's *A Description of Millenium Hall* (1762), and *The History of Sir George Ellison* (1766). These novels offer, I think, intriguingly different accounts of gender roles and of the problems raised by the instability of their definition, and while I do not want to suggest that they typify or represent the diversity of the mid century, I do think that the differences between them can help to indicate something of the cultural changes at issue in this period.

II

Sarah Fielding's *Adventures of David Simple* narrates the episodic adventures of its hero as he explores the contiguous worlds of fashion and trade in the microcosm of the "great Metropolis."[26] David Simple is determinedly idiosyncratic in his views, like so many of the narrator-editors of mid century periodicals, and like them he is largely preoccupied with observing the manifestations of commercial culture in the manners and morals of the middle classes. The keynote of this culture for him, as for the tatler and spectator earlier in the century, is struck by his observations on the Exchange, which he visits at the beginning of the book. For Simple, however, the visit to the Exchange does not provide matter for celebration; it is a "melancholy Prospect," a place "where Men of all Ages and all Nations were assembled, with no other View than to barter for Interest," where the "Countenances of most of the People, showed they were filled with Anxiety" (p. 28). Simple is the son of "a Mercer on *Ludgate-Hill*" (p. 9), and he accepts the primacy of commerce, the importance of visiting the Exchange before anywhere else as he sets out on his quest, but he is also hostile to this world of anxious competition, and excluded from it perhaps by his inherited wealth (though he loses that in *Volume the Last*). His leisure enables him to act as the exemplary embodiment of the private virtues of the Christian gentleman, but the narrator seems also to imply that he might be seen as the conscience of commerce and a paradigm of the sensibility it ideally produces. When Simple and his friends encounter a beggar, Fielding remarks that their response is "as much actuated by Compassion as ever a Miser was by Avarice, or an ambitious Man by his Pursuit of Grandeur" (p. 396); for their sentimental commerce is transacted in the parallel currency of feeling.

What is problematic about Simple's role in relation to the commercial strife that surrounds him is made most clearly apparent immediately after the woman he loves agrees to marry him. The narrator's comments are so striking that it is worth quoting the passage at length:

> If you are inclined to have an adequate Idea of *David's* raptures on that Confession, think what Pretty Miss feels when her Parents wisely prefer her in their Applause to all her Brothers and Sisters: Observe her yet a little older, when she is pinning on her first Manteau and Petticoat; then follow her to the Ball, and view her Eyes sparkle, and the convulsive Tosses of her Person on the first Compliment she receives: But don't lose sight of her, till you place her in a Room full of Company, where she hears her Rival condemned for *Indiscretion*, and exults in her *Loss of Reputation*. No matter whether she rivals her in my Lord ———— or Captain ———— or 'Squire &c. &c.—For as she is equally desirous of engrossing the Admiration of all, her Enmity is equal towards the Woman who deprives her of *such great Blessings*, which-ever she robs her of.— Imagine the joy of an ambitious Man, who has just supplanted his Enemy, and is got into his Place; imagine, what a young Lawyer feels the first Cause he gained; or a young Officer the first time he mounts Guard.—But imagine what you will, unless you have experienced what it is to be both a sincere and successful Lover, you have never imagined any thing equal to what *David* felt. (pp. 295–296)

Simple is compared to a spoiled child growing into the fashionable woman who cares only to be the center of admiration; he is like a ruthlessly competitive place-seeker or a lawyer, that stock figure for greed and self-interest, or an officer, frequently the type of male vanity. Perhaps there's some ambiguity about those last two figures, whom the narrative barely touches into satire, but on the whole the string of analogies seems free from hesitation or qualification. It is as though the narrative attempts to set up its hero as the exemplar of sincere feeling, the main stockholder of that currency, and must therefore embark on analogies that—almost incidentally, but nevertheless profoundly—destabilize his gendered and moral identity.

I can perhaps best explain why these troubling analogies seem almost inevitable to the narrative by looking briefly at the representation of women elsewhere in the novel. For the moral characters of middle-class women are represented as peculiarly soft and amorphous, only formed into some definite moral shape by the Pygmalion-like desires and projections of men. And the novel suggests two rather different accounts of the significance or the usefulness of this plasticity, accounts that imply that the feminization of the hero might be understood in two contrasting ways. In the first place, the softness of women or their lack of character, in Pope's famous terms, is important to the argument for the role of fashionable consumption in a providential distribution of wealth. Simple's friends discuss the specific and familiar example of the woman who buys fashionable fripperies, which she has been "brought to think she cannot do without, and is indulging her Vanity with the Thoughts of *out-shining* some other Lady." They comment that "the Tradesman who receives her Money in Exchange for those things which appear so trifling, to that Vanity perhaps owes his own and his Family's Support." The woman's purchases are not "necessary to Life or Health," but despite appearing "most useless," they "contributed to the general Welfare" (pp. 189–190). Fashion has a positive role in this providential (or perhaps Mandevillian) scheme.[27] The woman's malleable desires are shaped by fashion and custom, which make her no more than a channel for the business of exchange and distribution. Her desires and her desirability—for she purchases in order to shine—make her the central and admired figure for the fantasies that structure commerce and that produce its benefits to the common weal, for the anecdote on the woman of fashion illustrates the contention that "except all the World were so generous, as to be willing to part with what they think they have a right to, only for the pleasure of helping others; the way to obtain any thing from them is to apply to their Passions" (p. 189).

The consumer's passion, her desire and vanity, are represented here as amoral but nevertheless capable of supplying the place of philanthropy in the great providential scheme, and thus her desire is in a sense like the hero's. David Simple is a private man, and his philanthropy does not extend beyond the "little Society" (p. 304) of his family and friends. His inheritance places him beyond the need to work and thus in what was coming to seem by the mid century a position of feminized indolence.[28] As a dispenser of bounty, an idle consumer, and successful lover, he is central to those romantic exchanges of desire that structure the private worlds of commerce and fashion, and his position is very close to that of the fashionable woman. When he and his friends finally achieve domestic bliss (at the end of volume two) the narrator draws this moral from their ideal community:

> Let every Man, instead of bursting with Rage, and Envy, at the Advantages of Nature, or Station, another has over him, extend his Views far enough to consider, that if he acts his Part well, he deserves as much *Applause,* and is as useful a Member of Society, as any other Man whatever: for in every Machine, the smallest Parts conduce as much to the keeping it together, and to regulate its Motions, as the greatest. (p. 304)

The sentiment here is reminiscent of Lady Mary Wortley Montagu's reflections on greatness, in *The Nonsense of Common-Sense,* where she argued that:

> as much greatness of Mind may be shewn in submission as in command, and some Women have suffer'd a Life of Hardships with as much Philosophy as Cato travers'd the Deserts of Affrica, and without the support that the veiw of Glory afforded him. . . . A Lady who has perform'd her Duty as a Daughter, a Wife, and a Mother, appears to my Eyes with as much veneration as I should look on Socrates or Xenophon.[29]

For Montagu, of course, the notion that "real Distinction" lies in moral integrity and "consciousness of Virtue" is explicitly offered as consolation to those oppressed by differences of class and gender. In order to appreciate the pleasures of their private station, they do not need to make the effort of extending their views to encompass an idea of society but can simply resort to the alternative system of morality that allows them to compare their own integrity with that of the next person. Fielding's use of the familiar image of society as capitalist machine, however, in which the individual is unlikely to be able to extend their views beyond the horizons of their passions, works to obscure social differences as well as to ameliorate them. There is apparently no kingpin here, and no moral ascendancy either, for the image elides those moral differences that have been so important to the characterization of Simple as the hero and implies a common condition of submission that blurs differences of gender. It is not surprising, perhaps, that immediately after this passage Fielding turns to comparisons of society with the stage and the prospect view, where "every thing" is "kept in its proper Place," and which can more readily image the kinds of differences of class and of gender she sees as important to the social structure.[30] But in their roles as good cogs, Simple and the fashionable girl are equally useful and capable of that "equal and consistent" integrity of appearance or feeling that the *Connoisseur* saw as the mark of good taste and good morals.

I have suggested, however, that feminine softness seemed to have two different sets of meanings in this novel and two different sets of implications for the characterization of the hero. The second of these assumes particular importance in *Volume the Last*, published nearly a decade after the first two volumes of the novel. Montagu commented, rather acidly, that this volume was an improvement on the earlier two because it "conveys a useful moral (tho' she [Fielding] does not seem to have intended it)." Montagu thought that the third volume showed "the ill Consequences of not providing against Casual losses, which happen to almost every body."[31] The Simples should have been better insured, but the moral of the tale depends on the fact that they were not. For this imprudence places the hero in a position which resembles what his wife had experienced before her marriage in the second volume of the novel. In a striking episode Camilla attempts to support herself and her sick brother by begging, but the rich mistake her solicitings for those of prostitution, and when she resorts to the streets she is attacked by other beggars for "begging in their District" (p. 168). She concludes that if impoverished gentlewomen

> attempt getting our living by any Trade, People in that Station would think we were endeavouring to take their Bread out of their mouths, and combine together against us. . . . Persons who are so unfortunate as to be in this Situation, are in a World full of People, and yet are as solitary as if they were in the

wildest Desart; no body will allow them to be of their Rank, nor admit them into their Community. (pp. 169–170)

By some rather tenuous route, of course, she is allowed to retain her class status, her gentility, but the emphasis of the episode is on the extent to which she finds herself excluded from any rank or community as a result of her sudden poverty. Her inherited status turns out not to be inherent but to depend on her lover's recognition of her value. Simple's desire is necessary to reinstate her as someone whose softness and goodness is like "a great Stock in Trade" (p. 155).

In the last volume Simple has left the metropolis and become the victim of legal corruption: he has lost all his money and his poverty is carefully defined to be of the kind where "you pay *Cent. Per Cent.* for every Necessary of Life, by being obliged to buy everything by retail" (p. 351). This seems to mean that he is excluded from the economy of credit because he has lost that defining attachment to rank or community which credit recognizes. His position now is like that of Camilla, forced upon the town. In this situation it is difficult to distinguish between the domestic feminization of David and his wife; what is valuable in them is only their capacity for feeling, their capacity to act as the medium of sympathetic exchange. The Simples are exposed to the rigors of adversity, and on the death of their children Fielding writes of their feelings:

> The true Reason why I dwell not on that Concern, is, that Words cannot reach it—the sympathizing Heart must imagine it—and the Heart that has no Sympathy, is not capable of receiving it. *David* was, on every tender Occasion, motionless with Grief; and *Camilla*, although her Mind was too humble to distort her Countenance, yet did the Tears flow in Streams from her Eyes, and she was at once a Picture of the highest Sorrow and the highest Resignation; for Clamour is rather a Proof of Affectation than of a Mind truly afflicted; and tender Sorrow neither seeks nor wants Language to express itself. (p. 412)

The inexpensive responses of the Simples are contrasted with the behavior of the woman of the world who persecutes them. She displays equally noisy and impassioned grief for the anticipated death of her husband and for the loss of her lapdog, that quintessential fashion accessory, and her capacity for expression inhibits sympathy, inhibits those exchanges of ineffable feeling that structure domestic life in this novel. In this last volume Simple is much more markedly antagonistic to commercial culture and more explicitly feminized, and the contrast with the woman of the world suggests that his feminization is no longer the sign of his proximity to fashionable consumers, whose amoral subjection to custom greases the wheels of commercial exchange, but the sign of his affinity with social outcasts who are moral in adversity. In the first two volumes Simple and the fashionable woman had seemed analogous cogs in the social machine, but he had been moralized by his attachment to notions of private community. In the last volume the lack of community, the death of most of his family and friends, makes him an exemplary martyr. His capacity for sentiment makes him central to the commercial culture that the novel sets out to moralize and, I think, to celebrate, but this capacity seems also to make it impossible for him to speak in the languages of that culture. The hero argues, in volume two, that the anxious competition of the world would become morally acceptable if everyone would "fairly own when they were rowing against each other's Interest" (p. 252), but the conclusion of the novel implies that this sincerity is the prerogative of those who are made speechless, marginalized, and feminine.

III

David Simple represents a culture in which differences of gender seem unstable and ambivalent because there seems to be no room, in the insistently private and commercial culture which the narrative delimits, for the definition of unambiguously masculine character. This issue is, of course, central to the emergence in the mid century of the sentimental hero, and its implications structure the narratives of Sarah Scott's two novels of the 1760s, *A Description of Millenium Hall* and *The History of Sir George Ellison*. Scott's novels inhabit, I think, a rather different discursive context to that of *David Simple*. They are also concerned with private and commercial culture, but they indicate, I suggest, a much clearer awareness of the problematic relation between that culture and notions of public virtue and public life, notions that had seemed peripheral or even irrelevant to Fielding's novel. For that reason, perhaps, the instabilities of gender difference are more explicitly at issue in these later texts. In the second novel Ellison and his companion, Lamont reflect on their visit to the community of ladies at Millenium Hall, narrated in the earlier novel. Lamont observes that

> such a kind of life as they had been witnesses to, was very respectable in women, and was arriving at the highest excellence their sex could reach; but such retirement would be very unfit for man, who, formed with more extensive capacity, deeper penetration, and more exalted courage, was designed to govern the world, to regulate the affairs of kingdoms, and penetrate into the most mysterious arts of human policy.[32]

Lamont perceives the opposition between private retirement and public duty to be structured on gender difference. I want, in conclusion, to explore the significance of this structure in Scott's novels of the 1760s, but first I want to look briefly at the treatment of the relation between gender difference and the public/private axis in a few other texts of the period, for this is, I think, a relation that takes on a particular and troubled importance in these decades.

Lamont's argument resembles one developed in the periodical *Common Sense* which claimed in 1737 that

> Women are not form'd for great Cares themselves, but to soothe and soften ours; their Tenderness is the proper Reward for the Toils we under go for their Preservation; and the Ease and Chearfulness of their Conversation, our desirable Retreat from the Labours of Study and Business. They are confined within the narrow Limits of Domestick Offices, and when they stray beyond them, they move excentrically, and consequently without Grace.

The periodical, published nearly thirty years earlier, implies a similar sense that the proper retirement of women confirms their gendered identity; the essayist argues that women who "stray beyond" the "Bounds allotted to their Sex" should "declare themselves in form Hermaphrodites, and be register'd as such in their several Parishes."[33] The paper also suggests that the confinement of women within "narrow Limits" confirms, and perhaps even produces a properly protective and masculine identity in those engaged in the "Labours of Study or Business"—labors that might otherwise be seen as potentially feminizing. John Brown's sermon *On the Female Character and Education* (1765) echoes the sense that the subordination and domestication of women is necessary to masculine virtue. From his "View of the Female Character" he remarks, with an adroit use of the lexicon of cultivation, that he has "deduced those domestic and Christian Virtues which are naturally ingrafted on it by a Proper Education." But Brown characteristically takes a more apocalyptic line on the dangers of vagrant femininity. He claims that where women assume "masculine *Boldness* and indelicate *Effrontery*" and "affect a self-sufficiency and haughty Independency; assert an unbounded Freedom of Thought and Action; and even pretend to guide the Principles of Taste, and the Reins of Empire," it is inevitably the consequence that "the Reality of national Virtue vanisheth, and its Shadows occupy its Place; Sincerity is no more."[34]

These arguments depend on a conflation of the differences between what is private, domestic, apolitical, extracommercial, and feminine. That conflation makes it possible to describe the proper activities of men, which range from government to commerce, from military defense to scholarship and guiding the principles of taste, as though they were all forms of masculine public virtue. In an essay from *Sir Charles Grandison* (1753–1754) which has been attributed to Elizabeth Carter, she, in the character of Mrs. Shirley, reflects on the strategy of arguing as though masculine "superiority were entirely founded on a natural difference of capacity," which leads men to "Despise us *as* women, and value themselves merely *as* men." She points out that

> women have not opportunities of sounding the depths of science, or of acquainting themselves perfectly with polite literature: But this want of opportunity is not entirely confined to *them*. There are professions among the men

no more favourable to these studies, than the common avocations of women. For example; merchants, whose attention is (and perhaps *more* usefully, as to public utility) chained down to their accounts. Officers, both of land and sea, are seldom much better instructed, tho' they may, perhaps, pass through a few more forms: And as for knowledge of the world, women of a certain rank have an equal title to it with some of them.[35]

The point of Carter's argument is to rehearse the familiar mid-century theme of the need to educate women to be "fit companions for men of sense. A character in which they will always be found more useful than that of a plaything, the amusement of an idle hour."[36] Her way of making the case is more intriguing. For her claim that the education of women is no more limited than that of certain men picks up on the feminization of merchants and the officers of a standing army in the discourse of civic humanism.[37] The final comparison, in Carter's argument, between the "knowledge of the world" acquired by officers and "women of a certain rank" is echoed by Mary Wollstonecraft in her *Vindication of the Rights of Woman* (1792) and leads her to ask, "Where is then the sexual difference, when the education has been the same?"[38] Carter's language indicates that what she describes is not, as it were, a space that is neutral in gender but a set of occupations that are not fully masculine because they imply confined views and superficial knowledge.

Carter's argument suggests the precariousness of the identification of the masculine with the public and the feminine with the private. And the novel also hints at more radical possibilities, for Mrs. Shirley is responding here to an apparently flippant discussion of a topic referred to briefly as "Man's usurpation, and woman's natural independency."[39] The reference is an intriguing indication of the contemporary currency of arguments for women's rights, such as those articulated in the Sophia papers and other mid-century texts more or less directly indebted to Poullain de la Barre's *The Woman as Good as the Man, or, The Equality of Both Sexes* (first published in French in 1673).[40] These texts play on the notion that, on one hand, the gendering of the public/private divide removes any justification for excluding women from those employments characterized as private, such as learning, medicine, law, and commerce, and that, on the other, in a modern civilization where physical strength is less important or where the possession of landed estate and the right to bear arms are no longer central to the definition of public and masculine character, there is no longer any reason to exclude women from the more definitively masculine fields of politics, government, and war. They exploit, in other words, the unstable definition of public and private spheres in relation to gender difference, to indicate, broadly speaking, that the private now encompasses almost every sphere of activity and that the private can be identified with the range of activity appropriate to women.

The periodicals of the midcentury can also, I suggest, be understood to articulate and address the cultural nexus of instability formed by the complex of relations between the distinctions of public and private and those of gender. It is not something that they only respond to with hostility and alarm. So, for example, in a spirit of misogynistic banter, the author of *Common Sense* for February 26, 1737, prescribed that

> Ugly Women, who may more properly be called a Third Sex, than a part of the Fair one, should publickly renounce all Thoughts of their Persons, and turn their Minds another Way; they should endeavour to be honest good-humour'd Gentlemen, they may amuse themselves with Field Sports, and a chearful Glass; and if they could get into Parliament, I should, for my own Part, have no Objection to it.

Despite the explicit targeting of women here, there is clearly also a dig at the indolence and lack of masculine dignity shown by country gentlemen and parliamentarians, a suggestion, more fully explored in James Thomson's *Liberty* (1735–1736), that corruption has privatized their roles and made them potentially feminine.

In *The World* for July 3, 1755, the essayist described a dream in which Jupiter allocated people to the "proper calling" suited to their inclinations and abilities. Among the transpositions this involves, he sees the scarlet robes, which seem to be those of the lords spiritual, "put on by private gentlemen, who, lost in retirement and reserve, were little imagined to be qualified for such important posts"; he sees "princes and potentates" entering "with a good grace into private stations"; and "in a public assembly a junto of patriots, who while they were haranguing on the corruption and iniquity of the times, broke off in the middle, and turned stock-jobbers and pawn-brokers," while "many a man stept with a genteel air, from behind a counter, into a great estate, or a post of honour." Finally, he turns his gaze to women, and, he writes, "it was with a secret pride that I observed a few of my dear country-women quit their dressing-rooms and card-assemblies, and venture into the public, as candidates for fame and honours." It is important to the nature of this essay that these women do not secure the public roles he imagines for them. He sees a woman who clearly resembles the character usually attributed to Elizabeth Carter about to take office as the warden of an Oxbridge college, "but observing some young students at the gate, who began to titter as she approached, she blushed, turned from them with an air of pity unmixed with contempt, and retiring to her beloved retreat, contented herself with doing all the good that was possible in a private station."[41] In this rather Woolf-like vision, the permeability and progressive erosion of the division between public and private seems to be confirmed, as the dreamer recognizes in private men and women the virtues necessary to public office. The moral sphere, as it were, of the private seems to have expanded to absorb the public virtues, and the notion of the public seems to have become uncertain, for it is not clear here whether the "public assembly of patriots" refers to a corrupt legislative assembly that is nevertheless an exclusive public and political gathering, or to a party of coffeehouse politicians which is public only in the sense of its accessibility. But the essay reinstates the division of public and private even as it marks its blurring. It is here still the most important boundary, the axis in relation to which the virtues of the landed gentry and middle classes are plotted and measured, and in a sense this remains an essentially conservative vision that attempts to reappropriate virtue to public identity and to indicate that the public sphere is its natural and appropriate habitat. In order for that to be accomplished, women must remain private and retired, even though their ability to evince what are identified as public virtues is recognized.

IV

It is, I think, these instabilities and uncertainties in the relation between notions of public or private and gender difference that are, as it were, woven into the discursive tissue of Scott's novels of the 1760s. In response to Lamont's comments on the ways of life appropriate to men and women, George Ellison offers a long speech that might be understood, to some extent, as an elaboration of Carter's comments in *Grandison*. He points out that Lamont's notions of gender difference might have been appropriate to the "state of equality" that existed before "nature's Agrarian law" had "been abolished by political institutions" but that now "a great estate, or high birth" are necessary to his ideal of masculinity, though they "frequently exalt those who are . . . unfit" (1:110). He concludes that

> virtue creates the best superiority; therefore I shall not be ashamed of endeavouring to imitate the ladies [of Millenium Hall] . . . and do not fear, lest by so doing, I shall degrade my sex, though I confess to fall short of them may disgrace it; and yet I am very apprehensive that will be the case; for, the truth is, benevolence appears with peculiar lustre in a female form, the domestic cares to which the well educated have been trained, qualifies them better for discerning and executing the offices of humanity. . . . Our sex has long aped the most trifling part of the other in its follies; we are grown dissipated, puerile, vain, and effeminate; a sad abuse of talents, which I readily grant were given us for better purposes; so far I agree with you as to the dignity of man; but . . . the virtues are of no sex; and shall we less esteem any of them, because they are practised by women, when we are not ashamed . . . to adopt their follies! (1:111–12)

I have quoted this passage at some length because I am interested in its shifts, uncertainties, and hesitations; the way Ellison veers between the sense that for men not to outdo feminine virtue is a disgrace to their masculinity and the sense that virtue may be peculiarly feminine. Throughout the novel Ellison is represented as a resolutely private man, though one who is, of course, more fit for public office than most public men. More firmly than Grandison[42]—and this is clearly a novel that needs to be seen in the context of Richardson's work—he rejects public office because modesty is one of his virtues, and because he perceives it to be inevitably corrupt and corrupting. Most men, he argues, can do more to serve their country in "a private station" (2:28), and in his own private acts "the good of the public had no small share" (2:210). The virtues of a private man, his response to Lamont suggests, are those in which women excel and which I think John Brown is typical of the period in perceiving as having been "naturally ingrafted . . . by a proper education" on the female character. Ellison puts himself on the spot here, and his hesitations and qualifications indicate his attempts to suggest, on the one hand, that these are distinctively feminine virtues and, on the other, that they transcend gender and do not effeminate private men. But the follies or vices that have corrupted masculinity and reduced it to effeminacy are unambiguously those of women. Men can only ape them and be perversely feminized by them, for they are not natural to them, as they are, he clearly implies, to the "trifling part" of the other sex.

What I think is so interesting about poor Ellison's difficulties is that they indicate the extent to which the cultural hegemony of commercial capitalism produces a context in which virtuous masculinity seems an impossible ideal toward which men can only approximate themselves by emulating feminine virtue. The ladies of Millenium Hall, in the first novel, occupy a position that is analogous to that of the landed gentleman earlier in the century. Accounts of their interventionist brand of paternalism allude directly to the example of the heroes of Pope's third and fourth Moral Essays, and the account of their role in restoring an old mansion house for the use of "indigent gentlewomen," for example, is an elaborate paraphrase of Pope's passage on Old Cotta and his son in the "Epistle to Bathurst."[43] The description of their estate management is strongly reminiscent of the representations of virtuous public men in retirement in James Thomson's *Seasons*.[44] Observing the way they run their estate, Ellison remarks:

> I could not help exclaiming, "In what a heaven do you live, thus surrounded by people who owe all their happiness to your goodness! This is, indeed, imitating our Creator, and in such proportion as your faculties will admit, partaking of his felicity, since you can no where cast your eyes without beholding numbers who derive every earthly good from your bounty and are indebted to your care and example for a reasonable hope of eternal happiness." (p. 70)

Like Lyttelton in Thomson's "Spring," the ladies "taste / The Joy of GOD to see a happy World!"[45] The novel suggests, however, that this pseudo-public role is available to the women and has become problematic for men because the culture that makes this kind of benevolence possible has changed, as has the idea of the social structure that is implied by the exercise of virtue. This is not Fielding's machine, but it is in terms closer to that than to those of Thomson's virtuous polity that the women explain their understanding of society as "a state of mutual confidence, reciprocal services, and correspondent affections" (p. 61); they celebrate a more private and commercial view of society as bound together by exchanges of philanthropy and gratitude. Lamont is set up in this novel as a counterpart to the ladies' strange blend of gentlemanly, paternalist virtue and feminine moral strength; he is a feminized "coxcomb" for whom "Fashion . . . has been the guide" (p. 3), but he is also here, as in the second novel, occasionally the mouthpiece of a kind of classical republicanism, and this leads him to comment, when the ladies explain their view of society as a network of mutual dependence, that "you seem . . . to choose to make us all slaves to each other" (p. 62). In their retirement, the ladies combine financial independence with a kind of mutual slavery; they combine what is perceived as Godlike with what is perceived as most abject, and it is in these terms that they effect a kind of feminized moralization of commercial culture.

We could understand the role of the ladies of Millenium Hall in terms of the pre-Smithian formulation that "what oeconomy is in a family, political oeconomy is in a state."[46] In this novel and in *George Ellison* the notion of family extends to embrace almost everyone with whom the protagonists have any contact,[47] so that the family becomes a sort of alternative society of mutual interdependence and a prototype for the moralization of the expanding private sphere. The "families" in both of these novels interact through what is quite explicitly an affective commerce or economy in which benevolence is exchanged for gratitude, and a part of what is so powerful (as well as perhaps utopian) about this economy is its ability to accord value to unwaged as well as waged labor. The novels seem to endorse a kind of nostalgic feudalism, a society structured on affective ties of obligation and deference, but this is represented as an exchange of sentimental gratifications which is firmly identified as the pleasure of the retirement that industry and self-improvement affords. It is important to the virtue of the familial economies the two novels represent that they should be kept separate from the vices or the amoralism of worldly commerce and should be purely benevolent paternalist systems. Ellison comments that "as these ladies have no taste but what is directed by good sense, nothing found a place here from being only uncommon, for they think few things are very rare but because they are little desirable; and indeed it is plain they are free from that littleness of mind, which makes people value a thing more for its being possessed by no one but themselves" (p. 12). The ladies distance themselves from the world, which they perceive as resembling a Hobbesian state of nature, where "the same vanities, the same passions, the same ambition, reign in almost every breast; a constant desire to supplant, and a continual fear of being supplanted, keep the minds of those who have any views at all in a state of unremitted tumult and envy. . . . The love, as well as the pleasures, of society, is founded in reason, and cannot exist in those minds which are filled with irrational pursuits" (p. 61). The world they reject is that which, in *David Simple*, was represented or embodied in the figure of the fashionable woman: a world of passionate, amoral desires, justified by commerce and sanctified by adversity. The difficulty for the ladies of rejecting this world, of course, is that their own society of reciprocal obligation or mutual slavery exists precisely to help those who are in some way anomalous. They offer asylum for people who, "from some natural deficiency or redundancy" (p. 19), some difference of physical appearance, have been exhibited for profit as an "extraordinary spectacle" (p. 22), and for indigent gentlewomen who, like Camilla in *David Simple*, are excluded from the structures of rank or community. The narratives of the past histories of the ladies themselves make it clear that they too are unusual, most obviously in their rejection of marriage. People, if not things, repeatedly seem to find "a place here from being . . . uncommon" (p. 12), or as a result of their inability, whether willing or not, to participate in the "same vanities, the same passions, the same ambition" (p. 61) as everyone else. The narrative positions the women as desirable objects of emulation by emphasizing that they are uncommon, the rare manifestation of the ideal retreat from commerce, the ideal leisure and capacity for feeling that commercial culture affords.

The point is perhaps most succinctly expressed in one of the opening chapters of *George Ellison*, where the hero is in Jamaica, industriously occupied in making the fortune on which he will retire. Scott writes that

> business is a shield through which Love's arrows cannot easily penetrate. Amidst all the airs that coquetry could play off upon him, he was frequently computing the profits of his last embarked cargo of sugars and spices; and was in little danger of being captivated by the fairest form, except Commerce, as sometimes personified by the poets; the gums of Arabia, the gems of India, and in short the various riches of different climes, with which they deck her, would have greatly heightened her charms in his eyes; while the egrets, pompons, and bracelets of fashionable nymphs, appeared to him oftener burdensome than ornamental. (1:13)

The image of commerce here is most obviously reminiscent of Addison's reflections in *The Spectator* on visiting the Exchange. He writes that

> Nature seems to have taken a particular Care to disseminate her Blessings among the different Regions of the World, with an Eye to this mutual Intercourse and Traffick among Mankind, that the Nations of the several Parts of the Globe might have a kind of Dependance upon one another, and be united

together by their common Interest. . . . The single Dress of a Woman of Quality is often the Product of an hundred Climates. The Muff and the Fan come
together from the different Ends of the Earth. The Scarf is sent from the Tor-
rid Zone, and the Tippet from beneath the Pole. The Brocade Petticoat rises
out of the Mines of *Peru,* and the Diamond Necklace out of the Bowels of
Indostan.[48]

In Addison's famous celebration of trade, of course, the fashionable woman
is the emblematic figure of commerce, and there is no possibility of a choice
between the two. But Ellison is represented as though he makes the choice
of Hercules. His choice is not between pleasure and virtue, though the narrative does seem to strain after that possibility in passing, but between the
pleasure of sociability and the pleasure of profit, and even that is hardly
a choice. Addison's image of the "Woman of Quality" decked out in the
fruits of commerce emphasized the extent to which commercial gain was
regarded as a libidinized pursuit,[49] and, when Ellison does choose to marry,
only a couple of pages after his choice of the seductions of commerce, the
narrator comments that in his eyes "the lady was agreeable, her fortune
desirable" (1:16); the lady unites the barely distinguishable qualities of
pecuniary profit and fashionable femininity.

Once Ellison has retired to spend his fortune, he distances himself from
the commercial activity that had enabled him to acquire it. He tells his
cousin, a landed gentleman who is the less perfect foil for his virtues, that
riches cannot be the source of dignity because "the steps towards riches are
seldom virtuous." With a kind of aristocratic disdain, he explains that
wealth is "a thing industrious dulness may acquire, or dishonest arts"
(1:219). His Herculean choice is now perceived to be between what are represented as the thoroughly eroticized pleasures of philanthropy, and marriage, which he believes "would have degraded me into a mere infatuated
husband; and have substituted the ensnaring and intoxicating indulgences
of passion, to the calm and solid joys of conscious virtue" (1:172). His private retirement makes his position much closer to that of Thomson's patriots or their feminized counterparts at Millenium Hall. But the novel continues to imply that the virtues that make him an exemplary and "useful
member of society" (1:172) are best produced by involvement in commerce, however ambivalently that must be represented, rather than by the
inheritance of landed estate. And one of the ambivalent implications of that
commercial past is that it both produces the capacity to admire the virtues
of women and feminizes the hero. His cousin, aware that his own indifference toward the good of society and embittered disrespect for women set
off the virtues of Ellison, comments that "you are like a statuary who should
think the beauties of a Venus would not be sufficiently distinguished, if he
did not put a Sybil or a Tesiphone by her side" (1:174), implying that the
hero displays his own beautiful virtues as though they were a Venus, a figure

for desire not so far removed from the figures of commerce or the woman of fashion.

This group of novels, then, seems to indicate that the virtues associated with commercial culture are peculiarly appropriate to women; they are feminine and they feminize. That sense seems to combine two different aspects of the discursive terms in which the notion of commerce is most usually represented. On the one hand, commerce is feminizing because it demands or produces confined views and the endless pursuit of self-interested desires, qualities that characterize both Samuel Johnson's happy man and the woman of fashion. On the other hand, women can represent the moralized face of commerce because they are perceived to be excluded from it and, if they are affluent, confined to the leisure that it affords. Financially independent women can be represented as enjoying something like the retirement that could be perceived to be the condition of the disinterested virtue of Thomson's public heroes. The capacity of women, or notions of femininity, to be represented as at once central and peripheral to the workings of commerce gives them a kind of moral ascendancy. What seems to make it possible, if problematic, to represent feminine virtues as available to the sentimental hero might, in the context my essay has sketched, seem to be precisely those anxieties about the erosion of gender difference that appear to make trangression of gendered roles more difficult. Alarm at masculine women and effeminate men is clearly about the desire to return to an imagined golden age of stable differences, but it is also, and perhaps increasingly, a matter of such caricatural representations, such homophobic panic, that it enlarges the imaginary space in which gender difference is subject to renegotiation or in which shifts in the definition of gender roles are perceived as tolerable, acceptable, or even neutral. The imaginary space in which instability can be tolerated is most obviously defined by its location at what was beginning to seem the permeable periphery between public and private life, where philanthropy, benevolence, and sympathy seem to link domestic affections with concern for the general good of society. In that space it can seem permissible, or even desirable, for men and women of feeling to be barely distinguishable, united in their ambivalent relation to the commercial culture that produced them.

Body and Self

Bathing and Baptism

Sir John Floyer and the Politics of Cold Bathing

Mark Jenner

In recent years historians have increasingly turned their attention to what Marcel Mauss once termed "the techniques of the body."[1,2] Scholars have focused on the diverse histories of gesture, deportment, manners, and hygiene; many have emphasized the role of the somatic within the articulation of political and social power.[3]

This paper seeks to combine this approach with a more traditional contextual analysis of a number of books advocating the use of cold water in hygiene and medicine in what might be termed a technology of self.[4] I will examine the advocacy of cold bathing by the late seventeenth-century English physician, Sir John Floyer, offering a full contextualization of Floyer's practice and writing within contemporary political and religious debates. I will conclude by relating his work to the wider historiography that discusses Norbert Elias's theory of the civilizing process in early modern Europe.[5]

I

By 1700 balneology, particularly hot baths, had long been part of medical care. Around 1600, for instance, *A Description of a New Kinde of Artificiall Bathes* was published, showing them to be comparable in function with those of the Greeks and Romans, "though no way comparable to them for . . . vaine ostentation." In the mid-seventeenth century Peter Chamberlen engaged in an acrimonious dispute with the College of Physicians over the steam baths he was promoting. And in the 1680s several purpose-built commercial bagnios (steam baths) opened in Restoration London.[6] During the late seventeenth and early eighteenth centuries, however, cold bathing also became increasingly popular among English medical authors and their patients.

During the 1680s the physician and anatomist Edward Tyson began employing cold baths as a therapy in Bedlam,[7] and a decade later the natural historian and physician Charles Leigh devoted one section of his work on Lancashire mineral waters to the cures achieved by bathing in and drinking from cold springs.[8] In his highly influential *Some Thoughts Concerning Education* (1693) John Locke advised that the parent or tutor should have the pupil's "Shoes made so, as to leak Water; and his Feet washed constantly every Day in cold Water" in order to procure the boy's "Health and Hardiness."[9] This was both sensible and admirably stoic, Locke continued, for every one "is now full of the Miracles done by cold Baths on decay'd and weak Constitutions for the Recovery of Health and Strength."[10] Many advocates of cold bathing also recommended the benefits that could be obtained from drinking water as well as bathing in it. More generally they tended to prescribe a cooling regimen with fresh air, a light diet, and a regular course of exercise.

Sections of the public seem to have gone along with this enthusiasm. The Leeds antiquary Ralph Thoresby, for instance, records how his son's injured knee was treated with cold baths.[11] Many cold-bathing institutions were developed at springs to cater for this fashion. The facilities at Buxton in Derbyshire, for instance, were much improved during the 1690s, while new cold baths were constructed at Ilkley in Yorkshire, Quarndon in Derbyshire, and Cornhill in Northumberland.[12] Cold baths using pump water were established in London. In April 1701, for instance, the *Post Boy* carried a notice that "the Cold Bath . . . near Gray's Inn-Lane . . . in all Seasons . . . has been found . . . to be the best Remedy . . . [for] Dissiness, Drowsiness . . . Palsies, Convulsions . . . Vapours . . . Ruptures, Dropsies and Jaundice," to quote just a selection of the ailments it could cure.[13]

Scholars have established how these developments in advice and practice marked a significant point in the history of hygiene, but there is debate as to their ideological significance. The French historian Georges Vigarello has argued that the cult of cold bathing was a bourgeois reaction to the aristocratic cult of luxurious self-indulgence epitomized by the bagnio.[14] This class interpretation might be true of late eighteenth-century France but was not the case in late seventeenth-century England. Individual gentry and aristocrats were active in developing cold bathing establishments and wells, and medical men often sought their patronage and dedicated books to them.[15]

The historian of cleanliness, Virginia Smith, by contrast, has argued that influential English advocates of cold bathing such as Thomas Tryon and the Lichfield physician Sir John Floyer should be placed with a broad Protestant ascetic tradition, and Smith has written of Floyer's books on the benefits of cold bathing as a "plea for 'muscular Christianity.'"[16] Yet this description does not situate the practice within the religious and party politics of the 1690s or the early eighteenth century. The aim of this paper is therefore to extend Smith's and Vigarello's work and, in the spirit of many recent studies in the social history of medicine, to examine the religious and political dimensions of the advocacy of cold bathing.[17] John Floyer's medical work in particular makes most sense when looked at from this broader perspective.

Born in 1649 and educated at Queen's College, Oxford, Floyer pursued a career as a physician in Lichfield and was successful enough for the epitaph of his wife to claim (quite fictitiously) that he had been physician to Charles II.[18] It is clear that he prospered. His first wife, Sarah, was daughter of Sir Henry Archibold of that city, and his second spouse was a woman of independent means (and character); he owned an expensive town house.[19] In the absence of much correspondence and without the evidence of poll books, it is difficult to reconstruct Floyer's political preferences. Under Charles II and James II he seems to have been Tory in sympathy. In 1684–1685 he was active in Lichfield borough politics on behalf of the Tory earl of Dartmouth, to whom he was related by marriage, and it is likely that his knighthood in January 1685 was linked to these political services. When the corporation was reorganized early in the reign of James II, he was made a justice of the peace.[20] Floyer continued to play an active role in the city's society and government after 1688. He served as a trustee of the city's Conduit Lands during the 1690s, sat regularly on the grand jury in the late 1720s, and in 1729 (at the age of eighty) was made one of the trustees of the Lichfield turnpike trust.[21] Although Floyer addressed some of his printed work to Charles Stanhope, the Whig M.P. heavily implicated in bribery scandals involving the South Sea Company,[22] he remained fairly close to the Tory Dartmouth, and his "Essayes on Divine Subjects" reveal that his religious views were similar to those of his other High Church Tory friends (notably the Lichfield Jacobite bookseller Michael Johnson).[23]

Floyer's intellectual interests were as wide ranging as his social contacts and had a similar respect for traditional authority. He combined his medical work on balneology, the pulse, and asthma with a keen interest in contemporary natural philosophy.[24] The program of medical education he designed in later life recommended that after the aspiring doctor had immersed himself in the classics he should be trained in chemistry, anatomy, and natural philosophy, reading texts such as Boyle on the air pump, before going to the Netherlands in order to get two or three years' practical experience in hospitals until such time (as he devoutly hoped) such hospitals for the poor were built in England to act as centers for clinical training.[25]

On occasion Floyer chafed at the restrictions provincial medicine placed on his inquiries, complaining that the resistance of local people prevented him from dissecting bodies of people who had suffered from respiratory diseases in the way in which he had dissected cadavers of broken-winded horses.[26] As well as anatomies he performed quantitative experiments with the pulse, weighing machines, and thermometers.[27] Although on occasion expressing scepticism about the reliability of patients' accounts of their own condition, he avidly collected remedies from a variety of oral and written sources, from family and friends and also from the members of the lower orders, such as the farrier whose comments about the windpipe he transcribed into his copy of *Asthma*.[28]

We also know from Boswell that Floyer (in opposition to Whig physicians) advocated touching for the king's evil, recommending that the young Samuel Johnson be taken to London for the purpose.[29] In the 1720s he took up his pen not only in disputes over the correct form of baptism but also to attack smallpox inoculation as impious and sinful.[30] He was fascinated by Chinese medicine, especially Chinese methods of taking the pulse, and by studies of occult symbolism such as those of Athanasius Kircher. Later in life he developed an extensive study of biblical exegesis and chronology, publishing an anti-Newtonian account of the Mosaic system of the World and commentaries on Revelation and Esdras.[31] He also wrote a volume translating and defending the authenticity of the Sibylline Oracles, a topic on which he corresponded with the Socinian cleric and natural philosopher William Whiston.[32]

During the 1680s and 1690s Floyer became increasingly interested in the therapeutic possibilities of cold bathing and adopted the practice and a more temperate lifestyle for himself. With the assistance of neighboring gentry and what may have been a preferential lease from his fellow trustees of the Lichfield Conduit Lands, he established cold baths at St. Unite's Well just outside Lichfield.[33] In 1697 he published *An Enquiry into the Right Use and Abuses of the Hot, Cold, and Temperate Baths in England,* which surveyed the medical uses of all kinds of baths for diverse humors and conditions.[34] The most detailed sections of this work lauded the curative powers of Buxton and other cold baths, and the preface strongly recommended cold bathing as an ancient and highly efficacious form of therapy.

Five years later along with Edward Baynard, a London collegiate physician,[35] Floyer brought out *The Ancient Psychrolusia Revived, or An Essay to Prove Cold Bathing Both Safe and Useful.*[36] The title accurately expresses the main arguments of the volume, which are expressed in letter form. Cold bathing was practiced by the wisest of the ancients, he explained, and it was effective for a huge variety of afflictions of which he gave, if not an A-Z, then at least an A-W running from abortion and ague through gravel, gout, and hiccup to tetters, toothache, and windiness.[37] Cold bathing combined with an appropriate regimen would restore vitality and strength, particularly in cases of rheumatism and paralysis. It hardened the flesh and contracted the skin, making the bather clear-headed and hardy, capable of resisting all

inclement weather, whereas too many patients had injured their health by
an overheated lifestyle. In true Galenic fashion Floyer argued that cold
drove out hot.

In the second half of the book Baynard elaborated broadly similar
themes, recounting numerous cures he and others had obtained through
use of the cold bath. It was, he stressed, far preferable to "your *Nostrum-
munger,* Dr. *Stew-Toad,* one that sets up for *Miracle* and *Mystery,* and always
makes *Honey* of a *Dogs-Turd.*" Cold bathing could rejuvenate and could cure
venereal and hereditary disease. Periodically Baynard broke into his painful
verse.

> Cold Bathing has this Good alone,
> It makes Old John to hug Old Joan.
> And gives a sort of Resurrection
> To buried Joys, through lost Erection.[38]

Floyer's many multifaceted arguments in his books on cold bathing
reflected the eclecticism of his methodology, but he also repeatedly emphasized that he was reviving ancient medical practice rather than innovating.
He frequently criticized the presumption of the moderns and was highly
skeptical of the utility of either the microscope or chemical remedies.[39]
Indeed he argued that most of the new philosophy had done little more
than clarify and recover the wisdom of Hippocrates and Galen.[40] His medical associates and friends included many who resisted the College of Physicians' Dispensary in the 1690s; they tended also to have a taste for classical
learning as well as experimental knowledge.[41]

Some twentieth-century scholars have depicted Floyer as a figure of
fun and others have found him regrettably overenthusiastic in his claims,[42]
but despite initial opposition and amusement in some quarters his work
on cold bathing was highly influential and was reprinted six times by
1732.[43] It could "*never enough be admired,*" wrote the Norwich apothecary
John King in the 1730s. The Oxford antiquary Thomas Hearne recorded
how a clergyman drowned himself while putting Floyer's advice into practice.[44] He was joked about in the *Tatler,*[45] but his work on cold bathing was
translated into German and Latin. His reputation remained sufficiently
high for one nineteenth-century author to publish under the nom de
plume of Floyer's ghost.[46]

One striking facet of Floyer's writing (and the one satirized in the *Tatler*)
was his opinions about pediatrics. He considered cold bathing particularly
beneficial for infants and young children. It would combat rickets, skin diseases, and a variety of hereditary conditions that were exacerbated by the
luxurious and overheated lifestyle of their parents. It would also preserve
health, make the child's sinews strong, and make her or his animal spirits
vigorous.[47] Edward Baynard's essays, which Floyer appended to his own and

with which he presumably agreed, grew in the second edition into a fierce denunciation of other contemporary child-raising practices. The health of children was being undermined by the use of wet-nurses when maternal breast-feeding was morally and medically superior. Clothing ought to be loose, for swaddling crippled immature infants, producing physically stunted specimens.[48]

Such arguments, couched in terms of the need for a simpler and often more "natural" upbringing, will sound familiar to students of the mid- and late eighteenth century. A number of scholars have shown how William Cadogan and other Enlightenment authorities on child care emphasized the benefits and "naturalness" of maternal breast-feeding.[49] Others have demonstrated how influential mid-eighteenth-century medical advice authors like William Buchan and John Wesley stressed the need for a cool regimen to avoid the diseases brought on by the products of commercial society.[50] Clearly Floyer and Baynard anticipated such concerns. Yet they did so within a context and discourse that differed from most Enlightenment invocations of the natural.

One crucial difference is that Floyer argues that he is restoring the health care practices of the ancients rather than simply using the benefits of nature.[51] Moreover, as the proprietor of a cold-bathing establishment, he was anxious to control access to these curative establishments. Learned medical advice was vital—he was no apologist for quacks or indeed self-quacking, as physicians viewed self-medication. Second, Floyer's arguments are couched in a religious idiom very different from Cadogan's secular political arithmetic; as he wrote to the provost of the Queen's College, Oxford, in 1725, he "always made divine Subjects part of my study."[52] On one hand, Floyer sought to demonstrate the benevolence of divine providence by making use of the curative power of water and other natural resources as revealed by the human senses rather than the artifice of science. On the other, he was concerned to restore the authentic practices of the church.

Floyer believed bathing should start early in life; indeed, immersion should begin at baptism. As Floyer explained to John King in a letter reprinted in the *Gentleman's Magazine* in 1734, he dipped local children and thus cured them of childhood diseases.[53] Moreover, cold bathing at baptism was not just healthful, it was the sacramental practice of the ancient church. Indeed, Floyer's writings on cold bathing are as much about the sacrament as about medicine. They were thus inevitably politically controversial.

II

The third letter of *The Ancient Psychrolusia Revived* contained a lengthy historical exposition of Floyer's position on infant baptism, garnered from a wealth of biblical, patristic, and historical sources, many borrowed from Lichfield Cathedral Library and its canons.[54] Floyer cited Scripture and Tertullian to prove that baptism by immersion in rivers was the general practice of the primitive church, and he sought to demonstrate that baptisteries from the time of Gregory the Great to the twelfth century were designed for immersion. Bede, Erasmus, the canons of the English church, and the prayer books of Edward VI and Elizabeth I were all invoked "to prove, That Christianity was planted in *England* by the Use of the Immersion, and that was continued in *England* after the Reformation, during the Reign of *Edward* VI and Queen *Elizabeth.*"[55] It was only during the reign of James VI and I, Floyer continued, and under the malign influence of the Puritans that sprinkling had been introduced into the Church of England. The injunctions of the Presbyterian Directory of Worship of 1646 made sprinkling obligatory, and the habits this had formed caused the 1662 Prayer Book to soften the requirement for dipping in such a way as to permit it to go out of common usage. Yet as Floyer explained, if "Immersion continued in the Church of *England,* till about . . . 1600. And . . . if God and the Church thought that Practice Innocent for 1600 Years, it must be accounted an unreasonable Nicety in this present Age, to scruple either Immersion or Cold Bathing as dangerous Practices."[56]

Floyer felt passionately about this laxity and regularly reiterated his arguments in his later work. He avidly collected information about the dimensions of ancient fonts in order to prove that they had been designed for immersion.[57] He supervised immersion baptisms in Lichfield, and in 1722 he published a work devoted specifically to demonstrating that dipping was preferable to sprinkling.[58] His *Medicina Gerocomica* published two years later even contained a description of how to hold an infant for immersion.[59]

One does not have be a fervent structuralist to see striking parallels between Floyer's religious and medical opinions. The medical historian John Gabbay, for instance, described this as one example of the "deep structural homology . . . between Floyer's medical beliefs, and his political, philosophical, religious, and moral beliefs" and of the "explicit links" he drew between them.[60]

As Keith Thomas has recently emphasized, the parallel between bathing and baptism, between physical and spiritual cleansing, is an ancient one and was widespread in early modern England. The Anglican baptism service explained how at the baptism of Christ in the Jordan God had sanctified water "in the mystical washing away of sin," and the words of the service called on the Almighty to "wash" and "sanctifie" the child.[61] Many preachers developed this theme. In a sermon before the mayor and aldermen of London Philip Stubs explained that "Baptism signifies properly an Immersion, Dipping or Washing the whole Body in Water; and was a Ceremony used among the *Heathens,* as well as the *Jews,* upon the Admission of any new

Converts . . . By which Washing was signified, the Cleansing of the Persons, so baptized, from their former Pollutions; and their Resolution of continuing Pure and Unspotted for the future."[62]

Certain Baptist polemicists carried this metaphor to extremes, stating that an abundance of water was as necessary in baptism as it was in personal ablutions or housework. They labeled their pedobaptist opponents spiritual slatterns. "*Baptizo* signifies to dip or plunge," explained the Baptist Edward Paye in 1701, and "if you should bid your Maid wash a Pot, Glass, or Table, or her own Hands, and she only sprinkles them, or scatters some drops upon them, and then tells you she has washt them; I suppose you would suspect her to be a dirty Slut."[63]

This analogy, however, is not the whole story. There is an extensive anthropological literature that emphasizes the complex relations between sin and physical defilement. A venerable intellectual tradition, stretching from Sir James Frazer and Robertson Smith in the nineteenth century to Jean-Pierre Vernant and Paul Ricoeur in the twentieth, has argued that modern, internalized notions of sin developed from older religions preoccupied with taboo or physical defilement.[64] Such evolutionary theories have been severely criticized by more recent anthropologists. Mary Douglas, in particular, has shown how both Christian sacramental theories and the ritual prohibitions of African and Asian religions can be analyzed as similarly subtle systems of religious meaning.[65]

Regrettably historians have often been far less nuanced in writing about such "condensed symbols."[66] John Wesley's aphorism that cleanliness is next to godliness has had an extraordinarily malign effect on analysis, tempting scholars to adopt insufficiently historicized structuralist paradigms when discussing sin and dirt. Scholars have rarely thought through what might be meant by the terms "cleanliness" and "godliness" in particular contexts and have been too ready to assert that there was an equivalence between moral and physical purification in preindustrial England.[67] In part this kind of analysis reflects how many historians of early modern Europe continue (often unconsciously) to use theoretical models borrowed from structuralist/functionalist anthropology.[68] It also reveals the comparative neglect of ritual practice, ecclesiology, and liturgical issues within the historiographies of early modern religion, medicine, and science, all of which tend to work with a predominantly theological definition of religion.[69] No historian has discussed the links between bathing and baptism or those between sin and dirt with the epistemological subtlety or the attention to the nuances of language and metaphor which can be found in theological debates about the sacraments in the late seventeenth and early eighteenth centuries.[70]

Most early modern clerical commentators were careful to explain that one should not make any simple equivalence between spiritual and physical washing. In his highly influential history of infant baptism the Kentish clergyman William Wall took care to quote St. Cyprian's cautionary words: "For the Contagion, of Sin is not in the Sacrament of Salvation washed off, by same measures that the dirt of the Skin and of the Body is washed off, in an ordinary and secular Bath . . . It is in another way that the Breast of a Believer is washed; after another fashion that the mind of a Man is by Faith cleansed."[71] Moreover, contemporary discussions of baptism were not simply preoccupied with the metaphor of cleansing. Great attention was paid to the notions of death and rebirth, of deliverance and even of dyeing cloth implicit in the term "to baptize" and explicit in wording of the service. As we have already seen, Floyer was a highly educated man familiar enough with theological writings to compose his own history of baptism and commentaries on biblical and Apochryphal prophecies;[72] his understanding of the significance of the service was correspondingly sophisticated. Baptism, he wrote, "represents the death, and resurrection of christ, dipping, and Emersion."[73]

Consequently, Floyer's opinions about the links between bathing and a particular form of baptism should not be treated as a literal-minded equivalence or marginalized as one strand of what is defined as an intellectually conservative weltanschauung.[74] Floyer's opinions were part of his particular brand of natural philosophy and had a specific ideological and theological relevance at this time. His ideas should be treated as much as one aspect of the history of religion or politics as part of the history of hygiene or therapeutics. For he argued that the church had sagely annexed ancient medical practice and thus combined the physical and spiritual benefits of immersion within the sacrament of baptism. Floyer considered this association physiological in its nature. John the Baptist's initial baptism "had not only a natural Power for the Ablution of Corporeal Impurities, but also it prepared the Mind for Divine Illuminations and Government, by composing the Heat and irregular Motion of the Spirits, and all Corporeal Impressions of Love, Anger, and all other Excesses, which the natural Temperament produces."[75] In other words, cold bathing prepared the mind for spiritual illumination by helping to harness and restrain the animal spirits and unruly appetites. This elevated mental state was true rationality and Floyer argued that cold bathing was particularly efficacious for afflictions of the head and brain, including madness. Floyer was not alone in this last opinion. Indeed not only did a variety of late seventeenth-century medical writers recommend cold baths in cases of mental disorder[76] but there was a long popular tradition particularly in northern England and Scotland that immersion in particular wells would cure lunacy.[77]

Furthermore, in the early eighteenth century arguments such as Floyer's about the historicity of trine immersion within English Christianity were not antiquarian curios. This was an issue with profound ecclesiological implications. Baptisms had been the site of occasional but serious disputes between pastors and some of their congregations ever since the Reformation,[78] and there were at least four highly contentious (often interrelated) debates that raged around the institution of baptism in seventeenth- and eighteenth-century England. First, ever since the emergence of Baptist and Quaker congregations in the 1640s and 1650s the Church of England had engaged in repeated disputes about who ought to be baptized. Baptists restricted it to adult believers, while the Quakers denied all forms of ritual baptism in favor of baptism in the Holy Spirit.[79] These debates peaked during the Civil War and interregnum and intensified once more after the Toleration Act of 1689 when Baptists began openly to proselytize and baptize under the noses of outraged Anglican ministers. At Midden in Suffolk, for instance, a Baptist "set up . . . for making Proselites, by Re-baptizing them in a nasty Horse-pond; into which the filth of the adjacent Stable occasionally flows." When the local minister warned parishioners against his rival in catechism he was charged "with delivering Scriptureless Doctrine" and so entered into a public disputation with the Baptists in their meetinghouse in the nearby village of Lavenham.[80] As a loyal son of the church who stressed in correspondence that his son had been "bred up in the church interest," Floyer was entering controversial waters.[81]

Second, in the first decade of the eighteenth century the church was convulsed by the inflammatory writings of the High Church and nonjuror cleric Roger Laurence on the validity of lay baptism. In a widely read and often reprinted book Laurence argued that only those people who had been baptized by an episcopally ordained minister were true Christians. Those educated in dissenting academies were therefore to be denied the sacrament, occasional or otherwise, and many continental Protestants (including, crucially, members of the House of Hanover) were similarly to be excluded from the roll of true Christians.[82]

In addition, many within the Church of England were perturbed by the insidious spread of private baptism, which threatened to eclipse the traditional injunction that the ceremony ought to take place publicly before a congregation on Sundays or a holiday. The 1702 convocation, for example, complained of the "great neglect of bringing such infants as have been privately baptized, into the church . . . as the rubric directs; and that the unjustifiable use of the form of public baptism in private houses, hath lessened the reverence due to that holy office, and in some places hath . . . occasioned . . . undue practices of mutilating the public form."[83]

Finally, if Church of England Protestants were far from unanimous about who could perform valid baptism and on whom, they were at least as unsure about the appropriate way to carry out the actual act of baptism. Floyer's arguments were largely addressed to this debate. Although much less contentious than the issue of infant baptism itself, disputes about the form of baptism had crucial implications for every English parish and could even produce bitter disagreements around the font. Early in John Wesley's career as a minister, for instance, he was called on to baptize an infant. Wesley wished to follow the rubric of the 1549 Prayer Book (discussed in greater detail below) and to immerse the child. The parents and godparents would have none of it and demanded that the child be sprinkled instead. In the spirit of compromise Wesley asked if the child was too sickly to be dipped, for the Edwardian service contained provisions for aspersion if the infant was weak. He was told that the child was strong but should be sprinkled anyway, whereupon Wesley refused to baptize the child at all, leaving the rite to another minister to perform.[84]

Such a dispute could arise because the central documents of the history of the Church of England were characteristically ambiguous about the correct way in which to perform baptisms. The baptismal service enjoined in the first English Protestant prayer book stated that the minister should dip the child unless the parents certified that the infant was too weak to endure this ritual, in which case the child was to be sprinkled. This injunction was repeated in the 1552 Prayer Book and in that laid down in the Elizabethan service book.[85]

Such a liturgy was not the universal practice of Protestant churches. Although Calvin stated in the *Institutes* that the manner of baptism was a matter indifferent, the liturgy he established in the Genevan church was based on the practice of affusion. Many English reformers wished to follow its lead in this matter and to follow the Scots by adopting sprinkling.[86] Some, such as the Puritan Thomas Cartwright, saw the central role of the font in the baptismal service as idolatrous, and in 1644 Parliament ordered the removal of fonts from parish churches.[87] The directory of worship issued in 1646 at the end of the Westminster Assembly consequently recommended that children should be sprinkled and that ministers should use a basin, not a font.[88]

After the Restoration, of course, influential sections of the church reiterated the centrality of the sacraments. But the 1662 Prayer Book subtly altered the conduct of the baptismal service. The rubric prescribed that the godparents should bring the child to the font where they were to certify to the minister that the child was healthy enough to be dipped.[89] They had thus actively to opt for immersion. As the Kentish parish priest William Wall put it, the 1662 Prayer Book left "it wholly to the Judgment of the Godfathers and those that bring the Child, whether the Child may well endure dipping." Consequently, he continued, "in . . . *practice,* the Godfathers take so much advantage of the reference that is made to their Judgment, that they never . . . certifie the Priest *that the Child may well endure it:* And the Priests do now seldom ask that question."[90]

Such a trend did not go without opposition. Floyer was one of a long line of commentators from Joseph Mede to Jeremy Taylor who had called for the revival of immersion,[91] and Floyer's position seems to have been character-istic of High Churchmen at the time. Moreover, debates about the correct form of baptism had wider implications for the ecclesiastical polity. William Wall, the most authoritative Anglican historian of baptism of his time, noted how such arguments spilled over into more contentious areas, such as doubts about the institution of infant baptism itself, which of course had profound implications for the notion of a national church. More, he warned, "are brought . . . to doubt of the Validity of their Baptism for that they were not dip'd at the receiving it, than there are for that they received it in Infancy."[92]

When Church of England pastors debated with Quakers about the insti-tution of water baptism, they indeed found that their adversaries often exploited these uncertainties within the church about the correct form of baptism in order to undermine the whole institution of baptism. In 1714, for instance, Henry Stebbing, rector of Rickinghall Inferior, debated with Joseph Middleton in a Quaker meetinghouse in Suffolk over the institution of water baptism. At one point in the exchanges Middleton demanded that his opponent defend the manner in which the Church of England con-ducted water baptism. Clearly realizing that he was on more controversial ground, Stebbing refused to play into his opponents' hands by debating this point:

> For as I am a Church of *England*-man, [he stated] so thou art a Quaker; and consequently it must be very absurd for me to undertake to defend any par-ticular *Way* . . . of baptising with Water against thee, when thou denyest the Thing in gross . . . Before it can be proper to dispute *what Persons* are capable of being baptis'd with Water, and how, *i.e.* whether by *dipping* or by *sprinkling*, (which I perceive are the Points you would fain be at . . .) it is necessary to determine whether the Use of Water (*in general*) be essential to the Christian Baptism.[93]

As can readily be seen, Floyer's balneological work was inextricably linked with contemporary religious controversy and his own theories about the origin of natural religion and the history of baptism. This conclusion is further borne out if we look at the response to his work. People read Floyer for his opinions about baptism as well in the hope of improving their own or other people's health. In part this popularity is a testimony to the quality of Floyer's historical and patristic research. As one uncharitable opponent wrote of his book, he was "well vers'd in Authors *Antient* and *Modern, Popish* and *Reformed, Authentic* and *Legendary, Good* and *Bad*."[94] He clearly belonged in the *habitus* of Augustan antiquarians and scholars, reproducing, for instance, in the *Ancient Psychrolusia* a letter that one "eminent divine" had sent him about the saints after whom wells were named; that letter is studded with references to manuscripts in the Cottonian library and among the collections of Bishop Ussher.[95]

But Floyer's *medical* opinions about the benefits of immersion in cold water were also valuable weapons in these ecclesiastical debates about the appropriate form of baptism. For perhaps uniquely among the sacraments and services of the church, baptism could arouse fears about the health of the person undergoing the act: was the baby robust enough to be dipped? A regular line of argument in these debates was that there was a special dispensation for the church to safeguard the health of the child in cold climates such as the British Isles by sprinkling. As the Low Church bishop Gilbert Burnet argued, "The danger of *dipping* in cold Climates, may be a very good reason for changing the Form of Baptism to *Sprinkling.*"[96] The minister of Horsham in Sussex was more emphatic: "Suppose the *New-Testament* had expresly told us that every Person said there to be Baptized was Dipt, yet, even this would be no Obligation to dip in *Great Britain,* where not only the Climate is much colder, but also the Inhabitants are less accustomed to Washing, than the *Eastern Nations* were." He reiterated this warning, claiming that "we cannot Dip in Great Britain, but Myriads of Lives must be expos'd."[97]

It is not surprising that Floyer was cited by a variety of theological authors on precisely this point. Obviously Baptists found his arguments most useful, and several quoted him in works of controversy.[98] But William Wall, who was an exact contemporary of Floyer's at Queen's College, Oxford, devoted several pages of his 1705 *History of Infant Baptism* (for which he was thanked by Convocation) to enthusiastic summaries of Floyer's arguments.[99]

> And as for the Danger of the Infants catching cold by dipping, Sr. *John Floyer* has . . . evinced by Reasons taken from the Nature of our Bodies, from the Rules of Medicine, from modern Experiences, and from antient History, that washing or dipping Infants in cold Water is, generally speaking, not only safe but very useful . . .
>
> This learned Man prognosticates that the old Modes in Physic and Religion will in time prevail, when People have had more experience in cold Baths: and that the Approbation of Physicians would bring in the old use of Immersion in Baptism. If it do so, one half of the Dispute (which has caused a Schism) between the Paedobaptists and the Antipaedobaptists will be over.

Wall's optimism was not vindicated. Disputations between Anglicans and Baptists continued well into the eighteenth century. It is symptomatic that the Anglican clergyman who campaigned most vigorously to reconcile the baptismal services of both denominations to that of the "Primitive Church" was the highly individual Church of England minister William Whiston, who maintained that the Baptists were the only religious group to use "real

Baptism, or *Immersion into Water,*" but that they remained "very imperfect" in their services because they did not baptize children at around the age of three, did not anoint with oil, employ deaconesses for women's baptism, or dip naked.[100]

Moreover, by the 1720s Floyer's position in favor of immersion had become associated in Anglican circles with the sacramentalist and schismatic nonjurors and their High Church associates, whose services followed the 1549 Prayer Book in recommending dipping except in exceptional circumstances.[101] His 1722 pamphlet that sought to show that dipping was the authentic practice of the church contained a letter from George Osborne of Derby describing how his children had all been baptized by immersion without ill effect but noting that the ceremonies had been performed at home because he thought himself "oblig'd to join in Communion with the Successors of the deprived Bishops."[102] Significantly, the first issue of the Jacobite serial *Mitre and Crown* not only condemned excessive swaddling but noted:

> Were the Immersion in Baptism restor'd here according to the primitive Practice, and the Rubrick of the present Church; it would be more conformable to the primitive Institution, and more conducive to the Infants Health; the Rickets not being known in *England* until that Custom was omitted, which Immersion I have several times seen practis'd in this Church with great Safety and Success, and all the Infants enjoyed constant Health for many Years.[103]

III

Not all patients and practitioners shared Floyer's liturgical concerns, even if they were sympathetic to his therapeutic methods. The prose style, preoccupations, and self-presentation of his coauthor, Edward Baynard, who divided his practice between Bath in the summer and London (where he operated a cold bath) during the rest of the year, differed strikingly from the grave and measured manner of the Lichfield doctor. Irascible in his personal relations and fiercely satirical in his writing,[104] Baynard's acknowledgment that sprinkling was a liturgical novelty and his ridicule of the idea that it was dangerous betrayed a certain impatience with theological disputation. He wrote of those who thought dipping a health threat:

> I am apt to think the *Devil* has scatter'd some of his Hell Grubs in their Sculls, and fly-blown their *understanding* to a degree of *Lunacy,* least the old way of *Immersion* should come into the World again, not that I am an *Anabaptist,* for I was sprinkled my self, and a sprinkled *Christian* is better than none; for I put no great stress upon the form, provided a Man believes well, and lives well, for

he is my *Christian*, who shews me his *Christianity* by his Faith, his Faith by his good Works &c. But this being the *Parson*'s Province, I have done.[105]

Baynard tended to emphasize the secular advantages society would derive from the widespread adoption of cold bathing and a cool regimen. In politics he seems to have been a Whig (perhaps of country variety),[106] and his arguments form a trenchantly neo-Harringtonian denunciation of the enervating results of luxury and an overheated lifestyle among the middling and upper sort. He denounced the foolish fashion for high-heeled shoes among the wealthy and painted a vividly grotesque picture of "another nasty . . . Innovation . . . lately set on Foot, which is Snuff-taking, in the Nostrils . . . as if it were the Excrements . . . from the Head through the Nose." Worse still, these habits were, he maintained, being passed on from one generation to the next. "Proud, Haughty, Forward [people]," he wrote, "with their high savory Sauces, Wine, and strong Drink at every meal . . . bring forth a brood of miserable small King's-Evilly, Scabby, Ricketty, Infants."[107]

Such themes were present, though less prominent, in Floyer's arguments in favor of cold bathing. Floyer and indeed William Wall attributed the spread of sprinkling in part to the nicety and effeteness of recent generations of godparents.[108] Moreover, Floyer and Baynard mounted a fierce attack on the debilitating effect of imports and luxury. In 1697 Floyer denounced

the hot Regimen . . . as . . . Spirits, strong Wines, smoaking Tobacco, strong Ale, hot Baths, wearing Flannel and many Clothes . . . warming of Beds, sitting by great Fires, drinking continually of Tea and Coffee, want of due Exercise . . . by too much study or Passion of the Mind, by Marrying too young, or by too much Venery, which injures the Eyes, Digestion . . . and breeds Wind and Crudities, heats the Blood, and weakens the Nerves; for all the Effeminacy, Niceness, and Weakness of Spirits is produced in the Hysterical and the Hypochondriacal: I hope my count[ry]men will pardon my Freedom of Correcting these Vices or Errors when I shew them the only Remedies to prevent or cure these Disorders . . . which is by hardening their Bodies in the . . . cold Baths . . .[109]

Floyer returned to the fray in 1702, devoting a section of *Ancient Psychrolusia Revived* to

the vicious Diet . . . of Women, who are taught to Drink not only Strong Wines . . . but all sorts of sugared and spiced Liquors, Chocolate, Coffee, Tee, from their Youth; they are oft used to . . . High Sauces and Pickles, Oysters, Anchovies . . . and Meat full of Raw Blood; these Errors in Diet produce all the Female-fluxes, Scurfs, Leprosies, Consumptions, Hysterick Disorders . . . Decay of Appetite, and speedy Old Age. What Children are produced from Persons, who have thus by an ill management corrupted their Bloods and Spirits, must certainly inherit the Diseases of their Parents, and after, if bred up in the vicious way of Living, they will still increase the Propagation of the same Diseases, which are very much heightened in their Virulency by the continuance of the same ill Regimen for two or three Generations.[110]

Floyer and Baynard were not medical Jeremiahs ineffectually testifying to the path of good health and moral probity before an indifferent and self-indulgent public. Nor were they simply part of a broad tradition of Protestant asceticism. Historians are increasingly coming to realize that the 1690s and the first decade of the eighteenth century, when their books on cold bathing appeared, were years of grave disquiet about the social and moral order. For some, the supposedly providential success of the 1688 revolution indicated the need for thorough-going reformation; for others the accession of William and Mary was succeeded by an increasingly corrupt commercial order. Both political viewpoints were often articulated in a strikingly somatic manner.

Floyer's and Baynard's medical prescriptions should thus be placed alongside the campaigns for reformation of manners, the charity school movement, and the luxury debates of this period. Floyer's friend Frederick Slare was a founding member of both the Society for the Propagation of Christian Knowledge (SPCK) and the Society for the Propagation of the Gospel,[111] while the clergyman Nathaniel Ellison, whose letters about cold bathing Floyer incorporated into his text, was active in Newcastle in "discourageing Immorality and prophaneness" through the reformation of manners and corresponded with the SPCK for more than ten years.[112] Moreover, the diverse broadly "Country" interests which, as David Hayton has argued, underlay many of the protagonists of moral reform during this period could encourage collaboration between Whig and Tory just as seems to have happened between Baynard and Floyer.[113] Similarly, historians of ideas have demonstrated that the neo-Harringtonian critique of luxury and corruption was employed by radical Whig *and* Jacobite Tory alike in the late seventeenth and early eighteenth centuries.[114]

Moreover, Floyer and Baynard's concern about the raising and physical treatment of children echoed the marked emphasis on pedagogy in late seventeenth- and early eighteenth-century discourses on social problems. It would not be fanciful to draw parallels between their proposals for infant care and the many Anglican charity schools being founded in these decades for the education and training of older children, institutions that Floyer considered to be "the most effectuall method of Increaseing the number of church me[n] and lessening dissenters."[115]

Many sermons and pamphlets also echoed Floyer's and Baynard's concerns about the physical degeneration of the nation. In November 1697 the clergyman John Shower drew a picture of a nation losing its martial capacity through luxurious self-indulgence. "Great numbers of subjects that in time of war might defend their country are effeminated, debauched, diseased and made incapable of bearing arms; fitter for a hospital than an army, to be under a physician of [or?] chyrogean than a general." In a reformation of manners sermon a few years later Matthew Heynes lamented the "Luxury, Prodigality and Idleness . . . preying upon" and enervating the nation.[116]

Floyer's comments about luxury struck a chord in early eighteenth-century commentators. Many subsequent writers highlighted precisely those sections of his arguments which discussed luxury and national degeneration. The conservative physician Joseph Browne, for instance, wrote to Floyer agreeing that the disuse of cold baths

> may be attributed, in a great measure, to the Modern use of the hot *Regimen,* which, as you have justly observ'd, has increas'd with the Interest of Foreign Trade, which has introduc'd *Tobacco, Tea,* and *Coffee* with all the *Brandy, Spirits,* and *Spices.* And the Causes of all our *Rheumatisms, Defluctions, Intermitting-Fevers,* &c. are chiefly owing to the late Practice of Drinking hot Liquors, and the pernicious Use of *Flannel,* and *Woollen Shirts* next to the Skin, which always keep the Pores too open for the Climate we live in.[117]

In 1721 the Welsh physician Perrot Williams wrote to Floyer emphasizing exactly the same passage and picking up the gendered concerns the Lichfield physician had raised. Cold bathing, he wrote, was

> likely to prove the most Universal Antidote to the many growing Distempers of the Age; which are but the necessary and fatal Consequences of our Women's being (as you are pleas'd to express it, pag. the 75th of your Treastise of Cold Bathing) taught to drink, not only hot Liquors, but Coffee, Tea, &c. from their Youth, and that too in a most extravagant Manner. Which foolish and pernicious Custom (howsoever Advantageous to the Merchant) having now, like a spreading Contagion, prevail'd among even the common Sort, will doubtless, in Process of Time, greatly contribute towards the producing such a degenerate feeble Race of Mortals, as our more Temperate, and therefore Wiser Ancestors would have held with a just Commiseration, as unable to sustain the necessary Fatigues of Body and Mind.[118]

IV

Running through the concerns of Perrot Williams and similar authors is a strong sense of the past as something that had been lost or that was in danger of being swamped by commercial society. As Roy Porter and others have noted, the "consumer revolution" of the late seventeenth and eighteenth centuries provoked a succession of commentators, often doctors, who saw various diseases, including consumption, melancholy, drunkenness and even rickets, as the malign consequence of fashionably high living.[119] As can readily be seen in the passages quoted above, such authors often drew a parallel between the corrupting effect of imports on the nation and the deleterious results of exotic foods or drink imbibed by the individual.[120] They frequently articulated an aesthetic of (generally rustic) simplicity which was shared by many imaginative writers of the time. For many texts like Pope's "Epistle to Bathurst" hymned the way in which men lived a life of robust and healthy independence either in remote parts of the land or in times gone by.[121]

This appeal to the historical and frequently to the ancient historical permeated almost all late seventeenth- and early eighteenth-century discussions of cold bathing. As we have already seen, Floyer and Baynard saw themselves as reviving ancient medical and liturgical practices and the autochthonous cures of cold springs, not as introducing new remedies. Clearly it was difficult for any learned individual of the period to write about bathing without some reference to the Romans,[122] but this avowed retrospection went further. It encapsulated a nostalgic desire for the body of earlier, simpler cultures—Spartan, republican Roman, Celtic, or German—a longing that fractured the early modern discourse of civility.[123]

For one of the most striking aspects of these texts is the way in which reformers enthusiastically commended aspects of the body-care and child-rearing practices of the Irish, the Highland Scots, Muscovites, native Americans, and even the Scythians. Locke, for example, urged mothers not to be so tender of their children as to keep them from cold water but "let them examine what the *Germans* of old, and the *Irish* now do to them; and they will find that Infants . . . may . . . endure Bathing . . . of their whole Bodies in cold Water." Baynard asked mothers who swaddled their children to look and see how "the *Indians* . . . *Highlanders* . . . the Native *Irish* are proper, fair, [and] streight" because they had never been bound in infancy.[124] Yet these were exactly the groups from whom conduct manuals and other self-consciously "civil" texts argued that cultured Europeans should dissociate themselves. Indeed the process that made civility the basis of society legitimated English dominance in Ireland and other parts of the world.[125]

There are a number of possible explanations for this apparent paradox, none of which I can analyze exhaustively here. First, it may be that historians of civility have followed Norbert Elias's paradigms too closely. Like Elias, they have concentrated on conduct manuals and paid little attention to other discourses about the early modern body such as medicine and balneology.[126] It is clear that texts recommending cold bathing in this period (and indeed mid-eighteenth-century advice books advocating a cool regimen) complicate the generally accepted picture of the civilizing process.

Furthermore, historical discussions of civility have often blurred the distinction between body image and deportment. In tracing the increasing corporeal restraint of the early modern elite they have generally focused more on bodily behavior than on the kind of physical frame that was deemed desirable. In the late seventeenth century there seems to have been a bifurcation in the language of civility. A major theme in both Locke's educational writings and Floyer's books on cold bathing is that they recommend the hard, muscular body of the barbarians depicted in Tacitus's *Germania*, bodies toughened by physical exercise and by youthful immersion in cold water, but they also demand that such a body be governed prudently in a rational and civilized manner.[127] Indeed for reason to be strong, the body had to be vigorous.

There were many antecedents for these recommendations, not least among the authors of republican Rome and the satirists and historians of the early Empire—Tacitus, Horace, Juvenal—who were so widely read and imitated in the late seventeenth and early eighteenth centuries. From at least the sixteenth century the image of the strong and well-formed primitive haunted the discourses of civility and civic humanism. As John Sekora pointed out in his study of luxury, Ascham's *The Scholemaster* was gravely concerned about the debilitating effects of Italianate customs on English youth. In the early seventeenth century a number of moralistic commentators condemned fashionable foreign innovations (such as carriages) as effeminating and corrupting English bodies.[128] Late seventeenth-century advocates of cold bathing developed this tradition when (fifty years before Rousseau's noble savage) they held up the hard and healthy body of the barbarian as an ideal.

Discourses about cold bathing, however, were not *simply* reworking such Tacitean themes. Like all English discussions of health and hygiene they were also profoundly marked by the widening horizons offered by growth of international trade and the burgeoning world of goods. On the one hand, medicine dealt with and in new commodities, ranging from tobacco and sugar to quinine and tea; on the other, it was becoming aware of a far wider range of bodily practices.[129] The sheer diversity of reports about other cultures could undermine particular claims to superiority in hygiene, as in other areas of English life. Justin Champion has shown how translations of the Koran and of Aramaic gospels could be used by religious radicals such as John Toland to undermine the universalist claims of Christian dogma and to expose alleged priestcraft.[130] It has been argued that travelers' accounts of Moslem and Judaic hygiene laws helped to produce the relativism of Montesquieu's *Persian Letters* and the somatically satiric strategies of *Gulliver's Travels*. Certainly, the bagnios that opened in London were avowedly similar to those of the Ottoman empire, and their publicists went to some lengths to counter Orientalist prejudices about Turkish bodies and bodily practices, while, as we have seen, both Floyer and Baynard used travelers' reports to enhance the reputation of cold bathing.[131]

Texts recommending cold bathing therefore negotiated a complex relationship with the body of the Other, whether that body was separated by time or geography. The health care and regimen they prescribed inevitably set out a bodily aesthetic suffused with political meaning and in tension (but not necessarily incompatible) with the codes of polite and civil society. Although authors such as Floyer and Baynard cannot be fitted into a neat scheme whereby (say) cold baths were Tory and hot baths Whig, their somatic recommendations were clearly political. They offered both a critique of and remedy for the apparent luxury of English society. The religious dimensions of Floyer's writing, however, emphasize that we should not discuss the politics of late seventeenth- and eighteenth-century English culture in purely secular, market-oriented terms.[132] It is precisely in this confluence of concern about luxury and liturgy that the advocacy and practice of cold bathing should be discussed.

Medicine, Politics, and the Body in Late Georgian England

Roy Porter

The body has long been rendered problematic in our society, partly thanks to powerful religious and sexual constraints.[1] One consequence has been a disembodied historiographical tradition that tells us too little about the corporeal realities of the past and blinds us to the symbolic meanings of the body within culture.[2] This paper aims to make a small contribution toward rectifying this by examining visual representations of the human body, in health and sickness, in late Georgian England as icons in political debate.[3] I begin by presenting key elements of health and medicine at the time. I then tease out artists' deployment of medical themes for political purposes and conclude by tracing the political meanings of health and medicine as inscribed on the body.[4]

The ancient notion of the body politic played a crucial part in this story. An older school of historiography assumed that the "Elizabethan world picture," with its notion of a body politic sustained by ancient macrocosm/microcosm correspondences, was undermined by the Scientific Revolution. But that was not so.[5] In the light of recent thinking about stigmatization, the creation of "difference" and the "other," and the moral meanings of sickness, I focus attention on the enduring cultural symbiosis of medicine, the body, and politics.[6] In particular, I raise questions of *experience*. How did contemporaries regard their bodies? How did they conceive of disease and death? How did they feel toward medicine? And how did opinions about these life-and-death issues, as embodied in sayings, satires, and prints, define and express wider attitudes, notably about politics? In what ways, in short, did popular or common culture construct bridges between physic and politics?[7] My broader purpose is to heighten awareness of forms of representation and embedded meanings.[8]

WEALTH AND HEALTH

The decades around 1800 were times of intense turmoil in Britain: the Industrial Revolution, radical protest, the making of a class society, to say nothing of the cultural upheaval of romanticism. "A new world was opening to the astonished sight," declared the romantic critic William Hazlitt.[9] Those revolutionary years, however, brought no revolutions in medicine or in health. The old political and ecclesiastical order may have been shaken, but the biological ancien régime survived. "Scientific medicine" hardly began until the bacteriological revolution around 1870, and medical interventions did not dramatically improve survival rates until the development of antibiotics in the 1940s.

People died of all sorts of infections, from typhoid and typhus to what we today consider trivial complaints, like influenza. There were few improvements in treatment. With the exception of smallpox (for which inoculation was introduced around 1720 and vaccination by Edward Jenner in 1796), all other epidemic diseases remained as lethal as before.[10] Indeed, from the late 1820s, a terrible new plague arose, cholera, which moved from its traditional base in the Indian subcontinent and swept the globe in six catastrophic pandemics.[11]

After 1750 population grew rapidly, but this demographic surge was not a result of better medicine but a product of a rising birthrate, most likely a consequence of earlier marriage. For the years before the first national census of 1801 and the development around 1830 of vital statistics, quantifying the incidence of particular diseases is impossible; but there is ample evidence that air-, water-, and bug-borne fevers were ubiquitous and frequently lethal. Newly delivered mothers suffered from puerperal fever; infants and up to two-fifths of all children died before they reached their fifth year. Teenagers were particularly vulnerable to smallpox, and the rise of industrial towns led physicians to fear new "filth diseases."[12] The work of prison reformers, notably John Howard, and pioneer sanitarians like the London Quaker John Coakley Lettsom pointed to the evils of poor ventilation, overcrowding, dirt, and malnutrition and stressed the vulnerability of schools, jails, camps, barracks, and workhouses to "gaol fever" (typhus).[13] Tuberculosis ("the white plague") was becoming the greatest urban killer.[14]

What was to be done in the face of these health risks? An advice culture of health and sickness taught self-help. "Primary care" meant care by the head of the household, a cook, nursemaid, or neighbors or recourse to a "lady bountiful," perhaps the parson's wife.[15] The market was also growing for medical self-help books like William Buchan's *Domestic Medicine,* first published in 1769 and still in print seventy years later. John Wesley's *Primitive Physick* (1749) was also a bestseller, a book designed to show the poor that practically all diseases could be treated with the aid of onions, lemon, cold water, brown paper, and prayer.[16]

This flourishing medical self-help culture by no means precluded recourse to medical practitioners. Medical historians have recently shown that the Georgian era brought rapid expansion in the numbers of medical men (all regular practitioners *were* men: women were all but excluded from professional ranks). Their income and status were rising too—a fact to be explained not in terms of the profession's success in achieving cures but rather as a consequence of growing disposable income. A consumer boom was in progress, surplus income was being expended on all manner of goods and services, and seeking medical treatment was one way to display growing prosperity.[17]

Historians of eighteenth-century medicine used to picture a pyramidal medical profession, with elite physicians at the apex, surgeons in the middle, and apothecaries at the base, all regulated by corporations. Physicians commanded the greatest prestige because they had been trained at university, and "physick" was a science of the mind founded on book learning. Surgery, by contrast, carried less status because it was a manual art, involving the shedding of blood; the apothecary's trade was least dignified, being but shopkeeping. Recent research, however, has undermined such images of a hierarchical, closed profession. Medical practice was far more fluid and heterogeneous. Old regulations were being eroded and strict demarcations between physicians, surgeons, and apothecaries were challenged, circumvented, or ignored. This new fluidity owed much to the enormous popularity of Edinburgh University as the flagship of medical education. Its graduates learned not only physic but also surgical skills. Hence they tended to become general practitioners, combining all the medical functions in one person, the new "family doctor." Many set up in market towns and industrial centers, being the first medical graduates to venture into the provinces.[18] Not least, such surgeon-apothecaries or general practitioners practiced obstetrics. Traditionally, delivery of babies had been the work of village midwives, often ill educated. These women were increasingly elbowed out by the aspirant "man-midwife" (*accoucheur,* or obstetrician), whose claim to superiority hinged on possession of anatomical knowledge and forceps.[19]

The rise of well-trained rank-and-file practitioners threatened elite physicians and surgeons and sparked professional tensions. Some general practitioners demanded equality with their senior brethren, and they were driven to a radical critique of oligarchy and nepotism which found its weapon in the journal *Lancet,* set up in 1823 by Thomas Wakley, a pugnacious medical practitioner who lambasted the medical top brass.[20] Yet general practitioners were themselves being challenged from below. This challenge came partly from the rise of chemists and druggists, tradesmen without medical training who opened shop and sold medicines, thereby threatening the doctors' livelihood. But quacks and empirics also challenged the general practitioners.[21] As early as the 1760s Robert James, patentee of "Dr. James's Fever Powders," was able to sell millions of sachets of his powders; by the 1830s James Morison—part quack, part alternative healer—was peddling his "Special Vegetable Pills" in even larger quantities.[22]

Medical men were perturbed by such challenges. Some feared that medicine itself, far from being an ethical profession, had become perverted into a mercenary trade. Radical physicians like Thomas Beddoes, a supporter of the French Revolution, dubbed the profession a mere "sick trade," portraying a conspiracy between fashionable patients and toadying practitioners.[23] Yet it was not clear what could be done. In his pioneering *Medical Ethics* (1803), the Manchester physician Thomas Percival conceded that in medicine those who paid the piper called the tune. Only over charity patients could the physician command unchallenged authority. In many ways a medical politics thus emerged that mirrored the wider political struggles of the age of reform.[24]

Would there be medical reform or revolution? Should the medical profession aspire to be the legislators of mankind, vaunting a scientific expertise that would, as with Benthamite utilitarianism, dictate laws of well-being to the people and ensure the greatest health of the greatest number? Or was medicine to remain, in the fashion of the ancien régime, the lackey to the rich? These issues were not resolved in Britain. Medical revolution occurred elsewhere. The Jacobins had grandiose plans for the transformation of all medical institutions involving throwing the healing profession open to all. In Paris the medical corporations were dissolved and a new hospital system came into being, stressing anatomy, pathology, and statistics and therefore accentuating the scientific study of disease.[25] No such dramatic transformations, however, occurred in England. In medical politics, as in politics in general, the ancien régime survived its buffetings to live into the Victorian era. Mixed public feelings toward innovation were brilliantly sketched by George Eliot in *Middlemarch*, set in 1832, where the ambitious, idealistic young practitioner Tertius Lydgate, just returned from France with new medical ideas, is both fêted and hated by provincial society.[26] The core of this paper will address the public image of the medical profession in the context of a wider politics of protest.

But if the decades around 1800 brought no medical revolution, certain changes were taking place. Newly founded dispensaries provided outpatient services for the sick poor in London and elsewhere. The hospital movement, growing in the capital from the 1720s, reached the new industrial towns. Places like Nottingham and Hull (both in 1782) and Sheffield (in 1797) acquired their first infirmary.[27] One sphere saw striking growth: the treatment of mental disorders, spurred ironically by the madness of

George III. Before his accession, very few institutions specialized in mad-ness apart from Bethlem Hospital (Bedlam). From around 1760 charitable asylums were set up in Leicester, Newcastle, Manchester, and York, and pri-vate asylums were founded by enterprising medical men engaged in the "trade in lunacy." Many private madhouses were corrupt and brutal, but others were innovative, notably the York Retreat, opened in 1796 on the ini-tiative of Yorkshire Quakers and pioneering "moral therapy."[28] Its champi-ons argued that the insane must no longer be viewed as wild animals or as devoid of reason and human feelings. Such unfortunates should be treated with humanity, gentleness, and reason, argued Samuel Tuke's *A Description of the Retreat at York* (1813).[29]

In mental health the romantic movement brought a break with the past. Mary Wollstonecraft's *The Wrongs of Woman, or Maria, a Fragment* (published in 1798) invited the reader to identify with the madwoman as victim.[30] The Wordsworthian complaint that "the world is too much with us" assumed that sufferers were driven out of their minds by the market pressures of wealth, ambition, and emulation. Stress was laid on the healthiness of Rousseauian solitude.[31]

Romantic poets seized on the emblematic possibilities of the insane. William Blake rejoiced that he was himself divinely mad, while in his ode *On Melancholy* Keats aspired to the condition of a melancholiac, implying that depression was the wellspring of creativity and the deepest human experi-ence.[32] Ironically, it took another romantic, Charles Lamb, to challenge these attitudes. As the brother of one who in a mad fit had slain their mother with a bread knife, Lamb had no urge to glamorize madness. His essay "The Sanity of True Genius" refuted the romantic conceit that it was the mad who were the truly great poets.[33]

Many artists and writers were not only fascinated by madness but were also versed in medico-scientific knowledge.[34] They saw sickness not simply as a physical event, a breakdown of the body machine, but—crucially for cultural representations of illness and medicine—as an expression of the inner or essential self.[35]

The experience of illness enhanced the romantic exploration of uncon-scious processes and the dialectic of self, psyche, and soma.[36] Certain devel-opments in medical theory and on the medical fringes supported the romantic denial of the traditional mind-body dualism and pointed to a uni-tary self. Spreading in Scotland, medical theories associated with Robert Whytt, William Cullen, and their followers treated health and disease as functions of a nervous organization uniting body and brain or mind. By sug-gesting that disease was sympathetic, neurology provided explanations of hypochondria and hysteria.[37] Meanwhile, on the medical fringe, the popu-larity of Mesmerism, developed in Vienna by Franz Anton Mesmer, also resulted in the erosion of supposedly clear-cut distinctions between body and mind. Hypnotists were able to obtain control over their patients through fixing with the eye: such powers fanned fears of the destructive potential of medicine and science, anxieties also voiced in Mary Shelley's *Frankenstein* (1818).[38] The old Cartesian dogma of the mechanical body and the transcendent mind was challenged.[39] The dualism endorsed by the Scientific Revolution was replaced by the romantic belief in the unitary nature of human experience.[40] Hence while the late Georgian era neither revolutionized English medicine nor resulted in improved longevity, new representations of the body and of suffering formed an essential component in that journey into the self that constitutes the intense subjectivity of the romantic interlude.[41] And it is to the body and its fate that I now turn.

DISTRUSTING DOCTORS

Challenges to entrenched mind/body relations went with a deep sense of the vulnerability of the flesh and reinforced old suspicions of doctors themselves. "If the world knew the villainy and knavery (beside ignorance) of the physicians and apothecaries," the antiquarian John Aubrey was told by a doctor, "the people would throw stones at 'em as they walked in the streets."[42] Skepticism ran high: "God heals and the Doctors take the Fee," judged a proverbial wisdom that also warned that death and the doctors were thick as thieves, or at least they always conducted joint consultations.[43] Practitioners, it was alleged, fleeced the public first and slew them afterward. "When a Nation abounds in Physicians," bantered the *Spectator*, "it grows thin of people."[44]

Doctors were accused of caring only for their fees. Himself a practitioner, Bernard Mandeville versified this sneer:

Physicians valued Fame and Wealth
Above the drooping Patient's Health,
Or their own Skill: The greatest Part
Study'd, instead of Rules of Art,
Grave pensive Looks, and dull Behaviour;
To gain th' Apothecary's Favour,
The Praise of Mid-wives, Priests and all,
That served at Birth, or Funeral.[45]

Gravest of all was the charge that, by acts of commission or omission, physicians were fatal. Should one consult an old or a young physician? someone inquired of Dr. Frank Nicholls: "The difference," he replied, "is this: The former will kill you, the other will let you die."[46]

The faculty warned the public against imposters, but the retort was that the profession itself was quackery in camouflage. Doctors were seen as men on the make: "You tell your doctor, that y'are ill / And what does he, but write a bill."[47]

Figure 13. William Hogarth, *The Company of Undertakers*

Thus Matthew Prior put the matter in a nutshell—a point Hogarth figured in "The Company of Undertakers" (figure 13). Was there truly much
difference between the stately faculty physicians at the foot of the engraving
and the infamous quacks above—Joshua ("Spot") Ward, Sally Mapp the
bone-manipulator, and John ("Chevalier") Taylor the oculist? No: because
Hogarth's motto said: *Et plurima mortis imago*—everywhere the face of
death.[48]

People were, of course, always bellyaching. "Met Mr. Forbes the surgeon going to kill a few patients," Parson William Holland jotted in his diary.[49] Doctor distrust was bound to bubble up as the profession seemed to be aggrandizing itself yet health did not improve. Medical men commanded attention but elicited mixed feelings. Of the thirteen hundred satirical prints produced by the comic artist Thomas Rowlandson, up to fifty dealt directly with medical subjects.[50] The stereotypes created, however, were negative or equivocal. Doctor-bashing was, of course, nothing new: medieval illuminators depicted them as apes, and a donkey appears as a physician in Goya's "Capriccios." But there were also singular aspects of public disquiet that Georgian cartoonists exploited.

Strikingly prominent are violation and violence. Practitioners endlessly perform procedures that invade and pain their patients. They wield the lancet and let blood; they prescribe disgusting purges; they yank out teeth. In Rowlandson's 1823 print "The Tooth-Ache, or Torment and Torture" (figure 14), Barnaby Factotum, the village jack-of-all-trades, is portrayed drawing a fang, while an old lady suffering from a raging toothache awaits her turn. A testimonial pinned to the wall reads: "Draws Teeth, Bleeds and Shaves. Wigs made here, also Sausages, Wash Balls, Black Puddings, Scotch Pills, Powder for the Itch, Red Herrings, Breeches Balls and Small Beer by the Maker."[51]

Visual hints insinuate that medicine is a minefield or torture chamber. In one print a thin, young, bespectacled apothecary kneels in profile, his cocked hat has fallen to the ground as he applies a monstrous clyster (enema) syringe to an invisible lady—we see only her discarded shoe. The image conveys physical menace: he could be an infantryman preparing a fusillade. Illness is painful, but being physicked is no better.[52]

Moreover, artists wished to intimate an endemic fiendishness in medicine, a theater of cruelty. This is supremely expressed in the finale of Hogarth's *Four Stages of Cruelty* ("The Reward of Cruelty," figure 15), set literally in a London anatomy theater. Tom Nero is being dissected. In the first print he is caught red-handed tormenting a dog; he then descends to seducing a maidservant, later murdering her; and after his execution, he becomes a dissecting-room exhibit, being ritually disemboweled and having his eyes gouged out by surgeons and his guts guzzled by another dog, truly a *lex talionis*. Is there much to choose, ponders Hogarth, between the murderous malefactor and the dissecting doctors? Media stories about "resurrectionists," or grave robbers, and their links with anatomy schools further cemented unsavory popular associations between crime, capital punishment, and medicine: any body might be their victim.[53]

In prints and the press doctors thus posed threats to the body, not just through therapeutic violence but through sexual violation too, as hinted by the image of the apothecary. Scores of sketches feature the physician as

Figure 14. Thomas Rowlandson, *The Tooth-Ache, or Torment and Torture* (1823)

lecher and clinical consultations as erotic skirmishes. Often there's a hint of rape, though frequently the typically buxom patient is fantasized as eager to take her medicine. Rowlandson's doctors gawp, grope, and glyster their patients in a most un-Hippocratic manner. His "Medical Dispatch, or Dr. Doubledose Killing Two Birds with One Stone" (figure 16) shows the physician with one pudgy hand taking the pulse of a cadaverous, senseless invalid while draping his arm around the neck of the nubile maid. The "Composing Draught" and the opium pillbox on the table suggest the

Figure 15. William Hogarth, "The Reward of Cruelty," final print of *The Four Stages of Cruelty*

physician may be giving his patient a helping hand out of this world, the sooner to change the object of his medical ministrations.[54]

Sex and medicine coalesce; physical examination becomes a motif for fornication, and the practitioner's tools—his cane, enemas, lancets, squirts, and clyster pipes—assume an erotic air, sometimes bawdily comic, and lewd double entendres proliferate. Above all, the upstart profession of *accoucheur*—men like Sterne's Dr. Slop—became targets for prurient satire. The new male obstetrician challenging the old midwives' monopoly was portrayed as a hermaphroditic freak.[55]

Figure 16. Thomas Rowlandson, *Medical Dispatch, or Dr. Doubledose Killing Two Birds with One Stone*

Medical violation preyed on people's minds. It may therefore have been obliquely comforting to perceive that if the doctor was a threat, he was also a fool. The pedant doctor had long featured in the commedia dell'arte, offering models for Molière's satires and the prating, asinine doctors duped by their wives and apprentices in picaresque novels. The black humor of fatuous doctors physicking gullible patients to death never palled. Rowlandson's "A Visit to the Doctor" shows a rustic couple visiting a physician's book-lined consulting room. "Do you see, Doctor," the husband ventures, "my dame and I be come to ax your advice—we both of us eat well and drink well, and sleep well—yet still we be somewhat queerish." The bewigged physician can fortunately solve all their problems: "You eat well—you drink well, and you sleep well—very good—you was perfectly right in coming to me, for depend upon it, I will give you something that shall do away with all these things!"[56]

Sometimes doctors neglect, sometimes they kill: and whenever two or three are gathered together, they fight. In "The Chamber War," part of Rowlandson's "English Dance of Death" series, the fisticuffs among the physicians defy description.[57] And sometimes the cartoon doctor is more naive than his patients. In "Cunicularii, or The Wise Men of Godliman in Consultation" (1726) (figure 17), Hogarth mocked the noted *accoucheur* Sir Richard Manningham, the Princess of Wales's man-midwife. With other doctors, Manningham had testified on behalf of a peasant woman, Mary Toft, who claimed to give birth to litters of rabbits, enabling her to come to London, put herself on display, and so make a fast buck. Small wonder Manningham figured as "an occult philosopher searching into the depth of things."[58]

Not just fatuous, doctors were also depicted as pretenders to fashion. Dressed up to the nines in distinctive "physical wigs," sporting their gold-headed canes, all pomp and polish, prattling on, these practitioners were full of themselves—and mercenary too.[59] And if regulars suffered from such egregious faults, were not quacks ten times worse? Mountebanks in full cry offered artists the dream subject, a theater of illusion and delusion, comic and grotesque—an all-purpose allegory.[60] In Hogarth's "Southwark Fair," a quack appears promoting a pamphlet, puffing his nostrums and breathing fire to gain attention. Other artists also presented these charlatans as showmen, singling out their weird and wonderful contraptions, as in Gillray's terrifying exposé of Elisha Perkins's Metallic Tractors—brass and iron rods, united like a tuning fork, which concentrated galvanic electricity on affected areas to work dramatic cures.[61]

Cartoons played on the risqué aspects of the irregulars. The nerve doctor and pioneer sex therapist James Graham developed a mud-bathing establishment, employed scantily clad "goddesses of health" to arouse public curiosity (one being Emma Lyon, the later Lady Hamilton), promoted a "Celestial Bed" guaranteed to restore potency, and lectured on the restoration of national virility.[62] The quack who dominated the prints, however, was James Morison; his "Universal Pills" were early Victorian England's best-selling medicine: "My 'Universal Pills' are quite divine! / If one don't do, you may take nine." A caricature by George Cruikshank shows a huckster standing on a box of "Universal Vegetable Pills," Morison's brand-name, in a "before and after" scene, against the backdrop of his "British College of Health."[63]

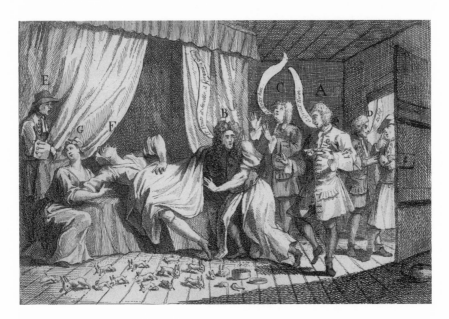

Figure 17. William Hogarth, *Cunicularii, or The Wise Men of Godliman in Consultation* (1726)

Contemporaries excoriated quackery. But we must be wary of hindsight, for our identifications of quack cures do not always coincide with theirs. Thus it was perfectly plausible around 1800 for Gillray to represent Edward Jenner's smallpox vaccination as balderdash.[64] Healers of all stripes, in other words, were portrayed in popular culture as menacing buffoons. What might render the comedy black was that disease was no joke. To be precise, Death was the satanic jester, the grave enemy, or bitter fool and medical humor the child of desperation. Diseases were Death's captains. Maladies were represented as sinister goblins, demons, and imps. Rowland-son excelled in personifying maladies. His "Ague and Fever" depicted a patient sitting, teeth chattering, holding his hands to a blazing fire. Ague— that is, malaria, in those days common in marshy areas—a sinuous, snaky monster, clings to him, while Fever, a furry fiend, stalks the room.[65] In prints like "The Blue Devils," George Cruikshank brought microbe men to life. A sufferer, lost in depression, dressed in nightgown, cap, and slippers, sits in a chair near a grate empty save for a huge bill. He is oppressed by sundry demons: a bailiff delivers a writ, a devil offers him a razor, a tiny fellow slips a noose around his neck. On the shelf lies Buchan's *Domestic Medicine*.[66]

The black comedy of these representations is the watermark of death. There was nothing new in this. From the medieval *danse macabre*, death had partnered life, and the *memento mori* taught that one lived to die and died to live. The shocking fact about these engravings is not Death's omnipresence but the role of doctors as Death's disciples. Medicine itself is a plague—a theme embroidered in Rowlandson's "English Dance of Death" sequence, where in dozens of images of Death stalking the living the doctor serves as his deputy. Death shadowed the anatomist in the mortuary and rode pillion with the undertaker. The image of Death as the doctor's overlord had enduring resonances.[67]

Maladies and medicine thus loomed large in premodern culture precisely because it was so near the bone. Disease, disfigurement, and death elicited anger, explosive laughter, and all the elemental passions. Medicine was a double agent: its ministrations desperately sought, it could also be accused of sleeping with the enemy. Doctors, Death, and the Devil so easily changed places. When we look at a print of a doctor—the Revd Dr. Francis Willis, the mad-doctor who treated King George III—it is disconcerting to spy that he sports not just a whip but maybe also a tail.[68]

BODIES POLITIC

Such representations of disease, doctors, and death provided a supple language for representing politics, for ours has been a culture incorporating contradictory attitudes toward the body. Bodies are emotional and cognitive resources. We feel and think through them; they mediate self and society, affording metaphors, models, and meanings. We anthropomorphize the external world (brow of a hill, head of state, footnotes), and philosophies have postulated correspondences between the body human, the body politic, and the body cosmic. Strong or weak, well or sick, the little world of man stood as an epitome of the macrocosm, and vice versa, from Livy's fable of Menenius Agrippa to Shakespeare and beyond. Language fleshes out the imaging of the world through the body and the body through the world: we speak of bodies of knowledge, body politics, and so forth. In the political arena centuries of allusion to members of Parliament and parliamentary motions, purges, and crises have left us practically oblivious to an omnipresent semantic topography of the body (deaf in part because bodily allusions suggest double entendre, smut, and shame).[69]

In our inherited culture the flesh bespeaks vile bodies. Powerful currents in Platonic, Pauline, and Puritan thinking, augmented by Cartesianism, have deemed the body inferior to the nobler faculties—soul, spirit, and consciousness. The body is theologically fallen: dirty, sordid, worm-eaten, too too solid, or sullied. While explaining our ambivalence and punitiveness toward the body and its sexuality, Freudians have reinforced feelings of defilement and denial. Small surprise then that political prints are fixated on the body.

This preoccupation grew out of artistic convention—before Cubism, the syntax of art was essentially that of the human form. But representing the body also follows from habits of mind and figures of speech: through metonymy, the body emblazons the people, the nation. When a cartoonist wants to depict a set-to between Britain and France, the idea is represented by contrasting physiques. When we see a citizen having his teeth yanked out by a politician—in one cartoon Pitt the Younger—we know the people are yet again being ripped off by Westminster. Cartographical wizardry easily turns Britain into a person: the map becomes human.[70] The point is obvious and the variations endless.

The body is deeply ambiguous. It may be the target of brutality, but it can also be the agent for expressing hatred and contempt. Hence the explosive power of the fart in low humor and other tropes of the "Kiss my arse" variety. The links between laughter and aggression have been explored notably in Freud's notion of humor as the vehicle of impermissible desires.

Early political prints were hieroglyphic and abstract, but during the Georgian century a new, punchy cartoon idiom emerged. Cartoons became barbed and biting, featuring identifiable individuals rendered bodily in a style trading on vulgarity and indecency. Offensive and scatological, cartoonists expressed the violent, slanderous, Swiftian deflating (or rather inflating) humor of "Magna Farta." Farts proved ever popular, and the British term "Broad Bottoms" to designate political coalitions also proved an irresistible prompt for visual punning, especially the notion that the one thing "Broad Bottom" politicians could always be relied upon to do was to shit upon the nation.[71]

Far more scandalous was the iconography of the royal rump, a vicious travesty of the Court ceremonials of His Highness, or rather His Backside, George II. In one print, Walpole, waving a wand of office, presides over the ceremony while Queen Caroline injects an enema into her bilious husband and courtiers worship in postures of fawning sycophancy. Backsides formed one of the great insignia in an era in which politics was public theater.[72] "Idol-Worship, or The Way to Preferment" (1740) contained a double assault. It showed one could get on only by kissing the prime ministerial arse, while its caption blamed it all on George II. But if Walpole's butt symbolized dirty power and filthy lucre, the prime minister was also portrayed on the receiving end of an "Up yours": in one print Cardinal Fleury administers a clyster from the rear, while Walpole's illegitimate daughter, Lady Churchill, toys with her father's privy purse.

Bums remained the most outrageous totems of power, the obscene might of ministers but also the instruments of impudent protest. An American cartoon of 1775, "The Congress of the Necessary Politicians," shows two men in a privy. One man is tearing up the resolutions of Congress for bum fodder while the other is reading a pamphlet refuting Samuel

Johnson's *Taxation No Tyranny*. Lord Chatham tarred and feathered serves as grafitti.[73]

Lavatory humor abounded. Ribald anti-Scot prejudice was maintained by images like the one of "Sawney in the Boghouse"—the stage Caledonian reveals himself to be a barbarian because he doesn't know what the outhouse holes are for and consequently shits himself. But this humor intensified the offense when the throne was occupied by none other than the monarch. In James Gillray's scatological "Taking Physick; or The News of Shooting the King of Sweden!" (1792) (figure 18), the royal couple are relieving themselves as a horrified Pitt, bearing the "News from Sweden," shrieks, "Another Monarch done over!" Wearing a crown that evokes a fool's cap, the king, with his distinctive tic of speech, can only utter: "What? Shot? What? what? what?—Shot! shot! shot!" while uncontrollably evacuating his bowels, as is treasonably mimed by the lion on the royal arms on the privy wall. In that surrealist subversive comedy perfected by Swift and Gillray, boghouse and palace dissolve, reminding us of Swift's jingle: "We read of kings, who in a fright, / Though on a throne, would fall to shite."[74]

In the cartoon cosmos the body—the body politic—is perpetually punished. Torsos serving as national emblems are racked and carcasses butchered. In "The Colonies Reduced" Britannia is mutilated by the loss of her limbs, the American colonies. Yet the political body may be a monster in itself, deformed and atrocious, and the grotesque body often signifies the mob or in revolutionary France the sansculottes. Ghoulish English audiences took horrified delight in spine-chilling images of the Terror, enabling George Cruikshank to produce deeply ambivalent images in which reform itself was sanguinary. "A Radical Reformer, i.e., a Neck or Nothing Man" shows the heads of the political nation—the Prince Regent, Liverpool, Castlereagh, and Eldon—abandoning their moneybags and fleeing from a grotesque monster whose body is a guillotine replete with daggers and flames. Sometimes it was the ministry that was the monster. In "The Ministerial Monster" Lord Bute appears as a grotesque winged hydra, devouring Habeas Corpus, tearing up Magna Carta, and trampling the people, to the accompaniment of prophecies from the Book of Revelation.[75]

Evocation of dismemberment could lead to the ultimate nightmare: public dissection. Execution was a calculated degradation. In the finale of Hogarth's "Four Stages of Cruelty," dissection acquired all the solemn and profaning connotations of the public execution (see figure 15). Rowlandson rang the changes on those macabre and gory elements. In "State Butchers," drawn during the Regency crisis, a ruthless Pitt occupies the throne as President of the Company of Surgeons and directs the anatomist to remove the Prince's heart, lest its "good qualities" ruin his plan.[76]

Political anatomy formed a favorite trope of political commentators. Perhaps the most striking example is "The Conduct of the Two B——rs," pub-

Figure 18. James Gillray, *Taking Physick, or The News of Shooting the King of Sweden!* (1792)

lished in 1749—there is of course a pun in the title, which may be "Brothers," "Butchers," what you will; Henry Pelham is shown performing an "anatomy" in which Britannia is disemboweled, while his elder brother, the duke of Newcastle, wears a ribbon identifying him as "Undertaker General" ("undertaker" meant a political manager as well as a funeral director).

The politician as state butcher received its most cutting treatment in 1832, the year not just of the great Reform Act but also of the Anatomy Act, which ended the Burke and Hare scandals of grave robbers and resurrectionists and permitted surgeons to dissect the unclaimed corpses of the hospital poor. Medically progressive, this measure was feared as offering the profession carte blanche to mutilate the populace, and, mutatis mutandis, the politicians to initiate carnage. In a 1832 print by Robert Seymour, Tory anatomist peers surround a body representing the Parliamentary Reform Bill. They dissect it, as the Tory peers were threatening to butcher the bill. Lord Harrowby amputates the left leg and exhibits it to Newcastle, Buckingham chops off the left arm, Wharncliffe severs the right, Cumberland excises the heart, while Wellington plunges a knife into the chest. In a nice touch Lord Eldon is picking the victim's pockets, while two bishops watch with an air of pious unconcern.[77]

If one thing was more sacrilegious than dissection it was cannibalism. The locus classicus was Gillray's "Petit Souper, à la Parisienne," prompted by the September massacres of 1792. Gillray depicts a hideous, subhuman anthropophagic sans-culottes family cramming themselves with human organs while basting a baby over an open fire—perhaps echoing Swift's *Modest Proposal*? As Ronald Paulson has shown, it was Gillray's genius to reduce the politics of revolution to the elemental: eating and being eaten, shitting and being shat upon.[78]

Cartoonists thus anatomized politics as a theater of cruelty against the body. But a more specific idiom was also being used in which politics was encoded through specific *medical* analogues, via those medical metaphors and models expressing distrust of doctors. Politicians were practitioners and the people patients, suffering from the diseases of war, impressment, taxation, and poverty. Sick and languishing, the body politic was being ruthlessly medicated by its doctor-leaders. Surgery was being performed, blood let, the patient purged or vomited; and, if all else failed, a postmortem was in order.[79]

The chief patient was John Bull. "Bull was portrayed as a stout countryman (usually a yokel)," John Brewer argues, "who laboured manfully beneath the burdens of British political life, while the sans-culottes, emaciated, fiendish, and with a grin that conveyed both concupiscence and folly, personified the threat of radical plebeian, looking utterly satanic or perhaps foolish and comic."[80] Unlike the confident, corpulent, mid-Victorian figure, Georgian political culture rarely sentimentalized John Bull. Typically coarse, often drunk, and endlessly put upon, his qualities were those of a dumb beast. Not surprisingly, therefore, he frequently appeared sick and afflicted. Above all, he is made to submit to the ministrations of the state physicians, Pitt, Wellington, Castlereagh, and later Peel, who treat him with bizarre nostrums like "Wellington Drops" and "Total Defeat for Bonaparte" pills.[81]

Taxation offered a prime medical metaphor. Sometimes, as in a 1786 print by William Dent, John Bull's very body is transformed into an anatomical chart for the multiple taxes levied by Pitt. There are other ways to wring the vitality out of a nation: "Johnny in a Flatting Mill" shows Bull being mangled for extra taxes in a year when war costs and inflation were emptying the treasury.[82] And a joke that never palled—obviously it rang true—was John Bull undergoing bloodletting, shown by Gillray's "Doctor Sangrado Curing John Bull of Repletion." Sangrado (literally Dr. Blood, the venesecting physician in Le Sage's *Gil Blas*), stands as a metaphor for the ministry, which, armed with lancets, is draining the nation of its lifeblood, that is, its guineas. A parallel appears in George Cruikshank's "State Physicians Bleeding John Bull." The sitting John gapes, while being bled of all his gold. "You have open'd so many veins," he complains, "and drained me so incessantly that I fear my constitution is impaired forever." John Bull bled dry was one of Cruikshank's chestnuts: in the 1810s he used the theme on at least six occasions.[83]

It was generally at ministerial hands that John Bull suffered medical violation, but not always. Popular politicians too could lend themselves to lampooning as performers of radical surgery. In "Radical Quacks Giving a New Constitution to John Bull," George Cruikshank sketched the national hero, with both legs amputated (one peg is inscribed "Universal Suffrage," the other "Religious Freedom"), being bled by the aristocratic Westminster radical Sir Francis Burdett while another radical M.P., John Cam Hobhouse, offers him a drink. They inform him: "M. Bull, you have lived too well, but when we have renovated your Constitution according to our plan the reform will be so complete —! that you will never again be troubled with any fullness whatsoever!"[84] Radicals might thus be no less bloody-minded than the ministers, and they were also vulnerable to a further device. Opposition politicians invited portrayal as quacks—a gag that ran and ran. In the context of Catholic emancipation, Cruikshank produced an engraving entitled "The Mountebanks, or Opposition Show Box," in which John Bull appears as a farmer and the mountebank doctors were the radical M.P. Samuel Whitbread, offering an "infallible panacea—reform," the Irish dramatist and politician Richard Sheridan (as a zany), and Lords Grenville and Grey, muzzling Bull with a "Catholic Emancipation" bandage. Whitbread's pockets were stuffed with nostrums, including "Whitbread's Intire," alluding of course to his other career as a brewer.[85]

Mountebanks tended to come from abroad, and for that reason non-English politicians were routinely depicted as quacks. The victim-in-chief in the 1760s was Lord Bute, the Scot who, as the favorite of young George III, was appointed First Lord of the Treasury. "The State Quack" was one of hundreds of attacks on this impostor and on his supposed mistress, George III's mother, the Princess Dowager, portrayed falling as rope-walker.[86]

Around 1800 satirists received a gift from the gods in the form of Henry Addington, later Lord Sidmouth, briefly prime minister and lengthily home secretary. The son of a physician who had once run a madhouse, Addington inevitably won the nickname of "political doctor." In over a hundred and thirty prints he featured in the guise of pharmacist, physician, apothecary, nurse, and mountebank. It is he who, in Gillray's "Doctor Sangrado Curing John Bull of Repletion," is the doctor bleeding John Bull who sits on a commode labeled "Reservoir for the Clysterpipe family!" The cartoon makes a double point. It protests against the exorbitant taxes levied to support the French war and it ridicules, via the "Clysterpipe family" associations, the sinecures Addington had swung for his teenage son.[87]

Cruikshank went to town at Addington's expense, drawing on the fact that there was something intrinsically ludicrous about a top politician being a doctor's son:

> My name's THE DOCTOR; *on the Berkshire hills*
> *My father purged his patients*—a wise man,
> Whose constant care was to increase his store,
> And keep his eldest son—myself—at home.
> But *I had heard of Politics, and long'd*
> *To sit within the Commons' House, and get*
> *A place*, and luck gave what my sire denied.[88]

In 1804 Gillray's "Britannia between Death and the Doctors" showed the nation being treated, or rather mistreated, by doctors.[89] Its aim was to crow over Addington's ignominious retirement. Gillray implied that Addington's medicines had left Britannia on the brink of the grave (death being equated with Napoleon). The body politic is relieved only by the return of her old physician Pitt, who is booting Addington out while also stamping on Fox's prostrate body. Pitt clutches a flask of "Constitutional Restorative" and "The Art of Restoring Health" pokes out of his pocket. Discarded on the ground are "Whig Pills" and in Fox's hand is "Republican Balsam," alongside panaceas and quack remedies.

Addington was also portrayed mishandling other diseases of state. In "Consultation on the Best Cure for the Gout," a critique of military expenditure, Sidmouth appears as physician examining the immensely enlarged hand—that is, patronage—of a gouty George IV. Sometimes he is ridiculed through wearing a mortar on his head labeled "Drugs for John Bull" and "Circular Pills," an allusion to an infamous circular issued in July 1819 by Home Secretary Sidmouth calling on lords-lieutenants to adopt all measures necessary for the preservation of order and to keep the yeomanry in readiness—actions later seen as precipitating the Peterloo Massacre. The name stuck and it appears in subsequent prints, as for instance where Addington is seen flying through the air in "A Kick Up in a Great House": "The ——d Bull has given my poor Brain such a Circular Twist—I fear all the Pills, Clysters, Emetics, Draughts, and Bolus's in my shop—will never put right again." Finally, in William Hone's pamphlet of 1819, *The Political House That Jack Built*, George Cruikshank showed Sidmouth, Castlereagh, and Canning in a woodcut, "The Doctor," that begins: "This is The Doctor of Circular Fame / A Driv'ller, A Bigot, A Knave without shame."[90]

If Addington was often portrayed as state physician or quack, other politicians figured as the sick men of Westminster. The classic instance was the radical M.P. Charles James Fox. He was the caricaturist's dream: his very name afforded Aesopian opportunities for animal physiognomy, while his gambling, drinking, libertinism, and demagogic predilections permitted artists to portray a double person, both patrician and plebeian, the member of Parliament turned into the "lost member" of some rake or roué. And as a lost member it was appropriate that in a William Dent print Fox's body was laid bare as if for dissection, being discovered to be riddled with every conceivable personal and political weakness. Not least, his disheveled locks and unkempt appearance and after 1789 his support for the French Revolution permitted cartoonists to represent him as not merely a lost member but a lost soul, fit for the madhouse.[91] Indeed, madness frames the tale I have been telling. This was, after all, the era in which George III lapsed into insanity, Edmund Burke was regarded as almost certifiable—"the most eloquent madman I know," quipped Gibbon—and Castlereagh, Romilly, and Whitbread all slit their throats, while the French Revolution and the Napoleonic eras were diagnosed as maniacal epidemics. Small surprise that the state was renamed Bedlam, not least by Hogarth, who in the finale of the "Rake's Progress" presented what looked like the interior of Bethlem but captioned it "Britannia."[92]

This essay has raised certain themes. It has argued for the importance of visual as well as verbal languages to the historian. It has maintained the need for the historian to break down specialized disciplinary boundaries—those between political history, cultural history, art history, medical history, and so forth—and recognize the common images, ideas, symbols, words, metaphors, and models linking them. Not least, it has insisted that the historian should think the body. Without attention to these issues, history remains blind and disembodied.

Nature and Culture

A Natural Revolution?

Garden Politics in Eighteenth-Century England

Stephen Bending

In other Lands let Trophies and Triumphal Arches be erected to their Kings, and Monuments of Slaughtering their own and other Nations; Let encreasing Riches, embellished Cities, and Millions of rising Subjects constitute the Glories of my Annals.

A HISTORY OF THE SUMATRANS

So says King Amurath III in John Shebbeare's most loosely veiled of allegories.[1] In Shebbeare's history Sumatra is seventeenth- and eighteenth-century Britain and Amurath is George III. Shebbeare, one-time Jacobite pilloried in the 1750s for anti-Hanoverian journalism, was a decade later an apologist for the king's ministers and soon to be pensioned.[2] Writing in 1760—with the Seven Years' War still far from its conclusion—he has his monarch reject a political aesthetic of imperial aggression, with its trophies and triumphal arches, in favor of commerce, increasing population, and an aesthetic of social utility. He also sketches a history of Britain that lays both aesthetic and political corruption at the door of a Whig oligarchy based on money, individualism, and selfishness. According to Shebbeare's account of the political nation, while the Tory party has always stood for the rights of kings and their lineal heirs and has observed a passive obedience to the Crown, Whig principles "foster the love of Power in Individuals" and a "Spirit of Arbitrariness" that inevitably raises the spectre of civil war. As a result of such Whig principles before the accession of the new king, political debate has become mere sophistry attempting to disguise impending ruin; religion has turned to the "boisterous Explosion of Turbulence and Nonsense" characteristic of Methodist prayer; empirical science has lost sight of its religious purpose and produces only "Raree show and Quirk"; literature (once great) now concerns itself with nothing more than mimicry and idle laughter, while for the arts as a whole,

That Contempt of Probity, which infected every Mind, stole into the Operations of their Fingers. Those Hands from which nothing formerly departed

241

without Truth of Workmanship, and strength of Constructure, were now fallaciously employed in concealing Imperfections with spurious Art, and dispatching Business with Expedition.

Foreign Nations, indeed, complained that the public Faith of the *Sumatrans* had degenerated with the private; and that their Treatise and Alliances were equally violated with the Probity and Honour of the Individuals.[3]

In the following pages I will be exploring one aspect of Shebbeare's polemic—the coopting of the aesthetic into the realms of factional party politics—and will be looking at one of the prime sites for that merging of political and aesthetic discourses: the English landscape garden. In particular, I will be turning to the royal gardens most personally associated with George III and the princess Augusta, those of Richmond and Kew, gardens that (despite Shebbeare's claims) were anything but free from monuments to military victories and the trophies of war and gardens where factional divisions over foreign and domestic policy were to become a central feature of both their design and interpretation.

Throughout the eighteenth century the English landscape garden was a contentious site for competing cultural concerns, acting as a locus for discourses in the period ranging from connoisseurship to radical politics and agricultural improvement, from antiquarianism and aesthetics to tourism and statistical surveys. In part this is bound to be so, for land represents here a site for both aesthetic intervention and political enfranchisement; the garden in turn, to borrow the language of civic humanism, embodies the right to vote while demonstrating—in its abstraction of the ideal from the particular—the owner's accuracy of perception, his judgment, and therefore his fitness to govern aesthetic and political realms. This latter, of course, is a matter of perspective, and for the nonlandowning the garden could look rather different; thus while I will begin by exploring these patrician accounts of the garden as an image of high politics, I will then turn to alternative accounts of the garden which begin to emerge noticeably from about mid century, accounts that make the garden a site for demonstrating membership of a polite culture far broader than the landed elite. In this respect, the garden acts as a venue for the polite battles within a society beginning to recognize divisions of class rather than rank; and part of that battle takes the form of the increasing number of garden histories that began to appear in the years after George III's accession. The garden's ability to naturalize political power in the eighteenth century makes it a space to be fought over all the more strongly.

One of the myths of the English landscape garden in the eighteenth century was of its almost miraculous "discovery" as a wholly native art in the early years of the Hanoverian succession. Modern garden historians have now shown such an account to be untenable and have mapped out various European influences;[4] but in the second half of the century a great deal of effort went into producing world histories of the garden which found their apotheosis in the newly discovered landscape style.[5] Many of these works were openly "Whiggish" in their historical methods and overtly patriotic in their claims: the "English" aesthetic of variety in the garden, the rejection of geometrical form, is to be recognized as an image of the constitution and of Britons' inherent liberty. The poet William Mason is characteristic in his claim that "Addison, Pope, Kent, &c. [are] the Champions of this true taste, because they absolutely brought it into execution. The beginning therefore of an actual reformation may be fixed at the time when the *Spectator* first appeared."[6] Indeed, both the 1710s, chosen by so many writers as the moment at which the landscape garden was conceived, and the period from the early 1760s in which the majority of such histories were produced are of central importance. While 1714 saw the establishment of the Hanoverian dynasty, the 1760s saw a generation of increasingly wealthy landowners who could finally put the Jacobite threat behind them. With the end of that threat of political upheaval came the end of an associated threat to property. But if there was a new monarch in the 1760s, cultivating a wholly British image and keen to assert dynastic stability, there was also a growing antagonism directed toward a landed ruling class deemed unpatriotically French in both manners and taste. It is at this point that we see a major surge in the publication of garden histories; aligning aesthetic with dynastic change, such histories reasserted the rights of property, the position of the great landowners as the natural leaders of society, and the Hanoverian monarchy as the natural rulers of the nation. As a number of historians have recently argued, the invention of Britishness is itself a central aspect of eighteenth-century culture, and that identity found its expression largely in opposition to France; but without a direct threat to mainland Britain for much of the century, it was to find a focus in broader, less material issues.[7] Garden histories, I suggest, are very much part of that project; they set about constructing the garden as an image of the nation, an image that attempted to restore the patriotic credentials of the landowning elite. Not only do we see the assertion of national identity in the writing of garden history—an identity associated directly with the arrival of the Hanoverians— but that sense of Englishness is defined quite openly against other cultures, most notably the French and that French style of gardening made famous by Louis XIV. I suggest further that this construction of garden history itself reinforces one of the central Hanoverian myths of the later eighteenth century, that of natural succession rather than revolution. In the lines from Mason quoted above, he carefully uses the word "reformation," with all its religious overtones, when he mentions 1714, and one of the tropes we see reappearing in such histories is the vacillation between "restoration" and "revolution" brought about by the recognition of their political charge. In Mason's account of garden history, as indeed in many others, what follows is a series of natural innovations that are at once revolutionary and carefully distanced from a sense of revolution. Emphasis falls both on a break with the past and on a series of inevitable changes growing one from the other, a rediscovery of the natural, but a rediscovery based firmly on established property rights that in turn guarantee that peculiarly English brand of liberty. In these terms garden history and dynastic rhetoric attempt to negotiate the same problems posed by restoration, reformation, and revolution: aligning dynasty with landscape, garden history's account of the nation becomes a means of naturalizing a Hanoverian succession supported by a landed elite.

While Horace Walpole's "Essay on Modern Gardening" (1770) proved to be one of the most influential histories of the English garden in the eighteenth century, it was not only overtly politically engaged writers like Walpole who turned to garden history; a wide range of authors chose to write on the establishment of the English garden style. The essay of William Falconer, a popular physician and a respected scholar, "Thoughts on the Style and Taste of Gardening among the Ancients" (1782), is typical of these efforts.[8] Like many, Falconer begins by likening ancient gardens to those of the East and associating both with forms of despotic government. Again in a move typical of such histories, when he then turns to England, Falconer traces the emergence of a polite culture with its "easy and natural style," where the history of England from the reign of Elizabeth to the late eighteenth century is that of a gradual removal of "stiffness" from the culture and, by implication, from government. The English garden becomes a shared national achievement open to all those of polite taste, and this stands in contrast to the cultural and political history of Britain's great rival, France, the regular gardens of which Falconer duly brings to the attention of the reader. One of the slights of hand being practiced here, again quite characteristically, is that the vast gardens of other ages and other cultures are equated with tyranny while English gardens—despite also being dependent on the amassing of both land and wealth at the expense of others—are characterized in terms of liberty. In this sense Falconer is quite openly an apologist for the landed elite at a time when that elite found such apologies more and more necessary. In the final decades of the eighteenth century and notably from the concluding years of the American war when Falconer published his essay, the landed classes came under far heavier criticism than ever before for being both exclusive and frivolous. Writers such as Thomas Paine and William Cobbett "treated the landed interest as a separate class parasitic on the nation, rather than as part of the nation and its natural leaders."[9] Faced by this challenge, the landed elite needed to find ways of reasserting its authority both socially and politically. As Linda Colley has argued, the need was to find indigenous forms of cultural expression which demonstrated patriotism but also their difference from those below them in society.[10] Falconer's essay can be understood as an attempt to meet this challenge. Histories of the landscape garden were histories of the kind of large-scale landowning open only to the aristocratic elite, but crucially they were based on the most patriotic of all things, the land itself. In the public gesture of gardening, landowners could equate themselves with the achievements of constitutional liberty and assert their dominance over aesthetic taste even as that taste was characterized as the shared property of the nation. In such histories the landed elite came to own one of the foremost expressions of national identity in the late eighteenth century. And within garden histories that ownership becomes both rational and natural.

At the head of such patriotic landowning stood the king himself, and the gardens at Richmond and Kew, with which George III was particularly involved, illustrate both the attempts to establish the monarch as patriotic leader of the nation and opposition attempts to challenge that status. Richmond gardens had been famous since the 1730s for the highly emblematic—and frequently ridiculed—designs of William Kent for Queen Caroline. It was at Richmond that Kent produced Merlin's Cave as a residence for Stephen Duck the Thresher Poet, complete with life-size wax statues including Merlin and his secretary; here also was a hermitage containing further busts of Newton and Locke, Wollaston and Boyle. The implications of these buildings as an attempt to link the Hanoverian with the Tudor court and the deliberate misinterpretation of that iconography from those in opposition to the Walpole administration has been explored elsewhere.[11] Here I want to consider the further iconographic battles that took place with the arrival of George III. Kew came into the hands of Prince Frederick at about the same time that his mother was involved with Richmond, and here Kent was to work also. Despite Frederick's death in 1751 his wife, Princess Augusta, continued the work on the gardens he had begun. In 1754 Kew Palace was allocated to Prince George, and under the advice of the Scottish peer Lord Bute the Scottish architect Sir William Chambers was made his architectural adviser, while another Scot, William Aiton, was appointed as gardener in 1759. This apparent predominance of Scottish interests in the royal gardens was itself to provide a point of contention that paralleled a similar concern about Scottish influence in the young George III's early ministries. With Chambers designing the gardens at Kew, most of Prince Frederick and Kent's works were replaced. During the 1750s and 1760s Chambers erected the Alhambra and Pagoda, a ruined Roman arch, and temples to Pan, Arethusa, and Aeolus among others. With the major success at Minden during the Seven Years' War he was asked to build a temple of Victory, while the Peace of Paris—despite its unpopularity—was also to be commemorated. Two years later, in 1764, 'Capability' Brown was appointed as Royal gardener, and he started work on the grounds at Richmond. By the early 1770s, while Chambers had been constructing a range of architectural features at Kew, Brown had largely removed the emblematic gestures of an earlier generation of royalty in favor of open park and woodland. Thus, while Kew continued to be controlled by Augusta and was heavily influenced by Bute into the early 1770s, Richmond, under Brown from 1764, was wholly at George III's command. With Bute's fall from favor by the mid-1760s this was a garden almost ostentatiously different from neighboring Kew. Equally, however, it was from about this date that the two gardens started to be linked, and with the death of Augusta in 1772 they were more fully merged.

In the year that the Seven Years' War finally reached its conclusion, Henry Jones, the bricklayer poet of Bristol, wrote a panegyric poem entitled *Kew Garden* (1763).[12] The poem celebrates both the garden and its owner, with Kew appearing as a representation of the nation—much as in the garden histories that started to appear from about this date—but also as an image of George III himself. Indeed much is made of George as a native king in a native garden. Opening with the accession of George, Jones celebrates the reinvigoration of arts and science and a youthful king "who cultivates the spot which gave him birth" (p. 6). As "the unquestion'd victor of the wat'ry world" George will reign over a nation that claims to be the true successor to the traditions of Greece and Rome: "The world shall wonder, GALLIA's self shall praise, / And LEWIS pine at GEOR[G]E's matchless fame" (p. 11). After a description of the new monarch with his "mild command," "righteous rule," and "godlike sway," Kew itself becomes the "image of his own accomplish'd mind," with the lake and never-failing stream as the "Best emblem of the king's rich heart diffus'd, / Which flows incessant on his people's Weal" (p. 12). Indeed, Kew and the lake become Egypt and the Nile, only better, for here are not the extremes of inundation and drought. In turn, the palace stands on a hill as a "lofty image of his own grand thought / . . . like his awful throne sublime" (p. 19). But this is a king who will also descend from his palace to the plain below; and in this sense walking in his garden becomes an image of the king as a man among his people, both physically and politically. Unlike Eastern tyrants, Jones assures us, "see, how like a royal friend he walks / Serene among us with a brother's smile" (p. 21). This then is a garden that naturalizes royal power. If for many it appears as an impenetrable maze, for George it contains a "royal plan":

> By seeming chance it looks! with incidents
> Judicious fraught, of mixt unequal kind,
> Where things in nature, far remote, conspire
> In just coincidence of just extreams,
> At once to please us, and at once improve,
> By art and genius drawn so close together.
> With what judicious pause, what piercing ken,
> Our young, our wise, illustrious, learned king
> Now travels thro' th'instructive moral maze

In rip'ning bloom, coeval with himself?
Where high and low, where great and small unite,
Where true magnificence and seeming scant
Where princely state, and rustic plainness verge,
In sweet vicinity for ever fixt,
For ever distant, and for ever near,
In one accomplish'd, one distinguish'd whole! (p. 21)

It becomes difficult here to distinguish between monarchy and garden as each becomes the ideal of nature and art combined. Extremes, confusion, injustice all disappear in the face of a monarchical vision that produces "one distinguish'd whole." Variety in the garden and variety in the political nation are legitimized in the person of the king; and as Jones continues, both George's actions and the national "garden" within which he acts demonstrate his liberal mind, his virtue, and his role as the bringer of concord and victory.

The death in 1772 of George III's mother, the princess Augusta, provided further opportunity for the celebration of Kew. Oliver Goldsmith's *Threnodia Augustalis,* "Sacred to the Memory of her late Royal Highness"— put together fairly hurriedly in the weeks after Augusta died—sets itself the task of praising Augusta's benevolence and "dignity of mind" and does so by drawing on a recognition of Kew as part of Augusta's public persona.[13] The work is composed of a series of songs and oratories of little original merit; as Goldsmith notes, it may "more properly be termed a Compilation than a Poem. It was prepared for the Composer in little more than two days; and may therefore rather be considered as an industrious Effort of Gratitude than of Genius." Indeed, the poem did not appear in Goldsmith's collected works until early in the nineteenth century, largely as a result of his attempt to keep his authorship a secret. In these terms, the poem is a fairly conventional piece of praise, a jobbing work articulating an apparently unproblematic and safely conventional view. Like Jones, Goldsmith sets royalty above the wranglings of party and faction. The death of the patient princess—who has stood "like some well-fashion'd arch" that "purchased strength from its encreasing load"—brings such disruptive elements to their senses. Party rage gives way to mourning, and Augusta's life is offered as a model for all to follow in a poem where the chorus joins in singing, "Let us, let all the world agree, / To profit by resembling thee."

After this opening section with its stress on sympathy of feeling, Christian fortitude, and disinterested virtue, Part II opens with a pastoral overture and a shift in location to the gardens at Kew. Goldsmith adopts the conventional language of garden description—"sweetly blending, still are seen / The wavy lawn, the sloping green"—and Kew becomes a site of mourning for the dead princess, with a "rural band" giving their speeches of praise. The group consists of those who have benefited from the benevolence of

Augusta: the "good old sire," the "modest matron," the "military boy," "orphan'd maid," and "shatter'd veteran." Each in turn sings her praises, the group as a whole—father, mother, child, and soldier—intimating a nation, domestic and military, mourning for a lost leader, a princess who has recognized her true role as the parent of her subjects. Royal benevolence is set against grudging masters and uncaring politicians; for the matron, Augusta takes on godlike powers with her omniscient care, while for the maid this death makes Kew a scene for eternal mourning. In the final chorus royal garden turns to royal graveyard and for the princess "the tears of her country shall water her tomb."

Goldsmith attempts to place Augusta and his own panegyric beyond the realms of politics by a metamorphosis of Kew into a site for patriotic mourning. But the claims made in *Threnodia Augustalis* for a princess above faction and free from party strife were to prove problematic by the 1770s as the physically and ideologically shifting grounds of Kew denied an easy patriotism rooted in the royal gardens. In the previous decade opposition factions had largely committed themselves to the myth of George III and his ministers as a puppet government run by Augusta and Lord Bute from the palace at Kew.[14] As a result, Goldsmith's treatment of Augusta and his choice of Kew inevitably implicated him in the factional skirmishes of the day, and his stance of disinterested patriotism became less easy to sustain. Certainly, in Thomas Chatterton's satire, "Kew Gardens," which he began sending to his publisher shortly after Augusta's death, the royal landscape is persistently articulated as a political space.[15] Indeed, one has to look hard for any appearance of Kew as a physical garden. Instead, Chatterton pointedly insists on a recognition of the physical landscape as a political entity. While the lake in Henry Jones's Kew acts as an image of a beneficent George and his nation, in Chatterton's poem "the sacred reservoirs of Kew" are drained to pay state pensions: Kew is the state, but the state is corrupt and its beauties are siphoned away. Where Jones has sheep feeding peacefully on the hillside, an image of lowly worth and happy sociability, in Chatterton they are marshaled by Augusta and Bute who plot and scheme as "the guiders of the tools who seem to guide." Jones himself is derided—somewhat inaccurately—for a poem in which

> Kitchen Gardens most luxuriant glow'd,
> With Flow'rs which ne'er in Mayo's Window blow'd:
> Where Cabbages exoticly divine,
> Were tagg'd in feet and measured with a Line.
> Ah! what invention grac'd the happy strain
> Well might the Laureat bard of Kew be vain.
>
> (ll. 115–20)

But the more serious charge than unfounded vanity on the part of Jones is that loyal panegyric sells out to a corrupt ministry intent on destroying the constitutional liberties of the state and pandering to the absolutism of monarchy. Thus while a Goldsmith or a Jones can indulge the politics of praise and attempt to naturalize the political both physically and intellectually, Chatterton's poem attempts to reverse that process in its flagrant disregard for its physical subject and its concentration on party issues and factional sniping. Chatterton himself looks back to an age before the present monarch and sees an almost prelapsarian Kew, "A place of Conversation for the Mind" now vitiated to "serve the purposes of Lust and Pride":

> But ah! how fallen from that better state!
> 'Tis now a heathen Temple of the great;
> Where sits the Female Pilot of the Helm
> Who shakes Oppression's fetters thro' the realm;
> Her name is Tyranny, and in a String,
> She leads the shadow of an infant King
>
> (ll. 175–86)

Jones's temples celebrating the victories of the Seven Years' War have become Chatterton's shrines to tyranny and oppression. And as the poet continues, the language of liberty so often applied to landscape design is transformed into the license of Augusta's lust for power and for Bute:

> Thy Garden's Elegance, thy Owner's State,
> The highest in the present List of Fate,
> Are Subjects where the Muse may *wildly range,*
> *Unsatiate in variety of Change.*
>
> (ll. 223–226; my emphasis)

Kew is transformed into a landscape of sexual and political excess as a lustful princess perverts the natural state. It is no longer the constitution of the state which demands variety but Augusta's sexual passion (see figures 19 and 20 for similar attacks from the popular press); the garden maps out not a stable if various order but an unquenchable thirst for frivolous novelty. That image of the garden as a false political state allows Chatterton to introduce all those other bugbears of the patriot opposition and of the poet in particular; his poem—loosely modeled on Charles Churchill's loosest of satiric forms—proceeds to inveigh against Bute, the Scots, Johnson, Shebbeare, North, Grafton, Mansfield, Sandwich, Fletcher Norton, and the entire population of Bristol.[16] There may well be an element of mere gesturing in all this, the attempt of a provincial poet to gain his own political patronage in opposition circles. Much of *Kew Gardens* consists of a minimal reworking of earlier poems, and the high incidence of missing names may suggest an attempt to trade off Whig paranoia and a consequent willingness to fill in the blanks rather than inside knowledge.[17] Certainly Horace Walpole, writing in 1778 and admittedly less than impartial at this point, could write admiringly of Chatterton's "strong vein of satire" but conclude, "He

Figure 19. "A View of Lord Bute's Erections at Kew; with some Parts of Kew Green, and Gardens," from the *Political Register*, 1767. "*I* A House built for lord Bute to *study in*, where none of his family resides. *K* A double row of trees, shading a gravel walk that leads down from lord Bute's house to *L*. *L* A door in the P.D. of Wales's garden-wall, which communicates with lord Bute's garden." British Library, PP3557ta. By permission of the British Library.

had no more principles than if he had been one of all our late administrations."[18] Nevertheless, Chatterton clearly picks up on one of the key points of sensitivity of the time, and in exploiting the relationship between Kew and faction he is not alone.

This conflict of opposing factions was to be played out more coherently in the clash between Sir William Chambers and the poet William Mason (aided by Walpole) which also took place in the year following the death of Augusta. The appointment of "Capability" Brown and his enormous popularity with the peerage in the 1760s was thought by many, including Horace Walpole, to be the stimulus for the attack on the modern landscape style—and Brown in particular—mounted by Chambers in his *Dissertation on Oriental Gardening* of 1772.[19] Given the hostile response to the *Dissertation* from Walpole and Mason, it is worth remembering that Chambers himself was characterized by Walpole as "a harmless Innovator of Taste": the attack on his Dissertation, as we will see, is overtly driven by political opportunism and the garden is claimed once again as a site for factional contest.[20] In 1773 Mason published *An Heroic Epistle to Sir William Chambers;* one of many replies to Chambers's *Dissertation*. The *Epistle* was produced in conjunction with Walpole, who provided copious manuscript note s to this and other satires by Mason (but these notes were to remain unpub-

Figure 20. "A View of the Princess Dowagers Palace at Kew," 1769. Augusta and the Earl of Bute can be seen embracing on the garden seat in the foreground to the right. British Museum, DG4330. Reproduced by courtesy of the Trustees of the British Museum.

lished until the 1920s).[21] Here Walpole spells out his own politics of taste, repeatedly merging the artistic, the economic, and the political into a single vision of culture, a culture that asserts property as the basis of constitutional and social stability. In this context, the years until the war with the American colonies are characterized in the popular if erroneous terms of an *"Empire of Freemen, an Empire formed by Trade, not by a military & conquering Spirit, maintained by the valour of independent Property, enjoying long tranquillity after virtuous struggles, & employing its opulence & good sense on the refinements of rational Pleasures."*[22] It is this very concatenation of terms—empire, freemen, trade, independent property, refinements, rational pleasures: the language of the "Old Whigs"—which drives Mason's satire and provides the coherence of focus for its attack. For Mason and Walpole, true taste in gardening is an expression of true politics, and the English garden's present perfection is the direct result of the progress of liberty, a progress now threatened by an encroaching monarchy. Walpole makes this point forcibly in a comment on Mason's major poem, *The English Garden:*

> The English Taste in Gardening is thus the growth of the English Constitution, & must perish with it. It must be rare under any arbitrary Government, because extensive property is possessed by very few, & by Those only while in favour . . .

Should Mr Mason's *English Garden* survive the Constitution it pictures, as it probably will for many ages, He will be the Second of our great Bards and Patriots, who has left a poem on *Paradise Lost.*[23]

Thus conceived, the English style of gardening is both a creation and a reflection of England's hard-won liberty and is set firmly against the false taste of the regular, indeed, according to this rhetoric, tyrannical designs characteristic of foreign, particularly French, gardens.

Mason's "Heroic Epistle" begins with an invocation to Chambers himself before moving on to George III, "Patron supreme of science, taste, and wit." Gathered around the monarch is his "chosen train," including Sir John Hill, Samuel Johnson, Shebbeare, and Tobias Smollett, all of whom Walpole characterizes in his notes as timeservers, charlatans, and hypocrites writing for the highest bidder or accepting government pensions. As the poem continues, it takes on that distinctly anti-Scottish bias prevalent in the 1760s and 1770s and focused on the apparently malign influence of Lord Bute. Thus "Mac-Ossian" joins Smollett, Hume, David Mallock, Robert and James Adam, and of course Chambers himself among the misguided circles of King George, and it is in this company that Chambers "Leap[s] each Ha Ha of truth and common sense" (l. 12) in his rejection of "Nature" both political and aesthetic. Quoting Pope's "Epilogue to the Satires," we are told "There was a time, 'in Esher's peaceful grove, / When Kent and Nature vy'd for Pelham's love'" (ll. 35–36), but with the arrival of Chambers that Whig magnate's garden—the product of nature—is rejected: Kent becomes "a Driveller" and Nature "a Drab." The attack continues by equating Chambers with Merlin's cave—recently removed from Richmond gardens by Brown—and so with the pretentious claims to learning and taste of Queen Caroline: his own pagodas and temples designed for the Princess Augusta are thus implicated as an attempt to restore the absurdities of an earlier generation (see figure 21). Indeed, in the final verse of this passage the message is made plain in a parody of Pope's line: "'A work to wonder at, perhaps a' Kew" (l. 70). Chambers's work becomes no more than a pompous rejection of Pope's acknowledged taste; with Pope's position as a founding father of the new style in gardening so firmly fixed in the eighteenth century, this perhaps was the greatest insult of all.

Continuing to follow Chambers's own *Dissertation*, Mason's poem moves on to the creation of sublime effects in the garden. But while following Chambers fairly closely with a garden full of snakes and lizards, prating parrots, and cats making "cruel love," the poem then turns from the sublime effects of the animal world to a social and ultimately political sublime. Thus, placed within a garden that should represent the beauties of constitutional politics we find the antisocial sublime of selfish political corruption. Rejecting the "foreign aid" of Chinese effects, Mason suggests the home-grown horrors of gibbets from Bagshot, powder mills from Hounslow, and, per-

Figure 21. "A View of the Wilderness with the Alhambra, the Pagoda, and the Mosque," from Sir William Chambers, *Plans, Elevations, Sections and Perspective Views of the Gardens and Buildings at Kew in Surry* (London, 1763). British Library, 649.c.25. By permission of the British Library.

haps most terrifying of all for George III, John Wilkes rattling his "gold chain" of office as the sheriff of London. Along with Newgate tales pinned to trees other horrors will include "B[u]te's confession, and his wooden head." Taking his lead from Chambers's assertion that the imperial Chinese gardens include a miniature version of the capital to amuse the emperor, Mason too will have a "mimic London," but one that at once recognizes the restricted view and the frivolity of royal designs. This monarch will be "Cast in the genuine Asiatic mould; / Who of three realms shall condescend to know, / No more than he can spy from Windsor's brow" (ll. 101–103). The microcosmic London is in fact the cue for a series of attacks on other individuals, "the minor plunderers of the age" (l. 93), many of whom are associated with Bute's brief administration or his continuing influence over the king. Thus the roll call includes the Adam brothers with their financially troubled Adelphi project; Samuel Martin, who dueled with Wilkes, and Jeremiah Dyson who rejected his republican upbringing for royalism, both of whom were in the service of Bute; Thomas Nowell, who in 1772 preached a sermon to the House of Commons in favor of royal prerogative; John Montagu, earl of Sandwich (alias Jemmy Twitcher), the one-time associate of Wilkes who later indicted him and Lord Chief Justice Mansfield, a friend of Bute's and frequently characterized as no friend of the jury system. It is the actions of these men which provide the "rural pastimes" of "Great B[ru]nw[ic]k's leisure" (ll. 135–136), but they do so while "Europe's balance trembles on its beam" (l. 140). The garden of King George is, then, an "Asiatic dream," a false paradise of leisure that prevents the king from taking up his true role within a constitutional monarchy. Indeed, the "Asiatic dream" points not simply to aesthetic taste but to a form of garden associated with the despotism of eastern monarchs. In this sense Chambers's Chinese style is claimed as a damningly appropriate representation of the false—despotic—political "style" of the garden's owner.[24]

For Mason, then, abuse of government and abuse of the garden are one. It is Chambers and his like—living by royal patronage and pandering to its whims—who represent an abuse of nature both aesthetic and political. Ironically exhorting Chambers to remodel Richmond gardens *à la chinois*, Mason assures him in the preface to the *Epistle*, that "under the auspicious patronage he now so justly enjoys, added to the *ready* vote of those who furnish ways and means, the royal work will speedily be compleated" (p. 4). Chambers, with his "unnatural" designs, deserves the patronage of a king whose government is equally unnatural. The "*ready* vote of those who furnish ways and means" is a misuse of that political power that has its basis in land; a misuse that may justly be termed corruption and that finds its image in the false ordering of the elements of nature. Chambers's designs are thus a debasement of "water, plants, and ground" (l. 46), and they produce a garden that is both unnatural and un-English. Indeed, the poem shows a suspicion of any garden system that attacks the Englishness of the English garden or seeks to replace it. To undermine the origin of the landscape garden is to deny the progression of English liberty from Saxon independence to a newly perfected—if threatened—constitutional system.

Shortly before the appearance of Mason's *Epistle*, Chambers published the *Explanatory Discourse* in order to defend his position from the numerous attacks it had already suffered.[25] As in his earlier work, the garden is treated as a formal problem; his design sets about producing "excitement" or "interest," but interest and excitement that appear not to be anchored, as in Mason's poems, to a particular political program. Thus, Chambers writes of "bridges, ruins, monumental urns, and other trifling decoration" or suggests that the gardener should open up recesses and "decorate them with objects."[26] In his earliest work, *Designs of Chinese Buildings* (1757), Chambers indeed likened architectural features to toys and the garden to an outdoor cabinet of curiosity; such "toys" are to be admired simply for their "oddity, prettyness, or neatness of workmanship," not for their role in part of a larger design.[27] In a letter defending the *Dissertation*, however, he argues that these architectural devices are merely "sportive episodes" and should be treated like "Interludes in a Drama." They are, he writes, "chiefly contrived to amuse the curious, the vulgar, or the childish," "great Nature, in various forms, & under various modifications, always appears triumphant."[28] Indeed, notwithstanding an apparently piecemeal approach to architectural features, Chambers's garden design contains notable similarities to that which Mason advocates. If one lays aside the somewhat overstrained attempts at sublimity, Chambers's designs recommend unexceptionably "English" features and are arguably more liberal in their construction than those of Mason. The *Explanatory Discourse* champions the removal of fences, the opening of gardens to the public (notably Richmond and Kew), the beauty of ordinary fields of corn being greater than that of the most carefully created lawn, and the recognition of "any tract of land . . . whose characteristic expressions have been strengthened by art" to be a garden.[29] Mason's attack, as a consequence, avoids recognizing such similarities and instead is aimed squarely at those political implications of Chambers's designs which pass beyond unproblematically patriotic features. By attacking the absurdities of the Chinese sublime, Mason attempts to enforce an interpretation of Chambers's work which denies those patriotic features and asserts a lack of moral value in the total design. It is this perceived lack of appropriate public meaning which provides a key element of Mason's *Epistle*. Without such meaning the garden becomes simply a playground for the emotions and loses any claim it may have to being a liberal art. Equally, the figures Mason enumerates in his satire, from George III to John Wilkes, represent that false political stance—whether radical or reactionary—which emphasizes the personal over the public. Those who fail in their public roles, by pandering to their personal natures, deserve and require such a garden as Chambers designs.

Some kind of response to this attack may be offered in a letter from Chambers to his Swedish friend, Count Scheffer. Writing of the recent political changes in Sweden, Chambers challenges the much vaunted political liberty of Britain and with it a form of landscape that claims itself as an image of that political aesthetic. He writes:

> I am fully persuaded, that perfect happiness cannot exist in any state, where liberty is stretched to its full extent, and power confined to its narrowest limits; wherever the balance is thus nicely poised, it never can be at rest; a breath of air, the weight of a feather makes it preponderate, and suffer a thousand vibrations before it fixes at the true point again.
>
> The English are for ever exulting in the Excellence of their constitution, and ever drawing haughty parallels between their liberty and the slavery of others, yet, there is not a more uneasy set of mortals upon the face of this little world. A spirit of general discontent rages through the Whole nation; they are; and at all times have been; dissatisfied with the prince, enraged at his ministers, displeased with their laws, disgusted with every thing about them: like children spoilt with too great indulgence, they cry for more while they have too much . . . [30]

English liberty is no longer an ideal balance, an ordered variety, but something dangerously close to chaos; the English may demand liberty but what they require is firm government.[31] And here it may become possible to map such a political vision of the nation against its aesthetic counterpart. If we return to Chambers's comments on the trivial nature of architectural ornament, we find the suggestion that variety of ornament serves merely to amuse "the curious, the vulgar, or the childish" while "great nature . . . always appears triumphant." In these terms, the variety inherent to the landscape garden's design—claimed by the likes of Mason in his long Georgic poem *The English Garden* to represent the variety of the constitution—dwindles into ornament, but ornament that may itself serve as a sop to the vulgar. Behind that ornament lies "great nature," the true state of things. And in the *Explanatory Discourse* Chambers offers us an image of this natural state as well. After all the suggestions for garden design in the Chinese style, Chambers continues:

> By these means this whole kingdom might soon become one magnificent vast Garden, bounded only by the sea; the many noble seats and villas with which it abounds, would give uncommon consequence to the scenery; and it might still be rendered more splendid, if, instead of disfiguring your churches with monuments, our Chinese manner of erecting mausoleums by the sides of the roads was introduced amongst you; and if all your public bridges were adorned with triumphal arches, rostral pillars, bas-reliefs, statues, and other indications of victory, and glorious atchievements in war: an empire transformed into a splendid Garden, with the imperial mansion [Windsor] towering on an eminence in the center, and the palaces of the nobles scattered like pleasure-pavilions amongst the plantations, infinitely surpasses any thing that even the Chinese ever attempted; yet vast as the design appears, the execution is certainly within your reach.[32]

It is an image of empire as garden and garden as empire, a whole nation formed into a spreading *ferme ornée*. Like that of Mason and Walpole, this garden, if not a result of *constitutional* growth, is yet an image of the political nation. But while Walpole and Mason's gardens seek to deny military spirit, this garden is made in the image of a nation building its wealth on military conquest. Indeed, that Tory polemic may extend further, for if Mason's landscape garden is an image of Whig oligarchy, Chambers's appears as that of Tory monarchism. In this vision of the garden the "imperial mansion" towers on an eminence at the center of the landscape. Chambers has produced a piece of Tory topography. It is a vision that looks from the center out, and what it sees from that position is not diverse centers of aristocratic power—not the aesthetic and political variety of Mason's mixed government—but mere pleasure palaces, palaces that gain their significance only as they relate to that single central eminence.[33]

As with Chatterton and Jones, both sides of the political debate of course maneuver to claim the natural as their own—to claim a kind of normative common sense so popular with modern governments—and both also set about constructing an appropriate tradition in which to ground such claims. If this reading of the Mason-Chambers debate suggests divisive factionalism, any threat to the established political system is far more apparent than real. As Colley has argued of parliamentary factionalism in the eighteenth century, while there was plenty of argument about detail, there was also a basic assumption that the system as a whole was beautiful, indeed, it was that very system that allowed for factional debate and had precluded the need for violent confrontation of the previous century.[34] At Kew the factional rivalries being fought within Parliament are played out also in a garden that claims to represent that Parliament. Crucially, then, Mason and Chambers are fighting over essentially the same space—both political and physical—and the arguments their texts employ are set strictly within the finite realms of a propertied political elite. There may be tensions, but they are tensions the gardens succeed in containing, indeed, tensions the garden is designed to contain. If, as Colley has argued, political elections served to reinforce a widespread confidence in the parliamentary system— despite that system's excluding the majority from its franchise—the political arguments engaged in within the garden reinforce that system in their fundamental assumptions about the importance of land. The design of the nation's gardens is important precisely because it is recognized as an image of the nation's politics: both have land as their basis, both place the landowner in his natural position as the leader of arts and men. Equally, however, both also make that crucial shift from physical struggle into safer realms of parliamentary and aesthetic debate.

But such a singularity of view, however internally contested, was itself to come under pressure, and the recognition of different modes of interpretation became an increasing source of anxiety in the final decades of the century. Arguably, the most influential garden in the eighteenth century continued to be the biblical Paradise, and this image of a lost garden was fundamentally moral and spiritual even as it lent itself to political interpretation. But that sense of the garden as a moral topos was to become problematic as designed landscape found itself increasingly immersed in the far less simply moral worlds of commerce, fashion, and politics. If there had been some possibility of the patrician elite's claiming the physical garden as a reclaiming of Paradise, not least with the growth of nonestablishment religions and the rise in economic power of different groups within society came an awareness that "culture" did not just belong to a landowning elite with a monopoly on moral and economic discourse: the garden was thus to be implicated in the politics of landowning and increasingly of class. It is in this context that we can turn to John Wesley and to the satires on Methodism.

Wesley's enormous travels gave him the opportunity to visit many of the great gardens of Britain, and he assiduously recorded his views about them in his journals. While he found much to admire and demonstrated his awareness of contemporary aesthetics, his response remained morally ambiguous, tempered as it was by an apocalyptic Christian faith. Quite typically, at Piercefield in South Wales, after describing the beauties of the embellished landscape, he concludes, "And must all these be burned up? What will become of us then, if we set our hearts upon them?"[35] While at Stourhead he records, "Others were delighted with the temples, but I was not: (1) Because several of the statues about them were mean; (2) because I cannot admire the images of devils, and we know the gods of the heathens are but devils; (3) because I defy all mankind to reconcile statues with nudities, either to common sense or common decency."[36] Such attacks on the triviality, indeed immorality, of physical gardens have an impact on those who own them: in questioning the aesthetic value of such design, a spiritual engagement with the garden here implicitly challenges landed culture's self-representation and justification. It is the kind of views expressed in these diary entries which become the stuff of Richard Graves's anti-Methodist satire, *The Spiritual Quixote, or The Summer's Ramble of Mr. Geoffry Wildgoose* (1773).[37] Graves had personal reasons for disliking Methodism, and his novel plays off an unsettlingly itinerant religion against the stable culture of the landowning elite. In fact his target is George Whitefield, in whose steps his eponymous hero attempts to follow, and it is Wildgoose's apparent Methodistical "enthusiasm" in the manner of Whitefield which is finally recognized as selfish and unsocial. Whitefield himself is not spared, appearing in person as nothing more than a self-serving, self-important spouter of "Gospel *lingo*" (7:1). And Graves's account of Methodism adopts the familiar approach of equating social and geographical movement with false religion and anarchic disrespect for the established order.[38] But what is of note for our purposes is that Graves chooses to play out a part of that attack in the context of the garden.

Indeed, Graves's novel forms one of the most extensive treatments of the garden in eighteenth-century fiction. Not only are the gardens of the famous considered—the poet William Shenstone's Leasowes receiving the greatest attention—but the smaller gardens of the middling sort are equally employed to claim a necessary relationship between the inner man and his restructuring of nature. Wildgoose, the hero of the novel, is a lay preacher, an enthusiast, and inevitably therefore a misguided soul. As an outsider to the conventional wisdom on garden design, Wildgoose allows Graves both to question and affirm its propriety. On reaching the famed Leasowes, Wildgoose, "with a truly enthusiastic spirit," observed that

> such gardens were the most innocent of any amusements; but that we should consider them as amusements only; and not let them engross much of our attention;—that we ought to spiritualize our ideas, not forgetting that the *fall* of our first parents was in the garden of Paradise—and that it was not worth while to enquire, how far too violent a fondness for these things might inter-

fere with our love of God; and attach us too strongly to the things of this world. (2:127)

The language is very close to that of Wesley's journals, but such notions are effectively discredited by Wildgoose's later action: in a fit of religious enthusiasm, he commits the heinous crimes of damaging property and invading the rights of others by breaking Shenstone's cisterns and toppling his statues (see figure 22). What we see in such moments is the recognition of a threat to the established order, even as that threat is shifted into the realms of the ridiculous. Wildgoose may be wrong, but he tramples on the roots of landed power in his rejection of established parochial religion and the aesthetics of the landowning elite. The kind of spiritual understanding of the garden we find in the diaries of Whitefield and Wesley becomes unsettlingly inappropriate for establishment culture. If Graves is close to Wesley in the spiritual language of his misguided hero, however, his narrator is closer to John Shebbeare's association of Methodism with the language of the mob, with selfishness, with a boisterous loss of control last seen during the Civil War; and in these terms Methodism's foray into the garden is a demagogic articulation of the dangerously misguided and disruptive voice of the people. The destruction of Shenstone's garden dramatizes the fear that wild spiritualism, itinerancy, and rejection of a settled parochial structure will ultimately destroy the established natural order. Indeed, Graves's position may be more conservative still in that the Shenstone myth, even by this time, is of a man living beyond his means in creating a garden that foolishly rejects georgic production for a frail pastoral fashion consciousness. Shenstone risks losing sight of the genuine moral claims of landowning and Wildgoose's attack, the physical articulation of a popular spiritualism, presages the resultant threat of social disorder. In *The Spiritual Quixote* these destructive forces can soon be annulled, and Shenstone quickly reerects his statues and mends his cisterns; but we have nevertheless been offered an alternative perspective to that of the dominant landowning culture, and this recognition of different modes of interpretation was to become an increasing source of anxiety in the final decades of the century.

It is these alternative claims for moral ownership of the landscape which Oliver Goldsmith was to explore in another poem of the early 1770s, his *Deserted Village.* A far more complex poem than the hurriedly composed *Threnodia Augustalis, The Deserted Village* laments the loss of an organic rural community and a countryside depopulated as a result of "luxurious" trade.[39] Goldsmith's poem is driven by the loss of a landscape and its culture and by their replacement with the alien values of a landscape garden that is the commercial vision writ large. The poem works in part by a very basic contrast of before and after ("A time there was . . . But times are altered" (ll. 57–63), one culture versus another, and it is this structure that allows the

Figure 22. Frontispiece to volume 3 of Richard Graves, *The Spiritual Quixote*, second edition (London, 1773). Cambridge University Library, 7720.d.186. By permission of the Syndics of Cambridge University Library.

variety and range of subjects Goldsmith covers—from the vicar and school-teacher to city life and the wilderness of foreign lands. Thus, while little is said about the aesthetics of the new physical landscape where "one master grasps the whole domain" (l. 39), the garden is defined by the absences it creates, the subjects of Goldsmith's poem representing all the things this garden destroys or fails to be. An important point to stress is that the term *garden* here encompasses not simply the physical or aesthetic but the social and political; and this in itself highlights the nature of the garden as an index of the culture that produces it. That is, it is a mistake to think of the garden simply as a physical object; rather, it is the site for a wide range of cultural concerns, social, political, and aesthetic. It is this which Goldsmith recognizes and explores in the wide range of subjects he represents as the negatives and absences the landscape garden engenders. Thus, in a poem ostensibly concerned with the sweeping away of a village in order to create a landscape park, Goldsmith is able to merge moral tropes and visual images of village life and depopulation, luxurious trade and agricultural prosperity, the evils of the city and the results of emigration; country virtue is challenged by commercial vice; time-honored land use bows to the pressure of fashionable aesthetics.[40] Finally, the story of Auburn comes to represent the age-old narrative of empires falling prey to decadence and decay. The "poor, houseless, shivering female" with "her virtue fled" is herself the image of such a society. Leaving her "wheel and robes of country brown" and "ambitious of the town" her fate presages that not only of Auburn but of a nation that rejects or enforces the rejection of country values for the false trading ambitions of the city (ll. 326–336).

As recent work has suggested, however, the distinction between country and city, land and trade, was never as firmly established as literary writing might suggest.[41] In contrast to that account of historical change which argues for a structural transformation of society from the feudal to the capitalist—with its need for neat oppositions—recent work has illustrated the extent to which members of the great landowning families were themselves involved in the city and large-scale commercial activity. Far from shunning that world of commerce and retreating to the doomed paradise of an outmoded country estate, many families were putting younger sons into the great commercial houses and reaping substantial financial benefits from that relationship to the point where "city" money became a crucial means of supporting the "landed" estate. What Goldsmith's poem points to with great clarity then is not a reality of opposition between land and trade but the need for the landowning interest to maintain such a fiction.[42] In claiming the country at the expense of trade, the landowning elite could neatly divert attention from their own economic activity while also claiming the traditional moral high ground of cultural debate. They emphasized in the land, that is, the one thing that established a sense of difference from other commercial adventures. In turn, this meant also the ability to maintain the social and political cachet of land as the basis of cultural values, itself articulated in terms of a liberal view and independence not available to the professional and trading classes.

But if Goldsmith's poem bewails the growth of a new commercial culture, it is also a poem in which the poetic voice is itself displaced, no longer neatly a part of the old patrician order. And while the poem may seem conservative in its reaction to commerce, it nevertheless lays stress on an individual sensibility quite distinct from the moral and aesthetic claims of ownership. In a move characteristic of sentimental writing, *The Deserted Village* offers scenes of individual suffering and individual loss which stand for much larger social and economic forces but which cannot adequately represent them. As in *The Vicar of Wakefield*, Goldsmith's benevolence is unable fully to imagine large-scale political ills or their redress. Instead, we are offered the plight of the lone figure, the "sad historian of the pensive plain," an image of conservative anger yet also of political impotence (see figure 23). In the face of that impotence, we are invited to indulge our sympathy, to experience the suffering of a figure who is at once the dispossessed woman telling her tale and a trope for the poet and his own sense of loss. The movement outward toward mankind as a whole finally returns us to a concern for self, both of poet and reader. Indeed, central to the construction of the poem is the reconstruction of a lost world around that individual sensibility, and in this sense the poem can be aligned with the growing challenge to aristocracy and its landscapes and in particular to the patrician reading of landscape gardens as an unproblematic image of Britain's constitutional liberties and of the landowner's right to rule. The increasing emphasis on the sensibility of the individual and the concomitant rise of a broader if vaguer polite language of the aesthetic could hint at the rejection of ownership as the arbiter of value. It is tempting to turn, as have many recent critics, to the rise of the picturesque as a fashionable mode of perception, or at least a fashionable mode of language, in order to suggest the growth of interest in an individual response to landscape unconstrained by the high politics of monarchy or by the class politics of the late eighteenth-century aristocracy. The picturesque scenes through which the fashionable traveler passes appear to offer a landscape of individual freedom of response where ownership, if not absent, is at least not apparent.

Even if freedom of response is a possibility for the feeling few, that sense of subjective response is as likely to be subsumed within the shared language of fashion and taste where different pressures impinge. Indeed, one way of making sense of the vast increase in travel and travel writing in the eighteenth century is in terms of a polite culture attempting to represent its communal concerns. As Paul Langford has pointed out, the term *polite* is itself ambiguous.[43] If it was associated with "the trappings of propertied life," it was also concerned with aping the manners and morals of social superiors, with aesthetic and intellectual taste, and notably in the later eighteenth century with sentiment and "feeling." As Langford writes, "The essence of politeness was often said to be that *je ne sais quoi* which distinguished the innate gentleman's understanding of what made for civilized conduct, but this did not inhibit others from seeking more artificial means of acquiring it."[44] Inevitably this meant also the constant application of double standards: to rise in society one aped the manners of one's social superiors but sneered at those lower on the social ladder attempting the same

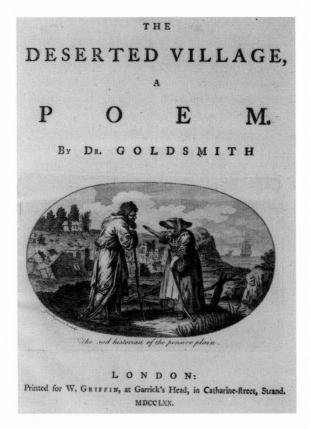

Figure 23. "The Sad Historian of the Pensive Plain," title
page of Oliver Goldsmith, *The Deserted Village: A Poem*
(London, 1770). Cambridge University Library,
7720.b.233. By permission of the Syndics of Cambridge
University Library.

thing. Hence in part the bickering in travel writing over how one should
describe a given scene. But if the large-scale landowner used the "natural"
garden to imply an equal naturalness in his social and political position,
others were to use that same space to assert their own membership in the
polite world. And part of the success of polite culture as a broad culture of
the propertied came from an increasing confidence in an equally broad language of taste, a language that remains very much in use today. In words
such as *beautiful, lovely, grand,* and *pretty* we see an aesthetic language that is
broad enough to include a wide range of responses and speakers within a
narrow range of terms. Whatever else it may be, such a language seems

inherently nonexclusive; it throws emphasis on a shared—if by definition banal—social response.

Indeed, this very lack of complication becomes a means of cementing the ties of polite culture: this is not the language of an elite connoisseurship, nor is it concerned with being overly precise. The interest of such language lies exactly in its quotidian nature. While the leisure activity of travel itself excluded the majority of eighteenth-century society outside of the proper-tied classes, within its own terms this language of taste became one of the means by which members of "respectable" society could demonstrate such membership: one may not *own* a landscape garden, but if one can appreci-ate its value then one can also make some claim to being a part of the cul-ture that produces it. Terms such as *lovely* and *beautiful* and the emphasis on nebulous private feeling allowed that claim to be made by a substantial sec-tion of society. In so doing they inherently challenged the claims of patri-cian culture to the singular control of aesthetic meaning.

In the widespread use of this language we see what one might term a democratization of aesthetic space, for the range of people claiming the garden as their own is massively broadened. As Ann Bermingham has argued more specifically in terms of the picturesque, "In aestheticising the natural and often commonplace scenery of Britain, the Picturesque awakened a large segment of the population to the realisation that aesthetic judgement was not the gift of the privileged few but could be learned by anyone and applied to just about anything."[45] One reaction to that democratization of the aesthetic can be seen in the large number of novels that satirized popu-lar "taste" while demonstrating their own good judgment and membership in the polite world. In *John Buncle, Junior,* of 1778, the famous gardens at Stowe become a site for the moral meditations of a group of fictional char-acters, and garden design offers the opportunity to demonstrate exclusions within an ostensibly egalitarian culture. Again, this sense of exclusion pivots on the notion of polite discourse itself. Considering the vogue for senti-mental publications, Buncle asserts that in the present age they are "pecu-liarly acceptable, as they neither require deep attention to investigate them, nor recollection to fix them in the mind"; instead they leave the sentimen-talist "happily exempt from the toil of study." As a result, "all our modern productions, whether sermons, essays, novels, romances, or comedies, are become so wonderfully sentimental! Nay our very news-papers, and the advertisements in them, abound with refined ideas, and affect to breathe a delicate sensibility."[46] The distaste toward the leveling—for Buncle, debas-ing—effect of sentimental discourse is here apparent, most notably in the final jibe over newspapers. Buncle aligns himself quite openly with the con-cerns of a literate and literary culture that seeks to differentiate itself from any kinship claims in the advertisements of mere tradesmen. It should be no surprise, then, that in the letter that follows—on "Affectations"—Buncle indulges in a tirade on the pretensions of a pair of gaudy countrywomen claiming to be nobility, and he does so in terms of their "vague ill directed applause, their extasy at trifles, and their insensibility to real beauties."[47] Real taste, and real feeling are set against the mere outward display of sentimental language; but the very pliability of that language is nevertheless recognized as a threat, for it allows the pretentiousness Buncle decries.

In the final decades of the century there was if anything an increasing insistence on both the Englishness of the landscape garden and the need for a "correct" understanding of its nature. While John Moore's *Zeluco* (1789) provided the famous example of Mr. Transfer, the city financier, filling his newly bought estate with statues he is unable to recognize,[48] by the late 1790s anti-Jacobin propagandists were turning once again to the patriotic Englishness of garden design. Arguably, accounts of gardens in the 1790s respond more to events in France than to the older factional divisions within British politics and claim the English garden as an unexceptionable emblem of English liberty.[49] In 1799 George Walker published his anti-Jacobin novel *The Vagabond*, a work that ridiculed the New Philosophy of Godwin and his followers. Early in the second volume of the work, the foolish and misled Doctor Alogos is forced to beat a hasty retreat to his country house after his audience of supposedly Jacobin country folk turn on him. As this "Church and King" mob rushes toward his house, the wish of Doctor Alogos for their further liberty rapidly evaporates, "'Oh! Curse it,' cried Doctor Alogos, 'they seem to have liberty enough; they are treading down my fine flower garden like a herd of swine: there go all my exotic shrubs!— I believe they are a troop of Goths and Vandals, who pay no regard to science.'" His niece replies in the voice of anti-Jacobin common sense: "My dear uncle they are all gone mad; they are talking about rights and liberties, and destroying every thing before them."[50] Set in an English estate, Walker's image of the destruction of "exotic shrubs" is less than subtle: fine flowers and foreign "science" contain the seeds of their own destruction and the false charms of the exotic, of that which is not native to Britain, should be eschewed by the responsible landowner. Walker insists throughout the novel that the common people are unworthy of that liberty the landowner possesses. Alogos's attempt to fire the mob with libertarian enthusiasm results in the destruction of all before them, both good and bad; his flower garden is trampled and his ancient house is destroyed by fire. For Walker, exotic flowers of any sort are out of place in the national garden, and the natural state—physical, political, social, and moral—must be defended from such foreign incursions.

If we cannot reclaim the private experience of the majority of garden visitors in the eighteenth century, we can look at the way in which a polite language of the aesthetic is claimed by various groups, at the fear of that kind of language expressed by some writers, and at the attempts of almost all to claim it for themselves at the expense of others. And in this we can see the growth of a polite—propertied—culture that challenges the aesthetic control of a patrician elite even as it seeks to become a part of that culture. The later eighteenth century presents a continuing series of battles for control over socioaesthetic space, and in these terms "aesthetic" texts (broadly defined) are an expression of class formation and the tensions within that formation. Equally it becomes impossible to *fix* the social groupings of the "polite" insofar as this sense of politeness is concerned as much with exclusiveness as it is with inclusiveness. Attempts to claim the language of taste are inevitably made at the expense of others, and while all stand to gain by this notion of an undifferentiated culture of the propertied classes—the middling in the possibility of moving up, the aristocracy in the ability to reassert their leadership of a society undergoing fundamental change—all are equally concerned with acts of differentiation. The linguistic infighting within even a single garden such as Kew itself points to the perceived importance of aesthetic *as* social and political space, the garden as a key meeting point of those spheres, and the importance therefore of claiming the garden as one's own. Thus, while the rise of sensibility and an increasing emphasis on feeling make it tempting to suggest a chronology of rediscovered aesthetic space replacing an older politicization of that space, in practice such a process was far from complete by 1800: in the late eighteenth century land was not to lose its political value, nor could the garden remain exempt from its claims.

The Pastoral Revolution

Michael McKeon

My subject in this essay is the ancient genre of pastoral poetry, the form "itself," and, more centrally, its transformation in England toward the end of the early modern period. I use quotation marks here because I believe generic form, although conceptually distinguishable from the historical existence of that genre, cannot be separated from it in analytic practice. And yet genre history—in fact, any history—can have no meaning if it does not attend both to the elements of discontinuity that signal change and to the thread of continuity by virtue of which we acknowledge that some integral and coherent entity has indeed changed. The history of pastoral in this period is a striking and problematic case in point. On the one hand, under the influence of fundamental material development, the ancient form might seem to undergo a transformation so great as to render questionable the very notion of its formal persistence. On the other hand, this generic transformation may be felt to be fully predicated on the plasticity of the ancient genre. By this understanding, pastoral attains a form that, always potential within it, by the end of the eighteenth century serves as a cultural screen against which material change itself acquires not only its meaning but its ongoing intelligibility.

In order to explicate the complexity of this movement, I will begin by making reference to the poetic practice of classical antiquity. I will then turn to the early modern context in an effort to suggest how deeply pastoral discourse and material experience—that is to say, economic, social, and political experience—are implicated in one another. Although my topic fully justifies the extended chronology of 1642–1789, for reasons of space I will largely confine my allusions to the discourse of eighteenth-century authors and texts.

WHAT IS PASTORAL?

It's evident enough that ancient pastoral is defined thematically by its celebration of rural life and rustic values. But this truth needs to be complicated
by the recognition—also evident enough—that the pastoral praise of the
country intimately and insistently invokes the counterstandard of the
"urban," the negative pole in opposition to which pastoral praise acquires
its meaning. This basic oppositional structure, grounded in a spatial or geographical antithesis between country and city, rural and urban, yields a
familiar series of value-laden extensions: simplicity versus sophistication,
innocence versus corruption (or experience), contemplation versus action,
contentment versus ambition, private retirement versus public activity,
otium versus *negotium,* peace versus war, communal affiliation versus individual aggression (or industry), and so forth. At the most fundamental level,
these analogous articulations are mutually translatable as the abstract opposition between nature and artifice (or simply art).

From this perspective, pastoral is also an ancient form of satirical or "political" poetry, because the praise of one term always carries a reciprocal, if
sometimes only implicit, critique of the latter. But as the need for doubling
(is it corruption or experience? aggression or industry? artifice or art?) suggests, the political charge of pastoral, the basic direction of its critique, is less
predictable than this implies. Doesn't pastoral also reflect on the rude and
uncultured way of life from the more refined and valorized vantage point of
cultivation? Received wisdom, referring us to the exemplary case of Virgil,
would argue that this perspective is the normative posture not of "pastoral"
but of "georgic." At the beginning of his career Virgil wrote "eclogues,"
which embody the basic value system I have just described and which posterity learned to call "pastorals." The *Georgics* are the work of Virgil's mid-career,
as distinct (in this view) from the *Eclogues* as labor is from leisure.[1]

Now, there is no doubt that the very purpose of the *Georgics*—they aim to
provide farmers hearty instruction in the science of productive husbandry—enjoins a very different relationship to nature than the humble
modes of habitation bespoken by the subtly modulated voice of the *Eclogues.*
Indeed, Virgil conceived the *Georgics* as an experimental poetic enterprise
implicitly analogous to the technological experiments that are the subject
of his poem (I, 40–42). Yet the *Georgics* and the *Eclogues*—vigorous land cultivation and tranquil animal herding—also operate within the same basic
scheme of oppositions, and each may be felt periodically to enact a value
reversal that runs counter to what appears to be its more customary com-
mitment. This can be seen in the space of a single book of the *Georgics.* The
second book begins by cheerfully instructing the industrious reader-farmer
to master nature and her lore, to domesticate and improve the wild through
hybrids, cuttings, grafts, transplants, and the like (II, 35–82). By the end of

the book, however, the terrifying specter of war has transformed the normative farmer into one who would shun the unnatural luxuries bred by foreign intercourse and the seductive perils of urban and courtly ambition.
The point is not to condemn culture and the mastery of nature's lore but to
validate as an equally blessed alternative a life lived at peace with a bountiful nature and her gods, a *locus amoenus* of uncultivated plenty that Virgil
compares to life in the Saturnian Golden Age (II, 458–542).[2]

This georgic vision recalls nothing so much as that of the famous fourth
eclogue, the rapt prophecy of a restored golden age predicated on perpetual peace and the autoproductivity of an unforced nature. But the reversal
of values can be seen to operate within the eclogues as well. In the second
eclogue Virgil impersonates the love-mad shepherd Corydon, whose naive
complaint to his beloved Alexis acutely internalizes the amused disdain of
the sophisticate for the humble bumpkin:

> If only paltry woods and fields could please you!
> We would dwell in lowly cottages, shoot deer,
> Drive herds of goats with switches cut from greenwood.
> . . . .
> Corydon, you country boy! Alexis scorns
> Your gifts—nor could they match Iollas'.[3]

In fact, the familiar topoi of the complaint and the contest remind us
that a species of ambition and *negotium* is inseparable from pastoral values
and that the *Eclogues* are insistent in their thematization of the normative
"artistry" of emulation, competition, and craftsmanship. Already in Theocritus, the capacity for artfulness was central to the characterization of natural humanity.

For these reasons, it seems to me important to recognize that the *Eclogues*
and the *Georgics* are opposed to each other in a way that is not dichotomous but continuous and dialectical. Recollecting his own youthful exercise in pastoral song, Virgil in fact ends the *Georgics* with the opening line
of the *Eclogues*. And this has significant implications for the basic oppositional structure that provides the foundation for pastoral poetry. To speak
(as I have done) of a periodic "reversal of values" in pastoral suggests that
we need to complicate our view of the function of the genre—the celebration of rural life and rustic values—at least by acknowledging how pastoral
also works on occasion to satirize these values according to the positive standard of urban cultivation. But my brief reading of ancient pastoral suggests
that a more fundamental reversal of values is also at work in these poems.
In conspicuously disclosing the art—of song, of husbandry, of emulation, of
identification—of which these artless herdsmen are capable, ancient pastoral does not so much devalue nature as relativize it, dispersing what has

already been posited as a unitary, discrete category into a plurality of more or less "natural" embodiments.

In the first eclogue Tityrus ruefully recalls his error in supposing life to be composed of just such a sliding scale of continuity:

> The city they call Rome, my Melibee,
> I like a fool thought like our own, where shepherds
> Drive down the new-weaned offspring of their sheep.
> Pups are like dogs, kids are like mother goats
> I knew, and thus compared great things and small.
> But she, among cities, holds her head aloft
> As cypresses among the creeping shrubs.
>
> (I, 19–25, pp. 10–11)

Tityrus discovers that Italy is divided into Rome on the one hand and the provinces on the other—although the figure by which Rome's utter difference is expressed ("as cypresses among the creeping shrubs") may be felt, in the near conflation of the natural, also to affirm a degree of similarity. And yet the force of his friend's lament is to destabilize this discovery. Evicted from his farm, Meliboeus confronts the prospect of exile to remote and alien lands, in absolute contrast to which his "country" now stands as a valorized and undivided emblem of home:

> Ah, but we others leave for thirsty lands—
> Africa, Scythia, or Oxus' chalky waves,
> Or Britain, wholly cut off from the world.
> Shall I ever again, within my country's borders,
> With wonder see a turf-heaped cottage roof,
> My realm, at last, some modest ears of grain?
>
> (I, 64–69, pp. 14–15)

Patriotism complicates pastoralism. The pun on "country" of which the English translation is capable (contrast Virgil's *patrios*) draws attention to the convertibility of terms, the way great things may indeed be compared with small: Rome is to the provinces as all of Italy is to foreign soil. But the pun also helps disclose the complexity of the proportional comparison as it really works here, the way its terms have been transvalued so as to insist that Rome is to the provinces as foreign lands are to all of Italy. Exile to the hinterlands, which in "strict pastoral" terms we might expect to see as a positive rustication, is figured instead as a loss. This sentiment in itself is not surprising. But in the immediate pastoral context the sentiment is expressed through the paradoxical implication that to leave the hub of civilization is to leave the rustic farm and homestead, the center of pastoral values.

On this basis one might say that Virgil's first eclogue tacitly teaches the lesson that the meaning of "nature" is always from a perspective, within a certain context. A similar lesson organizes more explicitly what may be for eighteenth-century readers the most influential of Horace's pastorals, the second epode. All but the last few lines of the poem are dedicated to the description of an idyllic rural retreat whose "georgic" concern with honest, strictly domestic, husbandry is preceded by the famous "pastoral" invocation of a life devoid of *negotium:*

> Happy the man who, far from business and affairs
> Like Mortals of the early times,
> May work his father's fields with oxen of his own,
> Exempt from profit, loss, and fee . . .

The end of the poem abruptly sets a framing context for this vision:

> Now with these words the money-lender Alfius,
> Soon, soon to be a country squire,
> Revoked all mid-month loans at interest,—
> But plans relending on the first.[4]

From this perspective, the genial georgic *otium* of the rural retreat (the epode's celebrated first line is *Beatus ille qui procul negotiis*) is suddenly rendered continuous with—financially dependent on and morally inseparable from—the urban *negotium* of the parvenu moneylender. If the ostensible reflection is on Alfius the moneylender, who lacks even the courage of his effrontery, the underlying (and rather more powerful) critique is of the simplicity with which "pastoral" oppositions between country innocence and city corruption are conventionally affirmed.

But my point, of course, is that pastoral works both to affirm and to suspend such oppositions—to conceive them, that is, not dichotomously but dialectically. Pastoral exists to oppose nature and art in such a way as to intimate simultaneously their interpenetration. This is recognizably the structural or presentational premise of the genre. Structural anthropology has made us mindful of the way dichotomous opposition works to help us think. Pastoral exploits and improves on this mechanism by incorporating into its operation the more or less explicit intuition that the oppositions on which it structures itself are potentially defective. As Frank Kermode remarks, "The first condition of Pastoral is that it is an urban product."[5] An artful impersonation of nature, pastoral deploys the sophisticated technology of poetic culture to represent its absence, and it is in the self-consciousness of this paradox that we recognize the characteristic complexity of the genre.

In Theocritus, and then quintessentially in Virgil, this is first of all a complexity of form and tone, a layering of lyric, dramatic, and narrative modes whose resulting multivocality both articulates and conflates the voices of which it is composed. By these means pastoral is felt to be inseparably "about" both nature and the poetic technique by which nature is enclosed and represented. But the formal and tonal complexity of the genre is the means by which its characteristic complication of geographical, cultural, and axiological relations is also ensured. Pastoral is the supreme poetic form of conventionality: not only because it presents itself as a critique of (social, political, poetic) convention; nor only because it (inevitably) elaborates this critique in conventional ways; but because, in seeking to be mindful of both these conditions at once, it takes as its subject the problem of conventionality itself. The instability of pastoral is therefore not an adventitious accident or a historical accretion but congenital and constitutive of it as a genre. Pastoral is a cultural mechanism whose poetic and ideological function is to test the dialectical fluidity of dichotomous oppositions.

PASTORAL AND PERIODIZATION

If the argument of pastoral is fundamentally one of location and geography, it is also, by a familiar and resonant extension, one of temporality and time. Pastoral's temporal dimension can be felt as a subtly emotional inflection of spatial detachment, the evocation of an immediacy that is nonetheless elusive, perhaps irreversibly unavailable. Like the *locus amoenus* of unmotivated—and therefore endless—delight, the pastoral countryside and its innocent dramas feel charmed into timelessness by the round of seasons that freeze nature apart from our flux of culture and change. Thus informed in a general way with the aura of a perpetual past "when life was simpler," pastoral also may render temporal detachment explicit, through a framing retrospection to the time when Daphnis still sang, or to the time before war and trade corrupted the land, or to the Age of Gold or the Garden of Eden. In all such retrospects, it is the past that is given the normative charge, even if it is "the past" as it is felt still to suffuse our present.

Yet the tacit implication of the temporal within the spatial is also available in a contrary, urbanist register, as in the suggestive opposition between "backwardness" and "development." And this suggests the way the temporal opposition in pastoral becomes hospitable to the sort of dialectical complication characteristic of its spatial analogue. If the *locus amoenus* is "now," how were things different "then"? In the fourth eclogue the initially intelligible distinction between past and present is quickly clouded not by the mildly paradoxical prospect of a golden age of the future—"redeunt Saturnia regna"—but because the narrative logic of this prospect leads Virgil's account of how we get there to run simultaneously both forward and backward through the history of civilization. The iron age both dies and converges with the golden, and the temporal borders erected to distinguish innocence from guilt, hope from desperation, helplessly bleed into one another. Just as ancient "pastoral" demonstrates its ready incorporation of "georgic" values, so this logic reveals the genre's capacity to celebrate at once the antithetical norms of a primitivist and a progressive historiography.

The fourth eclogue is also the supreme and concentrated instance of the more diffuse pastoral tendency to challenge the powers of normative periodization through, not skepticism, but a kind of supersaturation. The multiplication of retrospects and ruptures, some personal, some historical; the competition between alternative temporal divides, all of compelling authenticity for disparate speakers; these temporalizing projects need not accompany in any precise way the destabilizations of spatial opposition that I have already described as fundamental to pastoral, but they reinforce its basic dialectical tendency. The effect is to relativize periodization even as it is promoted. The sense of time as an apocalyptic watershed coexists with the sense of time as history, as a dialectical construct in which the past acquires meaning as a projection of the present's understanding of its own alterity. Although most pastoral poetry does not complicate its treatment of temporality to this degree, it is in this respect that I want to suggest that the genre takes as its subject the problem of periodicity itself.

There is another way in which Virgil's fourth eclogue paradigmatically enacts pastoral's concern with periodization. Here the concern is an "extrinsic" feature of the poem's interpretation which parallels the "intrinsic" preoccupation with temporal divisions that I have just discussed. The celebrated Christian allegorization of the fourth eclogue reconceived it for a new epoch according to the subtle teleology of typological thought. By this reading, pagan pastoral is subjected to a normative transvaluation, annulled and revived at a higher level. The interpretive history of the poem as proleptic sacred prophecy therefore recapitulates the history—of past as future, of the golden age as the time to come—it narrates. Once again, however, the fourth eclogue only concentrates a pervasive tendency of pastoral interpretation to repeat, in its generic histories, a temporalized version of the genre's constitutive instability. Theocritus is the unequaled founder of the form, but pious Virgil imitates him with such surpassing skill that he reinvents—or "institutionalizes"—the form in a new mode. In this familiar view, Theocritean origins are associated with a "natural" and relatively immediate rusticity that is both subsumed and preserved by the idealizing and sophisticated artifice of Virgil. And although this view invites us to oppose the nature of Theocritus to the art of Virgil, it also presupposes their unity under the aegis of a common pastoral purpose. Indeed, the opposition is recognizably a periodization of the singing contests whose modest emulativeness ruffles the rural calm in both poets. A yet subtler evocation of their debate may be sensed in the elegiac mode that sometimes colors those contests: Virgil's Menalcas is to his Daphnis not only as Theocritus's Thyrsis is to *his* Daphnis but also as Virgil is to Theocritus and as the Roman present is to the Greek past.[6]

Of course, the problem of periodicity is central to any essay in literary history that takes its task seriously. My aim here is not to claim its centrality to the interpretation of pastoral in particular but to exploit the striking way in which pastoral thematizes such disputes in order to illuminate what happens to the genre in the early modern period. I will approach this question by contrasting the viewpoints of two recent, powerful readers of early modern pastoral.

Focusing on Renaissance texts and concluding with Andrew Marvell, Frank Kermode's anthology of English pastoral poetry represents by its very selection the view that the great tradition comes to an end after the middle of the seventeenth century. What the Renaissance poets knew, Kermode says, is that artifice is vital to pastoral: close attention to its empirical accuracy misconceives its central purpose. In this view Samuel Johnson's complaint at the artificiality of *Lycidas* (1638, 1645) betrays his age's indifference to this central purpose, one of whose implications is that what pastoral poets imitate is less "nature" than the conventionality of their predecessors. Kermode wittily employs one such convention—the invocation of the Golden Age—to argue his periodization: after Marvell "the true impulse of rustic Pastoral petered out; it was something the Giant Race had understood." And he adds: "The eighteenth century excelled in the mock-Pastoral, which is a kind of pantomime following the great play."[7]

For Raymond Williams pastoral poetry owes its vitality to the tension the poet's effort to see "the real social conditions of country life" imposes on the poetic tendency toward abstraction and idealization. In Williams's history of pastoral, the Renaissance constitutes not a golden age but a fall into relatively uncomplicated artifice. The rural setting comes to be taken as no more than an allegorical mirror for an urban and courtly aristocracy—or for an emergent agrarian capitalism—and the ambition to see the countryside clearly is obscured by the counterambition to turn simple matter to other, "higher" ends. The point at which this fall is reversed is not precisely specified in Williams's literary history—for him Pope only extends the neoclassical idealizations of Renaissance practice—but it would seem to come somewhere in the middle of the eighteenth century. Williams associates with this period not the devolutionary "mock-pastoral" but the "counter-pastoral" of George Crabbe and others, which once again asks what the countryside is really like. In this context Johnson's impatience with Milton is deepened by his contribution to Crabbe's *The Village* (1783), which sharpens the poem's indignation at the mindless imitation of Virgilian convention.[8]

There is a sense in which both these apparently incompatible views of early modern pastoral are right. Williams is to Kermode as Theocritus is to Virgil, or as "pastoral" is to "georgic." That is, they occupy alternative and partial positions on a pastoral continuum that is defined not by the dichotomous opposition of nature to art but by the fluidity with which that differential may be variously enacted. Kermode, rightly insistent on the way "art" lies secreted at the heart of this putatively "natural" form, elevates Renaissance artifice; Williams, rightly mindful that the reflexive conventionality of the form exists to enable an account of the natural order of things, elevates eighteenth-century "realism." The terms of this debate are anticipated in the language not only of eighteenth-century poetry but also of contemporary prose controversy about pastoral. In the debate that occupied the pages of *The Guardian* in 1713, the antagonists Thomas Tickell and Alexander Pope agreed on the general necessity of pursuing the "design" of ancient pastoral poets. They disagreed on the extent to which modern poets might "deviate" from that design by naturalizing ancient pastoral to modern conditions.[9]

There is another important issue on which Kermode and Williams also agree. What they agree on is not only that pastoral poetry undergoes a fundamental change in the period from 1650 to 1800 but also that this change is related to a material transformation of the English countryside. Much of Williams's book is dedicated to disclosing, with consummate intelligence, the complex and powerfully determinate connections between a changing literature and a changing way of life. Kermode's aims are introductory and very different; still, he too remarks at one point that "certain things of importance had reduced the relevance of the old Pastoral. London had lost the country; its maypole, as Pope observed, had been taken down."[10] In Kermode's remarks there is, of course, the nostalgic implication that early modern material change rendered pastoral anachronistic. My own view is rather that it helped bring into relief—admittedly with an unprecedented sharpness—those problems that have always been constitutive of the form. Johnson signals not the demise of pastoral but its transfiguration.

PASTORAL PEOPLE:
MATERIAL CONDITIONS AS SOCIAL RELATIONS

Although it would represent not "culture" but "nature," pastoral inevitably presupposes people: voices speaking singly and in dialogue, figures populating the countryside in labor and leisure. What we take to be "natural" about these people is not an essential attribute but the way they live in relation to nature and one another. As Williams and others have observed with respect to Virgil, the depiction of these pastoral relations does not preclude rural disturbance and social change.[11] But the conventionality of the form after the Roman poets silently tends to assume a static social order against which more local and individual evocations of disorder—ambition, rivalry, death—may emerge with clarity. What does it mean to speak of fundamental material change in the early modern period and how might such change be related to the contemporary depiction of pastoral relations?

The capitalist revolution of English modernity began not in the industrial nineteenth century but in the "preindustrial" seventeenth-century countryside. During the past fifty years the consolidation of this crucial revisionist insight has made clear as well that the intricate and overdetermined story of the capitalist revolution cannot be told in any linear fashion. If we start with people at the most abstract level of analysis, we begin with a set of striking demographic figures. In the early modern period England's population rose by 280 percent, the urban percentage of its population quadrupled, its agricultural productivity more than doubled, and the proportion of its rural population that was engaged in agriculture fell by more than 50 percent.[12] These figures, all of which are exceptional when compared with those for other major European countries and for England's previous development, have an evident interdependence. The increase in the national population, especially in the urban sector, created an unprecedented demand for food. The resulting rise of a national market spurred both agricultural productivity and the growth of nonagricultural activities in the countryside—those directly associated with the agricultural market itself (like transport systems and commercial exchange), but also those stimulated by the availability of labor formerly concentrated in food production (small manufactures, specialist craft work, service industries). Yet urbanization and the general level of population growth could have been sustained only by increased rural productivity both inside and outside agriculture.

What are the implications of these developments for the relations between people viewed at a less elevated level of abstraction? First, at the beginning of this period the proportion of rural agricultural to rural nonagricultural employment was four to one; at the end these labor sectors were about equal.[13] In other words, industrious activities once experienced as relatively anomalous and marginal to the traditions of country life had come to be as unavoidable as herding and farming themselves. Second, the growth of a national commercial infrastructure brought rural England into intimate proximity and unavoidable interaction with elements of the burgeoning urban culture. Third, increased productivity required that agriculture be commercialized and capitalized on a scale never before experienced. In the famous and ethically resonant phrase, the ideology of agrarian "improvement" ensured that the technological "arts" of capitalist husbandry took ostentatious root within the "natural" countryside of early modern England.

Agrarian improvement required an increased access to capital, space, and time. That is, it depended on the capacity of landholders who had absolute property in relatively sizable plots of land to invest capital in relatively long-term agrarian experiments and projects. Money was needed for the consolidation of smaller holdings into larger units; for the enclosure of commons and wastes, as well as for the conversion of open fields to enclosed arable or pasture; for the adoption of new crops, fertilizers, and implements (like the seed drill), new kinds of livestock, and new methods of farming (like convertible husbandry); for the reclamation of heathlands, for marsh drainage, for disafforestation and the making of water-meadows. With the abolition of feudal tenures and the Court of Wards in 1646, large land-holders were freed from their dependence on the Crown and enabled to improve their estates by these and related methods. But since large holders did not lose the dependence of smallholders on themselves, these legal innovations of the Civil War years doubly facilitated the transfer of property in land from many hands to a few by aggravating the inability of smallhold-ers and tenant farmers to compete with large-scale capitalist farming.[14]

Having briefly summarized a complex set of demographic and socioeco-nomic developments, let me ask how these may have affected the custom-ary relations of people in the countryside. First, as I have already observed, agricultural activity now came face to face, as it never had been in the past, with alternative kinds of rural employment. Yet, second, within that agri-cultural arena the broad range of social relations conventionally enclosed by the category "feudalism"—a range subtly articulated by qualitative dif-ferences in station, kinds of service, and degrees of dependence—was sim-plified and starkly polarized into the increasingly quantitative and unitary opposition of large and small landholder. Involved in this process was the sacrifice of customary use rights (for example, to common and waste lands) and privileges (for example, to control the working conditions under which labor was accomplished). In the ultimate extension of this process, small renters who were obliged to forfeit their land became unpropertied wage laborers in contractual relation with large employers. What was new was not, of course, wage labor but the commodification of labor—wage labor on a scale and within a market context sufficient to color fundamentally its social meaning for contemporaries.

Under customary social relations, property—preeminently property in land—had been regarded as a matter of delimited rights rather than of dis-posable things, and the institution of a private, exclusive right to use prop-erty in prescribed ways coexisted with the institution of common property, whose use was available to all. The abolition of feudal tenures provided a symbolic sanction for the presuppositions of a capitalist market economy, a sanction to regard private property in land as constituting absolute posses-sion of it. If the market was to assume the responsibilities of economic allo-cation previously exercised by the Crown and the state, what was required was a conception of private property as an absolute, virtually unlimited, and salable right to things. "Common property" came to seem a contradiction in terms, and as customary use rights were increasingly subject to challenge, small farmers were seen to possess a property in nothing but their own labor.[15] At least since Adam Smith the market's complex administration of private property has been closely associated with the free pursuit of indi-vidual self-interest and located in a "private" realm of economic behavior unhindered by the "public" offices of the state. The locution has a certain irony. Not only does it identify as normatively "private" precisely those worldly activities that the "privacy" of pastoral rustics normatively eschew. It also names a behavior from which the contemporary embodiments of the pastoral rustic, the herders and farmers of eighteenth-century England, were systematically excluded.

Yet this process of social transformation was still incomplete in the eighteenth century. Tenants and the laboring poor had not yet exchanged the expectation of customary rights and privileges for the class consciousness of a rural proletariat.[16] The problematic social category of the improving landlord was composed neither of upwardly mobile commoners nor of paradoxically progressive aristocrats but was rather a complex amalgam of both. In *The Tatler* number 169 Richard Steele uses the tropes of the *beatus ille* to make a confident, and seemingly status-based, discrimination between good and bad landlords whose social identities are virtually indistinguishable.[17]

A traditional, status-based and an emergent, class-based model of social relations were locked in competition. At the end of the sixteenth century the traditional opposition between the antithetical status categories of land and trade was conventionally understood to provide an adequate summary of England's basic options in matters of national revenue. During the course of the seventeenth century, however, the conventional wisdom that land and trade were incompatible was challenged by the vigorous interpenetration of landed and trading families. And by the beginning of the eighteenth century the financial revolution had shifted the entire debate into an opposition between the landed and the moneyed interests— between a status-oriented belief in the fiscal purity of real estate and the conviction that the fortunes of land, trade, and all else besides were inextricably intertwined with the fate of the capitalist marketplace. Henceforth pastoral complaint would locate worldly corruption not only in trade and the city but also in the improved countryside—wherever the tentacles of exchange value had penetrated.[18]

Like the demographic, economic, and social factors I have already touched on, pastoral discourse was one among several interdependent links in the chain of circumstance that transformed the relations between people in the eighteenth-century countryside. The questions raised by these other factors in more implicit and experiential ways were articulated by pastoral in discursive form: What is becoming of the country way of work and life? What is rural labor? What happens when city dwellers move to the country and country people change their rural habits and stations or move to the city? How do you tell who is of the country and who is not? Are improving landlords the "natural rulers" of the countryside or interlopers from without? Where does the rural end and the urban begin? Where and how do we get our food? Who eats what we produce? Whose nature is improved by technology? What is the relationship between the right to work, to inhabit, and to own the land? How can what is held in common be possessed by a few? How can nature be improved by art?

Oliver Goldsmith's *The Deserted Village* (1770) asks many of these questions explicitly, but it is perhaps most plaintive in its unarticulated ambivalence about pastoral periodization. Although Goldsmith strains to capture the material conditions that precipitated the end of the rural English golden age, we slowly come to see that the crucial change is not in the land and its inhabitants but in the emotional experience of the poet himself—not in nature but in art. The subjectivity of individual history subsumes the objectivity of national material history at the very moment when the effort to do justice to the latter is most earnest and intense.

The contradictory doubleness of pastoral—its investment both in the establishment and in the complicating demolition of dichotomous opposition—is characteristically present in the eighteenth-century embodiment of that discourse. But this finely balanced doubleness is deranged by an apprehension of the increasing difficulty of finding, in country experience itself, the grounding structure of opposition that is prerequisite to any complication. Internalized within pastoral, the effect of this apprehension is to raise the power of pastoral exponentially: both to make it even more indubitably itself and to shift decisively its center of energy. One way of acknowledging this shift is to speak of the tendency of much eighteenth-century pastoral toward "realism." The tendency takes in a range of experimental poets—John Gay, Jonathan Swift, James Thomson, Stephen Duck, Mary Collier, Mary Leapor, Oliver Goldsmith, George Crabbe, William Wordsworth—self-consciously determined to disclose the underlying "reality" of the contemporary English countryside.

Another way of acknowledging this shift is to note a simple but monumental change in the conditions of poetic authorship. Although devoted to the depiction of the shepherd at song, the pastoral tradition had been equally devoted to the view that this rustic object of representation was by definition incapable of serving as its actual subject, its author. The appearance of pastoralists who were first of all rustic laborers revolutionized attitudes toward pastoral; but it also revolutionized attitudes toward agrarian social relations. Thus Stephen Duck, patronized by contemporaries as the Thresher Poet, came close to propounding the age-old antitheses of pastoral poetry in the as-yet-unformulated language of class conflict. Many modern pastoralists naturalized the traditional opposition between rural innocence and urban corruption through the static juxtaposition of landed simplicity and mercantile sophistication. Duck, however, enacted it as a dramatized spectacle of class conflict within the realm of the rural itself—as a confrontation between master and wage-earner, labor discipline and customary rights, profit and subsistence.[19]

PASTORAL PEOPLE:
MATERIAL CONDITIONS AS GENDER RELATIONS

If the conventional subject matter of pastoral poets is the natural existence of rustics both male and female, a common representation of that existence figures it as specifically female. This was true at least as early as the *Georgics,* which sometimes gender the inseminating cultivator male and nature a fecund female. And in an easy and traditional extension the art of husbandry might be analogized to the art of poetry. Yet eighteenth-century pastoral is unusual in having been written not only by rustics but even by female rustics, who played self-consciously with the double irregularity of their artifice. The extension of authorship to commoners and women at this time is, of course, part of a larger movement whereby authorship as such was institutionalized in the modern terms of print culture and the literary marketplace. In this context as in others, commoners and women were accorded an analogous significance by an eighteenth-century elite culture apprehensive both of their deficiencies and of their incipient challenge.

As with the fluid categories of social distinction, pastoral provided contemporaries with a mechanism for thinking about the limits of gender difference: between art and nature, between men and women.[20] And like their precursors, eighteenth-century pastoralists were preoccupied not simply with the orthodox correlation of male with culture and female with nature but also with its complications. First, as the pastoral context makes clear, the normative charge of the gender opposition is fundamentally unstable; if anything, it is positively weighted toward the female by virtue of her normative naturalness. Second, and even more unsettling, the very substance of the correlation is shaky. If female is predominantly nature, it is also significantly art. This complication is evident whenever social cuts across gender opposition, as in the artifice of female aristocracy when contrasted to the simplicity of the commoner. More generally, however, the association of the female with art or culture appears not only in the paradigmatically negative artifice of Eve (superficiality, deceit, corruption, and the lust for knowledge as power) but also in the positive arts of female cultivation, the female capacity to civilize the natural brutishness and savagery of men.

As in the case of social relations, early modern change rendered the field of gender relations more richly problematic than before, hence more than usually appropriate for pastoral exploitation. At the beginning of the sixteenth century economic production—which means in the main agricultural production—was dominated by a system in which the household was the major productive unit. The early modern "domestic economy" operated according to a schematic sexual division of labor—between female "inside" work and male "outside" work—that was in practice rather flexible and scarcely operative on smaller holdings. In such an economy husbands exercised the authority of the head of a household that was orga-nized as an integrated working partnership.[21]

The breakdown of the domestic economy and the concomitant with-drawal of women from work deemed economically productive was most immediately the result of capitalist improvement.[22] The flexibility of tradi-tional work relations depended on customary arrangements that capitalist innovation rendered unprofitable. Enclosure and the consolidation of large estates increasingly denied to lesser farmers the subsistence condi-tions on which their households had depended. The loss of commons rights—not only grazing but gathering fuel and gleaning harvest leav-ings—deprived women in particular of customary labor. When farmers lost access to land, their wives lost the means to keep a cow and practice dairy-ing, a common form of women's work. As a result, outside work tradition-ally available to women simply disappeared at the lower social strata. At the higher social strata increased sensitivity to price levels and market demand marginalized dairying (for example) in favor of more profitable produc-tion or transformed it into a commercial activity under the control of hired managers.[23]

What happened to that portion of the agricultural economy not orga-nized through the household? Over the course of the eighteenth century there was a general decrease in the agricultural employment of women, and work patterns for men and women outside the household diverged in a number of ways. Increasingly, female employment was concentrated in spring activities like dairying and calving, while male labor was specialized in the fall harvesting of cereal crops, which required heavier technology. Especially in the latter half of the century, moreover, male real wages rose as female real wages declined. By limiting quasi-independent domestic pro-duction, capitalist improvement exerted pressure on what was increasingly understood as "the labor market" so as to throw women into competition with men. This was most of all true in the fall, when the vulnerability of laborers in cereal production to structural unemployment put a premium on the availability of nonharvesting jobs. That men tended to prevail in this competition was both a cause and a consequence of developing concep-tions of familial income as primarily male income.[24]

At the higher social levels the differential process of class formation led women (and men) who aspired to a proto-"bourgeois" gentility to value idleness in women. In such households women's work was increasingly ori-ented toward female accomplishments, while cheap wage labor did what was once the inside work of wives. In more modest households husbands and wives turned increasingly to wage labor, seeking work outside the home. Both lost thereby the traditional liberty to define the tasks entailed in their work. But laboring women, as we have seen, were also losing the opportunity for this kind of employment as well. The decrease of female employment in the latter half of the eighteenth century is closely correlated with a rise in fertility, whose principal causes are a fall in the age of women at first marriage and a rise in the number of women who married. It seems plausible to connect these developments: "as female employment became more precarious and lowly paid, there were obvious motives to marry younger as defense against the unemployment which was increasingly the lot of women." Even as the incidence of marriage increased, however, wives were losing the flexibility once enjoyed in household labor, which was in the process of becoming "housework," the exclusive domain of women and increasingly denigrated as unproductive.[25]

This brief account of early modern changes in the sexual division of agricultural labor confirms other evidence that by the end of the eighteenth century England had gone a long way toward the familiar, culturally ramified opposition between the domestic or "private" and the public realms of experience. The completion of this process would entail not only a further rigidification and universalization of the division across class lines but also a revaluation of domestic work as not so much lesser as different: economically unproductive but charged with the office of spiritual cultivation and maternal nurture. But it would be a mistake to see the modern system of gender difference as an accomplished fact by 1800. Like the quantifying polarization of social distinction that would issue in Victorian class conflict, gender differentiation is a process whose ongoingness in eighteenth-century England is evident in the characteristically problematic approach taken toward it, within pastoral as without.[26] True, some eighteenth-century pastoral appears interested only in the dichotomizing articulation of gender categories. More often, however, it dedicates its energies to the experimental manipulation—whether anxious or playful—of gender difference, setting gender against pastoral categories in an effort to elicit their reciprocal intelligibility.

Throughout the century women of varied social strata (Anne Finch, countess of Winchilsea, Delarivier Manley, Mary Leapor, Lady Mary Wortley Montagu, Elizabeth Hands, Ann Yearsley) accommodated to women and commoners the Horatian topos of a gentlemanly retreat from the world. In this way the Horatian retreat was detached from its traditional social signification and made to stand by turns for the married state, the single state, freedom from male corruption, and the exclusive company of women. More abstractly, periodical essayists like Steele, Addison, Eliza Haywood, and Dr. Johnson self-consciously intermixed pastoral and gender types so as to underscore the intelligibility of women as both nature and art. In one *Spectator* paper, Addison depicts the idealized Aurelia as an amalgam of contradictory norms of the natural—nature as it informs not only the historically residual norm of domestic *economy* but also the historically emergent norm of domestic *ideology*.[27]

On the face of it (although at a high level of generalization), the retirement of women from what was deemed productive agricultural labor substantiated orthodox pastoral associations of the female with nature, retreat, and *otium* and the male with culture, activity, and *negotium*. Yet the contradictions engendered by social change are not far to seek. Pastoral "privacy" had been radically subdivided, identified both with the economically unproductive domesticity of women and (as we have seen) with the economically productive individualism of their antithetical male counterparts. I have already observed, moreover, how the depreciation of women as agricultural cultivators was inseparable from the inflation of their powers in the domestic cultivation of their spiritually boorish husbands. Buttressing this complicating reversal was the increasingly unequal sexual division of labor, which, because it made men more than before the principal visible inhabitants of the rural landscape, established them as heirs apparent to the role of pastoral personage whose natural authenticity was most persuasively gendered female. And yet the strongly felt disparity between the rationalized efficiency of modern men's labor and the customary conditions it was displacing inevitably aggravated the conventional (and parallel) disparity between such labor and the care of truly "pastoral" farmers and herdsmen.

Paradoxically, women, less visible on the land than before, for that very reason were less tainted by the industrious corruptions of modern productivity and better equipped to mediate the older, land-centered virtues. The meaning of this development was not easy to read. When in *The Thresher's Labour* Stephen Duck observes how his female counterparts resist the regimentation of the work week, he surprisingly and fatally condemns this behavior and thereby sides, against his own stated interest, with the efficient and oppressive employer. Yet, the leisure of the new protobourgeois "housewife" was not easily conflated with the *otium* of the pastoral maiden. If, as contemporaries recognized, the market was driven by the engine of consumption, it was the singular social role of the unproductive housewife to sustain the cycle of exchange by the perpetual desire for consumer goods and by the satisfaction of that desire.[28] This social role was understood to capitalize on women's inveterate thralldom to the artifice of appearance, ornamentation, and fashion. In the tradition of the Roman goddess Fortuna, the volatile instability and corruptibility of the capitalist market were often figured as female in the eighteenth century.[29] And an important contribution to this richly overdetermined figuration was made by the contradictory insight that the *negotium* of male marketplace activity was inseparably dependent on the *otium* of the retired housewife and her enforced leisure.

In summary, the question that pastoral helped to ask in this context was: What is the relationship between men and women under contemporary conditions of work and leisure? Behind this query, however, lies the yet more fundamental one: What, under such conditions, is the "nature" of men and women?

NATIONALISM AND IMPERIALISM AS MACRO-PASTORALISM

The fundamental structure of pastoral antithesis presumes a singular and integral countryside in opposition to the comparably monolithic culture of urbanity. The dialectical reversal that infiltrates this structure from the very start questions the unitary coherence of each pole, and the early modern developments that have been my subject in the last few pages made the internal divisions of country life more undeniably apparent. As unpropertied common laborers slowly separated out from improving landlords, as female supportiveness became distinguished from the heavily capitalized industriousness of men, the opposition of nature to art which was understood to define the difference between country and city seemed to be internalized and to take root within the rural itself.

This unsettling movement amounts to a respatialization of a geographical dispensation that formerly had appeared secure. A model for it may be found in the way Virgil invokes the realm of the barbarian in the first eclogue. Tityrus, it will be recalled, sadly testifies to the stability of the opposition between the city of Rome and its comparatively rural provinces. Meliboeus, under threat of exile, finds an analogous opposition between foreign soil and the Italian homeland. But as I have suggested, the analogy cannot work in any simple way because it involves a conflation of places—Rome and the provinces—whose very meaning within the pastoral context also requires their continuing opposition. In *London* (1738) Johnson establishes the familiar opposition between rural innocence and urban corruption only to transvalue this relationship by opposing the innocence of all of England to the corruption of the French. It's not that London loses her vices. It's rather that they are so relentlessly derived from a foreign source that London becomes a mere metonymy for England and England a land of innocent bumpkins ripe for the cultural imperialism of metropolitan France.

The destabilizing effect can operate in either direction. Both the internalization and the externalization of difference—the countryside as divided against itself, the countryside as conjoined with the city—are the result of transforming a structural unit of opposition into a linked chain of multiple and relative oppositions. In the early modern period this result was achieved with unparalleled force by the emergence of Britain as a national entity and an imperial power. The discourse surrounding this protracted emergence is so closely and intricately interwoven with the discourse of pastoral as to justify conceiving it as a species of "macro-pastoralism." For evidence of this connection one need look no further than the titles of some eighteenth-century Virgilian experiments, like William Collins's *Persian Eclogues* (1742), Thomas Chatterton's *African Eclogues* (1770), Edward Rushton's *West-Indian Eclogues* (1787), or Robert Southey's *Botany-Bay Eclogues* (1797). But the macro-pastoral impulse also permeates a diverse range of English texts of the period, hypostatizing the metropolitan unit of England against the underdeveloped rusticity of the colony. Macro-pastoralism therefore may be seen as a kind of "discursive" imperialism that proceeds in conjunction with the capitalist rationality and expansion with which imperialism in the more customary sense of the term is associated.[30]

The Navigation Acts of 1651 and 1660 may be seen as the macro-pastoral equivalents of such domestic legislation as the parliamentary enclosure acts—signal instances of protectionist policy that established the conditions for a subsequent laissez-faire. The two acts subordinated to the rule of Parliament all commercial relations undertaken by the American colonies and simultaneously established a national monopoly on all trade with those colonies. As articles both of imperial and of foreign policy, they helped constitute English national identity against two distinct sorts of geographical Other, the subordinate colony and the rival competitor. At first the colonies were most profitable to England as a source of "natural" raw materials; during the course of the eighteenth century they became more important for their "cultural" function, as a monopoly market for British commodities, compounding the population rise on the domestic front which was providing a spur to agricultural productivity for the home market. As early as the Age of Discovery Europeans had enthusiastically projected the aura of pastoral rusticity onto the Americas, at first onto its native population and then onto its European settlers as well. From the perspective of the colonial trade, however, the experiential basis for that aura—the difference between the English city and countryside—was invisible. By mid century the navigation laws had constrained the economic productivity of the colonies enough to provoke resistance and revolution against what was perceived as a unified system of metropolitan exploitation.

Contemporaries believed the slave trade to be the most profitable branch of English commerce. The capture of Jamaica in 1655 provided a base for its operations. The War of the Spanish Succession at the turn of the century won for England the monopoly of supplying slaves to the Spanish American empire; the South Sea Company was founded in 1711 to trade with that empire once peace had returned. The ultimate instance of the commodification of labor, slavery afforded a brutal analogy for capitalist employment which English people, nurtured in the republican language of antislavery, were not slow to make. Even with respect to sheer physical situation, enslaved people and wage laborers might be seen to share the fate of having been uprooted from their lands. Of course, the georgic aim of human "improvement" helped rationalize the temporary debasement of people who were patently inferior, although both domestic employers and colonial planters knew on pragmatic grounds to resist the educational "cultivation" of their workers. Yet in any case the analogy between slave and wage labor cut across social identities.[31] At the "pastoral" level of domestic relations, indignation at the "enslavement" of the laboring poor was complicated enough for those who found themselves in what was increasingly recognized as the "other" class, and pastoral discourse could always be made to construe impoverishment as freedom from care. But within the international, "macro-pastoral" context, even the laboring poor could be persuaded to regard colonized people as their essential Other, uncannily familiar in their subjection yet necessary both for economic reasons and as a negative ground against which the vaunted "English liberty" might be positively valued. It has been argued that the slave trade was a cause, not the consequence, of color racism in England. In the eighteenth century black people began to share the obloquy traditionally reserved for the "black Irish." The antislavery movement became an effective force only when England's special, colonial relationship with the Americas was in the process of being annulled.

Ireland was the prototypical English colony. Precisely because she shared with England a broad frame of cultural reference, Ireland's linguistic, religious, and ethnic deviations from the English norm aroused an absolute enmity, and the Irish were physically close enough (unlike the Americans) to suffer a perdurable policy of colonial exploitation. Solidified under Charles II, this policy was briefly suspended at the Glorious Revolution but rigorously reinforced thereafter through trading prohibitions and absentee landlordism. Yet physical proximity, because it made the process of exploitation so visible, also made the macro-pastoral ideology of a priori difference hard to sustain. This in turn aggravated the difficulty, inherent in the extension of pastoral ideology to the macro level, that what are locally viewed as innocence and corruption—small proprietorship, for example, versus unscrupulous rack-renting—are revalued as backwardness versus development when displaced onto the larger scene.

Scotland's story was very different. Bound to English political culture by a diversity of ties—the royal house of Stuart, but also the Solemn League and Covenant—Scotland enjoyed a free trade with England under Cromwell which was restricted under Charles II but restored in 1688 and ultimately codified in the Act of Union of 1707. The relationship of Scottish to English nationality had long exemplified one classic version of cultural opposition along the north-south axis.[32] The union of England and Scotland as "Great Britain" sought to dissolve the old quasi-colonial opposition within a singular national unit. In fact it had mixed results: the Scottish remained "North Britons," both familiar and estranged from English identity. And within Scotland the English connection helped ossify

the rivalry between the highlands and the lowlands into an internalized version of nationalist opposition, redolent of pastoral meaning. With the highlands stood "nature," the customary relations of feudal hierarchy, and a
"backward" way of life; with the lowlands stood "art," capitalist improvement, and modernization. Jacobitism and the defeats of 1715 and 1745
provided a pastoral theater in which was played out the inevitable corruption of nature by art, of the past by the present, engendering nostalgia for
a golden age enriched by the aesthetic distance of its political and cultural
relics.[33] Yet at the macro level the putative simplicity of England's northern
neighbor was profoundly complicated by the authentic aura of cultivation
conferred by the Scottish Enlightenment.

To aestheticize the past is to frame it as a pleasingly self-conscious fiction,
serviceable to present reality by virtue of its very detachment from it. The
antiquarian excavation of a native English past during the eighteenth century was tinged with this aesthetic regard, and it contributed importantly to
the growth of modern English nationalism. In the middle of the seventeenth century English or British "nationality" was still a manifold and contradictory idea, rooted as deeply in the sense of a strictly alternative past—
or of a radically oppositional outpost of the present—as in the reigning
institutional embodiments of sovereign authority and power. By the end of
the century a series of distinct but mutually reinforcing developments had
laid the ground for the modern conflation of the "nation" and the "state."[34]
The Hanoverian settlement propounded the British constitution as an all-
purpose explanatory myth plausible enough to suspend the disbelief of
those several interests crucial to the settlement compromise. In the space of
two generations the Whig "opposition" had engineered an efficient and
enduring working relationship with the monarchy and the fledgling financial forces of the City without entirely sacrificing its public persona as
defender of English liberties. Finally, the spectacular growth in taxation,
public deficit finance, and the vast bureaucratic infrastructure of fiscal
administration in the early eighteenth century centralized state power on
the unprecedented scale required to finance Britain's ostentatiously
"national" military, commercial, and imperial enterprise.[35]

The effect of these developments was to enforce the sense of Britain as a
homogeneous "nation-state" whose very diversity testified to the perpetually
inclusive consensus of its "Englishness." Thus cultural aberration and
regional recalcitrance might be read as the colorful precondition for an
irresistible and enlivening absorption, and the moldering remains of
ancient alterity could be figured as the enduring and legitimating sign of
national permanence—as "England's ruins"—rather than as a more ostensible emblem of the transience of all things.[36] Yet the complicating pastoral
countertendency was never absent. Even as antiquarian scholarship facilitated the sentimental accommodation of the Celtic, the Anglo-Saxon, and

the "gothic" past to the English present, it inevitably unearthed evidence of an ineluctable and unassimilable strangeness, an alien barbarity evocative of precisely that national foreignness against which the homogeneity of the English national tradition was seeking to define itself.

Along the East-West axis, eighteenth-century England's most significant foreign acquisition, in both material and symbolic terms, was India. Only toward the end of the century did England undertake the full governmental and administrative responsibility that stamped the face of Victorian India with an anglicized veneer. In the earlier period the East India Company exercised a trade monopoly that facilitated what contemporaries and historians agree in calling the "plunder" of India. The term bears a host of contradictory associations. Supine and defenseless in its natural feminine languor, the Orient was seen to submit to the piratical depredations of a criminal virility. India also bore a metonymic relation to the female. More than any other, the India trade dealt in articles of leisure and conspicuous consumption, exotic luxury goods whose "plunder" accentuated John Bull's hard-nosed practicality by indulging the splendid superfluousness of his women. But so far from being "raw material" extracted by European ingenuity from a native and primitive land, this Eastern plunder most famously consisted of the exquisitely artful fabrications of an ancient civilization. In these terms it was as though the rude hinterlands had plundered the metropolitan center of culture. In confronting the East, the West confronted not nature but an alien mode of cultivation: devious, "mysterious," unfathomable, yet possessed of an arcane wisdom that exposed to the West its own guileless innocence and vulnerability. From this perspective the Orient (India, Persia, Turkey, and to a lesser degree China) was the venerable artifice of urbane corruption—autocratic tyranny, diplomatic perfidy, religious hypocrisy, sexual perversity.

Ripe for exploitation, the East was by the same token seductive of English innocence—a means simultaneously of English aggrandizement and exculpation. "The East" was, in short, a way in which the English regulated their contradictory sense of national and imperial identity, and it bespoke in turn the contradictions of domestic, "pastoral" experience. The macro-pastoral, however, did not reflect the pastoral in any direct and consistent way. On the contrary, the structural effect of macro-pastoral was to unhinge the logic of pastoral opposition by expanding and imploding its terms: London is to its countryside as England is to the world. Thus the nabobs of the East India Company, laden with the fabled wealth of the East, returned to metropolitan England to purchase a seat in Parliament like nothing so much as parvenu City stockjobbers buying a country seat in rural Kent. Ultimately, macro-pastoral argued the evaporation of difference at the level of the international market, where everything—all nationality, all "natural" utility—seemed convertible and equalizable through the exchange mechanism. But macro-pastoral experience also sensitized English people to the indefinite internalizability of the north-south and east-west axes, their stealthy pertinence to the putatively irreducible, "micro-colonial" localities of the intranational domestic scene. In Tobias Smollett's *Humphry Clinker* (1771) this sensitivity is registered in the way incremental travel northward is experienced as a continuous chain of stereotypical movements from "south" to "north," each link plausible in itself but also radically relativized by its placement in a more comprehensive series.

In the foregoing pages I've argued that in early modern England and in conjunction with material change pastoral underwent a fundamental transformation that should be seen as a radical intensification of its basic generic character rather than as a qualitatively new departure. One aim of this argument has been to vindicate the elasticity and responsiveness of literary genres, their operation not simply as rule-bound regulators but as supple instruments for discerning and articulating change itself. A corollary of this argument has been that if the transformation of pastoral is an effect of material change, pastoral also operates as the lens through which material change is perceived and undertaken. In this interaction we can see not only the manifestly dialectical nature of the relationship between literary and material experience but also how the foundations of cultural life are laid by that interaction.

What happens to pastoral in the modern world? On the most immediate level, pastoral as a discipline of poetic technique might be said to die after 1800 only to be reborn as the prosaic and increasingly compelling and mandatory discourse of environmental politics. But it might also be objected that pastoral poetry didn't really die in 1800. Both the romantic poets and their heirs continue to write not only poetry they are content to call "pastorals" but also poetry that lacks the name yet bears the deep imprint of pastoral preoccupation—preoccupation with the dream of a direct apprehension of nature as well as with the inevitability of nature's imaginative construction. These days, the term *romanticism* is used to designate both a period discourse and a more general opening out into modernity. The complex logic that links modern romanticism to the traditionality of romance is powerful and undeniable. Nonetheless, there may be some value in seeing the poetic revolution sponsored by Blake, Wordsworth, and Coleridge as a movement not from romance to romanticism but from pastoral to pastoralism—in seeing romanticism, that is, as the profound assimilation of pastoral inquiry through its deliberate and increasingly imperceptible application to all experience.

NOTES

INTRODUCTION

1. K. Sharpe and S. N. Zwicker, eds., *Politics of Discourse: The Literature and History of Seventeenth-Century England* (Berkeley, 1987).

2. See, for classic examples of new historicism, S. Greenblatt, *Renaissance Self-Fashioning* (Chicago, 1980); *Shakespearian Negotiations* (Berkeley, 1988); and Greenblatt, ed., *Representing the English Renaissance* (Berkeley, 1988).

3. See J. Dollimore and A. Sinfield, *Political Shakespeare: New Essays in Cultural Materialism* (Ithaca and Manchester, 1985; 2d ed., Manchester, 1994); J. Drakakis, ed., *Alternative Shakespeares* (London, 1985). S. Mullaney, *The Place of the Stage: License, Play, and Power in Renaissance England* (Chicago, 1988); L. Marcus, *Puzzling Shakespeare: Local Reading and Its Discontents* (Berkeley, 1988); and J. Howard and M. O. O'Conner, eds., *Shakespeare Reproduced: The Text in History and Ideology* (New York, 1987).

4. Cf. K. Sharpe and P. Lake, "Introduction," *Culture and Politics in Early Stuart England* (Palo Alto and London, 1993); for other critiques of the methods of new historicism, see H. Veeser, ed., "Introduction," *The New Historicism Reader* (New York, 1994), E. Pechter, "The New Historicism and Its Discontents," *PMLA* 102, no. 3 (1987): 292–303, and Pechter, *What Was Shakespeare? Renaissance Plays and Changing Critical Practice* (Ithaca, 1995).

5. Greenblatt, *Renaissance Self-Fashioning*, chap. 1; J. Goldberg, *James I and the Politics of Literature* (Baltimore and London, 1983), chap. 2; D. Canadine, "Civic Ritual and the Colchester Oyster Feast," *Past and Present* 94 (1982): 107–130; see also C. Geertz, *The Interpretation of Cultures* (Chicago, 1975), G. Kipling, *The Triumph of Honour: Burgundian Origins of the Elizabethan Renaissance* (Leiden, 1977), and R. McCoy, *The Rites of Knighthood: The Literature and Politics of Elizabethan Chivalry* (Berkeley, 1989).

6. For a more sympathetic view of cultural studies, see the recent essays in *University of Toronto Quarterly* 64 (Fall 1995), "Cultural Studies in Canada," edited by the Toronto Cultural Studies Collective.

7. See, for example, H. Cixous, "The Laugh of the Medusa," in *The Hélène Cixous Reader,* ed. S. Sellers (New York, 1994); T. Moi, *Sexual/Textual Politics* (London, 1985); E. Meade, "Sexual Politics and Critical Judgement," in G. S. Jay and D. Miller, eds., *After Strange Texts: The Role of Theory in the Study of Literature* (Tuscaloosa, Ala., 1985); E. Showalter, ed. *The New Feminist Criticism: Essays on Women, Literature, and Theory* (New York, 1982); and C. Belsey and J. Moore, eds., *The Feminist Reader: Essays in Gender and the Politics of Literary Criticism* (Houndmills, U.K., and New York, 1989); and E. Said, *Orientalism* (London, 1978).

8. See C. Geertz, "Thick Description: Towards an Interpretive Theory of Culture," *The Interpretation of Cultures;* Geertz, *Negara: The Theater State in Nineteenth-Century Bali* (Princeton, 1980).

9. See K. V. Thomas, "History and Anthropology," *Past and Present* 24 (1964): 3–24; Thomas's anthropological approach has attracted the criticism that it is insufficiently sensitive to the moment and to short-term change. See too E. P. Thompson, "Anthropology and the Discipline of Historical Context," *Midland History* 3 (1972): 41–57.

10. For a classic case study, see C. Ginzburg, *The Cheese and the Worms: The Cosmos of a Sixteenth-Century Miller* (London, 1980); cf. R. Darnton, *The Great Cat Massacre and Other Episodes in French Cultural History* (New York, 1984).

11. See H. White, *Tropics of Discourse: Essays in Cultural Criticism* (1978; Baltimore, 1985); D. LaCapra and S. Kaplan, *Modern European Intellectual History: Reappraisals and New Perspectives* (Ithaca, 1982); LaCapra, *Rethinking Intellectual History: Texts, Contexts, Language* (Ithaca, 1983); and, more recently, P. Joyce, "History and Post Modernism," *Past and Present* 133 (1991): 204–209; Joyce, "The End of Social History?" *Social History* 20 (1995): 73–91.

12. Cf. Sharpe and Lake, "Introduction," *Culture and Politics.*

13. The readership of academic journals may be characterized in terms of Stanley Fish's "interpretive communities" (see S. Fish, *Is There a Text in This Class? The Authority of Interpretive Communities* (Cambridge, Mass., 1980). The fashionable revisionist history of the seventeenth century rigidly defines the (usually manuscript) sources suitable for political narrative.

14. On the coffeehouse, see B. Lillywhite, *London Coffee Houses* (London, 1963); see also J. Habermas, *The Structural Transformation of the Public Sphere* (Cambridge, Mass., 1989). The contemporary pamphlet literature on the coffeehouse begins early in the Restoration era; see, for example, *The Character of a Coffee-house* (London, 1665), *The Character of a Coffee-house With the Symptoms of Town-wit* (London, 1673), and *Coffee-houses Vindicated in Answer to the Late Published Character* (London, 1673).

15. See R. Strong, *The Cult of Elizabeth: Elizabethan Portraiture and Pageantry* (London, 1977), and Strong, *Art and Power* (Woodbridge, Conn., 1984).

16. The very titles of Strong's *Splendor at Court: Renaissance Spectacle and the Theater of Power* (Boston, 1973) and John Skelton's *Magnificence* testify to the aesthetic language associated with the Renaissance state.

17. See T. S. Eliot, "The Metaphysical Poets," in *Selected Essays, 1917–1932* (New York, 1932); for a more subtle discussion of aesthetics and politics see M. McKeon, "Politics of Discourse and the Rise of the Aesthetic in Seventeeth-Century

England," in Sharpe and Zwicker, *Politics of Discourse* (Berkeley, 1987); and Zwicker, *Lines of Authority* (Ithaca, 1993), chaps. 2–3.

18. Though see M. Aston, *England's Iconoclasts*, vol. 1 (Oxford, 1988), introduction and chap. 3, and John Phillips, *The Reformation of Images: Destruction of Art in England, 1535–1660* (Berkeley, 1973), 183–200.

19. Charles II's coronation is studied in G. Reedy, "Mystical Politics: the Imagery of Charles II's Coronation," in P. Korshin, ed., *Studies in Change and Revolution* (Menston, U.K., 1972), and in the introduction to R. Knowles's facsimile edition of *The Entertainment of His Most Excellent Majestie Charles II* (Binghamton, N.Y., 1988). There is no study of court ritual, entertainment, and pageantry, and biographies of Charles II pay little attention to such matters.

20. See E. Miner, "The 'Poetic Picture, Painted Poetry' of *The Last Instructions to a Painter,*" *Modern Philology* 63 (1966): 288–294; A. Patterson, *Marvell and the Civic Crown* (Princeton, 1978), 111–74; and S. Zwicker, "Virgins and Whores: The Politics of Sexual Misconduct in the 1660s," in Condren, Conal, and A. D. Cousins, eds., *The Political Identity of Andrew Marvell* (Aldershot, 1990), 91–105.

21. See "Introduction," this volume, p. 6 (on Rousseau).

22. For the revisionist narrative see J. C. D. Clark, *English Society 1688–1832: Ideology, Social Structure, and Political Practice during the Ancient Regime* (Cambridge, 1985); Clark, *Revolution and Rebellion: State and Society in England in the Seventeenth and Eighteenth Centuries* (Cambridge, 1986).

23. Though now see J. C. D. Clark, *Samuel Johnson: Literature, Religion, and English Cultural Politics from the Restoration to Romanticism* (Cambridge, 1994).

24. See J. Dollimore, *Radical Tragedy: Religion, Ideology and Power in the Drama of Shakespeare and His Contemporaries* (Chicago, 1984); Greenblatt, *Renaissance Self-Fashioning* and *Representing the English Renaissance.*

25. On the concept of fault lines, see A. Sinfield, *Faultlines: Cultural Materialism and the Politics of Dissident Reading* (Oxford, 1992).

26. Milton, of course, revealed a powerful sensitivity to that generic mixing in the preface to *Samson Agonistes*, "Of That Sort of Dramatic Poem Which Is Called Tragedy" (see Zwicker, *Lines of Authority*, 14); on the politics of the genre see N. K. Maguire, *Regicide and Restoration: English Tragicomedy, 1660–1671* (Cambridge, 1992); see K. Sharpe, "Religion, Rhetoric, and Revolution in Seventeenth-Century England," *Huntington Library Quarterly* 57 (1994): 255–299.

27. For the conventional histories of the genres and development of Restoration theater, see J. Loftis, *The Politics of Drama in Restoration England* (Oxford, 1963), G. Marshall, *Restoration Serious Drama* (Norman, Okla., 1975), and R. D. Hume, *The Development of English Drama in the Late Seventeenth Century* (Oxford, 1976).

28. See J. Phillips, *The Reformation of Images*, 198–200, and K. Sharpe, "'An Image Doting Rabble': The Failure of Republican Culture in Seventeenth-Century England," in this volume.

29. See S. Bending, "A Natural Revolution? Garden Politics in Eighteenth-Century England," and M. McKeon, "The Pastoral Revolution," both in this volume.

30. R. Hutton, *Charles II* (Oxford, 1991), 104, 403, and passim; see too R. Crawford, *The King's Evil* (Oxford, 1911).

31. Andrew R. Walkling and James A. Winn have begun to recover for us the

complex story of the Restoration masque and its transformation into opera: see Walkling, "Politics and the Restoration Masque: The Case of *Dido and Aeneas*," in Gerald Maclean, ed., *Culture and Society in the Stuart Restoration* (Cambridge, 1995), 52–69, and Winn, *"When Beauty Fires the Blood": Love and the Arts in the Age of Dryden* (Ann Arbor, 1992), 162–170.

32. On party definition in Andrew Marvell's *The Last Instructions*, see lines 105–372, *Poems on Affairs of State: Augustan Satirical Verse, 1660–1714,* vol. 1: 1660–1678, ed. George deF. Lord (New Haven and London, 1963), 105–117, and commentary; and John Wallace, *Destiny His Choice: The Loyalism of Andrew Marvell* (Cambridge, 1968), 173–178. The Kit Kat Club portraits endeavor to construct a political community through standardized forms. On Kneller see J. Stewart, "Sir Godfrey Kneller as a Painter of Histories and Portraits," in D. Howarth, ed., *Art and Patronage in the Caroline Courts* (Cambridge, 1993), 243–263; and Stewart, *Kneller and the English Baroque Portrait* (Oxford, 1983).

33. It is worth remarking here the powerful opposition to James II conducted in and through engravings that represented him in league with the devil as well as with the pope; see *Catalogue of Prints and Drawings in the British Museum,* Division I, Political and Personal Satires, Vol. 1: 1320–1689 (London, 1870), Vol. 2: 1689–1733 (London, 1873). That the art and industry of engravings was dominated by the Dutch gave William of Orange a political weapon, the importance of which awaits investigation.

34. As well as the mythological representations of William as Protestant Hercules, we must note the Toland edition of Milton which conscripted aesthetic authority to Whig politics; cf. S. Baxter, "William III as Hercules: The Political Implications of Court Culture," *The Revolution of 1688–89: Changing Perspectives,* ed. L. G. Schwoerer (Cambridge, 1992), 95–107, and Sharpe and Zwicker, *Politics of Discourse,* 13.

35. The classic exposition of the Augustan culture of commerce and politeness is P. Langford, *A Polite and Commercial People: England, 1727–1783* (Oxford, 1989); but see as well the recent studies, G. J. Barker-Benfield, *The Culture of Sensibility* (Chicago, 1992), and G. Dickie, *The Century of Taste* (Oxford, 1995).

36. Cf. above, "Introduction," pp. 14–16.

37. See P. G. M. Dickson, *The Financial Revolution in England* (London, 1967); N. McKendric, J. Brewer, and J. H. Plumb, *The Birth of a Consumer Society: The Commercialization of Eighteenth-Century England* (London, 1982); J. Brewer, *The Sinews of Power: War, Money, and the English State, 1688–1783* (Cambridge, Mass., 1988).

38. J. G. A. Pocock, *The Machiavellian Moment: Florentine Political Thought and the Atlantic Republican Tradition* (Princeton, 1975); Pocock, *Virtue, Commerce, and History* (Cambridge, 1985).

39. See the suggestive remarks in J. S. Adamson, "Chivalry and Political Culture in Caroline England," in Sharpe and Lake, *Culture and Politics,* 190–197; Mandeville referred to the "tokens" and "badges" of affluence; see E. J. Hundert, "Performing the Passions in Commercial Society," this volume, p. 147.

40. See L. Klein, "The Rise of Politeness in England, 1660–1715" (Ph.D. dissertation, Johns Hopkins University, 1983); Klein, *Shaftesbury and the Culture of Politeness: Moral Discourse and Cultural Politics in Early Eighteenth-Century England* (Cambridge, 1994); and M. Becker, *Civility and Society in Western Europe, 1300–1600* (Bloomington, 1988).

41. Voltaire, *Lettres philosophiques*, letter 6, cited in Hundert, "Performing the Passions in Commercial Society," p. 330n63.

42. D. Hayton, "The Country Interest and the Party System," in D. Jones, ed., *Party Management in Parliament, 1660–1784* (Leicester, 1984), 37–79; Pocock, *Machiavellian Moment*, chaps. 12–14.

43. Langford, *A Polite and Commercial People*, 77; cf. Langford, *Public Life and the Propertied Englishman* (Oxford, 1991), 1–14, on property as a "grand enchantress."

44. See D. Spadafora, *The Idea of Progress in Eighteenth-Century Britain* (New Haven, 1990); J. Malcolm, *Corruption and Progress: The Eighteenth-Century Debate* (New York, 1989); C. Vercher, *Eighteenth-Century Optimism: A Study of the Interrelations of Moral and Social Theory in English and French Thought between 1689 and 1789* (Liverpool, 1967); and L. Whitney, *Primitivism and the Idea of Progress in English Popular Literature of the Eighteenth Century* (New York, 1965).

45. See L. Klein, *Shaftesbury and the Culture of Politeness;* I. Hont and M. Ignatieff, *Wealth and Virtue: The Shaping of Political Economy in the Scottish Enlightenment* (Cambridge, 1983); and A. O. Hirschman, *The Passions and the Interests: Political Arguments for Capitalism before Its Triumph* (Princeton, 1977).

46. There has been a large and contentious debate about the openness of eighteenth-century society. See L. Stone and J. C. F. Stone, *An Open Elite? England, 1540–1880* (Oxford, 1984); J. Cannon, *Aristocratic Century: The Peerage of Eighteenth-Century England* (Cambridge, 1984); Langford, *Public Life and the Propertied Englishman, 1689–1789*. Our point here is that politeness at least appeared to open broader entry into an elite that defined itself in behavioral and cultural terms; for a critique of Langford, see N. Rogers, "Paul Langford's 'Age of Improvement,'" *Past and Present* 130 (1991): 201–209.

47. See J. Georgia, "Polite Literature: Conduct Books and the Novel in Eighteenth-Century England" (Ph.D. dissertation, Harvard University, 1994); on the growth of the industry of politeness see L. Klein, "The Third Earl of Shaftesbury and the Rise of Politeness," *Eighteenth-Century Studies*, vol. 18 (1984–1985); Klein, "Politeness for Plebes: Some Social Identities in Early Eighteenth-Century England," in J. Brewer and A. Birmingham, eds., *The Consumption of Culture* (New York and London, 1995); and N. Phillipson, ed., *Politics, Politeness, and Patriotism* (Washington, D.C., 1993).

48. See, classically, Richardson's *Pamela* or Austen's *Mansfield Park*, and see the discussion in N. Armstrong, *Desire and Domestic Fiction* (New York, 1987), and L. Klein, "Property and Politeness in the Early Eighteenth-Century Whig Moralists: The Case of the Spectator," in S. Staves and J. Brewer, eds., *Early Modern Conceptions of Property* (London, 1995).

49. See I. Kramnick, *Bolingbroke and His Circle: The Politics of Nostalgia in the Age of Walpole* (Cambridge, Mass., 1968), esp. chaps. 7 and 8; N. Everett, *The Tory View of Landscape* (New Haven, 1994).

50. E. P. Thompson, "The Moral Economy of the Crowd in the Eighteenth Century," *Past and Present* 50 (1971): 76–136; Thompson, "Eighteenth-Century English Society: Class Struggle without Class?" *Social History* 3 (1978): 382–406; Thompson, *Customs in Common* (London, 1991), esp. introduction and chaps. 3 and 5.

51. Cf. M. Jenner, "Bathing and Baptism," below in this volume; and D. Simpson, *Wordsworth's Historical Imagination* (New York, 1987); see also J. Raven, *Judging*

New Wealth: Popular Publishing and Responses to Commerce in England, 1750–1800 (Oxford, 1992); Gerald Izenberg argues that the old humanist language of civic virtue was reevoked to critique the corruption of commerce, this volume, pp. 117–18.

52. G. Harrison, *Wordsworth's Vagrant Muse: Poetry, Poverty, and Power* (Detroit, 1994); McKeon, "Pastoral Revolution," and D. Simpson, *Wordsworth's Historical Imagination* (New York, 1987).

53. See G. N. Izenberg, *Impossible Individuality: Romanticism, Revolution, and the Origins of Modern Selfhood, 1787–1802* (Princeton, 1992), chap. 3, and J. Bate, *Romantic Ecology: Wordsworth and the Environmental Tradition* (London, 1991).

54. See the beginnings of such a history in J. Brewer and R. Porter, eds., *Consumption and the World of Goods* (London, 1993).

55. The commercialization of literary culture has best been studied with reference to the emergence of journalism and the culture of Grub Street; see, for example, R. M. Wiles, *Freshest Advices: Early Provincial Newspapers in England* (Columbus, Ohio, 1987); M. Harris, *London Newspapers in the Age of Walpole* (Cranbury, N.J., 1987); W. A. Speck, *Society and Literature in England 1700–1760* (Dublin, 1983).

56. See, generally, P. Sheavyn, *The Literary Profession in the Elizabethan Age*, 2d rev. ed. (New York, 1967), and G. E. Bentley, *The Profession of the Dramatist in Shakespeare's Time, 1590–1642* (Princeton, 1971); for a study of Greene and Delaney as writers in the market, see D. Margolies, *Novel and Society in Elizabethan England* (London, 1985).

57. On Tonson's subscription edition of Milton, see K. Lynch, *Jacob Tonson, Kit-Cat Publisher* (Knoxville, Tenn., 1971), and on Dryden's financial relations with Tonson over the *Virgil,* see J. Barnard, "Dryden, Tonson, and the Subscriptions for the 1697 *Virgil,*" *PBSA* 57 (1963): 129–151; the contract between Dryden and Tonson and the accounting details on the project can be consulted in *The Works of John Dryden,* ed. Alan Roper (Berkeley and Los Angeles), vol. 6, appendix A, pp. 1179–1187.

58. See n. 55 above, this chapter; specifically on the culture of Grub Street, see P. Pinkus, *Grub St. Stripped Bare* (Hamden, Conn., 1968), and P. Rogers, *Grub Street* (London, 1972).

59. See S. Staves, "The Secrets of Genteel Identity in the Man of Mode: Comedy of Manners vs. the Courtesy Book," *Studies in Eighteenth-Century Culture* (East Lansing, Mich., 1989); R. Markley, "Credit Exhausted: Satire and Scarcity in the 1690s," in J. Gill, ed., *Cutting Edges: Postmodern Critical Essays on Eighteenth-Century Satire* (Knoxville, Tenn., 1995).

60. T. Raylor, *Cavaliers, Clubs, and Literary Culture* (Newark, N.J., 1994); C. Fox, *Locke and the Scriblerians* (Berkeley, 1988); P. Lewis, *John Gay and the Scriblerians* (Totowa, N.J., 1987); L. Curtis, *Esto Perpetua: The Club of Dr. Johnson and His Friends, 1764–1784* (Hamden, Conn., 1969). For contemporary commentary on the emergence of literary societies, see Charles Gildon, *The History of the Athenian Society* (London, 1691); Elkanah Settle, *The New Athenian Comedy* (London, 1693); Sir Richard Blackmore's *The Kit Cats* (London, 1708); and John Dunton, *A Supplement to the Athenian Oracle* (London, 1710).

61. See I. Kramnick, *Bolinbroke and His Circle* (Cambridge, Mass., 1968); S. Zwicker, "Lines of Authority: Politics and Literary Culture in the Restoration," *Politics of Discourse,* ed. Sharpe and Zwicker, 230–270; and, more recently, A. Goldgar,

Impolite Learning: Conduct and Community in the Republic of Letters, 1680–1750 (New Haven, 1995).

62. The classic scholarship on the battle of the books remains R. F. Jones, "The Background of the Battle of the Books," *Washington University Studies* 7 (1920): 99–162, and Jones's edition of *Ancients and Moderns* (St. Louis, 1961); see, more recently, J. M. Levine, *Humanism and History* (Ithaca and London, 1987), chap. 6, and Levine's *The Battle of the Books: History and Literature in the Augustan Age* (Ithaca, 1991).

63. For a brilliant study of the social and political performance of literature, see J. Bender, *Imagining the Penitentiary: Fiction and the Architecture of Mind in Eighteenth-Century England* (Chicago, 1987); see as well M. McKeon, *The Origins of the English Novel, 1600–1740* (Baltimore, 1987).

64. On Aphra Behn, see H. Hunter, *Rereading Aphra Behn: History, Theory, and Criticism* (Charlottesville, Va., 1993); on Mary Astell, see R. Perry, *The Celebrated Mary Astell* (New York, 1986). More generally, see I. Grundy and S. Wiseman, *Women, Writing, History, 1640–1740* (London, 1992); J. Pearson, *The Prostituted Muse: Images of Women and Women Dramatists, 1642–1737* (Cambridge, 1988); J. Spencer, *The Rise of the Woman Novelist: From Aphra Behn to Jane Austen* (Oxford, 1986); and L. Klein, "Gender, Conversation, and the Public Sphere in Early Eighteenth-Century England," in J. Still and M. Worton, eds., *Textuality and Sexuality: Reading Theories and Practices* (Manchester, 1993).

65. See M. Woodmansee, "The Genius and the Copyright: Economic and Legal Conditions of the Emergence of the 'Author,'" *Eighteenth-Century Studies* 17 (1984): 425–48; Mark Rose, *Authors and Owners: The Invention of Copyright* (Cambridge, Mass., 1993); M. Woodmansee, ed., *The Construction of Authorship: Textual Appropriation in Law and Literature* (Durham, N.C., 1994); and J. F. Loewenstein, *The Authorial Impression* (forthcoming).

66. See, most recently, H. Love, *Scribal Publication in Seventeenth-Century England* (Oxford, 1993). The fullest exploration of this subject has been for early modern France; see, for example, R. Darnton, "Reading, Writing, and Publishing in Eighteenth-Century France," *Daedalus* 100 (1971): 214–256; F. Furet and J. Ozouf, *Reading and Writing: Literacy in France from Calvin to Jules Ferry* (Cambridge, 1982); R. Chartier, *The Cultural Uses of Print in Early Modern France* (Princeton, 1989); and R. Chartier, ed., *The Culture of Print: Power and the Uses of Print in Early Modern Europe* (Princeton, 1989).

67. Isobel Rivers, *Books and Their Readers in Eighteenth-Century England* (Leicester, 1982); R. Chartier, *The Order of Books: Readers, Authors, and Libraries in Europe between the Fourteenth and Eighteenth Centuries* (Stanford, 1994); and the edited essay collections by R. Myers and M. H. Harris, *A Genius for Letters: Booksellers and Bookselling from the Sixteenth to the Twentieth Century* (New Castle, Del., 1995); *Series and Their Readers, 1620–1914* (New Castle, Del., 1993).

68. See *The Character of a Coffee-House* (London, 1671), 7–13, that "lay-convencticle . . . [where] each man has his news and his coffee for the same charge . . . the rendevous of idle pamphlets, and persons more idly employed to read them . . . and always shifting scene . . . [an] enchaned island . . . [where] they bring plays to repetition, sift each scene, examine every uncorrected line, and damn

beyond the fury of the rota"; or Rochester's brilliant cartoon of the Restoration wit aping the language and gestures of the theater:

> The second was a Grays Inn witt
> A great Inhabiter of the Pitt
> Where Crittick-like he sitts and squints
> Steales Pockett Handkerchers and hints
> From's Neighbour and the Comedy
> To Court and pay his Landlady.

from *A Ramble in Saint James's Parke*, ll. 63–68, *The Poems of John Wilmot, Earl of Rochester*, ed. K. Walker (Oxford, 1984). Here we see the value of the broader critical reconfiguration of text, and of Greenblatt's idea of the circulation of social energy between texts and in and out of texts. The coffeehouse questions the pervading tendency in historical studies to separate rigidly textual from other social practices.

69. The development of the printed key can be traced precisely to the Restoration collections of poems on state affairs; see the editorial apparatus of the modern Yale edition of *Poems on Affairs of State: Augustan Satirical Verse*, ed. George deF. Lord et al., 7 vols. (New Haven, 1963–1975), for lists of manuscript and printed keys.

70. Cf. J. Bender, *Imagining the Penitentiary: Fiction and the Architecture of Mind in Eighteenth-Century England* (Chicago, 1987), and M. McKeon, *The Origins of the English Novel, 1600–1740* (Baltimore and London, 1987).

71. See Zwicker, "Reading the Margins," below pp. 101–115; and W. Sherman, *John Dee: The Politics of Reading and Writing in the English Renaissance* (Amherst, 1995).

72. The Bible speaks powerfully to the politics of material form. James I's Authorized version was published to supplant the Geneva Bible with its (to him) dangerous marginalia.

73. R. Colie, *The Resources of Kind: Genre Theory in the Renaissance* (Berkeley and Los Angeles, 1973); A. Fowler, *Kinds of Literature: An Introduction to the Theory of Genres and Modes* (Cambridge, Mass., 1982); B. K. Lewalski, ed., *Renaissance Genres: Essays on Theory, History, and Interpretation* (Cambridge, Mass., 1986); and Sharpe and Zwicker, *Politics of Discourse*, 10–13.

74. Maguire, *Regicide and Restoration: English Tragicomedy, 1660–1671;* and McKeon, "The Pastoral Revolution," below in this volume.

75. See above, pp. 12 ff., and below, n. 81.

76. See G. H. Hartmann, *Wordsworth's Poetry, 1787–1814* (New Haven, 1964), for a radically ahistorical invoking of the imagination, and H. Bloom's *The Visionary Company: A Reading of English Romantic Poetry* (Ithaca, 1971), for stress on the atemporal transcendence of the romantic imagination.

77. See A. Liu, *Wordsworth: The Sense of History* (Stanford, 1989); D. Simpson, *Wordsworth's Historical Imagination* (New York, 1987); M. Levinson, *Wordsworth's Great Period Poems: Four Essays* (Cambridge, 1986); J. K. Chandler, *Wordsworth's Second Nature: A Study of the Poetry and Politics* (Chicago, 1982); and J. J. McGann, *The Romantic Ideology: A Critical Investigation* (Chicago, 1983).

78. See, for example, D. Landry, *The Muses of Resistance: Laboring-Class Women's Poetry in Britain, 1739–1796* (Cambridge, 1990), and D. Dugaw, *Warrior Women and Popular Balladry, 1650–1850* (Chicago, 1989).

79. See D. G. Hale, *The Body Politic: A Political Metaphor in Renaissance English Literature* (The Hague, 1971); L. Barkan, *Nature's Work: The Human Body as Image of the*

World (New Haven, 1975); and J. Sawday, *The Body Emblazoned: Dissection and the Human Body in Renaissance Culture* (London, 1995).

80. R. Strong, *The Cult of Elizabeth* (London, 1977); K. Sharpe, *Criticism and Compliment: The Politics of Literature in the England of Charles I* (Cambridge, 1987); see too T. Corns, *Uncloistered Virtue: English Political Literature 1640–1660* (Oxford, 1992), esp. chap. 7.

81. One suspects a relationship between Restoration politics and pornography, between the demystification of love and the female and of kingship and authority; see R. Braverman, *Plots and Counterplots: Sexual Politics and the Body Politic in English Literature, 1660–1730* (Cambridge, 1993); Kevin Sharpe is pursuing this twin subject for a book on images of power in England from 1500 to 1700.

82. For the Restoration (as indeed for the coronation and marriage) the verse panegyrics—which were produced in vast, unprecedented number—regularly twinned hopes of political harmony with sexual fecundity; the Exclusion Crisis was driven quite obviously by fears of a Catholic succession consequent, all too obviously, on the failure of royal fecundity.

83. See W. Cherniak, *Sexual Freedom in Restoration Literature* (Cambridge, 1995), and R. Weil, "The Politics of Legitimacy: Women and the Warming-Pan Scandal," in L. G. Schwoerer, ed., *The Revolution of 1688–1689*, 65–82; and Weil's "Sexual Ideology and Political Propaganda in England, 1680–1714" (Ph.D. dissertation, Princeton University, 1991).

84. On the 1650s see K. V. Thomas, "Women and the Civil War Sects," *Past and Present* 13 (1958): 42–62; P. Mack, "Women as Prophets during the English Civil War," *Feminist Studies* 8 (1982): 19–46; R. Tribowitz, "Female Preachers and Male Wives: Gender and Authority in Civil War England," in J. Holstun, ed., *Pamphlet Wars* (London, 1992) 112–133; and A. M. McEentee, "The [Un]Civill-Sisterhood of Oranges and Lemons: Female Petitioners and Demonstrators, 1642–1653," in Holstun, ed., *Pamphlet Wars*, 92–111.

85. There are many images of women with exotic fruits (lemons) and birds (parrots) in the Huntington Library's engravings collected by Richard Bull. See M. Pointon, *Hanging the Head: Portraiture and Social Formation in Eighteenth-Century England* (New Haven, 1993), chap. 2.

86. Cleland's *Fanny Hill* is of course the most famous of eighteenth-century novels celebrating female sexual desire, but equally Defoe's *Roxana* and *Moll Flanders* plot female sexual agency.

87. Bender, *Imagining the Penitentiary*, pp. 114–136; R. Paulson, *Hogarth's Graphic Works* (New Haven, 1965); Paulson, *Hogarth: His Life, Art, and Times*, 2 vols. (New Haven, 1971).

88. See above, "Introduction," p. 7; see H. Guest, "These Neuter Somethings," pp. 178–179.

89. Guest, "These Neuter Somethings," this volume, p. 185; McKeon, "The Pastoral Revolution," pp. 28off.

90. For the most obvious example, see Henry Mackenzie's *The Man of Feeling* (1771), but see as well Fanny Burney's *Evelina* (1778) or, for the valorization of feeling in the gothic novel, Anne Radcliffe's *The Italian* (1824), or Wordsworth himself in *The Prelude* or in the Lucy poems and Tintern Abbey. See also Barker-Benfield, *The Culture of Sensibility: Sex and Society in Eighteenth-Century Britain*.

91. See J. Sawday, "'Mysteriously Divided': Civil War, Madness, and the Divided Self," in T. Healy and J. Sawday, eds., *Literature and the English Civil War* (Cambridge, 1990), 127–46.

92. J. Locke, *An Essay concerning Human Understanding*, ed. P. H. Nidditch (Oxford, 1978), chap. 20, pp. 229–233; cf. pp. 128 ff.

93. See Locke, *An Essay concerning Human Understanding*, book 1, chapter 2, "No Innate Practical Principles," para. 8; see also K. Sharpe, "Private Conscience and Public Duty in the Writings of James VI and I," in J. Morrill, P. Slack, and D. Woolf, eds., *Public Duty and Private Conscience in Seventeenth-Century England* (Oxford, 1993), 77–78; K. Thomas, "Cases of Conscience in Seventeenth-Century England," in ibid., 53–56.

94. See M. Foucault, *Madness and Civilization: A History of Insanity in the Age of Reason* (London, 1967); *Discipline and Punish: The Birth of the Prison* (Harmondsworth, 1979); *The Order of Things: An Archaeology of the Human Sciences* (London, 1970).

95. See E. Hundert, *The Enlightenment's "Fable": Bernard Mandeville and the Discovery of Society* (Cambridge, 1994), and Hundert, "Performing the Passions," pp. 144–147.

96. Greenblatt's *Renaissance Self-Fashioning* inspired a whole new approach to Renaissance subjectivity.

97. See M. Featherstone, "The Body in Consumer Culture," *Theory, Culture, and Society* 1 (1982): 18–33.

98. The classic account of costume on the Restoration and early eighteenth-century stage is J. Genest, *Some Account of the English Stage from the Restoration in 1660 to 1830,* 10 vols. in 16 vols. (Chelsea, 1865)

99. See Hundert, "Performing the Passions," especially pp. 149ff.

100. See Porter, "Medicine, Politics, and the Body in Late Eighteenth-Century England," this volume, pp. 220–222; and G. S. Rousseau, ed., *The Languages of Psyche: Mind and Body in Enlightenment Thought* (Berkeley, 1990). See too C. Fox, ed., *Psychology and Literature in the Eighteenth Century* (New York, 1987), introduction, "Defining Eighteenth-Century Psychology: Some Problems and Perspectives."

101. On this theme see Izenberg, *Impossible Individuality,* chap. 3.

102. Izenberg, "The Politics of Song," pp. 124–125, 134–135.

103. See, for examples, D. Johnson, *Thomas Hobbes and the Politics of Cultural Transformation* (Princeton, 1986); and R. Prokhovnik, *Rhetoric and Philosophy in Hobbes' Leviathan* (New York, 1991); and cf. E. Skerpan, *The Rhetoric of Politics in the English Revolution, 1642–1660* (Columbia, Mo., 1992).

104. The most brilliant analysis and defusion of the failure of Charles II's fertility is of course Dryden's *Absalom and Achitophel:* see Zwicker, *Lines of Authority,* 133–136; on Queen Anne, see T. Bowers, *The Politics of Motherhood* (Cambridge, 1997); and Bowers, "Queen Anne Makes Provision," pp. 57–74.

105. The hive was an enduring trope from Virgil onward; see K. Sharpe, *Politics and Ideas* (London, 1989), 52–54.

106. John Barrell ("Sad Stories," in this volume) shows the persistence of the metaphors of body and father that shaped the discourse and perception of the state.

107. M. Butler, *Romantics, Rebels, and Reactionaries: English Literature and Its Background, 1760–1830* (New York, 1981).

108. See Izenberg, "The Politics of Song," pp. 134–135.

109. P. J. Marshall and G. Williams, *The Great Map of Mankind: British Perceptions of the World in the Age of the Enlightenment* (London, 1982); see C. Batten, *Pleasurable Instruction: Form and Convention in Eighteenth-Century Travel Literature* (Berkeley, 1978). We still await a good study of Enlightenment travel literature as exploration of the English imagination as well as overseas empire.

110. See P. Mitter, *Much Maligned Monsters: The History of European Reactions to Indian Art* (Oxford, 1977).

111. See M. Jenner, "Bathing and Baptism," pp. 212–213; on the exotic and Restoration and eighteenth-century literature and theater, see the essays in E. Dudley and M. Novak, eds., *The Wild Man Within* (Pittsburgh, 1972); Won-Moon Song, "Racial Otherness: The Representation of colored minorities in Shakespeare and Restoration Drama" (Ph.D. dissertation, University of Wisconsin, 1994); J. Clare, "The Production and Reception of Davenant's *The Cruelty of the Spaniards in Peru*," *Modern Language Review* 84 (1994): 832–841; W. Wilson, "Turks on the Eighteenth-Century Operatic Stage and European Political, Military, and Cultural History," *Eighteenth-Century Life*, vol. 9 (1985), and *Women, Race, and Writing in the Early Modern Period*, ed. P. Parker and M. Hendrix (London, 1994).

112. See Bending, "A Natural Revolution," pp. 244–245.

113. R. Armstrong, *The Atlantic Slave Trade and British Abolition, 1760–1800* (London, 1975); J. R. Oldfield, *Popular Politics and British Anti-Slavery: The Mobilisation of Public Opinion against the Slave Trade, 1787–1807* (Manchester, 1995); D. Turley, *The Culture of English Antislavery 1780–1860* (London, 1991); and Langford, *A Polite and Commercial People*, 515–518.

114. We owe this point to H. Guest, "Curiously Marked: Tattooing, Masculinity and Nationality in Eighteenth-Century British Perceptions of the South Pacific," in J. Barrell, ed., *Painting and the Politics of Culture: New Essays on British Art, 1700–1850* (Oxford, 1992); see, also, B. Smith, *European Vision and the South Pacific,* 3d ed. (South Melbourne, Australia, 1989).

115. Marshall and Williams, *The Great Map of Mankind*. The association of the East with sexual license and despotism had a long history; see P. Rycaut, *The Present State of the Ottoman Empire* (London, 1668); cf. J. Majeed, *Ungoverned Imaginings: James Mill's "History of British India" and Orientalism* (Oxford, 1992).

116. See Barrell, "Sad Stories," in this volume; and J. Mullan, *Sentiment and Sociability: The Language of Feeling in the Eighteenth Century* (Oxford, 1988).

117. It is not clear that J. Pocock and Q. Skinner fully negotiate the dimension we call here "latitude" as successfully as they indicate the "longitudinal" dimension of the languages and idioms whose histories they so brilliantly write.

118. See, for example, the discussion of "party" in Sharpe and Zwicker, *Politics of Discourse*, 7–8; for an excellent explication of the importance of changed electoral policies as a barometer of the broader shift from honor to commerce, see M. Kishlansky, *Parliamentary Selection: Social and Political Choice in Early Modern England* (Cambridge, 1986).

119. See *Catalogue of Prints and Drawings in the British Museum*, Division I, Political and Personal Satires, vol. 1: 1320–1689 (London, 1870), Vol. 2: 1689–1733 (London, 1873); it is worth reminding ourselves that even during the 1640s and 1650s there were no scatological cartoons depicting and denigrating the royal body.

120. See Porter, "Medicine, Politics, and the Body," pp. 230–232.

121. *OED*, s.v. "King's Evil"; J. C. D. Clark, *English Society, 1688–1832*.

122. Clark, *English Society, 1688–1832*.

123. See, for example, J. Toland, *Christianity not Mysterious* (London, 1696); *The Reasonableness of Assenting to the Mysteries of Christianity Asserted and Vindicated* (London, 1708); J. Dickinson, *The Reasonableness of Christianity in Four Sermons* (Boston, 1732); J. Locke, *A Second Vindication of the Reasonableness of Christianity* (London, 1736); G. Benson, *The Reasonableness of the Christian Religion As Delivered in the Scriptures* (London, 1743).

124. The English translation of Habermas, *Structural Transformation of the Public Sphere*, 1987, introduced to the world of Anglophone scholarship the idea of "public space" in the age of widening literacy and developing print culture; the past several years of scholarship have made clear both the importance of Habermas's term for the study of Restoration and eighteenth-century public and polite culture and the limitations of such terms as "public opinion" and "public space."

125. See Bending, "A Natural Revolution," pp. 241–266; and Guest, "These Neuter Somethings," pp. 173–194. For a similar argument about the Victorian Zoo, see H. Ritvo, *The Animal Estate: The English and Other Creatures in the Victorian Age* (Cambridge, Mass., 1987).

126. Sharpe and Zwicker, *Politics of Discourse*, 8–9.

127. *OED*, s.v. "Sublime."

128. L. Newlyn, *Paradise Lost and the Romantic Reader* (Oxford, 1993); P. Ackroyd, *Blake* (London, 1995); J. Wittreich, *Angel of the Apocalypse: Blake's Idea of Milton* (Madison, Wisc., 1975).

129. F. Fukuyama, *The End of History and the Last Man* (New York, 1992).

"AN IMAGE DOTING RABBLE"

1. E. M. W. Tillyard, *The Elizabethan World Picture* (1943, reissued to date); cf. A. O. Lovejoy, *The Great Chain of Being* (Cambridge, Mass., 1936).

2. P. Collinson, "The Monarchical Republic of Queen Elizabeth I," *Bulletin of the John Rylands Library* 69 (1987): 394–424.

3. J. H. Salmon, *The French Religious Wars in English Political Thought* (Oxford, 1959); J. E. Phillips, "George Buchanan and the Sidney Circle," *Huntington Library Quarterly* 12 (1948): 23–56.

4. M. Smuts, "Court-Centred Politics and the Uses of Roman Historians, c. 1590–1630," in K. Sharpe and P. Lake, eds., *Culture and Politics in Early Stuart England* (Stanford, 1994), 21–44; D. Norbrook, "Lucan, Thomas May, and the Creation of a Republican Literary Culture," in ibid., 45–66; B. Worden, "Classical Republicanism and the Puritan Revolution," in H. Lloyd-Jones, V. Pearl, and B. Worden, eds., *History and Imagination* (1981), 182–200; Worden, "The Commonwealth Kidney of Algernon Sidney," *Journal British Studies* 24 (1985): 1–40.

5. *An Act for Abolishing the Kingly Office in England, Ireland, and the Dominions thereunto Belonging*, British Library, Thomason Tracts, 669 f14/2.

6. I. Pennington, *The Fundamental Right, Safety, and Liberty of the People* . . . (1651), British Library, Thomason Tracts, E629/2.

7. J. Goodwin, *The Obstructors of Justice, or A Defence of the Honourable Sentence Passed upon the Late King* (1649), E557/2, dedication.

8. A. Warren, *The Royalist Reform'd* (1649), E582/4, pp. 20, 43.

9. [M. Nedham], *The Case of the Commonwealth of England Stated* (1650), E600/7, p. 93.

10. Panegyric to Cromwell in F. Peck, *Memoirs of the Life and Actions of Oliver Cromwell* (1740), p. 70.

11. *A Declaration of the Parliament of England Expressing the Grounds of Their Late Proceedings* (1649), E548/12.

12. Godwin, *Obstructors of Justice*, 46, 59.

13. See, for example, *The Bounds and Bonds of Publique Obedience* (1649), E571/26, p. 7. *Reasons Why the Supreme Authority of the Three Nations . . . Is Not in the Parliament* (1653), E697/19, p. 3, where it is claimed that "most of the Parliamentarian writers" make "Necessity . . . the main reason for turning the monarchy of this land into a state."

14. [Nedham], *Case of the Commonwealth*, 4.

15. See T. Corns, *Uncloistered Virtue: English Political Literature, 1640–1660* (Oxford, 1992), 208 and chap. 6.

16. *Bounds and Bonds of Publique Obedience*, 20–21.

17. *The Lawfulness of Obeying the Present Government* (1649), E551/22, pp. 6–8 and passim.

18. Nedham, *Case of the Commonwealth*, 23, 31.

19. R. Bennet, *King Charles' Trial Justified* (1649), E554/21, p. 4.

20. *The Government of the People of England Precedent and Present the Same* (1650), E594/19, p. 7.

21. *The True Portraiture of the Kings of England* (1650), E609/2, p. 15.

22. See pp. 30, 32–33.

23. *A Short Discourse between Monarchical and Aristocratical Government* (1649), E575/31, pp. 19–20, denounces Leveller arguments on these lines.

24. Nedham, *The Case of the Commonwealth;* on Nedham see J. G. A. Pocock, *The Machiavellian Moment: Florentine Political Thought and the Atlantic Republican Tradition* (Princeton, 1975), 379–384; J. Scott, *Algernon Sidney and the English Republic 1623–1677* (Cambridge, 1988), 110–112; and now B. Worden, "Marchamont Nedham and the Beginnings of English Republicanism, 1649–1656," in D. Wootton, ed., *Republicanism, Liberty, and Commercial Society, 1649–1776* (Stanford, 1994), pp. 45–81.

25. *A Short Discourse*, 12, 15.

26. For example, *Veni, Vidi, Vici: the Triumphs of the Most Excellent . . . Oliver Cromwell* (1652), E1298/1; *The Establishment* (1653), E720/1.

27. On pp. 52–53.

28. *A Logical Demonstration of the Lawfulness of Subscribing the New Engagement* (1650), E590/11, pp. 5–6.

29. *Monarchy No Creature of God's Making* (1652), E1238/1, dedication, p. 116 and passim. Cf. G. W., *The Modern Statesmen* (1653), E1542/2, p. 56.

30. *A Short Discourse*, 18.

31. B. Worden, "Providence and Politics in Cromwellian England," *Past and Present* 109 (1985): 55–99.

32. *A Letter from the Right Hon. the Lord Lieutenant of Ireland to . . . William Lenthall* (London, 1649), p. 2.

33. Worden, "Providence and Politics," passim.

34. E. Skerpan, *The Rhetoric of Politics in the English Revolution* (Columbia, Miss., 1992), 84, speaks of "the *opportunity* to create a new political community out of language." It was also a need.

35. I am grateful to Ross Parry for discussions of this subject.

36. *A Letter from the Lord Lieutenant of Ireland . . . 25 February 1649 / [50]*, p. 3.

37. *A Letter from the Lord Lieutenant of Ireland, 30 October 1649*, p. 8; *A Letter from the Lord General . . . 21 July 1650*, p. 5.

38. *Letter 21 July 1650*, p. 6; *A Letter from the Lord General Cromwell from Dunbar, 3 September 1650*, in *Original Memoirs during the Great Civil War, Being the Life of Sir Henry Slingsby* (Edinburgh, 1806), 302.

39. Ibid., 303.

40. British Library, Thomason tracts, 669 f13/77 (1649).

41. *The Government of the People of England*, 13; I. Pennington, *The Fundamental Right, Safety, and Liberty of The People . . .* (1651), E629/2, p. 17.

42. During the 1640s parliamentarians had endeavored to undermine the royalists' monopoly of this language with some measure of success. But it remained a language of monarchy, for all the differences about the nature of kingship. I am grateful to Joad Raymond for a discussion of this issue.

43. *Joyful News from Holland Showing the Royal Entertainment Given by the States of the United Provinces to the Lords Ambassadors of the Commonwealth of England* (1651), E626/18.

44. *Reasons Why the Supreme Authority . . . Is Not in the Parliament*, 11.

45. J. Milton, *History of Britain*, quoted in J. Scott, "The English Republican Imagination," in J. Morrill, ed., *Revolution and Restoration* (1992), 36.

46. Blair Worden, "Milton's Republicanism and the Tyranny of Heaven," in G. Bock, Q. Skinner, and M. Viroli, eds., *Machiavelli and Republicanism* (Cambridge, 1990), 231.

47. It is interesting that there was little translated from or written about Dutch or Venetian political debate.

48. Milton, *Eikonoklastes*, in W. H. Haller, ed., *The Works of John Milton* (New York, 1932), 5:309. See pp. 53–54.

49. Such portraits and engravings as there are depict members of the Council in sober, black dress, conveying a godly but not republican representation.

50. I spent several months with the large collection of engraved British portraits in the Huntington Library's Richard Bull copy of James Granger's *Biographical History of England*. All illustrations to this essay are reproduced with the kind permission of the Huntington Library. See M. Pointon, *Hanging the Head* (1993), chap. 2.

51. British Library, Thomason tracts, 669 f16/23. The engraving is based on a Robert Walker portrait, of which there are several variants and copies.

52. Huntington Library, Bull/Granger, vol. 10, no. 34.

53. Huntington Library, Bull/Granger, vol. 12, no. 34.

54. See M. Seymour, "Pro-Government Propaganda in Interregnum England, 1649–1660," (Ph.D. dissertation, Cambridge University, 1987), 125: "The badge of

a nation replaced the head of a king; the language of the people replaced the language of the law; the title of Commonwealth . . . replaced that of personal dominion; and the palm and laurel spoke of the peace brought by victory."

55. Most of the coins I have seen are from 1651 or later.

56. Seymour, "Pro-Government Propaganda," 120–124, quotation 120.

57. See pp. 45–46.

58. *A Second Part of the Religious Demurrer* (1649), E530/31, p. 7.

59. *Comparatio inter Claudium Tiberium Principem et Olivarium Cromwellium Protectorem* (1657) (Huntington Library not in Wing) p. 16. See K. Sharpe, "Private Conscience and Public Duty in the Writings of Charles I," *Historical Journal* 40 (1997): 643–665.

60. A. Evans, *The Euroclydon Winde Commanded to Cease* (1653), E1491/2, p. 6.

61. *The Life and Reign of King Charles, or The Pseudo Martyr Discovered* (1652), E1338/2, preface. Cf. *The Non Such Charles His Character* (1651), E1345, where after a damning condemnation of the monarchy the author acknowledges "the smile of a king can send comfort unto the very heart of men" (p. 182).

62. *A Short Discourse*, E575/31, p. 12.

63. *The Monument of Charles I* (1649), 669 f14/36.

64. See Skerpan, *Rhetoric of Politics,* chap. 5; Corns, *Uncloistered Virtue,* 80–91; K. Sharpe, "The King's Writ: Royal Authors and Royal Authority in Early Modern England," in Sharpe and Lake, *Culture and Politics,* 135; most of all the brilliant analysis in S. Zwicker, *Lines of Authority: Politics and English Literary Culture, 1649–1689* (Ithaca, 1993), chap. 2.

65. *An Elegie upon the Death of Our Dread Sovereign Lord King Charles* (1649), 669 f14/42.

66. *An Elegie on the Meekest of Men,* (London, 1649) 14.

67. *Psalterium Carolinum: The Devotions of his Sacred Majestie* (1657), E1076, an important and neglected work.

68. *Virtus Rediviva: A Panegyrick on Our Late King Charles I* (1660), E1806, p. 26.

69. See the appendix to *Monarchy or No Monarchy in England* (1651) (E638/17), especially pp. 81 ff.

70. *Eikon Alethine: The Portraiture of Truths Most Sacred Majestie* (1649), E569/16, pp. 2–6, p. 6.

71. Ibid., sig. [A1]: epistle to reader.

72. *The Life of King Charles* (1652), preface.

73. Ibid., 148–149.

74. Ibid., 178.

75. Huntington Library, Bull/Granger, vol. 6, nos. 23, 24.

76. *Eikon e Piste, or The Faithful Portraiture of a Loyal Subject* (1649), E573/11, an engraving of Charles writing, with accompanying verse.

77. H. Farquar, "Portraits of the Stuarts on the Royalist Badges," *British Numismatic Journal* 2 (1906): 23–30.

78. *Eikon Alethine:* see the verse "Presumptious priest to slip into the throne / And make his King his bastard issue owne," frontispiece.

79. *The True Manner of the Crowning of Charles the Second, King of Scotland* (1651), E669f15/82; R. Douglas, *The Form and Order of the Coronation* (Aberdeen, 1650), Wing 2030B.

80. R. W. K. Hinton, ed., *A Serious and Faithful Representation of Ministers of the Gospel* (Reading, 1949), 11.

81. Ibid., 12, 17.

82. *The Rebels Looking Glass* (1649), E554/23.

83. R. Sprye, *Rules of Civil Government Drawn from the Best Examples of Foreign Nations* (1653), E1484/3, sig. A3.

84. *A Brief Chronology of Great Britain* (1656), 669 f20/35; *Three Propositions* (1659), E985/17.

85. Nedham, we recall, took up a cyclical rather than linear view of history in *The Case of the Commonwealth*, 4.

86. *The True Portraiture of the Kings of England*, 11–15, quote 15.

87. J. T., *The Number and Names of All the Kings of England and Scotland* (1650), E1246/3.

88. N. Bacon, *The Continuation of an Historical Discourse of the Government of England* (1650), E624/1, p. 357.

89. *The Royalist Reform'd*, 10.

90. *A Short Discourse*, 18.

91. *Majestas Intemerata, or the Immortality of the King*, 118–119. We await a good study of the rhetoric and polemic of histories written and published during the civil war and interregnum.

92. W. J., *A Dissection of All Governments* (1649), E545/23, pp. 5, 12, and passim.

93. W. Juxon, *The Subjects Sorrow* . . . (1649), E546/16, p. 26.

94. *The Royal Legacies* (1649), E557/1, p. 49.

95. *An Exercitation concerning Usurped Powers* (1649), E585/2, p. 64: "We therefore swear to obey Princes . . . whilst it pleaseth God to continue them to us; and this tie a present interruption of government . . . cannot dissolve."

96. *Jeremias Redevivus* (1649), E556/33, p. 2.

97. See, for example, *Observations upon Aristotle's Politics,* sig A5; *God and the King* (1649), E550/2; *The Royal Legacies,* 78 and passim.

98. The photoarchives at the Huntington Library and Courtauld Institute reveal dozens of copies of the famous Van Dycks which are too often discussed as images seen only at Court.

99. Quite literally in the case of the engraving of Charles I surrounded by loyal supporters, sold by Sam Speed at the Rainbow in Fleet St. (Huntington Library, Bull/Granger, vol. 6, no. 26). Engravings were also made of statues that were removed during the Commonwealth: e.g., a Le Sueur statue preserved by a brazier in Holborne (ibid., vol. 6, no. 16).

100. *Mercurius Rusticus* (1647), E1099/1, pp. 203, 212–213.

101. Huntington Library, Bull/Granger, vol. 6, no. 20.

102. Ibid., vol. 6, no. 22.

103. *The Subjects Sorrow* (1649), E546/16.

104. Huntington Library, Bull/Granger, vol. 6, no. 25.

105. Huntington Library, Bull/Granger, vol. 7, no. 122; vol. 11, no. 38.

106. Ibid., vol. 10, no. 26, dated 30 January 1649, with verses from Job 14: 7–9. This is also British Museum, engraved portrait, no. 737.

107. Huntington Library, Bull/Granger, vol. 6, no. 30; vol. 12, no. 7.

108. B. L. Thomason tracts, 669 f12/88.

109. Huntington Library, Bull/Granger, vol. 10, nos. 3, 3v, vol. 12, no. 6.

110. Ibid., vol. 12, no. 31v.

111. Ibid., vol. 10, no. 26.

112. For example, ibid., vol. 10, no. 72v.

113. W. Sanderson, *Graphice: The Use of the Pen and Pencil, or The Most Excellent Art of Painting* (1658), E1077/2.

114. *The King's Last Farewell to the World* (1649), 669 f1/79.

115. *The Royal Charter* (1649), E1356/1, p. 18.

116. F. Peck, *Historical Pieces* (1740), 56; for information about the mace, I am grateful to Sean Kelsey.

117. H. W. Henfrey, *Numismata Cromwelliana: Coins, Medals, and Seals of Oliver Cromwell* (1877), 3–4.

118. See pp. 47–48.

119. *Monarchy or No Monarchy* (1651), E638/7, pp. 118–119.

120. N. G. Brett-James, *The Growth of Stuart London* (1935), 18, 43, 323.

121. O. Millar, *The Inventories and Valuations of the King's Goods*, Walpole Soc., no. 43 (1972); A. MacGregor, ed., *The Late King's Goods* (1989). Little attention has been paid to the purchasers of Charles I's goods (who include leading members of the Council of State) or to the significance of items with royal arms being distributed and displayed throughout the life of the republic.

122. *The Government of the People of England* (1650) was printed and sold at the King's Head!

123. See *Enthusiasm Displayed* (1743), 21; *The Right Picture of King Oliver* (1650), E858/7, p. 8.

124. Anon., *The Royal Game at Pickett* (1656), E886/4.

125. See K. Sharpe, "A Commonwealth of Meanings," in Sharpe, *Politics and Ideas* (1989), 50 ff. It is interesting that the Convention in France tried to change such symbols.

126. *A Short Discourse*, 19.

127. *The English Tyrants* (1649), E569/10, p. 12.

128. *An Act Establishing the Powers of Lord Admiral . . . as Lord Warden of the Cinque Ports upon the Council of State* (1651) 669/f15/80. In 1660 satires mocked Commonwealth proclamations; see, for example, *St. George and the Dragon* (1660), 669/f23/66.

129. *The Commonwealth Mercury*, 2–9 September 1658.

130. Peck, *Historical Pieces*, 60–61.

131. See D. Cressy, *Bonfires and Bells: National Memory and the Protestant Calendar in Elizabethan and Stuart England* (1989), chap. 9.

132. *Honor Redevivus* (1655), E1458/2, p. 61; cf. pp. 48, 62, and passim; *A New Catalogue of the Dukes, Marquesses, Earls, Viscounts, Barons . . .* (1652), E1238/2.

133. See R. Sherwood, *The Court of Oliver Cromwell* (1977).

134. J. S. A. Adamson, "Chivalry and Political Culture in Caroline England," in Sharpe and Lake, *Culture and Politics*, 194.

135. *The Card of Courtship* (1653), E1308/2; cf. K. Sharpe, *Criticism and Compliment: The Politics of Literature in the England of Charles I* (Cambridge, 1987), chap. 7.

136. *The Accomplished Courtier* (1658), E1824/1, title page.

137. *The Mysteries of Love and Eloquence* (1658), E1735, pp. 104, 155 ff, 176, and passim; cf. Corns, *Uncloistered Virtue*, 244–268, and D. Hirst, "The Politics of Literature in the English Republic," *The Seventeenth Century* 5 (1991): 135–155.

138. *Prologue to His Majesty at the First Play Presented at the Cockpit in Whitehall* (1660), 669/f26/26.

139. R. Brome, *Five New Playes* (1653), E1423.

140. *Hymen's Praeludia* (1655), E1459/2.

141. S. J. Wiseman, "History Digested: Opera and Colonialism in the 1650s," in T. Healy and J. Sawday, eds., *Literature and the English Civil War* (Cambridge, 1990) 189–204; J. Shirley, *Cupid and Death: A Masque* (1653), E690/4.

142. See J. Jacob and T. Raylor, "Opera and Obedience: Thomas Hobbes and *A Proposition for Advancement of Moralitie* by Sir William Davenant," *The Seventeenth Century* 6 (1991): 205–250. Cf. N. Smith, "Popular Republicanism in the 1650s: John Streater's 'Heroick Mechanicks,'" in Q. Skinner and D. Armitage, eds., *Milton and Republicanism* (Cambridge, 1995), pp. 137–155. I am grateful to Nigel Smith for his having allowed me to read this interesting essay in advance of publication.

143. *The Nuptials of Peleus and Thetis* (1654), E228/3.

144. See Seymour, "Pro-Government Propaganda," chap. 6.

145. Ibid., 224; cf. 229: "There was perhaps no convenient way to advertise the merits of a political collectivity."

146. Ibid., 196–199.

147. *London's Triumph, or The Solemn and Magnificent Reception of . . . Robert Tichborn, Lord Maior* (1656), E892/7, p. 9.

148. See Abbot, *Writings and Speeches of Cromwell*, 2:642–643.

149. *A Declaration of the Lord General and His Council . . .* (1653), E692/6, p. 4.

150. Peck, *Memoirs of Cromwell*, 122.

151. *A True State of the Case of The Commonwealth* E728/5 (1654), pp. 3, 28, 32 ff, 51, and passim.

152. *A Declaration concerning the Government of the Three Nations* (1653), E725/2.

153. Ibid.: E. J. Porter, "'Imperious Dictators and Masters of Words'": The Discourse of Legitimacy in Cromwell's England, 1653–1655 (Ph.D. dissertation, La Trobe University, 1992), 162–168.

154. *Declaration concerning the Government*, 6.

155. Ibid., 6.

156. *Reasons Why*, E697/19, pp. 7, 18; J. Cornubiensis, *The Grand Catastrophe* (1654), E726/12, pp. 7–8; J. Moore, *Protection Proclaimed* (1655), E860/5, To the Reader; S. Richardson, *Plain Dealing* (1656), E865/3, p. 10.

157. G. Wither, *The Protector: A Poem* (1655), E1565/2, "to the readers," pp. 17 ff.

158. *The Character of a Protector* (1654), E743/2.

159. S. Richardson, *An Apology for the Present Government* (1654), E812/18, p. 10; *Declaration of a Freeborn People* (1655), 669f19/70.

160. See *A Declaration of His Highness . . . 22 January 1654* (1655), E826/13, and Abbot, *Writings and Speeches of Cromwell*, 3:451–60.

161. *The Picture of a New Courtier* (1656), E875/6, p. 11. Smith suggests it may be by Streater ("Popular Republicanism," p. 139n4).

162. *Picture of a New Courtier*, 13.

163. S. Carrington, *The History of the Life and Death of . . . Oliver Late Lord Protector* (1659), E1787/1, p. 167; *Perfect Politician* (1660), E1869/1, pp. 253–254.

164. *The Perfect Politician*, pp. 265 ff.

165. *The Whole Manner of The Treaty . . . between His Highness the Lord Protector and the Lords Ambassadors of the United Provinces* (1654), E731/14, pp. 5–7; Sherwood, *Court of Oliver Cromwell*, 140–141.

166. For example, *The Unparalleled Monarch*, epistle to the reader; sig. [A6ᵛ], pp. 11, 51; P. Fisher, *Piscatoris Poemata Vel Panegyricum Carmen* (1656), Wing F 1034; J. Field, *Musarum Cantabrigiensium Luctus . . .* (1658), p. 1ᵛ; sig. H1, H4; G. Lawrence, *Peplum Olivarii* (1658), 12, 33.

167. Panegyric in Peck, *Memoirs*, 109.

168. *Unparalleled Monarch*, To the Reader.

169. Ibid., 42.

170. Ibid., sig. [A10].

171. Ibid., 61.

172. Ibid., 66.

173. Peck, *Historical Pieces* (1740), 56.

174. Huntington Library, Bull/Granger, vol. 10, no. 12. On the Garter, see K. Sharpe, *The Personal Rule of Charles I* (1992), 219–221.

175. Huntington Library, Bull/Granger, vol. 10, no. 22v.

176. Ibid., vol. 10, no. 17.

177. Ibid., vol. 10, no. 35; Henfrey, *Numismata Cromwelliana*, plate 8. See also K. Pearson and G. M. Morant, *The Portraiture of Oliver Cromwell* (Cambridge, 1935).

178. Peck, *Memoirs of Cromwell*, 130.

179. Henfrey, *Numismata Cromwelliana*, 219.

180. Ibid., 103.

181. *Unparalleled Monarch*, 8.

182. Ibid., 13.

183. C. Firth, "Cromwell and the Crown," *English Historical Review* 17 (1902): 429–442; 18 (1903): 52–80; Sherwood, *Court of Oliver Cromwell*, appendix A.

184. W. C. Abbott, *Writings and Speeches of Cromwell*, 2:589; Porter, "'Imperious Dictators,'" chap. 7.

185. Above, p. 47.

186. *The Only Right Rule* for *Regulating the Laws and Liberties of the People of England*, E684/33, p. 3.

187. Nedham, *True State*, 3–4, 47.

188. Cornubiensis, *Grand Catastrophe*, 11.

189. Ibid., 12–13, 15.

190. Wither, *The Protector*, "to the readers," and pp. 4, 17, 28, 31, and passim.

191. *For the Lord Protector* (1655), 669 f19/66.

192. Porter, "'Imperious Dictatours,'" 285.

193. *Copy of a Letter* (1656), E870/5, pp. 14, 20, 36–7.

194. J. Hall, *The True Cavalier* (1656), E885/10, preface, pp. 101–102.

195. *The Unparalleled Monarch, or The Portraiture of a Matchless Prince*, 50.

196. *A Modest Vindication of Oliver Cromwell* (1698), 60.

197. Abbott, *Writings and Speeches of Cromwell*, 1:527–528.

198. *Mercurius Politicus*, 25 June–2 July 1657; *Prestwich's Respublica*, 3–20.

199. Sherwood, *Court of Cromwell*, 163; see also 160–165.

200. See too *The Life and Death of Oliver Cromwell* (1659), E1787/1, pp. 202–203.

201. *The Tenth Worthy or Several Anagrams . . . upon the Name . . . Oliver* (1658), 669 f21/9.

202. *The Commonwealth Mercury*, 18–25 November 1657, p. 2; cf. *The True Manner of the Conveyance of His Highness's Effigies* (1658), E1866/2.

203. *Commonwealth Mercury*, 18–25 November 1658, p. 5, my italics. See Morant and Pearson, *Portraiture of Cromwell*, plate 8, for the effigy "standing in state."

204. Ibid., 5–6; Carrington, *The Life and Death of Oliver Cromwell*, 233–240; *The Perfect Politician*, 346.

205. See *Prestwich's Respublica*, 182–203, for the banners, escutcheons, and shields.

206. G. Lawrence, *Peplum Olivarii*, 31.

207. W. Prynne, *A Plea for the Lords* (1658) E944/1, "to the ingenuous reader."

208. Field, *Museum Cantab. Luctus et Gratulatio*, sig. G4^v; E. Waller, *Three Poems upon the Death of His Late Highness* (1659), Wing W526, p. 8.

209. *Eikon Basilike, or The True Portraiture of His Sacred Majesty Charles II* (1660), E1922/2, book 3, p. 4.

210. *A Brief Relation Containing an Abbreviation of the Arguments Urged by the Late Protector against the Government . . . by a King* (1659), E965/4, p. 7.

211. *History of the Life and Death of Cromwell*, 232.

212. Ibid., 164–165; *A Character of . . . King Charles II* (1659), E1836/3.

213. *A True Catalogue, or An Account of the Several Places and Most Eminent Persons . . . Where and by Whom Richard Cromwell was Proclaimed Lord Protector* (1660), E999/812.

214. *A True Catalogue*, 66.

215. Examples of lives of Charles I and Charles II: *The Faithful Yet Imperfect Character of a Glorious King* (1659), E1799/1; *A Dialogue between the Ghosts of Charles I . . . and Oliver* (1659), E985/24; *Bibliotheca Regia* (1659), E1718/1; *A Character of His Most Sacred Majesty King Charles II* (1659), E1836/2; L. Wood, *The Life and Reign of King Charles* (1659), E1760/2.

216. See, for example, *Monarchia Transformata in Respublicam Deformatam* (1649), 669 f14/75; cf. W. Prynne, *The Machiavellian Cromwellist* (1648), Wing P4007A; and see *Hypocrisie Discovered* (1655) Wing 3887.

217. *Declaration concerning the Government*, 6.

218. *An Honest Discourse* (1655), E840/10, p. 3.

219. Ibid., 13.

220. *The Picture of a New Courtier* (1656), E875/6. The author condemns the Protector's pomp and pride as worse than kings'.

221. *An Appeal from the Court to the Country*, E891/3, p. 6.

222. The campaign against the revival of royal government, however, was not a united campaign. See J. H. Hughes, "The Commonwealthmen Divided: Edmund Ludlow, Sir Henry Vane, and the Good Old Cause, 1653–1659," *The Seventeenth Century* 5 (1990): 55–70.

223. *English Liberty and Property Asserted* (1653), E905/2, pp. 6–7.

224. *To the Parliament . . .* (1657), E905/3, p. 1.

225. *A Narrative of the Late Parliament* (1658), E935/5, p. 28.

226. G. Wither, *Salt upon Salt* (1658), E1827/2, pp. 18, 31, 33–35, and passim.

227. See J. G. A. Pocock, *The Machiavellian Moment*, 384; Hughes, "Commonwealthmen Divided."

228. *A Secret Word to the Wise* (1659), E986/8.

229. See H. Erskine Hill and G. Storey, *Revolutionary Prose of the English Civil War* (Cambridge, 1983), 203–229.

230. Ibid., 211, 220.

231. Above pp. 30–31.

232. Pearson and Morant, *Portraiture of Cromwell*, plate 40.

233. *The Excellency of a Free State, or The Right Constitution of a Commonwealth* (1656), E1676/1, "to the reader."

234. Ibid., 6.

235. Ibid., 10.

236. Ibid., 14.

237. Ibid., 163. The criticism of Oliver Cromwell who had recently moved into royal palaces is obvious.

238. See MacGregor, *The Late Kings Goods*, chap. 1; see the list of goods reserved for Cromwell's use in Millar, *Inventories and Valuations of the King's Goods*, via index.

239. A. Short, *God Save the King, or A Sermon Preached at Lyme Regis May 18, 1660* (1660), E1919/2, "to the unprejudiced reader."

240. On the politics of silence, see Sharpe, "The King's Writ: Royal Authors and Royal Authority," 132–137.

241. I intend to explore this subject. For some evidence of such anxieties in the drama, see N. Maguire, *Regicide and Restoration: English Tragicomedy, 1660–1671* (Cambridge, 1992).

242. *No King but the Old King's Son* (1660), 669 f24/30.

243. See *A Sudden Flash* (1657), E1584/3, p. 18.

244. *The Speeches and Prayers of Maj. Gen. Harrison . . . Mr. John Carew . . . Mr. Justice Cooke, etc.* (1660), E1053/1, p. 13. The accounts of the executions and speeches skillfully blend the old Foxeian martyrology as deployed by Prynne, Burton, and Bastwick with motifs appropriated from Charles I's own trial.

245. Ibid., 13.

246. F. Phillips, *Veritas Inconcussa* (1661), E1925/2, "To Charles II." The quotation continues: "There are too many amongst those many that made acclamations and seemed to rejoice in your Majestie's return . . . who have not changed their spots."

247. See J. Ogilby, *The Entertainment of His Most Excellent Majestie Charles II* (1662), ed. R. Knowles (Binghamton, N.Y., 1988). I shall be discussing Restoration festival in the study *Images of Power in England, 1500–1700*.

QUEEN ANNE MAKES PROVISION

1. Queen Anne is generally recognized to have had five children, all of whom predeceased her by many years. Her daughters Mary (b. June 1, 1685) and Anne Sophia (b. May 12, 1686) both died, probably of smallpox, in February 1687—the "fatal February" when Anne also had a miscarriage. William Henry, propitiously born in 1689, was never healthy and died in 1700, to his mother's despair and Protestant alarm. Another Mary (b. October 14, 1690) lived for only a few hours; and a son George (b. April 17, 1692) died shortly after birth. In addition to all these bereavements, however, Anne also seems to have suffered at least thirteen mis-

carriages or stillbirths and at least two episodes of pseudocyesis. *The Dictionary of National Biography* (1:443 ff) provides what is probably the most accurate record of Queen Anne's many heartbreaking bereavements and goes so far as to attribute intellectual weakness to her maternal suffering (1:471).

Anne's maternal history, formidable though it is, might have appeared somewhat less extraordinary in her day than it does in ours. Many wealthy women of the time underwent twenty pregnancies, and at least one bore thirty children (see Dorothy McLaren, "Marital Fertility and Lactation, 1570–1720," in *Women in English Society*, ed. Mary Prior [New York, 1985], 22); but disease and cultural practices (e.g., sending out to nurse, feeding "by hand") often made it uncertain that even a single child would survive to adulthood.

2. Jonathan Swift, *Memoirs of the Last Four Years of the Reign of Queen Anne, from 1710, to Her Death* (London, 1742), 75.

3. Bishop Gilbert Burnet, *History of His Own Time*, 2d ed., 6 vols. (Oxford, 1833), 3:49, note y. The note, written by the earl of Dartmouth, presents a familiar picture of George as passive and dull, but its tone is unusually hostile. According to Dartmouth, George was not only "the most indolent of all mankind," but "could be made a tool of "; King William "treated him with the utmost contempt," "all foreign princes had him in very low esteem," and even Queen Anne "shewed him little respect." After repeating a nasty joke suggesting that George may have been inadequately equipped sexually, Dartmouth winds up by saying that George "died of eating and drinking" without having ever done anything of value.

4. Cf. "Mr. Marshall's Character of Her late Majesty," *The Loyal Mourner* (London, 1716), pp. 5–8; 10; Burnet, *History*, 2:391–392: George "lived in all respects the happiest with his princess that was possible."

5. Edward Gregg, *Queen Anne* (Boston, 1980), 35, 280 ff.

6. *The Parliamentary History of England, from the Earliest Period to the Year 1803*, 10 vols. (London, 1806–1820), 6:777.

7. *Journals of the House of Commons*, 16:72; cf. *Parliamentary History*, 6:778.

8. *Journals of the House of Commons*, 16:75; *Parliamentary History*, 6:778.

9. Gregg, *Queen Anne*, 213.

10. Burnet, *History*, 5:211, note s.

11. The seven were the archbishop of Canterbury, the lord chancellor, the lord treasurer, the lord president, the lord high admiral, the lord privy seal, and the lord chief justice (Gregg, *Queen Anne*, 212).

12. Gregg, *Queen Anne*, 210. For more on the politics of the Hanoverian invitation cf. Gregg, *Queen Anne*, 183–184, 209–214; John Churchill, Duke of Marlborough, Sidney Godolphin, et al., *The Marlborough-Godolphin Correspondence*, ed. Henry L. Snyder, 3 vols. (Oxford, 1975), 3:1217.

13. In eighteenth-century Britain, to "pretend" conveyed both our sense of fraudulent "pretense" and a now obsolete sense of (often justified) "hope" or "aspiration." The word's ambiguities make it a remarkably apt nickname for James Edward Stuart, son of Anne's father (the exiled James II) and his second wife (Mary of Modena), the competitor for Anne's throne throughout her lifetime and in the eyes of many the rightful heir.

For the widespread suspicion that Queen Anne might have harbored Jacobite sympathies, cf. James Macpherson, ed., *Original Papers*, 2 vols. (London, 1775) 2:288–289; Abel Boyer, *Memoirs of Queen Anne* (London, 1729), 36; Gregg, *Queen*

Anne, 83–84, 149–150, 363–366, 402; and especially Gregg, "Was Queen Anne a Jacobite?" *History* 57 (October 1972): 358–375.

14. Marlborough, 3:1217.

15. Cf. for example the Old Bailey *Proceedings* (London, 1680–1820) for 13–16 January 1720 (pp. 2–3), 30 August–1 September 1721 (p. 3), 11–14 October 1721 (pp. 3–4).

16. Peter C. Hoffer and N. E. H. Hull, *Murdering Mothers: Infanticide in England and New England, 1588–1803* (New York, 1981), 69.

17. Cf. John Dunton's *Ladies Dictionary* (London, 1694), which discusses "preparing *Child-bed-linnen*" as work that expectant mothers "are usually busie about" (p. 143). Dunton feels himself moved to "encourage" the practice (p. 143), not least by means of intimidation: "when we see a Poor Woman reduced to that miserable shift as to be Deliver'd in Rage," he observes, "we are apt to believe that the Woman misses somewhat of Matrimonies Pleasure . . . we take her for some forlorn Creature abandon'd by all Mankind" (p. 261).

18. Daniel Defoe, *Augusta Triumphans* (London, 1728), 9–10; cf. R. W. Malcolmson, "Infanticide in the Eighteenth Century," *Crime in England, 1500–1800*, ed. J. S. Cockburn (Princeton, 1977).

19. For a detailed examination of the scene in which Moll Flanders abandons the child for whom she has made provision, see my *The Politics of Motherhood: British Literature and Culture, 1680–1760* (Cambridge, 1996, pp. 104–111).

20. Other literary instances of "making provision" include Aphra Behn, *The Adventures of the Black Lady*, in *Oroonoko and Other Writings*, ed. Paul Salzman (Oxford, 1994), pp. 194–195; Delarivier Manley, *New Atalantis* (1709), ed. Rosalind Ballaster (New York, 1991), 83.

21. Such pamphlets came from both Whig and Tory directions. Cf. Charles Povey's Whiggish tract *An Enquiry into Miscarriages of the Four Last Years Reign* (London, 1714) and the anonymous Tory pamphlet *The Miscarriages of the Whig-Ministry* (London: 1714).

22. Boyer, *History of the Life and Reign of Queen Anne*, 2. William and Mary were childless.

23. Cf. Manley: at the time of her father's accession to the throne, the Princess Albania [Anne] "was certain in her self or Posterity to succeed her Father" (*The Secret History of Queen Zarah* [London, 1705], *The Novels of Mary Delarivier Manley*, ed. Patricia Koster, 2 vols. [Gainesville, 1971], :54).

24. My thanks to the staff of the Dutch Consulate's office in San Francisco for assistance with this translation.

25. For a few examples of Princess Anne's many strategic uses of her body's reproductive potential, see Henry Hyde, Earl of Clarendon, *Correspondence*, ed. Samuel W. Singer, 2 vols. (London, 1828) 2:196, 216; Macpherson 1:155; Gregg, *Queen Anne*, 51, 86–87, 123; Beatrice C. Brown, *The Letters and Diplomatic Instructions of Queen Anne* (London, 1935), 53; David Green, *Sarah, Duchess of Marlborough* (New York, 1967), 74–75; Gregg, "Was Queen Anne a Jacobite?" 368.

26. Cf. Clarendon, 2:196; Gregg, *Queen Anne*, 51.

27. Cf. Burnet, 3:318–323.

28. MacPherson, *Original Papers*, 1:155.

29. Burnet, 3:323.

30. Clarendon, 2:216.

31. Gregg, *Queen Anne*, 86–87. Cf. Brown, *Letters and Diplomatic Instructions*, 53; Green, *Sarah, Duchess of Marlborough*, 74–75.

32. Gregg, *Queen Anne*, 123; Gregg "Was Queen Anne a Jacobite?" 368.

33. Thomas Salmon, *The Life of Her Late Majesty*, 2 vols. (London, 1721), 1:30; Conyers Harrison, *An Impartial History of . . . Queen Anne* (London, 1744), 26; Gregg, *Queen Anne*, 72.

34. Burnet, *History*, 2:392; cf. Paul de Rapin-Thoyras, *Histoire d'Angleterre* (1724–1727), trans. Nicholas Tindal, *The History of England*, 4 vols. (London, 1732–1747), 4:534.

35. Anon., "The Generous Muse. A Funeral Poem in Memory of his late Majesty K. James the II" (London, 1701), 9.

36. Though, of course, Elizabeth also sent conflicting signals about her intentions. For over twenty years Elizabeth teased her realm with a large cast of possible husbands, effectively playing her potential maternity as a political trump card.

37. I quote Rapin's seventeenth-century paraphrase (Rapin-Thoyras, *Histoire d'Angleterre*, 2:53). For the text of Elizabeth's speech, see Allison Heisch, ed., *Queen Elizabeth I: Political Speeches and Parliamentary Addresses, 1558–1601* (MS in preparation): "The answere of the Quenes highnes to ye peticion proposed vnto hir by ye lower howse concerning hir mariage."

This first parliamentary address demonstrates the accuracy of Susan Frye's argument that what Elizabeth considered to be her "meetest ensign" was the figure of chastity (*Elizabeth I: The Competition for Representation.* [New York, 1993], 16, 15). The speech also shows that Elizabeth made use of other tropes alongside her central self-representation as virgin queen, including the figure of motherhood. Likewise at her coronation entry in 1559, the Virgin Queen participated in the simultaneous celebration of her body's procreative potential and the metaphorization of that potential, both of which were understood to be "versions of" her political authority (pp. 43–45). Though Elizabeth most frequently used the figure of motherhood during the early years of her reign, she continued to deploy the trope even much later, and she was often represented by her subjects in maternal terms (pp. 19, 25, 54–55, 70, 103).

Frye's *Elizabeth I* is the best study I know of the queen's changing and contested self-representations. My discussion is much indebted to Frye's important work.

38. *State Papers, Domestic Elizabeth*, 12.27.36; cf. Heisch, *Political Speeches*, 50.

39. Rapin-Thoyras, *Histoire d'Angleterre*, 2:57.

40. Gregg, *Queen Anne*, 152.

41. Ibid., 152.

42. Swift, *Memoirs*, 199.

43. Ibid., 295.

44. In the long view Elizabeth's failure bodily to secure the Protestant succession helped make inevitable the violence of the seventeenth century. The long-term results of Anne's maternal experience were arguably better: Britain got Hanoverians, not Stuarts, and enjoyed comparative stability and prosperity.

45. Frye, *Elizabeth I*, 39, quoting Heisch, *Political Speeches*.

46. Cf. Frye, *Elizabeth I*, 39.

47. Cf. the famous portrait attributed to Marcus Gheeraerts the Younger and now in Britain's National Portrait Gallery, where Queen Elizabeth is less an individ-

ual woman than a symbol, like the map on which she stands (reprod. Sarah Tyacke, *English Map-Making, 1500–1650* (London, 1983), fig. 8; Roy Strong, *Portraits of Queen Elizabeth* (Oxford, 1963), plate 15). Of this portrait, Tyacke notes, "the map of England" is "a symbol interchangeable for Queen and nation" (fig. 8, caption).

48. Margaret Homans, *Bearing the Word* (Chicago, 1989), 5, 10.

49. Cf. Catherine Gallagher, "Embracing the Absolute: The Politics of the Female Subject in Seventeenth-Century England," *Genders* 1:1 (1988): 38.

50. The figure of motherhood, however, continued to enhance Elizabeth's political authority for many years. Frye cites one Thomas Norton's address "To the queenes maiesties poore deceived subiectes of the northe contreye," written in the context of the rebellion of 1569, which calls Elizabeth "the most louing Mother and nourse of all her good subjects" (Frye, *Elizabeth I,* 55.)

51. Cf. Carolynn Van Dyke, *The Fiction of Truth* (Ithaca, 1985), esp. 165; D. J. Gordon, *The Renaissance Imagination,* ed. Stephen Orgel (Berkeley University of California Press, 1975), 18–23; James R. Siemon, *Shakespearean Iconoclasm* (Berkeley, 1985), 57–62. Siemon demonstrates a tension between continuity and change in attitudes toward representation during Elizabeth's reign: distrust of traditional understandings of "the timeless unity of physical element and spiritual reality" (p. 62) was for the first time a "truly popular worry" (pp. 57, 40). My thanks to Rose Zimbardo and Mary Claire Mulroney for enlightening conversations about the changing status of representation between Elizabeth's day and Anne's.

52. Steven Zwicker, "Politics and Literary Practice in the Restoration," *Renaissance Genres,* ed. B. K. Lewalski (Cambridge, Mass., 1986), 270.

53. Consider for example Locke's famous declaration that the supposedly inherent connection between words and the things they stand for is "a perfectly arbitrary imposition" (Locke, *Essay Concerning Human Understanding,* ed. Peter Niddich [Oxford, 1975], 408). Cf. Zwicker, "Politics and Literary Practice," 270, 275.

54. The arguments of this paragraph are expanded in Bowers, *The Politics of Motherhood: British Literature and Culture, 1680–1760* (Cambridge, 1996).

55. For the power of Roman Catholic images before the Reformation, see Margaret Aston, *England's Iconoclasts,* vol. 1: *Laws against Images* (Oxford, 1988), 20–34. For the continued power of Catholic dogma and iconography during the English Reformation, see Christopher Haigh, *The English Reformation Revised* (Cambridge, 1987). For the political power of Marian myth in Elizabeth's day, and for Elizabethan exploitations of that power, see Frances Yates, *Astraea* (London, 1975); Roy Strong, *The Cult of Elizabeth* (London, 1977), 114–116; Louis Montrose, "*A Midsummer Night's Dream* and the Shaping of Fantasies of Elizabethan Culture," *Rewriting the Renaissance,* ed. M. Ferguson (Chicago, 1986), 66.

56. C. L. Barber, "The Family in Shakespeare's Development," *Representing Shakespeare,* ed. M. M. Schwartz and C. Kahn (Baltimore, 1980), 96.

57. Anonymous, *Sorrowes Joy,* 2. My thanks to Kevin Sharpe for bringing this poem to my attention.

58. Gallagher, "Embracing the Absolute," 38.

59. A title frequently used for Anne by her supporters. Cf. Manley "Modest Enquiry" (1714); the anonymous drinking song "England's Triumph," n.p.; Richard Blackmore, *Eliza: An Epick Poem. In Ten Books* (London, 1705), 219–221. Mary Chudleigh "To the Queen's Most Excellent Majesty," *Poems on Several Occasions* (London, 1703), 122–124.)

60. Richard Steele, *Tatler* 83 (Oct. 18–20, 1709).

61. James Ralph, *The Other Side of the Question . . . By a Woman of Quality* (London, 1742), 243.

62. For a discussion of Anne's many efforts in support of the Hanoverian succession, see Gregg, "Was Queen Anne a Jacobite?" Considerable evidence supports Gregg's contention that the queen, though resolutely opposed to the invitation, was nevertheless dedicated to the Hanoverian succession.

63. Gregg seeks to assuage lingering suspicions about Anne's Jacobitism (*Queen Anne*, 83–84, 149–150, 364–366; Gregg, "Was Queen Anne a Jacobite?"). Among many possible citations exemplifying the traditional estimate of Queen Anne as a negligible political figure, see Henry L. Snyder's introduction to Marlborough and Godolphin, *The Marlborough-Godolphin Correspondence*, xvii; Brown, *Letters and Diplomatic Instructions*, vii; Gallagher, "Embracing the Absolute," 38.

SAD STORIES

1. Thomas Paine, *Rights of Man*, 3d ed. (London: J. S. Jordan, 1791), 24.

2. Edmund Burke, *Reflections on the Revolution in France* (1790), in *The Works of the Right Honourable Edmund Burke*, new ed., 14 vols. (London: F. C. and J. Rivington, 1815–1822), 5:151.

3. Burke, *Reflections*, 5:352.

4. John Whitaker, *The Real Origin of Government* (London: J. Stockdale, 1795), 42.

5. T. B. Howell and Thomas Jones Howell, eds., *A Complete Collection of State Trials*, 30 vols. (London: Longman et al., 1816–1822), 22:398–399.

6. Howell and Howell, *State Trials*, 22:818–819.

7. *A Letter from a Chancellor, Out of Office, to a King in Power* (London: D. I. Eaton, 1795), 52.

8. Howell and Howell, *State Trials*, 22:507.

9. See, in particular, Linda Colley, *Britons: Forging the Nation, 1707–1837* (New Haven and London: Yale University Press, 1992), 195–236.

10. Burke, *Reflections*, 5:183.

11. John Brewer, "This Monstrous Tragi-comic Scene: British Reactions to the French Revolution," in David Bindman, *The Shadow of the Guillotine: Britain and the French Revolution* (London: British Museum Publications, 1989), 23–24.

12. C. Sneyd Edgeworth, *Memoirs of the Abbé Edgeworth; Containing his Narrative of the Last Hours of Louis XVI* (London: Rowland Hunter, 1815), 61–62; M. Cléry, *A Journal of Occurrences at the Temple, during the Confinement of Louis XVI, King of France* (London: Baylis et al., 1798), 238. One lengthy report of the interview claimed to have been furnished by one of the municipal officers to "a Member of the late National Assembly," but as it describes Edgeworth himself as being present throughout the scene, its authenticity is questionable (*The Trial at Large of Louis XVI., Late King of France . . . as Communicated in a Series of Letters by a Member of the Late National Assembly, to a Member of the British Parliament* (London: W. Miller et al., 1793). In most newspaper reports, and in later narratives which derive from them, the impossibility of giving an accurate account of the interview is acknowledged: thus the *Morning Chronicle* (January 26) observed, "We may conceive what must have been the nature of the

scene—but a narrative of it is impossible." The *Morning Chronicle* described the interview as taking place only four hours before the execution, as did *The Times* of January 25.

13. As the one of the longest reports of the interview candidly admitted, in the absence of testimony from "a pure source," the historian could do no more than offer an account which appeared "most congenial to the truth," a phrase in which "truth" appears to be what ought to be the truth, or what we might wish it to be (Joseph Trapp, *Proceedings of the French National Convention on the Trial of Louis XVI* [London: by the author, 1793], 199).

14. Thus the *Morning Chronicle* (January 26) reported the "rumour" that "the QUEEN had been for some days in a state of distraction—that at times her mind was totally absent, and she was to be roused from lethargy to a sense of her sorrows." Elsewhere, however, the "distraction in her looks" is described as matching the "agitation in her manner"; she suffers "convulsive hysteric fits," she curses, she laments, and pours forth "all the effusions of agony which the very madness of grief and affliction could impell her to utter" (*The Trial at Large,* 119–120; Trapp, *Proceedings of the . . . Convention,* 199; *Description of the Picture of the Last Interview of Louis XVI. with His Family,* handbill describing Mather Brown's painting of the last interview, no publication details [1793]; *World,* January 26, 1793). The report in the *Gentleman's Magazine* represents Marie Antoinette as in such a "delirium of anguish" that she finally fainted, and had to be removed "in a state of insensibility" (January 1793, p. 85).

15. *The Accusation, Defence, Sentence, Execution, and Last Will, of Lewis XVI . . . Translated from the French* (Edinburgh: Thomas Brown [the same text is found credited to various booksellers], 1793), 95.

16. *The Times* merely reported that Louis had taken an "affectionate farewell" of his family, but believed that the meeting had taken place on the morning of his execution, and offered no account of what passed at the interview.

17. *The Trial at Large,* 120–121. This version of the scene may have achieved considerable currency; it was reproduced in a chapbook which made the pathos of the scene still more painful by eliminating the device whereby it is reported by a municipal officer, and by representing its author, a Mr. Johnson, as having been "an Eye-Witness of the Whole of the Transactions": *A Genuine Narrative of the Proceedings at Paris from the 16th of December, 1791, to the 1st of February, 1793: . . . to Which Is Annexed the Life, Trial, and Execution, of Louis XVI.* (London: Robert Turner, 1793).

18. Gillray's cartoon is reproduced in color in Bindman, *Shadow of the Guillotine,* between pp. 48 and 49; Bindman suggests (pp. 31 and 132) that the caricature was intended as a satire on catchpenny paintings and engravings of the last interview, such as those discussed below. It may have been so intended, but it is unlikely that it was so received.

19. William Preston, *Democratic Rage, or Louis the Unfortunate: A Tragedy* (Dublin: John Archer, 1793), 97.

20. John Bartholomew, *The Fall of the French Monarchy, or Louis XVI: An Historical Tragedy in Five Acts* (London: for the author, 1794), act 5, scene 2.

21. John Gifford, *The Reign of Louis the Sixteenth and Complete History of the French Revolution* (London: C. Lowdnes et al., 1794), 701.

22. That there is something of importance at stake here may be suggested by the fact that when the report in the *World* was reprinted in Edinburgh, where the

evidently Catholic concerns of the source on which it was based were unlikely to be popular, the "heavenly serenity" of Louis became simply a "great serenity" (*The Accusation*, 95). In the context of what will emerge as the far more evident competition to establish the significance of Louis's demeanor on the scaffold, this amendment, in a report otherwise reprinted almost verbatim, seems to mark a division between those reporters or their sources who interpret Louis's execution primarily in political, constitutional terms and wish to represent him as an exemplar of a more or less secular public virtue, and those for whom the great importance of the event lay in its implications for the future of the Catholic church in France.

23. There are versions of the interview among those apparently published immediately after the execution which treat it altogether more laconically: see H. Goudemetz, *Judgment and Execution of Louis XVI. King of France* (no publication details [1793]): "The interview lasted two hours. It is impossible to express the horror of the moment, when he was obliged to tear himself away from them." See also *The Trial of Louis XVI. Late King of France. Who Was Beheaded on Monday, January 21st, 1793 . . . To Which Is Added, the Demolition of the Bastille: Being a Full and Accurate Description of That Horrid State Prison* (London: "all the booksellers," 1793): "The interview lasted two hours and a half; their conversation was very earnest."

24. *The Will of Louis the Sixteenth, Late King of France / Testament de Louis Seize, Ci-devant Roi de France* (London: William Lane; Minerva Press, 1793).

25. Daniel Arasse, *The Guillotine and the Terror*, trans. Christopher Miller (London: Penguin Books, 1989), 65–70.

26. See especially Bindman, *Shadow of the Guillotine*, 50–51.

27. *The Trial at Large*, 120.

28. "Preface to the Edition of Shakespeare's Plays" (1765), in H. R. Woudhuysen, ed., *Samuel Johnson on Shakespeare* (London: Penguin Books, 1989), 140.

29. See the story communicated by the Commissaries of the Temple in a report to the Commune of Paris, printed in the *Morning Post*, January 28, 1793.

30. *Funeral Oration for Louis XVI.* (London: for J. Edwards, 1794), 17.

31. *Reflections, Moral, and Political, on the Murder of Louis the Sixteenth: In a Sermon, Preached on That Occasion, on Sunday, February 3d, 1793* (London: R. Edwards, 1793),

32. That Louis was mourned in Britain as a private man is exemplified almost everywhere in the writings about his death in 1793 and 1794; but see, for example, *A Short Account of the Character and Reign of Louis XVI, Shewing How Little He Deserved, from His Ungrateful People, the Name of Tyrant* (London: J. Downes, 1793); Ann Yearsley, *Reflections on the Death of Louis XVI.* (Bristol: the author, 1793), and *Sequel to Reflections on the Death of Louis XVI.* (Bristol: the author, 1793); anon., *A Ballad on the Death of Louis the Unfortunate, After the Manner of Chevy Chace, etc.* (Bristol: the Author, 1793); *English Review* 24 (August 1794): 147, review of Richard Hey's tragedy *The Captive Monarch.*

32. Henry Hunter, *A Sermon, Preached Feb. 3, 1793, at the Scots Church, London Wall, on Occasion of the Trial, Condemnation, and Execution of Louis XVI. Late King of France* (London: for the author, 1793), 14. Louis was an "enemy" insofar as "it was Louis who severed America from her, and thereby meant to enfeeble and humble her" (p. 14).

33. Helen Maria Williams, *Letters from France; Containing a Great Variety of Origi-*

nal Information Concerning the Most-Important Events . . . in the Years 1790, 1791, 1792, and 1793, 2 vols. (Dublin: J. Chambers, 1794), 2:137.

34. For an especially elaborate example, see the anonymous *Ballad on the Death of Louis the Unfortunate* (p. 12), published in Bristol later in 1793:

> Torn from his frantic Consort's heart,
>   His dying Daughter's face:
> Forc'd from his darling Son to part,
>   Without a fond embrace.
>
> Not tears of Sister, Child, or Wife,
>   Could move the savage crew:
> Behold them, then, depriv'd of life,
>   Refus'd one sad adieu.

35. Gifford, *Reign of Louis XVI*, 700. See also, for example, *The True and Remarkable Trial, Condemnation, and Execution of Louis the XVIth, Late King of France, Who Was on Monday Last Beheaded at Paris, upon a Scaffold* ("Printed and Sold in London" [1793]).

36. For the collaboration between Küchler and Boulton, see J. G. Pollard, "Matthew Boulton and Conrad Heinrich Küchler," *Numismatic Chronicle* (1970), 259–318; this medal of the last interview, and another by William Mossop or William Mainwaring, are illustrated and briefly discussed by Bindman, *Shadow of the Guillotine*, 51, 133–134.

37. Quoted in a review in the *Gentleman's Magazine*, February 1793, p. 161.

38. Wollstonecraft, *A Vindication of the Rights of Men* (1790), in Janet Todd and Marilyn Butler, *The Works of Mary Wollstonecraft*, 7 vols. (London: William Pickering, 1989), 5:27.

39. See the *Morning Chronicle*, January 26, the *Oracle*, January 28, the *World*, January 26, and the versions of the *World* report reprinted in Edinburgh.

40. *Reflections, Moral, and Political*, 26.

41. "The event," wrote Henry Hunter,

> has furnished an occasion of displaying . . . the different characters of the two rival nations, much to the advantage of our own. Britain mourns, sincerely mourns, the premature fall of a foreign prince against whom she had no small ground of offence. . . . She . . . loses all thought of the enemy and the king, in respect for the virtues, and sympathy in the suffering, of the man. France, on the contrary, revels in the blood of her native prince, once the pride and delight of every eye, and the theme of every tongue; exults in the miseries of him who, under Providence, conferred upon her that very liberty which she understands so ill, and is abusing shamefully. (*Sermon*, 14–15)

See also, for example, Thomas Moore, *An Address to the Inhabitants of Great Britain on the Dangerous and Destructive Tendency of the French System of Liberty and Equality* (York: Printed by G. Peacock; sold in London by R. Baldwin; in York by J. Todd), [1793]).

42. *Morning Post, World,* January 30, 1793.

43. *World,* February 9, 1793.

44. *Morning Chronicle, Times,* January 25, 1793.

45. *Gentleman's Magazine*, March 1793, 251. The liberal commentator Benjamin Vaughan, however, justifies the continuation of January 30 sermons, following the execution of Louis, as providing "a proper memento *both to prince* and people"

([Vaughan], *The Essence of the Calm Observer* [London: W. Williams et al., 1793], 93; my emphasis). John Brewer ("This Monstrous Tragi-comic Scene," 23) writes of the comparison between Charles and Louis:

> In 1792–3 numerous depictions of Louis's separation from his family reinforced the impression of a united family rent asunder. . . . They also reminded Englishmen of Charles I's final meeting with his youngest children before his execution in 1649. Louis's last words, "I forgive my enemies, I Die Innocent," . . . were also reminiscent of Charles's final statement on the scaffold at Whitehall. Louis's association with Charles lent him some of the English king's reputation as a devoted and doting parent. Both monarchs, by dwelling on the fate of their nations, also fulfilled in their final hours their allotted role as father of the people.

46. Eric Robinson, ed., *John Clare's Autobiographical Writings* (Oxford: Oxford University Press, 1983), 26.

47. *The Parish Register,* lines 43–50, in *Poems. By the Rev. George Crabbe, LL. B.* (1807), 3rd ed. (London: J. Hatchard, 1810).

48. The lead in this had been given by Tom Paine, who in his communication to the National Convention recommending that Louis should be imprisoned and subsequently exiled, but not executed, had suggested that had Louis been born in "an obscure condition . . . at liberty to practise the duties of domestic life," he would not have shown himself "destitute of social virtues" (Paine, *Reasons for Wishing to Preserve the Life of Louis Capet* [London: James Ridgway, n.d. (1793)], 6).

49. Williams, *Letters,* 2:2.

50. William Fox, *Thoughts on the Death of the King of France* (London: J. Ridgway et al., 1793), 4.

51. Fox, *Thoughts,* 16. George Colman the Younger's tragic opera *Inkle and Yarico,* first performed in 1787, was played in London every year thereafter until 1793. Thomas Southerne's *Oroonoko* had been revived on the London stage in 1792 and 1793; both works no doubt owed their popularity in part to the rise of the campaign to abolish the slave trade and to the appropriateness of that issue to sentimental tragic drama.

52. There are so many examples of writers who invoke particular tragedies to represent the death of Louis that it seems unnecessary to cite examples here; but a particularly interesting instance occurs in *A Tour through the Theatre of War, in the Months of November, and December, 1792, and January 1793,* 2d ed. (London: J. Bew, n.d. [1793]), 127, where the anonymous author invokes the ghost in Hamlet to describe the terrors unleashed by the execution: the phantasm of a murdered king stalks before our frighted imagination, and makes

> We fools of nature
> So horridly to shake our disposition,
> With thoughts beyond the reaches of our souls.

53. Tragedies written in 1793 and 1794 about the execution: Bartholomew's *Fall of the French Monarchy* and Preston's *Democratic Rage,* both discussed above, and *The Captive Monarch. A Tragedy. In Five Acts* (London: Vernor and Hood et al., 1794), by Richard Hey, an established loyalist writer.

54. Edmund Burke, *A Philosophical Enquiry into the Origin of Our Ideas of the Sublime and Beautiful,* ed. J. T. Boulton (London: Routledge and Kegan Paul, 1958), 47.

55. Joanna Baillie, *A Series of Plays,* 3d ed., 2 vols. (London: T. Cadell and W. Davies, 1800), 1:6.

56. Baillie, *Series of Plays,* 1:6.

57. Baillie, *Series of Plays,* 1:3–8.

58. Burke, *Philosophical Enquiry,* 67.

59. Something of the confusions this double identity could cause shows through in an intriguing poem published anonymously in early 1794, which accused the leaders of the popular radical movement of treason by imagining the king's death. The poet addresses these traitors as "heedless parricides," intent on the murder of their royal father; and then that father abruptly changes sex, as the poet demands that they "forbear / With blood-stain'd fangs, unnatural, to tear / The womb that bore you . . ." (*The British Patriot, to His Fellow Citizens. A Poem. Part the First* [London: Knight and Triphook et al., 1794], 8).

60. PRO TS11/944/3433, R. v. Edward Swift.

61. Howell and Howell, *State Trials,* 24:682–683; John Thelwall, "King Chauntinclere; or the Fate of Tyranny," in *Politics for the People* (London: D. I. Eaton, 1793), 8:102–107; the fullest version of Robert Crosfeild's song "Plant, Plant the Tree" is given in Howell and Howell, *State Trials,* 26:135–136.

62. Richard Brothers, *A Revealed Knowledge of the Prophecies and Times . . . Book the Second* (London: [George Riebau], 1794), 30, 116; Sarah Flaxmer, *Satan Revealed, or The Dragon Overcome* (London: the author, n.d. [1795]), 5.

READING THE MARGINS

1. Archibald Campbell, marquis and eighth earl of Argyll, *Instructions to a Son* (Edinburgh and London, 1661), 100–104.

2. Early modern habits of reading have been the subject of an increasingly sophisticated and detailed scholarship. The subject has had a longer history in France than in England; see, for example, R. Darnton, "Reading, Writing, and Publishing in Eighteenth-Century France: A Case Study in the Sociology of Literature?" *Daedalus* 100 (1971): 214–256; F. Furet and J. Ozouf, *Reading and Writing: Literacy in France from Calvin to Jules Ferry* (Cambridge, 1982); R. Chartier, *The Cultural Uses of Print in Early Modern France,* trans. Lydia G. Cochrane (Princeton, 1987); and, more recently, Roberta L. Krueger, *Women Readers and the Ideology of Gender in Old French Verse Romance* (Cambridge, 1995); Jean-Marie Goulemot, *Forbidden Texts: Erotic Literature and Its Readers in Eighteenth-Century France,* trans. James Simpson (Oxford, 1994).

Over the last several years Anthony Grafton and Lisa Jardine, "'Studied for Action': How Gabriel Harvey Read His Livy," *Past and Present* 129 (November 1990): 30–78; Margaret Spufford, *Small Books and Pleasant Histories: Popular Fiction and Its Readership in Seventeenth-Century England* (London, 1981); and Tessa Watt, *Cheap Print and Popular Piety, 1550–1640* (Cambridge, 1991), have opened the subject of habits of reading for early modern England. For other recent work see Timothy Hampton, *Writing from History: The Rhetoric of Exemplarity in Renaissance Literature* (Ithaca, 1990); Lorna Hutson, "Fortunate Travelers: Reading for Plot in Sixteenth-Century England," *Representations* 41 (1993); and William Sherman and Lisa Jardine, "Pragmatic Readers: Knowledge Transactions and Scholarly Services in Late Elizabethan England," *Religion, Culture, and Society in Early Modern Britain: Essays in Honour of Patrick Collinson,* ed. Anthony Fletcher and Peter Roberts (Cambridge: Cambridge University Press, 1994), 102–124.

3. On reading and self-fashioning, see Carlo Ginzburg, *The Cheese and the*

Worms: The Cosmos of a Sixteenth-Century Miller (London, 1976). The idea and the critical idiom of self-fashioning was made central to our readings of early modern culture by Stephen Greenblatt, *Renaissance Self-Fashioning* (Chicago, 1980).

4. The relation between polemic and literary production in the years of revolution and their aftermath has been the subject of recent work by Nigel Smith, *Literature and Revolution in England, 1640–1660* (New Haven, 1994); Thomas N. Corns, *Uncloistered Virtue: English Political Literature, 1640–1660* (Oxford: Clarendon Press, 1992); and Steven N. Zwicker, *Lines of Authority: Politics and English Literary Culture, 1649–1689* (Ithaca, 1993).

5. *Cobbett's Complete Collection of State Trials*, 33 vols. (London, 1809–1826), vol. 9 (1682–1684), p. 915.

6. *Cobbett's . . . State Trials*, 9:821.

7. J. Jane, *Salmasius His Dissection and Confutation of the Diabolical Rebel Milton* (London, 1660), A2r-A2v.

8. A transcript of the proceedings can be found in *An Exact Narrative of the Tryal and Condemnation of John Twyn* (London, 1664); on the trial and its implications for censorship, see Joseph F. Loewenstein, "Legal Proof and Corrected Readings: Press-Agency and the New Bibliography," *The Production of English Renaissance Culture*, ed. David Lee Miller, Sharon O'Dair, and Harold Webber (Ithaca, 1994), 93–122.

9. See, for example, the Folger Library (Washington, D.C.) copies: Folger D2212, D2216, D2204, vol. 4; the Clark Library (Los Angeles, Calif.) copies: *fPR 3419 A21 1681 and *fPR 3419 A21 1681A (copy 2); the Huntington Library (San Marino, Calif.) copy: HEH 135868; the Beinecke Library (Yale University, New Haven, Conn.) copies: Ij D848 C691, Ij D848 681aa, Ij D848 681ab, Ij D848 681ae; and the Michigan State University Library copy, PR 3412.D7.

On Jonson's veiling and satirizing of contemporaries in *The Alchemist*, see Margaret Cavendish, *The Description of a New World, Called the Blazing-World* (London, 1668), 65–66: "Dr. Dee, and one Edward Kelly . . . were described by one of their own Country-men, a famous Poet, named Ben. Johnson, in a Play call'd, *The Alchymist*, where he expressed Kelly by Capt. Face, and Dee by Dr. Subtle, and their two Wives by Doll Common, and the Widow; by the Spaniard in the Play, he meant the Spanish Ambassador, and by Sir Epicure Mammon, a Polish Lord."

10. *The Works of John Dryden*, ed. Sir Walter Scott, rev. and corrected by George Saintsbury, 18 vols. (London, 1882–1893), 8:209–210. An interesting parallel case can be found in John Banks's *The Innocent Usurper*, published in 1694; see the dedication to Richard Bently, the stationer (A2r):

> As to the Reflections about it, and its being prohibited the acting, you are an authentick Witness, and can clear me as to that Point; You know it was written Ten years since, just as it is now, without one tittle of Alteration, and therefore I cou'd have no other design in making choice of this Subject, but its being recommended to me by Friends, for the best Story that ever was put into a Play.

11. Preface to *Cleomenes*, in *The Works of John Dryden*, ed. Scott and Saintsbury, 8:219.

12. Compare Colley Cibber's and Thomas Shadwell's accounts of the suppression of Dryden's *Prologue to the Prophetess;* see *The Poems of John Dryden*, ed. J. Kinsley, 4 vols. (Oxford, 1958), 4:1997, and H. Macdonald, *John Dryden: A Bibliography of Early Editions and of Drydeniana* (Oxford, 1939), 305.

13. *Cobbett's . . . State Trials*, 9:918.

14. *Cobbett's . . . State Trials*, 9:921.

15. Sir Roger Twysden's marked copies of Philip Hunton's *A Treatise of Monarchie* (London, 1643) and Sir Robert Filmer's *Anarchy of a Limited or Mixed Monarchy* (London, 1648) are in the Victoria and Albert Museum, Foster and Dyce Collection, F. 48. D. 52.

16. William Prynne, *New Discovery of the Prelate's Tyranny* (London, 1641) [Folger Library, P4018]; see, for example, pp. 3, 4, 5, 33.

17. See, for example, *His Highnesse The Lord Protector's Speeches to the Parliament in the Painted Chamber* (London, 1654) [Folger Library, C7175], pp. 3, 5, 18, 28.

18. *Cabala, Mysteries of State* (London, 1654) [Folger Library, C183, copy 1], 108.

19. Richard Hawkins, *A Discourse of the National Excellencies of England* (London, 1658) [Folger Library, H 1178], 118.

20. Thomas Hardcastle, *A Sermon Preached at Shadwell-Chappell in Yorkshire. By Thomas Hardcastle Minister of the Gospell. Published by Some of the Hearers for Their Own Vindication and the Worlds Satisfaction* (London, 1665), A3r:

> Reader, This Sermon was preached at Shadwel Chappel in the West-riding of Yorkshire, June 18, 1665. . . . we not being conscious to our selves of any the least seditious design or practice against the King of his government, and desirous likewise to clear our innocency to the World, have printed the Sermon, as it was taken in short-hand by some of us, without any addition, alteration or correction by the Author, which we did purposely wave, that the matter might appear in greater simplicity and plainness.

21. See George Villiers, second duke of Buckingham, *The Rehearsal, As It Is Now Acted at the Theater Royal*, 3d ed. (London, 1675) [Folger Library, B5325, copy 2], front flyleaf: "In this Volume is a Key to the Duke of Buckingham's Rehearsal containing not only the Names of the Several Plays hinted at, but likewise the Passages themselves cited and faithfully transcrib'd and Compar'd by way of Paralell. By the Late Lord Marquis of Hallifax," signed "Ric. Evans. 1720."

22. Howard, *Poems and Essays* (London, 1674) [Folger Library, H2973a].

23. Clement Walker, *Compleate History of Independency* (London, 1661) [Folger Library, W2327].

24. The Bindley Pamphlets, a collection of Exclusion Crisis ballads, broadsides, and miscellaneous verse originally gathered by the eighteenth-century antiquarian James Bindley, are housed at the Huntington Library, San Marino, California, and the Clark Library, Los Angeles, California.

25. Sir Robert Filmer, *Patriarcha* (London, 1680) [Folger Library, F922], 46.

26. *Some Letters. Containing, An Account of What Seemed Most Remarkable in Switzerland, Italy, &c. Written by G. Burnet, D.D.* (Rotterdam, 1686), 38.

27. Ibid., 26.

28. Ibid., 37.

29. Ibid., 43.

30. Ibid., 39.

31. *Machiavel's Discourses upon the First Decade of T. Livius, Translated Out of the Italian . . . by E. D.* (London, 1674) [Folger Library, M135], front flyleaf.

32. See, for examples of such disinterested reading, John Wallace, "Dryden and History: A Problem in Allegorical Reading," *ELH* 36 (March 1969): 279–282, and "'Examples Are Best Precepts': Readers and Meanings in Seventeenth-Century Poetry," *Critical Inquiry* 1 (December 1974): 273–290; and Alan Roper, "Drawing Parallels and Making Applications in Restoration Literature," *Politics as Reflected in Literature* (Los Angeles, 1989), 29–65.

33. James Tyrrell, *Patriarcha non monarcha* (London, 1681), A1v [Folger Library, accession no. 146555].

34. *The Fourth Volume of the Works of Mr. John Dryden* (London, 1693) [Folger Library, D2208], 41.

35. Ibid., 41.

36. Ibid., 49.

37. William Prynne, *A New Discovery of the Prelate Tyranny* (London, 1641) [Folger Library, P4018].

38. *The Poems of John Dryden*, ed. James Kinsley, 1:217, ll. 1–18.

39. *The Works of John Dryden*, ed. E. N. Hooker and H. T. Swedenberg Jr., et al., 20 vols. (Berkeley and Los Angeles, 1953–), vol. 15, *Plays*, ed. E. Miner (1976), 71.

40. *The Poems of John Dryden*, 1:250.

41. *The Correspondence of Jonathan Swift*, ed. H. Williams, 6 vols. (Oxford, 1963), 3:293.

42. See Jonson's copy of Martial, *M. Val. Martialis nova editio. Ex Museo Petri Scriverii* (London, 1619), Folger Library, PA 6501 A2 1619 Cage.

43. See T. A. Birrell, *English Monarchs and Their Books: From Henry VII to Charles II* [The Panizzi Lectures, 1986] (London, 1987), 44–45.

44. *Paradise Lost: A Poem in Twelve Books* (London, 1678), Osborn Collection, pb 9, Beinecke Library, Yale University.

45. See Jonathan Swift, *Miscellaneous and Autobiographical Pieces, Fragments, and Marginalia*, ed. H. Davis (Oxford, 1962), 295–320.

46. *A Catalogue of the Library of Sir Edward Coke*, ed. W. O. Hassall, *Yale Law Library Publications*, no. 12 (New Haven, 1950), 61.

47. Defoe's copy of Bacon's *Advancement of Learning* is in the Robert H. Taylor Collection, Rare Books Division, Firestone Library, Princeton University.

48. *Bibliotheca illustris: Sive catalogus . . . November 21, 1687* (London, 1687), A1r.

49. Edward Clark, *The Protestant School Master* (London, 1680), and cf. *A Fannaticks Primmer* (London, 1660).

50. See Steven N. Zwicker, *Politics and Language in Dryden's Poetry: The Arts of Disguise* (Princeton, 1984), 177–205.

51. See James Toland, *Amyntor, or A Defence of Milton's Life* (London, 1699), and Bernard Sharratt, "The Appropriation of Milton," *Essays and Studies*, ed. S. Bushrui (London, 1982).

52. On Milton's eighteenth-century editors, see A. Oras, *Milton's Editors and Commentators from Patrick Hume to Henry John Todd, 1695–1801* (London, 1931).

53. See *Regular and Irregular Thoughts in Poets and Orators* (London, 1697), 33: "For Noble Thoughts, we might represent to our selves Milton, whose Paradise Lost is full of such."

54. *The Sorrows and Sympathetic Attachments of Werter; A German Story, By Mr. Goethe, Doctor of the Civil Law* (Philadelphia, 1784).

55. Ibid., 65.

THE POLITICS OF SONG
IN WORDSWORTH'S LYRICAL BALLADS

1. J. H. Averill, *Wordsworth and the Poetry of Human Suffering* (Ithaca, 1980).

2. William Hazlitt's classic interpretation of Wordsworth's inspiration as a

"leveling Muse" has been restated recently by Stephen Gill, who finds that *Lyrical Ballads* demonstrates the survival of the passion of Wordsworth's radical years: S. Gill, *William Wordsworth: A Life* (Oxford, 1989), 140. The most sophisticated modern version of this thesis is unquestionably still that of M. H. Abrams in *Natural Supernaturalism: Tradition and Revolution in Romantic Literature* (New York, 1971). The idea of "conservative apostasy" is associated with J. H. Thompson and recently with the more nuanced versions of the "new historicist" criticism of Jerome McGann, David Simpson, Marjorie Levinson, and Alan Liu.

3. E. de Selincourt, ed., *The Letters of William and Dorothy Wordsworth, vol. 1: The Early Years, 1787–1805* (Oxford, 1967), 314–315.

4. "Preface" to W. Wordsworth, *Lyrical Ballads* (1800), appendix 3, "*Lyrical Ballads and Other Poems, 1797–1800*," ed. J. Butler and K. Green (Ithaca and London, 1992), 746. All references to the "Preface" are to this edition.

5. See J. K. Chandler, *Wordsworth's Second Nature: A Study of the Poetry and Politics* (Chicago, 1982).

6. D. Simpson, *Wordsworth's Historical Imagination: The Poetry of Displacement* (New York and London, 1987), 3.

7. G. Harrison, *Wordsworth's Vagrant Muse: Poetry, Poverty, and Power* (Detroit, 1994), 17–23.

8. This is essentially Marjorie Levinson's argument, especially with regard to "Tintern Abbey" and "Michael," in *Wordsworth's Great Period Poems: Four Essays* (Cambridge, 1986).

9. "Michael," in W. Wordsworth, *Lyrical Ballads and Other Poems, 1797–1800*, p. 253, ll. 25–26, 37–39. All references to the poems in *Lyrical Ballads* are to this edition; after the first reference in each case only line numbers are given.

10. Ibid., pp. 133–139, ll. 97–101.

11. "Preface," p. 755.

12. Averill, *Wordsworth and the Poetry of Human Suffering*, 183.

13. "Hart-leap Well," ll. 179–180.

14. Ibid., l. 139.

15. Averill, *Wordsworth and the Poetry of Human Suffering*, 214.

16. "Hart-leap Well," ll. 32–33.

17. "Preface," p. 746.

18. Averill, *Wordsworth and the Poetry of Human Suffering*, 216–217.

19. I have discussed this in much greater detail in my book *Impossible Individuality: Romanticism, Revolution, and the Origins of Modern Selfhood, 1787–1802* (Princeton, 1992), 156–161. The argument of this essay is essentially a continuation, with some modifications and additions, of the analysis offered in the book.

20. Ibid., 154–155.

21. Ibid., 176–179.

22. W. Wordsworth, *The Prelude: 1799, 1805, 1850*, ed. J. Wordsworth, M. H. Abrams, and S. Gill (New York, 1979), Book X (1805), ll. 821–824. Italics added. Rivers in *The Borderers* uses almost exactly the same language.

23. W. Wordsworth, *The Borderers*, ed. R. Osborn (Ithaca, 1982), 3.2.92–95. The reference is to the early version of 1797–1799.

24. The phrase "defiance of law and custom" appears in the story "Vaudracour and Julia," the veiled account of Wordsworth's affair with Annette Vallon, in the 1805 version of *The Prelude*.

25. See the essay prefaced to the early version of *The Borderers,* 62–68, titled by the editor "On the Character of Rivers."

26. W. Wordsworth, *"The Ruined Cottage" and "The Pedlar,"* ed. J. Butler (Ithaca, 1979), MS B, ll. 520–524.

27. *The Prelude* (1805), X:818–824.

28. "Preface," p. 757. Italics added.

29. Ibid., p. 756.

30. Ibid., p. 745.

31. Harrison, *Wordworth's Vagrant Muse,* 18.

32. Certainly it is a contemporary political debate that animates Harrison's remark that Wordsworth's "idealization of rustic poverty . . . interferes with genuine concern over the welfare of the poor": Harrison, *Wordsworth's Vagrant Muse,* 18.

33. Izenberg, *Impossible Individuality,* 173.

34. W. Wordsworth, *The Prose Works of William Wordsworth,* ed. W. J. B. Owen and J. W. Smyser (Oxford, 1974), 1:43.

35. M. Jacobus, *Tradition and Experiment in Wordsworth's Lyrical Ballads* (Oxford, 1978), 237.

36. Simpson, *Wordsworth's Historical Imagination,* 155.

37. "Simon Lee, The Old Huntsman," *Lyrical Ballads and other Poems,* pp. 64–67, ll. 33–36, 45–48.

38. "Preface," p. 755.

39. Ibid. Inserted in the 1802 edition.

40. Ibid., 756.

41. The central thesis of Susan Eilenberg's *Strange Power of Speech: Wordsworth, Coleridge and Literary Possession* (Oxford, 1992), is Wordsworth's concern with literary property and his appropriation of *Lyrical Ballads* at Coleridge's expense. Again, however, the issue is put in terms of social class and its characteristic motives.

42. De Selincourt, *Letters,* I:210–212.

43. Izenberg, *Impossible Individuality,* 141.

44. M. Moorman, *William Wordsworth: A Biography.* vol. I, *The Early Years, 1770–1803* (Oxford, 1957), 427.

45. "Ruth," *Lyrical Ballads and other Poems,* pp. 191–200, ll. 27–30.

46. Ibid., ll. 122–127.

47. *The Prelude* (1805) XIII:86–90.

48. "Ruth," ll. 115–121.

49. Ibid., ll. 140–145.

50. Ibid., l. 162.

51. Ibid., ll. 193–198.

52. "A Fragment," *Lyrical Ballads and other Poems,* p. 241, ll. 57–66.

PERFORMING THE PASSIONS IN COMMERCIAL SOCIETY

1. Roy Porter, *English Society in the Eighteenth Century* (Harmondsworth: Penguin, 1982), 81.

2. Tom Paine, "The Rights of Man," in *Common Sense and Other Political Writings* (Indianapolis: Bobbs-Merrill, 1953), 120.

3. E. P. Thompson, "Patrician Society, Plebeian Culture," *Journal of Social History* 7, no. 4 (1974): 389.

4. See, for example, Jean-Marie Apostolides, *Le Roi-machine: Spectacle et politique au temps de Louis XIV* (Paris: Editions de Minuit, 1981).

5. John Brewer, "Theatre and Counter-Theatre in Georgian Politics," *Radical History Review* 22 (Winter 1979–1980): 7–40; Douglas Hay, "Property, Authority, and the Criminal Law," *Albion's Fatal Tree* (New York: Pantheon, 1975), 17–64; Peter Borsay, "'All the World's a Stage': Urban Ritual and Ceremony, 1660–1800," in Peter Clark, ed., *The Transformation of English Provincial Towns, 1600–1800* (Oxford: Oxford University Press, 1984), 228–258; Bob Bushway, *By Rite: Custom, Ceremony, and Community in England, 1700–1880* (Oxford: Oxford University Press, 1982), chap. 5; and Marc Baer, *Theatre and Disorder in Late Georgian London* (Oxford: Clarendon Press, 1992), 222–238.

6. Neil McKendrick, John Brewer, and J. H. Plumb, *The Birth of a Consumer Society* (London: Hutchinson, 1982).

7. On this subversive tradition in philosophy see Lionel Rothkrug, *Opposition to Louis XIV: The Political and Social Origins of the French Enlightenment* (Princeton: Princeton University Press, 1965), 52–54; Nannerl Keohane, *Philosophy and the State in France* (Princeton: Princeton University Press, 1980), 283–311; and Dale Van Kley, "Pierre Nicole, Jansenism, and the Morality of Enlightened Self-Interest," in Alan C. Kors and Paul Korshin, eds., *Anticipations of the Enlightenment* (Philadelphia: University of Pennsylvania Press, 1987), 69–85.

8. See the contemporary English translation of Pierre Bayle's *Pensées divers sur le comète* (1683), entitled *Miscellaneous Reflections on the Comet* (London, 1708), 212–225.

9. See particularly Pierre Nicole, "Of Grandeur" and "Of Christian Civility," in *Moral Essayes, Contain'd in Several Treatises on Many Important Duties* (London, 1696), 83–128 and 137–149. See too the Huguenot Jacques Abbadie, *The Art of Knowing Oneself, or An Inquiry into the Sources of Morality* (Oxford, 1695), 126–187, and Jacques Esprit, *Discourses on the Deceitfulness of Human Virtues* (London, 1706), preface and pp. 37–38.

10. All references placed parenthetically in the text refer to the volume and page number as they appear in the edition of F. B. Kaye, *The Fable of the Bees, or Private Vices, Public Benefits. By Bernard Mandeville. With a Commentary Critical, Historical, and Explanatory by F. B. Kaye*, 2 vols. (Oxford: Clarendon Press, 1924). For Mandeville's relationship to the theory of the passions in seventeenth-century Augustinian moral reflection, see Arthur O. Lovejoy, *Reflections on Human Nature* (Baltimore: Johns Hopkins, 1961), lectures 3–5, and, building on Lovejoy's work, Laurence Dickey, "Pride, Hypocrisy, and Civility in Mandeville's Social and Historical Theory," *Critical Review* 4, no. 3 (Summer 1990): 387–431. For a comprehensive account of Mandeville's eighteenth-century identity see E. J. Hundert, *The Enlightenment's "Fable": Bernard Mandeville and the Discovery of Society* (Cambridge: Cambridge University Press, 1984).

11. [Bernard Mandeville], *A Letter to Dion, Occasioned by His Book Call'd Alciphon, or The Minute Philosopher, by the Author of the Fable of the Bees* (London, 1732), 8.

12. Jacob Viner, *Religious Thought and Economic Society*, ed. Jacques Melitz and Donald Winch (Durham: Duke University Press, 1978), chap. 3, usefully explores the distinctions between a utilitarian conception of morals and an ethics of duty.

13. Thomas Hobbes, *Leviathan*, ed. C. B. Macpherson (Harmondsworth: Penguin, 1968), I.x.160.

14. See especially for the role of this French language of politeness, Maurice

Magendie, *La Politesse mondaine et les théories de l'honnêteté en France au XVIIe siècle, de 1600 à 1660* (1925) (Reprint, Geneva: Slatkine, 1970); Norbert Elias, *The Court Society* (Oxford: Blackwell, 1983); and Peter France, *Politeness and Its Discontents* (Cambridge: Cambridge University Press, 1992). For its transmission to England see L. Charlanne, *L'Influence française en Angleterre au XVIIe siècle* (Paris, 1906), chap. 3.

15. See especially Lawrence Klein, *Shaftesbury and the Culture of Politeness: Moral Discourse and Cultural Politics in Early Eighteenth-Century England* (Cambridge: Cambridge University Press, 1994).

16. Bernard Mandeville, *An Enquiry into the Origins of Honour, and the Usefulness of Christianity in War* (1732), ed. M. M. Goldsmith (Reprint, London: Cass, 1971), 8–9.

17. Pierre Bayle, *Nouvelles Lettres sur l'histoire du Calvinisme*, XVI, ix, p. 278b, cited in Elizabeth Labrousse, *Bayle* (The Hague: Nijhoff, 1964), 2:122, who provides a useful discussion of this point.

18. La Rochefoucauld, *Maxims*, trans. Leonard Tannock (Harmondsworth: Penguin, 1959), nos. 119 and 549. See La Rochefoucauld's teacher, Jacques Esprit, *The Falsehood of Human Virtue* (London, 1691), 40, for a description of the Court as the stage where affectation "acts her masterpieces."

19. Pierre Nicole, *Essais de Morale* (Paris, 1675), 421. In his *Traité de la Comedie* (1667), ed. Georges Couton (Paris: Société d'Edition "Les Belles Lettres," 1961), 49–59. Nicole argues that these passions are inherent in and promoted by theatrical entertainments themselves.

20. Thomas Hobbes, *Leviathan*, "Of Man," I. xvi, pp. 217–218.

21. For a discussion of the central place of theatricality in Augustinian moral psychology see E. J. Hundert, "Augustine and the Sources of the Divided Self," *Political Theory* 20, no. 1 (1992): 86–104.

22. Ernst Robert Curtius, *European Literature and the Latin Middle Ages*, trans. Willard Trask (London: Routledge and Kegan Paul, 1953), 140–142.

23. Miguel de Cervantes, *Don Quixote*, trans. J. M. Cohen (Harmondsworth: Penguin, 1958), II, iii, 12.

24. John Webster, *Complete Works*, ed. Frank L. Lucas (London: Chatto and Windus, 1924), 4:42–44.

25. Benjamin Boyce, *The Theophrastian Character in England to 1642* (Cambridge: Harvard University Press, 1947), 36–52.

26. The line of argument initiated by Stephen Greenblatt, *Renaissance Self-Fashioning: From More to Shakespeare* (Chicago: Chicago University Press, 1980), in part extended to a commercial context by Jean-Christophe Agnew, *World's Apart: The Market and the Theatre in Anglo-American Thought* (Cambridge: Cambridge University Press, 1986), and recently further developed by Katherine Eisamen Maus, *Inwardness and Theater in the English Renaissance* (Chicago: Chicago University Press, 1995), is suggestive rather than convincing as regards the portrayal of character since these works offer a secular and individualist perspective on what for contemporaries were essentially religious and metaphysical issues. For a powerful and historically sensitive investigation of character and the portrayal of individualism on the Renaissance stage, see Edward Burns, *Character: Acting and Being on the Pre-Modern Stage* (New York: St. Martin's Press, 1990).

27. David Berman, *A History of Atheism in Britain* (London: Croom Helm, 1988). See Berman's chapters 1 and 2 and, for example, G. Purshall, *Essay on the Mechanical Fabric of the Universe* (London, 1708).

28. Charles de Marguetel de Saint Denis, Seigneur de Saint-Evremond, *Works*, I, p. 158.

29. The most famous attack on the stage as immoral was Jeremy Collier, *A Short View of the Immorality and Profaness of the English Stage* (London, 1698). Sir Richard Blackmore, *Creation: A Philosophical Poem* . . . (1712), was the most thoroughgoing anti-Epicurean document of the eighteenth century. This poem is printed in his *Preface to Prince Arthur* (1695), in J. E. Springarn, ed., *Critical Essays of the Seventeenth Century* (Oxford: Oxford University Press, 1909), 3:230.

30. John Digby, *Epicurus's Morals* (London, 1712), 52.

31. Bernard Mandeville, *A Treatise on Hypochondriak and Hysterik Passions* (London, 1711), 34–37, 52–54, and 125.

32. Francis Bacon, "Of the Proficience and Advancement of Learning," in *The Works*, ed. J. Spedding, R. L. Ellis, and D. D. Heath (Reprint, New York: Longmans, 1963), 3:430.

33. David Hume, "Of Eloquence," *Essays: Moral, Political, Literary* (Oxford: Oxford University Press, 1963), 100.

34. Charles Gildin, *The Life of Thomas Betterton* (London, 1710), 86.

35. André Dacier, *The Preface to Aristotle's Art of Poetry* (1705) Augustan Reprint Society no. 76 (Los Angeles: William Andrews Clark Library, 1959), p. A3.

36. John Dennis, *The Advancement and Reformation of Poetry* (1701), in *Critical Works*, 2 vols. (Baltimore: John Hopkins University Press, 1939–1945), vol. 1.

37. René Descartes, *Philosophical Works*, trans. E. S. Haldane and G. R. T. Ross (Cambridge: Cambridge University Press, 1911), 1:373. See too Dennis, *The Advancement and Reformation of Poetry*, 364. For the conceptual dilemmas attendant on this view see Anthony Levi, *French Moralists: The Theory of the Passions, 1585–1649* (Oxford: Clarendon Press, 1964), 229–238.

38. Abel Boyer, *The English Theophrastus, or the Manners of the Age* . . . (London, 1702), 301.

39. Brewster Rogerson, "The Art of Painting the Passions," *Journal of the History of Ideas* 14, no. 1 (1953): 68–94, is a rich discussion of this subject. See too Lawrence Lipking, *The Ordering of the Arts in Eighteenth-Century England* (Princeton: Princeton University Press, 1970), esp. 38–65.

40. For Le Brun see Stephanie Ross, "Painting the Passions: Charles Le Brun's *Conférence sur l'expression*," *Journal of the History of Ideas* 45, no. 1 (1984): 25–47, and Jennifer Montagu, *The Expression of the Passions: The Origin and Influence of Charles Le Brun's "Conférence sur l'expression générale et particulière"* (New Haven: Yale University Press, 1994).

41. Henry Siddons, *Practical Illustrations of Rhetorical Gestury and Action*, 2d ed. (London, 1822), who compiles a list of fifty-eight passions and their appropriate expressions derived from Le Brun.

42. Anthony Ashley Cooper, earl of Shaftesbury, *A Notion of the Historical Draught of the Judgement of Hercules* (1732), in Benjamin Rand, ed., *Shaftesbury's Second Characteristics* (Cambridge: Cambridge University Press, 1914), 29–62. This point is discussed in Ronald Paulson, *Hogarth: His Life, Art, and Times* (New Haven: Yale University Press, 1972), 1:103–104. On the representation of the passions on the eighteenth-century stage, see William Worthen, *The Idea of the Actor* (Princeton: Princeton University Press, 1984), chap. 2. See, for example, Henry Home, Lord Kames, *Elements of Criticism*, 6th ed. (Edinburgh, 1785), 2 vols., parts 1–7, "Emotions and Passions."

43. Aaron Hill, *Essay of the Art of Acting* (London, 1746), first printed as essays in *The Prompter* (1734–1736); Samuel Foote, *A Treatise on the Passions, So Far as They Regard to the STAGE* (London, 1747); Marvin Carlson, *Theories of the Theater* (Ithaca: Cornell University Press, 1984), 138–139; Lewis [Luigi] Riccoboni, *A General History of the Stage . . .* (London, 1754), xvii and 177; and Antoine Sticcotti, *Garrick, ou Les acteurs anglais* (Paris, 1769).

44. See, in particular, Joseph R. Roach, *The Player's Passion: Studies in the Science of Acting* (Newark: University of Delaware Press, 1988), 58–115, and Richard Sennett, *The Fall of Public Man* (Cambridge: Cambridge University Press, 1974), 75–85. For a detailed account of these protocols, see the five-part essay by Dene Barnett, "The Performance Practice of Acting: The Eighteenth Century," *Theater Review International* 2–3 (1977–1978).

45. David Garrick, *An Essay on Acting* (London, 1744), 2.

46. J.-B. Du Bos, *Réflexions critiques sur la poésie et sur peinture* (Paris, 1719; 2d ed., rev., 1732); English translation, London, 1748. On Du Bos's importance see D. G. Charleton, "J.-B. Du Bos and Eighteenth-Century Sensibility," *Studies in Voltaire and the Eighteenth Century* 266 (1990): 151–162, and Peter Jones, *Hume's Sentiments: Their Ciceronian and French Context* (Edinburgh: Edinburgh University Press, 1982), chap. 3.

47. Du Bos, *Réflexions*, 3:179; see too, 1:10.

48. Ibid., 1:24.

49. Ibid., 2:xxii.

50. Ibid., 2:xxi; 3:xiii and xvi.

51. Ibid., 1:350.

52. *Spectator*, nos. 10, 274, 370.

53. Voltaire, *Lettres philosophiques*, lettre 6. See *Fable*, 1:343, where Mandeville claims that traders would have no more civility "than Bulls" had not interest brought them together.

54. Montesquieu, *The Spirit of the Laws*, trans. A. M. Cohen, B. C. Miller, and H. S. Stone (Cambridge: Cambridge University Press, 1989), VII.1; xix.8.

55. For other contemporary observers see, for example, the comments recorded in Harry W. Pedicord, "The Changing Audience," in Robert D. Hume, ed., *The London Theatrical World, 1660–1800* (Carbondale: Southern Illinois University Press, 1980), 239–246, and Leo Hughes, *The Drama's Patrons: A Study of the Eighteenth-Century London Audience* (Austin: University of Texas Press, 1971), 97 ff. See too Alexander Pope's satire of the stage in his "Project for the Advancement of the Stage," in *Peri Bathous* (1728), and his lament about audience behavior and public taste in the "First Epistle" of the *Second Book of Horace* (1732), II, 312–313.

John Dennis, *A Large Account of the Taste in Poetry* (London, 1702), in *The Critical Works of John Dennis*, ed. Edward Niles Hooker (Baltimore: Johns Hopkins, 1939), 1:293. See too, for example, the comments about the social composition of London audiences by Henri de Valbourg Misson, *Mémoires et observations faites par un voyage en Angleterre* (The Hague, 1698), 63–64. John Dennis, *Vice and Luxury Public Mischiefs* (London, 1724).

56. William Law, *The Absolute Unlawfulness of Stage-Entertainment Fully Demonstrated* (London, 1726), 9; see too Leo Hughes, *The Drama's Patrons*, 97 ff. In the pro-

logue Garrick spoke when the great actor began his career as manager of Drury Lane in 1747, Johnson wrote:

> Ah! let not Censure term our Fate our choice
> The Stage, but echoes back the publick Voice.
> The Drama's Laws the Drama's Patrons give
> For we that live to please, must please to live.

Quoted in James J. Lynch, *Box Pit and Gallery: Stage and Society in Johnson's London* (Berkeley: University of California Press, 1953), 204. For the audience as a participant in dramatic performance see Dane Farnsworth Smith and M. L. Lawhon, *Plays about the Theatre in England, 1737–1800* (Albuquerque: University of New Mexico Press, 1953).

57. James Boswell, *Boswell's London Journal*, ed. Frederick Pottle (New Haven: Yale University Press, 1950), 27. For other examples of responses like Boswell's see Hughes, *The Drama's Patrons*, 136–137.

58. Law, *The Absolute Unlawfulness of Stage-Entertainment*, 10.

59. Bernard Mandeville, *An Enquiry into the Frequent Executions at Tyburn* (London, 1725), Augustan Reprint Society no. 105 (Los Angeles: William Andrews Clark Memorial Library, 1964), 21, 26, and 40.

60. Mandeville, *Enquiry into the Origins of Honour*, 107, 149, 162, and 189.

61. George Bluett, *An Enquiry Whether a General Practice of Virtue Tends to the Wealth or Poverty, Benefit or Discouragement of a People?* (London, 1725), 216–218. Masquerades, as Bluett pointed out (pp. 143–149), had for some time been the fashion in London society and were denounced by a number of Mandeville's other clerical and lay adversaries. See, for example, the description of these events by Addison, in *Spectator* 8 and 14, as a "libidinous Assembly" of "Assignations and Intrigues."

62. Mandeville, *The Mischiefs that Ought Justly to Be Apprehended from a Whig-Government* [1714] (Reprint, Los Angeles: William Andrews Clark Memorial Library, 1975), 1–2.

63. See, particularly, Terry Castle, *Masquerade and Civilization* (Stanford: Stanford University Press, 1986), 1–56.

64. Mandeville, *A Modest Defense of Public Stews* (London, 1724), dedication.

65. Anon., *The True Meaning of the Fable of the Bees* (London, 1726), 27.

66. Eva Tabor, *Skepticism, Society, and the Eighteenth-Century Novel* (New York: St. Martin's, 1987), 54–77, discusses *The Fable*'s place in the eighteenth-century literary imagination and suggests that Mandeville served as an important point of departure for Richardson as well. See Henry Fielding, *Champion*, 22 January 1739/1740, in W. E. Henley, ed., *The Complete Works of Henry Fielding* (New York: Harper, 1903), 15:162; ibid., 11 December 1739, 15:94; and preface to *Miscellanies*, in Henley, *Complete Works of Fielding*, 12:243.

67. *Tom Jones*, in Henley, *Complete Works of Fielding*, 6:1.

68. Fielding, *Covent-Garden Journal*, 14 March 1752.

69. *Joseph Andrews*, I, xv.

70. *Covent-Garden Journal*, 14 January 1752; 25 April 1752.

71. See Bernard Harrison, *Henry Fielding's Tom Jones* (London: Sussex University Press, 1975), 39–48 and 70–88. Compare particularly Fielding's analysis of public executions in *Covent-Garden Journal*, 28 March 1752, and *An Inquiry into the* . . .

Causes . . . of the Increase in Robbers (1751) (Reprint, New York: AMS Press, 1975), 121, with Mandeville's in Tyburn. See too Hélène Desfond, "Tyburn chez Mandeville and Fielding, ou Le Corps exemplaire du pendu," in Paul-Gabriel Boucé and Suzi Halimi, eds., *Le Corps et l'âme en Grand-Bretagne au XVIIIᵉ siècle* (Paris: Sorbonne, 1985), 61–70.

72. P. P. Howe, ed., *The Complete Works of William Hazlitt,* cited in Homer Goldberg, *The Art of Joseph Andrews* (Chicago: Chicago University Press, 1969), 260.

73. *Tom Jones,* in Henley, *Complete Works of Fielding,* 6:1.

74. Ibid., 7:1: "A Comparison between the World and the Stage."

75. Fielding, *An Essay on the Knowledge and the Characters of Men,* 177–178.

76. Fielding's first publication, a poem, *The Masquerade* (1728), in Claude E. Jones, ed., *"The Female Husband' and Other Writings* (Liverpool: Liverpool University Press, 1960), was inscribed to "C—T H—D—G—R" and criticized his entertainments, "Because that thing, which we, in English, Do virtue call, is always took To hold its station in the look" (ll. 200–202). See Terry Castle's discussion of this theme in *Amelia* in her *Masquerade and Civilization,* 177–252.

77. Fielding, *An Essay,* 178.

78. John Brown, *A Dissertation on the Rise, Union and Power, the Progressions, Separations and Corruptions, of Poetry and Music* (London, 1763).

79. *An Essay,* 178. The characters Fielding names are stock figures of the Restoration stage.

80. *Joseph Andrews,* preface.

81. *An Essay,* 179.

82. Compare this quality with mere "good Breeding[,] the latter being the Art of conducting yourself by certain common and general Rules, by which Means, if they were universally observed, the whole world would appear (as all Courtiers actually do) to be, in their external Behavior at least, but one and the same Person," in Henry Fielding, *The Covent-Garden Journal* 55 (18 July 1752).

83. *Tom Jones,* 7:1.

84. *An Essay,* 187.

85. *An Essay,* 188.

86. *Joseph Andrews,* 3:10: A discourse between the poet and player.

87. Rameau's nephew to "Lui," in Denis Diderot, *Rameau's Nephew,* trans. L. W. Tancock (London: Penguin, 1966), 76 and 120. It is worthy of note that Rameau was referring to Noverre, the greatest contemporary teacher of dance, and that the dancing master was one of Mandeville's and Fielding's preferred images for the representation of deceit, a point made about Fielding by Claude Rawson in "Gentlemen and Dancing-Masters," in *Henry Fielding and the Augustan Ideal under Stress* (London: Routledge, 1972), 3–34.

88. *Joseph Andrews,* 1:7.

89. E. J. Hundert, "A Satire of Self-Disclosure: From Hegel through Rameau to the Augustans," *Journal of the History of Ideas* 47, no. 2 (1986): 235–248.

90. Alasdair MacIntyre, *After Virtue* (Notre Dame: Notre Dame University Press, 1981), 35–48, gives a brilliant account of the relation between Rameau's masquerades and eighteenth-century moral philosophy. For the decay of the behavioral styles represented by Fielding, see Charles Pullen, "Lord Chesterfield and

Eighteenth-Century Appearance and Reality," *Studies in English Literature, 1500–1800* 8 (1968): 501–515, and Michael Curtin, "A Question of Manners: Status and Gender in Etiquette and Courtesy," *The Journal of Modern History* 57 (September 1985): 395–423.

91. *Joseph Andrews*, preface.

92. Roger Shattuck, "The Prince, the Actor and I: The Histrionic Sensibility," in *The Innocent Eye* (New York: Farrar, Straus, and Giroux, 1984), 107–139.

93. *OED*, s.v. "identify," and see Marion Hobson, *The Object of Art: The Theory of Illusion in Eighteenth-Century France* (Cambridge: Cambridge University Press, 1982), 208.

94. Jean-Jacques Rousseau, *Discourse on the Origin and Foundations of Inequality* (1755), trans. Roger D. Masters (New York: St. Martin's Press, 1964), 130.

95. Jean-Jacques Rousseau, *Politics and the Arts: Letter to M. d'Alembert on the Theater* (1757), trans. Allan Bloom (Glencoe: The Free Press, 1960), 24. For Rousseau and the problem of the theater and theatricality, see Benjamin R. Barber, "Rousseau and the Paradoxes of the Dramatic Imagination," *Daedalus* 107 (1978): 79–92, and especially John Hope Mason, "The 'Lettre à d'Alembert' and Its Place in Rousseau's Thought," in M. Hobson, J. T. A. Leigh, and R. Wokler, eds., *Rousseau and the Eighteenth Century: Essays in Memory of R. A. Leigh* (Oxford: The Voltaire Foundation, 1992), 251–269.

96. E. Phillips, *An Appeal to Common Sense, or Some Considerations Offer'd to Restore Publick Credit. As Also the Means of Reviving It* (London, 1720), 4.

97. See especially David Hume, *A Treatise of Human Nature*, ed. L. A. Selby-Bigge (Oxford: Clarendon Press, 1955), I.iv.7, where he gives his famous account of personal identity as nothing but a heap of perceptions. At the same time, in *Treatise*, I.i.5, Hume continued to speak of "self, or that individual person," of whose actions and sentiments each of us is intimately conscious."

98. Hume, *Treatise*, xvii.

99. Ibid., III.iii.3.

100. Ibid., II.ii.5.

101. Ibid., I.iv.6.

102. E. J. Hundert and Paul Nelles, "Liberty and Theatrical Space in Montesquieu's Political Theory: The Poetics of Public Life in the *Persian Letters*," *Political Theory* 17, no. 2 (May 1989): 223–246.

103. Adam Smith, *The Theory of Moral Sentiments*, ed. D. D. Raphael and A. L. Macfie (Oxford: Oxford University Press, 1976), VII.2.4.10. Hereafter *TMS*.

104. Adam Smith, *An Inquiry into the Nature and Causes of the Wealth of Nations*, ed. R. H. Campbell and A. S. Skinner (Oxford: Oxford University Press, 1976), 124.

105. Smith, *TMS*, VII.2.4; III.4.6.

106. Ibid., I.3.2.3.

107. Ibid., I.3.2.1 and 4.

108. Ibid., III.1.3.

109. Ibid., III.1.5. Compare Rand, ed., *Shaftesbury's Second Characteristics*, 1:257, where the mind is referred to as "a spectator or auditor of other minds." See too Charles L. Griswald Jr., "Rhetoric and Ethics: Adam Smith on Theorizing the Moral Sentiments," *Philosophy and Rhetoric* 24, no. 3 (1991): 213–237; Jonah Barish, *The*

Anti-Theatrical Prejudice (Berkeley: University of California Press, 1981), 243–255, and Joseph J. Spengler, "Smith versus Hobbes: Economy versus polity," in F. R. Glahe, ed., *Adam Smith and the Wealth of Nations* (Boulder, Colo.: Associated University Press, 1978), 43, who points out that Smith's "invisible hand" was compared by Fontenelle in *Pluralité des mondes* (1686), a work Smith knew, to "that of an Engineer who, hidden in the pit of a French Theatre, operated 'the Machines of the Theatre' in motion on the stage."

110. *TMS,* II.2.3.2.

111. See, for this point, John Dunn, "From Applied Theology to Social Analysis: The Break between John Locke and the Scottish Enlightenment," in Istvan Hont and Michael Ignatieff, eds., *Wealth and Virtue* (Cambridge: Cambridge University Press, 1983), 119–136.

112. Immanuel Kant, *Anthropology from a Pragmatic Point of View,* trans. Mary J. Gregor (The Hague: Nijhoff, 1974), 14–15.

113. Immanuel Kant, *The Critique of Practical Reason,* trans. T. K. Abbott (London: Longmans, 1909), vol. 2, part 1, book 1, chap. 1, "Of the Principles of Pure Practical Reason," 129.

114. Kant, *Anthropology,* 14–15. Translation amended.

115. Rousseau, *Letter to d'Alembert,* 26.

116. A point developed in Mason, "The *Lettre à d'Alembert . . .*" 259–261.

117. Rousseau, *Letter to d'Alembert,* 16.

118. Charles E. Ellison, "Rousseau and the Modern City: The Politics of Speech and Dress," *Political Theory* 13, no. 4 (1985): 497–534.

119. Quoted in Hughes, *The Drama's Patrons,* 61.

120. Jean-Jacques Rousseau, *Narcisse, ou L'Amant de lui-meme,* in *Oeuvres complètes,* ed. Jean Starobinski (Paris: Gallimard, 1964), 966, 972.

121. *Letter to d'Alembert,* 22 and 25.

122. On this last point see Joseph W. Donahue Jr., *Dramatic Character in the English Romantic Age* (Princeton: Princeton University Press, 1970).

123. G. W. F. Hegel, *The Phenomenology of Spirit,* trans. A. V. Miller (Oxford: Clarendon Press, 1977), 103.

"THESE NEUTER SOMETHINGS"

1. *The World. By Adam Fitz-Adam,* no. 165, 26 February 1756.

2. *Common Sense, or The Englishman's Journal. Being a Collection of Letters, Political, Humorous, and Moral,* July 23, 1737. Compare Lady Mary Wortley Montagu, in *The Nonsense of Common-Sense,* no. 9, 12 March 1738: "Bravery and Chastity, the ancient Idols of the two Sexes, are not only left without Worshippers, but trampled on and despis'd . . . it is a Sort of Merit in People to get the better of natural Shame, when *Money* is in their Way."

3. Samuel Johnson, *The Adventurer,* no. 111, 27 November 1763.

4. *World,* no. 61, 28 February 1754; and [Moore], *World,* no. 1, 4 January 1753.

5. David Hume, "Of Essay Writing," in *Essays Moral, Political, and Literary,* ed. Eugene F. Miller (Indianapolis: Liberty Classics, 1985), 536. The essay was printed in Hume's *Essays: Moral and Political* (1742).

6. For further discussion of fashion see Neil McKendrick, "The Commercialisation of Fashion," in Neil McKendrick, John Brewer, and J. H. Plumb, *The Birth of a Consumer Society: The Commercialization of Eighteenth-Century England* (London: Europa, 1982), esp. 53–56. Complaints about the erosion of the social structure as a result of fashionable consumption and display had of course been common currency for several centuries, but see McKendrick's argument (pp. 34–56) that the situation of England in the mid to late eighteenth century was "unique as well as novel" (p. 55). See also Gerald Newman, *The Rise of English Nationalism: A Cultural History, 1740–1830* (London: Wiedenfeld: 1987), chap. 2.

7. *The Connoisseur. By Mr. Town, Critic and Censor-General*, no. 25, 18 July 1754.

8. Ibid., no. 44, 28 November 1754.

9. Catherine Talbot, *The Works*, ed. Montagu Pennington (London: Rivington, 1819), 62–63.

10. Henry Fielding, *The Covent-Garden Journal*, no. 37, 9 May 1752.

11. James Fordyce, *Sermons to Young Women* (1765), 2 vols. (London: Cadell, 1809) 1:193, 185. The first passage may be a paraphrase of *The Rambler*, no. 15, 8 May 1750.

12. [Cambridge], *World*, no. 118, 3 April 1755.

13. *Connoisseur*, no. 55, 13 February 1755; no. 46, 12 December 1754.

14. Ibid., no. 77, 17 July 1755.

15. [Moore], *World*, no. 18, 3 May 1753.

16. [J. Warton], *World*, no. 26, 28 June 1753. The sentiment is of course also common in other genres. Talbot comments in more directly moral terms that "the elegant beauty, whose fondest aim is to please and to be admired, has sometimes small regard to that complete harmony of manner and behaviour, which perfects the charm" (Essay 15 in Talbot, *Works*, 152).

17. *The Female Spectator*, book 12.

18. [?Marriott], *World*, no. 117, 27 March 1755.

19. I have in mind the processes Stephen Copley describes as evolving a bourgeois civic humanism: see the introduction to his anthology *Literature and the Social Order in Eighteenth-Century England* (London: Croom Helm, 1984).

20. *Connoisseur*, no. 65, 24 April 1755.

21. Henry Home, Lord Kames, for example, writing in the early 1770s, still saw foreign imports as both cause and evidence of effeminating luxury. See his *Sketches of the History of Man* (1774), book 1, sketch 8.

22. *Lichtenberg's Commentaries on Hogarth's Engravings*, trans. and introduction by Innes and Gustav Herdan (London: Cresset Press, 1966), 125.

23. Henry Fielding, *Covent-Garden Journal*, no. 42, 26 May 1752.

24. *Connoisseur*, no. 65, 24 April 1755.

25. Samuel Richardson, *The History of Sir Charles Grandison*, ed. Jocelyn Harris, 3 parts (Oxford: Oxford University Press, 1986), 3:247.

26. Sarah Fielding, *David Simple*, ed. Martin Kelsall (London: Oxford University Press, 1969); all further page references in text.

27. For a fuller discussion of these terms, see John Barrell and Harriet Guest, "On the Use of Contradiction: Economics and Morality in the Eighteenth-Century Long Poem," in Felicity Nussbaum and Laura Brown, eds., *The New Eighteenth Century: Theory, Politics, English Literature* (London: Methuen, 1987), 121–143.

28. See, for example, *Connoisseur,* no. 131, 29 July 1756, which describes the gentleman who is "not obliged to rise to open his shop or work at his trade" as the most "useless idle animal" and compares him to a "celebrated beauty."

29. *Nonsense of Common-Sense,* no. 6, 24 January 1738.

30. See John Barrell's discussion of an intriguingly similar passage in Smollett's *Ferdinand Count Fathom* (1753), in Barrell, *English Literature in History, 1730–1780: An Equal, Wide Survey* (London: Hutchinson, 1983), 185–187.

31. Lady Mary Wortley Montagu, *Complete Letters,* ed. Robert Halsband, 3 vols. (Oxford: Oxford University Press, 1967), 3:67.

32. [Sarah Scott], *The History of Sir George Ellison,* 2 vols. (London: A Millar, 1766), 1:108. All further page references in the text are to this edition.

33. *Common Sense,* 10 September 1737.

34. John Brown, *On the Female Character and Education: A Sermon, Preached on Thursday the 16th of May, 1765, at the Anniversary Meeting of the Guardians of the Asylum for Deserted Female Orphans* (London: L. Davis and C. Reymers, 1765), 15, 17, 18.

35. [Elizabeth Carter], in Samuel Richardson, *Sir Charles Grandison,* 3:243–244. On the attribution to Carter, see note at 3:508.

36. Ibid., 3:243.

37. See J. G. A. Pocock, *Virtue, Commerce, and History: Essays on Political Thought and History, Chiefly in the Eighteenth Century* (Cambridge: Cambridge University Press, 1985), 114.

38. Mary Wollstonecraft, *A Vindication of the Rights of Woman,* ed. Carol H. Poston (New York: Norton, 1975), 23.

39. Richardson, *Grandison,* 3:242.

40. See Francois Poullain de la Barre, *The Woman as Good as the Man; Or, the Equality of Both Sexes* (1673), trans. A. L., ed. with introduction by Gerald MacLean (Detroit, Mich.: 1988), introduction pp. 26 ff.

41. [Mulso], *The World,* no. 131, 3 July 1755.

42. See Richardson, *Sir Charles Grandison,* 3:439.

43. Sarah Scott, *A Description of Millenium Hall and the Country Adjacent Together with the Characters of the Inhabitants and Such Historical Anecdotes and Reflections as May excite in the Reader Proper Sentiments of Humanity, and Lead the Mind to the Love of Virtue* (1762), introduction by Jane Spencer (London: Virago, 1986), 174, 175–178. All further references in text to this edition.

44. On the significance of the retirement of Thomson's patriots, see Barrell, *English Literature in History . . . Equal, Wide Survey,* 56–78.

45. *The Seasons,* ed. James Sambrook (Oxford: Oxford University Press, 1981), "Spring," lines 902–903.

46. James Steuart, *Inquiry into the Principles of Political Oeconomy* (1767), quoted in Kathryn Sutherland's illuminating essay, "Adam Smith's Master Narrative: Women and the *Wealth of Nations,*" in Stephen Copley and Kathryn Sutherland, eds., *Adam Smith's Wealth of Nations: New Interdisciplinary Essays* (Manchester: Manchester University Press, 1995), 107.

47. See also Tony Tanner's comments on the "endless process of "familialization"" in *Sir Charles Grandison* in his *Adultery in the Novel: Contract and Transgression* (Baltimore: Johns Hopkins University Press, 1979), 178n.

48. *The Spectator,* no. 69, 19 May 1711.

49. For further discussion of this issue, see Laura Brown, *Ends of Empire: Women and Ideology in Early Eighteenth-Century English Literature* (Ithaca, N.Y.: Cornell University Press, 1993), chap. 4.

BATHING AND BAPTISM

1. I am grateful to the audiences in Lancaster, London, and Oxford who commented on versions of this paper and to Jonathan Andrews, Roger Cooter, Peter Goddard, David Harley, Penny Harvey, Scott Mandlebrote, John Pickstone, James Robertson, Frank Romany, Lyndal Roper, Bertrand Taithe, and Sir Keith Thomas, who read versions of the text and/or assisted with references and ideas. My thanks also to Justin Champion and Adrian Wilson, who provided detailed commentaries on a draft of the arguments, and above all to Patricia Greene for her perceptive observations and encouragement.

2. M. Mauss, "Techniques of the Body," in *Incorporations,* ed. J. Crary and S. Kwinter (New York, 1992), 455–477.

3. Recent studies include P. Brown, *The Body and Society* (London, 1989); J. Bremmer and H. Roodenberg, eds., *A Cultural History of Gesture* (Oxford, 1991); G. Vigarello, *Concepts of Cleanliness,* trans. J. Birrell (Cambridge, 1988); L. Roper, *Oedipus and the Devil* (London, 1994); D. Outram, *The Body and the French Revolution* (London and New Haven, 1989); L. Hunt, ed., *Eroticism and the Body Politic* (Baltimore, 1991).

4. This phrase is taken from L. H. Martin et al., ed., *Technologies of the Self: A Seminar with Michel Foucault* (Amherst, 1988).

5. N. Elias, *The Civilizing Process,* trans. E. Jephott, 2 vols. (Oxford, 1979–1982). Studies that discuss Elias's theoretical paradigms include A. Bryson, "The Rhetoric of Status: Gesture, Demeanour, and the Image of the Gentleman in Sixteenth- and Seventeenth-Century England," in *Renaissance Bodies,* ed. L. Gent and R. Llewellyn (London, 1990), 136–153; M. B. Becker, *Civility and Society in Western Europe* (Bloomington, 1988); F. Childs, "Prescriptions for Manners in English Courtesy Literature, 1690–1760, and Their Social Implications" (D.Phil. thesis, Oxford University, 1984). See also the far-ranging critique of H.-P. Duerr, *Nacktheit und Scham* (Frankfurt am Main, 1988).

6. *A Description of a New Kinde of Artificiall Bathes Lately Invented* (n.d. ca. 1600); *A Paper Delivered in by Dr. Alston . . . Together with an Answer Thereunto by Peter Chamberlen* (London, 1648); C. Webster, *The Great Instauration* (London, 1975), 261, 298; H. Cook, *The Decline of the Old Medical Regime in Stuart London* (Ithaca and London, 1986), 114–115; C. J. S. Thompson, *The Quacks of Old London* (1928), chap. 17.

7. J. Andrews, "'Hardly a Hospital, but a Charity for Pauper Lunatics'? Therapeutics at Bethlem in the Seventeenth and Eighteenth Centuries," in *Medicine and Charity before the Welfare State,* ed. J. Barry and C. Jones (London, 1991), 73, 80 n. 62.

8. C. Leigh, *Phthisiologia Lancastriensis, cui accessit tentamen philosophicum de mineralibus aquis in eodem comitatu observatis* (London, 1694), 140–143. See also Leigh, *The Natural History of Lancashire, Cheshire, and the Peak, in Derbyshire* (Oxford, 1700), 52–55. Leigh knew both Floyer and Edward Baynard, the main foci of this paper; Leigh, *Natural History,* 32; Leigh, *Phthisiologia,* 143. Tyson subscribed toward the publication of Leigh's *The Natural History.*

9. J. Axtell, ed., *The Educational Writings of John Locke* (Cambridge, 1968), 118–119.

10. Ibid., 120.

11. *The Diary of Ralph Thoresby, F.R.S.*, ed. J. Hunter, 2 vols. (London, 1830), 2:47, 53.

12. P. Hembry, *The English Spa* (London, 1990), 163, and chap. 10, passim. More generally, see C. E. Mullett, "Public Baths and Health in England from the Sixteenth to Eighteenth Century," *Bulletin of the History of Medicine,* suppl. 5 (1946); D. Harley, "A Sword in a Madman's Hand," in *The Medical History of Waters and Spas,* ed. R. Porter, *Medical History,* suppl. 10 (1990): 48–55.

13. *The Post Boy* 922 (15–17 April 1701). Cf. London, British Library (BL), Additional ms. 28276, *fol.* 220.

14. Vigarello, *Concepts of Cleanliness,* chap. 8.

15. Hembry, *The English Spa,* 167. The Devonshires, for instance, developed the waters at Buxton, and Floyer dedicated his *An Enquiry into the Right Use and Abuses of the Hot, Cold, and Temperate Baths in England* (London, 1697) to them.

16. V. S. Smith, "Cleanliness: The Development of the Idea and Practice in Britain, 1770–1850" (Ph.D. dissertation, University of London, 1985), 248, also 66–67.

17. Recent examples include C. Rose, "Politics and the London Royal Hospitals, 1683–1692," in *The Hospital in History,* ed. L. Granshaw and R. Porter (London, 1989), 123–148; M. Fissell, "Charity Universal? Institutions and Moral Reform in Eighteenth-Century Bristol," in *Stilling the Grumbling Hive,* ed. L. Davison et al. (Stroud, 1992), 121–144; D. Harley, "Mental Illness, Magical Medicine, and the Devil in Northern England, 1650–1700," in *The Medical Revolution of the Seventeenth Century,* ed. R. French and A. Wear (Cambridge, 1989), 114–144.

18. *Victoria County History of Staffordshire* (hereafter *VCH Staffs.*) (London and Oxford, 1908–), 14:21, 130; L. Lindsay, "Sir John Floyer," *Proceedings of the Royal Society of Medicine* 94 (1951): 43–48.

19. *VCH Staffs.,* 14:21, 107; "Dr. John Floyer and Dr. Edward Baynard on Cold Bathing," *The Palatine Notebook* 2 (1882): 208. For Floyer's relations with the family of his first wife, see Stafford, Staffordshire Record Office (hereafter Staffs. RO), D(W) 3222/170–171. Unusually, his second wife (who predeceased him) made a will disposing of her own property: London, Public Record Office (hereafter PRO), Prob11/631/197. See also J. Wilmot, *The Life of The Rev. John Hough* (London, 1812), 282; PRO C6/263/53 and 54 and C7/121/70.

20. *DNB,* s.n. "John Floyer"; *VCH Staffs.,* 14:79; *Elias Ashmole (1617–1692) His Autobiographical and Historical Notes . . . ,* ed. C. H. Josten, 5 vols. (Oxford, 1966), 4:1760–1764, 1766, 1768, 1779; B. D. Henning, ed., *The History of Parliament: The Commons 1660–1690,* 3 vols. (London, 1983), 1:385–387. A. L. Reade, *Johnsonian Gleanings,* 11 vols. (London, 1909–1952), 8:50.

21. Lichfield Joint Record Office, Lichfield Hall Book I (1679–1732) fol. 37; ibid., D68 (Lichfield Quarter Sessions Book 1726–1758) *fols.* 3, 3v, 6v, 7, 9, 13; H. Clayton, *Coaching City* (Bala, 1970), 5.

22. J. Floyer, *Medicina Gerocomica,* 2d ed. (London, 1725), contains as an appendix a letter addressed to Stanhope. For his involvement in the South Sea scandal, see

A. Newman, *The Stanhopes of Chevening* (London, 1969), 96–99; J. H. Plumb, *Sir Robert Walpole*, 2 vols. (London, 1956), 1:341–342, 365–366. Floyer had known members of the Stanhope family for many years: BL, Add. ms. 61620, *fol.* 230.

23. For continuing association with the Dartmouths, see Staffs. RO D1778/I/i/221 and D1778/III/152. Floyer's "Essayes" reveal him to be fiercely opposed to Presbyterians, Quakers, and Baptists and gravely concerned by the "many scandalous pamphlets, which expose the clergy to scorne, subvert the constitutions of the Christian Churche and ridicule the publicke offices of devotion . . ." (The Queen's College, Oxford, ms. 63, unfoliated). I am grateful to the provost and scholars of The Queen's College for allowing me to consult their manuscripts and to the librarian for expediting my visit. Floyer's friends included not only the near-Jacobite Johnson but also the Tory dean of Lichfield, Lancelot Addison (see J. I. A. Champion, *The Pillars of Priestcraft Shaken* [Cambridge, 1992], 114–115, and *DNB*), the Yorkshire Tory parish priest George Plaxton (BL, Ms. Stowe 748, *fol.* 142, and E. M. Walker, "Letters of the Rev. George Plaxton, M.A.," *Thoresby Society* 38 (1945): 30–104, esp. 63), the doctor Edward Tyson (allegiance learned from personal communication by Jonathan Andrews), and the physician Phineas Fowke, to whom he dedicated his book on asthma (see *DNB* for Fowke's views on passive obedience and the illegality of James II's deposition).

24. For a contemporary note of Floyer's publications, see Oxford, Bodleian Library, Ms. Rawlinson, J 40 4, *fols.* 69–71v.

25. D. D. Gibbs, "Recommendations of Sir John Floyer on the Education of a Physician," *International Congress of the History of Medicine Proceedings,* vol. 1 (London, 1974), pp. 367–370.

26. D. D. Gibbs, "Sir John Floyer, M.D. (1649–1734)," *British Medical Journal,* 21 January 1969, p. 244.

27. J. Floyer, *A Treatise of the Asthma* (London, 1698), 196–200, and *The Physician's Pulse-Watch* (London, 1707), esp. 298–337.

28. Lichfield Cathedral Library, Ms. 21 (a collection of "Country Receipts" belonging to and partly written by Floyer); autograph annotations at the end of the dedicatory preface to Phineas Fowke in the copy of *Asthma* in Lichfield Cathedral Library (shelf mark x77). For Floyer's opinion of the patient's narrative, see *Pulse-Watch,* preface. I hope to explore these aspects of his work in another context.

29. Reade, *Johnsonian Gleanings,* 3:61, 66; L. C. McHenry Jr. and R. Mac Keith, "Samuel Johnson's Childhood Illnesses and the King's Evil," *Medical History* 10 (1966): 390–391; J. Wiltshire, *Samuel Johnson in the Medical World* (Cambridge, 1991), 70–73. Floyer's opinion on the Royal Touch thus ressembles that of Jacobite Newtonian John Freind: R. J. J. Martin, "Explaining John Freind's *History of Physick,*" *Studies in History and Philosophy of Science* 19 (1988): 413.

30. J. Floyer, *An Essay to Restore the Dipping of Infants in Baptism* (London, 1722). Floyer would thus appear to conform to Adrian Wilson's argument that opposition to inoculation came from Tory circles, "The Politics of Medical Improvement in Early Hanoverian London," in *The Medical Enlightenment of the Eighteenth Century,* ed. A. Cunningham and R. French (Cambridge, 1990), 24–36.

31. J. Floyer, *The Physician's Pulse-Watch;* Floyer, *An Exposition of the Revelations, by Shewing the Agreement of the Roman, Saracen, and Ottoman Empires, and of the Popedom*

(London, 1719); Floyer, *The Prophecies of the Second Book of Esdras* (London, 1721). For contemporary commentary on Floyer's religious scholarship, see Walker, "Letters of the Rev. George Plaxton," 63.

32. J. Floyer, *The Sibylline Oracles Translated from the Best Greek Copies, and Compar'd with the Sacred Prophesies* (London, 1713). Whiston's heavily annotated copy of this work is in the British Library (shelf mark C.28 c.2) and he sent Floyer a copy of his own translation and interpretation of the Oracles, which Floyer acknowleged in a friendly letter further discussing the correct manner of interpreting these texts; BL, Egerton ms. 1963, *fols.* 6–7v. See also D. Katz, "Isaac Vossius and the English Biblical Critics, 1670–1689," in *Scepticism and Irreligion in the Seventeenth and Eighteenth Centuries,* ed. R. H. Popkin and A. Vanderjagt (Leiden, New York, and Koln, 1993), 161–164. For Whiston, see J. E. Force, *William Whiston, Honest Newtonian* (Cambridge, 1985); E. Duffy, "'Whiston's Affair': The Trials of a Primitive Christian, 1709–1714," *Journal of Ecclesiastical History* 27 (1976): 129–150.

33. *VCH Staffs.,* 14:130; Lichfield Joint RO, D16/2/54–55 (Conduit Lands Trust leases).

34. Floyer, *An Enquiry into the Right Use and Abuses of Hot, Cold, and Temperate Baths in England* (London, 1697).

35. Baynard was admitted to the College of Physicians in January 1684, London, Royal College of Physicians, Annals V, *fols.* 22v, 24v. It is not clear when he and Floyer first met, but Floyer acknowledged Baynard's assistance in his botanical work in 1687: John Floyer, *The Touch-stone of Medicines,* 2 vols. (London, 1687–1690), I sig. a3. For details of Baynard's life, see *DNB* s.n. and for his intellectual interests, *A Catalogue of the Libraries of Edward Baynard, M.D.* (London, [1721]).

36. Floyer and Baynard, *The Ancient Psychrolusia Revived, or An Essay to Prove Cold Bathing Both Safe and Useful* (London, 1702). Many authors have confused this book and Floyer's publication of 1697 (see note 34 above, this chapter).

37. Ibid., 22–23.

38. Ibid., postscript, 226, 292. For a more extensive example of Baynard's medical versifying, see his *Advice to Claret Drinkers* (London, 1709) and *Health: A poem* (London, [1716]). I discuss Baynard's verses more fully in "What You Write Is What You Drink? Selfhood, Style, and Diet in Restoration and Augustan Medicine," forthcoming.

39. J. Floyer, *Asthma,* 15–17, 40–41, and *Enquiry into the Right Use and Abuse of Hot, Cold, and Temperate Baths in England.* 37–39.

40. Floyer, *The Ancient Psychrolusia Revived,* 104–105. Cf. A. W. Franklin, "Clinical Medicine," in *Medicine in Seventeenth-Century England,* ed. A. G. Debus (Berkeley, Los Angeles, and London, 1974), 121–123.

41. J. Gabbay, "*Asthma* Attacked? Tactics for the Reconstruction of a Disease Concept," in *The Problem of Medical Knowledge,* ed. P. Wright and A. Treacher (Edinburgh, 1982), 35, 46 n. 42; H. Cook, *Decline of Old Medical Regime,* 222–240, esp. 235n.

42. G. I. Townsend, "Sir John Floyer (1649–1734) and His Study of the Pulse and Respiration," *Journal of the History of Medicine* 22 (1967): 286–316; G. Smerdon, "Four Seventeenth-Century Oxford Medical Eccentrics," in *Oxford Medicine,* ed. K. Dewhurst (Sandford-on-Thames, 1970), 18–20.

43. Floyer commented on the initial skepticism about his claims for cold baths in the preface to his *Physician's Pulsewatch* (unpaginated).

44. J. King, *An Essay on Hot and Cold Bathing* (London, 1737), sig. A3; *Remarks and Collections of Thomas Hearne, 1719–1722*, Oxford Historical Society (Oxford, 1906), 48:185.

45. *The Tatler*, ed. D. F. Bond, 3 vols. (Oxford, 1987), 1:127–128.

46. W. Perry ("Sir John Floyer's Ghost"), *A Dialogue in the Shades*, 8 parts (Uxbridge, 1805). In 1844 a fresh edition of Floyer on cold bathing was published in the publicity material of a hydrotherapy establishment. See also R. Price, "Hydropathy in England, 1840–1870," *Medical History* 25 (1981): 271.

47. *The Ancient Psychrolusia Revived*, 88–92, 109–113, 174–175, and passim.

48. J. Floyer, *Psychrolusia, or The History of Cold Bathing*, 2d ed. (London, 1706), part 2, passim. Note that this augmented second edition has this slightly different title.

49. On breast-feeding see, for example, L. Jordanova, *Sexual Visions* (London, 1989), esp. 30–32; L. Schiebinger, "Mammals, Primatology, and Sexology," in *Sexual Knowledge, Sexual Science*, ed. R. Porter and M. Teich (Cambridge, 1994).

50. C. Lawrence, "William Buchan: Medicine Laid Open," *Medical History* 19 (1975): 20–35; V. Smith, "Physical Puritanism and Sanitary Science: Material and Immaterial Beliefs in Popular Physiology, 1650–1840," in *Medical Fringe and Medical Orthodoxy, 1750–1850*, ed. W. F. Bynum and R. Porter (London, 1987), esp. 177–181.

51. There has been very little historical discussion of seventeenth- and eighteenth-century histories of health and medicine, but the Enlightenment's celebration of Hippocrates indicates that "ancient medicine" remained an important if contested source of cultural authority into the nineteenth century. See L. J. Jordanova, "Reflections on Medical Reform: Cabanis' *Coup d'Œil*," in *Medicine in the Enlightenment*, ed. R. Porter (Amsterdam and Atlanta, 1995).

52. J. Floyer, *A Comment on Forty-two Histories Described by Hippocrates* (London, 1726), 201. For an important discussion of the links between Puritan and Enlightenment recommendations for mothers to breast-feed, see David Harley, "From Providence to Nature: The Moral Theology and Godly Practice of Maternal Breast-Feeding in Stuart England," *Bulletin of the History of Medicine* 69 (1995): 198–223.

53. "A Letter from the Late Sir John Floyer to Mr. King of Bungay," *Gentleman's Magazine* 4 (1734): 197–198.

54. Floyer, *The Ancient Psychrolusia Revived*, 58–94. For another discussion of the religious significance of waters in the eighteenth century, see M. Benjamin, "Medicine, Morality, and the Politics of Berkeley's Tar Water," in *The Medical Enlightenment of the Eighteenth Century*, 165–193.

55. Ibid., 58–71. Quotation at p. 64.

56. Ibid., 59.

57. See Floyer, *Dipping of Infants*, 69.

58. Ibid., 14 and passim.

59. J. Floyer, *Medicina Gerocomica, or The Galenic Art of Preserving Old Men's Healths, Explain'd: In Twenty Chapters* (London, 1724), 113.

60. J. Gabbay, "*Asthma* Attacked?" 38.

61. K. V. Thomas, "Cleanliness and Godliness in Early Modern England," in *Religion, Culture, and Society in Early Modern Britain*, ed. A. Fletcher and P. Roberts

(Cambridge, 1994), 61–63; F. E. Brightman, *The English Rite*, 2 vols. (London, 1915), 2:729.

62. P. Stubs, *Of Public Baptism* (London, 1693), 3. For an identical exposition, see P. B., *A Discourse of Baptism, or An Answer to Mr. Stub's Sermon . . .* (London, 1705), 1.

63. E. Paye, *The Rector Corrected* (London, 1701), 17. Cf. W. Smith, *A Discourse concerning Baptism* (London, 1701), 42.

64. J.-P. Vernant, "The Pure and the Impure," in *Myth and Society in Ancient Greece*, trans. J. Lloyd (1974; Brighton, 1980), 110–129; P. Ricoeur, *The Symbolism of Evil*, trans. E. Buchanan (Boston, 1969).

65. M. Douglas, *Purity and Danger* (London, 1966); Douglas, *Natural Symbols* (London, 1970).

66. The phrase "condensed symbols" is taken from Douglas, *Natural Symbols*, 26.

67. Examples of the equation of sin and dirt include M. Fissell, *Patients, Power, and the Poor in Eighteenth-Century Bristol* (Cambridge, 1991), 82; R. Porter, "Reason and the Medicalisation of Order," *Journal of Historical Sociology* 5 (1992): 356; M. Ingram, "Ridings, Rough Music, and Mocking Rhymes in Early Modern Europe," in *Popular Culture in Seventeenth-Century England*, ed. B. Reay (London, 1988), 177–178.

68. For a more extensive discussion of this point, see M. S. R. Jenner, *Beyond Women on Top: Gender, Community, and Identity in Early Modern Europe*, York University History Department Occasional Paper (York, 1995).

69. It is notable that the index of J. Brooke's *Science and Religion: Some Historical Perspectives* (Cambridge, 1991) contains no entries under "sacrament" and only two under "transubstantiation." A fine example of the predominantly theological problematics that operate within the religious history of early modern England is the lengthy debate about attitudes to predestination in the Church of England before the Civil War.

70. For a discussion of the symbolism of baptism with reference to Locke's *Essay Concerning Human Understanding*, see "A Layman," *A Vindication of an Answer to a Late Pamphlet Entitled "The Validity of Baptism Administered by Dissenting-Ministers"* (Nottingham, 1714), 8.

71. W. Wall, *The History of Infant Baptism*, 2 parts (London, 1705), 2:294. Cf. P. King, *The Second Part of the Enquiry into the Constitution, Discipline, and Worship of the Primitive Church* (n.p., 1713), 75–77.

72. See the works cited in n. 31 above, this chapter. For a theological response to Floyer's arguments about dipping see J. Warden, *A Practical Essay on the Sacrament of Baptism* (Edinburgh, 1724), 194.

73. The Queen's College, Oxford, Ms. 63, unfoliated. This is not to suggest that Floyer did not also on occasion employ the metaphor of cleansing.

74. Gabbay, *"Asthma* Attacked?" 38.

75. Floyer, *The Ancient Psychrolusia Revived*, 79.

76. Ibid., 80–84; T. Tryon, *Pythagoras His Mystick Philosophy Reviv'd* (London, 1691), 297–298; Andrews, "Hardly a Hospital."

77. R. R. Reed, *Bedlam on the Jacobean Stage* (Cambridge, Mass., 1952), 10. For popular well lore, see A. Gribben, *Holy Wells and Sacred Water Sources in Britain and Ireland: An Annotated Bibliography* (New York and London, 1992). I hope to discuss the relations between early modern medical practitioners and popular attitudes to curative waters on another occasion.

78. On debates between pastors and their congregations, see M. K. McIntosh, *A Community Transformed: The Manor and Liberty of Havering, 1500–1620* (Cambridge, 1991), 182, 209–210, and J. Maltby, "'By this Book': Parishioners, the Prayer Book, and the Established Church," in *The Early Stuart Church, 1603–1642*, ed. K. Fincham (Basingstoke and London, 1993), 122–123. The fullest discussions of baptism in early modern Europe are those of John Bossy: *Christianity in the West, 1400–1700* (Oxford, 1985), 14–19, and "Blood and Baptism: Kinship, Community, and Christianity in Western Europe from the Fourteenth to the Seventeenth Centuries," in *Studies in Church History*, vol. 10 (Oxford, 1973), pp. 129–144. See also G. W. Bromiley, *Baptism and the English Reformers* (London, 1953); S. Cavazza, "La Doppia Morte: Resurrezione e battesimo in un rito del '600," *Quaderni storici* 50 (1982): 551–582; S. Smith-Bannister, "Names and Naming Patterns in England, 1538 to 1700," (D.Phil. dissertation, Oxford University, 1990), chap. 2. For the early medieval period, P. Cramer, *Baptism and Change in the Middle Ages, ca. 200–ca. 1150* (Cambridge, 1993), is indispensable.

79. B. R. White, *The English Baptists of the Seventeenth Century* (London, 1983); J. F. McGregor, "The Baptists: Fount of All Heresy," in *Radical Religion in the English Revolution,* ed. J. F. McGregor and B. Reay (Oxford, 1984), esp. 41–42; D. Featley, *The Dippers Dipt* (London, 1645). For the tensions produced by the Quakers' refusal to countenance water baptism, see A. Giardina Hess, "Midwifery Practice among the Quakers of Southern Rural England in the Late Seventeenth Century," in *The Art of Midwifery*, ed. H. Marland (London, 1993), 53. For a useful collection of defenses of infant baptism by early modern Church of England ministers, see W. Goode, *The Doctrine of the Church of England as to the Effects of Baptism in the Case of Infants*, 2d ed. (London, 1850).

80. W. Burkitt, *An Argumentative and Practical Discourse of Infant-Baptism*, 2d ed. (London, 1695), sig. A2. Cf. W. Russell, *True Narrative of the Portsmouth Disputation*, 3d ed. (London, 1699).

81. Staffs. RO, D1778/I/i/221, letter of 8 January 1710/11. See also D1778/III/152.

82. R. Laurence, *Lay Baptism Invalid* (London, 1708). This episode is discussed in G. V. Bennett, *The Tory Crisis in Church and State, 1688–1730* (Oxford, 1975), 150–156. For a Scottish perspective on this dispute, see *An Enquiry into the Doctrines of the High-Church concerning Ordination and Baptism* (Edinburgh, 1719). Some Anglicans had similar doubts about the validity of baptisms administered by non–episcopally ordained ministers during the interregnum: J. Spurr, *The Restoration Church of England* (London and New Haven, 1991), 159.

83. E. Cardwell, ed., *Synodalia: A Collection of Articles of Religion, Canons, and Proceedings of Convocation*, 2 vols. (Oxford, 1842), 2:709–710. See also N. Sykes, *From Sheldon to Secker* (Oxford, 1959), 25–26; D. A. Spaeth, "Parsons and Parishioners: Lay-Clerical Conflict and Popular Piety in Wiltshire Villages, 1660–1740" (Ph.D. dissertation, Brown University, 1985), 99–100, and A. Wilson, *The Making of Man-Midwifery* (London, 1995), 28. It is striking that although baptismal records are central to the work of English historical demographers, they have paid relatively little attention to the history of the practice; see, however, B. M. Berry and R. S. Schofield, "Age at Baptism in Pre-industrial England," *Population Studies* 25 (1971): 453–463.

84. *The Journal of . . . John Wesley*, ed. N. Curnock, 8 vols. (London, 1909–1916), 1:210–211. This episode is discussed in D. I. Naglee, *From Font to Faith: John Wesley on*

Infant Baptism and the Nurture of Children (NewYork, Bern, Frankfurt am Main, 1987), 138–139, and B. G. Holland, *Baptism in Early Methodism* (London, 1970), chap. 3.

85. *The First and Second Prayer-Books of Edward the Sixth,* Everyman Edition (London, n.d.), 240, 398; *Liturgical Services of the Reign of Queen Elizabeth,* ed. W. K. Clay (Cambridge: Parker Society, 1847), 203–204.

86. J. Calvin, *The Institutes of the Christian Religion,* trans. H. Beveridge, 3 vols. (Edinburgh: Calvin Translation Society, 1845–1846), 3:344. See also W. G. Naphy, "Baptisms, Church Riots, and Social Unrest in Calvin's Geneva," *Sixteenth Century Journal* 26 (1995), 87–97, and W. Balke, *Calvin and the Anabaptist Radicals,* trans. W. Heynen (Grand Rapids, Mich., 1981). For a later defense of the Church of Scotland's practice, see Warden, *A Practical Essay on the Sacrament of Baptism.*

87. Bromiley, *Baptism and the Anglican Reformers,* 141; J. Morrill, "The Church of England, 1642–1649," in *Reactions to the English Civil War,* ed. Morrill (Basingstoke and London, 1982), 94–95. See also D. Scott, "Politics and Government in York, 1640–1662," in *Town and Countryside in the English Revolution,* ed. R. C. Richardson (Manchester, 1992), 54.

88. This decision was taken after several days debate within the assembly. W. A. Shaw, *A History of the English Church during the Civil Wars and under the Commonwealth,* 2 vols. (London, 1900), 1:347; R. S. Paul, *The Assembly of the Lord: Politics and Religion in the Westminster Assembly and the Grand Debate* (Edinburgh, 1985), 374–375.

89. Brightman, *The English Rite,* 2:741. There was fresh debate about the manner by which to baptize infants during the attempt to revise the prayer book in the aftermath of 1688; see T. J. Fawcett, ed., *The Liturgy of Comprehension, 1689,* Alcuin Club Collections no. 54 (Southend-on-Sea, 1973), 163.

90. W. Wall, *History of Infant Baptism,* 2:303–304.

91. For Taylor, see H. B. Porter, *Jeremy Taylor Liturgist,* Alcuin Club Collections 61 (London, 1979), 32.

92. Wall, *History of Infant Baptism,* 2:309.

93. H. Stebbing, *A Short . . . Account of a Conference Held at a Quakers Meeting-House in Suffolk, with Joseph Middleton* (London, 1714), 15. For another example of this line of argument in Quaker polemic, see W. Salmon, *A Dissertation concerning Water-Baptism: The First Part,* 2d ed. (London 1710), sigs. A7–7v.

94. T. Guidott, *An Apology for the Bath* (London, 1705), 100.

95. J. Floyer, *The Ancient Psychrolusia Revived,* 202–206.

96. G. Burnet, *An Exposition of the Thirty-nine Articles of the Church of England* (London, 1699), 346. Cf. Featley, *The Dippers Dipt,* 38.

97. J. Stokes, *A Survey of Infant Baptism and the Mode of Baptizing* (1715), 28–29.

98. On the Baptists' use of Floyer see J. Gale, *Reflections on Mr. Wall's History of Infant-Baptism* (London, 1711), 194; J. Stennett, *An Answer to Mr. David Russen's Book* (London, 1704), 131–135.

99. Wall, *History of Infant Baptism,* 2:308.

100. W. Whiston, *Memoirs of the Life and Writings of Mr. William Whiston* (1749), 469; Whiston, *Primitive Infant-Baptism Reviv'd* (London, 1712), 46 and passim. It is perhaps not surprising that Whiston ended his days attending Baptist services.

101. W. Jardine Grisbrooke, *Anglican Liturgies of the Seventeenth and Eighteenth Centuries,* Alcuin Club Collections 40 (London, 1958), 119–121. Floyer never separated from the church, though his friend the earl of Dartmouth chose a nonjuror to edu-

cate his sons: P. K. Monod, *Jacobitism and the English People, 1688–1788* (Cambridge, 1989), 274.

102. Floyer, *Dipping of Infants*, 16–18, quotation at p. 18. In 1715 Osborne wrote to Bishop Hough announcing that he felt obliged to separate from the church: *Collecteana*, ed. W. D. Macray, Oxford Historical Soc., vol. 16 (1890), pp. 406–407. I owe this reference to J. C. Findon, "The Nonjurors and the Church of England, 1689–1716," (D.Phil. thesis, Oxford University, 1978), 92, 97, 214.

103. [G. Osborne], *Mitre and Crown* (1748), 1:3, printed in part in J. Wickham Legg, *English Church Life from the Restoration to the Tractarian Movement* (1914), 166–167.

104. For Baynard's stormy relations with the College of Physicians, see H. Cook, *Decline of the Old Medical Regime*, 226, 235.

105. Floyer, *The Ancient Psychrolusia Revived*, 303–304. In a mock epitaph that Baynard composed for himself he wrote he was "A foe to pope & superstition / And for his religion, he was a phisician." BL, Ms. Stowe, *fol.* 216. His library, however, contained many works of divinity and religious controversy ranging from the nonjuror George Hickes to the Presbyterian Richard Baxter. Baptist and Quaker publications are largely absent: see *A Catalogue of the Libraries of Edward Baynard, M.D.* (London, [1721]).

106. In the same manuscript mock epitaph Baynard styled himself "An Arch Williamite." BL, Ms. Stowe, *fol.* 216. In 1706 he listed the national heroes who could have been lost through the neglect of nurses and through swaddling in terms that do not suggest even a patriotic Tory: "How soon might a *Bacon*, a *Drake*, a *Rawleigh*, a *Camden*, a *MARLBOROUGH*, or a *Tillotson* have been *stifled* and *over-laid* by a sluggish and drousie *Nurse?*" Floyer, *Psychrolusia* 2d ed., 2:160. He described himself as an "old friend" of the Whig M.P. for Preston, Edward Rigby, and slipped criticisms of nonjurors into his work: ibid., 2:131, 268; W. Dobson, *History of the Parliamentary Representation of Preston* (Preston, 1856), 74; G. Holmes, *British Politics in the Age of Anne*, rev. ed. (London, 1987), 362–363.

107. Floyer, *Psychrolusia* (1706 ed.), 2:202–203, 198, 146–147. Baynard's naturalistic explanation of the king's evil would seem to differ from Floyer's advocacy of the royal touch.

108. Wall, *History of Infant Baptism*, 301; Floyer, *The Ancient Psychrolysia Revived*, 71.

109. Floyer, *Enquiry into the Right Use and Abuses of Hot, Cold, and Temperate Baths in England*, preface, sigs. c3v–4.

110. Floyer, *The Ancient Psychrolusia Revived*, 87.

111. E. McClure, *A Chapter in English Church History* (London, 1888), 2; *A Collection of Papers, Printed by Order of the Society for the Propagation of the Gospel in Foreign Parts* (1706), 6. For Floyer's friendship with Slare, see *Asthma*, 177 ff.

112. Floyer, *The Ancient Psychrolusia Revived*, 144–151; McClure, *Chapter in English History*, 65; Bahlman, *The Moral Revolution of 1688* (London and New Haven, 1957), 76. SPCK Archives, Abstract Letter Books, vol. 1, nos. 23, 36, 74, 97, 138, 152, 173, 188, 263, 315; vol. 2, no. 1010; vol. 4, no. 3058. (These mss. were consulted using microfilm copies in the John Rylands University Library, Manchester.) The SPCK seems also to have funded the publication of Ellison's sermon to mark the opening of a charity school in the city: vol. 3, no. 2011; N. Ellison, *The Obligations and Opportunities of Doing Good to the Poor* (Newcastle, 1710).

113. D. Hayton, "Moral Reform and Country Politics in the Late Seventeenth-Century House of Commons," *Past and Present* 128 (1990): 48–91. See also A. G. Craig, "The Movement for the Reformation of Manners, 1688–1715" (Ph.D. dissertation, University of Edinburgh, 1980); T. V. Hitchcock, "Paupers and Preachers: The SPCK and the Parochial Workhouse Movement," and R. B. Shoemaker, "Reforming the City: The Reformation of Manners Campaign in London, 1690–1738," in *Stilling the Grumbling Hive.*

114. J. G. A. Pocock, *Virtue, Commerce, and History* (Cambridge, 1985), part 3; M. Goldie, "The Roots of True Whiggism, 1688–94," *History of Political Thought* 1 (1980): 195–236.

115. Queen's College, Oxford, Ms. 63, unfolioed. In this passage Floyer proposed the closing of dissenting schools and barring from all positions of profit everyone educated in them. For the charity school movement and its Anglican character, see C. Rose, "Evangelical Philanthropy and Anglican Revival: The Charity Schools of Augustan London, 1698–1740," *London Journal* 16 (1991): 35–65; "'Seminarys of Faction and Rebellion': Jacobites, Whigs, and the London Charity Schools, 1716–1724," *Historical Journal* 34 (1991): 831–855; "London's Charity Schools, 1690–1730," *History Today* 40 (1990): 17–23. See also M. G. Jones, *The Charity School Movement: A Study of Eighteenth-Century Puritanism in Action* (Cambridge, 1938).

116. T. C. Curtis and W. Speck, "The Societies for the Reformation of Manners: A Case Study in the Theory and Practice of Moral Reform," *Literature and History* 3 (1976): 52; M. M. Goldsmith, "Liberty, Luxury, and the Pursuit of Happiness," in *The Languages of Political Theory in Early-Modern Europe,* ed. A. Pagden (Cambridge, 1987), 236.

117. J. Browne, *An Account of the Wonderful Cures Perform'd by the Cold Baths* (London, 1707), 5–6.

118. Floyer, *Dipping of Infants,* 69.

119. R. Porter, "Addicted to Modernity: Nervousness in the Early Consumer Society," in *Culture in History* (Exeter, 1992), 180–194; Porter, "Consumption: Disease of the Consumer Society," in *Consumption and the World of Goods,* ed. J. Brewer and R. Porter (London, 1993); G. Rousseau, "Immortal Doctor Cheyne," in *Millenarianism and Messianism in English Literature and Thought, 1650–1800,* ed. R. H. Popkin (Berkeley and Leiden, 1988), 81–126; *George Cheyne: The English Malady (1733),* fascimile reprint, ed. R. Porter (London, 1991). I intend to discuss this aspect of the history of rickets on another occasion.

120. Such concerns were an important strand in debates on the proper functioning of the economy in this period: see C. J. Berry, *The Idea of Luxury* (Cambridge, 1994), chap. 5.

121. C. Nicholson, *Writing and the Rise of Finance* (Cambridge, 1994), chap. 5. Fundamental to discussions of this theme are J. Sekora, *Luxury: The Concept in Western Thought, Eden to Smollett* (Baltimore and London, 1977), and R. Williams, *The Country and the City* (Oxford, 1973). The image developed by these authors is overwhelmingly of the paterfamilias. In the late eighteenth century, however, a number of feminist historians used Tacitus's *Germania* to argue that early Germanic societies accorded power and respect to women. See J. Rendall, "Tacitus Engendered: Gothic Feminism and British History," in *Imagining Nations,* ed. G. Cubitt (Manchester, forthcoming).

122. On the Romans and cold bathing see Glasgow University Library, Hunterian ms. 6 (an English translation of Antonio Cocchi, "A Dissertation on the Use of Cold Water"), esp. 11–12.

123. For the congruence seen between these very various cultures, L. E. Klein, "Liberty, Manners, and Politeness in Early Eighteenth-Century England," *Historical Journal* 32 (1989): 593–598.

124. Axtell, *Educational Writings of John Locke*, 116, 120; Floyer, *Psychrolusia* (1706 ed.), 152–153.

125. On civility and empire see, for example, P. Couglan, ed., *Spenser and Ireland* (Cork, 1989); K. V. Thomas, *Man and the Natural World* (London, 1983), 41–51.

126. N. Elias, *The Civilizing Process*. See also A. Bryson, "Concepts of Civility in England, ca. 1560–1685," (D.Phil. thesis, Oxford University, 1984).

127. For eighteenth-century discussion of the *Germania*, see H. D. Weinbrot, "Politics, Taste, and National Identity: Some Uses of Tacitism in Eighteenth-Century Britain," in *Tacitus and the Tacitean Tradition*, ed. T. J. Luce and A. J. Woodman (Princeton, 1993), 168–184. See also D. R. Kelley, "*Tacitus Noster:* the *Germania* in the Renaissance and Reformation," in *Tacitus and the Tacitean Tradition.* 152–167, and K. C. Schellhase, *Tacitus in Renaissance Political Thought* (Chicago, 1976).

128. Sekora, *Luxury,* 5; J. S. A. Adamson, "Chivalry and Political Culture in Caroline England," in *Culture and Politics in Early Stuart England*, ed. K. Sharpe and P. Lake (Basingstoke and London, 1994), 167–169; H. Peacham, *Coach and Sedan* (1636). Cf. O. Ranum, "Strengthening the Noble Male Body: Guillaume du Choul on Ancient Bathing and Physical Exercise," in *Politics, Ideology, and the Law in Early Modern Europe*, ed. A. E. Bakos (Rochester, N.Y., 1994).

129. See, for instance, Floyer's interest in Chinese medicine or the reports to the Royal Society on Japanese therapeutics involving the burning of moxa: B. Szczesniak, "John Floyer and Chinese Medicine," *Osiris* 11 (1954): 127–156; H. J. Cook, *Trials of an Ordinary Doctor* (Baltimore and London, 1994), 125 ff.

130. Champion, *The Pillars of Priestcraft Shaken.*

131. C. H. Hinnant, *Purity and Defilement in Gulliver's Travels* (London, 1987); S. Haworth, *A Description of the Duke's Bagnio* (London, 1683); Anon., *A True Account of the Royal Bagnio* (1680); S. Aravamudan, "Lady Wortley Montagu and Masquerade, Womanliness, and Levantization," *ELH* 62 (1995): 69–104. I intend to discuss this theme further in another paper.

132. Cf. I. Kramnick, *Bolingbroke and His Circle: The Politics of Nostalgia in the Age of Walpole* (Cambridge, Mass., 1968), and D. Solkin, *Painting for Money* (New Haven and London, 1992), introduction and chaps. 1–2.

MEDICINE, POLITICS, AND THE BODY
IN LATE GEORGIAN ENGLAND

1. The neglect of the body is explored in Barbara Stafford, *Imaging the Unseen in Enlightenment Art and Medicine* (Cambridge, Mass.: MIT Press, 1991).

This paper began as a profusely illustrated lecture. It has proved impossible here to reproduce more than a handful of the illustrations. By way of compensation, I emphasize that the prints referred to are merely representative of a genre: scores of other cartoons and caricatures would serve as substitutes, and works listed in the following notes contain illustrations similar to those mentioned in the text. See, for instance, Michael Duffy, ed., *The English Satirical Print, 1600–1832*, 7 vols. (Cambridge: Chadwyck-Healey, 1986); M. Dorothy George, *English Political Caricature, 1793–1832* (Oxford: Clarendon Press, 1959); George, *Hogarth to Cruikshank: Social Change in Graphic Satire* (London: Allen Lane, 1967); H. M. Atherton, *Political Prints in the Age of Hogarth: A Study of the Ideographic Representation of Politics* (Oxford: Oxford University Press, 1974); Brian Maidment, *Popular Prints, 1790–1870: Reading Popular Graphic Images* (Manchester: University of Manchester Press, 1996). Eirwen E. C. Nicholson's "English Political Prints and Pictorial Political Argument ca. 1640–ca. 1832: A Study in Historiography and Methodology" (Ph.D. dissertation, University of Edinburgh, 1994) is a superb critical account from which I have learned much.

2. See P. Stallybrass and A. White, *The Politics and Poetics of Transgression* (Ithaca, N.Y.: Cornell University Press, 1986); M. M. Bakhtin, *Rabelais and His World,* trans. H. Iswolsky (Cambridge, Mass.: MIT Press, 1968); and for further discussion Roy Porter, "History of the Body," in Peter Burke, ed., *New Perspectives on Historical Writing* (Cambridge: Polity Press, 1991), 206–232.

3. Barbara Duden, *The Woman beneath the Skin: A Doctor's Patients in Eighteenth-Century Germany,* trans. Thomas Dunlap (Cambridge: Harvard University Press, 1991), offers a marvelous exploration of the traditional "fluid" physiology and contains the stimulating "Toward a History of the Body." See also her "A Repertory of Body History," in M. Feher, ed., *Fragments for a History of the Human Body* (New York: Zone, 1989), 3:470–554.

4. E. M. Tillyard, *The Elizabethan World Picture* (London: Chatto and Windus, 1943). Physiognomy and phrenology allowed the body to be read within the genres of caricature and the grotesque. See E. H. Gombrich and E. Kris, *Caricature* (London: Penguin, 1940); Edward Lucie-Smith, *The Art of Caricature* (London: Orbis, 1981); Bevis Hillier, *Cartoons and Caricatures* (London: Studio Vista, 1970); Judith Wechsler, *A Human Comedy: Physiognomy and Caricature in Nineteenth-Century Paris* (Chicago: University of Chicago Press, 1982); Mary Cowling, *The Artist as Anthropologist: The Representation of Type and Character in Victorian Art* (Cambridge: Cambridge University Press, 1989).

5. For older views of the demise of the body politic see E. M. Tillyard, *The Elizabethan World Picture* (London: Chatto and Windus, 1934); Basil Willey, *The Eighteenth Century Background* (London: Chatto and Windus, 1962); for modern revisionism see Bryan S. Turner, "Recent Developments in the Theory of the Body," in Mike Featherstone, Mike Hepworth, and Bryan S. Turner, eds., *The Body: Social Process and Cultural Theory* (London: Sage, 1991), 1–35, and Arthur W. Frank, "For a Sociology of the Body: An Analytical Review," in *The Body,* 36–102; Bryan S. Turner, *The Body and Society: Explorations in Social Theory* (Oxford: Basil Blackwell, 1984).

6. Susan Sontag, *Illness as Metaphor* (New York: Farrar, Straus, and Giroux, 1978); Sontag, *AIDS as Metaphor* (Harmondsworth: Allen Lane, 1989); Charles E. Rosenberg and Janet Golden, eds., *Framing Disease: Studies in Cultural History* (New Brunswick, N.J.: Rutgers University Press, 1992).

7. See Dorothy Porter and Roy Porter, eds., *Doctors, Politics, and Society: Historical Essays* (Amsterdam: Rodopi, 1993), especially the introduction.

8. For the art of reading pictures see Peter Wagner, *Iconotexts* (London: Reaktion Books, 1995).

9. *Memoirs of the Late Thomas Holcroft, Written by Himself and Continued to the Time of His Death, from His Diary, Notes, and Other Papers*, ed. William Hazlitt, 3 vols. (London: Longman, 1816), 2:195.

10. W. F. Bynum, *Science and the Practice of Medicine in the Nineteenth Century* (New York: Cambridge University Press, 1994); Christopher J. Lawrence, *Medicine in the Making of Modern Britain, 1700–1920* (London and New York: Routledge, 1994); James C. Riley, *Sickness, Recovery, and Death: A History and Forecast of Ill Health* (Iowa City: University of Iowa Press, 1989); Alex Mercer, *Disease, Mortality, and Population in Transition: Epidemiological-Demographic Change in England since the Eighteenth Century as Part of a Global Phenomenon* (Leicester: Leicester University Press, 1990); Kenneth F. Kiple, ed., *The Cambridge World History of Human Disease* (Cambridge: Cambridge University Press, 1993); G. Miller, *The Adoption of Inoculation for Smallpox in England and France* (London: Oxford University Press, 1957).

11. M. Durey, *The Return of the Plague: British Society and the Cholera, 1831–1832* (Dublin: Gill and Macmillan, 1979).

12. For urban fevers see Anne Hardy, *The Epidemic Streets: Infectious Disease and the Rise of Preventive Medicine, 1856–1900* (Oxford and New York: Oxford University Press, 1993); F. B. Smith, *The People's Health, 1830–1910* (London: Croom Helm, 1979); Anthony S. Wohl, *Endangered Lives: Public Health in Victorian Britain* (Cambridge, Mass.: Harvard University Press, 1983).

13. Roy Porter, "Howard's Beginning," in R. Creese, W. F. Bynum, and J. Bearn, eds., *The Health of Prisoners: Historical Essays* (Amsterdam: Rodopi, 1995), 5–26.

14. F. B. Smith, *The Retreat of Tuberculosis, 1850–1950* (London and New York: Croom Helm, 1988).

15. Roy Porter and Dorothy Porter, *In Sickness and in Health: The British Experience, 1650–1850* (London: Fourth Estate, 1988); Dorothy Porter and Roy Porter, *Patient's Progress: Doctors and Doctoring in Eighteenth-Century England* (Cambridge: Polity Press, 1989).

16. Mary E. Fissell, "Readers, Texts, and Contexts: Vernacular Medical Works in Early Modern England," in Roy Porter, ed., *The Popularization of Medicine* (Routledge: London and New York, 1992), 72–96; C. J. Lawrence, "William Buchan: Medicine Laid Open," *Medical History* 19 (1975): 20–35.

17. I. S. L. Loudon, *Medical Care and the General Practitioner, 1750–1850* (Oxford: Clarendon Press, 1986); Anne Digby, *Making a Medical Living: Doctors and Patients in the English Market for Medicine, 1720–1911* (Cambridge: Cambridge University Press, 1994); for consumerism see John Brewer and Roy Porter, eds., *Consumption and the World of Goods* (London: Routledge, 1993); Neil McKendrick, John Brewer, and J. H. Plumb, *The Birth of a Consumer Society: The Commercialization of Eighteenth-Century England* (London: Europa, 1982).

18. For the modern view see Ivan Waddington, *The Medical Profession in the Industrial Revolution* (Dublin: Gill and Macmillan, 1984); for Scotland see C. Lawrence, "Medicine as Culture: Edinburgh and the Scottish Enlightenment" (Ph.D dissertation, University of London, 1984); Lisa Rosner, *Medical Education in the Age of Improvement: Edinburgh Students and Apprentices, 1760–1826* (Edinburgh: Edinburgh University Press, 1990).

19. J. Donnison, *Midwives and Medical Men: A History of Interprofessional Rivalries and Women's Rights* (London: Heinemann Educational, 1977); Irvine Loudon, *Death in Childbirth: An International Study of Maternal Care and Maternal Mortality,*

1800–1950 (Oxford: Clarendon Press, 1992); Adrian Wilson, *The Making of Man Midwifery* (London: University College Press, 1995).

20. Roger French and Andrew Wear, eds., *British Medicine in an Age of Reform* (London: Routledge, 1992).

21. S. W. F. Holloway, *Royal Pharmaceutical Society of Great Britain, 1841–1991: A Political and Social History* (London: Pharmaceutical Press, 1991).

22. R. Cooter, ed., *Studies in the History of Alternative Medicine* (London: Macmillan, 1988); W. F. Bynum and R. Porter, eds., *Medical Fringe and Medical Orthodoxy, 1750–1850* (London: Croom Helm, 1987).

23. Roy Porter, *Doctor of Society: Thomas Beddoes and the Sick Trade in Late Enlightenment England* (London: Routledge, 1991).

24. Thomas Percival, *Medical Ethics, or A Code of Institutes and Precepts Adapted to the Professional Conduct of Physicians and Surgeons* (Manchester: J. Johnson and R. Bickerstaff, 1803); Robert Baker, Dorothy Porter, and Roy Porter, eds., *The Codification of Medical Morality*, vol. 1 (Dordrecht/Boston/London: Kluwer Academic Publishers, 1993).

25. Dora Weiner, *The Citizen-Patient in Revolutionary and Imperial Paris* (Baltimore and London: Johns Hopkins University Press, 1993).

26. Miriam Bailin, *The Sickroom in Victorian Fiction: The Art of Being Ill* (Cambridge: Cambridge University Press, 1994), 25 f., 109 f.

27. I. S. L. Loudon, "The Origin and Growth of the Dispensary Movement in England," *Bulletin of the History of Medicine* 55 (1981): 322–342; E. G. Thomas, "The Old Poor Law and Medicine," *Medical History* 24 (1980): 1–19.

28. Roy Porter, *Mind Forg'd Manacles: Madness and Psychiatry in England from Restoration to Regency* (London, Athlone Press, 1987); Ida Macalpine and Richard Hunter, *George III and the Mad Business* (London: Allen Lane, 1969).

29. Anne Digby, *Madness, Morality, and Medicine: A Study of the York Retreat, 1796–1914* (Cambridge: Cambridge University Press, 1985).

30. Mary Wollstonecraft, *Mary and the Wrongs of Woman*, ed. J. Kinsley and G. Kelly (Oxford: The World's Classics, 1980); C. Tomalin, *Life and Death of Mary Wollstonecraft* (London: Weidenfield and Nicolson, 1974); Elaine Showalter, *The Female Malady: Women, Madness, and English Culture, 1830–1980* (New York: Pantheon Press, 1986); Sander L. Gilman, Helen King, Roy Porter, G. S. Rousseau, and Elaine Showalter, eds., *Hysteria beyond Freud* (Berkeley, Los Angeles, and London: University of California Press, 1993).

31. T. A. Markus, ed., *Order in Space and Society* (Edinburgh: Mainstream, 1982).

32. On romantic attitudes, see Helen Small, "Representing Madness: The Politics of Insanity in Nineteenth-Century English Novels and Medical Text, ca. 1800–1865" (Ph.D. dissertation, University of Cambridge, 1991); Allan Ingram, *The Madhouse of Language: Writing and Reading Madness in the Eighteenth Century* (London/New York: Routledge, 1991).

33. W. F. Courtney, *Young Charles Lamb, 1775–1802* (London: New York University Press, 1982).

34. N. Crook and D. Guiton, *Shelley's Venomed Melody* (Cambridge: Cambridge University Press, 1986); Hermione de Almeida, *Romantic Medicine and John Keats* (New York: Oxford University Press, 1991); D. C. Goellnicht, *The Poet-Physician: Keats and Medical Science* (Pittsburgh: University of Pittsburgh Press, 1984).

35. J. Engell, *The Creative Imagination* (Cambridge: Harvard University Press, 1981).

36. Roy Porter and Dorothy Porter, *In Sickness and in Health: The British Experience, 1650–1850* (London: Fourth Estate, 1988), chap. 12, pp. 201–233: "Creating Identity."

37. G. S. Rousseau, "Psychology," in G. S. Rousseau and Roy Porter, eds., *The Ferment of Knowledge* (Cambridge: Cambridge University Press, 1980), 143–210; C. J. Lawrence, "The Nervous System and Society in the Scottish Enlightenment," in B. Barnes and S. Shapin, eds., *Natural Order* (Beverly Hills and London: Sage Publications, 1980), 19–40; Roy Porter, "Addicted to Modernity: Nervousness in the Early Consumer Society," in J. Melling and J. Barry, eds., *Culture in History* (Exeter: Exeter Studies in History, 1992), 180–194.

38. Jonathan Miller, "Mesmerism," *The Listener,* 22 November 1973, pp. 685–690; Alan Gauld, *A History of Hypnotism* (Cambridge and New York: Cambridge University Press, 1992); Stephen Bann, ed., *Frankenstein: Creation and Monstrosity* (London: Reaktion Books, 1994).

39. Roy Porter, "Barely Touching: A Social Perspective on Mind and Body," in G. S. Rousseau, ed., *The Languages of Psyche: Mind and Body in Enlightenment Thought* (Berkeley, Los Angeles, London: University of California Press, 1990), 45–80; Andrew Cunningham and Nicholas Jardine, eds., *Romanticism and the Sciences* (Cambridge and New York: Cambridge University Press, 1990).

40. Roy Porter, "Civilization and Disease: Medical Ideology in the Enlightenment," in J. Black and J. Gregory, eds., *Culture, Politics, and Society in Britain, 1660–1800* (Manchester: Manchester University Press, 1991), 154–183.

41. M. Praz, *The Romantic Agony* (London: Oxford University Press, 1951).

42. Quoted in Porter and Porter, *Patient's Progress,* 54.

43. Benjamin Franklin, *Poor Richard's Almanack* (1744), quoted in Porter and Porter, *Patient's Progress,* 54.

44. D. Bond, ed., *The Spectator,* 5 vols. (Oxford: Clarendon Press, 1965), 1:88–90.

45. Bernard Mandeville, *The Fable of the Bees,* ed. P. Harth (Harmondsworth: Penguin, 1970), 65.

46. K. Garlick and A. Macintyre, eds., *The Diary of Joseph Farington,* vols. 1–6 (New Haven: Yale University Press, 1978–1979), 2:477.

47. Matthew Prior, *Alma,* canto 3, line 97, quoted in Porter and Porter, *Patient's Progress,* 57. "Bill" has the double sense of prescription and invoice.

48. See Norman B. Gwyn, "An Interpretation of the Hogarth Print 'The Arms of the Company of Undertakers,'" *Bulletin of the History of Medicine* 8 (1940): 115–277.

49. J. Ayres, ed., *Paupers and Pig Killers: The Diary of William Holland, a Somerset Parson, 1799–1818* (Gloucester: Alan Sutton, 1984), 24.

50. See T. G. H. Drake, "The Medical Caricatures of Thomas Rowlandson," *Bulletin of the History of Medicine* 12 (1942): 323–335; W. R. Bett, "The Medical Caricatures of Thomas Rowlandson, 1756–1827," *Alchemist,* August 1956, pp. 430–432; William C. Butterfield, "The Medical Caricatures of Thomas Rowlandson," *Journal of the American Medical Association* 224 (1973): 113–117, Ronald Paulson, "Thomas Rowlandson: His Medical Satire," *Hospital Update,* October 1974, pp. 619–628.

On general medical caricature, see Jean Avalon, "Malades, médecins, et charlatans dans la caricature anglaise au temps d'Hogarth et de Rowlandson," *Aesculape* 40 (1957): 2–62, W.-H. Hein, *Die Pharmazie in der Karikatur* (Frankfurt am Main: Govi-Verlag, 1964); E. Holländer, *Die Karikatur und Satire in der Medizin* (Stuttgart: Verlag von Ferdinand Enke, 1921); W. H. Helfand, *Drugs and Pharmacy in Prints* (Madison, Wisc.: American Institute for the History of Pharmacy, 1967); Helfand, "Medicine and Pharmacy in French Political Prints," *Pharmacy in History* 17 (1975): 119–131. The best analysis of the techniques of the comic, grotesque, and satirical is Ronald Paulson, *Representations of Revolution, 1789–1820* (New Haven: Yale University Press, 1983).

51. "The Toothache" is reproduced in J. G. L. Burnby, *Caricatures and Comments* (Staines, Middlesex: Merrell Dow Pharmaceuticals, 1989), upon which I have drawn heavily.

52. This illustration of the apothecary is reproduced in Kate Arnold-Forster and Nigel Tallis, comps., *The Bruising Apothecary: Images of Pharmacy and Medicine in Caricature* (London: Pharmaceutical Press, 1989), 13.

53. Ruth Richardson, *Death, Dissection, and the Destitute: A Political History of the Human Corpse* (London: Routledge and Kegan Paul, 1987).

54. Roy Porter, "Death and the Doctors in Georgian England," in R. Houlbrooke, ed., *Death, Ritual, and Bereavement* (London: Routledge, 1989), 77–94.

55. Jason S. Zielonka, "'A Man-Midwife': Etching, Hand Coloured, by S. W. Fores, London, 1793, New Haven, Yale Medical Library, Clements C. Fry Collection," *Journal of the History of Medicine* 30 (1975): 259; Roy Porter, "A Touch of Danger: The Man-Midwife as Sexual Predator," in G. S. Rousseau and R. Porter, eds., *Sexual Underworlds of the Enlightenment* (Manchester: Manchester University Press, 1988), 206–232.

56. T. G. H. Drake, "The Medical Caricatures of Thomas Rowlandson," *Bulletin of the History of Medicine* 12 (1942): 323–335, esp. 324.

57. Thomas Rowlandson, *Rowlandson's Drawings for the English Dance of Death* (San Marino: Huntington Library, 1966); Aldred Scott Warthin, "The Physician of the Dance of Death," *Annals of Medical History* n.s. 2 (1930): 351–371, 453–469, 697–710; n.s. 3 (1931): 75–109, 134–165.

58. Peter Wagner, "The Satire on Doctors in Hogarth's Graphic Works," in Marie Mulvey Roberts and Roy Porter, eds., *Literature and Medicine during the Eighteenth Century* (London and New York: Routledge, 1993), 200–225: an excellent discussion.

59. See W. H. Helfand, *Medicine and Pharmacy in American Political Prints (1765–1870)* (Madison, Wisc.: American Institute of the History of Pharmacy, 1978).

60. Roy Porter, *Health for Sale: Quackery in England, 1650–1850* (Manchester: Manchester University Press, 1989).

61. Theodore R. Simon, "'The Tractors': Engraving (1802) by Charles Williams, New Haven, Yale Medical Library, Clements C. Fry Collection," *Journal of the History of Medicine* 30 (1975): 61.

62. Roy Porter, "The Sexual Politics of James Graham," *British Journal for Eighteenth-Century Studies* 5 (1982): 201–206; Porter, "Sex and the Singular Man: The Seminal Ideas of James Graham," *Studies on Voltaire and the Eighteenth Century* 228 (1984): 3–24.

63. W. H. Helfand, "James Morison and His Pills: A Study of the Nineteenth-Century Pharmaceutical Industry," *Transactions of the British Society for the History of Pharmacy* 1, no. 3 (1974): 101–135.

64. See D. Baxby, "Gillray's 'Cowpock' Caricature," *Society for the Social History of Medicine Bulletin* 21 (1977): 60; A. W. Russell, "Ye Cow-Pock, Gillray, and Social Medicine—a Note on Gillray's Caricature of Jenner and the 'New Inoculation,'" *Society for the Social History of Medicine Bulletin* 20 (1977): 17–22.

65. Wolfgang Born, "The Nature and History of Medical Caricature," *Ciba Symposium* 6 (1944–1945): 1910–1924, esp. 1920.

66. Arnold-Forster and Tallis, comps., *The Bruising Apothecary,* 40. On George Cruikshank, see H. Evans and M. Evans, *The Man Who Drew the Drunkard's Daughter: The Life and Art of George Cruikshank* (London: Frederick Muller, 1978); Blanchard Jerrold, *The Life of George Cruikshank* (London: Chatto and Windus, 1882); John Wardroper, *The Caricatures of George Cruikshank* (London: George Fraser Gallery, 1977); Robert L. Patten, *George Cruikshank's Life, Times, and Art,* vol. 1: *1792–1835* (New Brunswick: Rutgers University Press, 1992).

67. Philippe Ariès, *The Hour of Our Death,* trans. H. Weaver (London: Allen Lane, 1981).

68. Sander L. Gilman, *Seeing the Insane* (New York: Brunner, Mazel, 1982); J. Kromm, "Studies in the Iconography of Madness, 1600–1900" (Ph.D. dissertation, Emory University, 1984).

69. Consult the cartoons reproduced in Paul Langford, *Walpole and the Robinocracy* (Cambridge: Chadwyck Healey, 1986); Peter D. G. Thomas, *The American Revolution* (Cambridge: Chadwyck Healey, 1986); H. T. Dickinson, *Caricatures and the Constitution* (Cambridge: Chadwyck Healey, 1986); J. A. Sharpe, *Crime and the Law in English Satirical Prints 1600–1832* (Cambridge: Chadwyck Healey, 1986); and Michael Duffy, *The Englishman and the Foreigner* (Cambridge: Chadwyck Healey, 1986).

70. John Brewer, *The Common People and Politics, 1750–1790s* (Cambridge: Chadwyck Healey, 1986).

71. Ibid.

72. John Brewer, *Party Ideology and Popular Politics at the Accession of George III* (Cambridge: Cambridge University Press, 1976); George Rudé, *The Crowd in History* (New York: Wiley, 1964); E. P. Thompson, *Customs in Common* (London: Merlin Press, 1991).

73. Thomas, *The American Revolution,* plate 46; Langford, *Walpole and the Robinocracy,* plate 67, 99, and passim.

74. Vincent Carretta, *George III and the Satirists from Hogarth to Byron* (Athens and London: University of Georgia Press, 1990), 297.

75. Dickinson, *Caricatures and the Constitution,* plate 4, 108.

76. Thomas, *The American Revolution,* plate 19; Burnby, *Caricatures and Comments.*

77. Dickinson, *Caricatures and the Constitution,* plate 145.

78. Draper Hill, *Mr. Gillray the Caricaturist* (London: Phaidon Press, 1965); Paulson, *Representations of Revolution, 1789–1820.*

79. For violence and the body, see H. M. Atherton, "The British Defend Their Constitution in Political Cartoons and Literature," *Studies in Eighteenth-Century Culture* 11 (1982): 3–31.

80. Brewer, *The Common People and Politics, 1750–1790s,* 41. The whole discussion is immensely valuable.

81. W. H. Helfand, "John Bull and His Doctors," *Veröffentlichungen der Internationalen Gesellschaft für Geschichte der Pharmazie* 28 (1966): 131–142, is a full survey.

82. Carretta, *George III and the Satirists.*

83. Duffy, *The Englishman and the Foreigner,* plate 132.

84. George Cruikshank, "Radical Quacks Giving a New Constitution to John Bull," in Dickinson, *Caricatures and the Constitution,* plate 118.

85. Cruikshank, "The Mountebanks, or Opposition Show Box," reproduced in W. H. Helfand, "John Bull and His Doctors," 139.

86. "The State Quack" is reproduced in John Brewer, *The Common People and Politics,* plate 101.

87. Gillray, "Doctor Sangrado Curing John Bull of Repletion," reproduced in W. H. Helfand, "Medicine and Pharmacy in British Political Prints—the Example of Lord Sidmouth," *Medical History* 29 (1985): 375–385.

88. See Helfand's admirable article mentioned in note 87, this chapter.

89. Gillray, "Britannia between Death and the Doctors," reproduced in Helfand, "Medicine and Pharmacy."

90. William Hone, *The Political House That Jack Built* (London: W. Hone, 1819).

91. Dickinson, *Caricatures and the Constitution,* plate 52.

92. Gilman, *Seeing the Insane.*

A NATURAL REVOLUTION?

1. John Shebbeare, *The History of the Excellence and Decline of the Constitution, Religion, Laws, Manners and Genius, of the Sumatrans. And of the Restoration Thereof in the Reign of Amurath the Third,* 2 vols. (London, 1760).

2. In 1758 Shebbeare was pilloried (for an hour) and sentenced to three years' imprisonment after a general warrant was issued over his polemical *Sixth Letter to the English People;* his *Seventh Letter* was suppressed. In 1764 he received a pension of £200 a year.

3. Shebbeare, *History of the . . . Sumatrans,* 285–286.

4. On the myth of a native English landscape garden, see notably, for example, Tom Williamson, *Polite Landscape: Gardens and Society in Eighteenth-Century England* (Stroud and Baltimore, 1995); Douglas Chambers, *The Planters of the English Landscape Garden: Botany, Trees, and the Georgics* (New Haven and London, 1993); John Dixon Hunt, *Garden and Grove: The Italian Renaissance Garden and the English Imagination, 1600–1750* (London, 1986).

5. See my "Horace Walpole and Eighteenth-Century Garden History," *Journal of the Warburg and Courtauld Institutes* 57 (1994): 209–226.

6. William Mason, *The English Garden: A Poem in Four Books. To Which Is Added a Commentary and Notes by William Burgh* (York, 1783), book 1, note 8.

7. See Linda Colley, *Britons: The Forging of a Nation, 1707–1837* (London, 1992), who argues that in the years after the Seven Years' War, and more particularly after the failures of the American war, the aristocracy made a series of (largely successful) attempts to legitimize their position in the face of increasing attacks from the middle class (p. 155). See also the influential account of E. P. Thompson, "Patri-

cian Society, Plebeian Culture," *Journal of Social History* 7 (1973–1974): 382–405; and for an emerging anti-French, anti-aristocratic nationalism from mid century, see Gerald Newman, *The Rise of English Nationalism: A Cultural History, 1740–1830,* chap. 4 and passim.

8. William Falconer, "Thoughts on the Style and Taste of Gardening among the Ancients," *Memoirs of the Literary and Philosophical Society of Manchester,* 2d ed. (London, 1789), 1:297–325.

9. Colley, *Britons,* 153.

10. Colley, *Britons,* 167.

11. Judith Colton, "Merlin's Cave and Queen Caroline: Garden Art as Political Propaganda," *Eighteenth-Century Studies* 10 (Fall 1976): 1–20; for Chambers at Kew see John Harris, *Sir William Chambers, Knight of the Polar Star* (London, 1970), chap. 3; see also Ronald King, *Royal Kew* (London, 1985).

12. Henry Jones, *Kew Garden: A Poem. In Two Cantos* (Dublin, 1763).

13. *Collected Works of Oliver Goldsmith,* ed. Arthur Friedman (Oxford, 1966), vol. 2, pp. 323–340.

14. Ian R. Christie, *Wars and Revolutions: Britain, 1760–1815* (London, 1982), 72–73.

15. *The Complete Works of Thomas Chatterton,* ed. Donald S. Taylor in association with Benjamin B. Hoover (Oxford, 1971), vol. 1, pp. 512–542.

16. For the influence of Charles Churchill, see Donald S. Taylor, *Thomas Chatterton's Art: Experiments in Imagined History* (Princeton, 1978), chap. 4.

17. Taylor, *Chatterton's Art,* 209–210.

18. *Horace Walpole's Correspondence,* ed. W. S. Lewis, 48 vols. (New Haven and London, 1937–1980), vol. 28, letter to Mason, 24 July 1778.

19. Sir William Chambers, *A Dissertation on Oriental Gardening* (London, 1772).

20. Here I am at variance with Alan Liu, who, citing George Mason's *Essay on Design in Gardening,* argues: "From the late 1760's through the 1780's, the picturesque must be said to have been politically preconscious—not because it had no politics, but because its understanding of freedom still reflected unthinkingly the principles fixed in the earlier landscapes of the Restoration and the Glorious Revolution. It was thus simply conventional to boast the traditional freedom or variety of English landscape." As the Mason-Chambers debate suggests, the "freedom" of British landscape was far from unthinking or uncontested in this period. See Liu, *Wordsworth: The Sense of History* (Stanford, 1989), 105–106.

21. "An Heroic Epistle to Sir William Chambers," in *Satirical Poems Published Anonymously by William Mason with Notes by Horace Walpole. Now First Published from His Manuscript,* ed. Paget Toynbee (Oxford, 1926), pp. 35–71.

22. Ibid., 44.

23. Mason, *Satirical Poems,* 45.

24. George III was frequently characterized at this time as an Eastern tyrant in satirical cartoons; see, for example, M. D. George, ed., *Catalogue of Prints and Drawings in the British Museum: Political and Personal Satires,* 11 vols. (London, 1935–1954), no. 5544, "The Patriot," and its various copies.

25. Sir William Chambers, *An Explanatory Discourse, by Tan Chet-qua, of Quangchew-fu,* published with the second edition of Chambers, *Dissertation on Oriental Gardening* (London, 1773).

26. Ibid., 129–130.

27. William Chambers, *Designs of Chinese Buildings* (London, 1757), preface.

28. John Harris, *Sir William Chambers, Knight of the Polar Star* (London, 1970), appendix 13, p. 192.

29. Chambers, *Explanatory Discourse*, 125–128.

30. Sir William Chambers correspondence, British Library Add. Ms. 41134 (copies of letters to and from Chambers in the early 1770s), Chambers to His Excellency Senator C. F. Scheffer at Stockholm, no date, 31–31v.

31. Cf. Mason's letter to Walpole, 23 November 1773, where he writes, "I always loved [a riot] as the only remaining vestige of English liberty, except that of the press."

32. Chambers, *Explanatory Discourse*, 133–134.

33. Again, for one of the fullest accounts of the English garden as an image of Britain's constitutional liberty, see William Mason, *The English Garden*.

34. Colley, *Britons*, 49–50.

35. *The Journal of the Rev. John Wesley, A.M., Sometime Fellow of Lincoln College, Oxford, Enlarged from Original Mss., with Notes from Unpublished Diaries, Annotations, Maps, and Illustrations*, standard edition, ed. Nehemiah Curnock, assisted by experts, 8 vols. (London, 1914), vol. 5, Friday, 25 August 1769, p. 337.

36. Wesley, *Journal*, vol. 6, Thursday, 12 September 1776, pp. 127–128.

37. Richard Graves, *The Spiritual Quixote, or The Summer's Ramble of Mr. Geoffry Wildgoose* (London, 1773).

38. For a useful account of early responses to Methodism and the frequent attacks on Wesley, see David Hempton, *Methodism and Politics in British Society, 1750–1850* (London, 1984), chap. 2; and for Wesley's use of sensational psychology and the tropes of sentimentalism, see G. J. Barker-Benfield, *The Culture of Sensibility: Sex and Society in Eighteenth-Century Britain* (Chicago, 1992), 65–77.

39. *The Poems of Thomas Gray, William Collins, Oliver Goldsmith*, ed. Roger Lonsdale (London, 1969).

40. While Goldsmith's poem was undoubtedly popular, it did not go unchallenged. See, for example, Anthony King, *The Frequented Village: A Poem. Inscribed to Dr. Oliver Goldsmith. By a Gentleman of the Middle Temple* (London, [1771?]). The debate continued in other minor poems, including John Robinson's *The Village Oppress'd* (London, 1771) and John Scott's "Armyn," in *Moral Eclogues* (London, 1778).

41. For this argument see P. J. Cain and A. G. Hopkins, "Gentlemanly Capitalism and British Expansion Overseas. I. The Old Colonial System, 1680–1850," *Economic History Review*, 2d ser. 39, no. 4 (1986): 501–525.

42. See also Langford, who marks Goldsmith's poem as itself a product of that perceived crisis of rural paternalism of the 1760s and 1770s: *Public Life and the Propertied Englishman, 1689–1798* (Oxford, 1991), 368, and, for a further discussion of this movement from the country, pp. 377–390.

43. Paul Langford, *A Polite and Commercial People: England, 1727–1783* (Oxford, 1992).

44. Ibid., 71.

45. Ann Bermingham, "The Picturesque and Ready-to-Wear Femininity," in *Politics of the Picturesque: Literature, Landscape, and Aesthetics since 1770*, ed. Stephen

Copley and Peter Garside (Cambridge, 1994), 81–119 (quote on p. 87). For the emergence of an aesthetic sphere distinct from aristocratic culture, see Jürgen Habermas, *The Structural Transformation of the Public Sphere: An Inquiry into a Category of Bourgeois Society,* trans. Thomas Burger and Frederick Lawrence (Cambridge: Polity Press, 1989), esp. 39–40.

46. Anon., *John Buncle, Junior, Gentleman,* 2 vols. (London, 1776–1778), 2:131–132.

47. Ibid., 2:140.

48. John Moore, *Zeluco: Various Views of Human Nature, Taken from Life and Manners, Foreign and Domestic* (London, 1789), 2:40 ff. For a discussion of Transfer's contemporary influence, see James Raven, *Judging New Wealth: Popular Publishing and Responses to Commerce in England, 1750–1800* (Oxford, 1992), 204.

49. But for the politicization of the picturesque along factional party lines and the relationship between Uvedale Price, Richard Payne Knight, and the parliamentary Whigs, see Sidney K. Robinson, *Inquiry into the Picturesque* (Chicago, 1991).

50. George Walker, *The Vagabond,* 2 vols. (London, 1799), 2:100–101.

THE PASTORAL REVOLUTION

1. At this point a few words on terminology are required. "Eclogue" means simply "selection." Virgil called his eclogues not "pastorals" (from the Latin "herdsman" or "shepherd") but "bucolics" (from the Greek "cowherd") after his master Theocritus. "Georgic" is a Latinization of the Greek for "the facts of farming." What we call Theocritus's "idylls" are not limited to themes of rustic life and were defined by him not thematically but metrically as a subcategory of "epos," which shared its hexameters.

2. Compare the useful discrimination between "hard" and "soft" primitivism: the former conceives natural existence as meager and arduous, the latter as indulgent and beneficent. See Arthur O. Lovejoy and George Boas, *Primitivism and Related Ideas in Antiquity* (Baltimore: Johns Hopkins University Press, 1935), 1:10–11.

3. Eclogue II, ll. 28–30, 56–57, trans. Paul Alpers, in Alpers, *The Singer of the Eclogues: A Study of Virgilian Pastoral* (Berkeley and Los Angeles: University of California Press, 1979), 16–19. Hereafter cited parenthetically in the text.

4. Horace, Epode 2, ll. 1–4, 67–70, in Charles E. Passage, trans., *The Complete Works of Horace* (New York: Frederick Ungar, 1983), 99–101.

5. Frank Kermode, *English Pastoral Poetry from the Beginnings to Marvell: An Anthology* (New York: Norton, 1972), editor's introduction, 14.

6. See, respectively, the fifth eclogue and the first idyll.

7. Kermode, *English Pastoral Poetry,* 42; see also pp. 11–13.

8. Raymond Williams, *The Country and the City* (New York: Oxford University Press, 1973), 13–22, 40.

9. See *The Guardian,* nos. 30, 40 (15, 27 April 1713), in *The Guardian,* ed. Alexander Chalmers, 2 vols. (London: Luke Hansard, 1806).

10. Kermode, *English Pastoral Poetry,* 42.

11. See Williams, *The Country and the City,* 16–17.

12. See E. A. Wrigley, "Urban Growth and Agricultural Change: England and the Continent in the Early Modern Period," in Wrigley, *People, Cities, and Wealth: The Transformation of Traditional Society* (London: Blackwell, 1987), 174, 177, 189–191, and passim. For the purpose of this data "the early modern period" ends around 1800 but has a terminus a quo that varies from 1520 to 1600. Correlations between these figures are therefore approximate.

13. Wrigley, "Urban Growth," 170, table 7.4.

14. For convenient guidance on these developments, see Christopher Hill, *Reformation to Industrial Revolution,* Pelican Economic History of Britain, vol 2: 1530–1780 (Harmondsworth: Penguin, 1969); H. C. Darby, "The Age of the Improver: 1600–1800," in Darby, ed., *A New Historical Geography of England after 1600* (Cambridge: Cambridge University Press, 1976); Keith Wrightson, *English Society, 1580–1680* (London: Hutchinson, 1982); Christopher Clay, *Economic Expansion and Social Change: England, 1500–1700,* 2 vols. (Cambridge: Cambridge University Press, 1984); Joan Thirsk, ed., *Agricultural Change: Policy and Practice, 1500–1750,* Agrarian History of England and Wales (Cambridge: Cambridge University Press, 1989).

15. On the transformation in attitudes toward property, see C. B. Macpherson, ed., *Property* (Toronto: University of Toronto Press, 1978), 1–13.

16. On the erosion of customary rights and its effect on social relations in the eighteenth century see, in general, E. P. Thompson, *Customs in Common: Studies in Traditional Popular Culture* (New York: New Press, 1991).

17. *The Tatler,* no. 169, (9 May 1710), in *The Tatler,* ed. Donald F. Bond (Oxford: Clarendon Press, 1987).

18. On these aspects of social transformation, see Michael McKeon, *The Origins of the English Novel, 1600–1740* (Baltimore: Johns Hopkins University Press, 1987), chap. 4.

19. See Stephen Duck, *The Thresher's Labour* (1736).

20. See Ludmilla Jordanova, *Sexual Visions: Images of Gender in Science and Medicine between the Eighteenth and Twentieth Centuries* (Madison: University of Wisconsin Press, 1989), chap. 2, who argues the connection between pastoral and gender oppositions (pp. 22–23).

21. See Susan Cahn, *Industry of Devotion: The Transformation of Women's Work in England, 1500–1660* (New York: Columbia University Press, 1987), 33, 46, 80–81, 89–90; Susan D. Amussen, *An Ordered Society: Gender and Class in Early Modern England* (Oxford: Blackwell, 1988), 43, 68–69; Bridget Hill, *Women, Work, and Sexual Politics in Eighteenth-Century England* (Oxford: Blackwell, 1989), 35.

22. Of course, such generalizations about how the domestic economy was undermined need to be complicated by crucial variations in households based on differences in region and social status.

23. B. Hill, *Women, Work, and Sexual Politics,* 36–37, 50–51; Cahn, *Industry of Devotion,* 38–39; K. D. M. Snell, *Annals of the Labouring Poor: Social Change and Agrarian England, 1660–1900* (Cambridge: Cambridge University Press, 1985), 22, 62.

24. See Snell, *Annals of the Labouring Poor,* 21–22, 37, 45, 51, 58–62, 157–158. Snell's data comes entirely from the south of England.

25. See B. Hill, *Women, Work, and Sexual Politics,* 47–48, 49–50; Cahn, *Industry of Devotion,* 43–44, 47, 99, 120, 158; Snell, *Annals of the Labouring Poor,* 53 n. 36,

215–218, 311–312, 348–349 (quotation on p. 348). On the rise in fertility see generally E. A. Wrigley, "The Growth of Population in Eighteenth-Century England: A Conundrum Resolved," in his *People, Cities, and Wealth*, 215–241.

26. For a treatment of this subject that goes beyond the pastoral context, see Michael McKeon, "Historicizing Patriarchy: The Emergence of Gender Difference in England, 1660–1760," *Eighteenth-Century Studies* 28, no. 3 (1995): 295–322.

27. See Addison, *The Spectator*, no. 15 (17 March 1711), in *The Spectator*, ed. Donald F. Bond (Oxford: Clarendon Press, 1965). Compare *Spectator*, nos. 41, 57, 66, 73, 104, 129, 435.

28. See Bernard Mandeville, *The Fable of the Bees* (1705, 1714), ed. F. B. Kaye (Oxford: Clarendon Press, 1924), vol. I, Remarks "M," "T"; Addison, *The Tatler*, no. 116 (5 January 1710), in *The Tatler*, ed. Bond; Addison, *The Spectator*, no. 69 (9 May 1711). On the preoccupations of the new "woman of leisure" see "Mrs. Crackenthorpe," *Female Tatler*, nos. 9, 67 (25–27 July, 7–9 December 1709), in *The Female Tatler*, ed. Fidelis Morgan (London: J. M. Dent, 1992); Johnson, *Rambler*, nos. 128, 191 (8 June 1751; 14 January 1752), in *The Yale Edition of the Works of Samuel Johnson*, vols. 4–5, ed. W. J. Bate and Albrecht B. Strauss (New Haven: Yale University Press, 1962).

29. See Daniel Defoe, *Review*, nos. 5, 55, 57, 59, 116 (10 January 1706; 1, 5, 10 August 1710; 21 December 1710).

30. My principal sources for the following several paragraphs are Christopher Hill, *Reformation to Industrial Revolution;* Charles Wilson, *England's Apprenticeship, 1603–1763* (London; Longman, 1965); Michael Hechter, *Internal Colonialism: The Celtic Fringe in British National Development, 1536–1966* (Berkeley: University of California Press, 1975); Gerald Newman, *The Rise of English Nationalism: A Cultural History, 1740–1830* (London: St. Martin's, 1987); James D. Tracy, ed., *The Rise of Merchant Empires: Long Distance Trade in the Early Modern World, 1350–1750* (Cambridge: Cambridge University Press, 1990).

31. On the analogy see in general Seymour Drescher, *Capitalism and Antislavery: British Mobilization in Comparative Perspective* (New York: Oxford University Press, 1987).

32. This opposition recapitulates the terms of a common version of East-West nationalist opposition. Below a certain latitude, however, the terms of the north-south opposition are inverted: England is to Scotland as England is to Spain.

33. For example, see William Collins, "An Ode on the Popular Superstitions of the Highlands of Scotland, Considered as the Subject of Poetry" (written ca. 1750), in Roger Lonsdale, ed., *The Poems of Gray, Collins, and Goldsmith* (London: Longman, 1969).

34. For an instructive comparison, see the two loco-descriptive poems of John Denham, *Coopers Hill* (1642–1650, 1655–1668), and Alexander Pope, *Windsor-Forest* (1713).

35. On this see John Brewer, *The Sinews of Power: War, Money, and the English State, 1688–1783* (New York: Knopf, 1989).

36. See Anne Janowitz, *England's Ruins: Poetic Purpose and the National Landscape* (Oxford: Blackwell, 1990).

CONTRIBUTORS

John Barrell, Professor of English, University of York • Stephen Bending, Lecturer in English, University of Southampton • Toni Bowers, Associate Professor of English, University of Pennsylvania • Harriet Guest, Lecturer in English, University of York • Edward Hundert, Professor of History, University of British Columbia • Gerald Izenberg, Professor of History, Washington University, St. Louis • Mark Jenner, Lecturer in History, University of York • Michael McKeon, Professor of English, Rutgers University • Roy Porter, Professor of History, Wellcome Institute • Kevin Sharpe, Professor of History, University of Southampton • Steven Zwicker, Professor of English, Washington University, St. Louis

INDEX

Page numbers in boldface refer to illustrations.

Absalom and Achitophel (Dryden), 103, 106, 107–8, 109
Act of Settlement (1701), 64
Act of Succession (1701), 58
Act of Union (1707), 286
acts, Commonwealth, 42
Adam brothers, 253
Addington, Henry, Lord Sidmouth, 235–36
Addison, Joseph, 147, 282; *Cato*, 85; *The Spectator*, 157, 192–93
Advancement of Learning (Bacon), 111
Adventures of David Simple, The (S. Fielding), 180–85, 192
"Adventures on Salisbury Plain" (Wordsworth), 123
aesthetic vs. political history, 3–5, 15, 20
"Ague and Fever" (Rowlandson), 229
Aiton, William, 245
Alchemist, The (Jonson), 322n.9
allegory, 10, 102, 103, 107–9
Alleyn, Edward, 152
American Revolution, 19, 78, 121
Americas, pastoral aura of, 285
Anatomy Act (1832), 233
Ancient Psychrolusia Revived, The (Floyer and Baynard), 200–201, 202–3
Anglicanism. *See* Church of England
Anne, Queen of England, Scotland, and Ireland, 57–74; accession to the throne, 66; and Elizabeth I, 66–68, 71; illness of, 62, 66; importance of producing an heir, 69; Jacobitism suspected of, 59, 73, 312–13n.13; longterm results of childlessness of, 73–74, 314n.44; marriage to Prince George, 57, 312n.3–4; motherhood of, political authority of, 62–64, **63**, 69, 313n.23; motherhood of, symbolic, 66, 67–74; opposes invitation to Hanoverian successor, 59–60, 64, 315n.62; pregnancies/children of, 57–58, 64–66, **65**, 311–12n.1; provision for succession of, 58–60, 61–62, 72–73; supports Hanoverian succession, 315n.62
annotations. *See* manuscript notations
aristocracy, 42–43
As You Like It (Shakespeare), 151
Ascham, Roger, 215
Aubrey, John, 222
Augusta, Princess of Wales, 245, 246, 247–49, **251**
authority: demystification of, 56; and language, 29, 54, 304n.34; maternal, 62–64, **63**, 69, 71, 313n.23

Bacon, Francis: *Advancement of Learning*, 111; *Great Instauration*, 111; "Of Truth," 153
Baillie, Joanna, 94–95
Ballad on the Death of Louis the Unfortunate, The, 318–19n.34
balneology, 197. *See also* cold bathing
Banks, John: *The Innocent Usurper*, 322n.10

baptism: and child's health, 209; cold bathing at, 202–3, 204–5; debates about, 205–9, 343n.82, 344n.89; history of, 203–4; methods of, 206–10, 344n.89; public vs. private, 206; records of, 343n.83
Baptists, 204, 206, 209–10
Bartholomew, John, 82
bathing, cold. *See* cold bathing
baths, therapeutic, 197. *See also* cold bathing
Bayle, Pierre, 142, 143, 146, 149, 151
Baynard, Edward, 340n.35; *The Ancient Psychrolusia Revived,* 200–201, 202–3; on baptism, 210–11; on the king's evil, 211, 345n.107; on luxury, 211, 216; politics of, 211, 345n.106; religious views of, 345n.105
Beddoes, Thomas, 220
Beggar's Opera, The (Gay), 151
benefit-of-linen defense (against infanticide charges), 60–61, 313n.17
Bermingham, Ann, 264
Bethlem Hospital (Bedlam), 221
Betterton, Thomas, 154
Bible, 298n.72
Bindley Pamphlets, 105
Blackmore, Sir Richard: *Creation: A Philosophical Poem,* 329n.29
Blackwell, Thomas, 163
Blake, William, 221
"Blue Devils, The" (Cruikshank), 229
Bluett, George, 159, 331n.61
body politic, 3, 11, 12, 15–16, 217; attitudes toward body, 230; cannibalism, 234; in cartoons, 18, 230–37, 301n.119; dissection, 233; and distrust of doctors, 234; and the French Revolution, 16; humor, 231–32; political anatomy, 232–35; politicians depicted as quacks, 235–37; representations in art/language, 230–31; the theologically fallen body, 230
Boleyn, Anne, 67
books. *See* reading
Borderers, The (Wordsworth), 122–23, 132–33, 325n.22
Boswell, James, 158
Bovi, M.: *The King's Departure from his Disconsolate Family,* 83–84, **84,** 89
Boyer, Abel, 155
breast-feeding, 202

"Britannia between Death and Doctors" (Gillray), 236
British people, as sympathetic, 79, 87
Brome, Richard, 43
Brothers, Richard, 97
Brothers, The (Wordsworth), 126
Brown, John, 163, 186, 190
Brown, Lancelot ("Capability"), 245–46
Browne, Joseph, 213
Buchan, William, 202, 218
Bull, John (personification), 234–35
Burbage, Richard, 152
Bürger, Gottfried August: *Wilde Jäger, Der,* 119–20, 132
Burke, Edmund: madness of, 237; on natural response to monarchy, 95; sentiment of, 75, 76, 78–79; as unsympathetic toward George III, 89
Burnaby, Thomas, 153
Burnet, Bishop Gilbert, 64, 105–6, 209
Burney, Charles, 127–28
Bute, John Stuart, 3rd Earl of, 235, 245, 246, 248–49, **250–51**

Cabala, 105
Cadogan, William, 202
Calvinists, 25, 164, 207
Campbell, Archibald, marquis and eighth earl of Argyll, 101
capitalism: and abolition of feudal tenures, 277; domestic economy undermined by, 281, 358n.22; and gender difference, 281, 283; and private property, 277–78. *See also* commercial society
Caroline, Queen of England, Scotland, and Ireland, 245
Carter, Elizabeth, 175; and *Sir Charles Grandison,* 186–87
Cartwright, Thomas, 207
case studies, 2–3, 20
Castiglione, Baldassare, Count, 147
Catholicism, 71
Cato (Addison), 85
Cavendish, Margaret, 322n.9
Cecil, William, Lord Burghley, 111
Cervantes, Miguel de: *Don Quixote,* 152
Chamberlen, Peter, 197
Chambers, Sir William: as architect of Kew Gardens, 245–46; criticism of, 250–55; *Designs of Chinese Buildings,* 254; *Dissertation on Oriental Gardening,* 250; on English

liberty, 255; *An Explanatory Discourse,* 254, 255, 256; on variety of ornament, 254, 256; *"A View of the Wilderness,"* **253**

"Chamber War, The" (Rowlandson), 228

Character of a Protector, 45

charity schools, 212, 346n.115

Charles I, King of England, Scotland, and Ireland: images of, **34, 37, 38,** 39–40, **40,** 306n.99; and Louis XVI, 90, 319–20n.45; martyrdom of, 32–34; sermons commemorating death of, 90, 319n.45; trial and beheading of, 26, 27, 32

Charles II, King of England, Scotland, and Ireland, 28; authority of, 5; coronation of, 35, 56; death of, 56; images of, 37, 39; pornographic court of, 12, 299n.81; on Prince George of Denmark, 57; and the republican cause, 56, 311n.246

Charles I on Horseback with Mr. St. Antoine (Van Dyck), 47–48

Chatterton, Thomas: "Kew Gardens," 248–50

chivalry, 7

Christianity: demystification of, 19; motives judged by God, 150; role-nakedness of persons, 152; self-love as underlying piety, 142–43 (see also *Fable of the Bees, The*)

Churchill, Sarah, 64

Church of England, 19, 206–7, 208, 209

citizenship, and family affection, 76

civility, 214–15. *See also* politeness

Clare, John, 91

Clarendon, Edward Hyde, first earl of, 64

class, 175–77, 278, 281

Cleland, John: *Fanny Hill,* 299n.86

Cleomenes (Dryden), 104

Cléry, M., 80, 89

Cobbett, William, 244

coffeehouse, Restoration, 3, 7–8, 10, 297–98n.68

coins and seals, 31–32, 48, 304n.54

Coke, Sir Edward, 111

cold bathing, 197–216; advocated by Floyer, 198, 200–202, 205, 215; at baptism, 202–3, 204–5; class interpretation of, 198; facilities for, 198; foreign influences on, 215; historical/ancient support for, 214, 215; vs. the hot regimen, 211, 213; for mental disorder, 205

Coleridge, Samuel Taylor, 132, 326n.41

Collier, Jeremy, 329n.29

Colman, George, the Younger: *Inkle and Yarico,* 93, 320n.51

colonies, pastoral aura of, 285–86

commemorations, 42

commercial society, 6–7; and class difference, 175–77; consumption in, 159, 177; criticisms of commerce, 8, 296n.51; as democratizing, 19; displays of wealth in, 144–45, 159; dynamics of, 144–45, 147; and fashion, 14, 175–78, 179, 193; and gambling, 177; and gender difference (*see* gender difference); politeness in, 7–8, 147; and progress, 7, 174; secularism of, 147; social bonds in, 143, 147–48, 157–58, 170; Tories on commerce in, 8

Common Sense, 186, 188

Commonwealth, 26–32; acts/proclamations of, 42, 307n.128; authority of, 26–30; cartoons of, 39, **41;** and foreign writings on civil virtues, 30, 304n.47; importance of, 55; and procession, 44, 308n.145; propaganda in defense of, 27–28; and royalist history, 36; and royalist language, 29–30, 37, 304n.42, 306n.95; Scriptural support for, 28, 37; seal/coins of, 31–32, 304n.54; symbols of, 41; theater during, 43–44; visual representations of, 30–32, **31,** 304n.49. *See also* monarchy

Compleat History of Independency (Walker), 105

"Conduct of the Two B——rs, The," 232–33

Conférence de M. Le Brun sur l'expression générale et particulière (Le Brun), 155

"Congress of Necessary Politicians, The," 231

Connoisseur, The, 175–78, 179, 336n.28

Cornubiensis, 49

courtesy books, 147, 155

courtly culture, 43, 46

Court of Wards, 277

Crabbe, George: *The Parish Register,* 91–92; *The Village,* 274

Creation: A Philosophical Poem (Blackmore), 329n.29

Critical Reflections on Poetry and Painting (Du Bos), 156–57

Cromwell, Oliver, 30–31, **31,** 105; ambitions/personality of, 52–53, 54; on the commonwealth, 28, 29; criticisms of, 52–53, 55, 311n.237; death/funeral of, 48–51, 53; de facto kingship of, 50–51;

Cromwell, Oliver (*continued*)
  images of, 32, 41, 47–48; on kingship, 48;
  Parliament dissolved by, 44–45, 52; Parlia-
  ment offers the crown to, 49–50; procla-
  mations of, 42; royal symbols used by,
  44–48, 54, 55; title of Protector, 45–46
Cromwell, Richard, 51–52
Crosfeild, Robert, 97
Cruikshank, George, 228, 236; "The Blue
  Devils," 229; "The Doctor," 236; "The
  Ministerial Monster," 232; "The Mounte-
  banks," 235; "Radical Quacks Giving a
  New Constitution to John Bull," 235; "A
  Radical Reformer," 232; "State Physicians
  Bleeding John Bull," 234–35
Cullen, William, 221
cultural studies, 1–2
Cuniculari (Hogarth), 228, **229**
Cyprian, Saint, 205

Dacier, André, 154
"Danish Boy" (Wordsworth), 136
Dante Alighieri: *The Inferno*, 115
Dartmouth, earl of, 59, 312n.3, 344–
  45n.101
Davenant, William, 43
David, Jacques-Louis, 84
death, representations of, 229–30
Defoe, Daniel, 7; on Bacon's *Advancement of
  Learning*, 111; *Moll Flanders*, 13, 61,
  299n.86; *Roxana*, 299n.86
degeneration: dissociation from commercial
  progress, 174; and fashionable society,
  174, 335n.6; inevitability of, 173; pam-
  phlets about, 212–13; sexual, 173–74,
  334n.2
Democratic Rage (Preston), 81
democratization, 19
Dennis, John, 154, 158
Dent, William, 234, 237
De Quincy, Thomas, 123
De Rerum Natura (Lucretius)
Descartes, René: mind-body dualism of, 14,
  222; on passions, 154–55, 157
description, thick, 2
Description of Millennium Hall, A (S. Scott),
  180, 185, 190–91
"Descriptive Sketches" (Wordsworth),
  121–22
Deserted Village, The (Goldsmith), 259–62,
  263, 279, 356n.40, 356n.42

Designs of Chinese Buildings (Chambers),
  254
Diderot, Denis, 165, 166, 332n.87
Digby, John, 153
Discourse of the National Excellencies of England
  (Hawkins), 105
Discourses (Machiavelli), 106
diseases, causes of, 213–14
Dissertation on Oriental Gardening (Cham-
  bers), 250
divine right, 35
"Doctor, The" (Cruikshank), 236
"Doctor Sangrado Curing John Bull of
  Repletion" (Gillray), 234, 235
domestic economy, 280–82, 358n.22
Don Quixote (Cervantes), 152
Don Sebastian (Dryden), 108–9
Douglas, Mary, 204
drama. *See* theater
Dryden, John, 9; *Absalom and Achitophel*,
  103, 106, 107–8, 109; *Cleomenes*, 104;
  Don Sebastian, 108–9; *The Medall*, 109; *Vir-
  gil*, 9
Du Bos, J.-B.: *Critical Reflections on Poetry and
  Painting*, 156–57
Duck, Stephen (the "Thresher Poet"), 279;
  The Thresher's Labour, 283
Dunciad, The (Pope), 110, 112–13
Dunton, 313n.17
Dyson, Jeremiah, 253

East India Company, 288
Eaton, Daniel Isaac, 77
Eclogues (Virgil), 268, 269–70, 272–73, 284,
  357n.1
Edgeworth, C. Sneyd, 80, 89, 316n.12
Edinburgh University, 219
egoism, 142–43, 146. See also *Fable of the
  Bees, The*
Eikon Basilike, 33–36, **34**
Eliot, George: *Middlemarch*, 220
Elizabeth I, Queen of England, 3, 11, 66–
  68, 69–71, 314n.44, 314n.47, 314nn.36–
  37, 315n.50
Ellison, Nathaniel, 212, 345.112
empirical research, 2–3
England: as commercial, 6–7; demographic
  changes in, 276–77, 358n.12; and Ireland, 286; land vs. trade, 276–78; nationalism of, 285–89; and Scotland, 286–87,
  359n.32. *See also* Great Britain

"English Dance of Death" (Rowlandson), 230

English Garden, The (Mason), 251–52, 256

engraving, Dutch dominance of, 294.n33

Enquiry into the Right Use and Abuses of the Hot, Cold, and Temperate Baths in England, An (Floyer), 200

Epicurus, 153

Erskine, Thomas, 78

"Essay on Modern Gardening" (H. Walpole), 244

etiquette. *See* politeness

Evans, Arise, 32

"Evening Walk, An" (Wordsworth), 119, 120, 124

Exclusion Crisis, 105, 106, 108

execution, pleasure of watching, 94–95

Explanatory Discourse, An (Chambers), 254, 255, 256

Fable of the Bees, The (Mandeville), 14, 16, 143–49; act vs. motive in, 150–51; approbation/flattery in, 148–49; criticism of, 143, 158, 161; dynamics of commercial society in, 144–45, 147, 170, 330n.53; moral virtue in, 145–46, 148–49; passions/egoism in, 143–44, 145, 148, 167–68, 170; "private vices, publick benefits" maxim of, 143, 163; satires of, 161; theatricality of, 152–53, 160

Faithorne, William, 47

Falconer, William: "Thoughts on the Style and Taste of Gardening among the Ancients," 244–45

Fanny Hill (Cleland), 299n.86

femininity: and literal meaning, 68–69; as nature and art/artifice, 280, 282, 283; in pastoral poetry, 280, 282–84; of sentiment, 76

fertility, 282

feudalism, 277

Fielding, Henry: on audience detachment, 166; on deceit, 165, 332n.82; on fashion, 176–77; on good breeding, 332n.82; on hypocrisy, 167; *Joseph Andrews*, 161, 165; opposition to Mandeville, 160–61, 163; on theater, 161–62; on the theatricality of public life, 163, 164–65, 166; theatrical representations used by, 165–66; *Tom Jones*, 161–62, 164–65; on virtue, 163, 164–65, 332n.76

Fielding, Sarah: *The Adventures of David Simple*, 180–85, 192; *Volume the Last*, 180, 183–85

Filmer, Sir Robert, 104; *Patriarcha*, 105, 106

Final Interview of Louis the Sixteenth, The (Tompkins), 84–85, **86,** 89

Firth, Sir Charles, 48

Fitz-Adam, Adam, 173, 177

Flaxmer, Sarah, 97

Floyer, Sir John: advocates cold bathing, 198, 200–202, 205, 215; on ancient medicine, 201, 205, 341n.51; *The Ancient Psychrolusia Revived*, 200–201, 202–3; background of, 199; on baptism, 202–3, 205, 207–8, 210; and Baynard, 200, 340n.35; on charity schools and dissenters, 212, 346n.115; on Chinese medicine, 200; on cold bathing for muscular Christianity, 198, 215; *An Enquiry into the Right Use and Abuses of the Hot, Cold, and Temperate Baths in England,* 200; establishes cold baths at St. Unite's Well, 200; friendships of, 339n.23; on inoculation, 200; on luxury, 211–12, 216; on medical education, 199; medical inquiries/experiments of, 199–200; *Medicina Gerocomica,* 203; on pediatrics, 201–2; religious views/studies of, 199, 200, 202–3, 205, 339n.23, 340n.32, 344n.101; reputation/popularity of, 201, 208–9; and Stanhope, 199, 338–39n.22; *Tatler* satirization of, 201; Tory sympathies of, 199, 339n.23; on touching for the king's evil, 200, 345n.107

Fontenelle, Bernard le Bovier de, 334n.109

Foote, Samuel, 155–156

Fordyce, James, 177

"Forsaken Indian" (Wordsworth), 123

Fox, Charles James, 236–37

Fox, William, 93–94

Fragments of Ancient Poetry (Macpherson), 114

France, and war with Great Britain, 90, 93

Frankenstein (Shelley), 222

Frederick Louis, Prince of Wales, 245

French Revolution: and the body politic, 16; and the individual, 136–37; influence on Wordsworth, 116, 118, 121–23,

French Revolution (*continued*)
124–25, 128, 134–36; representations
of, 232; the Terror, 122, 123
Freud, Sigmund, 130–31, 231
Frost, John, 78

gambling, 177
games, royal symbolism of, 42, 307n.125
gardens, English landscape, 241–66; and
the biblical Paradise, 257; and class difference, 242; discovery as native art,
242–43; and enfranchisement, 242; and
English liberty, 242, 251–52, 254, 255–
56, 265, 355n.20; vs. French gardens,
243, 252; and the Hanoverian monarchy,
243–44, 245–47; histories of, 242–45;
Kew Gardens (*see* Kew Gardens);
Mason–Chambers debate, 256–57 (*see
also* Chambers, Sir William; Mason,
William); and natural succession, 243–
44; and property rights/landowners,
243–45, 257, 262–63, 354n.7; Richmond
gardens (*see* Richmond gardens); Wesley
on, 257–58
Garrick, David, 156, 158, 171
Gay, John: *Beggar's Opera, The,* 151
gender difference, 11–12, 175–94; in *The
Adventures of David Simple,* 180–85, 192;
anxiety about, 179–80, 194; and domestic
economy, 280–81; dress/fashion, 175–
76, 178, 182; education of women, 187;
in *The History of Sir George Ellison,* 180,
185–86, 189–90, 191–94; independence
of women, 186, 194; in literature, 12–13;
moral ascendancy of women, 175, 194;
moral character of women, 181–82, 189;
in pastoral poetry, 280, 282–84; and pub-
lic/private spheres, 185–89, 190–91, 194;
subordination/domestication of women,
186; in wages, 281
gender history, 3
Gentleman's Magazine, 317.n14
George, Prince of Denmark, 57, 64,
312nn.3–4
George II, King of England, Scotland, and
Ireland, 231
George III, King of England, Scotland,
and Ireland: characterization as Eastern
tyrant, 254, 355n.24; imagined death of,
93, 96–97, 320–21n.59; madness of, 14–
15, 220–21, 237; and Richmond and Kew

gardens, 245–47; Scottish influence on,
245; sentimental language regarding ill-
ness of, 78–79, 88–89, 93, 96
Georgics (Virgil), 268–69, 280
Germania (Tacitus), 215, 346n.121
Gheeraerts, Marcus, the Younger, 314n.47
Gifford, John, 82, 87
Gilliver, Lawton, 110
Gillray, James, 228, 229; "Britannia between
Death and Doctors," 236; "Doctor Sangra-
do Curing John Bull of Repletion," 234,
235; *Louis XVI Taking Leave of His Wife and
Family,* 81, **82,** 317n.18; "Petit Souper, à la
Parisienne," 234; *Taking Physick,* 232, **233**
Glorious Revolution, 64, 66, 104
Godwin, William, 122, 265
Goethe, Johann Wolfgang von: *The Sorrows
and Sympathetic Attachments of Young Werter,*
113–15
Goldsmith, Oliver: *The Deserted Village,*
259–62, **263,** 279, 356n.40, 356n.42;
Threnodia Augustalis, 247–48
Good Old Cause, 52–54, 55
Goodwin, John, 26
"Goody Blake and Harry Gill"
(Wordsworth), 127–28
Goudemetz, H., 318n.23
Graham, James, 228
Graves, Richard: *Spiritual Quixote, The,*
258–59, **260**
Great Britain: imperialism of, 16–17,
284–86, 288; nationalism of, 285–89;
union of Scotland and England, 286–87;
war with France, 90, 93. *See also* England
Great Instauration (Bacon), 111
Great Reform Act (1832), 233
Guy Fawkes' Day, commemoration of, 42

Hall, John, 49
Hamlet (Shakespeare), 152
Hardcastle, Thomas: *A Sermon Preached at
Shadwell-Chappell in Yorkshire,* 105, 323n.20
Hardy, Thomas, 97
Harlot's Progress (Hogarth), 12–13
Harrington, James, 53
"Hart-leap Well" (Wordsworth), 119–20,
131–32, 133
Hawkins, Richard: *Discourse of the National
Excellencies of England,* 105
Haywood, Eliza, 178
Hazlitt, William, 116, 161, 218, 324n.2

health: and antibiotics, 218; asylums, 221; chemists/druggists, 219–20; cholera, 218; death, representations of, 229–30; diseases, 218, 229; family doctors, 219; fluidity within the medical profession, 219–20; hospitals, 220; hypochondria/hysteria, 221; illness and self, 221; infant mortality, 218; malaria, 229; mental disorders, treatment of, 220–21; Mesmerism, 221–22; midwives, 219; obstetrics, 219; physicians' authority, 220; physicians' prestige, 219; public feelings toward innovation, 220; quackery, 220; self-help books, 218–19; smallpox, 218; tuberculosis, 218; typhus, 218; and wealth, 218–22. *See also* medicine
Hearne, Thomas, 201
Hegel, G. W. F., 172
Heidegger, Count, 160
Henry VIII, King of England, 67
hero, sentimental, 185
Heroic Epistle to Sir William Chambers, An (Mason), 250–51, 252–55
Hett, William, 89
Heynes, Matthew, 213
Heywood, Thomas, 152
Hill, Aaron, 155
Hill, Sir John, 252
Hippocrates, 201, 341n.51
History of Sir George Ellison, The (S. Scott), 180, 185–86, 189–90, 191–94
History of the Sumatrans, A (Shebbeare), 241–42
hive trope, 16, 300n.105
Hobbes, Thomas, 13; *Leviathan*, 15–16; on the person as actor, 150; on politeness, 147
Hogarth, William: *The Company of Undertakers*, 223, **223**; *Cuniculari*, 228, **229**; *Harlot's Progress*, 12–13; *Marriage à la Mode*, 179; "Rake's Progress," 237; *The Reward of Cruelty*, 224, **226**, 232; "Southwark Fair," 228
Home, Henry, Lord Kames, 335n.20
homophobia, 179
Hone, William, 236
Horace, 215, 270
Howard, Edward: *Poems and Essays*, 105
Howard, John, 218
Hume, David, 153, 155; on identity/self, 167, 333n.97; on reason as the slave of

passions, 168; on self-interest and sympathy for others, 168–69; on women, 175
Humphrey Clinker (Smollett), 289
Hunter, Henry, 87, 318n.32, 319n.41
Hunton, Philip, 104
hygiene practices, foreign influences on, 215

iconoclasm, 4
"Idiot Boy" (Wordsworth), 123
"Idol Worship," 231
imperialism, 284–86, 288
imports, 179, 211, 214, 335n.20, 346n.120
India, colonial exploitation of, 17, 288
individual: conceptions of, 6; and the French Revolution, 136–37; and theater, 152, 328n.26; uniqueness of, 172; and the Whigs, 241
infanticide, 60–61, 72, 313n.17
Inferno, The (Dante), 115
Inkle and Yarico (Colman), 93, 320n.51
Innocent Usurper, The (Banks), 322n.10
inoculation, 200, 339n.30
interiority, 113–15
Ireland, colonial exploitation of, 286

Jacobins, 220
Jacobites, 210, 287
James, Robert, 220
James II, King of England, Scotland, and Ireland, 5, 63–64, 105, 294n.33
Jansenists, 142, 150, 164
Jenkins, Judge, 39
Jenner, Edward, 218, 229
John Bull (personification), 234–35
John Buncle, Junior, 264–65
John of Salisbury: *Polycraticus*, 151
Johnson, Samuel, 19; on Addison's *Cato*, 85; on commercial culture, 174; *London*, 284; on *Lycidas*, 274; on theater, 158, 331n.56; Walpole on, 252
John the Baptist, 205
Jones, Henry: *Kew Garden*, 246–47, 248
Jonson, Ben: *The Alchemist*, 322n.9
Joseph Andrews (H. Fielding), 161, 165
journals, academic, 3, 292n.13
Juvenal, 215

Kant, Immanuel, 170
Keats, John: *On Melancholy*, 221

Kent, William, 245
Kew Garden (Jones), 246–47, 248
"Kew Gardens" (Chatterton), 248–50
Kew Gardens (Royal Botanic Gardens), 242, **250–51;** Aiton as gardener, 245; Chambers as architect, 245–46; merges with Richmond gardens, 246; as a representation of Parliament, 257
King, John, 201
King's Departure from his Disconsolate Family, The (Bovi), 83–84, **84,** 89
king's evil. *See* touching for the king's evil
Kneller, Sir Godfrey, 5, 294n.32
Küchler, Conrad Heinrich, 88

Lamb, Charles, 221
Lancet, 219
landownership: and abolition of feudal tenures, 277; and enclosure, 281
landscape gardens. *See* gardens, English landscape
Lane, William, 89
language: and authority/power, 29, 54, 304n.34; longitude/lattitude of, 18, 301n.117; royalist, 29–30, 304n.42
La Rochefoucauld, François, 6th Duc de, 142, 149
Last Interview between Lewis the Sixteenth and his Disconsolate Family, The (Schiavonetti), 84, **85**
Laurence, Roger, 206
lavatory humor, 231
Law, William, 158
Le Brun, Charles: *Conférence de M. Le Brun sur l'expression générale et particulière,* 155
Leigh, Charles, 198
Letter to the Bishop of Llandaff (Wordsworth), 122
Lettsom, John Coakley, 218
Leviathan (Hobbes), 15–16
Lewis, Matthew Gregory, 132–33
literature: and authorship/copyright, 9; commercialization of, 8–9; and politics, 9, 11. *See also* reading practices
Locke, John, 315n.53; on cold bathing, 198, 214; on the individual, 6, 13–14; *Treatise on Education,* 14; *Two Treatises of Government,* 106
Lombart, Peter, 47–48
London (Johnson), 284
Louis XVI, King of France: affection for family, 83, 318n.23; ballad of the last inter-

view, 318–19n.34; British vs. French reactions to death of, 87–89, 318–19n.34, 318nn.31–32, 319n.41; and Charles I, 90, 319–20n.45; as Christian martyr vs. Roman hero, 83–86, 89; engravings of the last interview, 83–85, **84–86,** 94; execution of, 79; family relationships named in the last interview, 87–88; Fox's pamphlet on death of, 93–94; last interview with family, 79–80, 316nn.12–13; last words of, 83, 87; medal depicting the last interview, 87–88, **88;** pathos of death of, 86–87; political significance of death of, 90–93; public vs. private character of, 79–80, 82–83, 87, 317–18n.22; reports of the last interview/execution of, 79, 81–82, 316nn.12–13, 317nn.16–17, 318n.23; satire of the last interview, 81, **82,** 317n.18; tragedies written about the execution, 94, 320n.52; will, reading/publication of, 83
loyalist alarmism, 96–97
Lucretius, 156; *De Rerum Natura,* 153
Luttrell, Narcissus, 105
luxury, critique of, 212, 213, 216
Lycidas (Milton), 274
lyric, 11, 125, 129
Lyrical Ballads (Wordsworth), 116–37; "Adventures on Salisbury Plain," 123; attitude toward nature in, 117–18, 119, 124–25, 131–32, 137; *The Brothers,* 126; Coleridge's role in, 132, 326n.41; conservative apostasy of, 116, 324–25n.2; "Danish Boy," 136; democratic sympathies in, 116, 324n.2; "Descriptive Sketches," 121–22; "An Evening Walk," 121, 124; "Forsaken Indian," 126; "Goody Blake and Harry Gill," 127–28; "Hart-leap Well," 119–20, 131–32, 133; "Idiot Boy," 126; "Mad Mother," 126; "Michael," 118, 325n.8; "A Night on Salisbury Plain," 122; "Nutting," 127; passions in, 125–26; passivity vs. poetic absolutism in, 118; and pleasure, 119–20; "Preface," 119, 120, 124, 125–26, 132; "The Ruined Cottage," 123–24, 127; "Ruth," 133–35; and sensationalism, 120, 125, 126, 132; "Simon Lee," 127, 128–29; social vision in, 116–17, 127–28, 129, 136, 326n.32; song's power in, 125, 129–37; suffering in, 121–24, 126–27; "Tintern Abbey," 325n.8

Macdonald, Sir Archibald, 77
Machiavelli, Niccolò, 7; *Discourses,* 106
Macklin, Charles, 156
Macpherson, James: *Fragments of Ancient Poetry,* 114
macro-pastoral experience, 288–89
"Mad Mother" (Wordsworth), 123
making provision, legal concept of, 60–62, 72
Mandeville, Bernard: on doctors, 222; *The Fable of the Bees,* (see *Fable of the Bees, The);* Fielding's opposition to, 160–61; on hypocrisy, 167; influence of, 160, 331n.66; on passions, 157; on politeness, 147, 157; on reason, 168; on the theatricality of public life, 153–54, 158–60, 166–67
manners. *See* politeness
Manningham, Sir Richard, 228
Mansfield, Lord Chief Justice William Murray, 1st Earl, 253
manuscript notations, 10; for allegories, 102, 103, 107–9; in the Bible, 298n.72; contestation between, 107; decline of, 112–13; and gossip/scandal, 109–10; political commentary, 102, 103, 104–7; and printers' veiling of proper names, 109–10
marginalia. *See* manuscript notations
Marian mythology, 71
Marie Antoinette: execution of, 79; grief of before the execution, 81, 317n.14; last interview with family, 79–80, 316nn.12–13
Marie-Thérèse Charlotte, Princess, 80–81
Martin, Samuel, 253
Marvell, Andrew, 5
Mary II, Queen of England, 64, 104
masculinity: and fashion, 178–79, 182, 335n.20, 336n.28; and figural meaning, 68; in pastoral poetry, 280, 283; and the sentimental hero, 13
Mason, William, 243–44; *English Garden, The,* 251–52, 256; on English liberty, 356n.31; *An Heroic Epistle to Sir William Chambers,* 250–51, 252–55; and Walpole, 250–51
masque, 5, 293–94.31
masquerades, 159–60, 331n.61
maternal authority. *See* authority, maternal
Medall, The (Dryden), 109
Medical Dispatch (Rowlandson), 225–26, **227**
Medicina Gerocomica (Floyer), 203

medicine: ancient, 202, 341n.51; destructive potential of, 222; dissection, 224, 233; distrust of doctors, 222–30, 234; quackery, 222–23, **223,** 228–29; satire of, **223,** 223–30, **225–27, 229;** and violation/violence, 224–27. *See also* health
Mesmer, Franz Anton, 221–22
Methodism, 258–59
Method to Learn to Design the Passions, A (Le Brun), 155
"Michael" (Wordsworth), 118, 325n.8
Middlemarch (Eliot), 220
Middleton, John, 208
Milton, John: career of poetry of, 113; and *Eikon Basilike,* 33, 35, 54; on language and the commonwealth, 30; *Lycidas,* 274; on monarchy, 27, 54; *Paradise Lost,* 9; *Readie and Easie Way,* 54; on republicanism, 54; *Samson Agonistes,* 293n.26; *Tenure of Kings and Magistrates,* 27
mind-body dualism, 14, 221–22
"Ministerial Monster, The" (Cruikshank), 232
modernity, 8, 173
Moll Flanders (Defoe), 13, 61, 299n.86
monarchy: aesthetic language of, 3, 292n.16; campaign against revival of, 53–54, 310n.222; Christian foundation of, 36–37, 306n.95; historical importance of, 36–37; iconography of, 30–31; images of royalty, 37, **38,** 39, **40,** 306nn.98–99; language of sentiment used by loyalists, 76–78, 92–94, 96–98; pleasure in the suffering of, 94–96; rejection of, 27, 303n13; royal presence, 32–44, 305n.61; symbols of, 40–43, 307n.125. *See also* Commonwealth
Montagu, John, fourth Earl of Sandwich, 253
Montagu, Lady Mary Wortley, 182–83
Montesquieu, Charles de Secondat, Baron de la Brède et de, 157, 169
Moore, John: *Zeluco,* 265
morality, 146–47. See also *Fable of the Bees, The*
Morison, James, 220, 228
Morning Chronicle: on Louis XVI's last interview, 80–81, 316n.12; on Marie Antoinette's grief, 317n.14; on war between Britain and France, 90
Morning Herald, 87
"Mountebanks, The" (Cruikshank), 235

nationalism, 285–89
Navigation Acts (1651, 1660), 285
Nedham, Marchamont, 30; on the Commonwealth, 26; cyclical view of history, 306n.85; on monarchy, 27; on the Protectorate, 45, 49; on republican democracy, 28
New Discovery of the Prelates Tyranny (Prynne), 104
new historicism, 1, 2
Nicholls, Frank, 222
Nicole, Pierre, 142, 143, 146, 149–50, 151, 328n.19
"Night on Salisbury Plain, A" (Wordsworth), 121–22
Nowell, Thomas, 253
Nuptials of Peleus and Thetis, The, 43–44
"Nutting" (Wordsworth), 127

oaths, sanctity of, 35–36
obedience, duty of, 35
"Of Truth" (Bacon), 153
On Melancholy (Keats), 221
oratory, 154
Oroonoko (Southerne), 93, 320n.51
Osborne, George, 210, 345n.102

Paine, Tom: on the landed class, 244; on the language of sentiment, 75, 78, 94; on Louis XVI, 320n.48; trial of, 77; and Wordsworth, 127
Parish Register, The (Crabbe), 91–92
Parliament, 18; delays issuing seal/coins, 32; dissolution of, 44–45, 52; offers Cromwell the crown, 49–50; requests that Queen Anne remarry, 58, 59–60, 72; and royalist language, 29–30, 304n.42; symbols used by, 41; tries to establish a commonwealth, 26. *See also* Tories; Whigs
Parliamentary Reform Bill (1832), 233
passions: catalogs of, 155, 329n.41; Descartes on, 154–55, 157; in *The Fable of the Bees*, 143–44, 145, 148; in *Lyrical Ballads*, 125–26; and theater, 154–57; Wordsworth on, 125–26, 129–30
pastoral poetry, ancient, 267–73; country vs. city in, 268–69, 271, 284; the *Georgics* vs. the *Eclogues*, 268–70, 357n.1; patriotism in, 270; periodization of, 272–73; as satirical/political, 268, 269–70; and social relations, 275; value reversals in, 269

pastoral poetry, early modern, 274–89; artifice vs. realism in, 274–75; and gender relations, 280, 282–84; vs. georgic, 274; laborers as authors of, 279, 280; and the macro-pastoral, 288–89; periodization of, 274–75, 279; realism of, 279; and social relations, 277–79
pastoral poetry, modern, 289
Patriarcha (Filmer), 105, 106
patriarchal inheritance, 74
Patriarcha non Monarcha (Tyrrell), 105, 106–7
Paye, Edward, 204
Percival, Thomas, 220
Perfect List of All the Victories Obtained by Oliver Cromwell, 30–31, **31**, 304n.51
Perkins, Elisha, 228
Peterloo Massacre, 236
Peters, Hugh, 39
"Petit Souper, à la Parisienne" (Gillray), 234
Petronius Arbiter: *Satyricon*, 151
phrenology, 348n.4
physiognomy, 348n.4
Piercefield (South Wales), 258
Pious Instructions, 37, **38**, 39
Pitt, William, the Younger, 93
plays. *See* theater
Poems and Essays (E. Howard), 105
politeness, 7, 14; and aesthetic language, 263–64, 265–66; in commercial society, 7–8, 147; and concealment/hypocrisy, 147, 155, 167; courtesy books, 7, 147, 155; and entry into elite society, 7, 147, 155, 262, 295n.46; and virtue, 147
political vs. aesthetic history, 3–5, 15, 20
Polycraticus (John of Salisbury), 151
Pope, Alexander, 190; *Dunciad, The*, 110, 112–13; on pastoral poetry, 275
popular radical movement, 93, 97, 320–21n.59
pornography, Restoration, 12, 299n.81
Poullain de la Barre, François, 187
pregnancies of wealthy women, 312n.1
Prelude, The (Wordsworth), 125, 133–34
Preston, William: *Democratic Rage*, 81
primitivism, hard vs. soft, 357n.2
procession, 44, 308n.145
proclamations, Commonwealth, 42, 307n.128
property: and capitalism, 277–78; customary use rights to, 277, 281

prostitution, 60–61, 313n.17
Protectorate. *See* Cromwell, Oliver
Providence, argument from, 28
provision making, legal concept of, 60–62, 72
Prynne, William, 51; *New Discovery of the Prelates Tyranny,* 104; *Treachery and Disloyalty of Papists to their Soveraignes,* 107
psychology, 13–14
public space, 19, 302n.124
Puritans, 30

Quakers, 206, 208

racism, 286
"Radical Quacks Giving a New Constitution to John Bull" (Cruikshank), 235
"Radical Reformer, A" (Cruikshank), 232
radicals. *See* popular radical movement
"Rake's Progress" (Hogarth), 237
reading practices, 9–10, 101–15; and allegory, 103, 322.9; interiority/self-discovery, 113–15; and the printed key, 10, 298n.69; scriptural application in, 112; for study, 101–2; and treason/sedition, 102–3, 104; and variety of readers, 112. *See also* manuscript notations
Rebels Looking Glass, The, 35–36
Recluse, The (Wordsworth), 133
Regency Act (1706), 58, 59, 312n.11
religion: anthropological/historical study of, 204, 342n.69; Baptists, 204, 206, 209–10; Calvinists, 25, 164, 207; Catholics, 71; Church of England, 19, 206–7, 208, 209; demystification of, 19; Methodists, 258–59; Puritans, 30; Quakers, 206, 208; sin and dirt, 204. *See also* baptism; Christianity
Renaissance state, aesthetic language of, 3, 292n.16
republicanism, 25–26, 75; and the campaign against revival of the monarchy, 53–54; classical arguments for, 28, 128; Milton on, 54; republican cause, 55–56, 311n.246; Wordsworth and, 117, 118, 127. *See also* commonwealth
Republic of Letters, 142
Restoration, 3–5, 12, 13, 18; and theater, 5, 9, 11, 17, 103
Reward of Cruelty, The (Hogarth), 224, **226,** 232

Richardson, Samuel, 166, 179, 331n.66; *Sir Charles Grandison,* 186–87
Richmond gardens, 242, 245–46, 250
Rochester, John Wilmot, Earl of, 298n.68
Roman Catholicism, 71
romanticism, 8, 13, 15, 16, 19, 289
Rousseau, Jean-Jacques, 6, 16, 151, 166–67, 171–72
Rowlandson, Thomas: "Ague and Fever," 229; "The Chamber War," 228; "English Dance of Death," 230; *Medical Dispatch,* 225–26, **227;** "State Butchers," 232; "The Tooth-Ache," 224, **225;** "A Visit to the Doctor," 227–28
Roxana (Defoe), 299n.86
Royal Botanic Gardens. *See* Kew Gardens
royalty. *See* monarchy
"Ruined Cottage, The" (Wordsworth), 123–24, 127
Rump. *See* Parliament
"Ruth" (Wordsworth), 133–35

Salmon, Thomas, 64–65
Samson Agonistes (Milton), 293n.26
Satyricon (Petronius), 151
"Sawney in the Boghouse," 232
Schiavonetti, Luigi: *The Last Interview between Lewis the Sixteenth and his Disconsolate Family,* 184, **85**
Scotland, and England, 286–87, 359n.32
Scott, Sarah: *A Description of Millennium Hall,* 180, 185, 190–91; *The History of Sir George Ellison,* 180, 185–86, 189–90, 191–94
Scott, Sir John, 77
seals and coins, 31–32, 48, 304n.54
sedition, 96–97, 102–3
self, 13–14, 20, 118, 122, 123, 136–37, 172
self-discovery, 114–15
self-love, 144
sensationalist literature, 120, 125, 126
sentiment, language of, 75–98; about George III's illness, 78–79, 88–89, 93, 96; about Louis XVI (*see* Louis XVI, King of France); about Marie Antoinette (*see* Marie Antoinette); and family relations, 76, 79, 96, 98; as feminine, 76, 78, 81; loyalists' uses of, 76–78, 92–94, 96–98; as pathetic, 75–76
Serious and Faithful Representation of Ministers of the Gospel, A, 35

Sermon Preached at Shadwell-Chappell in York-shire, A (Hardcastle), 105, 323n.20
sermons, 105, 160, 323n.20
sexual difference. *See* gender difference
sexuality, 6, 12–13, 17, 20, 125, 130, 131–37
Seymour, Robert, 233
Shaftesbury, Anthony Ashley Cooper, 3rd Earl of, 147, 155, 167
Shakespeare, William: *As You Like It,* 151; *Hamlet,* 152; *Henry V,* 29; *Richard III,* 111
Shebbeare, John: *History of the Sumatrans, A,* 241–42; on Methodism, 259; Walpole on, 252
Shelley, Mary: *Frankenstein,* 222
Shirley, James, 43
Shower, John, 212–13
Siddons, Henry, 155, 329n.41
Sidmouth, Henry Addington, 1st Viscount, 235–36
Sidney, Algernon, 102–3, 104
Simon, Thomas, 48
"Simon Lee" (Wordsworth), 127, 128–29
sin and dirt, 204
Sir Charles Grandison (Richardson), 186–87
Slare, Frederick, 212
slave trade, 94, 285–86, 320n.51
Smith, Adam, 95, 169–70, 277, 334n.109
Smith, Virginia, 198
Smollett, Tobias George, 166, 252; *Humphrey Clinker,* 289
Society for the Propagation of Christian Knowledge (SPCK), 212, 345n.112
Society for the Propagation of the Gospel, 212
song, power of, 125, 129–37
Sophia, Electress of Hanover, 58, 59
Sorrows and Sympathetic Attachments of Young Werter, The (Goethe), 113–15
Southerne, Thomas: *Oroonoko,* 93, 320n.51
South Sea Company, 285
"Southwark Fair" (Hogarth), 228
Spanish Succession, War of the, 285
Spectator, The (Addison), 157, 192–93
Spectator, The, 222
Spiritual Quixote, The (Graves), 258–59, **260**
Stanhope, Charles, 199, 338–39n.22
"State Butchers" (Rowlandson), 232
"State Physicians Bleeding John Bull" (Cruikshank), 234–35

status vs. class, 278
Stebbing, Henry, 208
Steele, Sir Richard, 72, 147, 278
Stourhead (Wiltshire), 258
Stuart, James Edward (the Old Pretender), 59, 64, 312–13n.13
Stubs, Philip, 203–4
Subjects Sorrow, The, 39
sublime, 19, 121, 125–25
suffering, attraction of observing, 94–96, 153
Swift, Edward, 96–97
Swift, Jonathan, 57, 110, 232
symbols: in Elizabeth's vs. Anne's day, 70, 315n.51; maternal, 66, 67–74, 315n.50; representational instability of, 70–71, 315n.53; royal, 40–42, 307n.125

Tacitus: *Germania,* 215, 346n.121
Taking Physick (Gillray), 232, **233**
Talbot, Catherine, 176, 335n.16
Tatler, 201
taxation, 234–35
text: commercialization of, 8–9; recon-figuration of, 297–98n.68; scope of, 1
theater: acting technique, 154, 155–56; allegory in, 103–4; attacked as immoral, 153, 329n.29; audience's role in, 158, 162; during the Commonwealth period, 43–44; and the individual, 152, 328n.26; London stage, popularity of, 154, 158; masque, 5, 293–94n.31; and passions, 154–57; republican opposition to the stage, 171; Restoration stage, stock fig-ures of, 164, 332n.79; Restoration tragi-comedy, 5, 11, 293n.26
theatricality, 141–72; and acts vs. motives, 150–51; of elections, 141; of the elite, 149–50; masquerades, 159–60, 331n.61; moral codes as ceremonies, 149 (see also *Fable of the Bees, The*); the person as actor, 150; of public life, 14, 153–54, 158–60, 163–67, 169–71; world-as-stage metaphor, 151–53
Thelwall, John, 97
Theocritus, 271, 273
thick description, 2
Thomason, George, 28
Thomson, James, 188, 190
Thoresby, Ralph, 198
Thornton, Bonnell, 175, 177–78

"Thoughts on the Style and Taste of Gardening among the Ancients" (Falconer), 244–45

Threnodia Augustalis (Goldsmith), 247–48

Thresher's Labour, The (Duck), 283

Tickell, Thomas, 275

Times (London), 90, 316n.12, 317n.17

"Tintern Abbey" (Wordsworth), 325n.8

Tison (Marie Antoinette's maidservant), 89

Toft, Mary, 228

Toland, John, 215

Toleration Act (1689), 206

Tom Jones (H. Fielding), 161–62, 164–65

Tompkins, P. W.: *The Final Interview of Louis the Sixteenth*, 84–85, 86, 89

"Tooth-Ache, The" (Rowlandson), 224, **225**

Tories: on commerce, 8; and obedience to the king, 241; promote invitation to Hanoverian successor, 59

touching for the king's evil, 5, 19, 200, 211, 345n.107

Tour through the Theatre of War, A, 320n.52

travel/travel writing, 262–63, 264

Treachery and Disloyalty of Papists to their Soveraignes (Prynne), 107

Treatise on Education (Locke), 14

Trial at Large, The, 317n.17

Tricky, Christopher (acquaintance of Wordsworth), 128–29

Tryon, Thomas, 198

Tuke, Samuel, 221

Two Treatises of Government (Locke), 106

Twyn, John, 103

Twysden, Sir Roger, 104

Tyrrell, James: *Patriarcha non Monarcha*, 105, 106–7

Tyson, Edward, 198

Vagabond, The (Walker), 265

"Vale of Esthwaite, The" (Wordsworth), 121

Vallon, Annette, 134, 325n.24

Van Dyck, Sir Anthony, 306n.98; *Charles I on Horseback with Mr. St. Antoine*, 47–48

Vane, Henry, 53

"Vaudracour and Julia" (Wordsworth), 325n.24

Vaughan, Benjamin, 319n.45

"View of the Wilderness, A" (Chambers), **253**

Vigarello, Georges, 198

Village, The (Crabbe), 274

Villiers, George, second duke of Buckingham: *The Rehearsal*, 105, 323n.21

Virgil, 271; *Eclogues*, 268, 269–70, 272–73, 284, 357n.1; *Georgics*, 268–69, 280

virtue: and politeness, 147; and the soul, 164; vs. vice, 142–43 (see also *Fable of the Bees, The*)

"Visit to the Doctor, A" (Rowlandson), 227–28

Voltaire, François Marie Arouet de, 7, 157

Volume the Last (S. Fielding), 180, 183–85

Wakley, Thomas, 219

Walker, Clement: *Compleat History of Independency*, 105

Walker, George: *The Vagabond*, 265

Wall, William, 204–5, 207, 208, 209, 211

Walpole, Horace, 252; on Chambers, 250; on Chatterton, 249–50; "Essay on Modern Gardening," 244; and Mason, 250–51

Walpole, Sir Robert, Earl of Orford, 231

War of the Spanish Succession, 285

wealth, and health, 218–22

Webster, John, 152

Wesley, John, 202, 204, 207, 218–19, 257–58

Whigs, 5–6, 59, 241

Whiston, William, 200, 209–10, 340n.32, 344n.100

Whitaker, John, 76

Whitelocke, Bulstrode, 48

Whytt, Robert, 221

Wild, Jonathan, 165

Wilde Jäger, Der (Bürger), 119–20, 132

Wilkes, John, 253

William Henry, Duke of Gloucester, 62, 64–66, **65**

William III, King of England, Scotland, and Ireland (William of Orange), 58, 64, 294n.33

Williams, Helen Maria, 87, 92

Williams, Perrot, 213

Wilson, Adrian, 339n.30

Wither, George, 49, 53

Wollstonecraft, Mary, 89, 187, 221

women: exoticized/eroticized images of, 12, 299nn.85–86; visibility of, 12

Wordsworth, Dorothy, 124

Wordsworth, William, 15; affair with/child by Annette Vallon, 123, 134, 325n.24; on autonomy, 122–23, 124; *The Borderers,* 122–23, 132–33, 325n.22; and Coleridge, 132, 326n.41; French Revolution's influence on, 118, 121–23, 124–25, 134–36; on the individual, 6; *Letter to the Bishop of Llandaff,* 122; *Lyrical Ballads* (see *Lyrical Ballads);* on meter/poetry, 129–31; on nature, 16, 131; on passions, 125–26, 129–30; poetic persona of, 135–36; *The Prelude,* 125, 133–34; radicalism of, 122, 127; *The Recluse,* 133; on suffering, 116, 117; "The Vale of Esthwaite," 121; "Vaudracour and Julia," 325n.24

World (the): on fashion, 178; on Louis XVI's last interview/execution, 79, 82, 87; on Marie-Thérèse Charlotte, 81; on public/private spheres, 188–89

world-as-stage metaphor, 151–53

York Retreat, 221

Zeluco (Moore), 26